# Hotels and Country Inns of Character and Charm in France

Published in the United States by Fodor's Travel Publications, Inc.
Published in France by Payot/Rivages



ISBN 0-679-00206-5
Third Edition

**Hotels and Country Inns**
**of Character and Charm in France**

Translator: Anne Norris
Layout: Marie Gastaut
Cover design: Fabrizio La Rocca
Front cover photograph: Hostellerie le Maréchal (Alsace),
photo by François Tissier
Back cover: Château de la Treyne (Midi-Pyréenées)



Printed in Italy by Litho Service
10 9 8 7 6 5 4 3 2 1

**Fodor's** RIVAGES

# HOTELS AND COUNTRY INNS of Character and Charm IN FRANCE

*Conceived by*

Michelle Gastaut, Jean and Tatiana de Beaumont,
Anne Deren, Véronique de Andreis, Livia Roubaud
with Jean-Emmanuel Richomme

*Project editor*

Michelle Gastaut

*Fodor's Travel Publications, Inc.*

*New York • Toronto • London • Sydney • Auckland*

*www.fodors.com/*

# BIENVENUE

Welcome to the world of hotels with character and charm in France. This edition contains 585 hotels, including 33 small hotels in Paris and 130 properties that appear in the guide for the first time. All have been selected for charm, quality of service, food and location. They range from the comparatively simple to the luxurious.

When choosing among them, remember that you cannot expect as much of a room costing 200F as you can of one costing 600F or more. Please also note that the prices given were quoted to us at the end of 1997 and may change.

When you make your reservation be sure to ask for the exact prices for half board *(demi-pension)* or full board *(pension)* as they can vary depending on the number in your party and the length of your stay. Half board is often obligatory. Note that rooms are generally held only until 6 or 7PM; if you are going to be late, let the hotel know.

# STAR RATING

The government's hotel-rating organization assigns stars, from one to four, based on the comfort of a hotel, with special weight given to the number of bathrooms and toilets in relation to the number of rooms. This star rating has nothing at all to do with subjective criteria such as charm or the quality of the hospitality which are among our most important criteria. Some of the hotels in this guide have no stars because the hoteliers have never asked the government to rate them.

# HOW TO USE THE GUIDE

Hotels are listed by region, and within each region in alphabetical order by *département* and district. The number of the page on which a hotel is described corresponds to the number on the flag that pinpoints the property's location on the road map and to the numbers in the table of contents and index. The phrase "major credit cards" means that Diner's, Amex, Visa, Eurocard and MasterCard are all accepted.

# PLEASE LET US KNOW...

If you are impressed by a small hotel or inn not featured here, one that you think ought to be included in the guide, let us know so that we can visit it.

Please also tell us if you are disappointed by one of our choices. Write us at Fodor's Travel Publications, 201 E. 50th Str., New York, NY 10022.

# CONTENTS LIST

# CONTENTS

## ALSACE-LORRAINE

## A Q U I T A I N E

## B U R G U N D Y

## CHAMPAGNE - PICARDIE



## CORSICA

## FRANCHE-COMTÉ



## PARIS - ILE-DE-FRANCE

# L A N G U E D O C - R O U S S I L L O N

## MIDI-PYRENÉES

## NORD-PAS-DE-CALAIS



## NORMANDY

## PAYS DE LA LOIRE

## POITOU-CHARENTES

### CHARENTE



### CHARENTE-MARITIME



### DEUX-SEVRES



## PROVENCE-RIVIERA

### ALPES-DE-HAUTE-PROVENCE

## R H Ô N E - A L P E S

### AIN



### ARDÈCHE



### DROME

* Prices shown in brackets are prices for a double room, sometimes with half board. For precise details, go to the page mentioned.

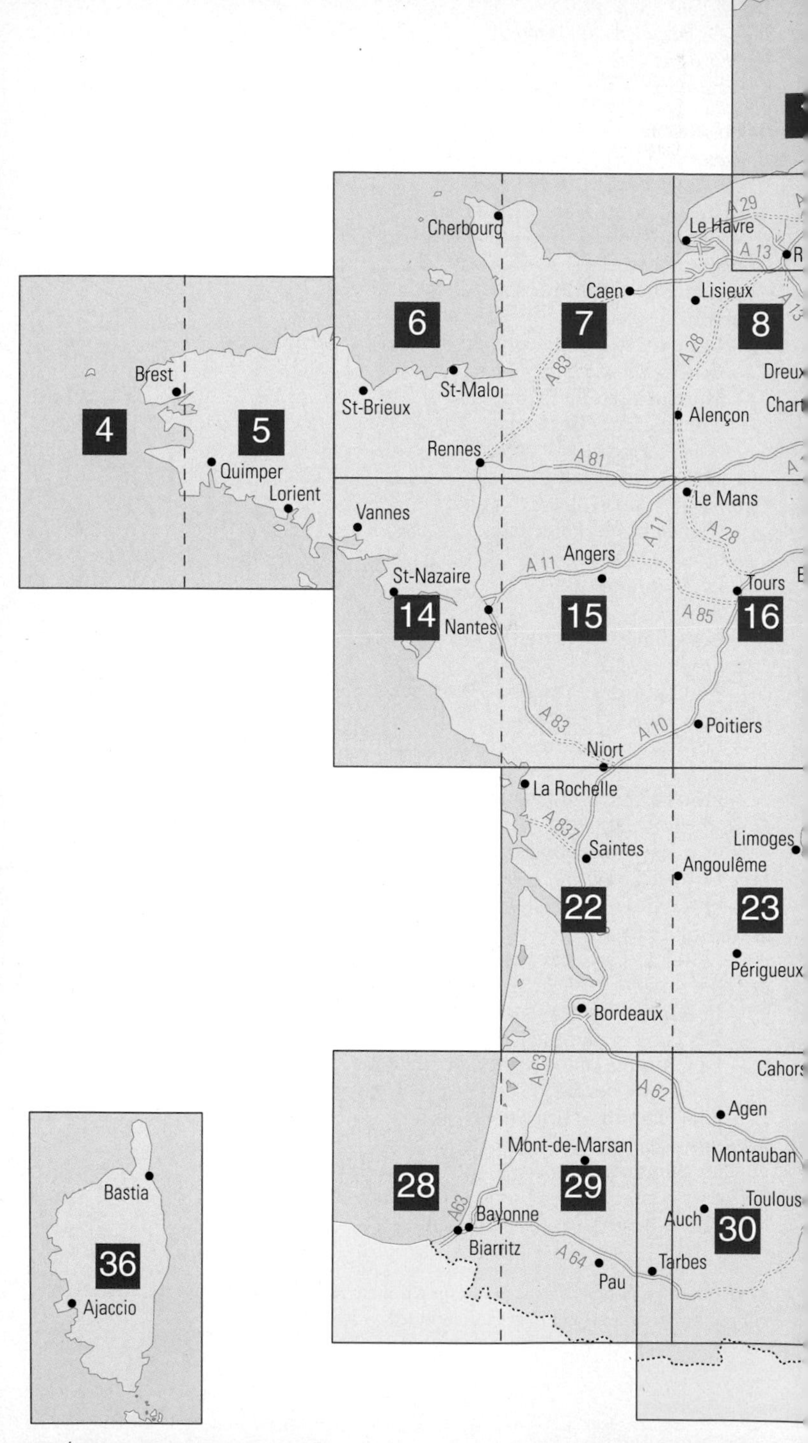

Cherbourg
Le Havre
A 29
A 13
Caen
Lisieux
6
7
8
A 28
A 83
Brest
St-Malo
Dreux
St-Brieux
Alençon
4
5
Rennes
A 81
Quimper
Lorient
Le Mans
Vannes
A 11
A 28
Angers
St-Nazaire
A 11
Tours
14
15
16
Nantes
A 85
A 83
Poitiers
A 10
Niort
La Rochelle
A 837
Saintes
Limoges
Angoulême
22
23
Périgueux
Bordeaux
Cahors
A 63
A 62
Agen
Mont-de-Marsan
Montauban
28
29
Bastia
A 63
Bayonne
Auch
30
Biarritz
A 64
Tarbes
Pau
36
Ajaccio

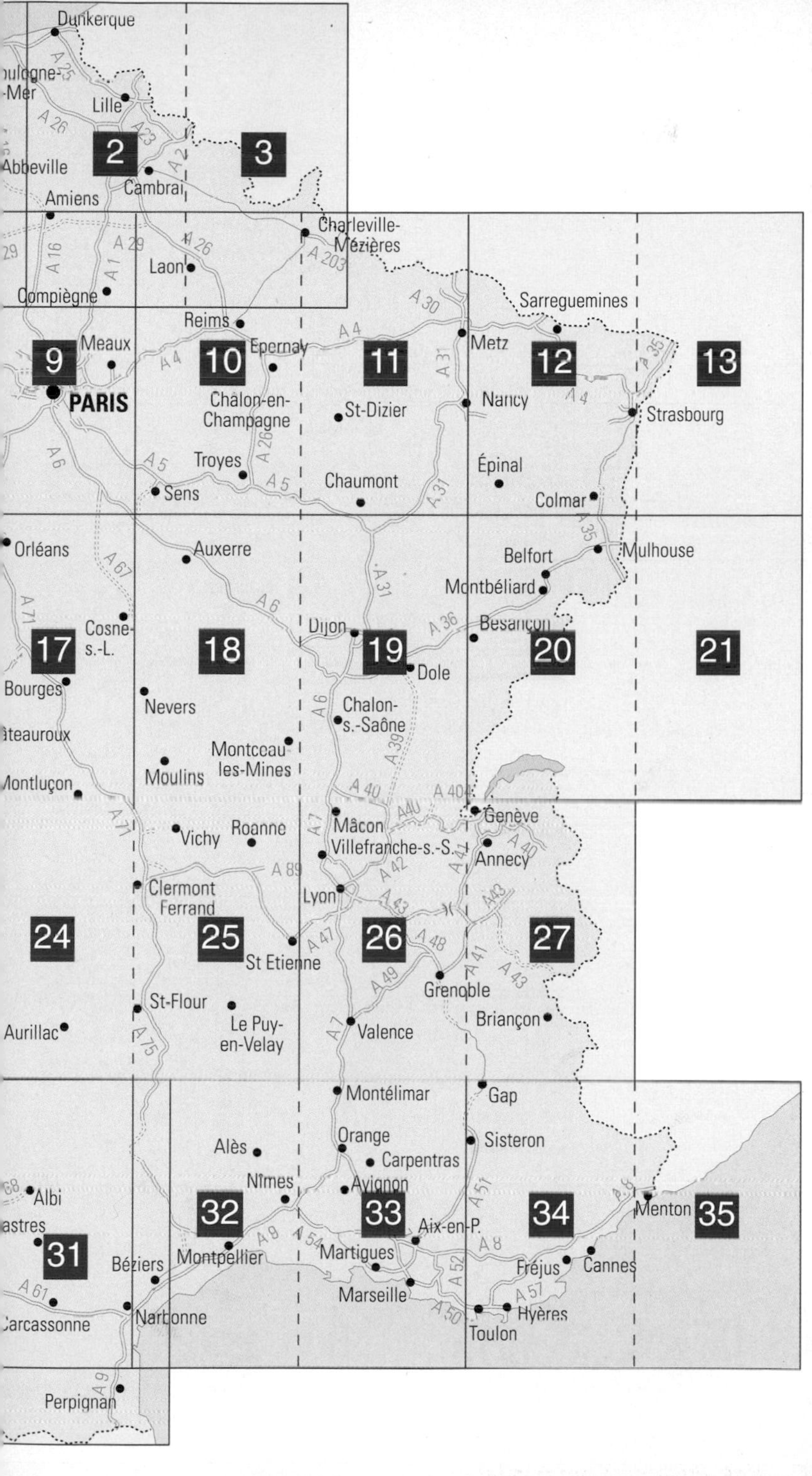

Dunkerque
Lille
Abbeville
Amiens
Cambrai
Charleville-Mézières
Laon
Compiègne
Sarreguemines
Reims
Meaux
Epernay
Metz
PARIS
Châlon-en-Champagne
St-Dizier
Nancy
Strasbourg
Troyes
Épinal
Sens
Chaumont
Colmar
Orléans
Auxerre
Belfort
Mulhouse
Montbéliard
Cosne-s.-L.
Dijon
Besançon
Bourges
Dole
Nevers
Chalon-s.-Saône
Montceau-les-Mines
Moulins
Genève
Mâcon
Vichy
Roanne
Villefranche-s.-S.
Annecy
Clermont Ferrand
Lyon
St Etienne
Grenoble
St-Flour
Le Puy-en-Velay
Briançon
Aurillac
Valence
Montélimar
Gap
Sisteron
Alès
Orange
Carpentras
Nîmes
Avignon
Albi
Menton
Aix-en-P.
Martigues
Montpellier
Béziers
Fréjus
Cannes
Marseille
Hyères
Narbonne
Carcassonne
Toulon
Perpignan
2
3
9
10
11
12
13
17
18
19
20
21
24
25
26
27
31
32
33
34
35

# KEY TO THE MAPS

Scale : 1:1,000,000

maps 30 and 31 : scale 1:1,200,000

**MOTORWAYS**

A9 - L'Océane

Under construction projected

**ROADS**

Highway

Dual carriageway

Four lanes road

Major road

Secondary road

**TRAFFIC**

National

Regional

Local

**JUNCTIONS**

Complete

Limited

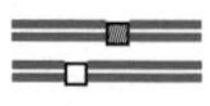

**DISTANCES IN KILOMETRES**

On motorway

On other road

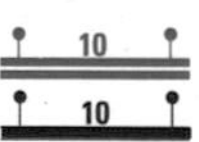


**BOUNDARIES**

National boundary

Region area

Department area

**URBAIN AREA**

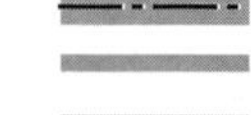

**Town**

**Big city**

**Important city**

Medium city

Little city

**AIRPORTS**

**FORESTS**

**PARKS**

Limit

Center

*Cartography*

*Created by*

1
PAS DE CALAIS
Dover
Folkestone
Hythe
New Romney
Lydd
Dungeness
Rye
Hastings
Ashford
Biddenden
Tenterden
Hawkhurst
Calais
Marck
Sangatte
Cap Blanc-Nez
Wissant
Cap Gris-Nez
Audinghen
Ambleteuse
Marquise
Guînes
Ardres
Audruicq
Licques
Nabringhen
Wimereux
Boulogne-s.-Mer
Le Portel
Desvres
Senlecques
Hardelot plage
Samer
Neufchâtel-Hardelot
Dannes
Camiers
Frencq
Hucqueliers
Maninghem
Le Touquet-Paris-Plage
Étaples
Cucq
Merlimont
Montreuil
Berck
Campagne-lès-H.
Hesdin
Fort-Mahon-Plage
Douriez
Quend
Rue
Labroye
Baie de la Somme
Crécy-en-P.
Le Crotoy
Nouvion
Cayeux-s.-Mer
St-Valéry
Canchy
Lanchères
Abbeville
St-Riquier
Ault
Friville
Mers-les-Bains
Moyenneville
Ailly
Le Tréport
Criel-s.-Mer
Eu
Flixecourt
Gamaches
St-Maxent
Hallencourt
Airaines
Dieppe
Varengeville-s.-Mer
Sept-Meules
Blangy-s.-Br.
Oisemont
Envermeu
Grandcourt
Sénarpont
Molliens-Dreuil
Offranville
Bourg-Dun
Londinières
Foucarmont
Lomer
Hornoy
Fontaine-le-D.
Bacqueville-en-C.
Torcy-le-Pt
Clais
Cany-Barville
Ste-Colombe
Longueville
Aumale
Poix
Mortemer
Doudeville
St-Laurent-en-C.
Ardouval
Neufchâtel-en-B.
Thieuloy
Seine-Maritime
76
Héricourt
Auffay
St-Saëns
St-Saire
Abancourt
Sarcus
Yerville
Tôtes
Grandvilliers
Feuquières
Formerie
Limésy
Crèvecoeur-le-Grd
Yvetot
Pavilly
Buchy
Forges-les-Eaux
Clères
Cailly
Argueil
Marseille-en-B.
Barentin
Montville
Songeons
Luchy
Caudebec-en-Caux
Duclair
Quincampoix
Gournay-en-Bray
Troissereux
Villequier
Mt-St-Aignan
Le Trait
Jumièges
Rouen
La Feuillie
Beauvais
Croisy
Bourneville
Sotteville-lès-Rouen
Lyons-la-Forêt
Neuf-Marché
Grand Couronne
Boos
Fleury-s.-And.
Charleval
Morgny
Bourg-Achard
Oissel
Montfort-s.-Risle
Elbeuf
Pont-de-l'Arche
Écouis
Étrépagny
Gisors
Léry
Seine
Somme
Bresle
353
208
391
390
387
389
388
370
2
8
9

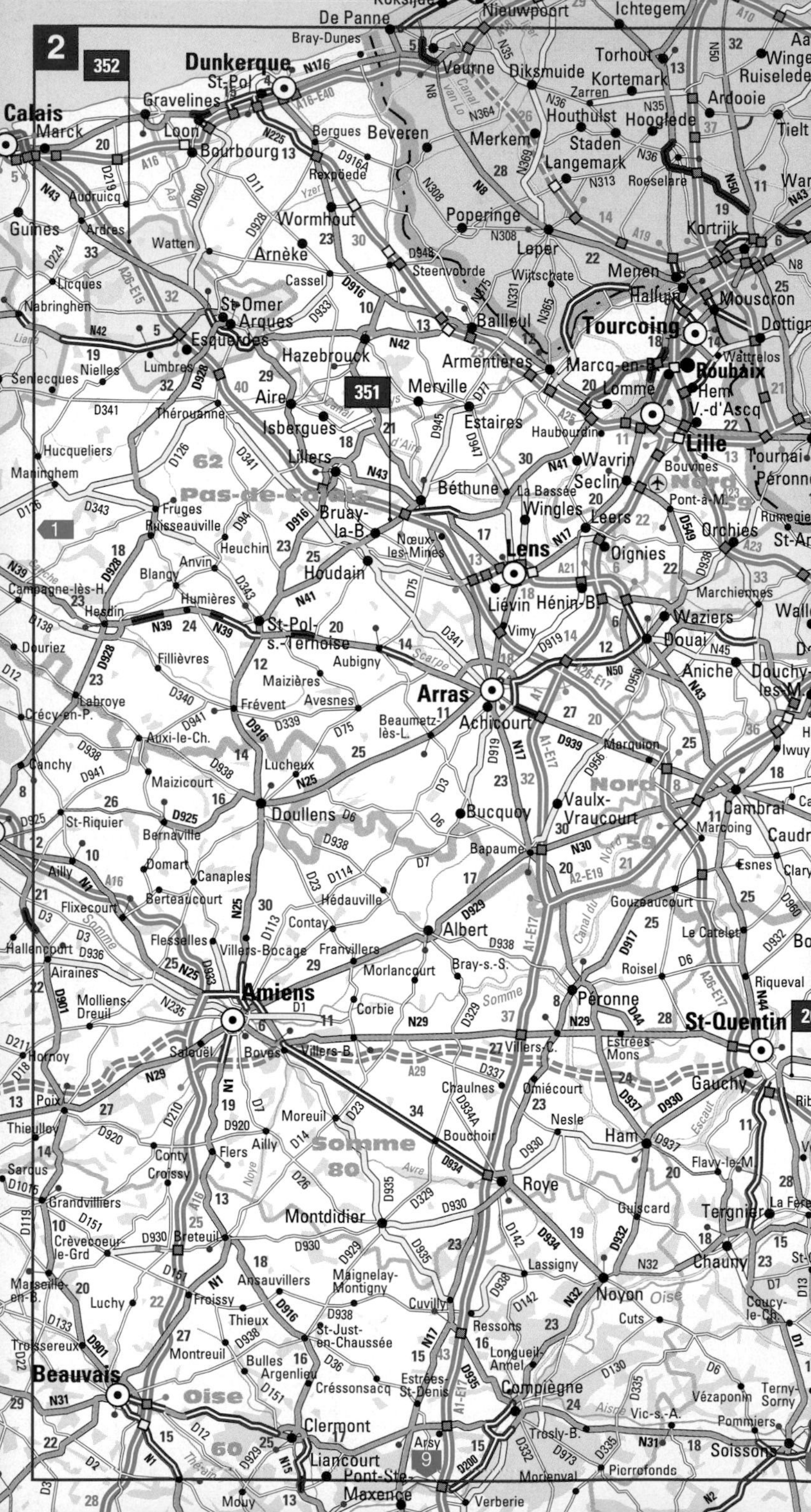

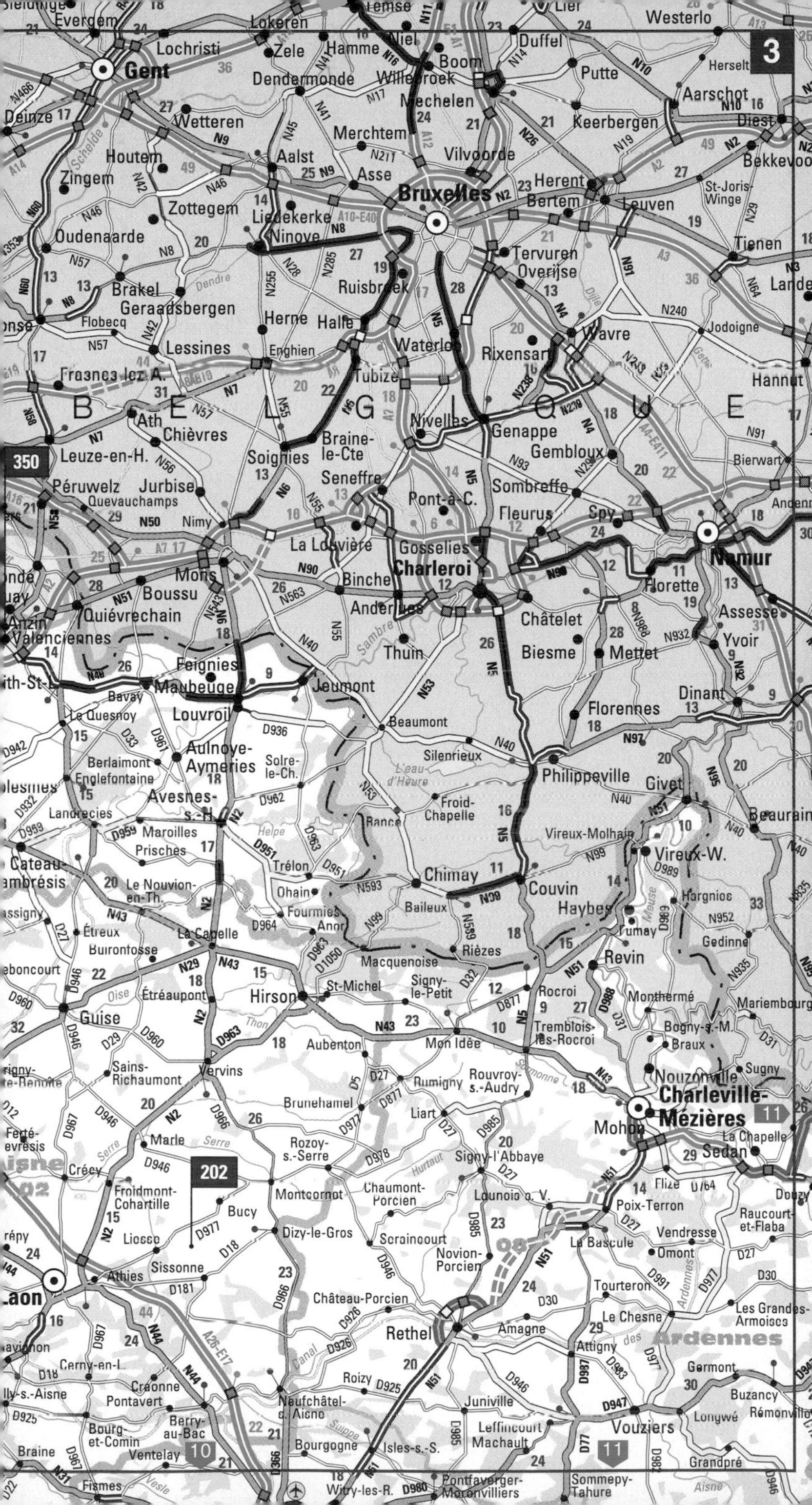

139
Plouguerneau
Lannilis
Ploudalmézeau
D28
Plouguin
D68
D26
Porspoder
D27
Plourin
Lampaul
Brélès
Bourg-B.
D13
D28
D5
Gouesnou
D67
St-Renan
Ile Molène
13
Brest
24
D789
Le Conquet
Pointe St-Mathieu
D8
Camaret-s.-Mer
Crozon
MER
D'IROISE
Cap de la Chèvre
Baie de
Pointe du Raz
D784
D765
Ile de Sein
Plogoff
Audierne
Plouhinec
Plozevet
Baie
d'Audierne
Pointe de Penmarc'h

Finistère
29
Côtes-d'Armor
22
Morbihan
Ile de Batz
Roscoff
St-Pol-de-Léon
Morlaix
Landivisiau
Landerneau
Châteaulin
Quimper
Concarneau
Lannion
Perros-Guirec
Tréguier
Paimpol
Guingamp
Carhaix-Plouguer
Gourin
Quimperlé
Lorient
Hennebont
Pontivy
Auray
Vannes
Quiberon
Belle-Ile
Ile de Groix
Iles de Glénan
Ile de Houat
Ile de Bréhat
6
14
140
129
130
125
131
124
135
121
123
142
136
163
143
155
162
132
133
137
164
158
159
165
156
153
152
160
157

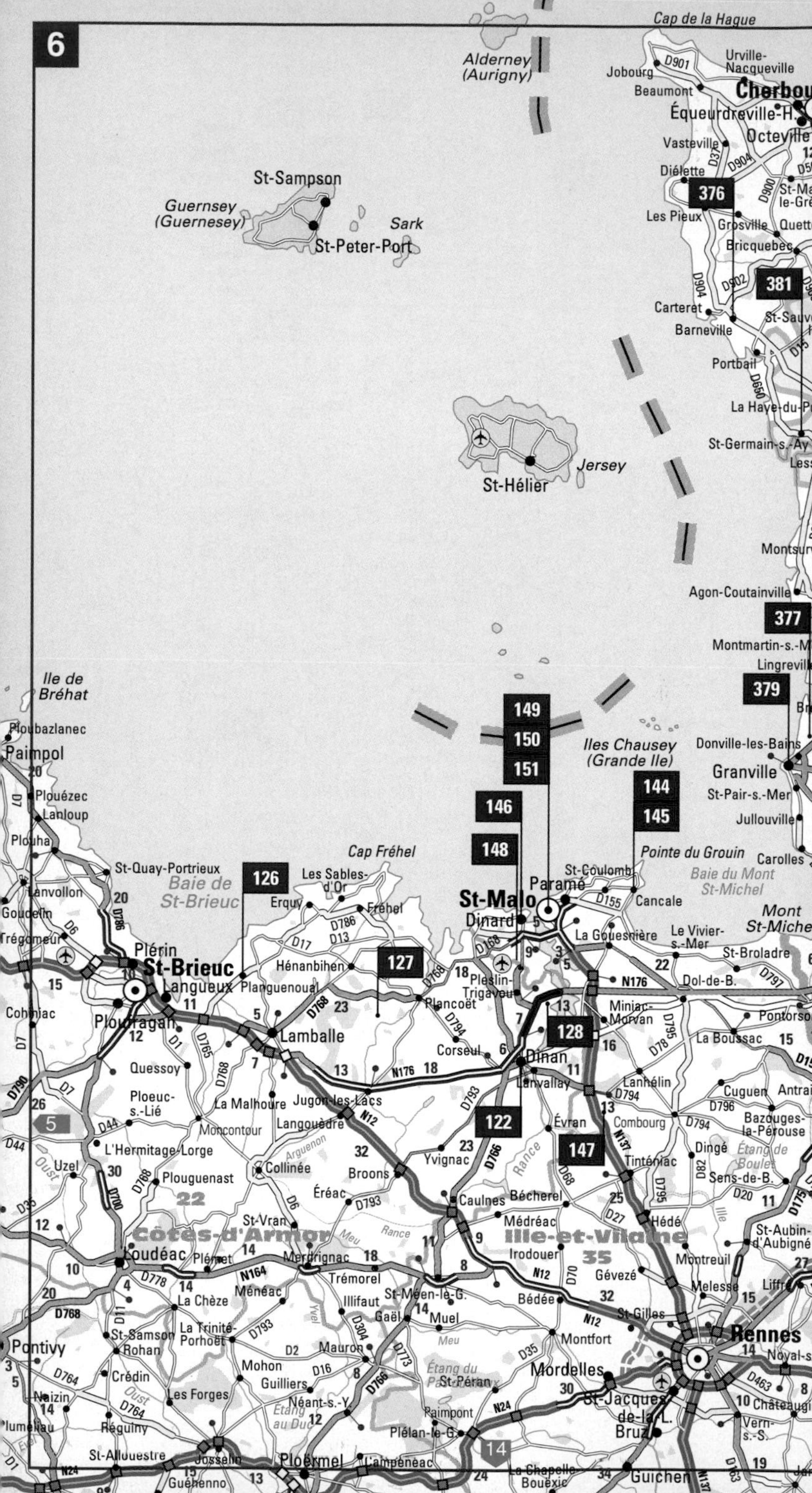

6
Cap de la Hague
Alderney
(Aurigny)
Jobourg
D901
Urville-
Nacqueville
Beaumont
Équeurdreville-H.
Octeville
Vasteville
Diélette
D904
D900
376
Les Pieux
Grosville
Bricquebec
D904
D902
381
Carteret
Barneville
Portbail
D650
La Haye-du-Pu
St-Germain-s.-Ay
St-Sampson
Guernsey
(Guernesey)
Sark
St-Peter-Port
Jersey
St-Hélier
Montsurv
Agon-Coutainville
377
Montmartin-s.-Me
Lingreville
379
Ile de
Bréhat
149
150
151
Iles Chausey
(Grande Ile)
Donville-les-Bains
Granville
St-Pair-s.-Mer
Jullouville
Carolles
144
145
146
148
Ploubazlanec
Paimpol
Plouézec
Lanloup
Plouha
St-Quay-Portrieux
Lanvollon
Goudelin
Trégomeur
Cap Fréhel
Les Sables-
d'Or
Erquy
Fréhel
126
Baie de
St-Brieuc
Pointe du Grouin
Baie du Mont
St-Michel
St-Coulomb
Paramé
St-Malo
Dinard
Cancale
Mont
Le Vivier-
s.-Mer
La Gouesnière
St-Broladre
Dol-de-B.
N176
D155
D786
D13
D17
D768
D786
Plérin
St-Brieuc
Langueux
Planguenoual
Hénanbihen
127
Pleslin-
Trigavou
Plancoët
Miniac-
Morvan
Pontorson
Cohiniac
Ploufragan
Lamballe
D768
D794
Corseul
Dinan
128
La Boussac
Quessoy
D765
D768
N176
Lanvallay
Lanhélin
D78
D795
Ploeuc-
s.-Lié
La Malhoure
Jugon-les-Lacs
D793
D794
Cuguen
D796
Bazouges-
la-Pérouse
5
D44
L'Hermitage-Lorge
Moncontour
Langouëdre
N12
122
Évran
Combourg
D794
Uzel
Oust
Arguenon
Yvignac
D766
Rance
147
Tinténiac
Dingé
Étang de
Boulet
D700
D768
Plouguenast
Collinée
Broons
Éréac
D793
22
D68
D82
Sens-de-B.
Caulnes
Bécherel
D795
D20
St-Vran
Médréac
Hédé
St-Aubin-
d'Aubigné
D175
Côtes-d'Armor
Meu
Rance
Ille-et-Vilaine
35
Ille
Loudéac
Plémet
N164
Merdrignac
Trémorel
Irodouer
Montreuil
D70
Gévezé
Melesse
Liffré
D778
La Chèze
Ménéac
St-Méen-le-G.
Illifaut
Bédée
N12
D768
D11
St-Samson
Rohan
La Trinité-
Porhoët
D793
Yvel
Gaël
D304
Muel
Meu
N12
St-Gilles
Rennes
Noyal-s.
Pontivy
D764
Crédin
D2
Mohon
Mauron
D773
D35
Montfort
D16
Guilliers
Étang du
Paimpont
St-Péran
Mordelles
D463
Naizin
D764
Oust
Les Forges
Néant-s.-Y.
Étang
au Duc
D766
N24
St-Jacques-
de-la-L.
Châteaugir
Vern-
s.-S.
Plumeliau
Réguiny
Paimpont
Plélan-le-G.
Bruz
14
St-Allouestre
Josselin
Ploërmel
Campénéac
La Chapelle-
Bouëxic
Guichen
N137
D163
D1
N24
Guéhenno

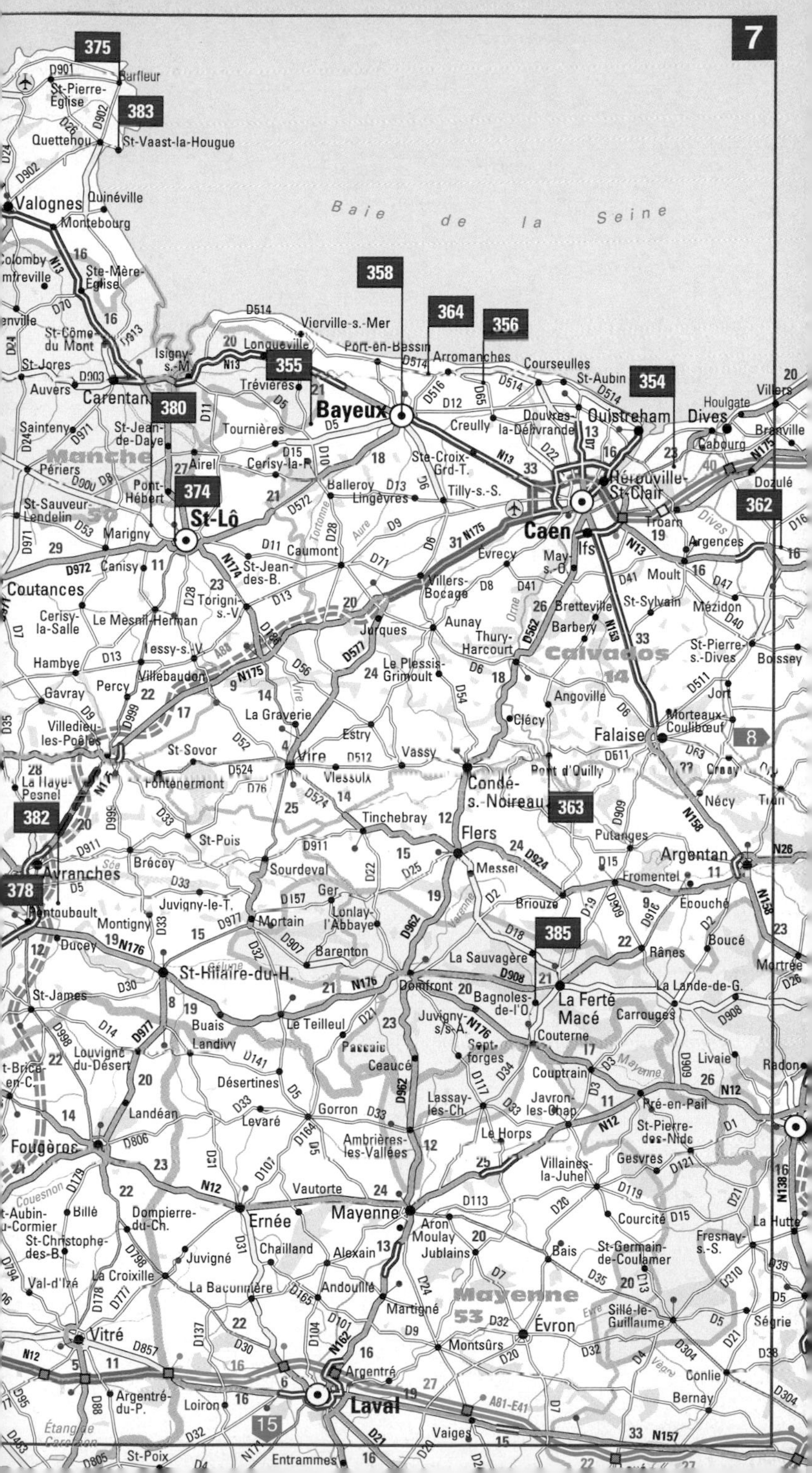

7

375 Barfleur
St-Pierre-Église
383
Quettehou
St-Vaast-la-Hougue
Valognes
Quinéville
Montebourg
Baie de la Seine
Colomby
Amfreville
Ste-Mère-Église
358
364
356
St-Côme-du Mont
Isigny-s.-M.
Longueville
Vierville-s.-Mer
Port-en-Bessin
Arromanches
Courseulles
St-Aubin
354
St-Jores
Carentan
Auvers
355
Trévières
Bayeux
Creully
Douvres-la-Délivrande
Ouistreham
Houlgate
Villers
Dives
Cabourg
380
Sainteny
St-Jean-de-Daye
Tournières
Ste-Croix-Grd-T.
Manche 50
Périers
Airel
Cerisy-la-F.
Balleroy
Lingèvres
Tilly-s.-S.
Hérouville-St-Clair
Dozulé
Pont-Hébert
374
St-Sauveur-Lendelin
St-Lô
Caen
Troarn
362
Marigny
Caumont
Évrecy
Ifs
Argences
Canisy
St-Jean-des-B.
May-s.-O.
Moult
Coutances
Torigni-s.-V.
Villers-Bocage
Bretteville
St-Sylvain
Mézidon
Cerisy-la-Salle
Le Mesnil-Herman
Jurques
Aunay
Barbery
Thury-Harcourt
Hambye
Tessy-s.-V.
Calvados 14
St-Pierre-s.-Dives
Boissey
Villebaudon
Le Plessis-Grimoult
Percy
Gavray
Angoville
Jort
Villedieu-les-Poêles
La Graverie
Clécy
Morteaux-Coulibœuf
Falaise
8
St-Sever
Estry
Vassy
La Haye-Pesnel
Vire
Fontenermont
Vessoux
Condé-s.-Noireau
Pont d'Ouilly
Crocy
Trun
Nécy
382
Tinchebray
363
St-Pois
Flers
Putanges
Argentan
Brécey
Sourdeval
Messei
Avranches
378
Ger
Fromentel
Écouché
Pontaubault
Juvigny-le-T.
Briouze
Montigny
Mortain
Lonlay-l'Abbaye
385
Ducey
Barenton
La Sauvagère
Rânes
Bouçé
St-Hilaire-du-H.
Mortrée
Domfront
Bagnoles-de-l'O.
La Ferté Macé
La Lande-de-G.
St-James
Juvigny-s/s-A.
Le Teilleul
Buais
Carrouges
Landivy
Couterne
Passais
Sept-forges
Louvigné-du-Désert
Ceaucé
Livaie
Radon
St-Brice-en-C.
Désertines
Couptrain
Lassay-les-Ch.
Javron-les-Chap.
Pré-en-Pail
Landéan
Gorron
Levaré
Le Horps
St-Pierre-des-Nids
Fougères
Ambrières-les-Vallées
Villaines-la-Juhel
Gesvres
Vautorte
Billé
St-Aubin-du-Cormier
Dompierre-du-Ch.
Ernée
Mayenne
Aron
Moulay
Courcité
La Hutte
St-Christophe-des-B.
Chailland
Alexain
Jublains
Fresnay-s.-S.
Juvigné
Bais
St-Germain-de-Coulamer
Val-d'Izé
La Croixille
La Baconnière
Andouillé
Mayenne 53
Martigné
Évron
Sillé-le-Guillaume
Ségrie
Vitré
Montsûrs
Argentré
Conlie
Argentré-du-P.
Loiron
Laval
Bernay
Étang de Carcraon
St-Poix
Vaiges
Entrammes
15

8
Fécamp
Le Havre
Honfleur
Trouville
Deauville
Lisieux
Bernay
Évreux
Rouen
Elbeuf
Louviers
Yvetot
Barentin
Lillebonne
Bolbec
Pont-Audemer
Brionne
Vimoutiers
L'Aigle
Verneuil-s.-Avre
Dreux
Chartres
Alençon
Mamers
Mortagne-au-Perche
Nogent-le-Rotrou
La Ferté-Bernard
Le Mans
Sées
Gacé
Seine-Maritime
Eure
Orne
Eure-et-Loir
Sarthe
357
359
360
361
371
372
373
388
389
368
367
366
386
384
405
171
370
7
1
16

9
Somme
80
Oise
60
Val-d'Oise
95
Yvelines
78
Essonne
91
Seine-et-Marne
77
Paris
Beauvais
Pontoise
Nanterre
Bobigny
Versailles
Créteil
Évry
Meaux
Melun
Compiègne
Clermont
Senlis
Fontainebleau
Rambouillet
Étampes
Pithiviers
Nemours
Montereau
Montdidier
Roye
Noyon
206
279
280
274
273
275
277
10
17

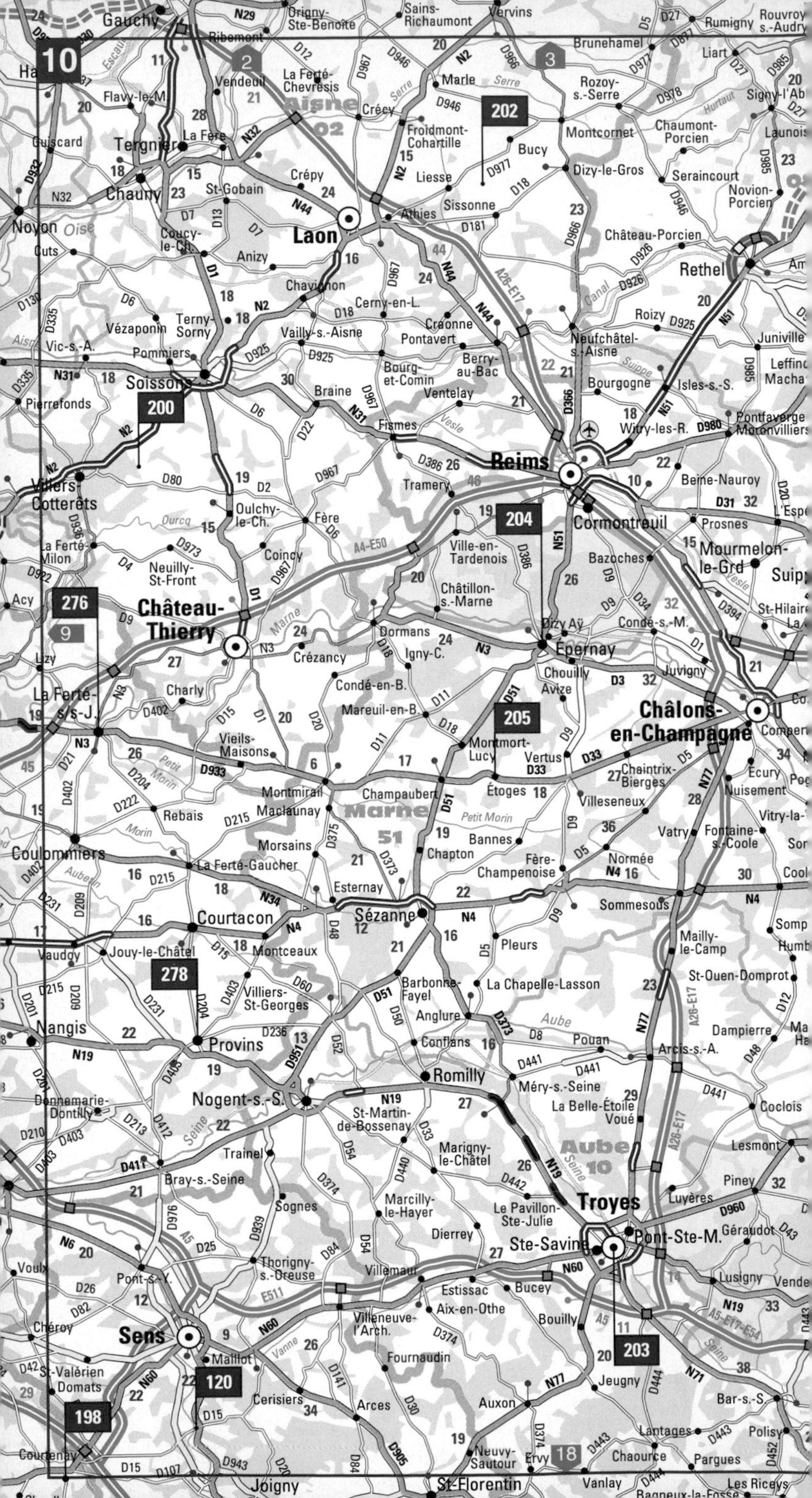

10
2
3
Gauchy
Origny-Ste-Benoite
Sains-Richaumont
Vervins
Rumigny
Rouvroy-s.-Audry
Ribemont
Brunehamel
Liart
La Ferté-Chevresis
Vendeuil
Marle
Rozoy-s.-Serre
Signy-l'Abbaye
Flavy-le-M.
Aisne
02
Crécy
202
Tergnier
La Fère
Froidmont-Cohartille
Bucy
Montcornet
Chaumont-Porcien
Launois
Guiscard
Crépy
Liesse
Dizy-le-Gros
Seraincourt
Chauny
St-Gobain
Novion-Porcien
Noyon
Laon
Athies
Sissonne
Oise
Coucy-le-Ch.
Anizy
Château-Porcien
Cuts
Rethel
Chavignon
Cerny-en-L.
Vézaponin
Terny-Sorny
Craonne
Roizy
Vic-s.-A.
Vailly-s.-Aisne
Pontavert
Neufchâtel-s.-Aisne
Juniville
Pommiers
Berry-au-Bac
Bourg-et-Comin
Soissons
Bourgogne
Isles-s.-S.
Leffincourt
Machault
200
Pierrefonds
Braine
Ventelay
Fismes
Witry-les-R.
Pontfaverger-Moronvilliers
Reims
Villers-Cotterêts
Tramery
Beine-Nauroy
Oulchy-le-Ch.
Fère
204
Cormontreuil
Prosnes
Ourcq
Coincy
Ville-en-Tardenois
Bazoches
Mourmelon-le-Grd
La Ferté-Milon
Neuilly-St-Front
Châtillon-s.-Marne
Suippes
Acy
276
Château-Thierry
St-Hilaire
9
Marne
Dormans
Dizy
Aÿ
Condé-s.-M.
Lizy
Crézancy
Igny-C.
Épernay
Chouilly
Juvigny
La Ferté-s/s-J.
Charly
Condé-en-B.
Avize
Châlons-en-Champagne
Mareuil-en-B.
205
Vieils-Maisons
Montmort-Lucy
Vertus
Chaintrix-Bierges
Étoges
Montmirail
Champaubert
Villeseneux
Écury
Nuisement
Rebais
Maclaunay
Marne
51
Petit Morin
Vitry-la-Ville
Vatry
Fontaine-s.-Coole
Morsains
Bannes
Chapton
Coulommiers
La Ferté-Gaucher
Fère-Champenoise
Normée
Esternay
Sommesous
Courtacon
Sézanne
Vaudoy
Jouy-le-Châtel
Montceaux
Pleurs
Mailly-le-Camp
278
Villiers-St-Georges
Barbonne-Fayel
La Chapelle-Lasson
St-Ouen-Domprot
Anglure
Aube
Nangis
Provins
Conflans
Pouan
Arcis-s.-A.
Dampierre
Romilly
Méry-s.-Seine
Donnemarie-Dontilly
Nogent-s.-S.
St-Martin-de-Bossenay
La Belle-Étoile
Voué
Coclois
Trainel
Marigny-le-Châtel
Aube
10
Lesmont
Bray-s.-Seine
Piney
Sognes
Marcilly-le-Hayer
Troyes
Luyères
Le Pavillon-Ste-Julie
Géraudot
Dierrey
Ste-Savine
Pont-Ste-M.
Voulx
Pont-s.-Y.
Thorigny-s.-Oreuse
Villemaur
Estissac
Bucey
Lusigny
Vendeuvre
Aix-en-Othe
Bouilly
Chéroy
Sens
Villeneuve-l'Arch.
Maillot
Fournaudin
203
St-Valérien
Domats
120
Cerisiers
Arces
Auxon
Jeugny
Bar-s.-S.
198
Lantages
Polisy
Courtenay
Neuvy-Sautour
Ervy
18
Chaource
Pargues
Joigny
St-Florentin
Vanlay
Bagneux-la-Fosse
Les Riceys

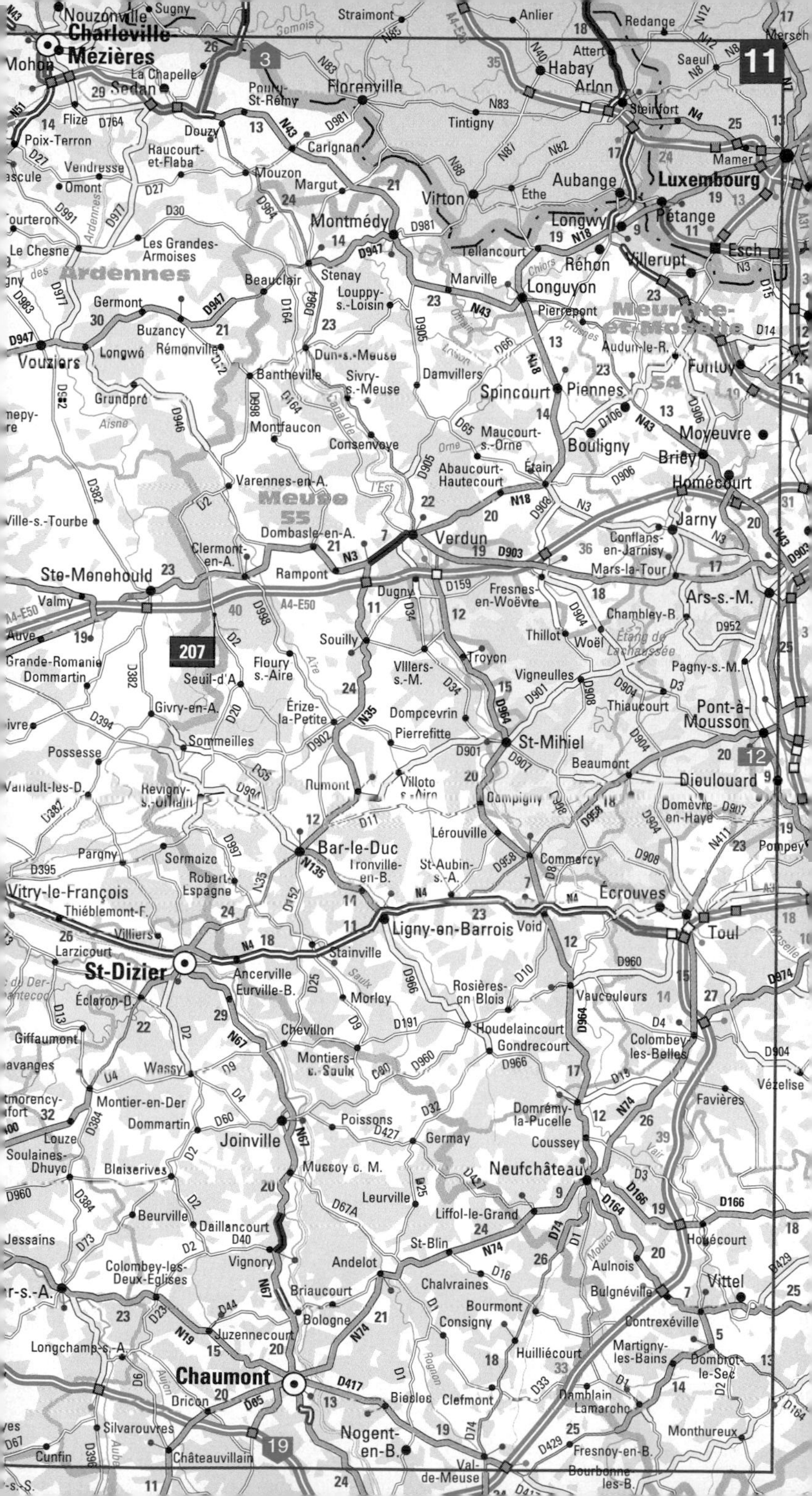

11
Nouzonville
Sugny
Straimont
Anlier
Redange
Charleville-Mézières
Mohon
3
Florenville
Habay
Attert
Saeul
Mersch
La Chapelle
Sedan
Pouru-St-Rémy
Arlon
Steinfort
Flize
Tintigny
Poix-Terron
Douzy
Carignan
Mamer
Raucourt-et-Flaba
Luxembourg
Vendresse
Mouzon
Aubange
Omont
Margut
Virton
Éthe
Tourteron
Montmédy
Longwy
Pétange
Le Chesne
Les Grandes-Armoises
Tellancourt
Esch
Ardennes
Stenay
Réhon
Villerupt
Beauclair
Louppy-s.-Loisin
Marville
Longuyon
Germont
Pierrepont
Meurthe-et-Moselle
Buzancy
Vouziers
Longwé
Rémonville
Dun-s.-Meuse
Audun-le-R.
Fontoy
Bantheville
Sivry-s.-Meuse
Damvillers
Spincourt
Piennes
54
Grandpré
Montfaucon
Consenvoye
Maucourt-s.-Orne
Bouligny
Moyeuvre
Briey
Aisne
Abaucourt-Hautecourt
Étain
Homécourt
Varennes-en-A.
Meuse
55
Verdun
Jarny
Ville-s.-Tourbe
Dombasle-en-A.
Conflans-en-Jarnisy
Clermont-en-A.
Ste-Menehould
Rampont
Mars-la-Tour
Valmy
Dugny
Fresnes-en-Woëvre
Ars-s.-M.
Auve
Chambley-B.
207
Souilly
Thillot
Woël
Étang de Lachaussée
Grande-Romanie
Dommartin
Floury s.-Aire
Troyon
Seuil-d'A.
Villers-s.-M.
Vigneulles
Pagny-s.-M.
Givry-en-A.
Érize-la-Petite
Dompcevrin
Thiaucourt
Pont-à-Mousson
Pierrefitte
St-Mihiel
Sommeilles
Possesse
Beaumont
12
Rumont
Villotte-s.-Aire
Dieulouard
Vanault-les-D.
Revigny-s.-Ornain
Campigny
Domèvre-en-Haye
Lérouville
Pompey
Pargny
Sermaize
Bar-le-Duc
Commercy
Robert-Espagne
Tronville-en-B.
St-Aubin-s.-A.
Vitry-le-François
Écrouves
Thiéblemont-F.
Ligny-en-Barrois
Void
Toul
Villiers
Larzicourt
Stainville
St-Dizier
Ancerville
Eurville-B.
Morley
Rosières-en-Blois
Vaucouleurs
Éclaron-D.
Chevillon
Houdelaincourt
Gondrecourt
Colombey-les-Belles
Giffaumont
Montiers-s.-Saulx
Wassy
Vézelise
Montier-en-Der
Domrémy-la-Pucelle
Favières
Dommartin
Poissons
Joinville
Germay
Coussey
Louze
Soulaines-Dhuys
Blaiserives
Mussey s. M.
Neufchâteau
Leurville
Beurville
Liffol-le-Grand
Jessains
Daillancourt
Houécourt
St-Blin
Vignory
Andelot
Aulnois
Colombey-les-Deux-Églises
Chalvraines
Vittel
Bulgnéville
Briaucourt
Bourmont
Bologne
Consigny
Contrexéville
Juzennecourt
Longchamp-s.-A.
Huilliécourt
Martigny-les-Bains
Dombrot-le-Sec
Chaumont
Dricon
Biesles
Clefmont
Damblain
Lamarche
Silvarouvres
Nogent-en-B.
Monthureux
Fresnoy-en-B.
Cunfin
Châteauvillain
19
Val-de-Meuse
Bourbonne-les-B.

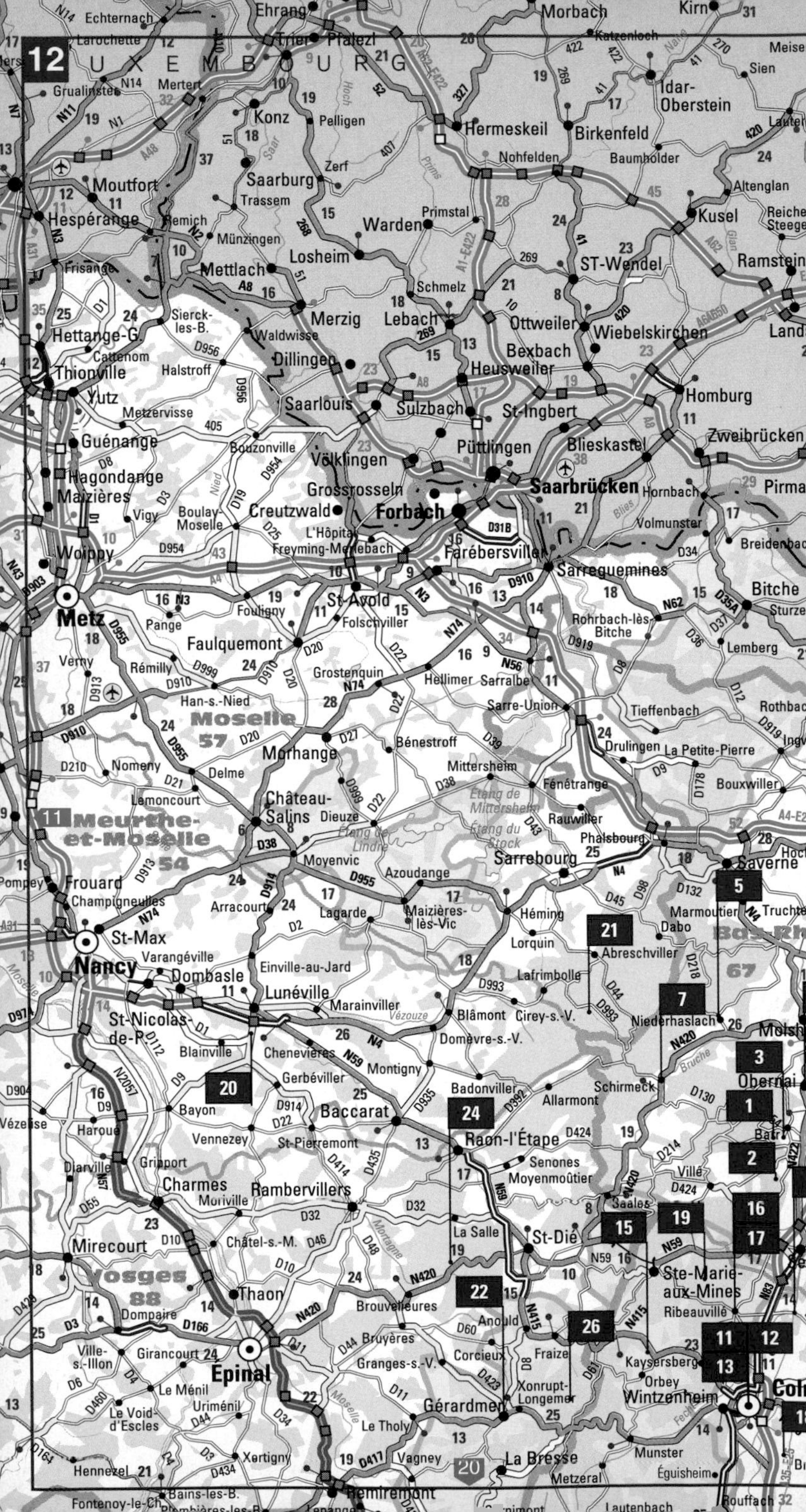
12
LUXEMBOURG
Trier
Konz
Saarburg
Mettlach
Merzig
Dillingen
Saarlouis
Völklingen
Forbach
Saarbrücken
St-Ingbert
Homburg
Zweibrücken
Kusel
Idar-Oberstein
Hermeskeil
Birkenfeld
St-Wendel
Ottweiler
Thionville
Metz
St-Avold
Sarreguemines
Bitche
Saverne
Sarrebourg
Château-Salins
Lunéville
Nancy
Moselle 57
Meurthe-et-Moselle 54
Vosges 88
Bas-Rhin 67
Baccarat
Raon-l'Étape
St-Dié
Épinal
Charmes
Mirecourt
Rambervillers
Gérardmer
Remiremont
Ste-Marie-aux-Mines
Colmar
Obernai
Sélestat
Kaysersberg
Munster
La Bresse

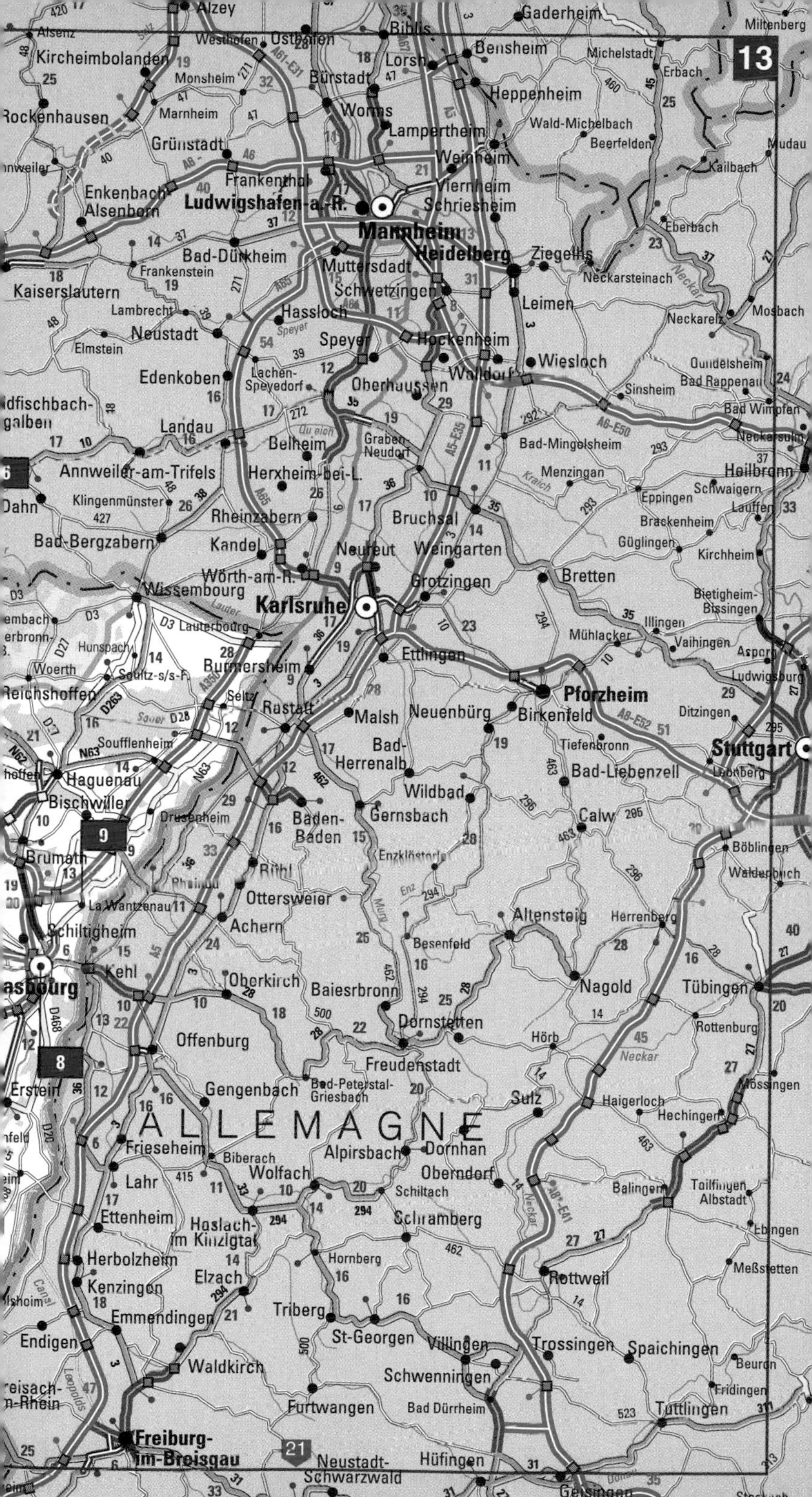
13
Alzey
Gaderheim
Miltenberg
Alsenz
Westhofen
Osthofen
Biblis
Bensheim
Michelstadt
Kirchheimbolanden
Monsheim
Bürstadt
Lorsh
Heppenheim
Erbach
Rockenhausen
Marnheim
Worms
Wald-Michelbach
Lampertheim
Beerfelden
Grünstadt
Weinheim
Mudau
Frankenthal
Kailbach
Enkenbach-Alsenborn
Ludwigshafen-a.-R.
Viernheim
Schriesheim
Mannheim
Eberbach
Bad-Dürkheim
Heidelberg
Ziegelhs
Frankenstein
Muttersdadt
Neckarsteinach
Kaiserslautern
Schwetzingen
Neckar
Leimen
Lambrecht
Hassloch
Neckarelz
Mosbach
Neustadt
Speyer
Hockenheim
Elmstein
Wiesloch
Edenkoben
Lachen-Speyedorf
Walldorf
Oberhausen
Sinsheim
Bad Rappenau
Bad Wimpfen
Landau
Belheim
Graben-Neudorf
Bad-Mingolsheim
Neckarsulm
Annweiler-am-Trifels
Herxheim-bei-L.
Menzingen
Heilbronn
Kraich
Schwaigern
Dahn
Klingenmünster
Eppingen
Lauffen
Rheinzabern
Bruchsal
Brackenheim
Bad-Bergzabern
Kandel
Neureut
Weingarten
Güglingen
Kirchheim
Wörth-am-R.
Grotzingen
Bretten
Wissembourg
Bietigheim-Bissingen
Karlsruhe
Lauter
Lauterbourg
Mühlacker
Illingen
Hunspach
Vaihingen
Asperg
Woerth
Buhmersheim
Ettlingen
Ludwigsburg
Soultz-s/s-F.
Pforzheim
Reichshoffen
Seltz
Rastatt
Malsh
Neuenbürg
Birkenfeld
Ditzingen
Sauer
Bad-Herrenalb
Tiefenbronn
Stuttgart
Soufflenheim
Leonberg
Haguenau
Bad-Liebenzell
Bischwiller
Wildbad
Baden-Baden
Gernsbach
Drusenheim
Calw
Böblingen
9
Brumath
Enzklösterle
Waldenbuch
Bühl
Rheinau
Ottersweier
La Wantzenau
Altensteig
Herrenberg
Schiltigheim
Achern
Murg
Besenfeld
Kehl
Oberkirch
Baiesrbronn
Nagold
Tübingen
Strasbourg
Offenburg
Dornstetten
Rottenburg
Hörb
8
Freudenstadt
Erstein
Gengenbach
Bad-Peterstal-Griesbach
Sulz
Haigerloch
Mössingen
Hechingen
ALLEMAGNE
Frieseheim
Alpirsbach
Dornhan
Biberach
Wolfach
Oberndorf
Lahr
Balingen
Tailfingen
Albstadt
Schiltach
Ettenheim
Haslach-im Kinzigtal
Schramberg
Ebingen
Herbolzheim
Hornberg
Rottweil
Meßstetten
Elzach
Kenzingen
Emmendingen
Triberg
Endigen
St-Georgen
Villingen
Trossingen
Spaichingen
Waldkirch
Beuron
Schwenningen
Fridingen
Breisach-am-Rhein
Furtwangen
Bad Dürrheim
Tuttlingen
Freiburg-im-Breisgau
21
Neustadt-Schwarzwald
Hüfingen
Geisingen
Stockach
Donau

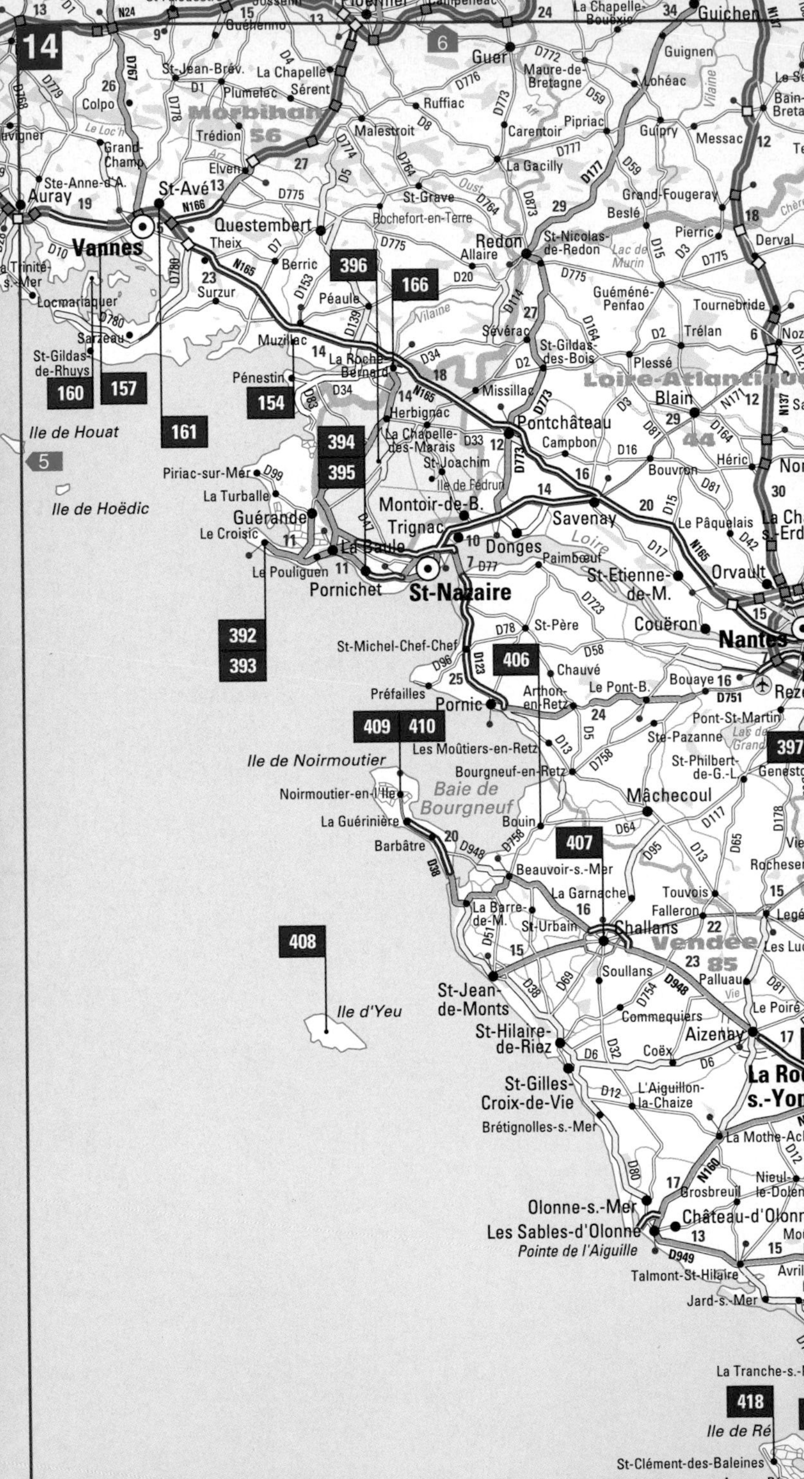
14
St-Allouestre
Josselin
Ploërmel
Campénéac
La Chapelle-Bouëxic
Guichen
Guer
6
Quelneuc
St-Jean-Brév.
La Chapelle
Sérent
Plumelec
Colpo
Morbihan
56
Trédion
Ruffiac
Malestroit
Maure-de-Bretagne
Lohéac
Guignen
Le Sel
Bain-de-Bretagne
Carentoir
Pipriac
Guipry
Messac
Pluvigner
Grand-Champ
Elven
La Gacilly
Ste-Anne-d'A.
Auray
St-Avé
St-Grave
Grand-Fougeray
Beslé
Questembert
Rochefort-en-Terre
Vannes
Theix
Berric
Redon
Allaire
St-Nicolas-de-Redon
Lac de Murin
Pierric
Derval
La Trinité-s.-Mer
Locmariaquer
Surzur
396
166
Péaule
Guéméné-Penfao
Tournebride
Sarzeau
Muzillac
Sévérac
Trélan
St-Gildas-de-Rhuys
La Roche-Bernard
St-Gildas-des-Bois
Plessé
Pénestin
Missillac
Loire-Atlantique
160
157
154
Blain
Ile de Houat
161
Herbignac
Pontchâteau
394
La Chapelle-des-Marais
Campbon
5
St-Joachim
Héric
Piriac-sur-Mer
395
Ile de Fédrun
Bouvron
La Turballe
Ile de Hoëdic
Guérande
Montoir-de-B.
Savenay
Le Croisic
Trignac
La Baule
Donges
Le Pâquelais
Le Pouliguen
Pornichet
St-Nazaire
Paimbœuf
St-Etienne-de-M.
Orvault
Loire
Couëron
Nantes
392
393
St-Père
St-Michel-Chef-Chef
406
Chauvé
Bouaye
Rezé
Préfailles
Pornic
Arthon-en-Retz
Le Pont-B.
Pont-St-Martin
409
410
Ste-Pazanne
Lac de Grand
397
Les Moûtiers-en-Retz
Ile de Noirmoutier
St-Philbert-de-G.-L.
Genestor
Bourgneuf-en-Retz
Baie de Bourgneuf
Noirmoutier-en-l'Ile
Machecoul
La Guérinière
Bouin
407
Barbâtre
Beauvoir-s.-Mer
Rocheservière
La Garnache
Touvois
La Barre-de-M.
Falleron
St-Urbain
Challans
Legé
Vendée
85
408
Soullans
Palluau
Les Lucs
St-Jean-de-Monts
Ile d'Yeu
Commequiers
Le Poiré
St-Hilaire-de-Riez
Aizenay
Coëx
St-Gilles-Croix-de-Vie
L'Aiguillon-la-Chaize
La Roche-s.-Yon
Brétignolles-s.-Mer
La Mothe-Achard
Grosbreuil
Nieul-le-Dolent
Olonne-s.-Mer
Château-d'Olonne
Les Sables-d'Olonne
Pointe de l'Aiguille
Talmont-St-Hilaire
Avrillé
Jard-s.-Mer
La Tranche-s.-M
418
Ile de Ré
St-Clément-des-Baleines
Ars-en-Ré

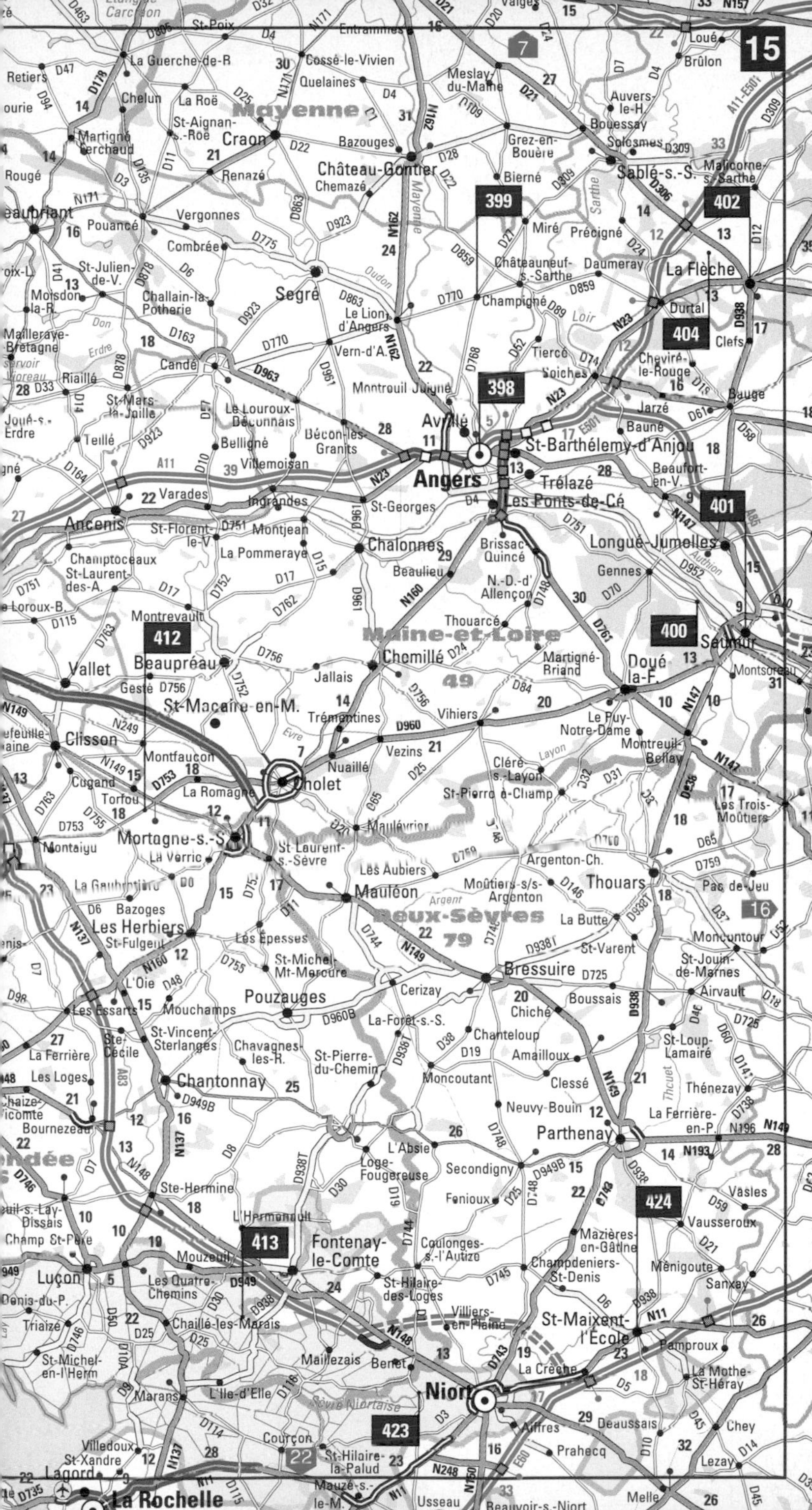
15
St-Poix
Entrammes
Loué
La Guerche-de-B
Cossé-le-Vivien
Brûlon
Retiers
Quelaines
Meslay-du-Maine
Chelun
La Roë
Mayenne
Auvers-le-H
St-Aignan-s.-Roë
Bouessay
Martigné Ferchaud
Craon
Bazouges
Grez-en-Bouère
Solesmes
Château-Gontier
Renazé
Chemazé
Bierné
Sablé-s.-S.
Malicorne-s.-Sarthe
Rougé
Vergonnes
Pouancé
Miré
Précigné
Combrée
Châteauneuf-s.-Sarthe
Daumeray
La Flèche
St-Julien-de-V.
Segré
Challain-la-Potherie
Champigné
Durtal
Moisdon-la-R.
Le Lion-d'Angers
Clefs
Meilleraye-de-Bretagne
Vern-d'A.
Tiercé
Cheviré-le-Rouge
Candé
Soiches
Riaillé
Montreuil-Juigné
Baugé
St-Mars-la-Jaille
Le Louroux-Béconnais
Avrillé
Jarzé
Joué-s.-Erdre
Baune
Teillé
Belligné
Bécon-les-Granits
St-Barthélemy-d'Anjou
Villemoisan
Beaufort-en-V.
Angers
Trélazé
Varades
Ingrandes
St-Georges
Les Ponts-de-Cé
Ancenis
St-Florent-le-V
Montjean
Longué-Jumelles
Champtoceaux
La Pommeraye
Chalonnes
Brissac Quincé
St-Laurent-des-A.
Beaulieu
Gennes
Le Loroux-B.
N.-D.-d'Allençon
Montrevault
Thouarcé
Saumur
Maine-et-Loire
Martigné-Briand
Doué la-F.
Vallet
Beaupréau
Chemillé
Montsoreau
Jallais
49
Gesté
St-Macaire-en-M.
Trémentines
Vihiers
Le Puy-Notre-Dame
Clisson
Montreuil-Bellay
Montfaucon
Vezins
Cléré-s.-Layon
Cholet
Nuaillé
Cugand
Torfou
La Romagne
St-Pierre-à-Champ
Les Trois-Moûtiers
Mortagne-s.-S.
Maulévrier
Montaigu
La Verrie
St-Laurent-s.-Sèvre
Argenton-Ch.
Les Aubiers
Thouars
Pas-de-Jeu
Moûtiers-s/s-Argenton
Mauléon
Bazoges
Deux-Sèvres
La Butte
Les Herbiers
79
St-Fulgent
Les Epesses
St-Varent
Moncontour
St-Michel-Mt-Mercure
Bressuire
St-Jouin-de-Marnes
L'Oie
Cerizay
Boussais
Airvault
Pouzauges
Mouchamps
Les Essarts
Chiché
La-Forêt-s.-S.
St-Vincent-Sterlanges
Chanteloup
St-Loup-Lamairé
Ste-Cécile
Chavagnes-les-R.
St-Pierre-du-Chemin
La Ferrière
Amailloux
Les Loges
Moncoutant
Clessé
Chantonnay
Thénezay
Chaize-Vicomte
Neuvy-Bouin
Bournezeau
La Ferrière-en-P.
L'Absie
Parthenay
Loge-Fougereuse
Secondigny
Vendée
Ste-Hermine
Fenioux
Vasles
Mareuil-s.-Lay-Dissais
Vausseroux
Champ St-Père
L'Hermenault
Mazières-en-Gâtine
Mouzeuil
Fontenay-le-Comte
Coulonges-s.-l'Autize
Ménigoute
Luçon
Champdeniers-St-Denis
Les Quatre-Chemins
St-Hilaire-des-Loges
Sanxay
Denis-du-P.
Villiers-en-Plaine
St-Maixent-l'École
Triaizé
Chaillé-les-Marais
Pamproux
St-Michel-en-l'Herm
Maillezais
Benet
La Crèche
La Mothe-St-Héray
Marans
L'Ile-d'Elle
Niort
Sèvre Niortaise
Aiffres
Deaussais
Chey
Villedoux
Courçon
St-Xandre
St-Hilaire-la-Palud
Prahecq
Lagord
Lezay
La Rochelle
Mauzé-s.-le-M.
Usseau
Beauvoir-s.-Niort
Melle
398
399
400
401
402
404
412
413
423
424
7
16
22

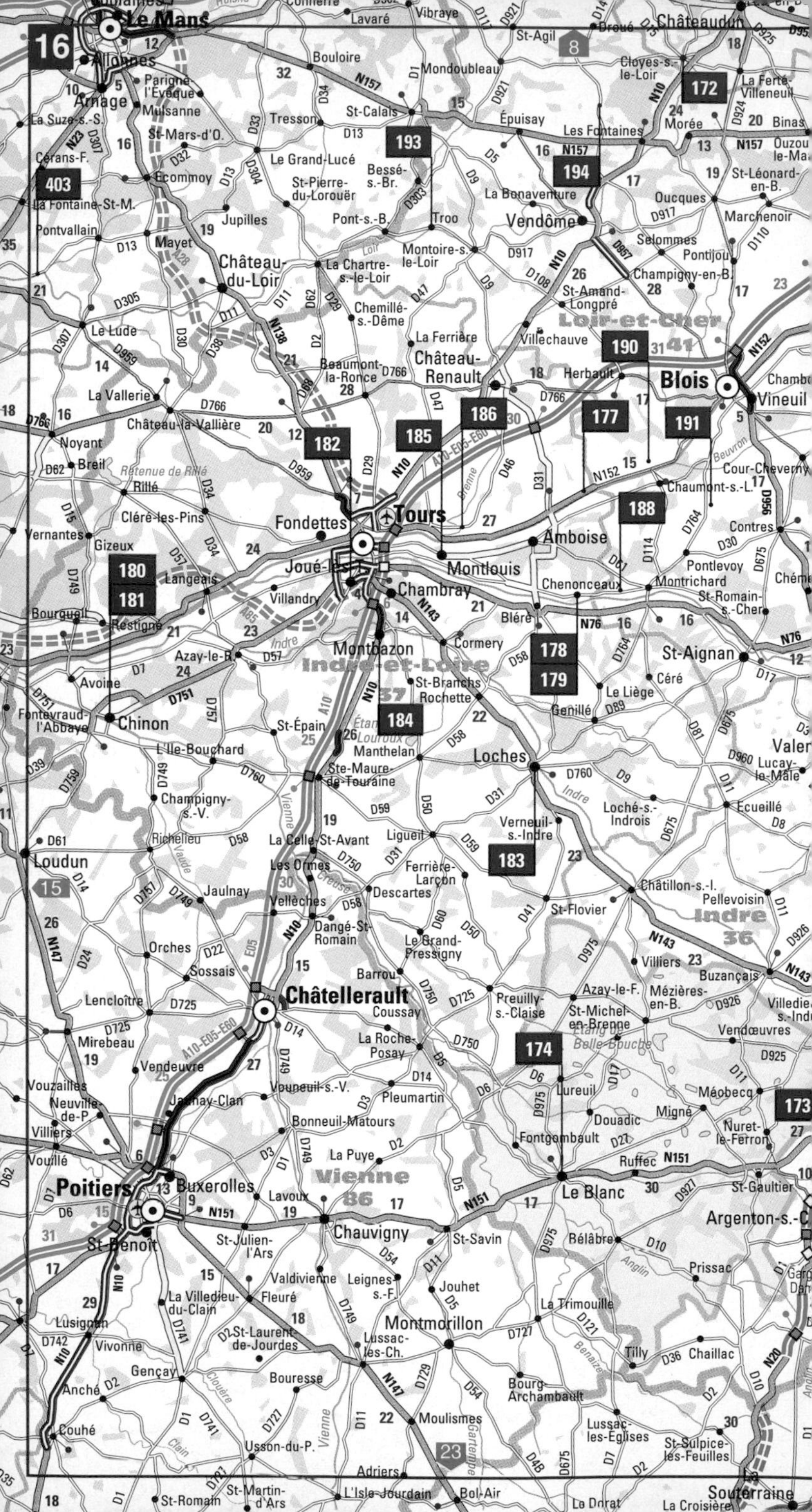
16
Le Mans
Allonnes
Arnage
Parigné-l'Évêque
Mulsanne
La Suze-s.-S.
St-Mars-d'O.
Cérans-F.
Écommoy
403
La Fontaine-St-M.
Pontvallain
Jupilles
Mayet
Château-du-Loir
Bouloire
St-Calais
Tresson
Le Grand-Lucé
St-Pierre-du-Lorouër
Bessé-s.-Br.
Pont-s.-B.
Troo
Montoire-s.-le-Loir
La Chartre-s.-le-Loir
Chemillé-s.-Dême
Lavaré
Vibraye
Mondoubleau
St-Agil
Droué
Châteaudun
8
Cloyes-s.-le-Loir
172
La Ferté-Villeneuil
Morée
Binas
Épuisay
Les Fontaines
193
194
La Bonaventure
Vendôme
Oucques
St-Léonard-en-B.
Marchenoir
Selommes
Pontijou
Champigny-en-B.
St-Amand-Longpré
Villechauve
Loir-et-Cher
41
190
Blois
Vineuil
Herbault
La Ferrière
Château-Renault
Beaumont-la-Ronce
Le Lude
La Vallerie
Château-la-Vallière
Noyant
Breil
Rillé
Retenue de Rillé
Cléré-les-Pins
Vernantes
Gizeux
182
185
186
177
191
Cour-Cheverny
Chaumont-s.-L.
188
Fondettes
Tours
Amboise
Montlouis
Contres
Pontlevoy
Montrichard
Chenonceaux
St-Romain-s.-Cher
180
181
Langeais
Joué-lès-T.
Chambray
Villandry
Bourgueil
Restigné
Azay-le-R.
Montbazon
Cormery
Bléré
178
179
St-Aignan
Céré
Le Liège
Indre-et-Loire
37
St-Branchs
Rochette
Genillé
Avoine
Chinon
Fontevraud-l'Abbaye
St-Épain
184
Manthelan
L'Ile-Bouchard
Ste-Maure-de-Touraine
Loches
Valençay
Lucay-le-Mâle
Champigny-s.-V.
Richelieu
La Celle-St-Avant
Ligueil
Verneuil-s.-Indre
Loché-s.-Indrois
Écueillé
Loudun
15
Les Ormes
Ferrière-Larçon
183
Jaulnay
Vellèches
Descartes
Châtillon-s.-I.
Pellevoisin
St-Flovier
Indre
36
Dangé-St-Romain
Le Grand-Pressigny
Orches
Sossais
Barrou
Villiers
Buzançais
Châtellerault
Lencloître
Coussay
Preuilly-s.-Claise
Azay-le-F.
Mézières-en-B.
St-Michel-en-Brenne
Étang de Belle-Bouche
Mirebeau
La Roche-Posay
174
Vendœuvres
Vendeuvre
Vouzailles
Neuville-de-P.
Vouneuil-s.-V.
Pleumartin
Lureuil
Méobecq
173
Jaunay-Clan
Bonneuil-Matours
Fontgombault
Douadic
Migné
Nuret-le-Ferron
Villiers
Vouillé
La Puye
Ruffec
Poitiers
Buxerolles
Vienne
86
Lavoux
Le Blanc
St-Gaultier
Argenton-s.-C.
Chauvigny
St-Savin
St-Benoît
St-Julien-l'Ars
Bélâbre
Prissac
Valdivienne
Leignes-s.-F.
Jouhet
La Villedieu-du-Clain
Fleuré
La Trimouille
Lusignan
Montmorillon
St-Laurent-de-Jourdes
Lussac-les-Ch.
Vivonne
Tilly
Chaillac
Gençay
Bourg-Archambault
Anché
Bouresse
Couhé
Moulismes
Lussac-les-Églises
St-Sulpice-les-Feuilles
Usson-du-P.
23
Adriers
St-Romain
St-Martin-l'Ars
L'Isle-Jourdain
Bel-Air
Le Dorat
La Croisière
La Souterraine

17
Sougy
Coudray
Corbeilles
Courtenay
Neuville-aux-Bois
Chambon-la-F.
Chevilly
Loury
197
199
Saran
Sully-la-Ch.
Ladon
Bellegarde
Montargis
Amilly
Fay-aux-Loges
Loiret 45
Thimory
Ingre
La Chapelle-St-M.
Orléans
Châtenoy
Châteaurenard
Lorris
Châteauneuf-s.-Loire
Montbouy
Charny
Cléry-St-André
Olivet
Jargeau
Nogent-s.-V.
Châtillon-Coligny
St-Maurice-s.-Aveyron
Meung-s.-L.
Beaugency
St-Benoît-s.-L.
Les Bordes
Les Choux
Tigy
Ouzouer-s.-L.
Champignelles
Lailly-en-Val
Marcilly-en-Villette
Sully-s.-Loire
187
La Ferté-St-Aubin
St-Aignan-le-Jaillard
La Bussière
Sennely
Gien
Isdes
189
Vouzon
168
Cerdon
Briare
St-Fargeau
La Marolle-en-S.
Lamotte-Beuvron
Coullons
Clémont
Argent-s.-S.
Châtillon-s.-L.
Bonny-s.-L.
Lavau
St-Amand-en-P.
Neung-s.-B.
Nouan-le-Fuzelier
Blancafort
Beaulieu
Neuvy-s.-L.
192
Aubigny-s.-Nère
Pierrefitte-ès-Bois
Alligny-Cosne
Marcilly-en-Gault
Souesmes
Vailly-s.-S.
Léré
Millançay
Salbris
Ménétréol-s.-S.
Savigny-en-Sancerre
Cosne-Cours-s.-L.
18
Romorantin-Lanthenay
La Ferté-Imbault
Nançay
La Chapelle-d'Angillon
Le Noyer
Ivoy-le-Pré
St-Satur
170
Villefranche
Theillay
Neuvy-s.-Barangeon
Henrichemont
Sancerre
Pouilly-s.-Loire
Garchy
Mennetou
Cher
Vierzon
Chabris
St-Martin-d'Auxigny
Les Aix-d'Angillon
Herry
La Charité-s.-Loire
Les Bertins
Graçay
Lury-s.-Arnon
Mehun-s.-Y.
Quincy
Bourges
St-Germain-du-Puy
Sancergues
Reuilly
Vatan
St-Pierre-de-Jards
Ste-Thorette
Baugy
Pougues-les-Eaux
Avord
Mornay-Berry
Fourchambault
Brion
Issoudun
Chârost
St-Florent-s.-Cher
Nérondes
La Guerche-s.-l'Aubois
Neuvy-Pailloux
Mareuil-s.-Arnon
Lovet
Dun-s.-Auron
Les Bourdelins
Blet
Déols
Châteauneuf-s.-C.
167
Chalivoy-Milon
Sancoins
Vouillon
Chezal-Benoît
Châteauroux
Pruniers
Le Pondy
St-Pierre-le-Moûtier
Ambrault
Ardentes
St-Août
Poinçonnet
Lignières
St-Amand-Montrond
82
Le Veurdre
Morlac
Orval
Charenton-s.-Cher
Ainay-le-Ch.
Lurcy-Lévis
176
St-Christophe-en-Boucherie
169
Limoise
175
St-Chartier
Le Châtelet
Couleuvre
Franchesse
Bouesse
Neuvy-St-Sépulchre
Thevet-St-Julien
Tronçais
Cérilly
Urçay
La Châtre
Châteaumeillant
Saulzais-le-Potier
La Croix-Cornart
Cluis
Culan
Bourbon-l'Archambault
Ygrande
Crevant
Ste-Sévère-s.-Indre
80
Cosne-d'Allier
Aigurande
Préveranges
Estivareilles
Chavenon
La Chapelaude
Le Montet
Genouillac
Domérat
Villefranche-d'Allier
Boussac
Treignat
Montluçon
Châtelus-Malvaleix
Commentry
Doyet
La Celle-Dunoise
Bonnat
Lavaufranche
Lamaids
Néris-les-Bains
Ladapeyre
24

18
Courtenay
Chuelles
117
Joigny
10
Neuvy-Sautour
Ervy
St-Florentin
Lantages
Chaource
Vanlay
Bagneux-la-Fosse
Migennes
116
Senan
Hauterive
Pontigny
Seignelay
Flogny-la-C.
Coussegrey
Arthonnay
Châteaurenard
Charny
Aillant-s.-Th.
Sommecaise
Appoigny
Ligny-le-C.
Yonne
Tonnerre
Cruzy-le-Châtel
Tanlay
St-Maurice-s.-Aveyron
Auxerre
Châblis
Lézinnes
Les Forges
Champignelles
Villiers-St-Benoît
Pourrain
St-Cyr-les-Colons
Ste-Vertu
Ancy-le-Franc
Toucy
119
89
Pasilly
Nuits
Ravière
Étivey
Mézilles
Vermenton
Nitry
Aisy-s.-Armançon
St-Fargeau
Ouanne
St-Sauveur-en-Puisaye
Courson-les-Carrières
Mailly-le-C.
Montbard
L'Isle-s.-Serein
Vassy
Lavau
St-Amand-en-P.
Druyes-les-Belles-Fontaines
118
Voûtenay-s.-Cure
Neuvy-s.-L.
Guillon
Coulanges-s.-Yonne
Alligny-Cosne
Clamecy
Vézelay
Avallon
Cussy-les-Forges
Semur-en-Auxois
Entrains-s.-Nohain
Dornecy
Chamont
Cosne-Cours-s.-L.
La Chapelle-St-André
Réservoir-du-Crescent
Nuars
Varzy
Quarré-les-Tombes
St-M.-du-Puy
Canal du Nivernais
Asnan
Pouilly-s.-Loire
Garchy
Châteauneuf-Val-de-Bargis
Champlemy
Lormes
Dun-les-Places
Saulieu
Corbigny
17
Brinon-s.-B.
Herry
Les Bertins
Ardan
Vauclaix
Montsauche
St-Révérien
La Charité-s.-Loire
Premery
Nièvre
L'Huis-Picard
Lac des Settons
Sancergues
Poiseux
Planchez
St-Saulge
58
Aunay-en-Bazois
Pougues-les-Eaux
Guérigny
Châtillon-en-B.
Anost
Lucenay-l'Évêque
Varennes-Vauzelles
Bona
Château-Chinon
La Petite-Verrière
Fourchambault
Nevers
Rouy
Tammay-en-Bazois
La Guerche-s.-l'Aubois
St-Bénin-d'Azy
Moulins-Engilbert
Autun
St-Léger-s/s-Beuvray
Challuy
Imphy
Vandenesse
St-Honoré-les-Bains
Étang-s.-Arroux
La Machine
Maison-de-Bourgogne
Cercy-la-Tour
Sancoins
La Chèvre
Decize
Luzy
Fours
St-Pierre-le-Moûtier
St-Hilaire-Fontaine
Neuville-lès-Decize
Canal latéral à la Loire
Saône-et-Loire
Le Veurdre
Lurcy-Lévis
Dornes
Cronat
Limoise
Lucenay-lès-Aix
111
Issy-l'Évêque
Toulon-s.-Arroux
Villeneuve-s.-Allier
Maltat
Couleuvre
Franchesse
78
Bourbon-Lancy
71
Perrecy-les-Forges
79
Chevagnes
Gueugnon
Bourbon-l'Archambault
St-Menoux
Yzeure
St-Aubin-s.-Loire
Moulins
Ygrande
Souvigny
St-Agnan
Dompierre-s.-Besbre
Digoin
Neuilly-le-Réal
Saligny-s.-Roudon
Vaumas
Paray-le-Monial
Bessay-s.-Allier
St-Yan
Chavenon
Le Montet
Châtel-de-Neuvre
Liernolles
Jaligny-s.-B.
Allier
Le Donjon
Bransat
Chazeuil
Neuilly-en-Donjon
Varennes-s.-Allier
03
Trézelles
25
Chambilly
Marcigny
St-Pourçain-s.-Sioule
St-Gérand-le-Puy
Lapalisse
Loire
Yonne
Cure
Cousin
Serein
Armançon
Ouanne
Allier
Besbre
Acolin
Bourbince
Arroux
Arconce

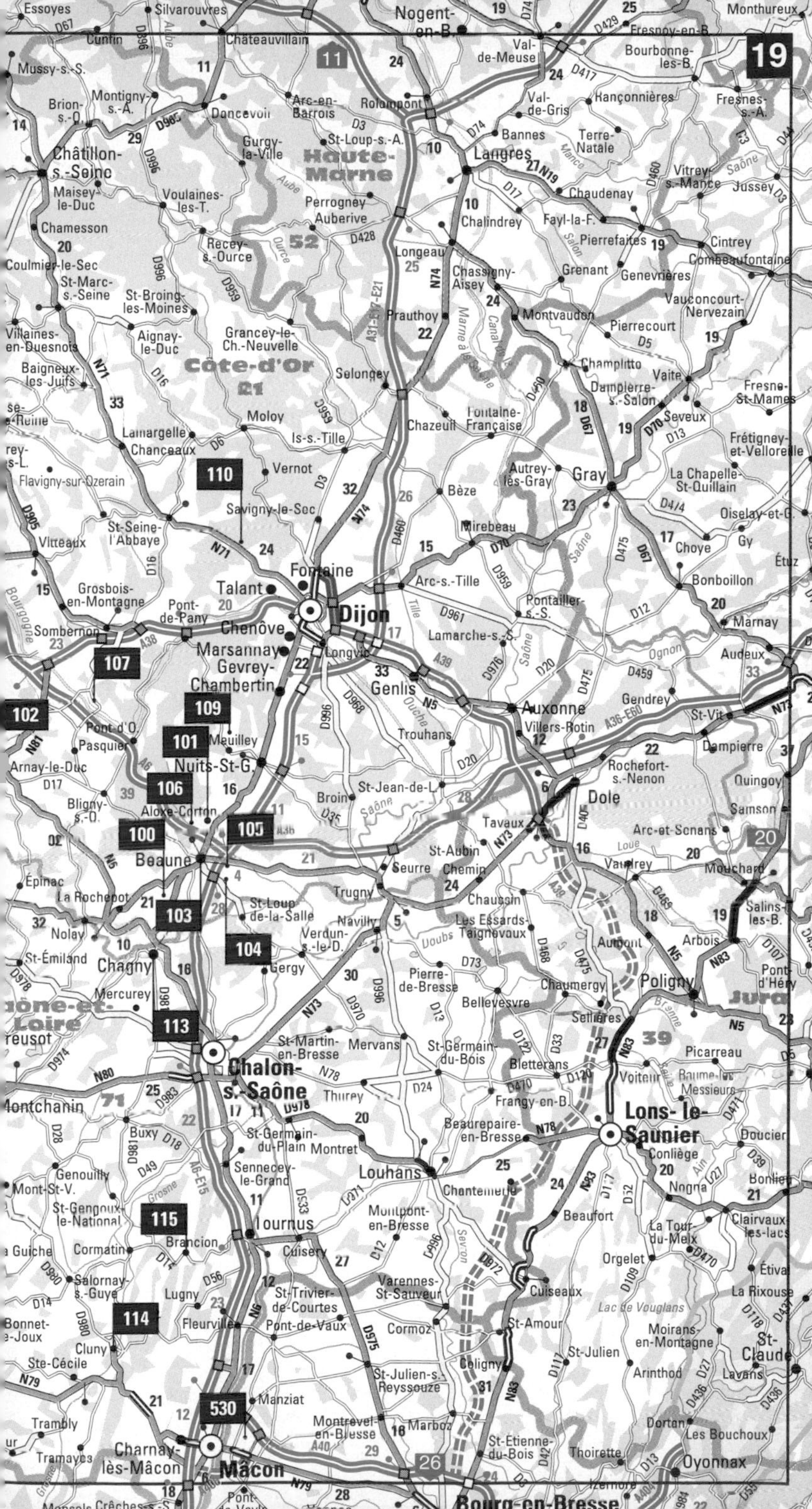
19
Essoyes
Silvarouvres
Nogent-en-B.
Monthureux
Cunfin
Châteauvillain
Val-de-Meuse
Fresnoy-en-B.
Bourbonne-les-B.
Mussy-s.-S.
Montigny-s.-A.
Arc-en-Barrois
Rolampont
Val-de-Gris
Rançonnières
Fresnes-s.-A.
Brion-s.-O.
Dancevoir
St-Loup-s.-A.
Bannes
Terre-Natale
Châtillon-s.-Seine
Gurgy-la-Ville
Haute-Marne
Langres
Vitrey-s.-Mance
Jussey
Maisey-le-Duc
Voulaines-les-T.
Perrogney
Auberive
Chaudenay
Chamesson
Chalindrey
Fayl-la-F.
Pierrefaites
Cintrey
Recey-s.-Ource
52
Longeau
Combeaufontaine
Coulmier-le-Sec
St-Marc-s.-Seine
Chassigny-Aisey
Grenant
Genevrières
St-Broing-les-Moines
Vauconcourt-Nervezain
Prauthoy
Montvaudon
Pierrecourt
Villaines-en-Duesnois
Aignay-le-Duc
Grancey-le-Ch.-Neuvelle
Côte-d'Or
21
Baigneux-les-Juifs
Selongey
Champlitte
Vaite
Dampierre-s.-Salon
Fresne-St-Mamès
Moloy
Chazeuil
Fontaine-Française
Seveux
Lamargelle
Chanceaux
Is-s.-Tille
Frétigney-et-Velloreille
Vernot
Autrey-lès-Gray
Gray
La Chapelle-St-Quillain
Flavigny-sur-Ozerain
110
Bèze
Savigny-le-Sec
Mirebeau
Oiselay-et-G.
St-Seine-l'Abbaye
Vitteaux
Choye
Gy
Étuz
Fontaine
Talant
Arc-s.-Tille
Bonboillon
Grosbois-en-Montagne
Pont-de-Pany
Dijon
Pontailler-s.-S.
Marnay
Sombernon
Chenôve
Lamarche-s.-S.
Audeux
107
Marsannay
Gevrey-Chambertin
Longvic
Genlis
Auxonne
Gendrey
St-Vit
102
109
Trouhans
Villers-Rotin
Dampierre
Pont-d'O.
Pasquier
101
Meuilley
Rochefort-s.-Nenon
Arnay-le-Duc
Nuits-St-G.
Quingey
Bligny-s.-O.
106
Aloxe-Corton
St-Jean-de-L.
Broin
Dole
Samson
100
105
Tavaux
Arc-et-Senans
Beaune
St-Aubin
Chemin
Seurre
Vaudrey
Mouchard
20
Épinac
La Rochepot
Trugny
Chaussin
Salins-les-B.
Nolay
103
St-Loup-de-la-Salle
Navilly
Les Essards-Taignevaux
Verdun-s.-le-D.
Aumont
Arbois
St-Émiland
104
Chagny
Gergy
Pierre-de-Bresse
Poligny
Pont-d'Héry
Mercurey
Bellevesvre
Chaumergy
Jura
Saône-et-Loire
113
Sellières
Creusot
Chalon-s.-Saône
St-Martin-en-Bresse
Mervans
St-Germain-du-Bois
39
Picarreau
Bletterans
Voiteur
Baume-les-Messieurs
Montchanin
71
Thurey
Frangy-en-B.
Lons-le-Saunier
Buxy
St-Germain-du-Plain
Montret
Beaurepaire-en-Bresse
Doucier
Conliège
Genouilly
Senneceyle-Grand
Louhans
Chantemerle
Mont-St-V.
St-Gengoux-le-National
115
Montpont-en-Bresse
Beaufort
Nogna
Bonlieu
Clairvaux-les-lacs
Tournus
Brancion
La Guiche
Cormatin
Cuisery
La Tour-du-Meix
Orgelet
Étival
Salornay-s.-Guye
Lugny
St-Trivier-de-Courtes
Varennes-St-Sauveur
Cuiseaux
La Rixouse
Lac de Vouglans
Bonnet-le-Joux
114
Fleurville
Pont-de-Vaux
Cormoz
St-Amour
Moirans-en-Montagne
St-Claude
Cluny
Ste-Cécile
St-Julien
Coligny
St-Julien-s.-Reyssouze
Arinthod
Lavans
Trambly
530
Manziat
Montrevel-en-Bresse
Marboz
Dortan
Les Bouchoux
Charnay-lès-Mâcon
Tramayes
St-Etienne-du-Bois
Thoirette
Oyonnax
Mâcon
26
Izernore
Crêches-s.-S.
Pont-de-Veyle
Bourg-en-Bresse
Saône
Ognon
Doubs
Loue
Aube
Ource
Tille
Ouche
Seille
Sevron
Ain
Grosne
Mance
Salon
Bourgogne
Canal de la Marne à la Saône

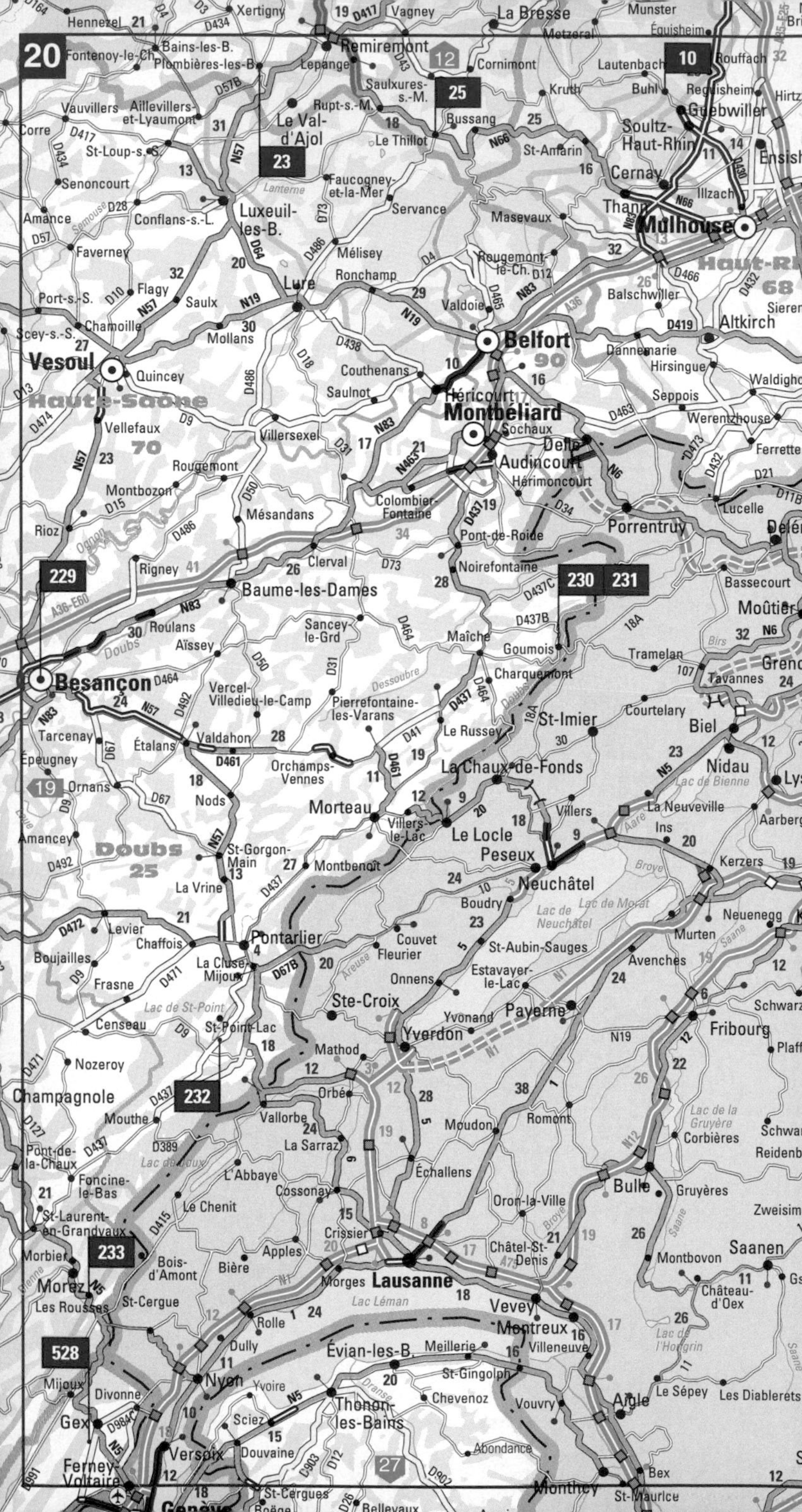
20
Vesoul
Haute-Saône
70
Luxeuil-les-B.
Lure
Belfort
90
Montbéliard
Héricourt
Mulhouse
Haut-Rhin
68
Remiremont
Le Val-d'Ajol
Besançon
Doubs
25
Baume-les-Dames
Pontarlier
Morteau
La Chaux-de-Fonds
Le Locle
Neuchâtel
Biel
Porrentruy
Yverdon
Lausanne
Vevey
Montreux
Fribourg
Bulle
Payerne
Nyon
Thonon-les-Bains
Évian-les-B.
Aigle
Monthey
Champagnole
Morez
Gex
Ferney-Voltaire
Versoix
Lac Léman
Lac de Neuchâtel
Lac de Bienne
Lac de St-Point
229
230
231
232
233
528
23
25
10
12
19
27

21
10
12
13
Freiburg-im-Breisgau
Neustadt-Schwarzwald
Hüfingen
Rouffach
Neuf-Brisach
Fessenheim
Bad-Krozingen
Staufen-im-Breisgau
Titisee
Rötenbach
Blumberg
Bonndorf
Guebwiller
Ensisheim
Hirtzfelden
Chalampé
Müllheim
Todtnau
Bernau
Schluch See
Ottmarsheim
Schliengen
Schönau-im-Schwarzw.
Todtmoos
Häusern
Mulhouse
Illzach
Haut-Rhin
68
Kembs
Kandern
Zell-im-Wiesental
Bannholz
Tiengen
Waldshut
Schopfheim
Lörrach
Wehr
Laufenburg
Sierentz
Altkirch
St-Louis
Rheinfelden
Döttingen
Hirsingue
Waldigholen
Basel
Bülach
Suppois
Reinach
Liestal
Gelterkinden
Sissach
Frick
Brugg
Baden
Kloten
Ferrette
Schlieren
Zürich
Lucelle
Laufen
Oberdorf
Aarau
Lenzburg
Suhr
Wohlen
Adliswil
Delémont
Olten
Aarburg
Zofingen
Séon
Muri
Bassecourt
Balsthal
Niederbipp
Murgenthal
Triengen
Moûtier
Dagmersellen
Cham
Solothurn
Langenthal
Hochdorf
Zug
Grenchen
Sursee
Tavannes
Biberist
Ettiswil
Biel
Utzenstorf
Huttwil
Willisau-Stadt
Ruswil
Luzern
Nidau
Lyss
Kirchberg
Burgdorf
Arth
Lac de Bienne
La Neuveville
Aarberg
Sumiswald
Ramsel
Gersau
Ins
Zollikofen
Bollingen
Stans
Kerzers
Langnau
Bern
Worb
Sarnen
Neuenegg
Köniz
Wigen
Eggiwil
Konolfingen
Murten
Belp
Münsingen
Schwarzenburg
Fribourg
Thun
Niederred
Meiringen
Plaffeien
Thuner-See
Spiez
Interlaken
Wimmis
Lac de la Gruyère
Corbières
Schwarzsee
Oberwil
Reidenbach
Lauterbrunnen
Frutigen
Gruyères
Zweisimmen
SUISSE
Saanen
Montbovon
Gstaad
Adelboden
Kandersteg
Château-d'Oex
Lac de l'Hongrin
Leukerbad Louèche
Rhône
Brig-Glis
Leuk
Le Sépey
Les Diablerets
Sierre
Visp
Stalden
Sion
Bex
St-Niklaus

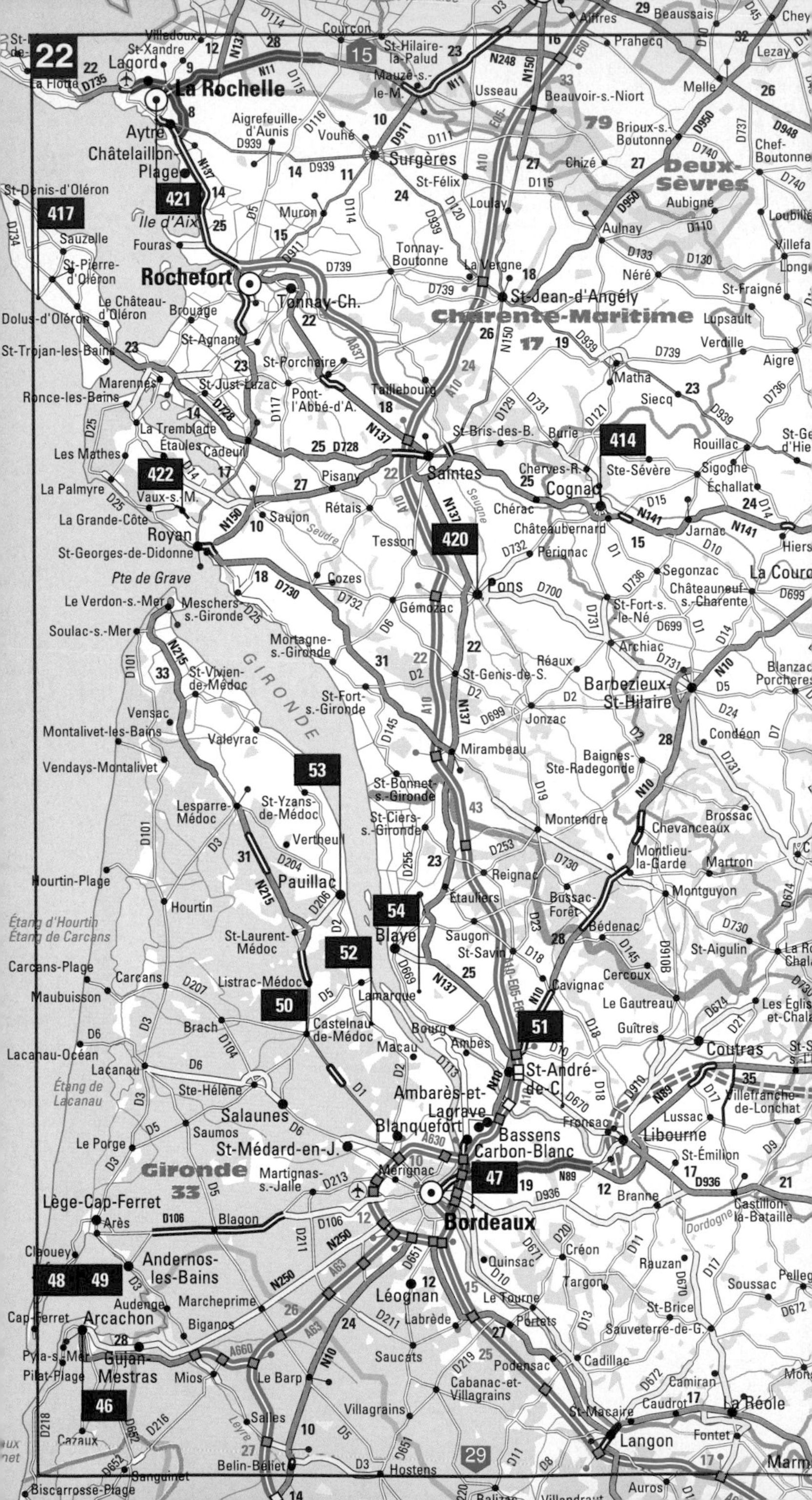
22
La Rochelle
Lagord
Aytré
Châtelaillon-Plage
Rochefort
Tonnay-Ch.
Surgères
St-Jean-d'Angély
Charente-Maritime
Deux-Sèvres
Saintes
Cognac
Royan
Pons
Barbezieux-St-Hilaire
Jonzac
Blaye
Pauillac
Libourne
Bordeaux
Arcachon
Langon
La Réole
Coutras
Gironde
Gironde
Andernos-les-Bains
Lège-Cap-Ferret
Gujan-Mestras
Mérignac
Blanquefort
Carbon-Blanc
Bassens
St-Médard-en-J.
Salaunes
Léognan
Lacanau
Lesparre-Médoc
Soulac-s.-Mer
Le Verdon-s.-Mer
Marennes
St-Georges-de-Didonne
Ile d'Aix
Fouras
Niort
Beauvoir-s.-Niort
Melle
Matha
Jarnac
Segonzac
Châteauneuf-s.-Charente
Archiac
Mirambeau
Montendre
Montguyon
St-Émilion
Castillon-la-Bataille
Branne
Créon
Cadillac
Podensac
St-Macaire
Belin-Béliet
Salles
Biscarrosse-Plage

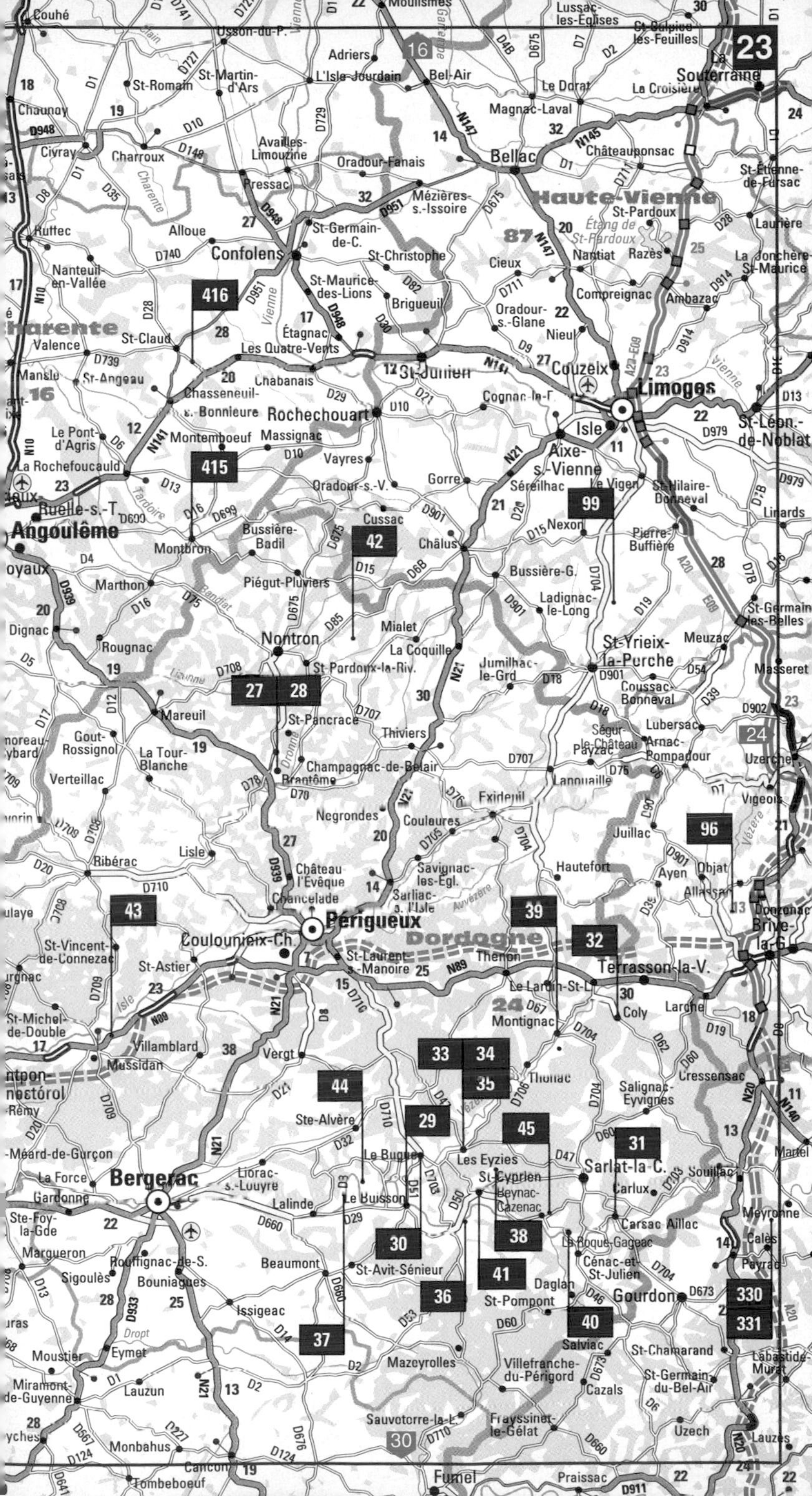

23
Couhé
Usson-du-P.
Moulismes
Lussac-les-Eglises
St-Sulpice-les-Feuilles
La Souterraine
Adriers
L'Isle-Jourdain
Bel-Air
Le Dorat
La Croisière
St-Romain
St-Martin-d'Ars
Magnac-Laval
Chaunay
Availles-Limouzine
Civray
Charroux
Oradour-Fanais
Bellac
Châteauponsac
St-Étienne-de-Fursac
Pressac
Mézières-s.-Issoire
Haute-Vienne
St-Pardoux
Laurière
Ruffec
Alloue
St-Germain-de-C.
Étang de St-Pardoux
Confolens
St-Christophe
Nantiat
Razès
La Jonchère-St-Maurice
Nanteuil-en-Vallée
Cieux
St-Maurice-des-Lions
Brigueuil
Compreignac
Ambazac
Charente
Oradour-s.-Glane
Étagnac
Nieul
St-Claud
Valence
Les Quatre-Vents
St-Junien
Couzeix
Mansle
St-Angeau
Chabanais
Limoges
Chasseneuil-s.-Bonnieure
Cognac-la-F.
Rochechouart
Isle
St-Léon.-de-Noblat
Le Pont-d'Agris
Montemboeuf
Massignac
Aixe-s.-Vienne
La Rochefoucauld
Vayres
Gorre
Séreilhac
Le Vigen
St-Hilaire-Bonneval
Oradour-s.-V.
Ruelle-s.-T.
Cussac
Nexon
Linards
Angoulême
Bussière-Badil
Châlus
Pierre-Buffière
Montbron
Marthon
Piégut-Pluviers
Bussière-G.
Ladignac-le-Long
St-Germain-les-Belles
Dignac
Nontron
Mialet
St-Yrieix-la-Perche
Meuzac
Rougnac
La Coquille
St-Pardoux-la-Riv.
Jumilhac-le-Grd
Masseret
Coussac-Bonneval
Mareuil
St-Pancrace
Thiviers
Ségur-le-Château
Lubersac
Gout-Rossignol
La Tour-Blanche
Payzac
Arnac-Pompadour
Uzerche
Verteillac
Brantôme
Champagnac-de-Belair
Lanouaille
Negrondes
Couleures
Exideuil
Vigeois
Juillac
Lisle
Hautefort
Ribérac
Château l'Évêque
Savignac-les-Egl.
Ayen
Objat
Allassac
Chancelade
Sarliac-s. l'Isle
Périgueux
Donzenac
Coulounieix-Ch.
Dordogne
Brive-la-G.
St-Vincent-de-Connezac
St-Laurent-s.-Manoire
Thenon
Terrasson-la-V.
St-Astier
Le Lardin-St-L.
Coly
Larche
St-Michel-de-Double
Montignac
Villamblard
Mussidan
Vergt
Thonac
Cressensac
Salignac-Eyvignes
Ste-Alvère
Le Bugue
Les Eyzies
Sarlat-la-C.
Souillac
St-Méard-de-Gurçon
St-Cyprien
Martel
La Force
Bergerac
Liorac-s.-Louyre
Beynac-Cazenac
Carlux
Gardonne
Lalinde
Le Buisson
Carsac Aillac
Meyronne
Ste-Foy-la-Gde
Margueron
La Roque-Gageac
Calès
Rouffignac-de-S.
Beaumont
St-Avit-Sénieur
Cénac-et-St-Julien
Payrac
Sigoulès
Bouniagues
Daglan
Gourdon
Issigeac
St-Pompont
Salviac
Eymet
Moustier
Mazeyrolles
Villefranche-du-Périgord
St-Chamarand
Labastide-Murat
Miramont-de-Guyenne
Lauzun
Cazals
St-Germain-du-Bel-Air
Sauveterre-la-L.
Frayssinet-le-Gélat
Uzech
Monbahus
Lauzès
Cancon
Tombeboeuf
Fumel
Praissac
416
415
42
99
27
28
96
43
39
32
33
34
35
44
29
45
31
30
38
41
36
40
37
330
331

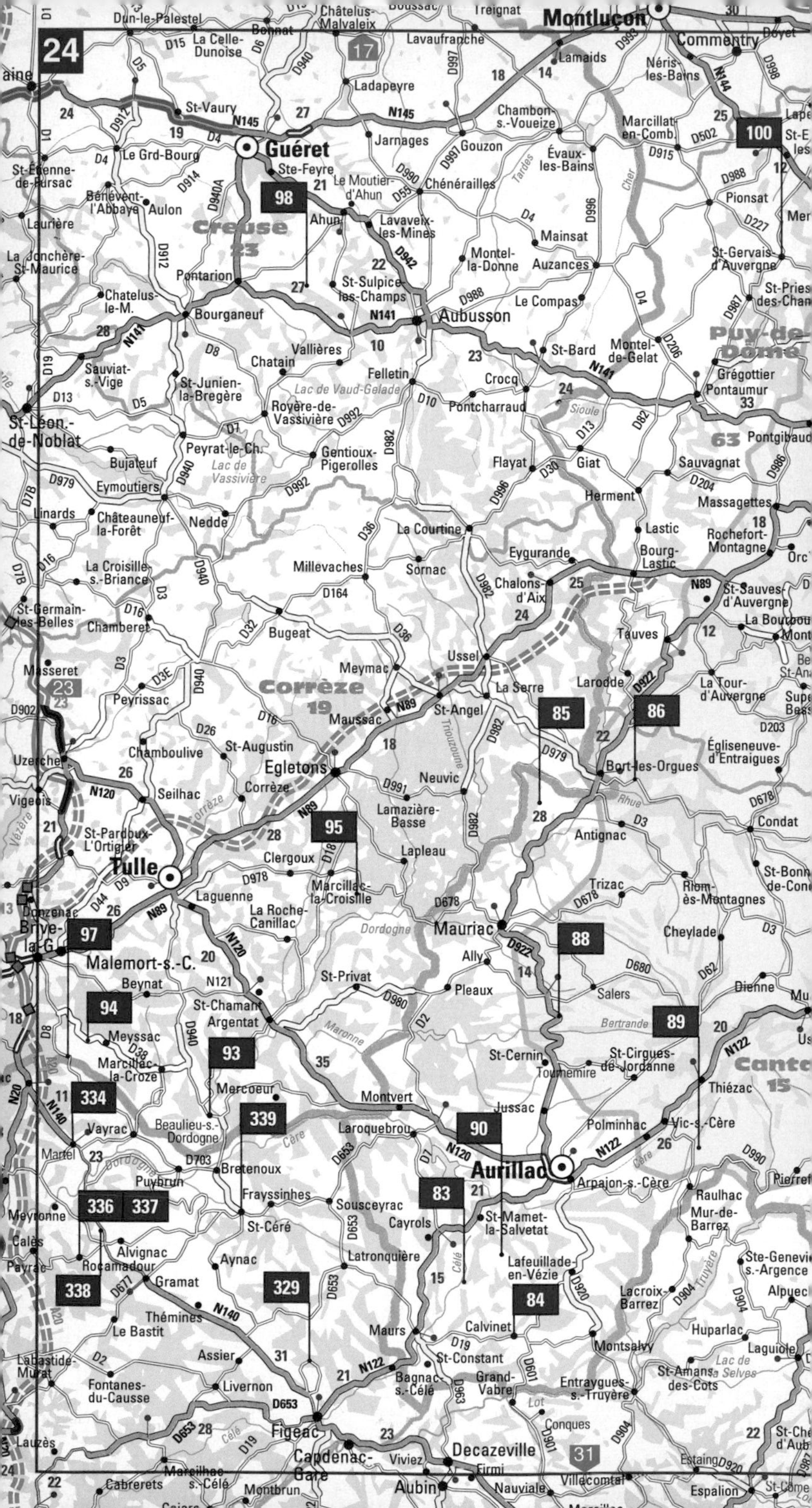

24
Montluçon
Commentry
Guéret
Creuse
23
Aubusson
Puy-de-Dôme
63
Corrèze
19
Ussel
Egletons
Tulle
Brive-la-G.
Mauriac
Aurillac
Cantal
15
Figeac
Decazeville
Bort-les-Orgues
Lac de Vassivière
Lac de Vaud-Gelade
Dordogne
100
98
85
86
95
97
94
93
88
89
90
83
84
334
339
336
337
338
329
17
31
23

25
81
112
18
91
92
26
32
Bransat
Chazeuil
Varennes-s.-Allier
03
Trézelles
Le Donjon
Neuilly-en-Donjon
Matour
St-Pourçain-s.-Sioule
St-Gérand-le-Puy
Lapalisse
Chambilly
Marcigny
La Clayette
La Chapelle-s/s-Dun
Chantelle
Brout-Vernet
St-Martin-d'Estreaux
La Pacaudière
Chauffailles
Charroux
Châtel-Montagne
Charlieu
Belmont-de-la-L.
Vichy
Cusset
St-Germain-Lespinasse
Pouilly-s/s-Charlieu
Gannat
Le Mayet-de-Montagne
St-Haon-Châtel
Mably
Roanne
Cours-la-Ville
Aigueperse
St-Yorre
Riorges
Le Côteau
Thizy
Randan
Ferrières-s.-S.
St-Priest-Laprugne
Amplepuis
Thuret
Limons
Regny
Puy-Guillaume
St-Just-en-Chev.
St-Polgues
St-Symphorien-de-Lay
Valsonne
Ennezat
Maringues
Chabreloche
Tarare
Joze
Thiers
Crézolles
Néronde
Clermont-Ferrand
Lezoux
Pont-de-Dore
Noirétable
St-Germain-Laval
Balbigny
Courpière
Loire 42
Panissières
Cournon-d'Auv.
Vollore-Montagne
Sail-s/s-C.
Boën
Feurs
Billom
Augerolles
Chalmazel
Ste-Foy-l'A.
St-Dier-D'A.
Olliergues
St-Georges-en-Couzan
Chazelles-s.-L.
Vic-le-Comte
Manglieu
Cunlhat
Bertignat
Montrond-les-B.
Montbrison
St-Galmier
Champeix
St-Amant-Roche-Savine
Ambert
Veauche
Perrier
Issoire
Sauxillanges
St-Anthème
Sury-le-Comtal
St-Étienne
Marsac-en-Livradois
St-Martin-des-Olmes
St-Jean-Soleymieux
Andrézieux-Bouthéon
Lac de Grangent
St-Germain-Lembron
Auzat
St-Germain-l'Herm
St-Just
Viverols
St-Bonnet-le-Château
Arlanc
Usson-en-Forez
Firminy
Ardes
Anzat-le-Luguet
Lempdes
Auzon
Champagnac-le-Vieux
Craponne-s.-Arzon
Monistrol-s.-Loire
Bas-en-Basset
St-Genest-Malifaux
La Chaise-Dieu
Brioude
Vieille-Brioude
Massiac
Haute-Loire 43
Bellevue-la-Mgne
Retournac
Riotord
Villeneuve-d'Allier
Paulhaguet
Vorey
Montfaucon-en-Velay
La Chapelle-Laurent
Fix-St-Geneys
St-Paulien
Tence
St-Bonnet-le-Froid
Vieillespesse
Lavoûte-Chilhac
Lavoûte-s.-L.
Yssingeaux
Langeac
Le Pertuis
Le Chambon-s.-Lignon
Loudes
Pinols
Le Puy-en-Velay
St-Julien-Chapteuil
St-Agrève
St-Flour
Ruynes-en-Margeride
Fay-s.-Lignon
St-Julien-Boutières
Montagnac
Faverolles
Monistrol-d'Allier
Saugues
Cayres
Le Monastier-s.-Gazeille
Paulhac-en-Margeride
Esplantas
Arlempdes
Le Cheylard
Chaudes-Aigues
Le Malzieu-Ville
Landos
Le Béage
Ancette
Mézilhac
Laval-Atger
St-Chély-d'Apcher
Lozère 48
St-Alban-s.-Limagnole
Grandrieu
Lanarce
Aumont-Aubrac
Langogne
Chastanier
Lesperon
Montpezat-s/s-Bauzon
Serverette
La Villedieu
St-Flour-de-Mercoire
Thueyts
Vals-les-Bains
Malbouzon
St-Amans
Ribennes
Rieutort-de-Randon
Châteauneuf-de-Randon
St-Étienne-de-Lugdarès
Aubenas
Valgorge
Marvejols
Pelouse
Belvezet
La Bastide-Puylaurent
Largentière
Sablières
Mende
Chirac
Barjac
Bagnols-les-Bains
Prévenchères
Allier
Dore
Ance
Truyère
Lignon
Loire

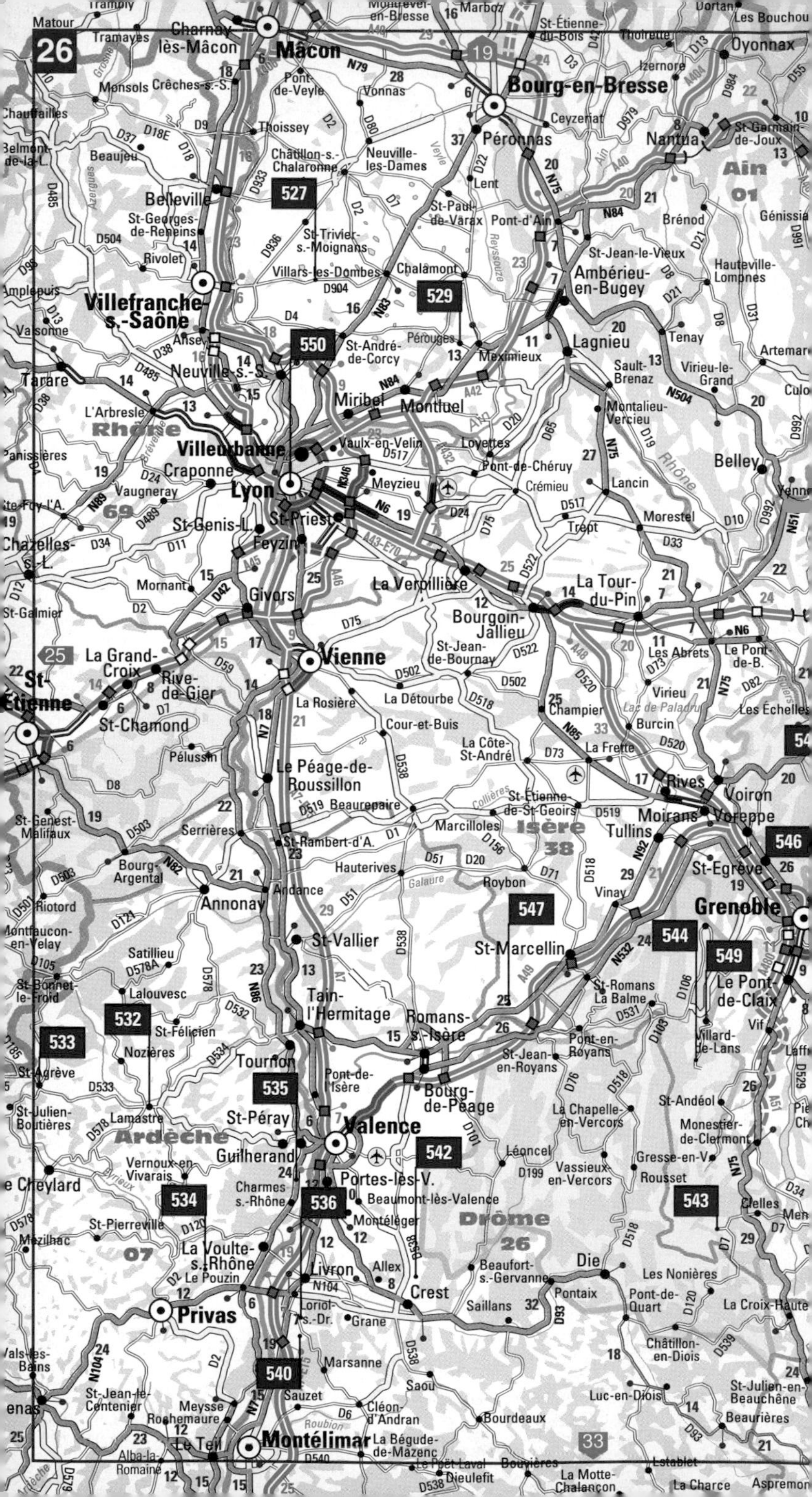
Mâcon
Bourg-en-Bresse
Oyonnax
Nantua
Péronnas
Ain
01
Villefranche-s.-Saône
Belleville
Châtillon-s.-Chalaronne
Villars-les-Dombes
Ambérieu-en-Bugey
Lagnieu
Meximieux
Miribel
Montluel
Villeurbanne
Lyon
Rhône
69
St-Priest
Feyzin
Givors
La Verpillière
Bourgoin-Jallieu
La Tour-du-Pin
Belley
Vienne
St-Etienne
St-Chamond
Rive-de-Gier
Tarare
L'Arbresle
Le Péage-de-Roussillon
Annonay
Isère
38
Voiron
Rives
Moirans
Voreppe
Tullins
Grenoble
St-Egrève
Le Pont-de-Claix
St-Marcellin
St-Vallier
Tain-l'Hermitage
Tournon
Romans-s.-Isère
Bourg-de-Péage
Valence
Guilherand
St-Péray
Portes-lès-V.
Ardèche
07
Privas
La Voulte-s.-Rhône
Livron
Crest
Die
Drôme
26
Montélimar
Le Teil
Roybon
Vinay
527
529
550
547
544
549
546
532
533
534
535
536
540
542
543
19
25
33

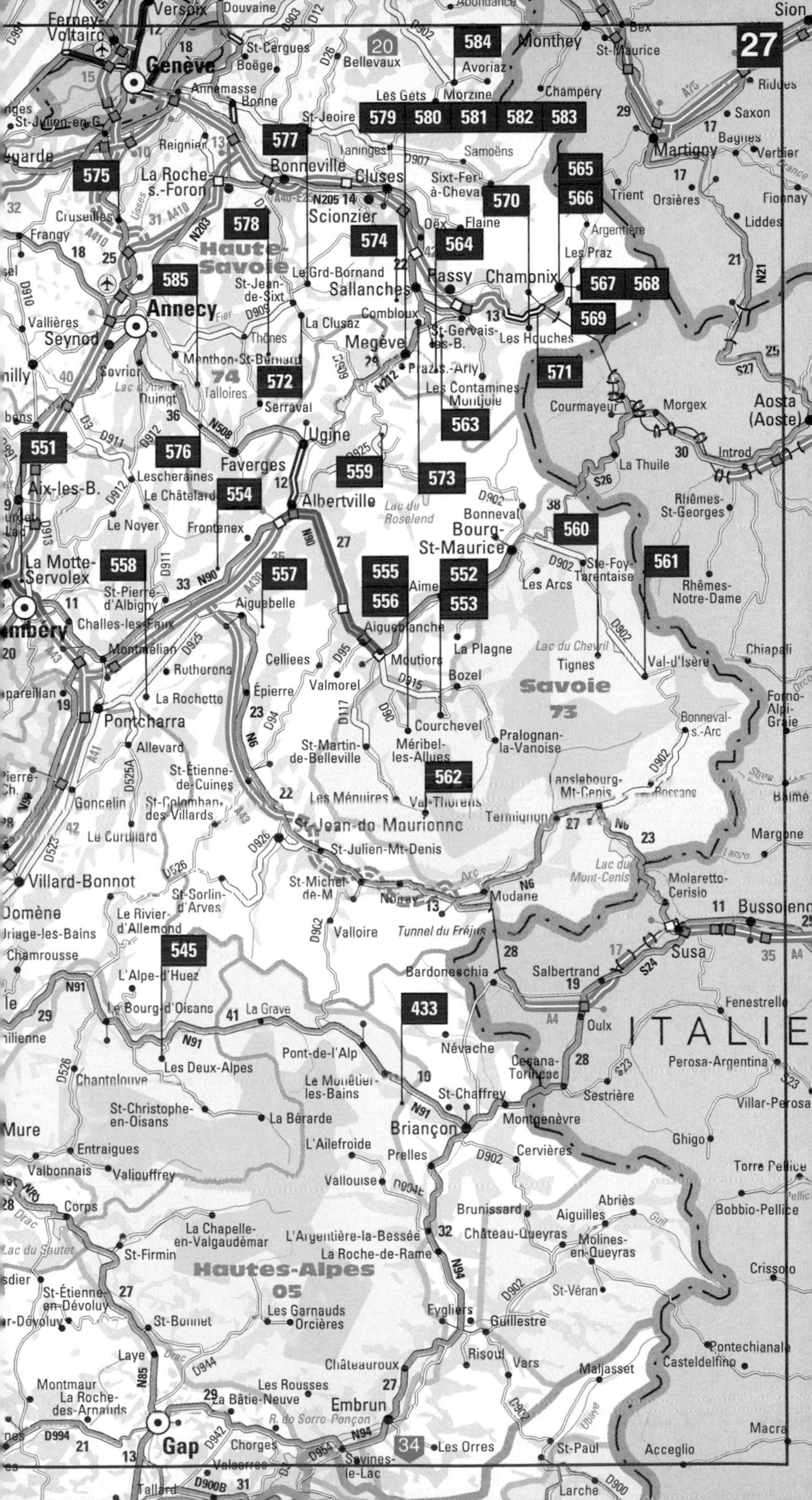

27
Versoix
Douvaine
Abondance
Sion
Ferney-Voltaire
Genève
Annemasse
Bonne
St-Cergues
Boëge
Bellevaux
20
584
Avoriaz
Monthey
Bex
St-Maurice
Morzine
Les Gets
Champéry
Riddes
Saxon
St-Jeoire
579
580
581
582
583
Martigny
Bagnes
Verbier
Reignier
577
Taninges
Samoëns
St-Julien-en-G.
575
La Roche-s.-Foron
Bonneville
Cluses
Sixt-Fer-à-Cheval
565
566
Trient
Orsières
Fionnay
Cruseilles
Frangy
Scionzier
570
Flaine
Liddes
578
Haute-Savoie
574
Oëx
564
Argentière
Les Praz
Le Grd-Bornand
Passy
Chamonix
Sallanches
St-Jean-de-Sixt
585
Annecy
567
568
569
La Clusaz
Combloux
St-Gervais-les-B.
Les Houches
Vallières
Seynod
Megève
Praz-s.-Arly
Thônes
Menthon-St-Bernard
572
571
Sevrier
74
Les Contamines-Montjoie
Lac d'Annecy
Duingt
Talloires
Serraval
Courmayeur
Morgex
Aosta (Aoste)
563
Ugine
551
576
Introd
Faverges
Aix-les-B.
Lescheraines
559
573
La Thuile
Le Châtelard
554
Albertville
Lac de Roselend
Rhêmes-St-Georges
Bonneval
Le Noyer
Frontenex
Bourg-St-Maurice
560
La Motte-Servolex
558
555
552
Ste-Foy-Tarentaise
561
557
Aime
Les Arcs
Rhêmes-Notre-Dame
St-Pierre-d'Albigny
556
553
Aiguebelle
Aigueblanche
Chambéry
Challes-les-Eaux
La Plagne
Montmélian
Lac du Chevril
Chiapali
Moûtiers
Celliees
Tignes
Val-d'Isère
Rotherens
Valmorel
Bozel
La Rochette
Épierre
Savoie
73
Pontcharra
Courchevel
Fono-Alpi-Graie
Allevard
St-Martin-de-Belleville
Méribel-les-Allues
Pralognan-la-Vanoise
Bonneval-s.-Arc
St-Étienne-de-Cuines
562
Goncelin
St-Colomban-des-Villards
Les Ménuires
Val-Thorens
Lanslebourg-Mt-Cenis
Bessans
Balme
Le Curtillard
St-Jean-de-Maurienne
Termignon
Margone
St-Julien-Mt-Denis
Lac du Mont-Cenis
Villard-Bonnot
St-Sorlin-d'Arves
St-Michel-de-M.
Modane
Molaretto-Cerisio
Domène
Le Rivier-d'Allemond
Valloire
Tunnel du Fréjus
Bussoleno
Uriage-les-Bains
Chamrousse
545
Susa
Bardonecchia
Salbertrand
L'Alpe-d'Huez
Le Bourg-d'Oisans
La Grave
433
Fenestrelle
Oulx
ITALIE
Pont-de-l'Alp
Névache
Les Deux-Alpes
Cesana-Torinese
Perosa-Argentina
Chantelouve
Le Monêtier-les-Bains
St-Chaffrey
Sestrière
Villar-Perosa
St-Christophe-en-Oisans
La Bérarde
Briançon
Montgenèvre
La Mure
Entraigues
L'Ailefroide
Prelles
Cervières
Ghigo
Valbonnais
Valjouffrey
Vallouise
Torre Pellice
Corps
Brunissard
Abriès
Aiguilles
Bobbio-Pellice
La Chapelle-en-Valgaudémar
L'Argentière-la-Bessée
Château-Queyras
Molines-en-Queyras
Lac du Sautet
St-Firmin
La Roche-de-Rame
Hautes-Alpes
05
Crissolo
St-Étienne-en-Dévoluy
St-Véran
Les Garnauds
Orcières
Eygliers
Guillestre
St-Bonnet
Pontechianale
Laye
Risoul
Vars
Châteauroux
Maljasset
Casteldelfino
Montmaur
La Roche-des-Arnauds
Les Rousses
La Bâtie-Neuve
Embrun
R. de Serre Ponçon
Macra
Gap
Chorges
34
Les Orres
Savines-le-Lac
St-Paul
Acceglio
Valserres
Tallard
Larche

Étang de Biscarrosse
Étang d'Aureilhan
Mimizan-Plage
Contis-Plage
St-Julien-en-Born
Lit-et-Mixe
St-Girons-Plage
St-Girons-en-Marensin
Étang de Léon
Léon
Messanges
Étang de Soustons
Vieux-Boucau
Soustons
Lac Blanc-Bidouze
St-Geours-de-Maremne
Soorts-Hossegor
Hossegor
Capbreton
St-Vincent-de-Tyrosse
Labenne
Tarnos
Boucau
Bayonne
Anglet
Biarritz
Adour
Briscous
Bidart
Guéthary
St-Jean-de-Luz
Ciboure
Hendaye
Hasparren
La Bastide-Clairence
Urrugne
St-Pée-s.-N.
Cambo-les-B.
Ainhoa
Espelette
Louhossoa
Irun
Oyartzun
Dancharia
Bidarray
Vera-de-Bidasoa
Lesaca
Nive
Irouléguy
Bidasoa
Baztan
St-Étienne-de-Baïgorry
St-Jean-Pied-de-Port
Santesteban
Zubieta
Irurita
Aldudes
Arnéguy
Roncesvalles
Orbaiceta
Burguete
Eugui
Zubiri
Erro
Arrieta
Arive
Enderiz
Villava
Egüés
Urroz
Itoiz
Aoiz
Pamplona
Lekeitio
Ondarroa
San Sebastian
Markina
Deba
Alzola
Zestoa
Zarauz
Usurbil
Hernani
Elgoibar
Eibar
Santuario de S. Ignacio de Loyola
Andoain
Azpeitia
Villabona
Bergara
Régil
Goizueta
Tolosa
Arrasate-Mondragon
Villafranca-de-Ordizia
Beasain
Leiza
Ezcurra
Oñati
Eskoriatza
Arantzazu
Betelu
Lecumberri
Jaunsaras
Ulzama
Larasa
Villanueva
Echarri-Aranaz
Alsasua
Olazagutia
Anoz
Goni
Olza
Echauri
Salinas-de-Oro
Astrain
Ega
Irati
69
70
74
72
71
75
68
66
73
77
A8
A63
A15
N1
N10
N240
N240A
N121A
N121B
NA403
NA120
NA172
NA232
N135
C130
C135
D4
D12
D79
D255
D932
D918
GI 627
GI 632
GI2634
BI638

29
Mestras
Mios
Le Barp
Podensac
Cadillac
Monségur
Cabanac-et-Villagrains
Villagrains
22
St-Macaire
Caudrot
La Réole
Langon
Fontet
Marmande
Salles
Cazaux
Belin-Béliet
Hostens
Sanguinet
Biscarrosse-Plage
Balizac
Villandraut
Auros
Biscarrosse
St-Symphorien
Bazas
Bouglon
Préchac
Grignols
Gironde
33
Liposthey
Sore
Lucmau
Casteljaloux
Pissos
Callen
Captieux
Lerm-et-Musset
Luxey
St-Michel-de-Castelnau
Lot-et-Garonne
47
Pontenx-les-Forges
St-Paul-en-Born
Labouheyre
Trensacq
Fargues-s.-O.
Escource
Sabres
Allons
Houeillès
Durance
Labrit
Landes
40
60
Onesse-et-Laharie
Garein
Brocas
Lapeyrade
Morcenx
Roquefort
Sos
Ygos-St-Saturnin
Villenave
St-Justin
Créon-d'Armagnac
Gabarret
Rion-des-Landes
St-Martin-d'Oney
Labastide-d'Armagnac
Cazaubon
Castelnau-d'Auzan
Taller
Laluque
Mont-de-Marsan
Villeneuve-de-Marsan
Bougue
Estang
Eauze
Tartas
Meilhan
58
325
324
Pontonx-s.-l'Adour
Souprosse
Grenade-s.-l'Adour
Manciet
Péré
Le Houga
Dax
St-Paul-lès-Dax
St-Sever
Cazères-s.-l'Adour
323
Nogaro
Mugron
Urgosse
Hinx
Montfort-en-Chalosse
Eugénie-les-Bains
Aire-s.-l'Adour
Aignan
Hagetmau
Lupiac
Pomarez
Samadet
55
Geaune
St-Mont
Riscle
Cahuzac-s.-l'Adour
Pouillon
Habas
Tilh
Amou
56
30
Sault-de-Navailles
Monget
Sarron
Plaisance
57
Puyoô
Ramous
Garlin
Castelnau-Riv.-Basse
Bellocq
Orthez
Arzacq-Arraziguet
Cadillon
Marciac
Bidache
Salles-de-Béarn
Escos
Thèze
Sévignacq-Thèze
Maubourguet
Arthez-de-B.
Sauveterre-de-B.
Maslacq
Lacq
Artix
Lembeye
Villecomtal-s.-Arros
Vic-en-Bigorre
Garris
Mourenx
St-Jammes
Baleix
Rabastens-de-Bigorre
St-Palais
Charitte-de-Bas
Morlaàs
Sedzère
Montaner
Uhart-Mixe
67
Navarrenx
Moneinn
Lons
Billère
Pau
Andrest
Gelos
Soumoulou
Ibos
Aureilhan
Tarbes
St-Just-Ibarre
Mauléon-Licharre
L'Hôpital-St-Blaise
Oloron-Ste-M.
Lasseube
76
Pyrénées-Atlantiques
64
Mendive
Barcus
Nay-Bourdettes
Coarraze
Pontacq
Ossun
Tardets-Sorholus
Aramits
Ogeu
Rébénacq
St-Pé-de-Bigorre
Montgaillard
Arudy
Lourdes
Licq-Athérey
Montory
Arette
Asasp-Arros
Louvie-Juzon
Bielle
Larrau
Bagnères-de-Bigorre
Argelès-Gazost
Ferrières
Ste-Engrâce
Arette-Pierre-St-Martin
Bedous
Arbéost
Laruns
Eaux-Bonnes
Les Eaux-Chaudes
Gourette
Pierrefitte-Nestalas
Ste-Marie-de-Campan
Escaroz
Etsaut
Barèges
Isaba
Urdos
Artouste
Cauterets
La Mongie
Luz-St-Sauveur
Pont-d'Espagne
Güesa
A62-E09-E72
A64-E80
N10
N124
N134
N117
D932
D933
D934
D935
D626
D651

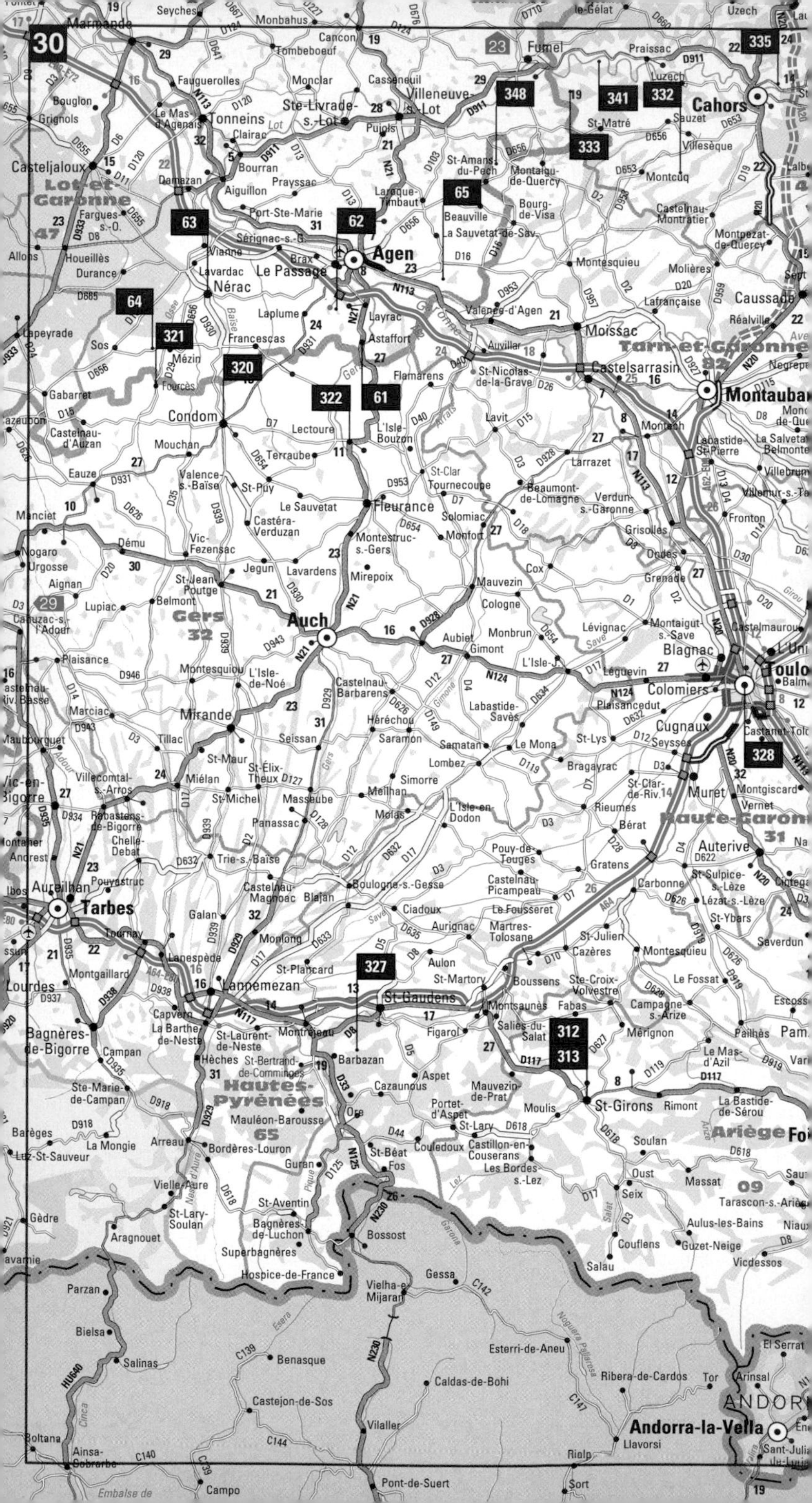
30
Marmande
Seyches
Monbahus
Cancon
Fumel
le-Gélat
Uzech
Tombeboeuf
Praissac
Luzech
Fauguerolles
Monclar
Casseneuil
Villeneuve-s.-Lot
Cahors
Bouglon
Grignols
Le Mas-d'Agenais
Tonneins
Ste-Livrade-s.-Lot
Pujols
St-Matré
Sauzet
Villesèque
Clairac
Lot
Casteljaloux
Damazan
Bourran
Aiguillon
Prayssac
St-Amans-du-Pech
Montaigu-de-Quercy
Montcuq
Lot-et-Garonne
47
Fargues-s.-O.
Port-Ste-Marie
Laroque-Timbaut
Beauville
Bourg-de-Visa
Castelnau-Montratier
Sérignac-s.-G.
La Sauvetat-de-Sav.
Montpezat-de-Quercy
Allons
Houeillès
Vianne
Brax
Agen
Durance
Lavardac
Le Passage
Montesquieu
Molières
Nérac
Caussade
Laplume
Layrac
Valence-d'Agen
Lafrançaise
Réalville
Lapeyrade
Francescas
Astaffort
Moissac
Sos
Mézin
Auvillar
Tarn-et-Garonne
82
Flamarens
St-Nicolas-de-la-Grave
Castelsarrasin
Montauban
Gabarret
Fourcès
Condom
Lectoure
L'Isle-Bouzon
Lavit
Montech
Castelnau-d'Auzan
Mouchan
Terraube
Larrazet
Labastide-St-Pierre
Eauze
Valence-s.-Baïse
St-Puy
St-Clar
Tournecoupe
Beaumont-de-Lomagne
Verdun-s.-Garonne
Villebrumier
Manciet
Le Sauvetat
Fleurance
Solomiac
Fronton
Castéra-Verduzan
Monfort
Grisolles
Nogaro
Urgosse
Dému
Vic-Fezensac
Montestruc-s.-Gers
Ondes
Aignan
Jegun
Lavardens
Mirepoix
Cox
Grenade
St-Jean-Poutge
Mauvezin
Lupiac
Belmont
Cologne
Cazaubon
Cauzac-s.-l'Adour
Gers
32
Auch
Aubiet
Monbrun
Lévignac
Montaigut-s.-Save
Castelmaurou
Gimont
Blagnac
Plaisance
Montesquiou
L'Isle-de-Noé
L'Isle-J.
Léguevin
Colomiers
Toulouse
Balma
Castelnau-Barbarens
Labastide-Savès
Plaisancedut
Marciac
Mirande
Héréchou
Cugnaux
Castanet-Tolosan
Maubourguet
Tillac
Seissan
Saramon
Samatan
Le Mona
St-Lys
Seysses
St-Maur
St-Élix-Theux
Lombez
Bragayrac
Villecomtal-s.-Arros
Miélan
Simorre
St-Clar-de-Riv.
Muret
Montgiscard
Vic-en-Bigorre
St-Michel
Masseube
Meilhan
Molas
L'Isle-en-Dodon
Rieumes
Vernet
Rabastens-de-Bigorre
Haute-Garonne
31
Chelle-Debat
Panassac
Bérat
Montaner
Andrest
Pouy-de-Touges
Auterive
Trie-s.-Baïse
Gratens
Pouyastruc
Castelnau-Magnoac
Boulogne-s.-Gesse
Castelnau-Picampeau
Carbonne
St-Sulpice-s.-Lèze
Cintegabelle
Aureilhan
Tarbes
Blajan
Lézat-s.-Lèze
Galan
Ciadoux
Le Fousseret
St-Ybars
Aurignac
Martres-Tolosane
Tournay
Monlong
St-Julien
Saverdun
Lanespède
Cazères
Montesquieu
Lourdes
Montgaillard
St-Plancard
Aulon
Le Fossat
Lannemezan
St-Martory
Boussens
Ste-Croix-Volvestre
St-Gaudens
Montsaunès
Fabas
Campagne-s.-Arize
Escosse
Capvern
La Barthe-de-Neste
Montréjeau
Figarol
Salies-du-Salat
Mérignon
Pailhès
Pamiers
Bagnères-de-Bigorre
St-Laurent-de-Neste
Campan
Barbazan
Le Mas-d'Azil
Hèches
St-Bertrand-de-Comminges
Aspet
Hautes-Pyrénées
65
Cazaunous
Mauvezin-de-Prat
Ste-Marie-de-Campan
Portet-d'Aspet
Moulis
St-Girons
Rimont
La Bastide-de-Sérou
Mauléon-Barousse
Ore
St-Lary
Barèges
La Mongie
Arreau
Bordères-Louron
Couledoux
Castillon-en-Couserans
Soulan
Ariège
Foix
Luz-St-Sauveur
St-Béat
Fos
Guran
Les Bordes-s.-Lez
Vielle-Aure
Oust
Massat
09
Seix
St-Aventin
Tarascon-s.-Ariège
Gèdre
St-Lary-Soulan
Aulus-les-Bains
Aragnouet
Bagnères-de-Luchon
Bossost
Couflens
Guzet-Neige
Superbagnères
Vicdessos
Salau
Hospice-de-France
Gessa
Parzan
Vielha-e-Mijaran
Bielsa
Esterri-de-Aneu
El Serrat
Salinas
Benasque
Ribera-de-Cardos
Tor
Arinsal
Caldas-de-Bohi
ANDORRA
Castejon-de-Sos
Vilaller
Andorra-la-Vella
Llavorsi
Boltana
Ainsa-Sobrarbe
Rialp
Sant-Julià-de-Lòria
Campo
Pont-de-Suert
Sort
Embalse de
348
341
332
335
333
65
63
62
64
321
320
322
61
328
327
312
313
23
29

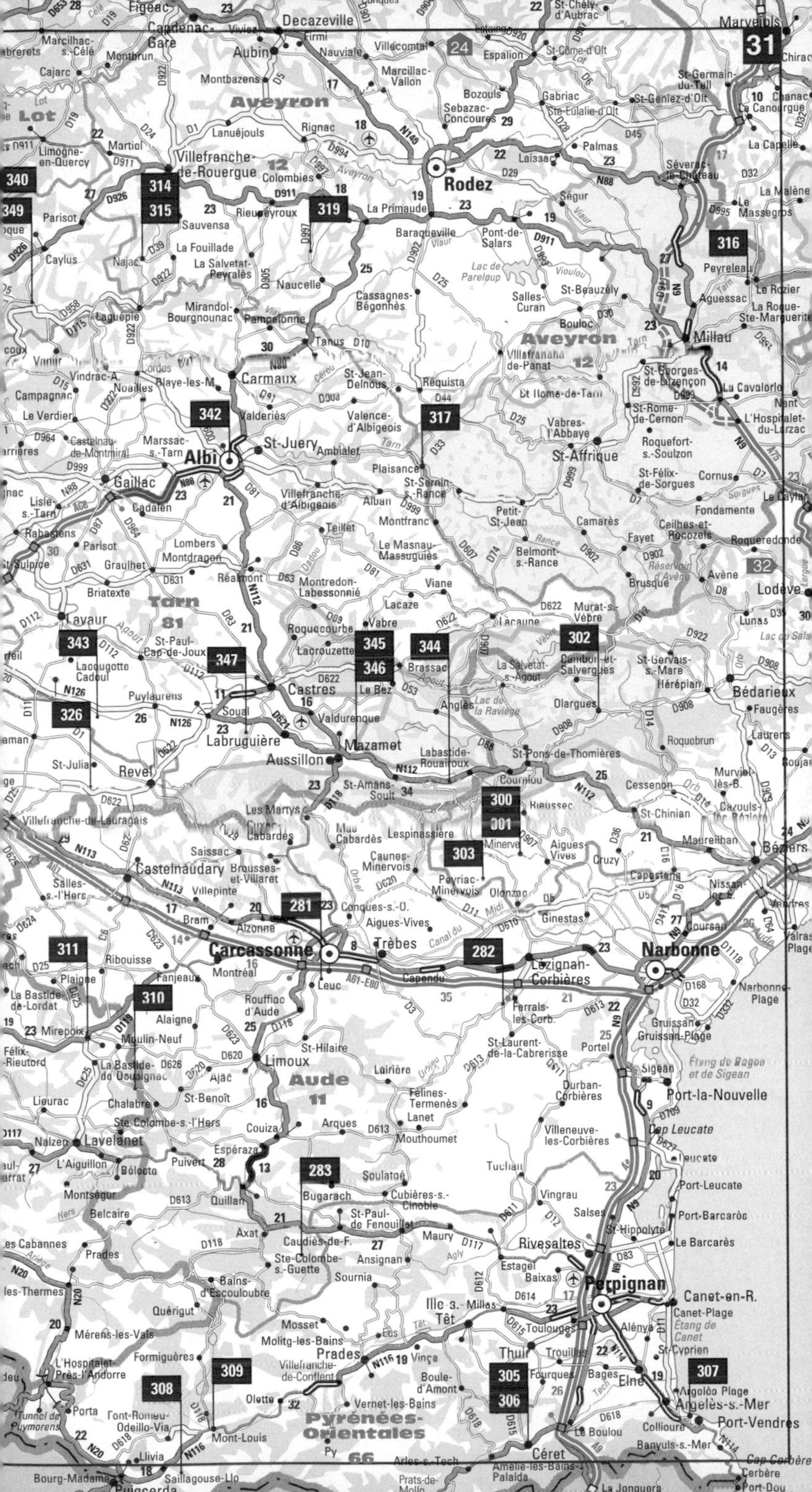

32
Malbouzon
Nasbinals
Serverette
La Villedieu
St-Amans
St-Flour-de-Mercoire
Thueyts
Vals
Ribennes
Rieutort-de-Randon
25
Châteauneuf-de-Randon
St-Étienne-de-Lugdarès
Aubenas
Pelouse
Valgorge
Marvejols
Belvezet
La Bastide-Puylaurent
Sablières
Largentière
Mende
Chirac
Barjac
Bagnols-les-Bains
Prévenchères
St-Germain-du-Teil
Balsièges
Le Bleymard
Altier
Joyeuse
St-Geniez-d'Olt
Chanac
La Canourgue
304
Lablachère
Ruoms
Lozère
Villefort
Les Vans
48
La Capelle
Ispagnac
Le Pont-de-Montvert
Séverac-le-Château
Ste-Enimie
St-Maurice-de-Ventalon
Génolhac
531
La Malène
St-Chély-du-Tarn
Florac
St-Julien-d'Arpaon
Le Massegros
Le Mazel
Ste-Cécile-d'Andorge
Bessèges
St-Ambroix
Barjac
316
La Parade
Barre-des-Cévennes
St-Germain-de-Calberte
La Grd-Combe
Peyreleau
Le Rozier
Meyrueis
St-Étienne-Vallée-Fr.
St-Martin-de-Val.
Navacelles
Aguessac
La Roque-Ste-Marguerite
St-André-de-Valborgne
Salindres
Millau
St-Jean-du-Gard
Alès
Seynes
Trèves
L'Estréchure
L'Espérou
Valleraugue
296
St-Georges-de-Luzençon
318
Gard
30
Anduze
Vézénobres
La Cavalerie
Nant
St-Jean-du-Bruel
Lasalle
291
292
St-Rome-de-Cernon
L'Hospitalet-du-Larzac
Sauclières
St-Hippolyte-du-Fort
Lédignan
Alzon
Le Vigan
St-Chaptes
Roquefort-s.-Soulzon
Montdardier
Ganges
Sauve
St-Félix-de-Sorgues
Cornus
Pompignan
Quissac
Montmirat
La Calmette
Le Caylar
St-Maurice-Navacelles
St-Bauzille-de-Putois
St-Mamert-du-Gard
Fondamente
Nîmes
Ceilhes-et-Rocozels
294
Roqueredonde
St-Pierre-de-la-Fage
299
Tréviers
Calvisson
St-Martin-de-Londres
Sommières
Galargues
Vergèze
Réservoir d'Avène
Avène
Boisseron
Brusque
31
Lodève
St-Guilhem-le-Désert
Viols-le-Fort
Les Matelles
Vauvert
Lunas
Castries
Lunel
Aimargues
Aniane
Montarnaud
Lac du Salagou
Clermont-l'Hérault
Gignac
Montpellier
Marsillargues
St-Gervais-s.-Mare
St-André-de-S.
Vendargues
Hérépian
Bédarieux
Juvignac
Hérault
34
St-Jean-de-Védas
Mauguio
Faugères
Paulhan
Fabrègues
Pérols
Aigues-Mortes
La Grande-Motte
Sylvéréal
Roquebrun
Laurens
Villeveyrac
Gigean
Palavas-les-Flots
Le Grau-du-Roi
Étang du Roi
Roujan
Montagnac
Murviel-lès-B.
Pézenas
Frontignan
Pointe de l'Espiguette
285
286
Cessenon
Cazouls-lès-Béziers
Golfe d'Aigues-Mortes
St-Chinian
Montblanc
St-Thibéry
Mèze
Sète
Maureilhan
Florensac
Béziers
Bassin de Thau
Bessan
Marseillan
Capestang
Vias
Nissan-lez-E.
Vendres
Agde
Le Cap-d'Agde
Cap d'Agde
Coursan
Valras-Plage
Narbonne
Narbonne-Plage
Gruissan
Gruissan-Plage
GOLFE DU LION
Étang de Bages et de Sigean
Sigean
Port-la-Nouvelle
Cap Leucate
Leucate
Port-Leucate

33
Marsanne
Saou
Châtillon-en-Diois
St-Julien-en-Beauchêne
Beaurières
Veynes
Aspres
Luc-en-Diois
St-Jean-le-Centenier
Meysse
Rochemaure
Sauzet
Cléon-d'Andran
Bourdeaux
Montélimar
Le Teil
Alba-la-Romaine
La Bégude-de-Mazenc
Le Poët-Laval
Dieulefit
Bouvières
La Motte-Chalançon
Establet
La Charce
Aspremont
Ardèche
Hautes-Alpes
Donzère
Grignan
Valréas
Rémuzat
Rosans
Serres
St-Remèze
Pierrelatte
St-Paul-Trois-Ch.
Nyons
Verclause
Montjay
Eyguians
Bourg-St-Andéol
St-Martin-d'A.
Drôme
Laragne-Montéglin
Bollène
Tulette
Buis-les-Baronnies
Montauban-s.-l'O.
Pont-St-Esprit
Ste-Cécile-les-V.
Vaison-la-Romaine
St Léger-du-Ventoux
Séderon
Curel
Ribiers
Malaucène
Montbrun-les-B.
Bagnols-s.-Cèze
Orange
Les Omergues
Vaucluse
84
Sault
Revest-du-Bion
St-Étienne-les-Orgues
Gard
Châteauneuf-du-P.
Carpentras
Pernes-les-Font.
St-Christol
Roquemaure
Simiane-la-Rotonde
La Bastie
Sorgues
Villeneuve-lès-A.
Le Pontet
Forcalquier
Remoulins
Avignon
L'Isle-s.-la-Sorgue
Gordes
Roussillon
Rustrel
Reillanne
St-Michel-l'Ob.
Aramon
Le Coustellet
Apt
La Bégude
Céreste
Manosque
Marguerittes
Cavaillon
Ménerbes
Bonnieux
Beaucaire
Maillane
Plan-d'Orgon
Oppède-le-V.
Tarascon
St-Étienne-du-Grès
St-Rémy-de-Prov.
Eygalières
Orgon
Lauris
Lourmarin
Cadenet
Bellegarde
Fontvieille
Les Baux-de-P.
Maussane-les-A.
Sénas
Mallemort
Mirabeau
Fourques
Arles
Salon-de-P.
Lambesc
Pertuis
St-Cannat
Peyrolles-en-P.
Rians
Le Merle
St-Martin-de-Crau
Miramas
La Fare-les-Oliviers
Éguilles
Vauvenargues
St-Chamas
Ventabren
Aix-en-Provence
Pourrières
Étang de Vaccarès
Istres
Étang de Berre
Rognac
Vitrolles
Trets
Bouches-du-Rhône
13
Berre
Marignane
Stes-Maries-de-la-Mer
Fos
Port-de-Bouc
Martigues
Septèmes-les-Vallons
St-Zacharie
Salin-de-Giraud
Port-St-Louis-du-Rhône
Lavéra
Allauch
Auriol
Golfe de Fos
Aubagne
Carro
Carry-le-Rouet
Marseille
Cap Couronne
Gémenos
Ile Pomègues
La Penne-s.-H.
Cassis
Cap Croisette
Cap Canaille
Ile de Riou
La Ciotat
St-Cyr-s.-M.
Sanary-s.-Mer
MER
MÉDITERRANÉE

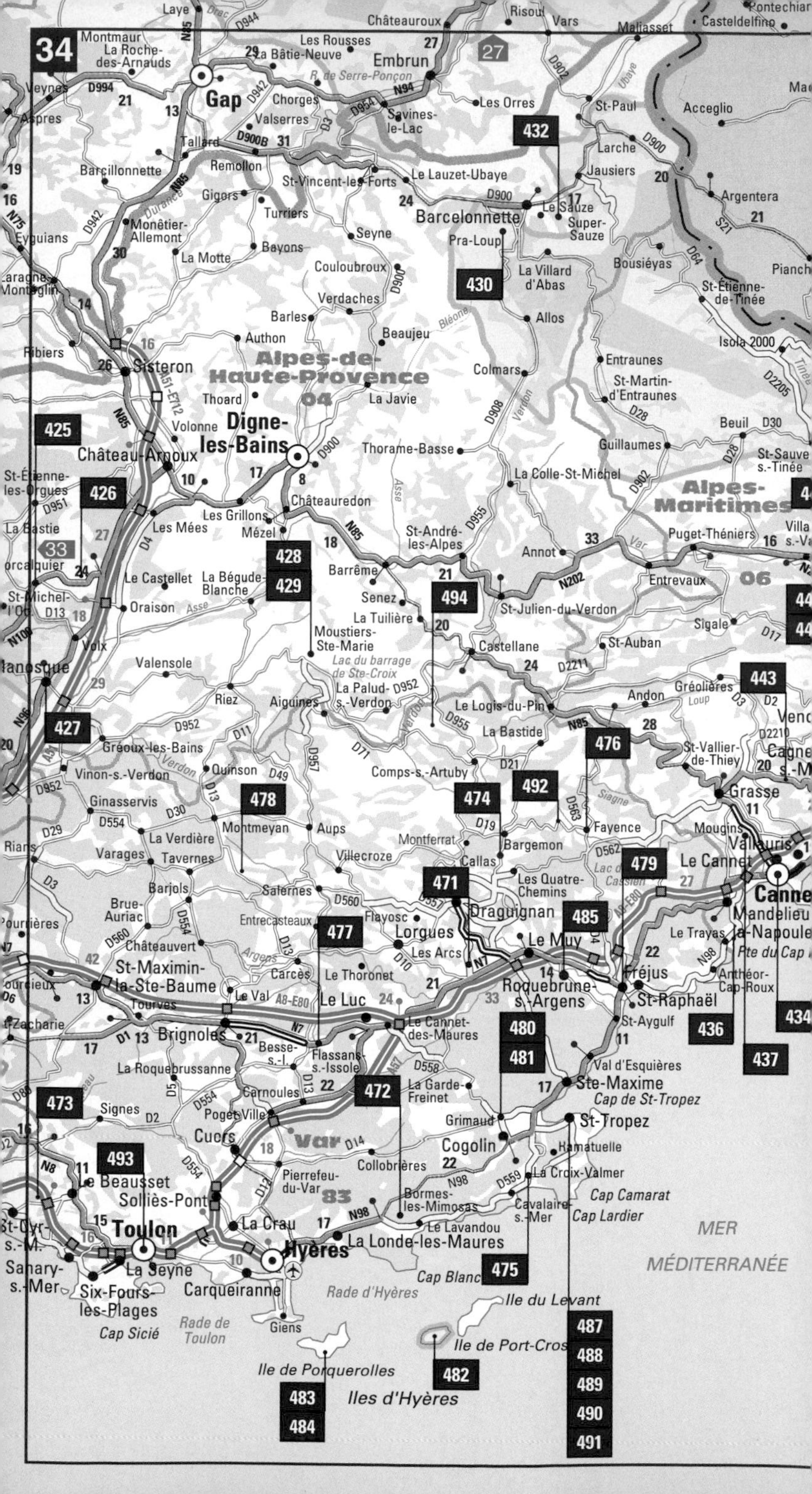

Gap
Embrun
Sisteron
Digne-les-Bains
Barcelonnette
Alpes-de-Haute-Provence
04
Alpes-Maritimes
06
Var
83
Draguignan
Toulon
Hyères
Fréjus
St-Raphaël
St-Tropez
Ste-Maxime
Grasse
Brignoles
St-Maximin-la-Ste-Baume
Castellane
Manosque
Le Luc
Lorgues
Le Muy
Cannes
Mandelieu-la-Napoule
Moustiers-Ste-Marie
Lac du barrage de Ste-Croix
Ile de Porquerolles
Ile de Port-Cros
Ile du Levant
Iles d'Hyères
Rade d'Hyères
Rade de Toulon
Cap Sicié
Cap Blanc
Cap Camarat
Cap Lardier
Cap de St-Tropez
MER MÉDITERRANÉE
425
426
427
428
429
430
432
434
436
437
443
471
472
473
474
475
476
477
478
479
480
481
482
483
484
485
487
488
489
490
491
492
493
494

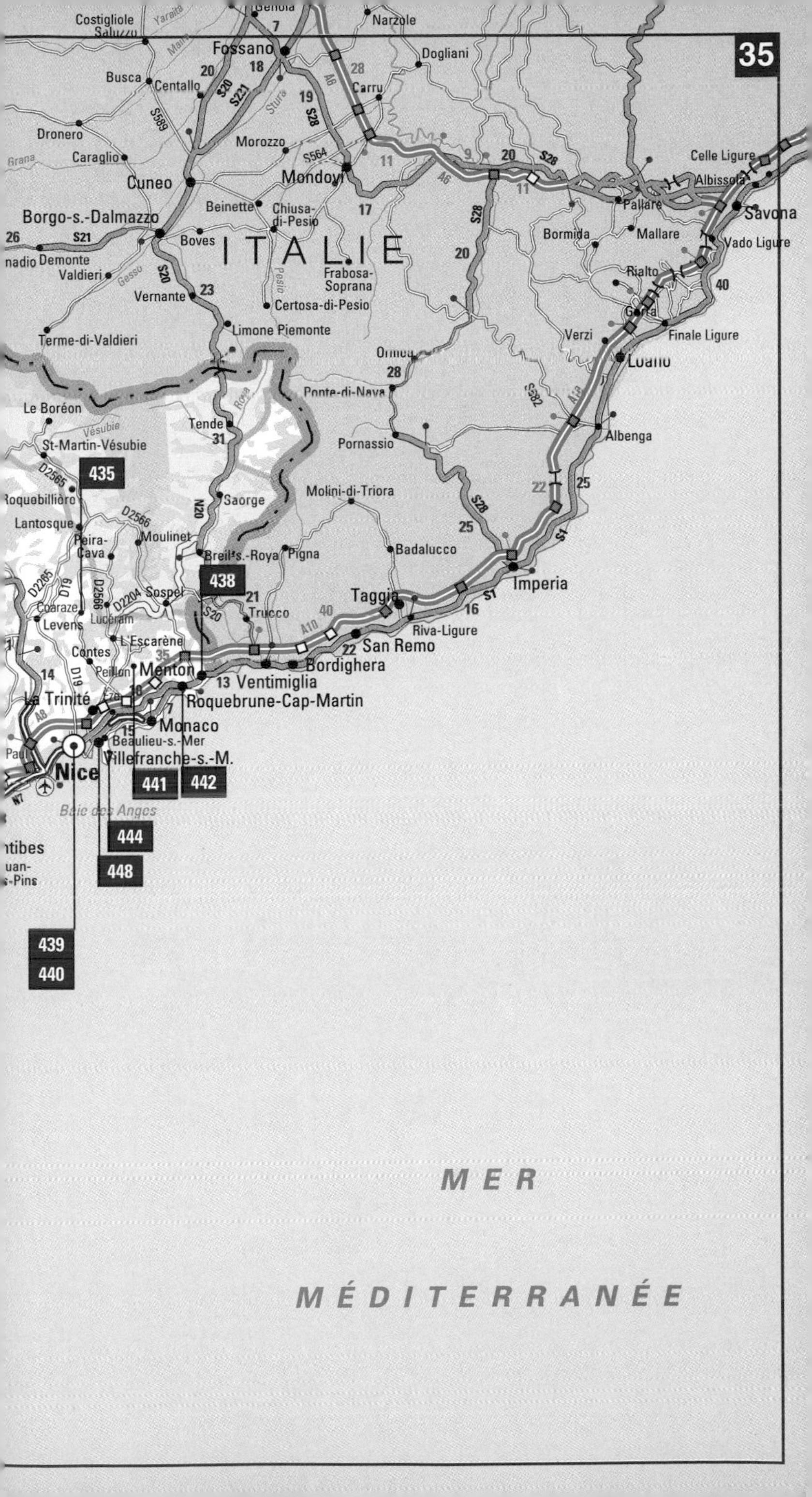

Costigliole Saluzzo
Genola
Narzole
Fossano
Dogliani
Busca
Centallo
Carru
Dronero
Morozzo
Caraglio
Cuneo
Mondovi
Celle Ligure
Albissola
Savona
Borgo-s.-Dalmazzo
Beinette
Chiusa-di-Pesio
Pallare
Mallare
Bormida
Vado Ligure
Demonte
Valdieri
Boves
ITALIE
Frabosa-Soprana
Rialto
Vernante
Certosa-di-Pesio
Terme-di-Valdieri
Limone Piemonte
Verzi
Finale Ligure
Loano
Ponte-di-Nava
Le Boréon
Tende
Albenga
St-Martin-Vésubie
Pornassio
435
Roquebillière
Saorge
Molini-di-Triora
Lantosque
Peira-Cava
Moulinet
Breil-s.-Roya
Pigna
Badalucco
438
Imperia
Taggia
Sospel
Coaraze
Levens
Lucéram
Trucco
Riva-Ligure
L'Escarène
San Remo
Contes
Bordighera
Peillon
Menton
Ventimiglia
La Trinité
Èze
Roquebrune-Cap-Martin
Monaco
Beaulieu-s.-Mer
Villefranche-s.-M.
Nice
441
442
Baie des Anges
444
Antibes
448
439
440
MER
MÉDITERRANÉE

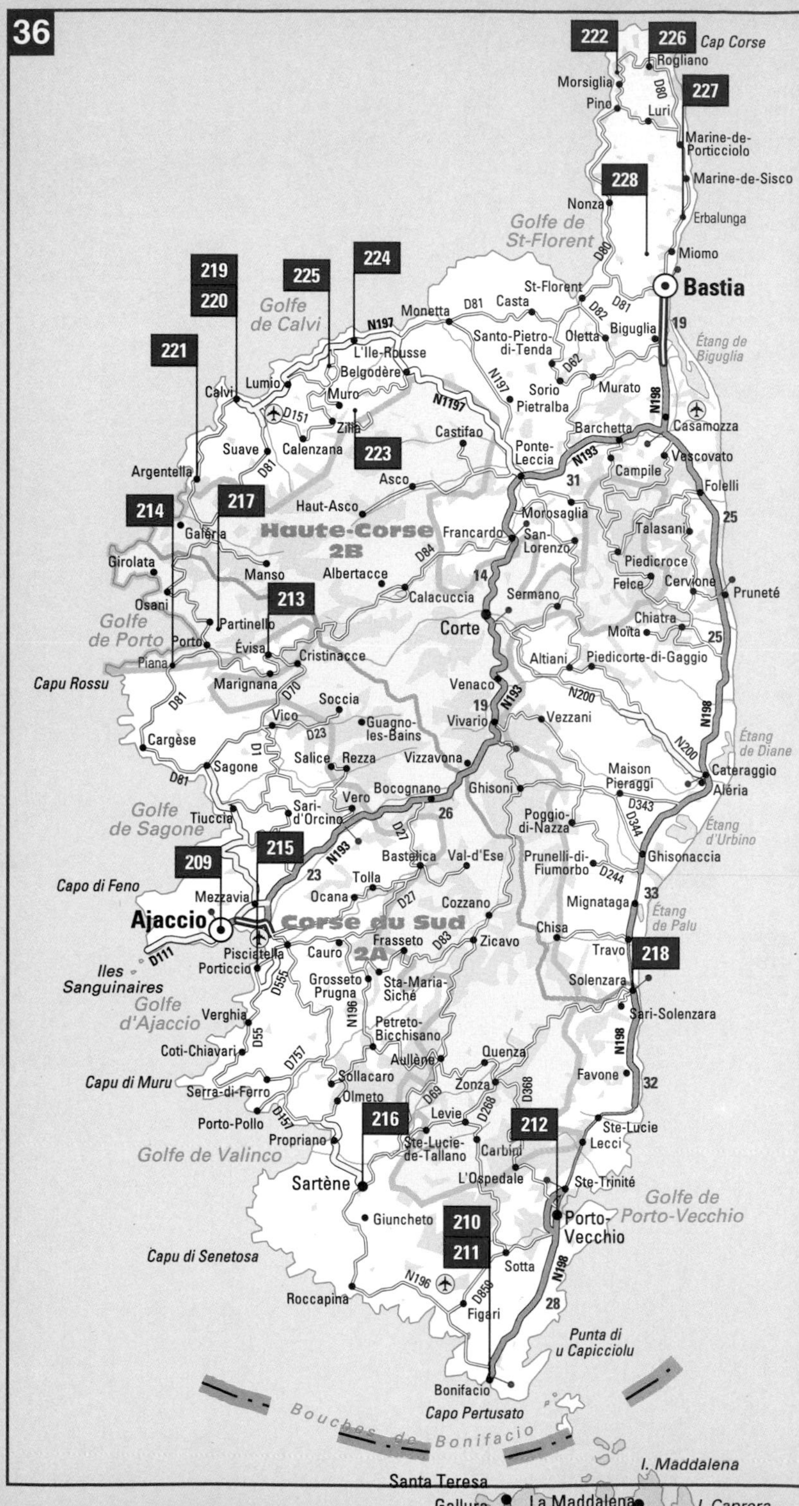

Cap Corse
Rogliano
Morsiglia
Pino
Luri
Marine-de-Porticciolo
Marine-de-Sisco
Nonza
Golfe de St-Florent
Erbalunga
Miomo
Bastia
St-Florent
Casta
Monetta
Santo-Pietro-di-Tenda
Oletta
Biguglia
Étang de Biguglia
Golfe de Calvi
L'Ile-Rousse
Belgodère
Lumio
Calvi
Muro
Zilia
Calenzana
Suave
Sorio
Pietralba
Murato
Casamozza
Barchetta
Castifao
Ponte-Leccia
Vescovato
Campile
Folelli
Argentella
Asco
Haut-Asco
Morosaglia
Galéria
Haute-Corse 2B
Francardo
San-Lorenzo
Talasani
Girolata
Manso
Albertacce
Piedicroce
Felce
Cervione
Pruneté
Osani
Calacuccia
Sermano
Golfe de Porto
Partinello
Corte
Chiatra
Moïta
Porto
Évisa
Cristinacce
Altiani
Piedicorte-di-Gaggio
Piana
Capu Rossu
Marignana
Venaco
Soccia
Vivario
Vezzani
Vico
Guagno-les-Bains
Étang de Diane
Cargèse
Salice
Rezza
Vizzavona
Sagone
Maison Pieraggi
Cateraggio
Aléria
Ghisoni
Bocognano
Golfe de Sagone
Tiuccia
Sari-d'Orcino
Vero
Poggio-di-Nazza
Étang d'Urbino
Bastelica
Val-d'Ese
Prunelli-di-Fiumorbo
Ghisonaccia
Capo di Feno
Tolla
Mezzavia
Ocana
Mignataga
Étang de Palu
Cozzano
Ajaccio
Corse du Sud 2A
Chisa
Zicavo
Frasseto
Cauro
Pisciatella
Travo
Iles Sanguinaires
Porticcio
Grosseto Prugna
Sta-Maria-Siché
Solenzara
Sari-Solenzara
Golfe d'Ajaccio
Verghia
Petreto-Bicchisano
Coti-Chiavari
Aullène
Quenza
Favone
Capu di Muru
Sollacaro
Zonza
Serra-di-Ferro
Olmeto
Porto-Pollo
Levie
Ste-Lucie
Lecci
Propriano
Ste-Lucie-de-Tallano
Carbini
Golfe de Valinco
L'Ospedale
Ste-Trinité
Sartène
Golfe de Porto-Vecchio
Porto-Vecchio
Giuncheto
Capu di Senetosa
Sotta
Roccapina
Figari
Punta di u Capicciolu
Bonifacio
Capo Pertusato
Bouches de Bonifacio
I. Maddalena
Santa Teresa
Gallura
La Maddalena
I. Caprera
222
226
227
228
219
220
225
224
221
223
214
217
213
209
215
218
216
212
210
211

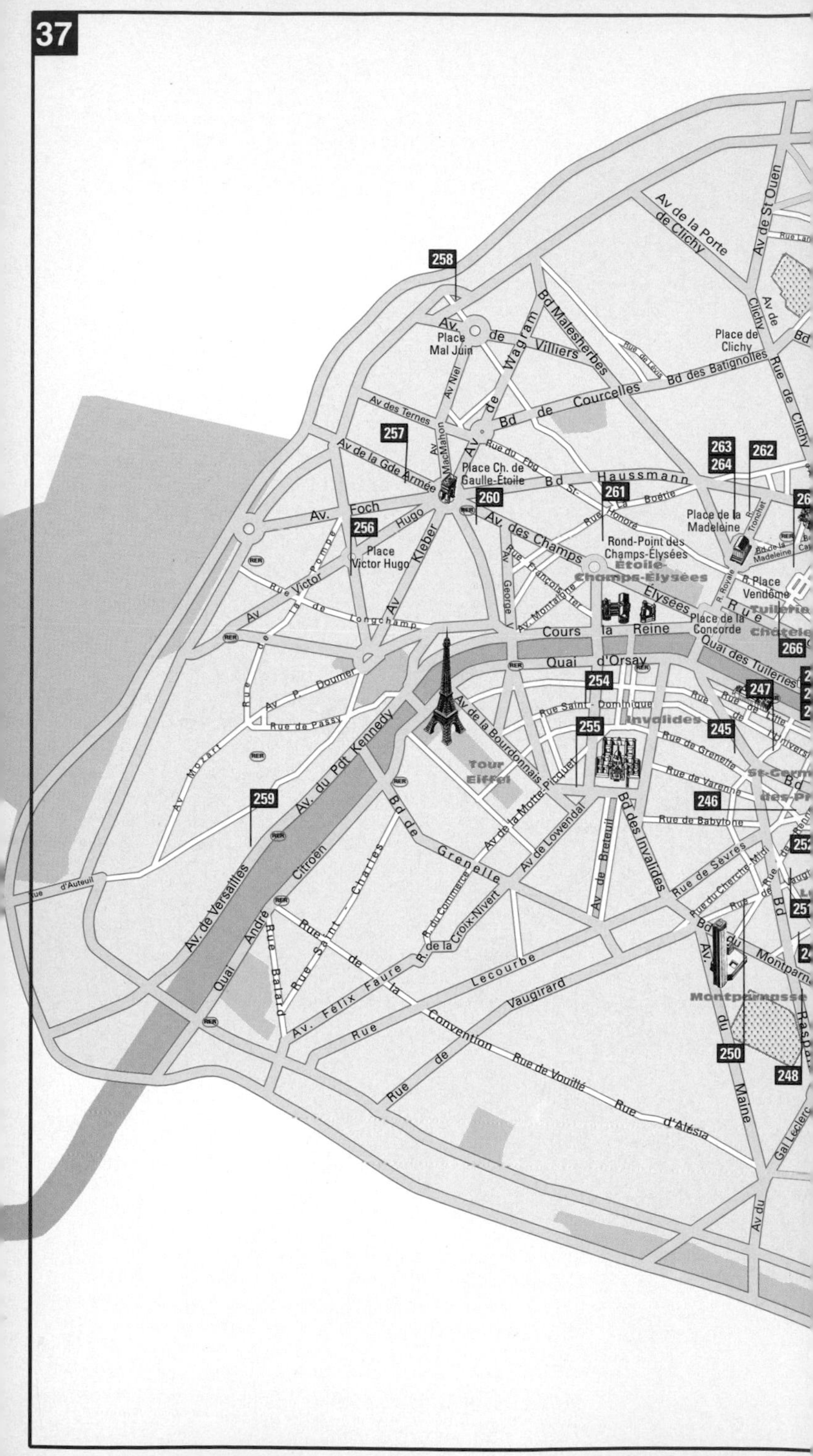
Av de la Porte de Clichy
Av de St Ouen
Av de Clichy
Place de Clichy
Rue de Clichy
Bd des Batignolles
Bd Malesherbes
Av. de Villiers
Place Mal Juin
Av. de Wagram
Av Niel
Bd de Courcelles
Av des Ternes
Av de la Gde Armée
Av MacMahon
Place Ch. de Gaulle-Étoile
Bd Haussmann
Rue du Fbg St-Honoré
La Boétie
Place de la Madeleine
Bd de la Madeleine
R. Tronchet
Rond-Point des Champs-Élysées
Étoile-Champs-Élysées
Av. des Champs Élysées
Av. Foch
Hugo
Place Victor Hugo
Av Victor Hugo
Kleber
Rue de la Pompe
Av de Longchamp
Av George V
François-1er
Av. Montaigne
R. Royale
R. Place Vendôme
Rue
Tuileries
Place de la Concorde
Cours la Reine
Quai d'Orsay
Quai des Tuileries
Rue de Lille
Rue de l'Université
Av. P. Doumer
Rue de Passy
Av Mozart
Av. du Pdt Kennedy
Av de la Bourdonnais
Rue Saint-Dominique
Invalides
Rue de Grenelle
Rue de Varenne
Rue de Babylone
Tour Eiffel
Av de la Motte-Picquet
Av de Lowendal
Av de Breteuil
Bd des Invalides
Bd de Grenelle
Rue de Sèvres
Rue du Cherche-Midi
Bd du Montparnasse
Montparnasse
Av. du Maine
Rue d'Auteuil
Av. de Versailles
Quai André Citroën
Rue Balard
Rue Saint-Charles
R. du Commerce
R. de la Croix-Nivert
Av. Félix Faure
Rue de la Convention
Rue Lecourbe
Rue de Vaugirard
Rue de Vouillé
Rue d'Alésia
Gal Leclerc
RER
258
257
256
260
261
263
264
262
266
254
255
245
247
246
259
250
248

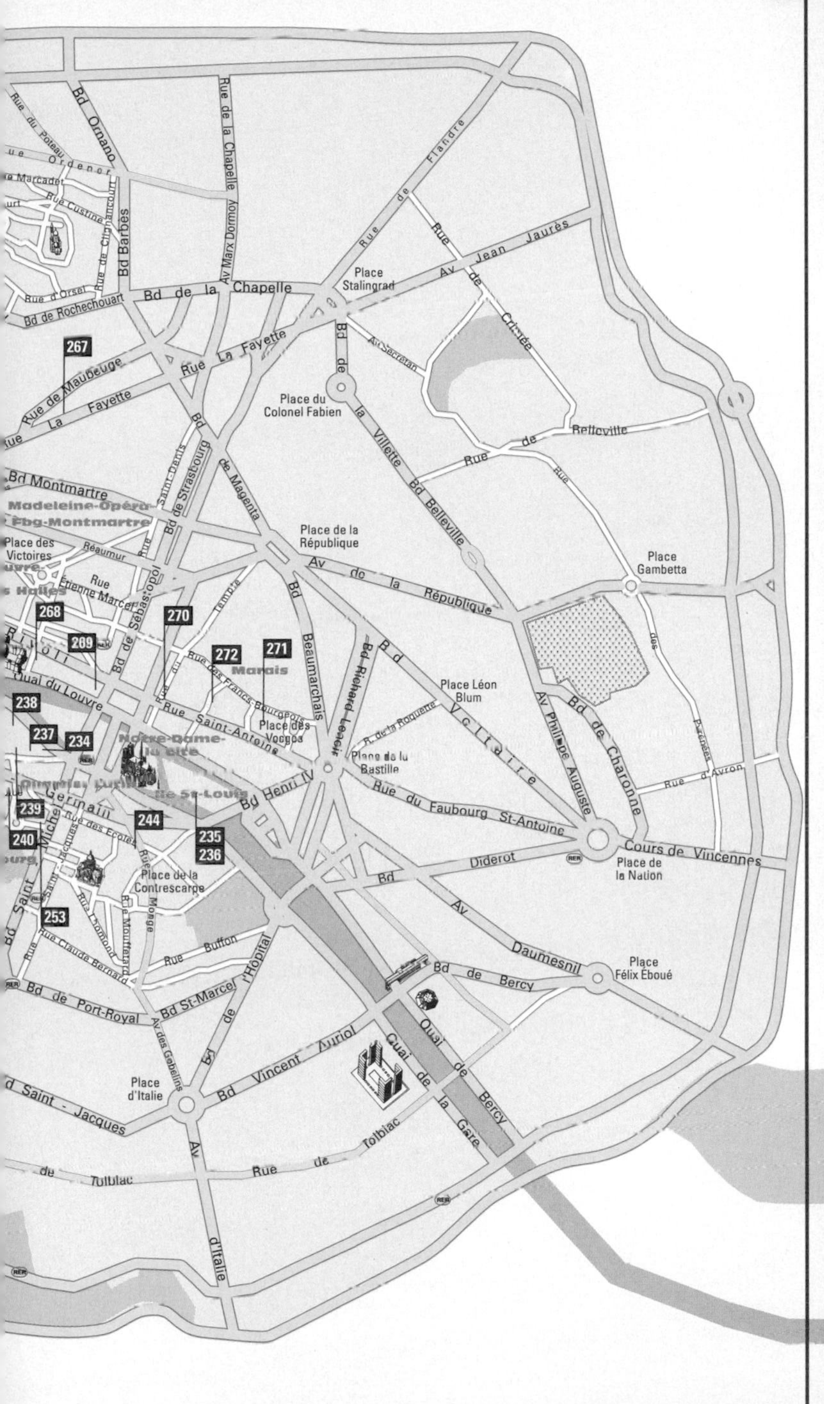
Bd Ornano
Rue de la Chapelle
Rue du Poteau
Ordener
Marcadet
Rue Custine
Rue de Clignancourt
Bd Barbès
Av Marx Dormoy
Rue de Flandre
Rue de Crimée
Av Jean Jaurès
Place Stalingrad
Rue d'Orsel
Bd de Rochechouart
Bd de la Chapelle
267
Rue La Fayette
Rue de Maubeuge
Av Secrétan
Bd de la Villette
Place du Colonel Fabien
Rue de Belleville
Bd Montmartre
Madeleine-Opéra
Fbg-Montmartre
Bd de Strasbourg
Rue de Magenta
Place des Victoires
Réaumur
Rue Etienne Marcel
Place de la République
Bd Belleville
Place Gambetta
Av de la République
268
269
270
272
271
Marais
Rue des Francs-Bourgeois
Rue du Temple
Bd Beaumarchais
Bd Richard-Lenoir
Bd Voltaire
Place Léon Blum
Quai du Louvre
238
Rue Saint-Antoine
Place des Vosges
R. de la Roquette
Av Philippe Auguste
Bd de Charonne
Rue des Pyrénées
Rue d'Avron
237
234
Notre-Dame-Île de la Cité
Place de la Bastille
Bd Henri IV
Rue du Faubourg St-Antoine
239
Rue des Ecoles
244
Île St-Louis
235
236
240
Rue St-Jacques
Bd Diderot
Cours de Vincennes
Place de la Nation
Place de la Contrescarpe
Rue Monge
Rue Mouffetard
Rue Lhomond
253
Rue Claude Bernard
Rue Buffon
Av Daumesnil
Bd de l'Hôpital
Bd de Bercy
Place Félix Éboué
Bd de Port-Royal
Bd St-Marcel
Av des Gobelins
Quai de Bercy
Bd Vincent Auriol
Quai de la Gare
Place d'Italie
Bd Saint-Jacques
Rue de Tolbiac
Av d'Italie

## ZinckHôtel

13, rue de la Marne
67140 Andlau (Bas-Rhin)
Tel. (0)3.88.08.27.30 - Fax (0)3.88.08.42.50 - M. and Mme Zinck

**Category** ★★★ **Rooms** 14 with telephone, bath or shower, WC and 4 with TV - 1 for disabled persons. **Price** Single and double 295-600F. **Meals** Breakfast 40F, served 8:00-10:00. No restaurant. **Credit cards** Visa, Eurocard and MasterCard. **Pets** Dogs not allowed. **Facilities** Parking. **Nearby** Alsace Wine Route, from Marlenheim to Thann, church in Andlau and church of Sainte-Marguerite in Epfig. **Open** All year.

Installed quite recently in an old mill which until 1945 was also a sock factory, this hotel is a good reflection of the owners' fantasy and love of their job. They have opened 14 rooms here, whose names give you a good idea of their diversity: the *Coloniale, Jazzy* and *Baroque* rooms are full of humor and color; the *Japonaise* is more sober, and the *Alsacienne* very warm. All have ultra-modern amenities. Breakfast is served in an immense room of the converted factory or, in good weather, on the terrace in front of the hotel. A few steps away, a delightful small enclosed orchard makes a quiet place to relax in the summer. If you wish, Monsieur and Madame Zinck will be pleased to give you information on the wine cellars in this region of great vineyards, or the places they love visitors to see in Roman Alsace. For restaurants, we recommend *Le Relais de la Poste* and *Le Caveau Val d'Eléon* (two *winstubs*), and *Au Boeuf Rouge.*

***How to get there*** *(Map 12): 39km south of Strasbourg via A 352, exit Barr-Obernai, then dir. Selestat; in Saint-Pierre, turn right in dir. of Andlau.*

## Hôtel Arnold

98, route du Vin
67140 Itterswiller (Bas-Rhin)
Tel. (0)3.88.85.50.58 - Fax (0)3.88.85.55.54 - Mme Arnold
Web: http://ww.oda.fr/aa/arnold

**Category** ★★★ **Rooms** 28 and 1 apartment (2-5 pers.) with telephone, bath or shower, WC, TV and minibar. **Price** Double 270-595F; apart. 600-1200F. **Meals** Breakfast 48F, served 7:30-10:30; half board and full board 350-525F (per pers.). **Restaurant** Service 11:30-14:30, 19:30-21:00 (closed Sunday evening and Monday); menus 130-365F. Seasonal carte. Specialties: Noisette de chevreuil, civet de sanglier, choucroute, baeckeoffe, foie gras. **Credit cards** Visa, Eurocard and MasterCard. **Pets** Dogs not allowed. **Facilities** Parking. **Nearby** Alsace Wine Route from Marlenheim to Thann, church in Andlau, church of Sainte-Marguerite d'Epfig. **Open** All year.

The Hôtel Arnold lies in the heart of the Alsatian vineyards at the foot of the Vosges Mountains. It is composed of three buildings in the most traditional Alsatian style. Windows and balconies overflow with flowers. The bedrooms, which are decorated in a standard, functional style, are very comfortable, bright and quite large. The great attraction of most rooms is their large balcony and view over the vineyards. The entrance, hallways, breakfast room and lounge (upstairs) are warm and prettily decorated. On the *Réserve* side, the bedrooms are more attractive but the view is not as good. Intent on maintaining Alsatian traditions, the Arnold family will invite you to try the regional specialties in the restaurant. You can also buy them in the hotel's shop, which offers wines, *foie gras* and other products from the family estate.

***How to get there** (Map 12): 41km south of Strasbourg via A35; Obernai exit; then N422 to Epfig; turn right on D 335 to Itterswiller.*

# Hôtel Gilg

1, route du Vin
67140 Mittelbergheim (Bas-Rhin)
Tel. (0)3.88.08.91.37 - Fax (0)3.88.08.45.17 - M. Gilg

**Category** ★★ **Rooms** 15 with telephone, bath, WC and TV. **Price** Single 215-350F, double 250-400F. **Meals** Breakfast 35F, served 7:30-10:00. **Restaurant** Service 12:00-14:00, 19:00-21.00, menus 125-325F, also à la carte. Specialties: Filet de sandre et langoustines poêlées servis en ravioles ouvertes. **Credit cards** All major. **Pets** Dogs allowed. **Facilities** Parking. **Nearby** Barr, church in Andlau, church of Sainte-Marguerite in Epfig, Mont Sainte-Odile. **Open** Jan 30 – June 28, July 16 – Jan 8 (closed Tuesday evening and Wednesday).

This imposing *winstub* is located on the corner of two small streets in a lovely village whose principal activity is winegrowing. The rooms here are quiet, warm and cozy, with furniture that is somewhat old-fashioned but charming in the oldest rooms. Comfortable and well decorated, those rooms which have just been renovated are the best (it's a good idea to reserve one of these). Meals are served in a large dining room with handsome traditional decor; the excellent cuisine is flavorsome and delicate. The hospitality and the many qualities of this hotel make it a noteworthy place to stay not far from the vineyards and the splendid villages of Alsace.

***How to get there*** *(Map 12): 37km north of Colmar via N83 to Sélestat and N422 towards Barr.*

# Hôtel A la Cour d'Alsace

3, rue de Gaie
67210 Obernai (Bas-Rhin)
Tel. (0)3.88.95.07.00 - Fax (0)3.88.95.19.21 - Mme Hager and M. Hartleyb
Web: http://www.strasbourg.com/cour-alsace

**Category** ★★★★ **Rooms** 43, with telephone, bath or shower, WC, TV and Minibar - Elevator. **Price** Single and double 470-780F, 730-800F. **Meals** Breakfast 55F, 75F (Buffet), served 7:00-10:00; half board 1095-1300F (per pers., in double). **Restaurant** Service 12:00-15:00, 19:00-22:00; menus 195-390F, also à la carte. **Credit cards** All major. **Pets** Dogs not allowed. **Facilities** Parking. **Nearby** Alsace Wine Route, church in Andlau, church of Sainte-Marguerite in Epfig, Mont-Saint-Odile; Barr – Wantzenau golf course. **Open** Jan 24 – Dec 22.

This magnificent hotel is composed of several adjoining houses grouped around a very old courtyard and built against the ramparts of Obernai. Whether you are in the *Petite France* or the *Petite Suisse*, the bedrooms are elegant, very comfortable and of varying sizes (which justifies the price differences). The style is light colors with pale or beige tints, paneling and furniture of natural wood and white eiderdowns, all contributing to a refined ambiance. For lunch or dinner you have a choice between the gastronomic restaurant or the charming *winstub*. You can have a drink in the garden at any time, which has lovely flowers and is niched among the old moats running the length of the hotel. This is an impeccable, genuinely luxurious hotel where you can be assured of excellent cuisine and professional, attentive service.

***How to get there*** *(Map 12): 24km south of Strasbourg.*

## Relais des Marches de l'Est

24, rue de Molsheim
67280 Oberhaslach (Bas-Rhin)
Tel. (0)3.88.50.99.60 - Fax (0)3.88.75.68.88 - Mme Weber

**Category** ★★ **Rooms** 9, with telephone, bath or shower, WC and TV. **Price** Single and double 170F, 190-230F. **Meals** Breakfast 30F, served 7:00-10:30; half board 230F (per pers.). **Restaurant** For residents only, by reservation. Service from 19:00; menus 60-160F. Specialties: Tarte flambée, choucroute, bacleolle. **Credit cards** Not accepted. **Pets** Dogs allowed. **Facilities** Parking. **Nearby** Alsace Wine Route, Mont Sainte-Odile, Barr, church in Andlau, church of Sainte-Marguerite in Epfig – Wantzenau golf course. **Open** All year.

Sculptors as well as hoteliers, Bénédicte and Sylvain have succeeded in creating a personal, warm atmosphere here. On the street side, however, the hotel is unremarkable, with its pink Alsatian sandstone, and unobtrusive, as if it were afraid to be discovered too easily. Inside, the rooms on the ground floor have a "refined bistrot" ambiance, with the bread oven as the central element. On weekends, guests can observe as *baeckeoffe* and flamed tarts come out of the oven (reserve two days in advance). Upstairs, the bedrooms have old stone walls and the antique beds have been modernized for comfort; an old wardrobe, pretty fabrics and impeccable bathrooms complete the furnishings. The result is simple and charming; only the tiled floors could do with a few rugs. In the morning, you have a choice of two kinds of breakfast, which is served in the garden in good weather. This is a very pleasant hotel, and ideal for discovering the Hasel Valley and the Nideck region. Prices are more than reasonable.

***How to get there*** *(Map 12): 24km south of Strasbourg.*

# Hôtel Anthon

40, rue Principale
67510 Obersteinbach (Bas-Rhin)
Tel. (0)3.88.09.55.01 - Fax (0)3.88.09.50.52 - Mme Flaig

**Category** ★★ **Rooms** 9 with telephone, bath (1 with shower) and WC (7 with minibar). **Price** Double 290-320F. **Meals** Breakfast 55F, served 8:00-10:00. **Restaurant** Service 12:00-14:00, 18:30-21:00; menus 270-360F (also 120F weekdays), also à la carte. Specialties: Foie gras frais de canard, game in season. **Credit cards** Visa, Eurocard and MasterCard. **Pets** Dogs allowed. **Facilities** Parking. **Nearby** Lake at Hanau, Châteaux of Lutzelhardt and Falkenstein – 18-hole golf course in Bitche. **Open** Feb – Dec. Closed Tuesday and Wednesday.

The hotel-restaurant Anthon, in a small picturesque village in the heart of the Vosges du Nord Park, has nine pleasant, renovated bedrooms, all overlooking the surrounding countryside as far as the wooded slopes of the Vosges. The dining room is spacious; it is circular in shape and its large bay windows give the impression of dining in a garden full of flowers: perfect surroundings for the very high-quality food. The hotel also has a lively bar and a quiet lounge. The hotel itself, surrounded by extensive grounds, is very quiet.

***How to get there*** *(Map 13): 66km north of Strasbourg via A4 and D44 to Haguenau, then D27 to Lembach, and D3 to Obersteinbach.*

## Hôtel Neuhauser

Les Quelles
67130 Schirmeck (Bas-Rhin)
Tel. (0)3.88.97.06.81 - Fax (0)3.88.97.14.29 - M. Neuhauser

**Category** ★★ **Rooms** 14 and 3 chalets with telephone, bath or shower, WC and TV. **Price** Single and double 300-320F; chalet 700F (2 pers.), 800F (3 pers., 900F (4 pers.). **Meals** Breakfast 48F, served 8:00-10:00; half board 340-360F, full board 390-410F (per pers., 3 days min.). **Restaurant** With air conditioning. Service 12:00-14:00, 19:00-21:00 (closed 10-31 Jan), menus 110-300F, also à la carte. Specialties: Foie gras maison, filet de lapereau farçi, noisette de chevreuil forestière. **Credit cards** Visa, Eurocard and MasterCard. **Facilities** Heated swimming pool and parking. **Nearby** Belvédère de la chatte pendue. **Open** All year.

The Neuhauser and the few small houses in this tiny hamlet are ringed on all sides by fields and forest, an isolated location ensuring total peace and quiet. The few bedrooms are comfortable, well kept, and tastefully appointed in traditional style with rustic furniture and beams. There are three small Scandinavian chalets now, which have been arranged as suites, each with a lounge and terrace; they are ideal for families who need extra space. Served in a huge panoramic dining room decorated like a winter garden, the cuisine is varied and well prepared. The wine list, too, deserves your attention, as do the liqueurs and *eaux de vie*. This is an attractive hotel with reasonable prices—there's even a swimming pool you can enjoy with the first rays of sunshine.

***How to get there*** *(Map 12): 56km southwest of Strasbourg via A35 and A352, then N420 or D392 to Schirmeck, then Les Quelles.*

## Hôtel du Dragon

2, rue de l'Ecarlate - 12, rue du Dragon
67000 Strasbourg (Bas-Rhin)
Tel. (0)3.88.35.79.80 - Fax (0)3.88.25.78.95 - M. Iannarelli
Web: http://www.alsanet.com/dragon

**Category** ★★★ **Rooms** 32 with telephone, bath, WC and TV - Wheelchair access. **Price** Single 430-635F, double 495-675F, suite 795-895F. **Meals** Breakfast 60F, served 6:45-10:00. No restaurant. **Credit cards** All major. **Pets** Dogs not allowed. **Nearby** La Wantzenau, Alsace Wine Route – 18-hole golf courses in Illkirch-Graffenstaden and Plobsheim. **Open** All year.

We tend to equate charming with picturesque and old; and yet the 17th-century Hôtel du Dragon, which has been done in a very modern style, certainly has its own charm. The grey tones of the interior decoration and the designer furniture create a somewhat cold atmosphere, but the friendly, welcoming staff and the beautiful contemporary paintings quickly compensate. The very comfortable bedrooms face onto one of the quiet streets of the historic quarter. There is no restaurant, but delicious breakfasts are served on pretty china from the Café Coste. (If you admire the paintings, some are for sale.) For restaurants, M. Iannarelli will give you good recommendations, but be sure to visit *Chez Yvonne*, one of the most popular wine bars in the city; the *Pont Corbeau*, as well as the *Strissel* for outstanding sauerkraut. The atmosphere of the Dragon and Monsieur Iannarelli's courteous management make the hotel a favorite with the European Community officials who come to Strasbourg frequently.

***How to get there*** *(Map 13): In the center of Strasbourg via the Quai Saint-Nicolas and the Quai Ch. Frey.*

1998

## Relais de la Poste

21, rue du Général de Gaulle
67610 La Wantzenau (Bas-Rhin)
Tel. (0)3.88.59.24.80 - Fax (0)3.88.59.24.89 - M. Daull

**Rooms** 19 (8 with air-conditioning) with telephone, bath or shower, WC and TV - 1 for disabled persons - Elevator. **Price** Single and double 300-650F, 475-655F. **Meals** Breakfast 50F, served 7:00-10:00; half board 580-700F (per pers.). **Restaurant** Service 12:00-14:00, 19:00-22:00 (closed Saturday lunchtime, Sunday evening and Monday); menus 275-395F - also à la carte - Specialties: Aumonière de foie d'oie à la truffe, filet de rouget aux épices, farçi de pigeon aux petits légumes, tartelette tiède aux griottes et glace cannelle. **Credit cards** All major. **Pets** Dogs allowed. **Facilities** Parking. **Nearby** Strasbourg, Alsace Wine Route, local festivities - 18-hole La Wantzenau golf course. **Open** All year except the 3 first weeks of Jan and the 2 last weeks of July, Sunday evening and Monday.

North of Strasbourg in a village of charming half-timbered houses, this former postal-relay station and country bistrot, built in 1789, has today added an inn to its gastronomic restaurant: Since 1986, under the direction of the owner and impassioned chef Jérôme Daull, the Relais de la Poste has been one of the outstanding gourmet tables of the region. The small bedrooms, which Monsieur Daull is progressively arranging, are decorated in rustic Alsatian style, with fabric-covered walls and floral wallpaper; some have a small television alcove, while others enjoy a small living room and a balcony. All the bathrooms are equipped with a hairdryer and an enlarging mirror, but they could do with a more modern facelift. There is a restful bar with honey-colored panelling and Spanish-style fabrics, and for intimate dinners, you can ask for a private dining room decorated with Alsatian frescos.

***How to get there*** *(Map 13): 15km northeast of Strasbourg via A4 exit Reichett, then N 363 towards Lauterbourg, exit Wantzenau.*

## Hostellerie Saint-Barnabé

Buhl
68530 Murbach (Haut-Rhin)
Tel. (0)3.89.62.14.14 - Fax (0)3.89.62.14.15 - M. and Mme Orban

**Category** ★★★ **Rooms** 27 with telephone, bath or shower, WC, TV and minibar. **Price** Single and double 450-610F, suite 695-765F. **Meals** Breakfast (buffet) 60F, 70F (in room), served 7:30-10:30. **Restaurant** Service 12:00-14:00, 19:00-21:00 (closed Sunday evening Nov – Mar and Apr – Oct); menus 128-348F, also à la carte. Specialties: Triologie de foie gras, variante de l'ocean, pigeon rotie au miel de lavande. **Credit cards** All major. **Pets** Dogs allowed (+30F). **Nearby** Lauch Valley, Murbach Abbey, Unterlinden Museum in Colmar, Automobile and Rail Museums in Mulhouse, Alsace Wine Route – 9-hole Rouffach golf course. **Open** Mar 6 – Jan 10. Closed Sunday evening Nov – Mar.

Now that the Saint-Barnabé has been beautifully refurbished, we are pleased to put it it back into the Guide. The Hostellerie has several dining rooms, lounges, and smoking rooms with beautiful views of its forest setting. The atmosphere is tranquil and the decoration is classic. The bedrooms are attractive and very comfortable, with elegant bathrooms. (Rooms 11, 16 and 20 can be noisy during meal times). Certain suites are ideal for families, and nature lovers will enjoy the Pavillon Vert rooms on the ground floor. Note also the irresistible Chalet room with a cheerful fireplace. The fabrics throughout have been beautifully chosen. The regional cuisine is excellent - you are served on the terrace in summer - and there is a delightful choice of Alsatian wines. The owners are young and friendly.

***How to get there*** *(Map 20): 3km from Guebwiller. Go straight through the center of town to Bulh; then turn left for Murbach.*

## Hostellerie Le Maréchal

4-6, place des Six Montagnes Noires
68000 Colmar (Haut-Rhin)
Tel. (0)3.89.41.60.32 - Fax (0)3.89.24.59.40 - M. and Mme Bomo

**Category** ★★★★ **Rooms** 30 with air-conditioning, telephone, bath or shower, WC and TV. **Price** Single 450-500F, double 550-1200F, suite 1500F. **Meals** Breakfast 75F, served 7:30-10:00, half board 650F, full board 800F (per pers., 3 days min.). **Restaurant** Service 12:00-14:00, 19:00-22:00; menus 195-380F, also à la carte. Specialties: Terrine de foie de canard à la gelée au Muscat d'Alsace, salade de homard et queue de lotte vinaigrette à l'essence de truffes, choucroute Barholdi en feuilleté à l'escalope de foie de canard frais. **Credit cards** All major. **Pets** Dogs allowed (+35F). **Facilities** Parking (+35F). **Nearby** Issenheim altarpiece at the Unterlinden Museum in Colmar, Alsace Wine Route, Neuf-Brisach, Trois-Epis, Munster – 18-hole golf course in Ammerschwihr. **Open** All year.

Well located in the old quarter of Petite Venise (Little Venice) in Colmar, the Hostellerie Le Maréchal occupies four old houses on the edge of the canals. The interior is delightful. Beams and stone go well with the Louis XIII furniture in the lounge and dining room. Each bedroom has its own style, and you can choose between medieval or 18th-century decor. They are elegant, comfortable and well equipped, and though some are rather small, this fits in perfectly with the cozy atmosphere of the hotel. Ask for a room on the canal side. The candlelit dinners in the long dining room beside the Lauch, the specialties offered there, and the warm, solicitous welcome make the Hostellerie Le Maréchal the best hotel in Colmar.

*How to get there (Map 12): In the center of old Colmar.*

## Le Colombier

7, rue Turenne
68000 Colmar (Haut-Rhin)
Tel. (0)3.89.23.96.00 - Fax (0)3.89.23.97.27 - Mme Lejeune

**Category** ★★★ **Rooms** 24 with air-conditioning, telephone, bath (some with whirlpool) or shower, WC, safe, minibar and cable TV - Elevator - 2 for disabled persons. **Price** Single 420-540F, double 540-930F, suite 1050-1300F. **Meals** Breakfast 60F, served 7:30-11:30. **Credit cards** All major. **Pets** Dogs allowed. **Nearby** Issenheim altarpiece at the Unterlinden Museum in Colmar, Alsace Wine Route, Neuf-Brisach, Munster, Trois-Epis - 18-hole golf course in Ammerschwihr. **Open** All year.

Located in the old quarter of La Petite Venise criss-crossed by several canals, the beautiful Le Colombier is installed in a large Renaissance building with its original winding stone staircase, surprisingly graceful and light. Shapes, materials and colors have been tastefully combined in decorating the bedrooms, which are equipped with modern amenities. Italian furniture lends the rooms a note of elegane and refinement. Located on four floors, the charming rooms range from small to very large; some are beneath the eaves and overlook the street or the inner courtyard with its old half-timbering and a cool fountain. In winter, a large fire crackles in the lounge fireplace. The breakfasts are excellent. Good restaurants include: *Caveau Saint-Jean, Winstub Brenner, Brasserie Koïsbu*s. For more gastronomic fare: *Le Fer Rouge, La Maison des Têtes.*

***How to get there** (Map 12): In the center of Old Colmar.*

1998

# La Maison des Têtes

19, rue des têtes
68000 Colmar (Haut-Rhin)
Tel. (0)3.89.24.43.43 - Fax (0)3.89.24.58.34 - M. and Mme Rohfrisch

**Category** ★★★★ **Rooms** 18 with telephone, bath (wirlpool in some rooms) or shower, WC, satellite TV, safe and minibar - Elevator - 1 for disabled persons. **Price** Double 550-950F; 3 pers. 1000 and 1250F; duplex 1250-1500F. **Meals** Breakfast 60F, served 7:15-10:00/11:00; half board 650-850F (per pers., 3 days min.). **Restaurant** Service 12:00-14:00, 19:00-21:30 (closed Sunday evening and Monday); menus 120-330F, also à la carte - Specialties: Foie gras frais au riesling, gibier en saison, turbot, rouget, homard, choucroute. **Credit cards** All major. **Pets** Dogs allowed (+60F). **Facilities** Parking. **Nearby** Issenheim altarpiece at the Unterlinden Museum in Colmar; Alsace Wine Route; Neuf-Brisach; Munster; Trois-Epis - 18-hole golf course in Ammerschwihr. **Open** All year except Feb vacations.

In the heart of Colmar between the Domenican Church and the Unterlinden Museum, the Maison des Têtes is the former Wine Exchange, a beautiful Rhine Renaissance building with a façade of 105 masks of grotesque figures. Last year, this restaurant famed for its regional cuisine and its magnificent, late 19th-century wood panelling added a hotel which, though entirely new, is well integrated into the old part of the building. The lobby stands on the vestiges of the Colmar wall, built between 1216 and 1220. The eighteen bedrooms surround a small paved courtyard with a young climbing vine. They contain a small corridor leading to the toilet, the storage space, and finally to the bedroom with white cob-style walls and mat-varnished pine furniture. The bathrooms feature a pink sandstone floor, and a bathtub and independent shower in the largest rooms. Those on the *premier étage* are the smallest. Note also the duplexes with a small lounge below and the bedroom upstairs. Gourmets will love a few meals--and henceforth a room--at the Maison des Têtes.

***How to get there*** *(Map 12): In town center.*

## Les Hirondelles

33, rue du 25 janvier
68970 Illhaeusern (Haut-Rhin)
Tel. (0)3.89.71.83.76 - Fax (0)3.89.71.86.40 - Mme Muller

**Category** ★★ **Rooms** 14 with air-conditioning, telephone, shower, WC and TV. **Price** Double 260-280F. **Meals** Breakfast 35F, served 8:00-10:00; half board 255-280F (per pers.). **Restaurant** For residents only. Service from 19:30 (closed Nov 1 – Easter). Specialties: Traditional country cooking, Alsatian specialties. **Credit cards** Visa, Eurocard and MasterCard. **Pets** Small dogs allowed. **Facilities** Parking. **Nearby** Colmar, Alsace Wine Route from Marlenheim to Thann, Haut-Koenigsbourg – 18-hole golf course in Ammerschwihr. **Open** Mar – Jan.

Les Hirondelles is an ancient farm of vast dimensions lying near the famous Auberge de l'Ill restaurant and the lovely Ill River. The bedrooms are located in a large outbuilding which has been entirely refurbished. Decorated for comfort and practicality, they are furnished with new but typically Alsatian wardrobes of polychromed wood. You may choose between rooms giving onto flowery balconies and the courtyard, or a more rural view over small vegetable gardens. There is a welcoming lounge on the ground floor where breakfast is served, along with good dinners based on regional cooking. The welcome is charming and informal at this pleasant hotel near the vineyards, and the prices are very reasonable.

***How to get there*** *(Map 12): 12km north of Colmar via RN83 in the Strasbourg towards.*

## Auberge Les Alisiers

5, rue Faude
68650 Lapoutroie (Haut-Rhin)
Tel. (0)3.89.47.52.82 - Fax (0)3.89.47.22.38 - M. and Mme Degouy

**Category** ★★ **Rooms** 16 with telephone, bath or shower and WC. **Price** Single and double 190-365F. **Meals** Breakfast (buffet) 44F, served 7:30-10:00, half board 280-370F. **Restaurant** Service 12:00-13:45, 19:00-20:45 (closed Monday evening except for guests on half board, and Tuesday); menus 79-189F, also à la carte. Specialties: Pigeonneau rôti, truite saumonée à la crème de lard, cervelas rôti sur salade de choucroute, pommes de terre coiffées de munster fondu. **Credit cards** Visa, Eurocard and MasterCard. **Pets** Dogs allowed. **Facilities** Parking. **Nearby** Colmar, Alsace Wine Route from Marlenheim to Thann – 18-hole golf course in Ammerschwihr. **Open** All year except in Jan.

The Auberge Les Alisiers lies 700 meters up in the mountains; the view from it over the Hautes Vosges and the Béhine Valley is stunning, and the hotel itself is very pleasant. The small bedrooms are intimate, comfortable and well kept; one has a small private terrace. A warmly decorated lounge is at your disposal where, in winter, you can enjoy the beautiful fireplace before dinner. The dining room is delightful, with several pieces of antique furniture and an impressive panoramic view. You will enjoy excellent, very reasonably priced cuisine. From your table in the evening, you might see several deer grazing at the edge of the woods, a bird of prey circling over the valley and the chef's assistant fishing a beautiful trout out of the fishtank. This is a very friendly hotel whose relaxed and informal atmosphere is largely created by the hospitable owners.

***How to get there*** *(Map 12): 19km northwest of Colmar via N415; at Lapoutroie go left in front of the church and follow the signs for 3km.*

## Hôtel Le Clos Saint-Vincent

Route de Bergheim
68150 Ribeauvillé (Haut-Rhin)
Tel. (0)3.89.73.67.65 - Fax (0)3.89.73.32.20 - M. Chapotin

**Category** ★★★★ **Rooms** 12, and 3 apartments, with telephone, bath, WC, TV, safe and minibar. **Price** Single 650F, double 700-935F, apart. 1000-1100F. **Meals** Breakfast incl., served 8:15-10:30. **Restaurant** Service 12:00-14:00, 19:00-20:30 (closed Tuesday and Wednesday); menus 260F, also à la carte. **Credit cards** Visa, Eurocard and MasterCard. **Pets** Dogs allowed (+30F). **Facilities** Covered swimming pool, parking. **Nearby** Hunawihr, swan reproduction center, ruins of the Château of St-Ulrich, Riquewihr, Alsace Wine Route from Marlenheim to Thann, Le Haut-Koenigsbourg; local festivities: Wine Festival in July-Aug, Minstrel Festival in Sept, Baroque Music Festival in autumn – 18-hole golf course in Ammerschwihr. **Open** Mar 15 – Nov 15.

In the heart of the Riesling wine country, the three-storey Clos Saint Vincent looks out on the Alsace plateau, the Black Forest, and to the east, the Alps. On the *premier étage* there is a lobby and a pleasant restaurant with a panoramic view. The bedrooms, with Directoire-style or rustic furniture, are bright, very comfortable and totally quiet. The tasteful fabrics lend much to the decoration. There is a very beautiful covered swimming pool.

***How to get there*** *(Map 12): 19km north of Colmar via N83 and D106 towards Ribeauvillé, then D1b towards Bergheim (follow the signs).*

## Hostellerie des Seigneurs de Ribeaupierre

11, rue du château
68150 Ribeauvillé (Haut-Rhin)
Tel. (0)3.89.73.70.31 - Fax (0)3.89.73.71.21 - Mmes Barth

**Category** ★★★ **Rooms** 10 with telephone, bath or shower and WC. **Price** Doubles 590-700F, suite 700-880F. **Meals** Breakfast incl., served 8:00-11:00. No restaurant. **Credit cards** Amex, Visa, Eurocard and MasterCard. **Pets** Dogs not allowed. **Nearby** Hunawihr, swan reproduction center, ruins of the Château of Saint-Ulrich, Riquewihr, Alsace Wine Route from Marlenheim to Thann, Le Haut-Koenigsbourg; local festivities: Wine Festival in July-Aug., Minstrel Festival in Sept., Baroque Music Festival in autumn – 18-hole golf course in Ammerschwihr. **Open** Mar 6 – Jan 4.

The Hostellerie des Seigneurs de Ribeaupierre is a remarkable small hotel in one of the most beautiful villages of Alsace. There are several delicious rooms in this 18th-century auberge, which is located outside the town center. All are charming and comfortable, with beautiful old regional furniture, soft beds, light-colored woodwork and half-timbering, and ravishing fabrics. The bathrooms are superb and there is a lovely corner sitting area in many rooms. On the ground floor, there is a small lounge where a fireplace is often blazing; several steps down, you come to the breakfast room. Breakfasts are delicious and copious and you may also ask for brunch, with cold cuts, eggs and, as this is Alsace, a slice of *foie gras*. This is a magnificent hotel, where you are greeted warmly by the owners, two very dynamic sisters. For restaurants, we suggest the gastronomic *La Winstub Zum Pfifferhüs*, reserved for non-smokers;; and the simpler *La Flammerie* (delicious *jambonneau*) and *L'Auberge Zahnacker*. And three kilometers out of town, the *Winstub du Sommelier*.

***How to get there** (Map12): 19km north of Colmar via N83 and D106 towards Ribeauvillé.*

## Hôtel Au Moulin

68127 Sainte-Croix-en-Plaine (Haut-Rhin)
Tel. (0)3.89.49.31.20 - Fax (0)3.89.49.23.11
M. and Mme Wœlffle

**Category** ★★ **Rooms** 16 and 1 suite with telephone, bath, WC and TV - Elevator - Wheelchair access. **Price** Single and double 220-390F, suite 420F. **Meals** Breakfast 45F, served 7:30-10:00. No restaurant. **Credit cards** Visa, Eurocard and MasterCard. **Pets** Dogs allowed (+30F). **Facilities** Parking. **Nearby** Colmar, Neuf-Brisach, Munster, Trois-Epis, Alsace Wine Route from Marlenheim to Thann – 18-hole golf course in Ammerschwihr. **Open** End Mar – Nov 2.

This former flour mill was built in the 16th-century by a colony of Mennonites and was converted into a hotel in 1982. It is a large white building with windows brightened by geraniums. The owners, the Wœlffle family, live in adjoining buildings, the ensemble forming a pretty courtyard with banks of flowers surrounding an old stone well. Spread over three floors, the bedrooms face either west, towards the Vosges, or across the fields. Most are spacious and all have well equipped bathrooms. (There is no television, as peace and quiet are the main concern). Finally, there are three further rooms in another building facing onto the courtyard, where breakfast can be enjoyed to the sound of water flowing down the Thur River, also called the "canal of the twelve mills" (two still work). This is a hotel with a very friendly atmosphere and very attractive prices. For fine dining, we recommend *Le Caveau d'Eguisheim* and *Hostellerie du Pape* in Eguisheim, and *La Maison des Têtes* and *Au Fer Rouge* in Colmar.

***How to get there*** *(Map 12): 6km south of Colmar via N422, then D1 towards Sainte-Croix-en-Plaine. On motorways exit 27, toward Herrlisheim.*

## Auberge La Meunière

30, rue Sainte-Anne
68590 Thannenkirch (Haut-Rhin)
Tel. (0)3.89.73.10.47 - Fax (0)3.89.73.12.31 - M. Dumoulin

**Category** ★★ **Rooms** 20 with telephone, bath or shower, WC and TV - Elevator. **Price** Double 390F. **Meals** Breakfast 35F, served 8:00-9:30; half board 240-300F, full board 310-370F. **Restaurant** Service 12.15-14:00, 19:15-21:00; menus 95-235F, also à la carte. Specialties: Cassolette d'escargots à la fondue de poireaux et tomates, aiguillettes de pigeon aux épices caramelisées, filet de canard à la cannelle, jarret de porcelet à la leppe sur lit de choucroute. **Credit cards** Amex, Visa, Eurocard and MasterCard. **Pets** Dogs allowed (+20F). **Facilities** Health center and sauna (150F for 2 pers.), mountain bikes, billiard and parking. **Nearby** Haut-Koenigsbourg, Ribeauvillé, Riquewihr, Kaysersberg – 18-hole golf course in Ammerschwihr. **Open** Mid. Mar – beg. Dec.

It is impossible not to notice the typically Alsatian facade of this lovely auberge in the little village of Thannenkirch in the foothills of the Vosges. You will find the same charm in the dining room, with its almond-green table linens and low ceilings and the wooden partitions that create several little intimate corners. The bedrooms, some furnished with antiques and some in more modern style, all have the same cozy and comfortable feel. Instead of numbers, the bedroom doors have enameled plaques inscribed with women's names. We particularly liked the *Sophie* and *Josephine* rooms with their glassed-in balconies looking over the countryside towards the fortress of Haut-Koenigsbourg in the distance. The view is superb from the large terrace, where meals are also served.

***How to get there*** *(Map 12): 25km north of Colmar via N83 to Guémar, N106 and D42.*

# Château d'Adoménil

Rehainviller
54300 Lunéville (Meurthe-et-Moselle)
Tel. (0)3.83.74.04.81 - Fax (0)3.83.74.21.78 - M. Million

**Category** ★★★ **Rooms** 8, and 4 duplex (some with air-conditioning) with telephone, bath, WC, TV and minibar. **Price** Single and double 500-850F, suite 1200F, duplex 1050F. **Meals** Breakfast 70F, served 8:00-10:30; half board 735F (per pers., 3 days min.). **Restaurant** Service 12:15-14:00, 19:30-21:30 (closed Sunday evening, Monday and Tuesday lunchtime Nov 1– Apr 15, and Monday and Tuesday lunchtime Apr 16 – Oct 31); menus 245-460F, also à la carte. Specialties: Sandre aux lardons, gris de Toul, foie gras poêlé, assiette lorraine, omelette de grenouilles au beurre d'herbes. **Credit cards** All major. **Pets** Dogs allowed. **Facilities** Swimming pool and parking. **Nearby** Château de Lunéville, Crystal Museum in Baccarat, Place Stanislas, School of Nancy Museum and Emile Gallé Museum in Nancy, Saint-Etienne Cathedral in Toul. **Open** All year.

Some ten years ago, M. Million left his restaurant in Lunéville to move into this beautiful château. He has opened a successful restaurant here, and the old stables have been converted into five spacious rooms which open onto the orchard. They all have beautiful tiled floors, modern Italian furniture and decorative objects, and luxurious bathrooms. In the château there are three other rooms of a more classical charm. The château is on a beautiful 17-acre estate which is disturbed only occasionally by a little railway nearby. The cuisine lives up to its strong reputation, and you will enjoy delicious breakfasts with croissants and assorted pastries.

***How to get there*** *(Map 12): 30km southeast of Nancy via N4 to Lunéville; 3km south of Lunéville via D914.*

## Auberge du Kiboki

Route du Donon (D993)
57560 Turquestein (Moselle)
Tel. (0)3.87.08.60.65 - Fax (0)3.87.08.65.26 - M. Schmitt

**Category** ★★ **Rooms** 16 with telephone, bath or shower, WC and TV. **Price** Double 450-500F, suite 600F. **Meals** Breakfast (buffet) 60F, served 8:00-10:00, half board 450F (per pers., 3 days min.). **Restaurant** Service 12:00-14:00, 19:00-21:00; à la carte 150-220F. Regional cooking. **Credit cards** Visa, Eurocard and MasterCard. **Pets** Dogs not allowed. **Facilities** Covered swimming pool, whirlpool, sauna, tennis and parking. **Nearby** Dabo Rock, crystal factories, potteries in Niderviller. **Open** Mar 2 – Nov 15 (closed Monday, Tuesday, Wednesday Nov 15 – Jan 15).

In the middle of the forest in the Turquestein-Blancrupt Valley lies the traditional Auberge du Kiboki. A very cozy atmosphere is created by the warm decor in this hotel. The dining rooms are very appealing: one is bright with checked tablecloths, matching curtains and lampshades; the other is decorated in soft colors and has a handsome, large china cabinet filled with local pottery. The comfortably furnished bedrooms reflect the same style, with warm beige and brown tones, canopied beds and antique wardrobes. This authentic forest inn is an ideal place for a restful stay. The cuisine is excellent and the owners are very hospitable, all making the Kiboki one of the outstanding hotels in this guide.

***How to get there*** *(Map 12): 73km west of Strasbourg via A35 and D392 towards Saint-Dié; at Schirmeck D392 towards Donon and D993 towards Turquestein-Blancrupt.*

## Hostellerie des Bas-Rupts et Chalet Fleuri

Les Bas-Rupts
88400 Gérardmer (Vosges)
Tel. (0)3.29.63.09.25 - Fax (0)3.29.63.00.40 - M. Philippe

**Category** ★★★ **Rooms** 32 with telephone, bath or shower, WC and TV. **Price** Single and double 380-780F, suite 900F. **Meals** Breakfast 80F, served 7:00-10:00; half board 580-750F. **Restaurant** Servic 12:00-14:00, 19:00-21:30; menus 160-450F, also à la carte. Specialties: Tripes au riesling, aiguillette de canard, andouille fumée sur choucroute. **Credit cards** Amex, Visa, Eurocard and MasterCard **Pets** Dogs allowed (+50F). **Facilities** Swimming pool, tennis, garage, parking. **Nearby** Les Cuve Waterfall, Longemer Lake, Retournemer Lake, Epinal – 18-hole golf course in Epinal. **Open** All year.

The Hostellerie des Bas-Rupts, with its flower-bedecked chalet and famou restaurant, is located just outside Gérardmer, once a favorite Alsace-Lorraine resort where the well-heeled enjoyed spending time (and money in th casino). The nostalgic town was almost completely destroyed at the end o World War II. The Hostellerie des Bas-Rupts is a veritable celebration of flowers, which are found painted on beams, doors, bedsteads; and in fresh an dried bouquets throughout, adding much charm to the comfortable bedroom in the annex. Some rooms in the hotel itself are more ordinary. The service i both professional and extremely courteous.

***How to get there*** *(Map 12): 56km west of Colmar via D417 and D486 toward La Bresse.*

## Hôtel de la Fontaine Stanislas

Fontaine-Stanislas
88370 Plombières-les-Bains (Vosges)
Tel. (0)3.29.66.01.53 - Fax (0)3.29.30.04.31 - M. and Mme Bilger

**Category** ★★ **Rooms** 19 with telephone, 14 with bath or shower, 11 with WC and 8 with TV. **Price** Single 140-205F, double 195-310F. **Meals** Breakfast 39F, served 7:30-9:30; half board 250-320F, full board 300-380F (per pers., 3 days min.). **Restaurant** Service 12:00-13:30, 19:00-21:00; menus 90-270F, also à la carte. Specialties: Truite à la crème et noisettes, faux filet aux cinq baies, ice cream. **Credit cards** Amex, Visa, Eurocard and MasterCard. **Pets** Dogs allowed (+25F). **Facilities** Parking. **Nearby** Epinal, Augronne and Semouse Valleys, Guéhand Waterfall, la Feuillée Nouvelle – 18-hole golf course in Epinal. **Open** Apr 1 – Oct 14.

Since 1933, four generations have successively run this hotel which could do with some improvement of late. Among its attractions are the excellent hospitality and a splendid forest setting which you can enjoy from the sloping terraces and the panoramic bay windows of the dining rooms. There is a charming, old-fashioned atmosphere here, with 1950s furniture in pale wood, parquet ceilings and beautiful table linens. You will enjoy the ambiance and the menu prices are reasonable. As for the bedrooms, they are old-fashioned and sparsely furnished, and could do with more tasteful decoration. However, many rooms have a lovely view and are reasonably priced. The renovations underway should continue at a regular pace. For the moment, we recommend the rooms in the annex, and Numbers 2, 3, and 11, which have small terraces. Meals are made with fresh products and you'll enjoy homemade ice cream and pastries.

***How to get there*** *(Map 20): 30km south of Epinal via D434 to Xertigny, then D3, D63 and D20; at Granges-de-Plombières take the forest road on the right.*

## Auberge de la Cholotte

Les Rouges-Eaux 88600 Bruyères (Vosges)
Tel. (0)3.29.50.56.93 - Fax (0)3.29.50.24.12
Mme Cholé

**Rooms** 5 with bath or shower and WC. **Price** Double 400F. **Meals** Breakfast incl.; half board 350F, full board 450F (per pers., 3 days min.). **Restaurant** Service 12:00-14:00, 19:00-21:00 (closed Sunday evening and Monday); menus 150F, also à la carte. Specialties: Jambon cuit au foin, rapées de pomme de terre, tarte aux myrtilles. **Credit cards** Visa, Eurocard and MasterCard. **Pets** Dogs allowed. **Facilities** Parking. **Nearby** Skiing in winter, Cathedral and Cloisters of Saint-Dié, Epinal, Gérardmer Lake – 18-hole golf course in Epinal. **Open** Mar 1 – Dec 31 (closed Sunday evening and Monday).

Nestled in a small valley, the Auberge de la Cholotte is an irresistibly charming 18th-century farmhouse. In the bedrooms, which have been carefully restored, fabric and wall colors are tastefully coordinated in shades of yellow, blue and soft green, with an occasional brighter color. There are permanent art exhibits on view and a collection of regional objects, along with 19th-century furniture and handsome old Alsatian pieces in polychromed wood. All combine to create a cheerful, refined atmosphere in the comfortable lounges and the two small dining rooms. Concerts are often given in a third, larger dining room with 18th-century paneling and a Steinway piano. The simple bedrooms are charming, and one has a whirlpool bath. All have a pretty view of the flower garden and the pines which cover this magnificent countryside. The seasonal cuisine is succulent and healthy, and the welcome is very friendly.

***How to get there*** *(See Map 12): 15km west of Saint-Dié via D420, towards Bruyères.*

## Chalets des Ayes

Chemin des Ayes
88160 Le Thillot (Vosges)
Tel. (0)3.29.25.00.09 - Fax (0)3.29.25.36.48 - M. Marsot

**Category** ★★★ **Rooms** 2 and 17 chalets (4-10 pers.), with bath or shower, WC and TV - Wheelchair access. **Price** Double 340-420F. Chalets 1200F (4 pers.) 4800F (10 pers.). **Meals** Breakfast 55F, served 8:00-10:00. No Restaurant. **Credit cards** Visa, Eurocard and MasterCard. **Pets** Dogs allowed only in the chalets. **Facilities** Swimming pool, tennis (38F) and parking. **Nearby** Cross-country and downhill skiing, riding, mountain bikes, walks. **Open** All year.

The Chalets des Ayes is not actually a hotel. It does however provide a practical and pleasant solution to the problem of lodging in the wild and seductively beautiful Vosges region, where it is sometimes hard to find a hotel with rural charm. Two comfortable bedrooms are at your disposal (we prefer the one overlooking the valley), along with very well-equipped, pleasantly appointed small chalets, which won the First Prize in the Vosges *département* for houses with beautiful flower gardens. Strictly speaking, they are rented by the week but, like the bedrooms, may be reserved for several nights. You can enjoy a magnificent view from the garden and the swimming pool. And if you wish to go out for dinner, you can choose between the *Vicenza,* a pleasant farm/pizzeria, or the more gastronomically sophisticated *Restaurant des Sapins.*

***How to get there*** *(Map 20): 51km west of Mulhouse via N66 towards Remiremont and towards Mulhouse to Le Thillot.*

# Auberge du Val Joli

88230 Le Valtin (Vosges)
Tel. (0)3.29.60.91.37 - Fax (0)3.29.60.81.73
M. Laruelle

**Category** ★★ **Rooms** 16 with telephone, 6 with bath, 7 with shower, 12 with WC and TV, 8 with mini bar. **Price** Single and double 150-380F. **Meals** Breakfast 38F, served 8:00-10:00; half board 241 610F, full board 346-750F. **Restaurant** Service 12:30-14:00, 19:30-21:00; menus 60-230F, also à la carte. Specialties: Truite fumée maison, pâté lorrain, tarte aux myrtilles. **Credit cards** Visa, Eurocard and MasterCard. **Pets** Dogs allowed (+20F). **Facilities** Tennis and parking. **Nearby** Saint-Dié Cathedral, Gérardmer Lake – 18-hole golf course in Epinal. **Open** All year (closed Sunday evening and Monday except during vacancies).

The little village of Valtin has only 99 inhabitants, and the mayor is also the owner of this auberge which stands at the bottom of one of the prettiest valleys of the Vosges. You only have to open the door to feel its character: low ceilings, beams, flagstones and fireplace create a completely authentic atmosphere. The dining room is very attractive with its many small windows and particularly its carved wood ceiling which is the work of an Alsatian carpenter. The comfort of the bedrooms and their bathroom facilities are vary. They would be improved with more decoration. Fortunately, the bedrooms have just been extensively enlarged: the four new bedrooms with balcony are the best in the place. Even though the hotel is on the road, there is not much noise; if in doubt reserve a room overlooking the mountain, such as numbers 16, 5, or 4 This is an unpretentious hotel in a very well preserved village.

***How to get there*** *(Map 12): 40km west of Colmar via D417 (by the Schluch pass) to le Collet, then right on D23 to Le Valtin.*

## Le Chatenet

Le Chatenet
24310 Brantôme (Dordogne)
Tel. (0)5.53.05.81.08 - Fax (0)5.53.05.85.52 - M. and Mme Laxton

**Category** ★★★ **Rooms** 10 with telephone, bath and shower, WC and TV. - 1 for disabled persons (–20%). **Price** Double 490-590F, suites 790F. **Meals** Breakfast 60F, served 8:30-10:00. No restaurant. **Credit cards** Visa, Access, Eurocard and MasterCard. **Pets** Dogs allowed. **Facilities** Heated swimming pool, tennis, billard, parking at hotel. **Nearby** Bell tower of the abbey church in Brantôme, "Peiro-Levado" dolmen, châteaux of Hierce, Puymarteau and Saint-Jean-de-Côle, Chancelade Abbey, Saltgourde estate, Marsac - 18-hole golf course in Périgueux. **Open** April - Nov.

Le Chatenet, which owner Philippe Laxton describes as "a family house open to friends and to friends of friends" in the pretty countryside of Brantôme, is a very pleasant place to stay. It is composed of two buildings in the beautiful regional architectural style. You will find superb bedrooms with upholstered walls, very tasteful furnishings and modern bathrooms. The lounge and dining room are inviting but in summer, guests often prefer the loggia, mainly because of the excellent breakfasts served there. There is no restaurant but there are many good ones nearby, including *Le Moulin de l'Abbaye, Les Frères Charbonnel* (highly rated in Michelin and Gault-Millau), and *Le Saint Marc*. This is a beautiful and very welcoming hotel.

***How to get there*** *(Map 23): 27km north of Périgueux, 1.5km from Brantôme via D78 towards Bourdeilles.*

## Domaine de la Roseraie

24310 Brantôme (Dordogne)
Tel. (0)5.53.05.84.74 - Fax (0)5.53.05.77.94
M. Roux

**Category** ★★★ **Rooms** 7 with telephone, bath or shower, WC and TV - Wheelchair access. **Price** Double 400-680F, suite 750F. **Meals** Breakfast 50F, served 7:30-10:30. Half board 370-590F. Tea room. **Restaurant** Service 12:00-15:00, 19:00-21:00; menus 145-225F, also à la carte. Specialties: Foie gras mi cuit "maison" - Sanit Jacques aux cèpes, spavé de saumon à la crème d'oseille, pavé de chevreuil aux truffes. **Credit carts** All major. **Pets** Dogs allowed. **Nearby** Bell tower of the abbey church in Brantôme, "Peiro-Levado" dolmen, châteaux of Hierce, Puymarteau and St-Jean-de-Côle, Chancelade Abbey, Saltgourde estate, Marsac – 18-hole golf course in Périgueux. **Open** Mar 14 – Jan 10.

Nestled in the countryside outside Brantôme, La Roseraie is composed of two buildings set at an angle and a Perigourdine tower where breakfasts and drinks are served here with the first sunny days. Inside, the Roseraie is very inviting. There are two lounges (one is brightened with a lovely log fire in winter) which are furnished with pleasant, comfortable period furniture and decorated with Impressionist-style paintings. The bedrooms and baths are equally attractive and impeccably clean. Families should note the splendid duplex suite. All rooms are on the ground floor and have independent entrances. Last but not least, it is beautifully quiet here.

***How to get there*** *(Map 23): 27km north of Périgueux via D939; in the center of the town, 1km in the towards of Angoulême.*

## Hôtel du Manoir de Bellerive

Route de Siorac
24480 Le Buisson de Cadouin (Dordogne)
Tel. (0)5.53.27.16.19 - Fax (0)5.53.22.09.05 - M. Clevenot

**Category** ★★★ **Rooms** 6 in park and 16 in château with air-conditioning, telephone, bath or shower, WC, TV and minibar. **Price** Single and double 500-700F and 430-850F (château). **Meals** Breakfast 50-70F, served 8:00-11:00. **Restaurant** Service 19:30-22:00, menus 115-280F, also à la carte. Specialties: "Cuisine inventive" and regional cooking. 12:00-14:00 menus 95-145F. **Credit cards** Visa, Eurocard and MasterCard. **Pets** Dogs allowed. **Facilities** Swimming pool, tennis, sauna (100F), parking. **Nearby** Le Bugue, cave of Bara-Bahau and Proumeyssac chasm, Limeuil, National Museum of Prehistory in Les Eyzies – 18-hole golf course in la-Croix-de-Mortemart. **Open** Mar 1 – Dec 15.

Situated off the road in beautiful English parklike grounds, this 19th-century manor borders the Dordogne. It has been delightfully converted by two interior decorators. On the ground floor, the lounge, bar and dining room open off a vast central colonnaded hall, from which a double staircase sweeps up to the *premier étage* bedrooms. The pervading atmosphere of aestheticism and refinement has been created by a sensitive and masterly combination of colors, fabrics and *trompe l'œil* marble. There are also antiques, beautiful carpets, and engravings. Among the bedrooms, you can choose between those in the manor house and others in a small chateau, which are just as comfortable.The bathrooms are luxurious. In good weather breakfast is served on the terrace, which overlooks the Dordogne. You will find a very hospitable welcome. The restaurant has just opened a new dining room with varied menus.

***How to get there*** *(Map 23): 47km southeast of Périgueux via N89 to Niversac, D710 to Le Bugue, and D31.*

1998

## Domaine de la Barde

Route de Périgueux
24260 Le Bugue (Dordogne)
Tel. (0)5.53.07.16.54 - Fax (0)5.53.54.76.19 - M. Darnaud

**Category** ★★★ **Rooms** 18 with telephone, bath or shower, WC and TV on request - 2 for disablec persons. **Price** Double 425-940F. **Meals** Breakfast (buffet) 65F, served 8:00-10:30. No restaurant Diner only for residents, by reservation. **Credit cards** Visa, Eurocard and MasterCard. **Pets** Dogs allowed on request (+50F). **Facilities** Swimming pool, Tennis, Sauna (60F) - Parking. **Nearby** Le Bugue: cave of Bara-Bahau and chasm of Proumeyssac; Limeuil; Museum of Prehistory in Eyzies abbey of Cadouin; *bastides* of Belvès tour in Montferrand-du-Périgord (130 km) - 18-hole Croix-de-Mortemart golf course. **Open** Mid. Apr – Oct.

The new owners of this 14th-century estate have just converted it into a hotel designed for comfort and pleasure. The Domaine's bedrooms, all different, are named after plants: *Bleuet, Les Physalis*; the history of the estate *Le Colombier, Maître Pierre*, and *La Belle Meunière*, located in the mill; or after the hill that can be seen from the window: *Bara-Bahau*. The rooms are located in three different buildings: in the manor house, containing the smallest room to the most luxurious; in the old nut-oil mill, featuring more rustic but thoroughly delightful rooms with modern accommodations (some have an independent entrance overlooking the garden); and the most recent bedroom *La Forge*, which is located in a small, Mansart-style house. Then there is the beautiful park with many pleasant spots for relaxation and the replanted formal garden that looks as it must have centuries ago. There is no restaurant but guests can request dinner, which is served in a lovely dining room. The owners are as charming as the Domaine de la Barde is beautiful.

***How to get there*** *(Map 23): 47km southeast of Périgueux via N89 to Niversac, D710 to Bugue.*

## Le Relais du Touron

Le Touron
24200 Carsac-Aillac (Dordogne)
Tel. (0)5.53.28.16.70 - Fax (0)5.53 28 52 51 - Mme Carlier and M. Amriah

**Category** ★★ **Rooms** 12 with telephone, bath or shower and WC. **Price** Double 265-375F, triple 390-485F. **Meals** Breakfast 38F, served 8:00-10:00; half board 293-340F. **Restaurant** Closed Tuesday (lunchtime) and Friday in high season (except half board); menus 92-270F, also à la carte. Specialties: Foie gras d'oie poêlé aux pommes caramélisées, feuilleté d'escargots aux cèpes, filet d'agneau au beurre de foie gras, sandre à l'orange. **Credit cards** Visa, Eurocard and MasterCard. **Pets** Dogs allowed. **Facilities** Swimming pool, parking. **Nearby** Walk along the valley of the Enéa from Carsac to Sainte-Nathalène, old town and house of La Boétie in Sarlat, Château de Puymartin – 9 hole golf course in Vitrac. **Open** Apr 1 – Nov 14.

The Relais du Touron is a peaceful country inn at the end of the village. The rustling leaves of the poplar trees and the murmuring of the Enea as it flows tranquilly along create a romantic pastoral atmosphere. The comfortable bedrooms are in the building facing the swimming pool. In the neighboring Périgourdine house, you will find No. 11 and No. 12, which is the best of the two and is reserved for parties of 3 or 4 people. (It has a beautiful high ceiling and exposed beams.) A beautiful swimming pool, surrounded by shady trees and lawns and a terrace where meals and breakfasts are served facing the garden: contribute to making the Touron a delightful place to stay.

***How to get there*** *(Map 23): 75km southeast of Périgueux to Sarlat, then D704 towards Gourdon (600m before the village of Carsac).*

## Manoir d'Hautegente

24120 Coly (Dordogne)
Tel. (0)5.53.51.68.03 - Fax (0)5.53.50.38.52
Mme Hamelin

**Category** ★★★ **Rooms** 10 and 4 duplex, with telephone, bath, WC, TV and minibar. **Price** Double 520-970F. **Meals** Breakfast 65F, served 8:30-10:00; half board 510-750F (per pers.). **Restaurant** Service from 20:00; menus 220-380F (at lunchtime 150F), also à la carte. Specialties: Brasière de ris de veau aux écrevisses, poêlée de cèpes sur son foie gras et sauce aux truffes. **Credit cards** Visa, Eurocard and MasterCard. **Pets** Dogs allowed. **Facilities** Heated swimming pool, fishing, parking. **Nearby** Lascaux caves, Abbey of Aubazines, Argentat, Collonges-la-Rouge. **Open** Apr 1 – Nov 11.

Formerly a mill and forge of the warrior monks of Saint Amand-du-Coly and the property of the Hamelin family for almost three centuries, this Perigord manor has been an elegant hotel for several years now. It is in a beautiful valley where graceful old walnut and oak trees line the roads. Ducks roam freely along the banks of the winding, babbling brook in front of the manor. The rooms and lounges have all been tastefully decorated with the family furniture in a perfect blend of style and comfort. The fabric wall drapes and curtains are splendid, especially in the *Liserons* room, which is very large and has a private balcony overlooking the river. You will receive a warm and attentive welcome at this very charming hotel.

***How to get there*** *(Map 23): 30km southwest of Brive-la-Gaillarde via N89 towards Périgueux to Le Lardin-Saint-Lazare, then D704 and D62 towards Sarlat-Souillac.*

# Hôtel Cro-Magnon

24620 Les Eyzies-de-Tayac (Dordogne)
Tel. (0)5.53.06.97.06 - Fax (0)5.53.06.95.45
M. and Mme Leyssales

**Category** ★★★ **Rooms** 18 and 4 apartments, with telephone, bath or shower and WC (TV on request). **Price** Double 350-550F, suite 600-800F. **Meals** Breakfast 50F, served 8:00-10:00; half board 350-505F (per pers., 3 days min.). **Restaurant** Service 12:00-14:00, 19:00-21:15 (closed Wednesday lunchtime except national holidays); menus 140-280F, also à la carte. Specialties: Escalopes de foie de canard aux pignons de pin, millefeuille d'agneau sauce poivrade, truffe en croustade. **Credit cards** All major. **Pets** Dogs allowed (+30F). **Facilities** Swimming pool, parking. **Nearby** Le Bugue, Bara-Bahau cave and Proumeyssac chasm, Limeuil, National Museum of Prehistory in Les Eyzies – 18-hole La-Croix-de-Mortemart golf course in Le Bugue. **Open** May 8 – Oct 10.

This old coaching inn has been in the family for generations. The two reception rooms, whose colors harmonize with the open stonework and old furniture, are charming. There is a small museum in one. You can choose between a pretty dining room in local style or another, more modern, one which opens onto a shady terrace. Excellent regional cuisine is complemented by a well-chosen wine list. The bedrooms are comfortable and elegantly decorated; for peace and quiet, we prefer those in the annex, which look out onto a very large park with a swimming pool. The staff is very friendly.

***How to get there*** *(Map 23): 45km southeast of Périgueux via N89 and D710, then D47.*

# Hôtel Les Glycines

24620 Les Eyzies-de-Tayac (Dordogne)
Tel. (0)5.53.06.97.07 - Fax (0)5.53.06.92.19
M. and Mme Mercat

**Category** ★★★ **Rooms** 23 with telephone, bath and WC. **Price** Single 315-390F, double 360-410F. **Meals** Breakfast 50F, served 8:00-10:00; half board 395-450F and 493-550F (per pers., 3 days min.). **Restaurant** Service 12:00-14:00, 19:30-21:30 (closed Saturday lunchtime except national holidays and July, Aug. and Sep.); menus 140-290F, also à la carte. Specialties: Pavé de bœuf fourré de son escalope de foie frais et sa sauce truffes, pain perdu à la gelée d'abricot aux amandes. **Credit cards** All major. **Pets** Dogs allowed. **Facilities** Swimming pool, park, parking. **Nearby** Le Bugue, cave of Bara-Bahau and Proumeyssac chasm, Limeuil, National Museum of Prehistory in Les Eyzies – 18-hole La-Croix-de-Mortemart golf course in Le Bugue. **Open** Apr 15 – End Oct.

Dating back to 1862, this old coach inn is a large house where stone, wood and prolific vegetation blend happily together. As the name indicates, there is a pergola covered with an abundance of wisteria; trimmed lime trees shade the terrace. The lounge and bar have a restful atmosphere and are furnished and decorated with great care. The lovely dining room opens onto the garden, but meals may also be taken on a new veranda that opens onto the lawn. All the bedrooms are very comfortable and the furnishings have been well selected; fabrics, papers and colors are in a contemporary style. The cuisine makes good use of fresh produce from the garden.

***How to get there*** *(Map 23): 45km southeast of Périgueux via N89 and D710, then D47.*

## Moulin de la Beune

24620 Les Eyzies-de-Tayac (Dordogne)
Tel. (0)5.53.06.94.33 - Fax (0)5.53.06.98.06
M. and Mme Soulié

**Category** ★★ **Rooms** 20 with telephone, bath or shower and WC. **Price** Single and double 260-400F. **Meals** Breakfast 40F, served 8:00-10:30; half board 320F, full board 420F (per pers., 2 days min.). **Restaurant** Service 12:00-14:30, 19:00-21:30 (closed Tuesday lunchtime); menus 95-280F, also à la carte. Specialties: Saint-Jacques aux truffes, raviolis de foie gras, pigeonneau roti en cocotte, cêpes et ail. **Credit cards** Amex, Visa, Eurocard and MasterCard. **Pets** Dogs allowed. **Facilities** Parking. **Nearby** Le Bugue, cave of Bara-Bahau and Proumeyssac chasm, Limeuil, National Museum of Prehistory in Les Eyzies – 18-hole la-Croix-de-Mortemart golf course in Le Bugue. **Open** Mar – Nov.

When you arrive at this old mill, it is hard to believe that you are in one of the most popular tourist areas of France. The River Beune runs quietly at your feet and the small garden dotted with tables is a peaceful haven. In the lounge, beside the large fireplace, there are armchairs and little tables arranged comfortably for reading and writing. To one side there is a room where drinks and breakfast are served. The decor of the recently refurbished bedrooms has been tastefully chosen. The restaurant, Le Vieux Moulin, occupies another adjacent mill, and is also charmingly decorated. In the large dining room with its exposed stonework and beams, or in the garden at the foot of the ancient cliffs, truffle-based Périgourdine specialties are served.

***How to get there*** *(Map 23): 45km southeast of Périgueux via N89 and D710, then D47; in the middle of the village.*

## La Grande Marque

24220 Marnac-Saint-Cyprien (Dordogne)
Tel. (0)5.53.31.61.63 - Fax (0)5.53.28.39.55
Mme Terracol

**Category** ★★ **Rooms** 16 (4 duplex) with telephone, bath or shower, WC and TV - 1 for disabled persons. **Price** Single and double 260F, duplex 400F. **Meals** Breakfast 35F, served 8:30-11:30; half board and full board 250-285F. **Restaurant** Service 12:30-13:30, 19:30-21:00; menus 75-150F, also à la carte. Specialties: Foie gras, cuisine du terroir. **Credit cards** Visa, Eurocard and MasterCard. **Pets** Small dogs allowed. **Facilities** Swimming pool, tennis, parking. **Nearby** Châteaux of Veyrignac, Les Milandes and Montfort, Beynac and Cazenac, Domme – 9-hole Rochebois golf course in Vitrac. **Open** Apr – Nov 1.

Set on a hillside in the heart of the countryside, the Grande Marque is a landmark site that offers an extraordinary panoramic view over the Dordogne. You enter by a modern, soberly furnished lounge that is illuminated by immense bay windows. The bedrooms upstairs are also simple. In the 17th-century house, four duplexes for families or groups of friends have just been opened. The garden is a mass of flowers and the shady terrace has several tables where guests can enjoy breakfast in summer. Excellent dinners are served in a pleasantly rustic dining room with a big fire in winter.

***How to get there*** *(Map 23): 57km southeast of Périgueux via N89 to Niversac, D710 to Le Bugue, D31 to Le Buisson, then Siorac and D703. Turn left in 1km.*

## La Métairie

24150 Mauzac (Dordogne)
Tel. (0)5.53.22.50.47 - Fax (0)5.53.22.52.93
M. Heinz Johner

**Category** ★★★ **Rooms** 10 with telephone, bath, WC and TV (7 with minibar). **Price** Double 450-600F (low season), 500-650F (high season), suite 950-1110F. **Meals** Breakfast 60F, served 8:00-11:00, half board 450-550F (per pers., 2 days min.). **Restaurant** Service 12:30-13:45, 19:30-21:00; menus 150-300F, also à la carte. Specialties of Périgord. **Credit cards** Visa, Eurocard and MasterCard. **Pets** Dogs allowed (+30F). **Facilities** Swimming pool, parking. **Nearby** Les Eyzies, Limeuil, Le Bugue, Bergerac – 18-hole la-Croix-de-Mortemart golf course in Le Bugue. **Open** Apr 1 – Oct 30.

A few kilometers from the famous horseshoe-shaped Cingle de Trémolat, in a beautiful valley where great loops of the Dordogne River wind through a mosaic of cultivated fields, lies La Métairie. It is a charming and beautiful house converted with comfort, delicacy and good taste. The garden is also very well done. At the same level as the lawn a pleasant terrace runs along the side of the house, and in summer there is a grill near the swimming pool. The aroma from the cuisine is very appetizing. Finally, it is worth noting that the hotel is close to a superb lake where every type of water sport is available.

***How to get there*** *(Map 23): 68km south of Périgueux via N89 and D70 to Le Bugue, then D703 and branch off for Mauzac.*

# Hôtel de la Ferme lamy

24220 Meyrals (Dordogne)
Tel. (0)5.53.29.62.46 - Fax (0)5.53.59.61.41
M. Bougon

**Rooms** 12 with telephone, bath or shower, WC and TV (10 with minibar) - 1 for disabled persons. **Price** Double 310-800F. **Meals** Breakfast 40F. No restaurant. **Credit cards** All major. **Pets** Dogs allowed (35F). **Facilities** Swimming pool - Parking. **Nearby** Sarlat, Valley of Vézère (Prehistory route), Dordogne Valley (castles), vineyard of Bergerac, Les Eyzies, museum of Tobacco in Bergerac, Limeuil, Le Bugue - 18-hole Croix-de-Mortemart golf course in Bugue. **Open** All year.

As its name indicates, this hotel is an old farmhouse, close to the the magnificent sites of the Dordogne and the Vézère Valleys and reflecting their remote, ethereal atmosphere. Standing on a shady, green hilltop where you will enjoy a beautiful panorama of the region, the Ferme Lamy offers peace and quiet, and total relaxation. Located in various buildings, the twelve recently opened bedrooms have comfortable amenities while retaining their original charm. There is a wide choice of rooms, depending on whether they are located in the outbuildings or in the main house: we prefer the latter. There is no restaurant in the hotel but two neighboring restaurants (one is a three-minute walk away) offer half-board, making the Ferme Lamy an attractive place to stay in many ways.

***How to get there*** *(Map 23): 12km west of Sarlat to Périgueux via D6 then D47, in Bénivès, take the road to the left via C3 towards Meyrals.*

1998

## La Roseraie

11, Place d'Armes
24290 Montignac-Lascaux (Dordogne)
Tel. (0)5.53.50.53.92 - Fax (0)5.53.51.02.23 - M. Guimbaud

**Category** ★★★ **Rooms** 14 with telephone, bath or shower, WC and TV. **Price** Double 350-490F. **Meals** Breakfast 45F; half board 350-440F (per pers., obligatory in summer). **Restaurant** Closed 1 Nov – Easter. Service 12:00-14:00, 19:00-21:30; menus 100-250F; also à la carte. Specialties: Foie gras frais chaud aux fraises, confit, tournedos sauce Périgueux, tartes aux fruits. **Credit cards** All major. **Pets** Dogs allowed. **Facilities** Swimming pool. **Nearby** Lascaux, abbey of Saint Amand-de-Coly, Sarlat, manor of Eyrignac, Hautefort – 18-hole golf course in Brive-la-Gaillarde. **Open** 6 Apr – 1 Nov.

On the outskirts of the famous Lascaux prehistoric caves, the Roseraie is a big, beautiful 19th-century townhouse with, on the edge of the Vézère River, a delicious flower garden where meals are served in summer; large, cool shade trees; and the roseraie, rose garden, which gives the hotel its name. Fourteen comfortable, colorfully decorated, intimate bedrooms have been tastefully arranged. The two most beautiful rooms are very large, with lovely parquet floors and windows overlooking the river. The young owner makes his own preserved Périgord specialties, which are used abundantly in the hotel's gourmet cuisine.

***How to get there*** *(Map 23): 37km southwest of Brive-la-Gaillarde via N89 in to Périgueux to Condat; follow towards Lascaux.*

## La Plume d'Oie

Au Bourg 24250 La Roque-Gageac (Dordogne)
Tel. (0)5.53.29.57.05./53.28.94.93 - Fax (0)5.53.31.04.81
M. and Mme Walker

**Rooms** 4 with telephone, bath and shower, WC, TV and minibar. **Price** Single 350F, double 400-450F. **Meals** Breakfast 55F, served 8:00-9:30. **Restaurant** Service 12:15-13:30, 19:30-21:00; menus 195F, 295F, 395F, also à la carte. Specialties: Lasagnes à la purée de mais et aux truffes de pays, grenadins de veau aux giroole fraîches, filet de bar à la tomate et au basilic. **Credit cards** Visa, Eurocard and MasterCard. **Pets** Dogs allowed (+25-40F). **Nearby** Old Town and La Boétie's house in Sarlat, châteaux of Puymartin and Commarques, Carsac, Lascaux – 9-hole golf course in Vitrac. **Open** Mar – Jan (closed Monday). By reservation.

La Plume d'Oie is a restaurant with an excellent reputation to which four charming bedrooms have just been added. Light and bright, comfortably modern, they are decorated with pretty chestnut furniture and cream-colored fabrics with occasional splashes of color; the bathrooms are impeccable. Three rooms open onto the river, which is just across the narrow street. Built on the flank of a gigantic cliff right on the Dordogne, La Roque-Gageac is a superb site. There's another side to the coin, however: you hear the traffic a little, which can be a problem in the high season – July and August. If you want complete silence, it's best to reserve the bedroom looking out on the cliff. Breakfast is served in your room when you wish. The jovial, thoughtful owners will welcome you warmly.

***How to get there*** *(Map 23): 8km south of Sarlat-la-Canéda.*

## Hôtel L'Abbaye

Rue de l'Abbaye
24220 Saint-Cyprien-en-Périgord (Dorgogne)
Tel. (0)5.53.29.20.48 - Fax (0)5.53.29.15.85 - Yvette and Marcel Schaller

**Category** ★★★ **Rooms** 24 with telephone, bath or shower and WC (TV on request). **Price** Single 340-400F, double 550-680F, suite 680-700F. **Meals** Breakfast 55F, brunch in July and Aug 60F, served 8:00-10:00; half board 390-560F (per pers.). **Restaurant** Service 12:00-14:00, 19:30-21:30; menus 75F (lunch), 145-320F, also à la carte. Specialties: Foie gras frais, poulet sauté aux langoustines, escargots à la crème de persil. **Credit cards** Amex, Visa, Eurocard and MasterCard. **Pets** Dogs allowed. **Facilities** Swimming pool, parking. **Nearby** Cave of Proumeyssac, Le Bugue, Château de Campagne, Les Eyzies – 18-hole La-Croix-de-Mortemart golf course in Le Bugue. **Open** Apr 15 – Oct 15.

The exterior of this large house in the pretty village of Saint-Cyprien has been left untouched, so that the local stone acts as decoration. The same feeling is echoed in the lounge, with its stone walls and fireplace and original stone floor. The bedrooms are all comfortably appointed; some are more luxurious than others. In one of the annexes, some bedrooms can be combined to form a family apartment, and the bedrooms in the new building are very elegant. A lovely terrace and pleasant gardens with swimming pool add to the charm of L'Abbaye, where the cuisine is very good and the owners warm and welcoming.

***How to get there*** *(Map 23): 54km southeast of Périgueux via N89 and D710 to Le Bugue, then D703 and D35 to St-Cyprien.*

## Hostellerie Saint-Jacques

24470 Saint-Saud-Lacoussière (Dordogne)
Tel. (0)5.53.56.97.21 - Fax (0)5.53.56.91.33
M. and Mme Babayou

**Category** ★★★ **Rooms** 18 and 3 apartments, with telephone, bath or shower and WC, TV and minibar, radio. **Price** Single 250F, double 350-450F, suite 700F. **Meals** Breakfast 50F, brunch by the swimming pool; half board 300-400F, full board 400-500F (per pers., 2 days min.); in apart. (family with 2 children) 1190F and 1390F. **Restaurant** Service 12:00-13:30, 19:00-21:00, 22:00 in July and Aug (closed Sunday evening and Monday except for residents, and Oct 31 – Easter except Sunday and national holidays); menus 100-217F, also à la carte. Specialties: Crêpe de maïs aux langoustines, trilogie de foie gras de canard maison (aux figues, naturel, magret), terrine chaude de cèpes de pays aux coquilles Saint jacques. **Credit cards** Visa, Eurocard and MasterCard. **Pets** Dogs allowed. **Facilities** Heated swimming pool, tennis, riding (2km), parking. **Nearby** Brantôme Abbey, Villars caves, Saint-Jean-de-Côle – 18-hole Saltgourde golf course in Marsac. **Open** Apr 1 – Oct 31 (closed Sunday night and Monday in low season).

The Hostellerie Saint-Jacques has the generous proportions of an 18th-century Périgourdine house. The bedrooms all have different fabrics and furniture and are comfortable, cheerful, bright and decorated with a great amount of taste and imagination. Some have a small corner lounge where the bookshelves (worthy of Arsène Lupin), open up to give access to the luxurious bathroom. Downstairs, the dining room has a Provençal air with its elegant yellow and blue decor, but the cuisine is nevertheless authentically Périgourdine. Made with local farm products, it is excellent and light. In the summer, a few tables are set out beneath the maples. Note the special Weekend and Country Vacation package rates.

***How to get there*** *(Map 23): 58km north of Périgueux via N21 to La Coquille, then D79.*

## Le Chaufourg en Périgord

24400 Sourzac (Dordogne)
Tel. (0)5.53.81.01.56 - Fax (0)5.53.82.94.87
M. Dambier

**Rooms** 10 (2 suites) with telephone, bath, WC and TV (4 with minibar). **Price** Double 700-1200F, suite 1500F. **Meals** Breakfast 80F, served 8:00-11:00. **Restaurant** For residents only. By reservation. **Credit cards** Amex, Visa, Eurocard and MasterCard. **Pets** Dogs allowed on request. **Facilities** Swimming pool, parking. **Nearby** Saint-Emilion, Brantôme, Bergerac, Périgueux, Echourgnac and forest of la Double, Chancelade Abbey, Saltgourde estate, Marsac – 18-hole golf course in Périgueux. **Open** All year.

This very beautiful and elegant 17th-century family mansion is not really a hotel: Le Chaufourg en Périgord is M. Dambier's childhood home, which he has restored "to create the elegant decor I dreamed of for entertaining." You will, not surprisingly, find everything here you could wish for when you travel: very comfortable accommodations, the tasteful furnishings (featured in many French interior-decoration magazines) warm hospitality, and those extra details that make all the difference. There is a billiard table at your disposal, and a wealth of information on making the most of your visit to this enchanting part of the Périgord. The garden overlooking the Isle River is heavenly. You can relax around the swimming pool, stroll in the shady park or take a boat ride down the river. Served on reservation, dinners highlight the specialties of the Périgord's renowned cuisine.

***How to get there*** *(Map 23): 30km southwest of Périgueux via N89, towards Mussidan.*

## Le Vieux Logis

24510 Trémolat (Dordogne)
Tel. (0)5.53.22.80.06 - Fax (0)5.53.22.84.89 - M. Giraudel
E-mail: le.vieux.logis@wanadoo.fr

**Category** ★★★ **Rooms** 24 with telephone, bath, WC, TV, and minibar. **Price** Single and double 750-1390F, suite 1640F. **Meals** Breakfast 85F, served 8:00-11:00. **Restaurant** Service 12:00-14:00, 19:30-21:30, carte. 400F; Menus 185F, 245F, 390F. **Credit cards** All major. **Pets** Dogs allowed. **Facilities** Swimming pool, parking. **Nearby** Tobacco Museum in Bergerac, Lanquais, bastide town of Sainte-Foy-la-Grande. **Open** All year.

For four centuries, the same family has lived on this superb estate, which was made into a hotel by M. Giraudel's mother. The different buildings are all charming: In addition to the main building, there is the tobacco barn, the lodge, and the gardener's house. No two bedrooms are alike but they have one point in common:, they are extremely comfortable, quiet and elegantly decorated down to the last detail; the antique furniture and the *souleiado* Provençal fabrics go together beautifully. The two dining rooms are magnificent. One is small, with pale wood paneling; the other is immense, overlooked by a balustraded lounge (the former hayloft). Gourmets will love it, and so will those who appreciate interior design.

***How to get there*** *(Map 23): 54km south of Périgueux via N89 to Niversac. D710 to Le Bugue and D81.*

# Manoir Hôtel de Rochecourbe

Rochecourbe 24220 Vézac (Dordogne)
Tel. (0)5.53.31.09.84 - Fax (0)5.53.28.59.07
M. Roger

**Rooms** 6 with telephone, bath, 5 with WC. **Price** Single and double 260-500F. **Meals** Breakfast 39F, served to 10:30. No restaurant. **Credit cards** All major. **Pets** Dogs allowed by reservation. **Facilities** Swimming pool, parking. **Nearby** Sarlat, châteaux de Beynac and de Castelnaud, canes of Eyzies – 9-hole golf course in Vitrac. **Open** Apr – 14 Nov

Surrounded by the prehistoric and historic treasures of the Périgord, this traditional manor house, which has been in the same family for generations, has recently been converted into a hotel. The friendly atmosphere is that of a home. Six rooms, five of which are beautifully spacious, have been discreetly decorated and equipped with modern baths. They overlook the surrounding countryside, some enjoying an incomparable view of the Château of Beynac spectacularly silhouetted against the sky. Breakfast is served in a large dining room with a stone fireplace. Guests may relax in a pleasant salon or, in summer, in a small shady garden in front.

***How to get there*** *(Map 23): 75km southeast of Périgueux to Sarlat, then D57 towards Bergerac.*

## Villa Térésa-Hôtel Semiramis

4, allée de Rebsomen
33120 Arcachon (Gironde)
Tel. (0)5.56.83.25.87 - Fax (0)5.57.52.22.41 - M. and Mme Baurès

**Category** ★★★ **Rooms** 20 with telephone, bath, WC and TV on request. **Price** Double 400F, 630-680F. **Meals** Breakfast 63F; half board 550F. **Restaurant** By reservation. Service 20:00-21:00; menu 180F. Specialties: regional cooking. **Credit cards** Visa, Eurocard and MasterCard. **Pets** Small dogs allowed (+35F) except in the restaurant. **Facilities** Swimming pool, parking. **Nearby** Bassin d'Arcachon: dune du Pyla; Cap Ferret; lakes of Hourtins-Carcans, Lacanau; Bordeaux; Le Bordelais. **Open** All year.

In 1860, the Pereire banking family had the idea of building a vast "urban park" on the dune belt of Arcachon. It was a fabulous ensemble of neo-Gothic, Moorish, Colonial, Swiss and other villas which were frequented by the aristocracy, the *haute bourgeoisie* and the high flyers of the medical world. Saved from seemingly inevitable ruin and classed as a historic monument, Thérésa has been brilliantly restored. In the lobby, wood paneling runs around vast decorative compositions in earthenware tiles, continuing up the stairway and onto a gallery upstairs. The comfortable bedrooms, located in the Villa and in a small house near the swimming pool, are for the most part very old-fashioned and not well soundproofed. Those in the Villa are soberly decorated in tones of pearl grey and pink. The room in a small turret is surrounded by windows in arcades and enjoys an immense terrrace. The pavilion bedrooms have prettier fabrics and beautiful carpets. There is also a pleasant salon decorated with squat armchairs. The dining room is bright and elegant, and each evening on reservation a set menu is served, based on fresh market produce. Elegantly enhanced by pretty dishes and embroidered tablecloths, the breakfasts are outstanding and original. For a fish dinner in town, try *Chez Yvette*.

***How to get there*** *(Map 22): 60 km southwest of Bordeaux. In the "winter city".*

## Hauterive Hôtel Saint-James

3, place Camille-Hostein
33270 Bouliac (Gironde)
Tel. (0)5.57.97.06.00 - Fax (0)5.56.20.92.58 - M. Amat

**Category** ★★★★ **Rooms** 18 (10 with air-conditioning) with telephone, bath, WC, TV and minibar **Price** Single 500-900F, double 550-950F, suite 1250-1550F. **Meals** Breakfast 80F, served from 7:00. **Restaurant** Service 12:00-14:00, 20:00-22:00; menus 255F, also à la carte. Specialties: Fondant d'aubergine au cumin, pigeon aux épices et sa pastilla, salade d'huîtres au caviar et sa crépinette. **Credit cards** All major. **Pets** Dogs not allowed. **Facilities** Swimming pool, tennis, parking. **Nearby** Museum of Contemporary Art, Museum of Fine Art, Port-de-la-Lune Theatre, Cité Mondiale du Vin (25, quai des Chartons) in Bordeaux; Le Bordelais (renowned world-wide for its wines) – 18-hole Cameyrac golf course, 18-hole Bordelais golf course. **Open** All year.

To include this ultra-modern place in this chapter means that it must be out of the ordinary. And so it is, due to the immense talents of two people: the owner and chef, Jean-Marie Amat, and the architect Jean Nouvel. The result of their combined efforts is amazing. Occupying three buildings, all the bedrooms have picture windows with extensive views over vineyards and the plain of Bordeaux. The decor is in tones of white and cream, broken by brightly-colored carpets or the flash of steel grey. This high-tech approach combines with bunches of flowers, sculptures and books to create the intimacy of a private house: what could have been cold, is warm instead. There is no need to describe the famous cuisine of Jean-Marie Amat. His celebrated restaurant and an excellent bistro adjoin the hotel.

***How to get there*** *(Map 22): 5km east of Bordeaux. On Bypass, Bouliac exit (number 23).*

1998

## La Maison du Bassin - Le Bayonne

5, rue des Pionniers
Lège 33950 Cap Ferret (Gironde)
Tel. (0)5.56.60.60.63 - Fax (0)5.56.03.71.47 - Mme Desfayes

**Rooms** 7 with telephone, shower and WC. **Price** 450, 550 and 700F. **Meals** Breakfast 50F, served until 11:30. **Restaurant** *Le Bistrot du Bassin.* Service 19:00-23:00 (closed Tuesday except July and Aug); menus 170-200F. **Credit cards** Amex, Visa, Eurocard and MasterCard. **Pets** Dogs allowed. **Nearby** Bordeaux, Le Bordelais (renowned world-wide for its wines) - 18-hole Lacanau golf course. **Open** Apr 1 – 2 Jan.

After Saint Tropez and the Island of Ré, now it's Cape Ferret, the summer vacation spot popular with Bordeaux families that has become the fashionable new resort of France. The Maison du Bassin looks like something out of an interior decoration magazine: the building itself with its beautiful wood façade in the tradition of this oyster-farming area, the bedrooms with objects and old furniture evoking a theme: *Louisiane, Cabane de Pêcheur, Maison du Bassin....* Our favorite is Room 3, *Cabine de Bateau*, which overlooks the water. Each room is supplied with elegant dressing gowns and toiletry articles. The charm of this small hotel also lies in its restaurant looking out over the water, which features local specialties and a magnificent dessert trolley. Its colonial bar, "Le Tchanqué", is delightful, too, and the young staff is efficient and friendly. The Maison du Bassin is an appealing spot for those who love ocean beaches--and who have nothing against being in the latest trendy resort. Other musts: on Cape Ferret, *Fredelian,* for its famous ice cream and *cannelet* pastry; *Chez Hortense,* for a special mussel recipe; *Le Sail Fish,* with excellent cuisine and a popular night-owl atmosphere; the *Hôtel de la Plage* in L'Herbe; and in La Vigne, the *Wharrfzazate.* Don't miss a drink at the *Pinasse Café* or *L'Escale.*

***How to get there*** *(Map 22): 65km southwest of Bordeaux.*

1998

## Hôtel des Pins

23, rue des Fauvettes
33950 Cap Ferret (Gironde)
Tel. (0)5.56.60.60.11 - Fax (0)5.56.60.67.41 - M. Rohr

**Category** ★★ **Rooms** 14 with telephone, bath or shower, WC, TV and minibar. **Price** Single and double 255-345F, 288-418F. **Meals** Breakfast 38F, half board and full board 285-310F, 289-344F (per pes.). **Restaurant** Open 15 June – 30 Sep. Service 19:00-23:00, menus 90-120F, also à la carte. Specialties: pavé de morue fraîche à l'aïoli, thon grillé à la bordelaise, brochette de magret à l'orange, agneau de Pauillac, assiette aux trois saumons, escargots. **Credit cards** Visa, Eurocard and MasterCard. **Pets** Dogs allowed by reservation. **Facilities** Parking. **Nearby** Dune du Pyla, fishing, réserve banc d'Arguein, Bordeaux, le Bordelais – 18-hole Cameyrac golf course, 18-hole bordelais golf course. **Open** 22 Mars – 11 Nov

Located in a quiet quarter in the heart of Cape Ferret, the Hotel des Pins is a charming small turn-of-the-century hotel built in the Arcachon style and renovated in its original spirit. Set in the midst of a garden full of hydrangeas and roses, it is midway between the beaches of the Arcachon Basin, 50 yards away, and those of the Atlantic, 700 yards distant. It has the atmosphere of a traditional family home, with panelled walls in the old-style bedrooms. Dinners, offering several excellent specialties, are served in summer on the terrace high above the shady garden. On your return from the beach, be sure to stop off *Fredelian,* Cape Ferret's famous spot for homemade pastries and ice cream.

***How to get there*** *(Map 22): 65km southwest of Bordeaux via D106 to Lège, Cap Ferret.*

# Château du Foulon

33480 Castelnau-de-Médoc (Gironde)
Tel. (0)5.56.58.20.18 - Fax (0)5.56.58.23.43
M. and Mme de Baritault du Carpia

**Rooms** 5 with bath and WC. **Price** Double 450F, suite 500-600F. **Meals** Breakfast incl. No restaurant. **Credit cards** Not accepted. **Pets** Dogs not allowed. **Facilities** Parking. **Nearby** Médoc peninsula on the left bank of the Garonne, then the Gironde (day trip, 150km), Mouton-Rothschild Museum in Pauillac – 18-hole Bordelais golf course, 18-hole Bordeaux-le-Lac golf course. **Open** All year.

The very elegant Château du Foulon stands at the end of a long avenue of trees which leads into a wood and then an immense park where you will discover magnificent peacocks and snow-white swans. M. and Mme de Baritault, who will greet you with great hospitality, have tastefully decorated each bedroom with beautiful antique furniture. There are also two charming apartments, ideal for a long stay. Breakfasts are served at a large table in the magnificent dining room, a model of elegance and refinement. For dinner or for discovering the region, your hosts will give you a wealth of good advice.

***How to get there*** *(Map 22): 28km northwest of Bordeaux via D1 to Le Verdoux, then go south to Foulon.*

# Hostellerie du Vieux Raquine

Lugon
33240 Saint-André-de-Cubzac (Gironde)
Tel. (0)5.57.84.42.77 - Fax (0)5.57.84.83.77 - Mme de Raquine

**Category** ★★★ **Rooms** 10 with telephone, bath or shower and WC (5 with TV). **Price** Single 440 700F, suite 650F. **Meals** Breakfast 55F, served 8:00-10:00. No restaurant. **Credit cards** Visa, Eurocard and MasterCard. **Pets** Dogs not allowed. **Facilities** Parking. **Nearby** Church of Saint-André-de-Cubzac, château de Bouilh, Bourg, Saint-Emilion – 18-hole Bordeaux golf course. **Open** Feb 11 - Jan 11.

The ground floor of this hotel covers the whole top of a hill. Completely renovated, it is furnished in an old-fashioned style. The bedrooms are impeccably kept and all are at ground level. There are two reception rooms including the one used as the dining room; it has windows all along one side opening onto a large terrace with an outstanding view of the vineyards of Fronsac, bordered by the Dordogne in the distance. Mme Raquine makes the hotel feel like a family house. Tranquillity and fresh air are guaranteed. For fine dining, try a restaurant near the hotel or *Au Sarment* in Saint-Gervais.

***How to get there*** *(Map 22): 23km northeast of Bordeaux; A10 St-André-de-Cubzac exit, D670.*

## Le Pavillon de Margaux

33460 Margaux (Gironde)
Tel. (0)5.57.88.77.54 - Fax (0)5.57.88.77.73
Mme Laurent and Mme Gonzalez

**Rooms** 14 with telephone, bath, WC, TV and minibar - 1 for disabled persons. **Price** Single and double 350-550F. **Meals** Breakfast (buffet) 50F, served 7:30-10:00; half board and full board 330F, 470F (per pers.). **Restaurant** Service 12:00–14:00, 19:30-22:00 (closed Monday evening, Tuesday and Jan); menus 90-270F, also à la carte. Specialties: Poêlée de langoustines au jambon de canard fumé et dés de foie gras chaud, crépinette de daurade rôtie aux champignons. **Credit cards** Amex, Visa, Eurocard and MasterCard. **Pets** Dogs allowed. **Facilities** Parking. **Nearby** Le Médoc; Le Bordelais; Bordeaux - 36-hole Médoc golf course. **Open** All year except in Jan.

The name Château Margaux alone is enough to bring to mind the entire noble family of the great Médoc wines. And there is nothing like staying at the Pavillon de Margaux when you tour the cellars of the château (open every day except Saturday, Sunday and holidays). Built two years ago on the site of the former village school, the hotel exemplifies the 19th-century architecture of the village of Margaux. Classically decorated and restful, the bedrooms offer comfortable accommodations. Chef Frank Launay's specialties, genuine and without frills, are served in a beautiful dining room, but with the first good weather, you can enjoy meals on the shady terrace overlooking the famous vineyards. The dynamic young staff is attentive to your every need.

***How to get there*** *(Map 22): 30km northwest of Bordeaux, A 10 to Mérignac, exit number 7 towards Pauillac.*

## Château Cordeillan-Bages

33250 Pauillac (Gironde)
Tel. (0)5.56.59.24.24 - Fax (0)5.56.59.01.89
M. Rabier

**Category** ★★★★ **Rooms** 25 with telephone, bath, WC, TV and minibar - Wheelchair access. Elevator. **Price** Single and double 900-1200F. **Meals** Breakfast 65F, 95F (buffet), served 7:30-10:30; half board 1150-1550F. **Restaurant** Closed Saturday lunchtimes and Monday. Service 12:15-14:00, 19:30-21:30, menus 185-240-380F, also à la carte. Specialties: Foie chaud poélé, pêche confite, cordon de porto réduit, agneau de pauillac rôti à la broche, gâteau chaud au cacao, crème chocolat aux épices. **Credit cards** All major. **Pets** Dogs allowed. **Facilities** Parking. **Nearby** Le Médoc; Le Bordelais; Bordeaux. **Open** All year except in Dec and Jan.

On the left bank of the Garonne, this 17th-century charterhouse stands on the small Médoc peninsula which is strung out with hundreds of world-famous wine chateaux and vineyards: Château Margaux, Château Lafite, Mouton Rothschild, to mention only the three *premiers grands crus classés* of the tiny village of Pauillac. Renovated in 1989, Château Cordeillan-Bages has retained its original Médoc character, while offering modern amenities. The twenty-five bedrooms, located in the recently built wings around a quiet, inner garden, are elegantly decorated in cheerful colors. The salons are lovely and the large dining room, whose terrace overlooks the vineyards, reminds us that this is where the Bordeaux School of Oenology gives courses in wine tasting to amateurs and professionals alike. An expert *sommelier* will advise you on wines to accompany your meal, and the best ones to buy.

***How to get there** (Map 22): 45km northwest of Bordeaux, A 10 dir. Mérignac, exit number 7 to Le Verdon; on leaving Ezines, take D1, Route des Châteaux.*

## La Closerie des Vignes

Village des Arnauds
33710 Saint-Ciers-de-Canesse (Gironde)
Tel. (0)5.57.64.81.90 - Fax (0)5.57.64.94.44 - Mme Gladys Robert

**Category** ★★ **Rooms** 9 with telephone, bath, WC and TV. **Price** Double 390F. **Meals** Breakfast 40F, served 8:00-10:00; half board 360F (per pers., 3 days min.). **Restaurant** Service 12:00-13:30, 19:30-21:00 (closed Sunday evening and Tuesday in low season); menus 120-170F, also à la carte. Specialties: Gambas flambées au whisky, saumon à l'orange, magret confit, foie gras, clafoutis. **Credit cards** Visa, Eurocard and MasterCard. **Pets** Dogs allowed. **Facilities** Swimming pool, parking. **Nearby** Citadel in Blaye, Bourg, cave of Pair-non-Pair near Prignac, Château de Bouilh, Church of Saint-André-de-Cubzac. **Open** May 1 – Oct 31.

The Closerie des Vignes is not an old building but this small auberge is truly delightful and the ambience so welcoming and friendly that it cries out to be included in this guide. Lying amid vineyards, it is very comfortable and admirably well cared for. Its decor includes modern furniture, soft pastel colors, pretty floral fabrics and comfortable sofas and chairs. The dining room opens onto the vineyards and there is a pleasant swimming pool for summer visitors. Ask for a room away from the kitchen, which is somewhat noisy.

***How to get there*** *(Map 22): 8km southeast of Blaye via D669 to Villeneuve, then D250.*

## Le Couvent des Herbes

40320 Eugénie-les-Bains (Landes)
Tel. (0)5.58.05.06.07 - Fax (0)5.58.51.10.10
M. and Mme Guérard

**Category** ★★★★ **Rooms** 8 with telephone, bath, WC, TV and minibar. **Price** Double 1000-1700F, suite 1500-2000F. **Meals** Breakfast 120F, served 7.30 10.30 - "semaine à thèmes" 9900-14900F. **Restaurant** "Les Prés d'Eugénie". Service 12:00 14.30, 19:00-22:30 (closed Wednesday and Thursday lunchtime); menus 590-750F, also à la carte. Specialities: Foie gras confit dans sa graisse, poitrine de poulette grillée au lard, fine tarte chaude aux fraises. **Credit cards** All major. **Pets** Dogs allowed (+150F). **Facilities** Swimming pool, tennis, sauna, health center, parking. **Nearby** Aire-sur-Adour, Mont-de-Marsan, Samadet, Saint-Sever – 18-hole golf course in Mont-de-Marsan. **Open** Feb / – Jan. 5.

This village in the heart of Gascony which was made famous in the 19th-century by Empress Eugénie, who came here to take the waters. Le Couvent aux Herbes is a former 18th-century convent and girls' boarding school lying on the edge of a lovely park lush with magnolias, palms and banana trees. It has been exquisitely restored by Christine Guérard of *Les Prés d'Eugénie* in the village, which is famous for the cuisine of her husband, Michel, as well as for her own gracious hospitality and decorative talents. Mme Guérard has decorated the *Couvent aux Herbes* with soft, refined, harmonious touches throughout the eight exquisite bedrooms/salons. They are so beautiful we wanted to try them all: *Le Temps des Cerises* for its delicious scent of old roses; *Belle Nonnette* for its magnificent oak beams; or, *Jardin Secret,* which opens onto the luscious herb garden for which the hotel is named. If a week's slimming and exercising is part of your vacation plan, this is the place to come.

***How to get there*** *(Map 29): 25km south of Mont-de-Marsan via D124 towards*

## La Maison Rose

40320 Eugénie-les-bains (Landes)
Tel. (0)5.58.05.05.05 - Fax (0)5.58.51.10.10
M. and Mme Guérard - M. Hardy and M. Leclercq

**Category** ★★ **Rooms** 32 and 5 suites, with telephone, bath, WC and TV. **Price** Single 400-500F, double 480-580F, suite with kitchen 550-850F. **Meals** Breakfast 70F (Buffet), served 8:00-9:30; full board 620-850F (per pers., 3 days min.). **Restaurant** "Cuisine minceur" Service 13:00 and 20:00; menu 185F. "Ferme aux Grives" meals 185F. **Credit cards** All major. **Pets** Dogs allowed (+60F). **Facilities** Swimming pool, tennis, sauna, health center, parking. **Nearby** Aire-sur-Adour cathedral and organs, Mont-de-Marsan museums and keep, Samadet pottery museum, Saint-Sever Dominican monastery. **Open** Feb 8 – Dec 1, Dec 18 – Jan 4.

Michel and Christine Guérard have always been successful at combining their respective arts. There is Michel's gastronomic art, of course, which has made his Prés d'Eugénie into one of the greatest restaurants in France. And Christine's art of gracious hospitality has made the couple's three houses in Eugénie into models of charm. While Les Prés has a colonial touch and Le Couvent des Herbes has become one of their prettiest hotels, La Maison Rose is decorated in a more country manner. We especially like this one for its "Feather Weight, Feather Price" menu, with five daily thermal treatments and the possibility of following a slimming regime, for a reasonable full-room-and-board price. Throughout your stay, you can enjoy the master's famous *Cuisine Minceur*, or a rustic festive meal at *La Ferme aux Grives*, the couple's third auberge. Be prepared for a week-long dream in a charm place.

***How to get there*** *(Map 29): 25km south of Mont-de-Marsan via D124 towards Pau. Pau Airport 45km away, Bordeaux 150km.*

## La Ferme aux Grives

40320 Eugénie-les-Bains (Landes)
Tel. (0)5.58.51.19.08 - Fax (0)5.58.51.10.10
M. and Mme Guerard

**Category** ★★★ **Logis-suites** 4 with telephone, bath, WC, TV and minibar. **Price** Double 700-850F. **Meals** Breakfast in lounge 70F, served 8:30-10:00. 1 week 4380-7950F (per pers.). **Restaurant** Service 12:00-14:00, 20:00-22:30 (closed Mon. evening, Tues. lunchtime except July 12 - Sep 12); menus 185F. **Specialties:** tarte feuilletée à la paysanne de légumes, volaille du jour rôtie à la broche, cochon de lait comme en castille, millassou caramélisé à l'armagnac. **Credit cards** Visa. **Pets** Dogs allowed (+60F). **Facilities** Swimming pool, tennis, sauna, health center, parking. **Nearby** Aire-sur-Adour, Mont-de-Marsan, Samadet, Saint-Sever, Mauriac Festival. **Open** Fev 6 - Jan 5.

La Ferme aux Grives is yet another of our newly selected hotels in the small village of Eugénie-les-Bains. We have included this rustic auberge because it offers real quality and country charm at affordable prices. This old farmhouse has been entirely restored in the finest regional tradition: its walls of large rocks are from the Adour River, its big stone fireplaces and terra cotta floors have been charmingly renewed. There are two dining rooms: the Café du Village, where you can sample the excellent wines of the region and enjoy the chef's special; and the large auberge dining room where a beautiful menu highlights authentic family recipes of this gastronomic region. Here, plump, farm-raised Landes chickens turn roasting on the spit and hams are hung from the ceilings to cure, while fresh seasonal vegetables and magnificent country breads are displayed on a large butcher block in the center. There are several bedrooms in a small building, which have all the delightful rusticity and charm of the country.

***How to get there*** *(Map 29): 25km south of Mont-de-Marsan via D 124, dir. Pau. Pau Airport 45km away, Bordeaux 150km.*

## Pain, Adour et Fantaisie

7, place des tilleuls
40270 Grenade-sur-Adour (Landes)
Tel. (0)5.58.45.18.80 - Fax (0)5.58.45.16.57 - M. Garret

**Category** ★★★ **Rooms** 11 with air-conditioning, telephone, bath (9 with whirlpool), WC, TV, safe and minibar - Wheelchair access. **Price** Double 380-700F, apart. 1200F. **Meals** Breakfast 75F; "Week-end de charme" 2750F (per 2 pers.); "Soirée Fantaisie" 1430F (per 2 pers.). **Restaurant** Service 12:00-14:15, 20:00-22:30 (closed Sunday evening and Monday except national holidays); menu 150-350F, also à la carte. **Credit cards** All major. **Pets** Dogs allowed (+50F). **Facilities** Parking, garage (+50F). **Nearby** Landes de Gascogne Regional Park, Bastides tour; 9- and 18-hole golf courses in Mont-de-Marsan. **Open** All year.

On the village side, this superb, half-timbered 17th-century auberge looks out onto the arcades of the large public square. On the river side, a cool, shady terrace (a summer dining spot), the large traditional balconies and certain bedrooms look out directly onto the river Adour. Here is a place of peace and pleasure. The bedrooms, with evocative names from nature, are vast and bright. Decorated with great talent, they all have charm and character; and the bathrooms are well equipped. Original old wood paneling graces the the dining room. You will enjoy the culinary specialties of Philippe Garret, who brings off the *tour de force* of offering excellent cuisine at astonishingly reasonable prices. This is yet another very good auberge, and is reason enough to make the trip to the Landes.

***How to get there*** *(Map 29): 15km south of Mont-de-Marsan via N 124. Pau Airport 45km away, Bordeaux 150km.*

## La Vieille Auberge

Port-de-Lanne - 40300 Peyrehorade (Landes)
Tel. (0)5.58.89.16.29 - Fax (0)5.58.89.12.89
M. and Mme Lataillade

**Category** ★★★ **Rooms** 10 with telephone, bath or shower and WC (2 with TV). **Price** Single and double 230-450F, suite 500-600F. **Meals** Breakfast 40-50F, served 8:30-10:30; half board 320-450F (per pers.). **Restaurant** Service 12:00-13:30, 19:30-21:00, menus 120-250F, also à la carte. Specialties: Magret, saumon à l'oseille, confits de canard et de porc à l'ail, matelote d'anguilles, filets de sole aux cèpes. **Credit cards** Not accepted. **Pets** Dogs allowed. **Facilities** Swimming pool, fishing, parking. **Nearby** Biarritz, Peyrehorade, abbey of Arthous, Sorde-l'abbaye, Romanesque church in Cagnotte, Bonnat and Basque museums in Bayonne; Hossegor golf course (18-hole) . **Open** May 1 – Oct 21 (closed Monday).

Both M. Lataillade and his father were born in this old coaching inn whose rustic beams, walls and floors bear the imprint of time. The inviting reception rooms are disturbed only by the slow rhythm of an antique pendulum clock or occasional music from an old piano. The bedrooms, located in the former stables and barns, are charming and comfortable, and there is a lovely garden with a swimming pool. M. Lataillade has built up an interesting museum, which is in the old hay barn. It contains objects retracing the history of the port of Lanne and its seafarers, who were known as *Gabariers.* La Vieille Auberge is a friendly Gascon inn, where you will enjoy Mme Lataillade's homemade preserves at breakfast.

***How to get there*** *(Map 29): 30km northwest of Bayonne via N117; on the church square.*

## Auberge des Pins

Route de la Piscine
40630 Sabres (Landes)
Tel. (0)5.58.07.50.47 - Fax (0)5.58.07.56.74 - M. and Mme Lesclauze

**Category** ★★ **Rooms** 24 with telephone, bath (8 with wirlpool) or shower and WC (21 with TV). **Price** Single and double 230-450F, suite 500-600F. **Meals** Breakfast 40-50F, served 7:30-10:00; half board 230-450F (per pers., 3 days min.). **Restaurant** Service 12:00-14:00, 19:30-21:00; menus 100-350F, also à la carte. Specialties: Soupe de pêche, foie gras poêlé pointe d'asperges, filets de rouget, langoustines aux cèpes, pigeon roti et farci. **Credit cards** Visa, Eurocard, MasterCard and Amex. **Pets** Dogs not allowed. **Facilities** Parking. **Nearby** Church in Sabres, local history museum in Marquèze, Les Landes de Gascogne Regional park. **Open** All year (closed Sunday evening and Monday in low season).

You will be enchanted by this hotel amid the pines on the way out of the village of Sabres. Generations of good hotel keeping ensure high-quality service and a faultless welcome. The bedrooms in the main building have every comfort and an old-fashioned charm, but the bedrooms in the newer building blend very well with the old ones and are our favorites. They are large, light, airy and elegantly modern, with lovely fabrics, superb bathrooms and a small terrace. The dining room, with its antique furniture, copperware, ceramics and fireplace laden with a collection of rare old Armagnacs, is a place to linger in over the beautiful cooking of Michel Lesclauze, who uses the best local produce to make truly memorable meals.

***How to get there*** *(Map 29): 40km east of Mimizan via D44.*

## Le Square

5, place de la Craste
47220 Astaffort (Lot-and-Garonne)
Tel. (0)5.53.47.20.40 - Fax (0)5.53.47.10.38 - M. Cabrel

**Category** ★★★ **Rooms** 8 with air-conditioning, telephone, bath, WC, TV and minibar - 1 for disabled persons. **Price** Single and double 350F. **Meals** Breakfast 32F, served 8:00-10:00. **Restaurant** Closed Sunday evening and Monday. Service 12:00-14:00, 19:30-22:00; menu 92F, also à la carte. Specialties: Regional cooking. **Credit cards** All major. **Pets** Dogs allowed. **Nearby** Agen, bastides of Villeneuve-sur-Lot and of Beauville, Prades, Auvillar, Nérac, market "fermier" Monday in Astaffort. **Open** All year (except 2-3 weeks in Jan; Sunday evening and Monday).

The pretty pink and blue façade of Le Square seems to beckon you to this brand-new village hotel which is surprisingly refined and comfortable. The ravishing bedrooms are decorated with tasteful combinations of colors and prints, while the bathrooms, in the same color schemes, are superb. There are two dining rooms where you are served the delicious cuisine of the Southwest, which is both traditional and inventive. One dining room opens onto a small terrace where you can have your meals in summer; in the other, which is cool and informal, you are served on warmly colored enameled-lava tables. Guests enjoy the friendly atmosphere of Le Square, a charming hotel very near Agen.

***How to get there*** *(Map 30): 16km south of Agen via RN 21. Via A62, number 7 Agen exit.*

## Château de Lassalle

47310 Moirax-Laplume/Agen (Lot-et-Garonne)
Tel. (0)5.53.95.10.58 - Fax (0)5.53.95.13.01
M. and Mme Laurens

**Category** ★★★ **Rooms** 10 with telephone, bath, WC and TV. **Price** Single and double 400-600F, 450-700F, suite 850-950F. **Meals** Breakfast 60F; half board 450-700F (per pers., 3 days min.). **Restaurant** Closed Thursday in low season. Service 12:00-15:00, 20:00-22:00, menus 150-250F. Specialties: œufs coque aux cèpes, foie gras cru au pacherenc, terrine de pommes de terre à la crème d'aïl, bavaroise à la réglisse et au floc, huitres à la gelée de concombres. **Credit cards** Visa, Eurocard, MasterCard, Amex. **Pets** Dogs allowed in kennel. **Facilities** Swimming pool, Ball-Trap, parking. **Nearby** Agen; Bastides of Condom, Fourcès, Lectoure; Prades; Auvillar; Nérac. **Open** on request.

Standing at the end of a lane of large oaks, this beautiful country house is surrounded by a large park where you can enjoy sun or shade, sports or just relaxation. Built in a U-shape around a patio-courtyard, the chateau has two magnificent suites, tastefully and comfortably appointed. The other bedrooms are of different sizes but all have their own charm and are equipped with pleasant baths. A large dining room overlooking the park and comfortable lounges create a homey atmosphere. Jacqueline and Jean-Pierre Laurent are hard-working, hospitable owners, and the region, too, is most welcoming.

***How to get there*** *(Map 30): 7km south of Agen. In Agen, towards. trafic circle on highway, then towards Auch for 3km. Turn right to Moirax; on leaving Moirax, go 5km.*

1998

## Les Terrasses du Petit Nérac

7, rue Sédérie
47600 Nérac (Lot-et-Garonne)
Tel. (0)5.53.97.02.91 - Fax (0)5.53.65.65.98 - Mme Kuiper

**Rooms** 4 with telephone, bath, WC and TV. **Price** Single and double 240-350F. **Meals** Breakfast 30-40F; half board 420F (per 2 pers.). **Restaurant** Service 12:00 15:00, 19:00-22:00, menus 100-150F, also à la carte. Specialties: fish and foie gras maison. **Credit cards** Amex, Visa, Eurocard and MasterCard. **Pets** Dogs allowed. **Nearby** Agen; Bastides of Villeneuve-sur-Lot, of Beauville; Prades; Auvillar; Nérac. **Open** All year.

A stone's throw from the chateau where Henri IV stayed as a youth, this restaurant with several rooms is installed in a small house in the old part of Nérac on the banks of the Baïse, a lovely river offering popular sightseeing cruises. Two dining rooms spill over to the river's edge in good weather. There, you'll have a front-row seat for watching the boats, the old houses on the opposite bank, and the summer sky. And then, there are four colorfully decorated bedrooms to prolong the pleasure (early birds should ask for a room on the street.) Add delicious cuisine and charming hospitality, and you will have an idea of the delightful stay that awaits you at the Petit Nérac.

***How to get there*** *(Map 30): 28km west of Agen via D 656, towards Nérac; on the edge of the Baïse River.*

## A la Belle Gasconne

47170 Poudenas (Lot-et-Garonne)
Tel. (0)5.53.65.71.58 - Fax (0)5.53.65.87.39
Mme Gracia

**Rooms** 7 with telephone, bath or shower and WC (3 with TV). **Price** Single 410F double 530-580F, suite 650F. **Meals** Breakfast 60F; half board 590-650F (per pers.) **Restaurant** Service 12:00-14:00, 19:30-21:30; menus 185-290F, also à la carte. Specialties: Foie gras frais, civet de canard au vin vieux de Buzet. **Credit cards** All major. **Pets** Dogs allowed. **Facilities** Heated swimming pool. **Nearby** Beauville, Auvillar (pottery museum), Nérac – 18-hole golf courses in Albret and Barbaste. **Open** Mar 1 – Dec 31 (closed Sunday evening and Monday in low season).

Who hasn't dreamed of spending a few romantic days in an old mill lulled by the sound of water trickling beneath the window? Lying at the foot of a stunningly beautiful medieval village, A la Belle Gasconne offers comfortable, beautifully appointed bedrooms whose colors are tastefully coordinated with the elm furniture; the bathrooms are decorated with Salernes tiles and even the dressing gowns are changed daily. The dining room still has the original beams, stones and old machinery from the mill. Further atmosphere is lent by a log fire, a large bay window overlooking the water, and elegant table linens. The esthetic pleasures are enhanced by those of the table, for the cuisine is one of the finest in France; each dish is a veritable enchantment. Mme Gracia, the chef, oversees the dining room and her kindness adds a lovely touch to the meal. In good weather, you can relax on the leafy island, enjoy the swimming pool and have breakfast by the waterside. A la Belle Gasconne is truly marvelous.

***How to get there*** *(Map 30): 47km southwest of Agen via D656 towards Nérac.*

## Les Loges de l'Aubergade

52, rue Royale
47270 Puymirol (Lot-et-Garonne)
Tel. (0)5.53.95.31.46 - Fax (0)5.53.95.33.80 - M. Trama

**Category** ★★★★ **Rooms** 10 with air-conditioning, telephone, bath, WC, TV, safe and minibar - 1 for disabled persons. **Price** Double 750-1410F. **Meals** Breakfast 90F, served 8:00-10:00; half board 2100F (2 pers., 3 days min.). **Restaurant** Service 12:00-14:00, 19:30-21:30 (closed Sunday evening and Monday); menus 180F (lunch except weekend anf national holidays), 280-680F, also à la carte. Specialties: Papillottes dc pommes-de-terre à la truffe, hamburger de foie gras chaud aux cèpes, double corona trama et sa feuille de tabac au poivre. **Credit cards** All major. **Pets** Dogs allowed (+100F). **Facilities** Swimming pool, jacuzzi, mountain bikes - Parking (70F). **Nearby** Agen, Villeneuve-sur-Lot, Beauville; Prades, Auvillar (pottery museum), Nérac – 9-hole Saint-Ferréol golf courses. **Open** Mid Mar – mid Feb (closed Sunday evening and Monday in low season).

First and foremost here, this place is home to the restaurant of the great chef Michel Trama, whose outstanding cuisine is given top ratings throughout France. His taste for beautiful things inspired him, with the help of Mme Trama, to decorate eleven spacious bedrooms in an old house which belonged to the Counts of Toulouse in the 13th-century. All enjoy the most elegant modern conveniences and bathrooms where the everthing is provided for relaxation and pleasure. The rooms are arranged around a patio, the center of which is occupied by a large outdoor jacuzzi. In the heart of the fortified village of Puymirol, this is a welcoming place, as renowned for its rooms as for its cuisine.

***How to get there** (Map 30): 20km east of Agen. Via A62 exit Valence-d'Agen, towards Golfech le Magistère, turn right, follow signs.*

1998

## Hôtel Ithurria

64250 Aïnhoa (Pyrénées-Atlantiques)
Tel. (0)5.59.29.92.11 - Fax (0)5.59.29.81.28
Isabal Family

**Category** ★★★ **Rooms** 27 with telephone, bath, WC and TV. **Price** Single and double 400-600F. **Meals** Breakfast 50F, served 8:00-10:30; half board 520-600F (per pers., 3 days min.). **Restaurant** Service 12:00-14:00, 19:00-21:00; menus 170-250F, also à la carte. **Credit cards** All major. **Pets** Dogs allowed. **Facilities** Parking. **Nearby** Biarritz, Anglet and forest of Chiberta, Forest of Iraty, Arcangues, Bidart, Saint-Jean-de-Luz - 18-hole Biarritz golf course - 18-hole Chiberta golf course in Anglet. **Open** Apr – Oct. Closed Wednesday except in July and Aug.

Nestling among the gentle rolling hills of the Basque Country and in the heart of Aïnhoa, rated "One of the Most Beautiful Villages of France", the Hôtel Ithurria is a big inn which opens onto the Place de l'Eglise, where Basque *pelote* is played. It is a traditional family hotel where guests can enjoy a quiet vacation, pleasant hospitality, and gourmet cuisine. You will find a large choice of comfortable bedrooms, all attractive while differing in size and decoration. In the spacious dining room, where delicious, creative Basque cuisine is served with a smile, local color is created by traditional floor tiles, the fireplace, and the sculptured wood door lattices. Add a delightful small bar and an immense swimming pool at the back of the garden and you'll understand why the Ithurria is a favorite spot with those who love the good life.

***How to get there*** *(Map 28): 25km south of Saint-Jean-de-Luz via D918.*

## Chez Chilo

64130 Barcus (Pyrénées-Atlantiques)
Tel. (0)5.59.28.90.79 - Fax (0)5.59.28.93.10
M. and Mme Chilo

**Category** ★★ **Rooms** 10 and 1 apartment (2 rooms) with telephone, bath or shower, WC and TV. **Price** Single 200-450F, double 250-650F. **Meals** Breakfast 45F; half board 300-730F, full board 400-900F (2 pers., 3 days min.). **Restaurant** Service 12:00-14:00, 19:30-22:00 (closed Sunday and Monday in low season); menus 90-300F, also à la carte. Specialties: Tarte de thon en pipèrade, carré d'agneau de lait "Axuria" aux raviolis de fromage de brebis, pèche blanche farcie à la glace pistache au sabayon de Jurançon mœlleux. **Credit cards** All major. **Pets** Dogs allowed. **Facilities** Swimming pool, parking. **Nearby** Châteaux of Moumour and Aven, Saint-Blaise-Hospital, Pau – Golf course in Artiguelouve. **Open** Feb 4 – Jan 14 (closed last week in Mar, Sunday evening and Monday in low season).

You have to have an adventurous spirit to turn off onto this tiny winding road in the heart of the green Béarn mountains. Yet it's only a few kilometers from the villages of Aramits and Lanne, immortalized in Alexandre Dumas's *The Three Musketeers*. You won't regret your detour. Awaiting you in this beautiful countryside is a restaurant offering sumptuous cuisine and a hotel worthy of the most discriminating tastes. This family auberge has recently been enlarged and redecorated with taste and originality by young Mme Chilo, whose husband is the chef. The bedrooms, all now renovated, combine charm with simplicity. And the welcome is extremely courteous.

***How to get there*** *(Map 29): 16km west of Oloron-Sainte-Marie via D24; towards Mauléon-Licharre.*

## Hôtel Laminak

Route de Saint-Pée
64210 Artonne (Pyrénées-Atlantiques)
Tel. (0)5.59.41.95.40 - Fax (0)5.59.41.87.65 - M. and Mme Cauderlier

**Category** ★★★ **Rooms** 10 with telephone, 6 with bath, 4 with shower, WC, TV and minibar - Wheelchair access. **Price** Double 350-560F. **Meals** Breakfast 50F, served 8:00-11:00. No restaurant. Snacks available in evening on request. **Credit cards** Amex, Visa, Eurocard and MasterCard. **Pets** Dogs allowed. **Facilities** Parking. **Nearby** Biarritz, Anglet and the forest of Chiberta, Arcangues, Bidart, Saint-Jean-de-Luz – 18-hole golf courses in Arcangues and Bussussary. **Open** Mar 15 - Nov 15.

Perched on a hilltop on the edge of Biarritz between the Atlantic and the Pyrenees, this 18th-century Basque farmhouse has just been entirely converted into a charming small hotel. Surrounded by hilly countryside, the Laminak is calm and peaceful. The bedrooms have been carefully decorated, combining the latest amenities with original touches which lend an individual character to each. Some are larger and have corner sitting areas, but all are in exquisite taste. You can enjoy a copious, elegant breakfast in the colonial-style winter garden, which also serves light snacks. There are many good restaurants nearby, including *L'Epicerie d'Ahetze* and *Les Frères Ibarboure* in Bidart; in Biarritz, *Campagne et Gourmandise is famous* for its cuisine, its charm, and its view, and *La Tantine de Burgos* for its Basque and Spanish ambiance.

***How to get there*** *(Map 28): 4km south of Biarritz. On A 63 exit Biarritz-La Négresse, then D 255 towards of Arbonne.*

## Le Château du Clair de Lune

48, avenue Alan-Seger
64200 Biarritz (Pyrénées-Atlantiques)
Tel. (0)5.59.41.53.20 - Fax (0)5.59.41.53.29 - Mme Beyrière

**Category** ★★★ **Rooms** 16 with telephone, bath, WC, TV and minibar. **Price** 450-700F (2 pers.), 350 and 700F (3 pers.), 750F and 800F (4 pers.). **Meals** Breakfast 60F, served 8:00-11:00. No restaurant. **Credit cards** All major. **Pets** Dogs allowed (+45F). **Facilities** Parking. **Nearby** Rock of the Virgin, Anglet and the Forest of Chiberta, Arcangues, Bidard – 18-hole Biarritz golf course, 18-hole Chiberta golf course in Anglet. **Open** All year.

This turn-of-the-century house stands in a very quiet park above Biarritz. It is the sort of house which conjures up nostalgic memories of childhood. The bathrooms and bathtubs have the huge proportions of another era, and the floor tiles and basins are antique. The large lounge on the ground floor opens onto and merges with the garden: cheerful, airy and bright, it is furnished with yellow sofas and a grand piano. The dining room is where guests breakfast together around a large table. This lovely family house on the Basque coast, though a hotel, feelsl as if it were your own. At the edge of the property, you will find a restaurant on an 18th-century farm. We also recommend *Campagne et Gourmandises*, for its cuisine and lovely view.

***How to get there*** *(Map 28): 4km south of the town center via the Pont de la Négresse and D255 (Arbonne route).*

## Hôtel Villa L'Arche

Chemin Camboénéa
64210 Bidart (Pyrénées-Atlantiques)
Tel. (0)5.59.51.65.95 - Fax (0)5.59.51.65.99 - Mme Salaignac

**Category** ★★★ **Rooms** 8 with telephone, bath or shower, WC, TV and minibar. **Price** Double 450-800F. **Meals** Breakfast 60F, served to 12:00. No restaurant. **Credit cards** Visa, Eurocard and MasterCard. **Pets** Dogs allowed (+30F). **Facilities** Covered parking. **Nearby** Biarritz, Anglet and the Forest of Chiberta, Arcangues, Bidart, Saint-Jean-de Luz – 18-hole Arcangues golf course, 18-hole Bussussary golf course. **Open** Feb 15 - Nov. 15

This small hotel alone is worth making a long detour for. For how is it possible to find a more enchanting location than this flower-covered cliff with a stairway leading directly to the beach? When Bernadette Salaignac transformed her house into a hotel, she might have been content with simply the location, but she also put an enormous amount of talent into decorating the comfortable bedrooms. A bay window opens onto each terrace where you can have breakfast (delicious) and, from six terraces, there is a view of the ocean. Those who prefer breakfast in the salon enjoy the same view with classical music in the background. Here too, the decoration is very tasteful, with blue and white checkered sofas, chairs painted in pearl grey, old paintings, collector's objects, all slyly observed through the window by a pig and a saddle horse. This very homey atmosphere is echoed at the reception and you will certainly leave the Villa with a promise to return. There is no restaurant in the hotel, but there are good addresses nearby, including *La Tantina della Playa, Les Frères Ibarboure, La Ferme de l'Ostalapia* and *La Cucaracha*.

***How to get there*** *(Map 28): RN 10 between Biarritz (7 km) and Saint-Jean-de Luz. In Bidart center, rue de l'Ouhabia to Embruny.*

## Hôtel du Pont d'Enfer

64780 Bidarray (Pyrénées-Atlantiques)
Tel. (0)5.59.37.70.88 - Fax (0)5.59.37.76.60
Mme Gagnant

**Category** ★★ **Rooms** 17 with telephone, 12 with bath and WC, 10 with TV. **Price** Single and double 135-250F, 150-340F. **Meals** Breakfast 30F, served 8:00-9:00; half board and full board 215-280F, 285-370F (per pers., 3 days min.). **Restaurant** Service 12:00-13:30, 19:00-20:30, menu 70-168F. Specialties: foie gras, torrine de cèpes, soufflé basquaise, filet d'ombrine au basilic, merlu Koskera, zorzuela, salmis et civet de gibier. **Credit cards** Amex, Visa, Eurocard and MasterCard. **Pets** Dogs allowed. **Facilities** Parking. **Nearby** Biarritz; Anglet and forest of Iraty; Arcangues; Bidart; Saint-Jean-de-Luz – 18-hole Biarritz and Le Phare glof course – 18-hole Chiberta golf course in Anglet. **Open** 2 March – 30 Sep, closed Wednesday, Tuesday until 17:30 except June – Sep.

You go across the old Pont d'Enfer bridge over the Nive River to get to this hotel, named after the bridge but popularly called "Chez Anny" after the delightful owner who loves to regale guests with stories of her region and the time the novelist Pierre Loti once stayed here. Located at the foot of a hill, the hotel is old but comfortable. We loved the huge dining room, faithfully furnished in Basque country style, and the atmosphere of the bedrooms. Some are located in an independent house, with Numbers 14, 16 and 18 directly overlooking the river. In summer, meals are served on the terrace over the Nive.

***How to get there*** *(Map 28): 35km southeast of Bayonne via D 932 and D 918.*

## Lehen Tokia

64500 Ciboure (Pyrénées-Atlantiques)
Tel. (0)5.59.47.18.16 - 05 59.47.38.04
M. Taboulet

**Rooms** 6 with telephone, bath or shower, WC and TV. **Price** Single and double 500-800F, suite 1200F. **Meals** Breakfast 50F, served 8:30-10:00. **Restaurant** Only for residents and by reservation. Menu. Specialties: Turbot au jus de viande, foie gras à la mousse d'aïl, paëlla impériale. **Credit cards** Visa, Eurocard and MasterCard. **Pets** Dogs not allowed. **Facilities** Swimming pool, sauna, parking. **Nearby** Saint-Jean-Baptiste church in Saint-Jean-de-Luz, coast road, Ciboure, Bayonne, Biarritz – 18-hole Nivelle and Chantaco golf courses. **Open** All year.

Built in 1925, this splendid Basque villa has recently been classed as a Historic Monument, notably because of its remarkable stained glass. The original owner used to come here on vacation with his family. Today, two of his grandchildren have opened Lehen Tokia to guests. The interior has been refurbished, but the original decoration is intact. There is a subtle combination of magnificent objects and Art Deco furniture with antique regional furniture and family paintings (which explains why young children, are not admitted). The rooms are of superb size. You enter the vestibule, then go up several steps to the salon, which in turn is surrounded by an elegant curving stairway leading to the bedrooms. Ravishingly beautiful and very comfortable, most have a marvelous view out over the Atlantic. The bedroom in the garden near the swimming pool has only a few pieces of Art Deco furniture but is not lacking in charm. From the suite and the lounge, you can see the entire harbor of Saint-Jean-de-Luz. A beautiful spot, indeed.

***How to get there*** *(Map 28): 2km from Saint-Jean-de-Luz. On A 63, exit Saint-Jean-de-Luz south.*

# Hôtel Arcé

64430 Saint-Etienne-de-Baïgorry (Pyrénées-Atlantiques)
Tel. (0)5.59.37.40.14 - Fax (0)5.59.37.40.27
M. Arcé

**Category** ★★★ **Rooms** 22 with telephone, bath or shower, WC and TV. **Price** Single and, double 310-715F, suite 1080F. **Meals** Breakfast 50F, served 7:45-10:30; half board 420-565F, 765F in suite (per pers., 3 days min.). **Restaurant** Service 12:30-13:45, 19:30-20:30 (closed Monday lunchtime in low season except national holidays); menus 110-215F, also à la carte. Specialties: Truite au bleu du vivier, tête de veau vinaigrette, foie chaud aux goldens. **Credit cards** Visa, Eurocard and MasterCard. **Pets** Dogs allowed. **Facilities** Heated swimming pool, tennis, parking. **Nearby** Adudes valley, Saint-Jean-Pied-de-Port, dolmens, Cromlechs – 18-hole Souraïde golf course. **Open** Mid. Mar – mid. Nov.

This old inn, typical of the region and luxuriously restored, has been managed by the same family for the last five generations. The large picture windows are in keeping with the beautiful proportions of the dining room, and outside, long terraces are laid out at the water's edge. The bedrooms are extremely comfortable, newly decorated and overlook the river and the Pyrenees. A variety of reading matter is even supplied. Bouquets of flowers are placed all over the hotel. The little annex is a pleasing addition, with its balconies overhanging the river: you can fish without even leaving your bedroom! You will enjoy classic regional cooking and a very friendly welcome.

***How to get there*** *(Map 28): 50km southeast of Bayonne via D932 and D918 to Saint-Martin d'Arossa, then D948 to St-Etienne-de-Baïgorry.*

## La Devinière

5, rue Loquin
64500 Saint-Jean-de-Luz (Pyrénées-Atlantiques)
Tel. (0)5.59.26.05.51 - Fax (0)5.59.51.26.38 - M. Carrère

**Category** ★★★ **Rooms** 8 with telephone, bath and WC. **Price** 500-650F (+100F hight season). **Meals** Breakfast 50F, served all morning. No restaurant. **Credit cards** Visa, Eurocard and MasterCard. **Pets** Dogs allowed on request (+50F). **Facilities** Tea salon 16:00-19:00.**Nearby** Saint-Jean-Baptiste Church in Saint-Jean-de-Luz, Basque coast road, Ciboure, Bayonne, Biarritz – 18-hole Nivelle and Chantaco golf courses. **Open** All year.

There is no obvious reason why M. and Mme Carrère should have taken on and renovated this residential family hotel – he is a lawyer and she an antiques dealer – other than the pleasure of opening a charming place in the heart of Saint-Jean-de-Luz. Good taste and discernment are apparent everywhere. The eight bedrooms are ravishingly pretty and are furnished with beautiful antiques, as are the music room and library, which are open for the use of the guests. The pedestrian street and the garden ensure quiet nights even in the heart of the town. The welcome is warm. Breakfast is served in the tea room, which offers homemade pastries, teas and old-fashioned hot chocolate. For fine dining, try *Chez Pablo (piperades* and *chipirons), Kaïku* for shellfish; and *La Taverne Basque*, offering cuisine made with market-fresh seasonal produce. In the immediate environs, don't miss the *magret de canard* at the *Ferme Penzia* (open only in summer); *Chez Mattin*'s *ttorro*; or the grilled fish at *Chez Pantxoa* in Ciboure.

***How to get there** (Map 28): 15km southwest of Biarritz via A63.*

## Hôtel Arraya

Place du village
64310 Sare (Pays Basques)
Tel. (0)5.59.54.20.46 - Fax (0)5.59.54.27.04 - M. Fagoaga

**Category** ★★★ **Rooms** 20 with telephone, bath or shower, WC and TV. **Price** Single 395-400F, double 480-540F, suite 755-855F. **Meals** Breakfast 50F, served 8.00-10:30. **Restaurant** Service 12:00-14:00, 19:30-22:00; menus 130-190F, also à la carte. Specialties: Méli-mélo de gambas et ris d'agneau aux girolles, chipirons entiers poêlés et marmelade de crabe, gratin de fraises et framboises au sabayon à l'orange. **Credit cards** Amex, Visa, Eurocard and MasterCard. **Pets** Dogs not allowed. **Facilities** Parking. **Nearby** Villa Arnaga in Cambo, Espelette, Ascain, Saint-Jean-de-Luz, Bonnat and Basque museums in Bayonne – 18-hole La Nivelle and Chantaco golf courses. **Open** Apr. 15 – Nov 12.

Do not be put off by the Arraya's somber facade, which is typical of the region. This superb Basque hotel, set on the corner of two streets in the center of the village, is made up of three old houses; the garden, invisible from the street, effectively screens out the noise. On the ground floor, the lovely lounges and the comfortable dining room are charming with rustic furniture and bright bowls of flowers. The bedrooms are all different butequally attractive: the prettiest is on the garden side. There is a boutique selling regional delicacies which you can eat on the spot or take away. The restaurant menu is long and varied, but regional dishes remain the specialties of the house.

***How to get there*** *(Map 28): 28km south of Bayonne via A63, Saint-Jean-de-Luz exit, D918 to Ascain and D4 to Sare.*

# Les Bains de Secours

64260 Sévignac-Meyracq (Pyrénées-Atlantiques)
Tel. (0)5.59.05.62.11 - Fax (0)5.59.05.76.56
M. Jean-Pierre Paroix

**Category** ★★ **Rooms** 7 with telephone, bath or shower, WC, TV and 2 with minibar. **Price** Single and double 270-350F. **Meals** Breakfast 36F; half board 240F **Restaurant** Closed Sunday for diner and Monday except for residents. Service 12:30-13:30, 19:30-21:30, menus 80-150F, also à la carte. Specialties: salade de soles aux cèpes, calamars farcis au foie gras, assiettes de poires à toutes les façons. **Credit cards** Amex, Visa, Eurocard and MasterCard. **Pets** Dogs allowed by reservation. **Facilities** Parking. **Possibilités** Parc National des Pyrénées; Pau; vignobles du Jurançon; Lescar. **Open** All year. Closed Sunday evening and Monday in low season.

A stone's throw from the Jurançon vineyards and the lush Ossau Valley, the tranquil Bains de Secours is still only twenty or so kilometers from Pau. It has been renovated by the young chef Jean-Pierre Paroix, whose ancestors used to welcome curistes to take the waters at the small thermal establishment nearby called Les Bains de Secours, "Therapeutic Baths", (which is still open.) The auberge today has seven simple but quiet rooms with comfortable amenities; the high point, however, is Paroix's regional cuisine, combining tradition with innovation. Meals are served in two beautifully rustic dining rooms, one with a cheerful fireplace, the other with warm wood paneling on the walls. This is a wonderful place to stay in a magnificent region off the beaten track.

***How to get there*** *(Map 28): 20km south of Pau, dir. Saragosse. In Gan, take dir. Laruns. After Rébénacq, go 2km, then follow signs on left.*

# Hôtel La Patoula

64480 Ustaritz (Pyrénées-Atlantiques)
Tel (0)5.59.93.00.56 - Fax (0)5.59.93.16.54
M. Guilhem

**Category** ★★★ **Rooms** 9 with telephone, bath or shower and WC. **Price** Double 350-470F. **Meals** Breakfast 60F; half board 350-430F, full board 450-530F (per pers., 3 days min.). **Restaurant** Service 12:00-14:00, 20:00-22:00; menus 100F, 150F, 200F, also à la carte. Specialties: Alose grillée, saumon sauvage, gibier, agneau de lait des Pyrénées, tarte fine aux pommes chaudes caramélisées. **Credit cards** Visa, Eurocard and MasterCard. **Pets** Dogs allowed (+35F). **Facilities** Parking. **Nearby** Villa Arnaga in Cambo, Biarritz, Bonnat and Basque museums in Bayonne – 18-hole Biarritz golf course, 18-hole Chantaco golf course in Saint-Jean-de-Luz. **Open** Feb 15 – Jan 5 (closed Sunday evening and Monday in low season).

This hotel is set back from the road in a park bordered by the tranquil waters of the River Nive. This romantic view can be enjoyed either from the dining room, from the pergola where breakfast tables are laid in summer, or from the chaise longues in the garden. In the winter, when there are fewer tourists, the dining room with its open fire provides an intimate setting, and people come for the cooking from all over the region. The bedrooms are spacious, comfortable and very prettily decorated. We preferred the two which overlook the river and the four which overlook the garden. The modest number of rooms and Mme Guilhem's friendliness give La Patoula a very pleasant atmosphere.

***How to get there*** *(Map 28): 11km south of Bayonne via A63, Bayonne-sud exit number 5, towards Cambo-les-Bains, then D982; in the center of Ustaritz, opposite the church.*

## Grand Hôtel Montespan Talleyrand

2/4, place des Thermes
03160 Bourbon L'Archambault (Allier)
Tel. (0)4.70.67.00.24 - Fax (0)4.70.67.12.00 - M. Livertout

**Category** ★★ **Rooms** 58 with telephone, bath or shower, WC and TV - Elevator - 1 apartment with bath. **Price** Single 175-190F, double 285-360F; apart. 500F. **Meals** Breakfast 42F, served 7:30-10:00; half board 295F, full board 330F (per pers., 3 days min.). **Restaurant** Service 12:30-13:30, 19:30-21:00; menus 100-220F, also à la carte. Specialties: Lapin à la moutarde de Charroux, pièce de boeufs façon Ducs de Bourbon, Vacherin Montespan, nougat glacé aux trois épices. **Credit cards** Amex, Visa, Eurocard and MasterCard. **Pets** Dogs allowed. **Facilities** Swimming pool, parking. **Nearby** Bourbon; Souvigny priory, châteaux of the Besbre Valley and of Lapalisse in Dompierre (half day's journey), triptych of the Maître de Moulins at Notre Dame cathedral in Moulins – 9-hole Avenelles golf course in Moulins. **Open** Apr – end Oct.

This hotel derives its name from the illustrious guests who came here for the famous thermal baths. It is made up of four adjoining town houses with well appointed bedrooms. The *Sévigné* and *Talleyrand* rooms are vast, decorated with antique furniture and some have a balcony. The *Capucine* room, with a view over the gardens, is decorated with rattan furniture and elegant floral fabrics. The *Montespan* bedroom is reserved for guests taking the waters. On the ground floor, comfortable reception rooms and a large dining room (good family cooking) look out onto the greenery where in summer you can have breakfast. Another attractive feature of the Grand Hôtel is its immense terrace-garden built against the wall and surrounded by a medieval tower. It has a swimming pool, several flower-covered rock gardens, and tables and chaises-longues. This is a very pleasant hotel with extremely reasonable prices.

***How to get there*** *(Map 18): 20km west of Moulins.*

# Le Chalet

03000 Coulandon (Allier)
Tel. (0)4.70.44.50.08 - Fax (0)4.70.44.07.09
M. Hulot

**Category** ★★★ **Rooms** 28 with telephone, bath or shower, WC and TV. **Price** Single 310-350F, double 370-480F. **Meals** Breakfast 48F, served 7:00-11:00; half board 355-420F, full board 480-520F (per pers., 3 days min.). **Restaurant** Service 12:30-13:30, 19:30-21.00; menus 120-250F, also à la carte. Specialties: Fresh local produce. **Credit cards** All major. **Pets** Dogs allowed. **Facilities** Lake, fishing, swimming pool, parking. **Nearby** Souvigny priory, châteaux of the Besbre Valley and of Lapalisse in Dompierre (half a day's journey), triptych of the Maître de Moulins at Notre Dame cathedral in Moulins; 18 hole Avenelles golf course in Moulins. **Open** Feb 1 – Dec 15.

This turn-of-the-century hotel is set in the hilly Bourbonnais countryside. The bedrooms are located in the main house and the outbuildings: numbers 8, 3 and 4, which still have the charm of the past, are beautifully spacious and they have pretty balconies. Numbers 16, 17 and 19, which have been renovated, are comfortable and well-decorated. Avoid number 1, which is too close to the parking lot. The other rooms have varying amenities but are all pleasant, with prettily coordinated wallpapers and fabrics. The restaurant is in a building somewhat too new for our taste. In summer, tables are set out on the terrace, where traditional, somewhat rich meals are served. There is a beautiful view over the swimming pool and a landscape of fields and trees all around. The staff is very courteous, but an additional person would perhaps improve the service. This is a lovely country setting just several minutes from Moulins.

***How to get there*** *(Map 18): 6km west of Moulins via D945.*

# Le Grenier à Sel

10, rue Sainte-Anne
03100 Montluçon (Allier)
Tel. (0)4.70.05.53.79 - Fax (0)4.70.05.87.91 - M. Morlon - M. Bourhy

**Rooms** 4 with telephone, bath or shower, WC and TV. **Price** Single and double 350F, 500F. **Meals** Breakfast 55F, served from 7:30; half board on request (3 days min.). **Restaurant** Service 12:30-14:00, 19:30-22:00 (closed Sunday evening and Monday except in July and Aug); menus 120-390F, also à la carte. Specialties: Chausson de morilles, canette fermière à la Duchambais. **Credit cards** All major. **Pets** Dogs allowed (+25F). **Facilities** Parking. **Nearby** Oak forest of Tronçais, Evaux-les Bains, Château of Boussac, Château of Culan. **Open** All year. Closed Sunday evening and Monday except in July and Aug.

Like a small haven of greenery and tranquillity in the heart of old Montluçon, this large hotel with its pointed roofs dates from the 16th century, which perhaps explains the majesty of the great trees shading the delicious small garden which the dining room overlooks. In fact, the Grenier à Sel is known especially for its restaurant, which was taken over several years ago by Jacky Morlon on his return to his native region after stints with several leading French chefs. Morlon and his brother-in-law, the maître d', have had the hotel decorated very tastefully: antique furniture, decorative objects, and paintings create an atmosphere of charming comfort and discreet luxury. The two bedrooms on the *premier étage* upstairs are spacious and bright, with ultra-modern bathrooms. The rooms on the last floor have mansard roofs but are equally well equipped. A pleasant stay awaits you in this beautiful hotel.

***How to get there*** *(Map 17): 332km south of Paris via A 10 until Orléans and A 71, to Bourges. In the old town, beside the theater.*

## Château de Boussac

Target
03140 Chantelle (Allier)
Tel. (0)4.70.40.63.20 - Fax (0)4.70.40.60.03 - M. and Mme de Longueil

**Rooms** 5 with bath and WC. **Price** Single and double 600-800F, suite 950-1100F. **Meals** Breakfast 55F, served 8:00-10:00; half board 1100F (per pers., 5 days min.). **Restaurant** Set meal in the evening only and on reservation; menu 260-320F incl. wine and alcohol. **Credit cards** Amex, Visa, Eurocard and MasterCard. **Pets** Dogs allowed (fee). **Facilities** Parking. **Nearby** Church of Sainte-Croix and museum of the Vine in Saint-Pourçain-sur-Sioule, priory in Souvigny, triptych of the Maître de Moulins at Notre Dame cathedral in Moulins – 18-hole golf course in Montluçon. **Open** Apr 1 – Nov 15.

The many faces of this beautiful château blend medieval austerity with the grace of the 18th-century. The owners receive you like friends and spontaneously include you in their aristocratic country life. Each very comfortable bedroom is superbly furnished with antiques (often Louis XV or Louis XVI), family mementos, and beautiful fabrics. The lounges have been charmingly restored. Finally, the large dining room table sets the scene for festive dinner parties which are very popular with sportsmen in the hunting season. The elegant silverware, the conversation, and the cuisine all contribute towards making each evening a lovely and memorable event.

***How to get there*** *(Map 25): 40km south of Moulins via A71, number 11 Montmarault exit, then D42 to Boussac (between Chantelle and Montmarault).*

## Le Tronçais

Avenue Nicolas-Rambourg
Tronçais - 03360 Saint-Bonnet-Tronçais (Allier)
Tel. (0)4.70.06.11.95 - Fax (0)4.70.06.16.15 - M. and Mme Bajard

**Category** ★★ **Rooms** 12 with telephone, bath or shower, WC and TV. **Price** Single 210F, double 268-354F. **Meals** Breakfast 36F, served 8:00-10:30; half board 251-295F, full board 306-350F (per pers., 3 days min.). **Restaurant** Service 12:00-13:30, 19:30-21:00; menus 98-180F, also à la carte. Specialties: Terrine d'anguille aux mûres, sandre au gratin, côte de veau aux cèpes, game. **Credit cards** Visa, Eurocard and Mastercard. **Pets** Dogs allowed only in bedrooms. **Facilities** Tennis, parking. **Nearby** Oak forest of Tronçais, château d'Ainay-le-Vieil, Château Meillant – 18-hole Nassigny golf course. **Open** Mar 15 – Dec 15 (closed Sunday evening and Monday in low season).

Once the private house of a forge owner, the Tronçais is located at the edge of the forest in a garden bordered by a lake. From the entrance steps to the bedrooms, the hotel is calm, comfortable and civilized. The bedrooms are tastefully appointed, comfortable, and many are huge. There are rooms also in a small annex; we find them small, but they have just been redone.The graveled garden in front of the two buildings serves as the terrace and bar in the summer. The meals are excellent, light, and appetizing (the portions are on the small side) and are served in a charming dining room. The hotel grounds stretch all the way to the banks of the lake, in which you can fish.

***How to get there*** *(Map 17): 45km north of Montluçon. On A71 Forêt-de-Tronçais exit, then N144 and D978A to Tronçais.*

## Auberge de Concasty

15600 Boisset (Cantal)
Tel. (0)4.71.62.21.16 - Fax (0)4.71.62.22.22
Mme Causse

**Category** ★★★ **Rooms** 16 with telephone, bath, WC and TV. **Price** Single 290-310F, double 340-500F. **Meals** Breakfast 50F, brunch 80F, served 9:00-11:30; half board 340-450F (per pers., 2 days min.). **Restaurant** By reservation; closed Wednesday except for residents. Service 12:30-13:30, 20:00-21:30; menus 150-200F. Specialties: Fresh local produce. **Credit cards** All major. **Pets** Dogs allowed (+40F). **Facilities** Heated swimming pool, whirlpool, Turktish bath, billard, parking. **Nearby** Audillac, valleys of the Lot and the Truyère, Champollion museum in Figeac, Haute Auvergne golf. **Open** Feb 1 - Nov 15 and Nov 30 - Jan 16.

The Auberge de Concasty is an old family mansion surrounded by its farm and fields. It has been completely restored and equipped with a swimming pool and whirlpool. Around the inn you will find many marked hiking paths and a beautiful golf course, which has just opened. The inn nonetheleess looks like a traditional family vacation house. It is very comfortable, the rooms have again been improved, and the reception rooms are pleasantly decorated. At Concasty, Mme Causse will delight you with fine seasonal cuisine featuring local specialties, (*cèpe* mushrooms, *foie gras*). You can also enjoy a good Auvergnat breakfast in this lovely vacation spot.

***How to get there*** *(Map 24): 25km southwest of Aurillac. In Aurillac via Cahors/Montauban by N122 for 20km; then in Manhes, turn left on D64 and follow signs.*

# Hôtel Beauséjour

15340 Calvinet (Cantal)
Tel. (0)4.71.49.91.68 - Fax (0)4.71.49.98.63
M. Puech

**Category** ★★ **Rooms** 12 with telephone, bath or shower, WC and cable TV. **Price** Single and double 250F, 300F. **Meals** Breakfast 40F, auvergnat 60F, served 9:00-11:30; half board 250-300F (per pers.). **Restaurant** Closed Sunday evening and Monday in low season, Monday lunchtime in hight season (except national holidays). Service 12:30-14:00, 20:00-21:30 by reservation, menus 95-140-205-300F. Market cooking. **Credit cards** Visa, Eurocard and MasterCard. **Pets** Dogs allowed. **Facilities** Parking. **Nearby** Audillac, valleys of the Lot and the Truyère, Champollion museum in Figeac, Conques. **Open** Beg Mar – 14 Jan. Closed Sunday evening and Monday in low season.

The Pueches are natives of this region and despite his growing reputation as a gourmet chef, Louis-Bernard preferred renovating this hotel, which was built by his parents, rather than setting up in a more prestigious place or a more accessible region but far from his roots. The building is nothing special but the modern interior is pleasant. It is discreet and perfectly well-kept, as are the bedrooms, which offer excellent value for the price when you consider their size and comfort. The outstanding features of the Beauséjour begin with the restaurant and the big, bright dining room overlooking greenery and a few village houses. Gourmets come from far and wide to savor the chef's fine, imaginative cuisine in a friendly atmosphere. There are superb culinary discoveries in the offing, and the prices are reasonable.

***How to get there*** *(Map 24): 32km south of Aurillac via RN 122 to Maurs, then D19.*

## Château de Lavendès

15350 Champagnac (Cantal)
Tel. (0)4.71.69.62.79 - Fax (0)4.71.69.65.33
M. and Mme Gimmig

**Category** ★★★ **Rooms** 7 with telephone, bath or shower, WC and TV. 1 junior 's suite. **Price** Double 440-595F. Suite 660F. **Meals** Breakfast 55F, served until 10:00; half board 435-510F (per pers, 3 days min.). **Restaurant** Service 12:30-13:45, 19:30-20.45; menus 135-198F, also à la carte. Specialties: Filet de bœuf pays vert, fomble de fontaine, truite Fario. **Credit cards** Visa, Eurocard and MasterCard. **Pets** Dogs not allowed. **Facilities** Swimming pool, parking. **Nearby** Bort-les-Orgues, Bort dam and château de Val, gorges of the Dordogne from Bort to the Aigle dam (2 hours) – 9-hole Mont-Dore golf course. **Open** Mar 1 – Nov 15 (closed Sunday evening and Monday in low season).

This manor house from the 14th century is set in the middle of a 2 1/2-acre park. The lobby, with its imposing fireplace, is also used as a tea room. In the château's two dining rooms—one Louis XV and the other Louis XIII in style—you can enjoy the gastronomic specialties of the Auvergne, which are prepared by Madame Gimmig. For lunch, you can also go to the hotel's other restaurant, *La Corniche,* which is above the dam at Bort-les-Orgues and where the chef is Jean-Christophe Gimmig. A splendid staircase, on which you will find many curiosities such as old wooden mechanisms and children's furniture, leads to the comfortably furnished bedrooms. The only sound you will hear is the tinkling of cow bells in the surrounding meadows. (Salers beef is a prized regional specialty).

***How to get there*** *(Map 24): 78km north of Aurillac via D922 to Ydes via Mauriac, then left on D12 or D112 to Champagnac; (the château is on D15). At the village exit, towards Neuvic, 1km after the church.*

## Auberge du Vieux Chêne

34, route des Lacs
15270 Champs-sur-Tarentaine (Cantal)
Tel. (0)4.71.78.71.64 - Fax (0)4.71.78.70.88 - Mme Moins

**Category** ★★ **Rooms** 15 with telephone, bath or shower, WC and TV. **Price** Double 320-420F. **Meals** Breakfast 45F, served 8:00-10:00; half board 280-300F, full board 320-380F (per pers., 3 days min.). **Restaurant** Service 12:00-13:30, 19:00-20:30; menus 130-230F, also à la carte. Specialties: Foie gras d'oie maison, confit de canard aux lentilees vertes du Puy, escalope de saumon à l'oseille. **Credit cards** Visa, Eurocard and MasterCard. **Pets** Dogs allowed. **Facilities** Parking. **Nearby** Bort-les-Orgues, Bort dam and château de Val, gorges of the Dordogne from Bort to the Aigle dam (3 hours)–9-hole Mont-Dore golf course. **Open** Mar 15 – Nov 15 (closed Sunday evening and Monday except July and Aug).

This old stone and timber farmhouse, which is set well away from the road, has been charmingly restored and enlarged. The bedrooms have been beautifully renovated with cheerful, refined colors, coordinated fabrics and wallpapers and many charming decorative details. At one end of the ground floor, there is a pleasant bar, while the rest of the area is occupied by a salon and a vast dining room whose end wall is one immense fireplace. Outside, a new terrace has just been added, where breakfast and meals are served, further enhancing the country character of the "Old Oak Inn." The hospitality is warm and the cuisine excellent.

***How to get there*** *(Map 24): 93km north of Aurillac via D922 to Bort-les-Orgues, then D979.*

# Auberge du Pont de Lanau

Lanau
15260 Chaudes-Aigues (Cantal)
Tel. (0)4.71.23.57.76 - Fax (0)4.71.23.53.84 - M. Cornut

**Category** ★★ **Rooms** 8 with telephone, bath, WC and TV. **Price** Single and double 270-350F. **Meals** Breakfast 36F; half board 270-300F, full board 350-400F (per pers., 3 days min.). **Restaurant** Service 12:30-14:00, 19:30-21:30; menus 95-300F, also à la carte. **Credit cards** Visa, Eurocard and MasterCard. **Pets** Dogs allowed (+35F). **Facilities** Parking. **Nearby** Saint-Flour, gorges of the Truyère. **Open** All year (except in Jan and Feb. Monday evening and Tuesday in low season).

Courtesy is the tradition in this old farmhouse-auberge built in 1855. In the past, clients were served meals on the left (today the restaurant) and horses were stabled on the right (today the lounge, breakfast room and bar). The beautifully decorated rustic restaurant has stone walls and is dominated by an immense fireplace. Guests once slept in bed recesses close to the fireplace to keep warm, and you can still see traces of the original wooden partitions. Today the inn is primarily a restaurant serving very good, refined regional cooking. M. Cornut often prepares specialties which are little known today, or delicious new versions of traditional regional dishes. The eight bedrooms are pleasant, some decorated in floral motifs while others are drenched in salmon pink. They have fabric-covered walls and are well insulated with double windows. The auberge is located beside a country road and is a lovely place to stay.

***How to get there*** *(Map 25): 20km south of Saint-Flour via D921.*

# Hostellerie de la Maronne

Le Theil
15140 Saint-Martin-Valmeroux (Cantal)
Tel. (0)4.71.69.20.33 - Fax (0)4.71.69.28.22 - Mme Decock
E-mail: hotel.de.la.maronne@wanadoo.fr

**Category** ★★★ **Rooms** 21 with telephone, bath, WC, minibar and TV. **Price** Single and double 350-600F, suite 700F. **Meals** Breakfast 40-50F, served 8:30-10:00; half board 440-520F. **Restaurant** Service 19:30-21:00; menus 140-300F, also à la carte. Specialties: Escalope de sandre aux mousserons, foie gras chaud au caramel de porto, gâteau tiède aux marrons et chocolat amer. **Credit cards** Visa, Eurocard and MasterCard. **Pets** Dogs allowed. **Facilities** Swimming pool, tennis, parking. **Nearby** Medieval city of Salers, basilica of Notre-Dame-des-Miracles in Mauriac, Puy Mary. **Open** April 3 – Nov 5.

M. and Mme Decock have marvelously transformed this 19th-century Auvergnat house into a hotel. Everything has been provided for guests' entertainment and rest: for example, guests watching television sets are provided with headsets so as not to disturb others. The living room, reading room and bar have been elegantly decorated with comfortable armchairs and some antique furniture. The elegantly modern, comfortable bedrooms are decorated in pale shades, our preferences leaning toward those with a view, which is splendid, particularly from the rooms with large terraces and balconies. (There is also an apartment, which families will enjoy). The cuisine is increasingly renowned and the dining room is beautiful, with a lovely view over the countryside. Walking in the area is a pleasure, and there are tennis courts and a swimming pool. Last but not least, the hospitality and service are charming.

***How to get there*** *(Map 24): 33km north of Aurillac via D922 to Saint-Martin Valmeroux, then D37 towards Fontanges.*

## Auberge des Montagnes

15800 Pailherols (Cantal)
Tel. (0)4.71.47.57.01 - Fax (0)4.71.49.63.83
M. Combourieu

**Category** ★★ **Rooms** 26 with telephone, bath or shower, WC (7 with TV and minibar). **Price** Single and double 212-270F. **Meals** Breakfast 28F, served 8:00-9:30; half board 235-280F (per pers., 2 days min.). **Restaurant** Service from 12:30, from 19:30; menus 75-125F, also à la carte. Specialties: Truite saumonée feuilletée, chou farci, truffade, noisetier sous la neige, croustine au praliné. **Credit cards** All major. **Pets** Dogs allowed. **Facilities** Swimming pool, courses in cross-country skiing and horse-drawn mountain carriages, parking. **Nearby** Medieval city of Salers, basilica of Notre-Dame-des-Miracles in Mauriac, Puy Mary. **Open** Dec 21 – Oct 13.

The Auberge is located in the center of this village which lies between the mountains of Les Puys and L'Aubrac. A countryside of holes and hollows, low stone walls, cropped grass and woods, the Pailherois plateau has a wild kind of beauty. The hotel consists of several buildings fairly far apart. The main building includes the restaurant, a bar-lounge and bedrooms which we do not recommend. Across the street, you will find two swimming pools, one of which is heated and is installed in a barn adjacent to a game room. Finally, 200 meters farther on, the Clos des Gentiannes annex has just been built, offering vast, very comfortable bedrooms decorated in a modern, cheerful style. They offer unbeatable value for the money and all overlook a sublime landscape; some are ideal for families. M. and Mme Cambourieu are especially friendly and turn out regional cuisine whose reputation is known throughout the valleys. You will enjoy a family-style, informal atmosphere here.

***How to get there*** *(Map 24): 21km east of Aurillac via Vic-sur-Cère.*

## Auberge de la Tomette

15220 Vitrac (Cantal)
Tel. (0)4.71.64.70.94 - Fax (0)4.71.64.77.11
M. and Mme Chausi

**Category** ★★ **Rooms** 15 with telephone, bath or shower, WC and TV. **Price** Single and double 250-320F, suite 390-460F. **Meals** Breakfast 43F; half board 246-314F, full board 336-404F (per pers., 3 days min.). **Restaurant** Service 12:00-14:00, 19:00-20:30; menus 68-185F, also à la carte. Specialties: filet de truite aux noisettes, magret au vinaigre de cidre, caille forestière, ris de veau crémaillère, tartes maison, crépinette de pied de cochon. **Credit cards** Amex, Visa, Eurocard and MasterCard. **Pets** Dogs allowed in bedrooms only. **Facilities** Swimming pool, sauna (45F). **Nearby** Conques, Salers, Rocamadour, monts du Cantal, château d'Anjony, Vic-sur-Cère. **Open** Apr 1 – Dec 31.

Vitrac, surrounded by chestnut plantations, is a beauty spot in the south of the Cantal, and the Auberge de la Tomette is right in the heart of the village. The restaurant is located here and in the evening, you can have dinner in the delicious garden behind the inn. The bedrooms are a few steps away in a vast flowery park with a very beautiful view of the countryside. The bedrooms are comfortable, impeccably kept and decorated in a sober, modern style, brightened with pretty fabrics. Note the duplex, which is ideal for families. The atmosphere in the rustic dining room, with its exposed beams and wood paneling, is very friendly, and the cuisine is excellent. Mme Chausi will greet you charmingly and advise you on what to do and where to go in the region. This is a picturesque place to stay, where you become part of the village life.

***How to get there*** *(Map 24): 25km south of Aurillac via N122 towards Figeac; at Saint-Mamet-La Salvetat take D66.*

## Hôtel de l'Echo et de l'Abbaye

Place de L'Echo
43160 La Chaise-Dieu (Haute-Loire)
Tel. (0)4.71.00.00.45 - Fax (0)4.71.00.00.22 - M. Degreze

**Category** ★★ **Rooms** 11 with telephone, bath or shower, 9 with TV. **Price** Single 260-300F, double 300-350F. **Meals** Breakfast 50F, served 7:30-9:30; half board 320-350F (per pers., 3 days min.). **Restaurant** Service 12:00-14:00, 19:30-21:00, menus 90-250F, also à la carte. Specialties: Flan aux cèpes sauce forestière, mignon de porc à la crème de myrtilles, tournedos de saumon aux lentilles vertes du Puy, entrecôte à la fourme d'Ambert, tarte aux fruits des bois. **Credit cards** All major. **Pets** Dogs not allowed. **Nearby** Basilica of Notre-Dame du Puy, church of Saint-Laurent and Aiguille au Puy, Mont Mezenc, Mont Gerbier-de Jonc, village of Arlempdes. **Open** Apr 5 – Nov 10.

This auberge is part of the enclave formed by the splendid La Chaise Dieu Abbey, and is the ideal place for visiting the historic village. Its name refers to the "Room of Echoes" nearby, which is known for its strange acoustical phenomenon. It is a very old, remarkably well-kept hotel, which has just changed management, but you will still be hospitably welcomed by Madame Chirouzé. The small bedrooms are charming and comfortable, and some have a view of the cloister. There is always a contemporary painting exhibit on view in the restaurant dining room, which is decorated in Haute Epoque style. Often complimented in the guest book, the regional Auvergnate cuisine is excellent. Cocktails and refreshments can be served outside on the terrace, which is reserved exclusively for the hotel.

***How to get there*** *(Map 25): 35km north of Le Puy-en-Velay.*

## Le Pré Bossu

43150 Moudeyres (Haute-Loire)
Tel. (0)4.71.05.10.70 - Fax (0)4.71.05.10.21
M. Grootaert and Mme Moreels

**Category** ★★★ **Rooms** 10 with telephone, bath or shower and WC. **Price** Double 370-475F. . **Meals** Breakfast 55F, served 8:00-10:00; half board 430-590F (per pers. in double room). **Restaurant** Closed lunchtime except Saturday and Sunday. Service 12:00-13:30, 19:30-21:00; menus 170-360F (child 65F), also à la carte. Specialties: Ecrevisses aux petits légumes, andouillette d'escargot au coulis de céleri. **Credit cards** All major. **Pets** Dogs allowed in bedrooms (+35F). **Facilities** Parking. **Nearby** Basilica of Notre-Dame-du-Puy in Puy-en-Velay, Gerbier-des-Joncs, Mézenc forest – 9-hole Chambon-sur-Lignon golf course in Romières. **Open** Apr 1 – Nov 2.

Located in the lovely village of Moudeyres, this old thatched cottage built in local stone is named for the meadow which surrounds it. The atmosphere is cozy and welcoming. To one side there is a reception room with a large fireplace, TV and library. In the beautiful stone dining room with its smartly set tables, you will be served outstanding regional gourmet specialties, which are made with fresh produce from the kitchen garden. The bedrooms are very comfortable and attractively furnished, and the garden and terrace overlook the countryside. If you wish to go out for the day, picnic baskets can be prepared, and the welcome is very friendly.

***How to get there*** *(Map 25): 25km east of Le Puy via D15 to Les Pandreaux, then D36 to Moudeyres via Laussonne.*

## Le Turenne

1, boulevard Saint-Rodolphe-de-Turenne
19120 Beaulieu-sur-Dordogne (Corrèze)
Tel. (0)5.55.91.10.16 - Fax (0)5.55.91.22.42 - M. Cavé

**Category** ★★ **Rooms** 15 with telephone, bath or shower, TV and WC. **Price** Double 270-280F; half board 260-280F. **Meals** Breakfast 40F. **Restaurant** Service 12:15-13:30, 19:30-21:00 (closed Sunday evening and Monday in low season); menus 75F(lunch in week) 96F, 140F, 350F (wine toasting incl.), also à la carte. Specialties: Croustillant de foie gras et cèpes sauce banuyls, Filet de perche en matelotte, crépinette de pied de porc à la moutarde violette, assiette aux noix. **Credit cards** All major. **Pets** Dogs allowed. **Facilities** Parking. **Nearby** Collonges, Turenne, Argentat – 18-hole Coiroux golf course in Aubazines. **Open** Mid Feb – mid Jan (closed Sunday evening and Monday in low season).

There are so many superb houses in Beaulieu because in the 13th century a powerful abbey was built here. This hotel occupies a part of its venerable walls, 100 meters from the banks of the Dordogne River. Inside, various vestiges are reminders of the ancient age of the building: many monumental fireplaces, a superb spiral staircase, parts of age-old doors. All confer special charm to the place. Pascal Cavé, the chef, respects the Quercy culinary traditions while lending them a lighter and more delicate touch. His cuisine is marvelous. In winter, there is always a fire crackling in the immense fireplace of the restaurant, while in summer the large ogival French doors open onto a leafy terrace with a few tables. The bedrooms are being renovated in pastel colors with classic furniture. Some look out on the medieval city, others onto the square; all are very quiet. Overall, the hotel is simple, family-style and the prices are very reasonable.

***How to get there*** *(Map 24): 39km south of Tulle via D940.*

## Relais de Saint-Jacques-de-Compostelle

19500 Collonges-la-Rouge (Corrèze)
Tel. (0)5.55.25.41.02 - Fax (0)5.55.84.08.51
M. Guillaume

**Category** ★★ **Rooms** 24: 14 in the annex, 10 with telephone, bath or shower and WC (4 with TV.) **Price** Double 170-310F. **Meals** Breakfast 40F. **Restaurant** Service 12:30-13:30, 19:30-21:00; menus 100-250F, also à la carte. Specialties: Feuilleté de Saint-Jacques, filet de bœuf fourré au foie gras, terrine de cèpes au coulis de jambon de pays, crème brulée aux noix. **Credit cards** All major. **Pets** Dogs allowed. **Facilities** Parking. **Nearby** Collonges, Turenne, church in Beaulieu-sur-Dordogne, Argentat – 18-hole Coiroux golf course in Aubazines. **Open** Mid-Mar – mid-Nov.

Its fascinating medieval houses in red sandstone make Collonges-la-Rouge a very beautiful and much visited place. Located in the heart of the village, the hotel has just been very tastefully restored; the general effect is light and flowery. On the ground floor are two dining rooms, a small reception room furnished with amusing "toad" armchairs, and an intimate bar. The small bedrooms are all very attractive. Excellent cooking is served with a smile. In summer, tables are laid on three lovely shaded terraces. M. and Mme Guillaume's welcome, even in this tourist-ridden town, is reason enough for a visit.

***How to get there*** *(Map 24): 45km south of Tulle via D940 and D38 towards Meyssac. The hotel is in the village.*

## Au Rendez-Vous des Pêcheurs

Pont du Chambon
19320 Saint-Merd-de-Lapleau (Corrèze)
Tel. (0)5.55.27.88.39 - Fax (0)5.55.27.83.19 - Mme Fabry

**Category** ★★ **Rooms** 8 with telephone, bath or shower, WC and TV. **Price** Single and double 240F, 270F. **Meals** Breakfast 38F, served 8:00-9:30, half board 240-270F, full board 295-345F (per pers., 3 days min.). **Restaurant** Service 12:15-13:30, 19:45-21:00; menus 78-210F, also à la carte. Specialties: Sandre au beurre blanc, ris de veau aux cèpes, mousse de noix glacée, marbré de foie gras et magret aux pruneaux. **Credit cards** Visa, Eurocard and MasterCard. **Pets** Dogs allowed. **Facilities** Parking. **Nearby** Merle, château of Sédières, viaduc des Rochers Noirs. **Open** Dec 23 - Jan 7 and Feb 16 - Nov 11. (closed Friday evening and Saturday lunchtime Oct 1 – Mar 30).

Built on the banks of the Dordogne, this large house has a backdrop of wooded hills and owes much of its appeal to its exceptional location. On the ground floor, a light, large and well-decorated dining room with flowered curtains and pretty tables has beautiful views across the river. On one side, a small lounge and bar give access to a lovely terrace overlooking the river. The bedrooms have been renovated, with improved amenities and soundproofing, but again, the view is the highlight of the decor. There is good fishing here, and you can try the local perch, pike and trout cooked by Elise. Pedalboats are for rent at the hotel, and you can also cruise on the Dordogne in a traditional *gabare*. This is a good hotel, and very moderately priced.

***How to get there*** *(Map 24): 45km east of Tulle via D978 to Saint-Merd-de-Lapleau via Marcillac-la-Croisille, then D13 to Pont-du-Chambon.*

# Auberge des Prés de la Vézère

19240 Saint-Viance (Corrèze)
Tel. (0)5.55.85.00.50 - Fax (0)5.55.84.25.36
M. Parveaux

**Category** ★★ **Rooms** 11 with telephone, bath, WC and TV. **Price** Single and double 250-350F. **Meals** Breakfast 35F, served 7:30-10:00; half board 31-360F (per pers.). **Restaurant** Service 12:00-14:00, 19:30-21:00; menus 88-155F, also à la carte. Specialties: Tourtou au saumon fumé, civet de vin de Cahors, parmentier de confit de canard, flognarde aux pommes. **Credit cards** Visa, Eurocard and MasterCard. **Pets** Dogs allowed. **Facilities** Parking. **Nearby** Abbey of Aubazines, Uzerches, Argentat, Collonges-la-Rouge, Pompadour stud farm, Beaulieu-sur-Dordogne – 18-hole Coiroux golf course in Aubazines. **Open** May to Oct.

Saint-Viance is a very well-preserved small town, with its old houses and the lovely bridge that spans the Vézère, a river very popular with fishermen. The hotel is at the entrance to the village beside a quiet road. There is a large dining room which extends onto a beautiful shaded terrace. On the *premier étage*, although the corridor is somewhat dark, you will be agreeably surprised by the bedrooms, which have lovely pale wallpapers and pretty curtains matching the bedcovers. The rooms are cheerful and well-kept and all have well-equipped bathrooms. This is a good place for a family holiday.

***How to get there*** *(Map 23): 11km northwest of Brive-la-Gaillarde, towards Objat then Allassac.*

## La Maison des Chanoines

Route de l'Église
19500 Turenne (Corrèze)
Tel. (0)5.55.85.93.43 - M. and Mme Cheyroux

**Rooms** 6 with bath and WC and 1 suite. **Price** Double 330-600F. **Meals** Breakfast 40F, served 7:30-10:00; half board 340F. **Restaurant** Service 12:00-14:00, 19:30-21:00; menus 140-195F, also à la carte. Specialties: Escalope de foie gras frais mariné de canard, filet de sandre à l'étuvée de concombres, moules de bouchot au jus de noix vertes, médaillon de veau du limousin aux girolles à la saison. **Credit cards** Visa, Eurocard and MasterCard. **Pets** Dogs allowed. **Nearby** Abbey of Aubazines, Uzerches, Argentat, Collonges-la-Rouge, Pompadour stud farm, Beaulieu-sur-Dordogne – 18-hole Coiroux golf course in Aubazines. **Open** Apr 1 – Nov 16 (closed Tuesday evening and Wednesday except July 1 – Sept ).

Turenne is one of the most beautiful villages of France and this old house is a good illustration of the architectural richness of the town. La Maison des Chanoines is basically a small restaurant to which three bedrooms have been added. Totally renovated, the rooms are elegant and tastefully decorated with antiques. To the great pleasure of their dinner guests, M. and Mme Cheyrou have given quality priority over quantity. There is a reasonable number of dishes on the menu, a maximum of 16 diners in the beautiful vaulted dining room, and no more than 25 when meals are served outdoors beneath the honeysuckle trellis. Strictly fresh products, reliable gastronomic quality and very friendly service are guaranteed. We will long remember the *foie gras* simply marinated with truffle and *girolle* vinegar.

***How to get there*** *(Maps 24): 14km south of Brive-la-Gaillarde. Highway A 20, exit number 52 in Noailles; Turenne 10 mn.*

# Domaine des Mouillères

Les Mouillères
Saint-Georges-la-Pouge - 23250 Pontarion (Creuse)
Tel. (0)5.55.66.60.64 - Fax (0)5.55.66.68.80 - Mme Thill-Blanquart

**Category** ★★ **Rooms** 7 with telephone (3 with bath, 4 with WC). **Price** Single and double 200-380F. **Meals** Breakfast 40F, served 8:00-9:30. **Restaurant** For residents only. Service 20:00-20:30; menus 90-150F, also à la carte. Specialties: Filet de truite rose au beurre blanc, feuilleté aux cèpes, tournedos forestier aux cèpes. **Credit cards** Visa, Eurocard and MasterCard. **Pets** Dogs not allowed. **Facilities** Parking. **Nearby** Hôtel de Moneyroux and Guéret Museum, abbey church of Moutier-d'Ahun – 18-hole la Jonchère golf course in Montgrenier-Gouzon. **Open** Apr – Oct 1.

This old farmhouse is set in an absolutely magnificent countryside of valleys, pastures, small rivers, birch groves, conifer-covered hills and large trees. The lovely small lounge has a mixture of furniture and old-fashioned objects. We prefer the bedrooms with bathrooms, but the others have been totally refurbished and are equipped with basins. They are all pretty and pleasant, many with satin bedcovers and small, round, skirted tables. Dinners are served in a rustic dining room and feature good first courses, salads and excellent meats (ask for the meat dishes with little sauce.) The owners rent bikes for exploring the superb surrounding countryside. Drinks and meals can be served on the lovely garden terrace. The staff is very courteous.

***How to get there*** *(Map 24): 34km south of Guéret via D942 towards Limoges to Pontarion; then towards La Chapelle-Saint-Martial, D3.*

## Au Moulin de la Gorce

87800 La Roche l'Abeille (Haute-Vienne)
Tel. (0)5.55.00.70.66 - Fax (0)5.55.00.76.57
Bertranet-Bremont Family

**Category** ★★★ **Rooms** 9 and 1 apartment, with telephone, bath, WC and TV. **Price** Single 350F, double 700-950F, suite 1300F. **Meals** Breakfast 75F, served from 8:00, half board 1450-1550F, full board 1850-1980F (2 pers., 3 days min.). **Restaurant** Service 12:00 13.30, 19:30-21:00; menus 180-380F, also à la carte. Specialties: Œufs brouillés aux truffes dans leur coque, foie poêlé aux pommes, lièvre à la royale. **Credit cards** All major. **Pets** Dogs allowed. **Facilities** Parking. **Nearby** Saint Etienne cathedral and Adrien-Dubouché ceramics museum in Limoges, abbey of Solignac, church of Saint-Léonard-de-Noblat – 18-hole Porcelaine golf course in Limoges. **Open** Mar 1 – Dec 31 (closed Sunday evening and Monday Sept 20 – Apr 30).

Converted into a sumptuous hotel-restaurant by a family of pastry cooks/caterers from Limoges, this flour mill dates back to 1569. Today, entirely renovated, it consist of several buildings set around a beautiful lake with a stream that tumbles down into the garden. The interior decoration is very tasteful, intimate and comfortable. The bedrooms are pleasant and elegantly furnished. Drinks are served on the terrace overlooking the lake and garden, and there is fine, gourmet cuisine with an interesting "Saint Jacques de Compostelle" menu. This is a luxurious, professionally run hotel which has nevertheless retained its family-style hospitality.

***How to get there*** *(Map 23): 30km south of Limoges via D704 then D17.*

## Castel-Hôtel 1904

Rue du Castel
63390 Saint-Gervais-d'Auvergne (Puy-de-Dôme)
Tel. (0)4.73.85.70.42 - Fax (0)4.73.85.84.39 - M. Mouty

**Category** ★★ **Rooms** 17 with telephone, bath or shower, WC, TV and minibar. **Price** Single and double 295-320F. **Meals** Breakfast 45F, served 7:30-10:00; half board 270F, full board 340F (per pers., 3 days min.). **Restaurant** Service from 12:30 and 19:30; menus 75-269F, also à la carte. Specialties: Tournedos roulé au hachis de pieds de porc, sandre, crêpe Céline. **Credit cards** Visa,Eurocard and MasterCard. **Pets** Dogs not allowed. **Facilities** Parking. **Nearby** Gorges of the Sioule, church in Ménat, Fades viaduct, Mandet museum and museum of the Auvergne in Riom – 9- and 18-hole Volcans golf course in Orcines. **Open** Easter – Nov 11.

This ancient château, built in 1616, was converted into a hotel in 1904 and has been run by the same family ever since. All the charm of an old French hotel is to be found in its warm and welcoming rooms, bar and above all its large dining room, whose parquet floors gleam. The fireplaces, the antique furniture and the ochre tones of the walls and curtains all contribute to the old-fashioned but very charming character of the hotel. The comfortable bedrooms are all different and in keeping with the spirit of the hotel. You have the choice of two restaurants: the *Castel,* which has an inventive menu, and the *Comptoir à Moustache*, an authentic country bistro. The Castel is welcoming and friendly - the kind of place you become attached to.

***How to get there*** *(Map 24): 55km northwest of Clermont-Ferrand via N9 to Châtelguyon, then D227 to Saint-Gervais-d'Auvergne via Manzat.*

## Villa Louise

21420 Aloxe-Corton (Côte-d'Or)
Tel. (0)3.80.26.46.70 - Fax (0)3.80.26.47.16 - M. Voarick
E-mail: villalou@iafrica.com - Web: www.villalouix.com

**Category** ★★★ **Rooms** 10 with telephone, bath, WC, TV and minibar. **Price** Single 500F, double 600-800F. **Meals** Breakfast 75F, served 8:00-13:00. No restaurant. **Credit cards** Visa, Eurocard and MasterCard. **Pets** Dogs allowed. **Facilities** Parking. **Nearby** Hôtel-Dieu, basilica of Notre Dame in Beaune, Hôtel de la Rochepot and Bourgogne Wine museum in Beaune, Côte de Beaune between Serrigny and Chagny, château du Clos-Vougeot, Nolay, Rochepot – 18-hole Beaune-Levernois golf course. **Open** All year.

If you enjoyed the former Hôtel Clarion, you'll be happy to know that it is still here, now called Villa Louise. Monsieur Voarick has tastefully combined modern comfort with the beauty of nature, creating a hotel of character and charm only three kilometers from Beaune, just behind the famous winegrowing village of Aloxe-Corton. The Villa Louise is a converted country mansion bordered by a large lawn that eventually disappears into the vines. But behind this traditional appearance, there is a tastefully decorated contemporary interior, which combines old exposed beams and fireplaces with the clean lines of a simple modern design. The result is a warm, intimate atmosphere. The rooms have soft lights, antique furniture, comfortable armchairs and magnificent bathrooms. The breakfasts are marvelous, and you can have brunch anytime next to the fireplace or under the linden trees in the garden. The service and reception are casual. For restaurants in Beaune, we recommend the elegant *Le Jardin des Remparts,* near the Hospices de Beaune; the charming *Le Bénaton*; and Le *Gourmandin,* for its bistrot atmosphere.

***How to get there*** *(Map 19): 5km north of Beaune via N74. and Beaune nord exit A 6 (2km).*

## Chez Camille

1, place Edouard-Herriot
21230 Arnay-le-Duc (Côte-d'Or)
Tel. (0)3.80.90.01.38 - Fax (0)3.80.90.04.64 - M. and Mme Poinsot

**Category** ★★★ **Rooms** 14 with telephone, bath and TV. **Price** Double 395F. **Meals** Breakfast 50F served 7:00-12:00; half board 400F (per pers.). **Restaurant** Service 12:00-14:30, 19:30-22:00; menus 80-450F, also à la carte. Specialties: Rissoles d'escargots aux pâtes fraîches et champignons, le charolais. **Credit cards** All major. **Pets** Dogs allowed. **Facilities** Garage. **Nearby** Basilica of Saint-Andoche in Saulieu, château de Commarin, Châteauneuf – 18-hole Château de Chailly golf course. **Open** All year.

This charming hotel is peaceful and quiet despite its town location in small Arnay-le-Duc. There is a large, comfortable lobby with a piano, and a lovely 17th-century stairway that leads to the bedrooms. The rooms are restful, comfortable and some come with antique furniture. We especially liked Number 17 (reserv it ahead of time). Chez Camille is also a famous restaurant. The ravishing dining room is set in a winter garden with a glass roof: a perfect setting for trying the fine specialties of Burgundy, made with products from the Poinsots' farm. The regional cuisine is light and inventive, making Chez Camille a Burgundian must. Note that children under eleven are guests of the hotel.

***How to get there*** *(Map 19): 28km northeast of Autun via N81.*

## Hôtel Le Home

138, route de Dijon
21200 Beaune (Côte-d'Or)
Tel. (0)3.80.22.16.43 - Fax (0)3.80.24.90.74 - Mme Jacquet

**Category** ★★ **Rooms** 23 with telephone, bath or shower and WC (8 with TV). **Price** Single and double 325-450F **Meals** Breakfast 35F. No restaurant. **Credit cards** Visa, Eurocard and MasterCard. **Pets** Dogs allowed. **Facilities** Garage. **Nearby** Hôtel Dieu, basilica of Notre-Dame in Beaune, Côte de Beaune between Serrigny and Chagny, château du Clos-Vougeot, Nolay, Rochepot – 18-hole Beaune-Levernois golf course. **Open** All year.

The inspiration for this small hotel, at the entrance to Beaune, is definitely English. The Virginia-creeper–covered house is surrounded by a flowery garden where breakfast is served. Well-chosen antiques, lamps and carpets give a personal touch to every room. The bedrooms are pretty, comfortable and quiet; the living room inviting. The proximity of the road is noticeable only from outside as the interior is well-insulated from noise. The hospitable Mme Jacquet loves her house, which explains why you will be received here as a friend. For restaurants see page 133.

*How to get there (Map 19): In Beaune, on the Dijon road; beyond the church of Saint-Nicolas. Exit Autoroute north, and Beaune north.*

## Hôtel Le Parc

Levernois – 21200 Beaune (Côte-d'Or)
Tel. (0)3.80.22.22.51/(0)3.80.24.63.00 - Fax (0)3.80.24.21.19
Mme Oudot

**Category** ★★ **Rooms** 25 with telephone and TV (19 with shower, 6 with bath and 24 with WC). **Price** Double 200-490F. **Meals** Breakfast 36F, served 7:30-9:30. No restaurant. **Credit cards** Visa, Eurocard and MasterCard. **Pets** Dogs allowed (extra charge). **Facilities** Parking. **Nearby** Hôtel Dieu, basilica of Notre-Dame in Beaune, Côte de Beaune between Serrigny and Chagny, château du Clos-Vougeot, Nolay, Rochepot – 18-hole Beaune-Levernois golf course. **Open** Jan 15 - Dec 1.

The Hôtel Le Parc is an old, ivy-covered Burgundian house on the doorstep of the charming international wine capital of Beaune. It has a flowery courtyard where breakfast is served, and a garden with huge, ancient trees. Hôtel Le Parc has the feel of a much smaller hotel despite the number of bedrooms. The atmosphere of every bedroom is different, created in one by the wallpaper, in another by a chest of drawers and in yet another by a quilt. M and Mme Oudot refurbish the rooms regularly. Those which have just been redecorated have pretty floral-bordered English wallpapers coordinated with the curtains and bedspreads. Some of them are very large and luxurious, and all are in good taste. Although not far from the town, you will feel as if you are in the country, and, most importantly, you will feel most welcome. For restaurants, try the famous *Hostellerie de Levernois*, or in Beaune the elegant *Jardin des Remparts*, the charming *Le Bénaton*, or *Le Gourmandin*.

***How to get there** (Map 19): 4km southeast of Beaune via D970, towards Verdun, Lons-le-Saulnier.*

## Château de Challanges

Rue des Templiers
Challanges 21200 Beaune (Côte-d'Or)
Tel. (0)3.80.26.32.62 - Fax (0)3.80.26.32.52 - M. Schwarz

**ategory** ★★★ **Rooms** 9 and 5 suite with telephone, bath or shower, WC and TV. **Price** Double 530F, uite 800F. **Meals** Breakfast 60F (buffet), served 8:00-10:00. No restaurant. **Credit cards** Amex, iner's, Visa, Eurocard and MasterCard. **Pets** Dogs allowed. **Facilities** Tennis, hot air balloon, wine asting, parking. **Nearby** Hôtel Dieu, basilica of Notre-Dame in Beaune, Côte de Beaune between Sergny and Chagny, château du Clos-Vougeot, Nolay, Rochepot – 18-hole Beaune-Levernois golf course. **pen** Mar – Dec.

When you arrive at the Château de Challenges, don't worry about the proximity of the autoroute because it is hidden by a 17-acre park. The noise f the cars sounds only like a faraway murmur; but ask for the bedrooms overooking the entrance to the park. The hotel is decorated in classical, tasteful tyle with straw-yellow walls, a great amount of blue and sober, contemporary urniture. The breakfast buffet is prettily presented in a pleasant, bright dining oom. The bedrooms and suites are all attractive, each with their own color and andsome fabrics in the same tones. The adjoining bathrooms all have white iles with a coordinated frieze. The bedrooms are not all very large; ask for hose with a king-size bed (160 centimeters wide). This is a very comfortable otel from which to visit Beaune and its environs.

***low to get there*** *(Map 19): On A6, take the Beaune exit towards Dole; turn ight in 2km to Challanges.*

1998

## Le Hameau de Barbaron

Rue des Templiers
21420 Savigny-les-Beaune (Côte d'or)
Tel. (0)3.80.21.58.35 - Fax (0)3.80.26.10.58 - Mme Nomine

**Rooms** 9 with telephone, bath or shower, WC, TV and minibar. **Price** Single and double 450-500F, 550-900F; suite 1000-1200F. **Meals** Breakfast (buffet) 65F, served until 12:00. **Restaurant** By reservation. **Credit cards** Visa, Eurocard and MasterCard. **Pets** Dogs allowed. **Facilities** Garage. **Nearby** Hôtel-Dieu, basilica of Notre-Dame in Beaune, Côte de Beaune between Serrigny and Chagny, Côte de Nuits, château of Clos-Vougeot, Nolay, Rochepot - 18-hole Beaune-Levernois golf course. **Open** All year.

Originally a monastery, the Barbaron is set in a remote valley, isolated from the world in keeping with Cistercian tradition. Here too, following the French Revolution in 1789, farming families settled on this immense estate devoted to hunting, cattle grazing, and agriculture. Meticulously restored, the 16th-century buildings, built around a small courtyard, look austere and serious. But once you're inside, the atmosphere is one of warmth, refinement, and conviviality. You might prefer the large suites like *Les Cousins* or *Le Guet du Loup* with their gleaming blue and white bathrooms. Or the more intimate rooms like *Lucien*, which overlooks the orchard and is equipped with a large shower rather than a bathtub. With a sweeping view of the countryside and classical music in the background, the breakfast room has a very charming décor with a fireplace and a floor of wood and ceramic tiles. You will enjoy absolute peace and quiet on this estate inhabited by birds, hares, and even the Barbaron's wild boars.

***How to get there*** *(Map 19): A 6 Beaune exit, to the town center. Take the road N74 to Dijon then to Savigny-les-Beaune.*

1998

## Hostellerie du Château

Rue du Centre
21230 Châteauneuf-en-Auxois (Côte-d'Or)
Tel. (0)3.80.49.22.00 - Fax (0)3.80.49.21.27 - M. and Mme Hartmann

**Category** ★★ **Rooms** 17 with telephone, bath or shower and WC - 1 for disables persons. **Price** Single 270F, double 270-430F. **Meals** Breakfast (buffet) 50F, served 8:00-9:45; half board from 370F (per pers., 2 days min.). **Restaurant** Service 12:00-13:30, 19:00-21:00 (closed Monday evening and Tuesday except in July and Aug); menus 140-220F, also à la carte. Specialties: Filet de charolais au foie gras de canard poêlé, filet de rougel pôêlée aux poivrons doux et olives noires. **Credit cards** All major. **Pets** Dogs allowed. **Nearby** Château of Commarin, basilica of Saint-Andoche in Saulieu, Hôtel Dieu and basilica of Notre-Dame in Beaune - 18-hole Château de Chailly golf course. **Open** Feb – Nov.

Perched on the hilltop of this fortified village, the Hostellerie is adjacent to a very beautiful château, built in the 12th century and restructured in the 15th, which has been photographed and filmed many times. The hostelry has all the character and charm of old inns. The bedrooms are progressively being restored to their original simplicity under the direction of a hard-working young Alsatian couple, André Hartmann and his wife. The rooms are located in two buildings: in the inn itself, offering a pleasant small suite in blue; and in a late 17th-century building a few steps away, where some rooms have a loft and others a roof window to provide light in addition to that of the small windows of the epoch. Guests can enjoy drinks on the terrace--and a beautiful view of the château turrets.

***How to get there*** *(Map 19): 30km northwest of Beaune via A 6 Pouilly-en-Auxois exit, then towards Vandenesse; after the cemetery at the left.*

# Hôtel Les Magnolias

8, rue Pierre-Joigneaux
21190 Meursault (Côte-d'Or)
Tel. (0)3.80.21.23.23 - Fax (0)3.80.21.29.10

**Rooms** 11 and 1 suite with telephone, bath or shower and WC. **Price** Double 400-620F; suite 750F. **Meals** Breakfast 48F, served 8:00-10:00. No restaurant. **Credit cards** Amex, Visa, Eurocard and MasterCard. **Pets** Dogs not allowed. **Facilities** Parking. **Nearby** Château of Commarin; basilica of Saint-Andoche in Saulieu; Hôtel Dieu and basilica of Notre-Dame in Beaune - 18-hole château de Chailly golf course. **Open** Mar 16 – Nov 30.

In this Burgundian village famed for its great Meursault, an amusing Englishman has converted an old winegrowing family's house into into a hotel of character and charm. Surrounded by a lush garden of old roses, sweet william, honeysuckle, and magnolias, the outbuilding offers four bedrooms, including a suite with a small private terrace on the ground floor. The other rooms are located in the house, each decorated with a special touch, antique furniture, and floral wallpaper, and all redolent of fragrant pots-pourris. Most of the baths are of average size, with a small tub, but they are relaxing and attractively fitted out in grey tones and white marble. You can enjoy breakfast outside in the sun (hoping that the vineyard tractors are not too busily at work.) Good restaurants nearby include *Le Chevreuil* and *Le Bouchon* in Meursault; *Lameloise* in Chagny; and the splendid restaurants of Beaune are only six kilometers away.

***How to get there*** *(Map 19): 6km south of Beaune via A 6, Beaune-sud exit or Chalon-nord.*

## Le Manassès

21220 Curtil-Vergy (Côte-d'Or)
Tel. (0)3.80.61.43.81 - Fax (0)3.80.61.42.79
M. Chaley

**Rooms** 7 (5 with air-conditioning) with telephone, bath, WC, TV and minibar. **Price** Single and double 400F **Meals** Breakfast 50F, served 7:45-10:00. No restaurant. **Credit cards** Visa, Eurocard and MasterCard, Diners and Amex. **Pets** Small dogs allowed. **Facilities** Parking. **Nearby** Abbey of Saint-Vivant in Curtil-Vergy, abbey of Cîteaux, château du Clos-Vougeot, Côte de Nuits – 18-hole Dijon-Bourgogne golf course. **Open** Mar – Nov 31.

To reach this small, quiet hotel you go under a little porch and then across an inner courtyard. M. Chaley is a wine grower and, as a jovial host, he well upholds the profession's reputation. References to wine abound: in the barn which houses an interesting wine museum, in the big room where breakfast is served and in the corridors and bedrooms – each picture is a reminder. From the cellars close by comes the faint aroma of casks in which the wine is kept. You will be served breakfast of coffee and croissant or a Burgundian buffet with Morvan ham, Burgundian parsleyed ham, sausage with *marc* brandy, and a small surprise for wine lovers. The communal rooms are brightened with beautiful antique furniture and a The comfortable bedrooms are more modern, with pretty color combinations and marble-lined bathrooms. The view over the wild green valley is superb. Good restaurants include *La Ruellée* in Curtil-Vergy; *L'Auberge du Coteau* in Villars-Fontaine; *La Ferme de Rolle* in Ternant; *La Sommelerie* in Gevrey-Chambertin; and *Chez Robert Losset* in Flagey-Echezeaux.

***How to get there*** *(Map 19): 24km northwest of Beaune. A31, Nuits-Saint-Georges exit, D25 and D35.*

## Hostellerie du Val-Suzon

R.N. 71 - 21121 Val-Suzon (Côte-d'Or)
Tel. (0)3.80.35.60.15 - Fax (0)3.80.35.61.36
M. and Mme Perreau

**Category** ★★★ **Rooms** 17 with telephone with bath and WC, TV, safe and minibar. **Price** Single 300-350F, double 450-520F, suite 650-980F. **Meals** Breakfast 60F, served 7:30-9:30; half board 485-520F, full board 685-720F (per pers., 3 days min.). **Restaurant** Closed Sunday noon and Monday Oct - Apr. Service 12:00-14:00, 19:30-21:45; menus 130-420F, also à la carte. Specialties: Œufs coque homard et foie gras, millefeuille d'escargots au beurre de persil. **Credit cards** All major. **Pets** Dogs allowed (+50F). **Facilities** Parking. **Nearby** Dijon, Carthusian monastery in Champmol, Côte de Nuits – 18-hole Dijon-Bourgogne golf course. **Open** Dec 7 - Nov 11 (closed Sunday evening and Monday Oct – Apr).

The Hostellerie is composed of two houses separated by a ravishing, vast garden laid out on a slight rise. The restaurant is located in the main house; a fireplace, a few prettily set tables and thick draperies add to the enjoyment of Yves Perreau's delicious, creative cuisine. The other house resembles a chalet and overlooks the garden. The bedrooms are located here. All are comfortable, bright and decorated in a somewhat strict modern style, with a traditional note added by 19th-century style armchairs or antique tables. The staff is warm and welcoming.

***How to get there*** *(Map 19): 15km northwest of Dijon via N71 towards Troyes.*

## Manoir de Sornat

Allée de Sornat
71140 Bourbon-Lancy (Saône-et-Loire)
Tel. (0)3.85.89.17.39 - Fax (0)3.85.89.29.47 - M. Raymond

**Category** ★★★ **Rooms** 13 with telephone, bath or shower, WC, TV and minibar. **Prices** Single and double 350-700F. **Meals** Breakfast 60F, served 7:30-11:00; half board 450-700F, full board 550-850F (per pers., 3 days min.). **Restaurant** Closed Monday lunchtime. Service 12:00-14:00, 19:30-21:30; menus 160-400F, also à la carte. Specialties: Galette d'escargots de Bourgogne, filet de bœuf. **Credit cards** All major. **Pets** Dogs allowed (+30F). **Facilities** Parking. **Nearby** Château de Saint-Aubin-sur-Loire, church in Ternant, abbey at Paray-le-Monial. **Open** All year but closed 3 weeks between mid Jan and mid Feb. (closed Sunday evening in low season).

This house was built in the 19th-century at the whim of an affluent Lyonnais who was fond of horse racing at Deauville. He chose a pure Anglo-Norman style of architecture which, though common in Deauville, is unusual here. Adjoining the Manoir are the remains of a racecourse where up to World War II the Bourbon Lancy stakes race was run. Many bedrooms are spacious; all are comfortably appointed and tastefully decorated. On the park side, some rooms have a terrace where you can enjoy a copious breakfast overlooking large trees often inhabited by scampering squirrels. The gastronomic reputation of the Manoir de Sornat needs no introduction (Michelin gives it a star) and many gourmets make a special trip here for Gérard Raymond's cuisine. You will be served in a large dining room, which is pleasant enough but it could do with a touch more heat. This small reservation aside, the Manoir, whose owners are courteous and competent, is one of the loveliest hotels in the center of France.

***How to get there*** *(Map 18): 30km northeast of Moulins via N79 towards Chevagnes.*

## Château de la Fredière

La Fredière 71110 Céron (Saône-et-Loire)
Tel. (0)3.85.25.19.67 - Fax (0)3.85.25.35.01
Mme Charlier

**Rooms** 10 and 1 suite with telephone, bath or shower, WC and TV. **Price** Single and double 290F, 480-620F; suite 750F. **Meals** Breakfast 55F; half board and full board 610-1070F, 820-1280F (per 2 pers.) **Restaurant** Service 12:00-14:00, 19:30-21:30 (closed Nov 16 – Mar 15 and Wednesday in low season); menu, also à la carte. Specialties: Terrine de queues de bœuf, charolais, charlotte aux fraises **Credit cards** Visa, Eurocard and MasterCard. **Pets** Dogs allowed on request (+50F). **Facilities** Swimming pool, 18-hole golf course and parking. **Nearby** Château of Lapalisse, Romanesques churches (Brionnais). **Open** All year except in Jan.

This small château looks out over a large park surrounded by an 18-hole golf course. Most of the bedrooms and the suite are spacious and bright and all are quiet and comfortably appointed. The rooms on the *second étage* have been recently renovated and decorated with bright fabrics, while the period furniture in those on the *premier étage* lends them the charm of the past The large salon and fireplace offer a relaxing place to read. Breakfast is served in the bright dining room with a blond parquet floor, or on the terrace in good weather. We had a lovely impression of relaxation and tranquillity in this beautiful hotel and its country setting. Just a few steps away from the château, you will find the pretty dining room, which overlooks a lake and the garden. The Frédière is a beautiful place to stay for a weekend in the country, and Madame Charlier and her family will greet you like a personal friend.

***How to get there*** *(Map 25): 40km north of Roanne to Marcigny, towards Le Donjon, Lapalisse and follow signs for the golf course.*

# Hostellerie du Château de Bellecroix

71150 Chagny (Saône-et-Loire)
Tel. (0)3.85.87.13.86 - Fax (0)3.85.91.28.62
Gautier-Crinquant Family

ategory ★★★ **Rooms** 21 with telephone, bath or shower, WC, TV and minibar. **Price** Single and ouble 580-1000F. **Meals** Breakfast 68F, served 7:30-10:00; half board 590F, full board 690-950F (per ers., 3 days min.). **Restaurant** Service 12:00-13:30, 19:30-21:00; menus 260-350F, also à la carte. pecialties: Escargots en cocotte lutée, filet de charollain et foie gras chaud. **Credit cards** All major. **ets** Dogs allowed (+50F). **Facilities** Swimming pool, parking. **Nearby** Hôtel-Dieu in Beaune, Côte de eaune between Serrigny and Chagny, château du Clos-Vougeot, Nolay, Rochepot – 18-hole Beaune-evernois golf course. **Open** Feb 15 – Dec 18 (closed Wednesday except Jun to Aug).

Built in the 12th-century and modified in the 18th, the Hostellerie, which is just out of the town, was once the *commanderie* of the Knights of Malta. At the entrance, a large, beautifully decorated, panelled room serves as recep-ion hall and dining room. It is decorated with lovely flowered draperies, com-ortable Louis XV-style chairs, elegantly laid tables, and reproductions of Old Master paintings on the walls. Next to it, in a turret, there is a small, intimate ounge. The comfortable bedrooms occupy two buildings, with some over-ooking the five-acre park with a swimming pool, terraces, and shady lawns. The rooms in the first building are tastefully furnished, often in 18th-century tyle (some are very small). The rooms in the first building are small but well lesigned; many are done in a handsome 18th-century style. Those in the other uilding, which is magnificent, with old walls and mullioned windows, are ast, superbly Haute Epoque in decor, but of course more expensive. Some edrooms are on the ground floor and open onto the garden. The Bellecroix is a pleasant hotel which constantly strives to improve—and succeeds.

*How to get there (Map 19): 15km south of Beaune via N74, then N6.*

## Hôtel de Bourgogne

Place de l'Abbaye
71250 Cluny (Saône-et-Loire)
Tel. (0)3.85.59.00.58 - Fax (0)3.85.59.03.73 - Mme Gosse

**Category** ★★★ **Rooms** 15 with telephone, bath or shower, WC, TV and tel. **Price** Single and double (apart.) 450-1000F, suite 890-920F. **Meals** Breakfast 60F, served 7:30-9:30; "Soirée étape gourmande" 990-1550F (2pers.). **Restaurant** Service 12:00-14:00, 19:30-21:00; menus 85F (lunchtime)–220-350F, also à la carte. Specialties: Foie gras frais de canard, volaille de Bresse à la vapeur de truffes. **Credit cards** All major. **Pets** Dogs allowed (+60F). **Facilities** Garage (+45F). **Nearby** Abbey and Ochier museum in Cluny, caves in Azé, arboretum in Pézanin, château de Chaumont – 18-hole Château de la Salle golf course in Lugny. **Open** Mar 5 – Nov 26 (closed Tuesday evening).

This hotel was built on part of the site of the ancient Cluny Abbey. However the number of rooms and the arrangement of the rooms around a small inner garden ensure peace and quiet. There is a pleasantly proportioned living room, where several styles are nicely combined; a large dining room, and gourmet cooking that lives up to its excellent reputation. The comfortable bedrooms have the old-fashioned charm of provincial hotels, including an inviting bar where breakfasts are served. Everything, including the welcome, contributes to the pleasure of your stay. The 19th-century poet Alphonse de Lamartine enjoyed the hotel, as did the many famous people who have signed the Guest Book for the past thirty years.

***How to get there*** *(Map 19): 24km northwest of Mâcon via N79 and D980.*

## La Montagne de Brancion

Brancion
71700 Tournus (Saône-et-Loire)
Tel. (0)3.85.51.12.40 - Fax (0)3.85.51.18.64 - M. and Mme Million

**ategory** ★★★ **Rooms** 20 with telephone, bath or shower (hairdryer), WC, TV, minibar, and safe. **rice** Single 460F (3 rooms) 650F, double 650-760F. **Meals** Breakfast 75F, served 8:00-9:30 or 10:00 room and garden. **Restaurant** Service 12:00-13:30, 19:30-21:00; menus 180F (lunch except week-nd), 290-330F, also à la carte. Specialties: regional. **Credit cards** All major. **Pets** Dogs allowed -50F). **Facilities** heated swimming pool, parking. **Nearby** Church of Saint-Philibert in Tournus, hurch in Chapaize, Blanot, Cluny, Taizé, château de Cormatin – 9- and 18-hole Château-la-Salle olf course. **Open** Mar 14 – Nov 16.

Located in very well-preserved countryside, this recently built hotel is perched on a hilltop and enjoys a sweeping view over the vineyards and he pretty village of Martilly-les-Brancion. The interior is modern. The bed-ooms are regularly redecorated and are pleasant and simple with coordinated abrics. They are exposed to the morning sun over the countryside and four ave a small balcony. The newer rooms with warmer colors are especially heerful, and the bathrooms have modern conveniences. While the dining oom is somewhat too modern, the service there is professional and pleasant, eaturing gourmet cuisine made with local farm products. You will also enjoy he swimming pool and the overall peaceful setting. The staff is hospitable and iendly and the countryside beautiful.

*How to get there (Map 19): 13km west of Tournus ; A 6 exit Tournus; via D14 ir. Briancion. After Martailly-lès-Brancion, follow signs and turn on the left.*

## La Fontaine aux Muses

89116 La Celle-Saint-Cyr (Yonne)
Tel. (0)3.86.73.40.22 - Fax (0)3.86.73.48.66
Pointeau-Langevin Family

**Category** ★★ **Rooms** 17 with telephone, bath or shower, minibar and WC (4 with TV). **Price** Single 345F, double 405F, suite 525-630F. **Meals** Breakfast 38F, served 8:00-10:00; half board 375-525F (per pers., 3 days min.). **Restaurant** Service 12:30-13:45, 20:00-21:15; menu 185F, also à la carte. Specialty: Ragoût de homard au foie gras, brasillade de pigeonneaux. **Credit cards** Visa, Eurocard and MasterCard. **Pets** Dogs allowed. **Facilities** Swimming pool, golf (50F), tennis (35F), parking. **Nearby** Joigny, Othe forest, St-Cydroine, church of St-Florentin, Auxerre. **Open** All year, by reservation in Jul and Aug. Closed Monday 11:00 to Tuesday 17:00.

The charm of certain hotels is largely due to their owners and that is certainly the case with the Fontaine aux Muses, which was created by a family of artists, whence the name. Today son Vincent is the dynamic spirit of the place. Obviously in love with this tiny hamlet, he decided to indulge his passion for the country and to share it with his clients. He loves wine and has his own vineyard; he loves to hunt, with the exception of Toto the wild boar who is a great favorite of city children. Vincent also loves music and often invites his musician friends to enliven weekend dinners with ballads and bossa-novas during the meal, finishing with a veritable professional jazz session. Comfortable armchairs await you beside the fire in the lounge-bar, and the bedrooms all have a beautiful view of the countryside. Several more comfortable rooms are located in a small house at the entrance to the golf course. We are delighted that this traditional auberge spirit is being maintained, even if the lessons given in hotel schools are sometimes forgotten.

***How to get there*** *(Map 18): 36km northwest of Auxerre via N6 to Joigny, D943 for 7km, then D194. By A6, Joigny (North)), Auxerre-nord (south) exit.*

## Château de Prunoy

Prunoy
89120 Charny (Yonne)
Tel. (0)3.86.63.66.91 - Fax (0)3.86.63.77.79 - Mme Roumilhac

**ooms** 11 and 8 suites with telephone, bath and WC (9 with TV) - 3 with wheelchair access. **Price** ouble 700F, suite 850-1200F. **Meals** Breakfast 50F, served 8:00-10:30. **Restaurant** Service 12:00 nd 20:00; menus 190-220F, also à la carte. Family cooking. **Credit cards** Amex, Visa, Eurocard and lasterCard. **Pets** Dogs allowed. **Facilities** Swimming pool, tennis, parking. **Nearby** Saint-Fargeau, outissaint animal park, château de Ratilly, cathedral of Saint-Etienne d'Auxerre – 18-hole de Ron-emay golf course in Chassy. **Open** May 1 – Jan 1.

Surrounded by 250 acres of parks, the Château de Prunoy was built in the purest 17th-century architectural style. Inside, the beautiful reception ooms on the ground floor, with stunning 18th-century sculptured woodwork, eflect the rare nature of this setting, which has been entirely designed and dec-rated by Madame Roumilhac. (During dinner, she goes from table to table to nake sure that guests are enjoying their meal.) In one wing, the dining room, ecorated in a cheerful country style, gives onto a terrace dominated by the reat trees in the park. The cuisine is healthful and good, although perhaps omewhat expensive compared to other meals we have tasted in the region. ut the outstanding feature of Prunoy is the bedrooms, many of which are tandouts for the quality and originality of their décor, their spaciousness, and heir modern amenities. The view is magnificent, from the bedrooms over-ooking the main courtyard as well as from those on the park, whose immense erspective seems to penetrate right into the forest. This beautiful château still eems to have much of the atmosphere of a private residence.

***ow to get there*** *(Map 18): 4 km northwest of Auxerre via A6, exit Joigny, rom Lyon N6 to Joigny), then D943 towards Montargis and D16 to Prunoy owards Charny).*

# Le Castel

Place de l'église
89660 Mailly-le-Château (Yonne)
Tel. (0)3.86.81.43.06 - Fax (0)3.86.81.49.26 - M. and Mme Breerette

**Category** ★★ **Rooms** 12 with telephone, of which 8 with bath, 3 with shower and 8 with WC **Price** Single 160F, double 230-340F. Apart. 400F. **Meals** Breakfast 37F, served 8:00-9:30. **Restauran** Service 12:15-13:30, 19:15-20:30; menus 75-170F, also à la carte. Specialties: Escargots au noisettes, pavé de charolais, coq au vin traditionnel, filet de perche aux baies de groseille, gratin d framboises. **Credit cards** Visa, Eurocard and MasterCard. **Pets** Dogs allowed (+25F). **Nearby** Basil ica of Sainte-Madeleine in Vézelay, Saussois rocks, cathedral of Saint-Etienne in Auxerre, Arc caves – 18-hole Roncemay golf course in Chassy. **Open** Mar 16 – Nov 14 (closed Wednesday).

A pretty garden with a lime-shaded terrace awaits you in front of this lat 19th-century house. The arrangement of the ground floor means that th lounge lies between the two dining rooms, the whole forming a single area Around the fireplace are Empire tables and armchairs, and although the furni ture in the dining rooms is in a different style, the ensemble is tasteful an effective. Several bedrooms have been renovated and until the others follov suit, we recommend rooms 6, 9 and especially number 10, which is very hand some with its blue Jouy fabric and corner lounge. Despite several new carpets the others are still too lackluster for our taste. Located in a historically pre served site in front of the church of this tiny, typical village, Le Castel is a quie hotel with a very good restaurant, and a bar on the terrace. The owners an friendly and informal.

***How to get there*** *(Map 18): 30km south of Auxerre via A6 exit Auxerre-suc then N6 dir. Avallon until D 100 on the right via Bazarnes, Mailly-la-ville e Mailly le-Château.*

## Auberge du Château

3, rue du Pont
89580 Val-de-Mercy (Yonne)
Tel. (0)3.86.41.60.00 - Fax (0)3.86.41.73.28 -L. and J. Delfontaine

**Rooms** 4 and 1 suite with telephone, bath or shower, WC and TV. **Price** Double 350-400F, suite 550-650F. **Meals** Breakfast 50F. **Restaurant** Service 12:00-14:00, 19:30-22:00 (closed Sunday evening and Monday except reservation); menus 170-350F, also à la carte. Specialties: Dos de bar grillé aux senteurs forestières riz basmati, chausson saint-jacques au beurre d'escargots, moscovite à la vanille, crème anglaise au café. **Credit cards** Visa, Eurocard and MasterCard. **Pets** Dogs allowed. **Nearby** Cathedral Saint-Etienne and abbey of Saint-Germain in Auxerre; Cure valley; Ouanne valley. **Open** Feb 28 – Jan 15.

This lovely inn recently opened in the quiet Burgundian village of Val-de-Mercy. It is made up of several exposed-stone buildings which are connected by a flowery courtyard, extending into a pleasant garden. The bedrooms are upstairs and are very tastefully decorated with parquet floors (in all but one), white walls which show off the old-pink of the drapes and bedcovers, and some antique furniture. In good weather, the room with an immense terrace is especially in demand. The restaurant is located in two small lounges and the dining tables are set with rare elegance; only the lighting is somewhat cold. Jacques Delfontaine mans the kitchen stoves and the result is quite delicious, for simple dishes as well as more sophisticated cuisine. Breakfasts are served either in a lovely corner bar, the garden, or beneath the beautiful roof beams of a room which serves as an art gallery and tea room. This is a charming inn offering reasonable prices and friendly service.

***How to get there*** *(Map 18): 18km south of Auxerre via A6, Auxerre Sud exit; then N6 towards Avallon, D85 towards Coulanges-la-Vineuse, D165 to Val-de-Mercy.*

# La Lucarne aux Chouettes

14, Quai Bretoche
89500 Villeneuve-sur-Yonne (Yonne)
Tel. (0)3.86.87.18.26 - Fax (0)3.86.87.22.63 - Mme Leslie Caron

**Rooms** 4 with telephone, bath and WC. **Price** Double 490F, suite 720F, loft and duplex 830F. **Meals** Breakfast 85F, served 8:30-10:30. **Restaurant** Closed Sunday evening and Monday in winter. Service 12:00-14:00, 19:00-22:00; menu 98F (weekday lunch) - 178F, also à la carte. Specialties: Terrine de chévre aux artichauts et son bouquet de salade à l'huile de noix, petite marmite de ris d'agneau et pleurottes, pavé de boeuf foie gras et jus au porto, souflé glacé au pruneaux et à l'armagnac. **Credit cards** Amex, Visa, Eurocard and MasterCard. **Pets** Dogs allowed. **Facilities** Parking. **Nearby** Cathedral and Synod Palace, the municipal greenhouses in Sens, Joigny: church of Saint-Florentin, cathedral Saint-Etienne d'Auxerre, Avarollais museum. **Open** All year (closed 3 weeks in Feb.).

Originally four village houses, the Lucarne aux Chouettes has recently been converted into a very charming auberge by Leslie Caron herself. On the ground floor, there is a bar-veranda and a superb dining room whose beams and half-timbering create the essential part of the decor. The cuisine is delicious, inventive, light and refined. (Marc Daniel used to be the chef at Paris's famous restaurant *Lasserre*). The service is attentive and in summer meals are served on the lovely terrace overlooking the quay. The bedrooms are upstairs and all have a beautiful view over the river. Priority has been given to spaciousness, modern amenities and charm in the bedrooms, where there are antique-style beds, pretty fabrics, family furniture and paintings. The welcome is very hospitable and friendly, making the Lucarne aux Chouettes a delightful place to stay.

***How to get there*** *(Map 10): 15km south of Sens. Via A6 exit Courtenay/ Sens, then D15 towards Piffonds and Villeneuve-sur-Yonne.*

## Château Hôtel de Brélidy

Brélidy - 22140 Bégard (Côtes-d'Armor)
Tel. (0)2.96.95.69.38 - Fax (0)2.96.95.18.03
Mme and M. Yoncourt-Pemezec

**Category** ★★★ **Rooms** 14 with telephone, bath and WC (4 with TV). **Price** Single 380-450F, double 420-790F, suite 1130-1215F. **Meals** Breakfast 50F, served 8:00-10:00; half board 400-605F. **Restaurant** Service 19:30-21:00; menus 145-185F. Specialties: Panaché de poissons, aiguillettes de canard aux pommes caramélisées. **Credit cards** All major. **Pets** Dogs allowed in room (+50F). **Facilities** Fishing, Mountain bikes, jacuzi, parking. **Nearby** Saint-Tugdual cathedral in Tréguier, basilica of Notre-Dame-de-Bon-Secours in Guingamp, château de Tonquedec, Kergrist, Rosambo – 18-hole Ajoncs d'or golf course in Saint-Quai-Portrieux. **Open** Easter – Nov 1.

From this old Breton château buried in the countryside you can see woods, wild hedgerows and deep lanes criss-crossing the hills. The granite walls rise out of banks of hydrangeas. The bedrooms are as comfortable as those of a good hotel. A set menu is served in one of two beautiful dining rooms, featuring cuisine which, like the welcome and the service, is friendly and family-style. After dinner you can retire to the lounge or take advantage of the billiard room. Both are vast and, though a little bare, welcoming. The bedrooms are named after flowers and the suite has a canopied bed and beautiful views; but for less money you might prefer the *Jasmine* or *Iris* rooms. This is a place to treasure in the most unspoiled Breton countryside.

***How to get there*** *(Map 5): north of Guingamp; on N12 after Guingamp, Lannion-Bégard exit, 300m after the first trafic circle, take D712 towards Tréguier, then 11km on left Brélidy.*

# Hôtel d'Avaugour

1, place du Champ-Clos
22100 Dinan (Côtes-d'Armor)
Tel. (0)2.96.39.07.49 - Fax (0)2.96.85.43.04 - Mme Quinton

**Category** ★★★ **Rooms** 27 with telephone, bath, WC and TV. **Price** Single 350-480F, double 400-650F. **Meals** Breakfast (Buffet) 48F, served 7:00-10:00. No restaurant. **Credit cards** All major. **Pets** Dogs allowed. **Nearby** Léhon, Pleslin, Pleslin, Pléven, château de la Hunaudaie, St Malo – 18-hole Dinard golf course in Saint-Briac-sur-Mer. **Open** All year.

The beautiful grey stone façade of the Avaugour overlooks the ramparts in the middle of the town. Inside, you will find the comfortable, intimate atmosphere of a family home. All the bedrooms are charming and some look out onto a beautiful garden. They are all comfortable but we prefer those which have been recently redecorated, which are more attractive, brighter and have pretty fabrics. The hotel is very pleasant throughout and it is lovely to stroll in the garden, which is laid out on the old cannon emplacement on the ramparts, and to enjoy the beautiful view out over the château of Duchess Anne. Last but not least, Mme Quinton is a very warm hostess. At the back of the garden, in the constable's tower, there is the restaurant *La Poudrière*. In the center of town, try *La Caravelle, Les Grands Fossés,* or *Chez la Mère Pourcel.*

***How to get there** (Map 6): 29km south of Saint-Malo (in the center of the town).*

## Manoir du Cleuziou

22540 Louargat (Côtes-d'Armor)
Tel. (0)2.96.43.14.90 - Fax (0)2.96.43.52.59
M. and Mme Costan

**Category** ★★ **Rooms** 28 with telephone, bath (1 with shower) and WC. **Price** Single and double 320F, 380-480F. **Meals** Breakfast 40F, served 8:00-10:00; half board from 335F (per pers.). **Restaurant** Closed Wednesday and Saturday lunchtime. Service 12:00-13:30, 19:00-21:30; menus 90-225F, also à la carte. **Credit cards** Amex, Visa, Eurocard and MasterCard. **Pets** Dogs allowed. **Facilities** Swimming pool, Tennis (30F), lounge, billard, lake, mountain bikes, parking. **Nearby** Basilica of Notre-Dame-de-Bon-Secours in Guingamp, Menez-Bré – 18-hole Saint-Samson golf course in Pleumeur-Bodou. **Open** Mar 1 – Jan 31.

The oldest part of the manor dates back to the 15th century. It is a beautiful building, the interior a match for its elegant façade. There are magnificent carved stone fireplaces, lovely doors and tapestries. The small bedrooms have less character but they are quite comfortable and offer families good value for money: Many of them have bunk beds or a mezzanine. The cuisine is now under the direction of a new chef, Joseph Traon; guests will surely enjoy it, along with the guidance of the new *maître sommelier,* Nöel Constan. They can also enjoy the bar which has been attractively installed in the old wine cellars. We should point out the presence of a small deluxe camping site a little way away which belongs to the manor and has the use of its leisure facilities.

***How to get there*** *(Map 5): 14km west of Guingamp via N12; in the village follow signs.*

## Le Repaire de Kerroc'h

29, quai Morand
22500 Paimpol (Côtes-d'Armor)
Tel. (0)2.96.20.50.13 - Fax (0)2.96.22.07.46 - M. Broc

**Category** ★★★ **Rooms** 13 with telephone, bath, WC, TV and minibar. **Price** Single and double 290-580F, suite 580-990F. **Meals** Breakfast 50F, served 8:00-12:00; half board 370-515F (per pers.). **Restaurant** Service 12:15-14:00, 19:15-22:00; "Le Bistro" menus 98F, also à la carte 150F. "Le Restaurant" menu 125F (lunch except Sunday and national holidays), 185-325F. Specialties: Tronçon de turbot au lard et aux pommes de terre, chartreuse de rouget au foie gras, soufflé au citron et à l'estragon. **Credit cards** Visa, Eurocard and MasterCard. **Pets** Dogs allowed. **Facilities** Ocean fishing (150F per pers.). **Nearby** Abbey of Beauport, Guilben Point, l'Arcouest Point, Lanieff, Kermaria-an-Iskuit chapel, Lanloup, Plouézec, Bilfot Point; Bréhat. **Open** All year.

Bréhat and Plougescant are only a few kilometers from the small town of Paimpol. On the quayside stands this very charming hotel, built in 1793 in typical St. Malo style. The pretty bedrooms are named after islands off the Brittany coast and are well furnished in old-fashioned style. The hotel has been enlarged by the acquisition of another part of this former pirate's house. There the bedrooms are larger and decorated with wallpapers and chintzes in bright, cheerful colors. The windows are double , which together with the thick walls of the old house ensures a peaceful night's sleep. Kerroc'h is also a gourmet's hotel with the arrival of the prestigious chef Louis Le Roy. Note also a simpler restaurant, *Le Bistro*. The Repaire is a pleasant hotel in town, which evokes the sea and Brittany.

***How to get there*** *(Map 5): 33km east of Lannion via D786 to Paimpol.*

## Le Manoir du Sphinx

67, chemin de la Messe
22700 Perros-Guirec (Côtes-d'Armor)
Tel. (0)2.96.23.25.42 - Fax (0)2.96.91.26.13 - M. and Mme Le Verge

**Category** ★★★ **Rooms** 20 with telephone, bath, safe, WC and TV - Elevator - Wheelchair access. **Price** Double 520-600F. **Meals** Breakfast 48F, served 7:30-9:30; half board 540-600F (per pers.). **Restaurant** Closed Monday lunchtime except holidays. Service 12:30-14:00, 19:30-21:30; menus 130-280F, also à la carte. **Credit cards** Amex, Visa, Eurocard and MasterCard. **Pets** Dogs not allowed. **Facilities** Direct access to the sea, parking. **Nearby** Footpath to Ploumanac'h, pink granite coast (chapel of Notre-Dame-de-la-Clarté), Sainte-Anne-de-Trégastel, boat excursions to the Sept Iles (Ile aux Moines) – 18-hole Saint-Samson golf course in Pleumeur-Bodou. **Open** Feb 21 – Jan 5.

Located on a small road along the pink granite coast, overlooking the Bay of Trestrignel, this hotel has an exceptional site with a garden going all the way down to the sea, a warmly decorated bar-lounge and adjoining dining room jutting out over the Channel. The owners are very hospitable. The bedrooms, decorated with English-style furniture, are comfortably appointed and all enjoy a marvelous view over the bay. Our favorites are those with a small lounge next to tall bay windows high above the sea. They are modern, of course, but elegant and cheerful. Monsieur Le Verge's fine cuisine adds a delicious finishing touch.

***How to get there*** *(Map 5): 11km of Lannion, along the coast.*

## Domaine du Val

22400 Planguenoual (Côtes-d'Armor)
Tel. (0)2.96.32.75.40 - Fax (0)2.96.32.71.50
M. Hervé

**Category** ★★★ **Rooms** 38 and 2 apartments (4-6 pers.) with telephone, bath, WC and TV. **Price** Single and double 450-1000F, apart. 760-1150F. **Meals** Breakfast 45-55F; half board 480-660F. **Restaurant** Service 12:30-14:00, 19:30-21:30; menus 140-350F, also à la carte. Specialties: Saumon fumé maison, homard breton à l'armoricaine, pigeonneau à la Valoise, foie gras poêlé aux pommes. **Credit cards** Visa, Eurocard and MasterCard. **Pets** Dogs allowed. **Facilities** Covered and heated swimming pool, sauna, squash, covered tennis, covered and heated balnéo, parking. **Nearby** Château de Bienassis, stud farm and church of Saint-Martin in Lamballe – 18-hole Val d'Armor golf course. **Open** All year.

Set in large grounds stretching down to the sea, the Château du Val is well camouflaged. The covered tennis courts, squash courts, gymnasium, covered swimming pool and whirlpool bath are virtually hidden from sight. Amidst the greenery only a pretty Renaissance style building is visible. The numerous bedrooms are similarly concealed, with some located in the chateau and others in one-story granite houses, each with a small terrace but often separated from its neighbor by only a low wall; the two apartments are thus in fairly close contact. The bedrooms in the chateau are classic and more elegant, with Plancöet tiles in the baths. On the ground floor the dining room is comfortable and decorated in Neo-Gothic style. Beside it is an attractive verandah where in summer you can dine under bunches of grapes hanging from the vine. In all, the pleasant welcome and the many leisure activities available make the Domaine du Val a good place to stay.

***How to get there*** *(Map 6): 27km northeast of Saint-Brieuc, exit autoroute a Le Val-André; 1km from Planguenoual.*

## Manoir du Vaumadeuc

22130 Pleven (Côtes-d'Armor)
Tel. (0)2.96.84.46.17 - Fax (0)2.96.84.40.16
M. O'Neill

**Category** ★★★★ **Rooms** 14 with telephone, bath or shower and WC. **Price** Single and double 490-1050F, suite 1050F. **Meals** Breakfast 50F, served 8:00-10:00; half board 450-720F (per pers., 3 days min.). **Restaurant** Diner by reservation 195F. **Credit cards** All major. **Pets** Dogs allowed (+50F). **Facilities** Fishing in the lake, parking. **Nearby** Château de la Hunaudaye, Dinan, Saint-Malo, Léhon – Pen Guen golf course (9-hole), 18-hole Briac-sur-Mer golf course. **Open** Easter – Jan 5.

Dating from the end of the 15th century, this manor house has survived unscathed. In the main building are the dining room, a huge lounge and delightful bedrooms, immaculately decorated and furnished. To one side there are two small houses in the same style, also comfortably arranged. In front of the manor, in the 16th-century dovecote, is the bar. Set in woods, but only 18km from the sea, this is an excellent place to stay. As the restaurant is open only in season, it is difficult for us to comment on the cuisine. Note however that in the low season you can order a seafood platter (the day before).

***How to get there*** *(Map 6): 37km east of Saint-Brieuc via N12 to Lamballe; in the village, D28 to Pléven via La Poterie and the Hunaudaye Forest.*

## Manoir de Rigourdaine

22490 Plouër-sur-Rance (Côtes-d'Armor)
Tel. (0)2.96.86.89.96 - Fax (0)2.96.86.92.46
M. Van Valenberg

**Category** ★ **Rooms** 19 with telephone, bath or shower, WC and TV - Wheelchair access. **Price** Double 290-390F, suite 420F (2 pers.) +70F extra pers. No restaurant. **Meals** Breakfast 38F, served 8:00-10:30. No restaurant. **Credit cards** Visa, Eurocard and MasterCard. **Pets** Dog allowed at the ground floor. **Facilities** Parking. **Nearby** Saint-Malo; Dinan; Léhon; Pays de Rance and Aguenon – 18-hole Saint-Cast golf course, 18-hole Ormes golf course. **Open** Apr 3 – Nov 15

The location of this old, extensively renovated farmhouse combines the charms of the country with a sweeping view over the blue waters of the Rance Valley 200 meters below. The bedrooms, all of which enjoy this panorama, are new, with English-style wallpaper and a pleasant decor. An old wardrobe here, a chest-of-drawers there and numerous paintings lend a personal touch. Those on the ground floor have a private terrace and are perfect for summer. For families, we recommend the suites, which are especially well-suited to groups. Breakfast is served in a large, rustic-style dining room or on the leafy terrace. Despite decoration which is still somewhat stiff (and which we are sure will improve with time), the general ambiance is very pleasant, as is M. Van Valenberg's youthful and attentive hospitality. Recommended restaurants: nearby, *Le French Connection*, which serves good local and Anglo-Saxon cooking; *La Grève*, a gastronomic restaurant in Saint Suliac; and in Dinard, *Le Canterbury*, offering good value for the price.

***How to get there*** *(Map 6): 15km northeast of Dinan. On N176 between Do[illegible] and Dinan, take the Plouër exit towards Langrolay. Signposted.*

## Ti Al-Lannec

Allée de Mezo-Guen
22560 Trébeurden (Côtes-d'Armor)
Tel. (0)2.96.15.01.01 - Fax (0)2.96.23.62.14 - M. and Mme Jouanny

**Category** ★★★ **Rooms** 29 with telephone, bath, WC and satellite TV. **Price** Single 410-460F, double 650-1100F. **Meals** Breakfast 70-90F, served 7:15-10:30; half board 605-820F, full board 760-975F. **Restaurant** Service 12:30-14:00, 19:30-21:30; menus 110-390F, also à la carte. Specialties: Noix de coquilles Saint-Jacques dorées sauce curry, caneton rôti aux baies de cassis, la tentation de l'écureuil. **Credit cards** All major. **Pets** Dogs allowed (+45F). **Facilities** Fitness-beauty center, parking. **Nearby** Le Castel, Bihit point, the Breton corniche from Trébeurden to Perros-Guirec – Saint-Samson golf course in Pleumeur-Bodou. **Open** Mid. Mar – mid. Nov.

Ti Al-Lannec is exceptionally well decorated and the hotel has a wonderful view of the sea (which is easily accessible by a small path) and terraced gardens. The very comfortable bedrooms are beautifully furnished and decorated, some with English fabrics and wallpaper; most have a sitting area, a charming verandah or terrace. The same care in decoration is evident in the lounges and in the dining room, which extends onto a large verandah overlooking the bay. The service here is perfect and the cuisine excellent. Also worthy of note is the fitness center.

***How to get there*** *(Map 5): 9km northwest of Lannion via D65.*

# Manoir de Crec'h-Goulifern

Beg Leguer-Servel
22300 Lannion (Côtes-d'Armor)
Tel. (0)2.96.47.26.17 - Fax (0)2.96.47.28.00 - Mme Droniou

**Rooms** 8 with telephone, bath or shower and WC. **Price** Single and double 300F, 380-450F. **Meals** Breakfast incl., served 8:00-10:00. No restaurant. **Credit cards** Not accepted. **Pets** Dogs allowed (+40F). **Facilities** Tennis, parking. **Nearby** Chapel of Kerfons, châteaux de Tonquédec, de Kergrist and de Rosambo, chapel of the Sept-Nains – Saint-Samson 18-hole golf course in Pleumeur-Bodou. **Open** All year.

The manor of Crec'h-Goulifen, originally an 18th-century farm, has been lovingly renovated. The main room on the ground floor is arranged with regional country furniture, and on the terrace you will be served a copious breakfast, which always includes a homemade pastry. The bedrooms, some of which are rather small and dark, are rustic in style and have thick carpets. All are comfortably appointed, but we prefer those with a bathroom and tub. Madame Droniou is very hospitable and has a great sense of humor: we immediately felt at home here. For meals, you might try the gastronomic restaurant *Ville Blanche*, five kilometers away in the town of Ville Blanche; or *La Tourelle* in Trébeurden.

***How to get there*** *(Map 5): 6km northwest of Lannion via D21, then towards Servel.*

# Kastell Dinec'h

22200 Tréguier (Côtes-d'Armor)
Tel. (0)2.96.92.49.39 - Fax (0)2.96.92.34.03
M. and Mme Pauwels

**Category** ★★★ **Rooms** 15 with telephone, bath and WC (9 with TV). **Price** Double 440-520F. **Meals** Breakfast 60F, served 8:00-10:00; half board 435-495F. **Restaurant** Service 19:30-21:30; menus 130-310F, also à la carte. Specialties: Bar en croûte de sel, cassolette de moules aux mousserons, crêpes de seigle au homard. **Credit cards** Visa, Eurocard and MasterCard. **Pets** Dogs allowed (+30F). **Facilities** Heated swimming pool (May 15 – Sept 15), parking. **Nearby** Cathedral of Saint-Tugdual and the house of Ernest Renan in Tréguier, Pleubian, chapel of Saint-Gonéry in Plougescrant, château de la Roche-Jagu – 9-hole Saint-Samson golf course in Pleumeur-Bodou. **Open** Mar 20 – Oct 11 and Oct 27 – Dec 31 (closed Tuesday evening and Wednesday in low season).

In the countryside 2km from Tréguier stands this 17th-century manor-farm. The main building – housing a beautiful dining room, a small comfortable lounge and some of the bedrooms – has two annexes containing the other bedrooms. Together they look onto a lovely garden where drinks and breakfast are served in summer. The bedrooms are small but tastefully decorated, some with antique furniture. The overall effect is simple and elegant. Mme de Pauwels is very hospitable, and her husband's cooking is delicious.

***How to get there*** *(Map 5): 16km east of Lannion via D786, 2km before Tréguier; follow the signs.*

# Le Minaret

Corniche de l'Estuaire
29950 Bénodet (Finistère)
Tel. (0)2.98.57.03.13 - Fax (0)2.98.66.23.72 - Mme Kervran

**Category** ★★ **Rooms** 20 with telephone, bath or shower, WC and TV - Elevator. **Price** Double 260-430F **Meals** Breakfast 45F, served 8:00-10:00; half board (obligatory in high season) 270-420F. **Restaurant** Closed Tuesday in Apr and May. Service 12:30-14:00, 19:30-22:45; menus 90-210F, also à la carte. Specialties: Le couscous de la mer, gigot de lotte au poivre vert, pavé de poisson grillé à la façon des îles, homard grillé à la crème d'estragon. **Credit cards** Visa, Eurocard and MasterCard **Pets** Dogs allowed except in the restaurant. **Facilities** Parking. **Nearby** Quimper, boat trip on the Odet from Quimper to Bénodet, Breton museum and villages, Notre-Dame de Quilinen chapel. **Open** Apr 3 – Sep 30.

An oasis in the midst of traditional Brittany: That is what Le Minaret looks like! It is a large white house designed in the 1920s by the architect Laprade; from the top of its real minaret, there's a breathtaking view out over the estuary of the River Odet, where sailboats pass regularly on their way in and out of the port. Even more than the exterior, the interior of the house reminds you of its Oriental character. The bright rooms, three of which have a small terrace, have a view of the sea or the charming small inlet bordering the town of Sainte-Marine. The great curiosity of the house is the Pacha bedroom, decorated in pure Moroccan style with wide windows opening onto the estuary. The mixture of the styles is attractive and lends unusual charm to the hotel. A pretty garden surrounds the house, and the terrace on the seafront also affords a superb view.

***How to get there*** *(Map 5): 16km south of Quimper.*

## Domaine de Kéréven

29950 Bénodet (Finistère)
Tel. (0)2.98.57.02.46 - Fax (0)2.98.66.22.61
Mme Berrou

**Category** ★★ **Rooms** 16 with telephone, bath or shower and WC. **Price** Double 280-390F. **Meals** Breakfast 39F, served 8:30-10:00; half board 310-345F. No restaurant. **Credit cards** Not accepted. **Pets** Dogs not allowed. **Facilities** Parking. **Nearby** Boat trip on the Odet from Quimper to Bénodet, chapels of Gouesnac'h and le Drennec, châteaux of Bodinio and Cheffontaines, Quimper, îles de Glénan – 18-hole l'Odet golf course in Bénodet. **Open** Easter – Oct 14 (by reservation Easter – May 20 and Sept 22 – Oct 15).

Surrounded by fields and farmland, the vast Domaine de Kéréven and its contiguous old farm buildings are eloquent examples of the unspoiled traditional charm you will still find in this part of the Breton countryside (and yet it is still near the sea and beaches). The family atmosphere and the hospitality of the domaine are very pleasant. The bedrooms here are small and very simply furnished. Outside, a sunny terrace where you can have breakfast in summer is a beautiful spot from which to enjoy the leafy surroundings. On another part of the property, there are several guest houses for longer stays but their predominantly beige and brown decor is no longer terribly tasteful. Madame Berrou's hospitality, however, is delightful. In the delicious village of Bénodet, you will find many pleasant restaurants; and we also recommend *La Ferme du Letty* two kilometers away, which rates one Michelin star; and *La Forge d'Antan* in Clohars-Fouesnant three kilometers away.

***How to get there*** *(Map 5): 16km south of Quimper via D34.*

## Hôtel Ty Mad

Plage Saint-Jean
29100 Douarnenez (Finistère)
Tel. (0)2.98.74.00.53 - Fax (0)2.98.74.15.16 - Mme Martin

**Category** ★★ **Rooms** 23 with telephone, bath or shower and WC (TV on request). **Price** Single and double 240-330F. **Meals** Breakfast 39F, served 8:00-11:00. **Restaurant** Service 12:30-14:00, 19:30-21:30; menus, also à la carte. Specialties: fish, seafood. **Credit cards** All major. **Pets** Dogs allowed (+25F). **Facilities** Parking. **Nearby** Douarnenez (port-musée), coast paths of Plomarc'h and Roches Blanches, Beuzec point, Cap Sizun, Quimper, Locronan, church of Confort, Pont-Croix and Sainte-Anne-la-Palud – 18-hole l'Odet golf course in Bénodet. **Open** Easter – Nov 1.

What famous guests for such a small hotel! Many renowned people in search of peace and quiet have sought refuge in this house, including Christopher Wood and Max Jacob, who lived here for more than two years. Located twenty minutes from the house of Françoise Gilot, Picasso's companion, Ty Mad has bedrooms which, from its three upper floors, look out over a countryside beautiful enough to be painted. Meals are served in a large, bright room with white tablecloths and a glossy parquet floor, which gives onto a terrace. Nearby, there is a small 17th-century chapel and a beach for the clients of the hotel. The Ty Mad is right out of a Jacques Tati film, – an excellent small hotel.

***How to get there*** *(Map 5): 18km northwest of Quimper via D765; at the Tréboul Yacht Harbor, the hotel is signposted.*

1998

# Grand Hôtel des Bains

15 bis, rue de l'Eglise
29241 Locquirec (Finistère)
Tel. (0)2.98.67.41.02 - Fax (0)2.98.67.44.60 - M. Van Lier

**Category** ★★★ **Rooms** 36 with telephone, bath, WC, TV - 2 for disabled persons - Elevator, **Price** Double with half board or full board 375-550F, 475-650F (per pers., 3 days min.). **Meals** Breakfast incl., served 8:00-11:00. **Restaurant** Service 12:30 14:00, 19:30-21:30; menu 140F, also à la carte. Specialties: Fish, shellfish. **Credit cards** All major. **Pets** Dogs allowed (+50F). **Facilities** Covered and heated swimming pool, whirlpool, sauna, massage and parking. **Nearby** Church and tower of La Pointe de Locquirec; Côte de Granit rose, Côte sauvage, Regional Park of Armorique - 18-hole golf course in Lannion. **Open** All year.

Built on one of the most beautiful spots of the Breton Coast, this imposing turn-of-the-century hotel has just had a face lift. Its park on the waterside, which served as a setting for the film *L'Hôtel de la Plage*, is as elegant as in its heyday except that today, it boasts a big plus: a beautiful covered swimming pool. Exposed to the morning sun, almost all the bedrooms overlook the sea (some have a large terrace) and afford guests the spectacle of the clear waters crashing against the rocks, or of the beach, immense at low tide. The rooms are of variable sizes, their extremely comfortable arrangement reminiscent of the 1900s beach-house style. The beautiful decor includes walls painted in delicate shades of grey or grey-beige; lovely pale-blue, old-rose or lime-green fabrics, white painted furniture....The excellent cuisine is served in a huge, elegant dining room which opens wide onto the garden. After long years of neglect, the superb rebirth of the Grand Hôtel des Bains should quickly meet with great success.

***How to get there*** *(Map 5): 79km east of Brest via E50 to Morlaix, then D796 to Plestin-des-Grèves and Locquirec.*

## Manoir de Moëllien

29550 Plonévez-Porzay (Finistère)
Tel. (0)2.98.92.50.40 - Fax (0)2.98.92.55.21
M. and Mme Garet

**Category** ★★ **Rooms** 10 with telephone, bath, WC and TV. **Price** Double 360-740F. **Meals** Breakfast 45-60F, served 8:00-9:30; half board and full board 370-570F, 460-650F (per pers.). **Restaurant**. Closed Tuesday, Wednesday, Thursday lunchtime except Jun 15 - Sep 15 and national holidays and Service 12:30-14:00, 19:30-21:00; menus 126-285F, also à la carte. Specialties: Fish and shellfish. **Credit cards** All major. **Pets** Dogs allowed (+30F). **Facilities** Parking. **Nearby** Saint-Corentin cathedral and art museum in Quimper, Locronan, Sainte-Anne-la-Palud, church in Ploéven – 18-hole l'Odet golf course in Bénodet. **Open** Mar 20 – Nov 1 and Dec 15 - Jan 2.

Invisible from the little road leading to it, this château is hidden by a pine forest. The dining room is on the ground floor of the main building, built of stone in the 17th century. It is very Haute Epoque in style and is pleasantly decorated with antique Breton furniture, fresh flowers, pale table linens, and pictures. Next door is a small, intimate bar. In the relaxing first-floor lounge a stone fireplace is pride of place. Opposite the noble facade of the manor is a building housing bedrooms at ground-floor level. They are comfortable, pretty, quiet and well-kept, with a beautiful view of the surrounding countryside. This is an excellent hotel just several minutes from the superb Finistère coastline.

***How to get there*** *(Map 5): 20km northwest of Quimper via D63 to Locronan at the first traffic circle, take Plonévez-Porzay exit.*

## Moulin de Rosmadec

Venelle de Rosmadec
29930 Pont-Aven (Finistère)
Tel. (0)2.98.06.00.22 - Fax (0)2.98.06.18.00 - Sébilleau Family

**Category** ★★ **Rooms** 4 with telephone, bath, WC and TV. **Price** Double 470F. **Meals** Breakfast 44F. **Restaurant** Service 12:30-14:00, 19:30-21:30; menu 165F, 300F, 400F with lobster, also à la carte. Specialties: Fish, homard grillé Rosmadec. **Credit cards** All major. **Pets** Dogs allowed (+25F). **Facilities** Parking. **Nearby** Gauguin Museum in Pont-Aven, Saint-Corentin cathedral and museum fine arts in Quimper, Tremal chapel, Nizon, Kérangosquor, the enclosed city of Concarneau, boat ride down Odet River – 18-hole Odet golf course in Bénodet. **Open** All year except 2 weeks in Nov, Feb and Wednesday (Sunday evening exept hight season).

You will find the Moulin de Rosmadec at the end of a small lane in the charming village of Pont Aven, immortalized by Paul Gauguin. Nestling between two branches of a pretty river, this 15th-century mill is an ideal place to stay in order to explore this marvelous Breton village with fifteen mills in all. The Moulin's four small bedrooms, which are located in the building adjacent to the hotel, are all comfortable, and from them you will hear the peaceful sound of water tumbling through the wheel, which is still in operation. The hotel's Michelin-starred restaurant, which is run by the owners' son, has been here for more than sixty years, its reputation deservedly extending beyond Brittany. The beautiful dining room has great character, spilling over into a ravishing veranda which is perfect for breakfast in the sun (unless you prefer the patio with its old moss-covered well.) This is an exceptionally friendly and lovely hotel where you just might be tempted to stay on a while.

***How to get there*** *(Map 5): 32km southeast of Quimper via D783, towards Concarneau.*

## Château de Kernuz

29120 Pont-L'Abbé (Finistère)
Tel. (0)2.98.87.01.59 - Fax (0)2.98.66.02.36
M. and Mme du Chatellier

**Category** ★★ **Rooms** 19 with telephone, bath and WC. **Price** Single 370F, double 370-450F and 600F. **Meals** Breakfast 40F, served 8:00-10:00; half board 370-450F, full board 510-600F (per pers.). **Restaurant** Service 12:00-13:30, 19:30-21:30; menu 150F (children 80F), also à la carte. **Credit cards** All major. **Pets** Dogs not allowed. **Facilities** Swimming pool, tennis and parking. **Nearby** Cathedral Saint-Corentin and fine arts museum in Quimper, Breton villages, Pont-Aven, Concarneau, boat ride down Odet River – 18-hole Odet golf course in Bénodet. **Open** Mar – Sept 30.

This is a family home and a beautiful château which became a hotel out of necessity but which has maintained itself proudly and nobly in its park, surrounded by a dovecote, a chapel and a watchtower. There is a very charming lounge whose beautiful dark woodwork is brightened by beige-grey sofas, and farther on a very handsome bar with two Renaissance pillars of painted sculpted wood. The bedrooms are also striking, although not so alluring as the rooms on the main floor. These are very charming, each with different colors and decor. Everything here is in good taste, and the welcome is friendly.

***How to get there*** *(Map 5): 20km south of Quimper; 1km south of Pont-L'Abbé, take D785, towards Plomeur, then the road for Penmarc'h.*

## La Demeure Océane

29830 Portsall (Finistère)
Tel. (0)2.98.48.77.42 - Fax (0)2.98.80.52.64
M. and Mme Richard

**Rooms** 6 and 2 duplex with shower and WC. **Price** Double 270-350F, duplex 450F. **Meals** Breakfast 35F, served 8:30-10:00. No restaurant but evening meal for residents only on request. Service from 20:00; menu 95-180F. **Credit cards** Visa, Eurocard and MasterCard. **Pets** Dogs allowed (+35F). **Facilities** Parking. **Nearby** "Côte des abers" from Conquet to Brignognan (120km); Guiligui Dolmen. **Open** Mar – Oct except national holidays.

This large, somewhat ordinary village house is surrounded by a garden and is very well-located a hundred meters from a small bridge. You will find family-style hospitality, half-way between that of a bed-and-breakfast and a hotel. Recently renovated, the bedrooms are simple, pleasant, impeccably maintained and very bright. On the *premier étage* upstairs, they are classic and decorated with period furniture. On the *second étage,* there is a younger ambiance and some duplex rooms which are ideal for families. A dinner menu is posted in the lobby every day (on reservation). The cuisine is traditional and of course regularly features fish and shellfish. A great wine lover, M. Richard has built up a very interesting cellar of estate-bottled wines and *grands crus*. This is an occasion to make interesting discoveries, although it is a shame that the decoration of the dining room is not of the same quality as the wines. Larger tables with more space between them and prettier tablecloths would fit the bill. Apart from that, the "Ocean Residence" is pleasant, the prices are reasonable and you shouldn't miss a walk to the highly scenic port.

***How to get there*** *(Map 4): 30km north of Brest towards Saint-Renan. In Ploudaimézeau, take the road to Portsall. Signposted.*

# Le Brittany

Boulevard Sainte-Barbe
29681 Roscoff (Finistère)
Tel. (0)2.98.69.70.78 - Fax (0)2.98. 61. 13. 29 - Mme Chapalain

**Category** ★★★ **Rooms** 25 with telephone,bath or shower,WC and TV - wheelchair access. **Price** Single 400-590F, double 540-820F, apart. 720-1100F. **Meals** Breakfast 58F, served 7:00-10:30; half board 420-680F. **Restaurant** "Le Yachtman". Service 12:15-14:00, 19:15-21:30 (closed Monday, except for residents); menus 130-320F, also à la carte. Specialties: Fish and shellfish. **Credit cards** Amex, Visa, Eurocard and MasterCard. **Pets** Dogs allowed except in restaurant. **Facilities** Covered and heated swimming pool, sauna, parking. **Nearby** Balz island (15 min. by boat), Saint-Pol-de-Léon, tour of châteaux of Léon (château of Kérouzéré, manoir of Tronjoly, château of Kerjéan). **Open** Apr – Oct.

In the delightful small town of Roscoff, the Brittany Hotel is the last rampart against the winds that beat in from the Atlantic. The bedrooms are decorated with beautiful old furniture and white fabric wall coverings; they are calm and pleasant, with well equipped bathrooms. You might want to have breakfast in your room because the breakfast room near the swimming pool can be noisy. The dining room, which is located in a 17th-century manor house, is the most charming and pleasant part of the hotel: Facing due west, it looks out over the sea and its large bay windows bathe the room with light. The hospitality is very British, and the cuisine is typical of the region, with lots of fresh fish; and there is a very good wine list. The bar has the discreet atmosphere of a great hotel. The last stop on the way to Ireland and England, this auberge combines the pleasures of a comfortable stopover with the tranquillity of an old Breton house.

***How to get there*** *(Map 5): 25km north of Morlaix.*

## Hotel de la Plage

Boulevard Sainte-Barbe
29550 Sainte-Anne-la-Palud (Finistère)
Tel. (0)2.98.92.50.12 - Fax (0)2.98.92.56.54 - M. and Mme Le Coz

**Category** ★★★★ **Rooms** 30 with telephone, bath or shower, WC, TV and minibar - Elevator. **Price** Single and double 800-1400F, suite 1000-1350F. **Meals** Breakfast 75F, served 8:00-10:00; half board 350F (per pers. 2 days min.). **Restaurant** Service 12:30-13:30, 19:30-21:00; menus 220-400F, also à la carte. Specialties: Fish and shellfish. **Credit cards** All major. **Pets** Dogs allowed except in restaurant. **Facilities** Swimming pool, tennis, sauna, parking. **Nearby** Saint-Corentin cathedral and art museum in Quimper; Locronan; church in Ploéven – 18-hole l'Odet golf course in Bénodet. **Open** End-Mar – beg-Nov.

The small road that leads to this hotel goes right up to the sandy beach facing a superb bay. The hotel thus well deserves its name, "The Beach". Luxurious without being stuffy, it takes maximum advantage of its exceptional location. The comfortable bedrooms are classically decorated overall, with beautiful period furniture, paintings, and carpets. Others have been recently appointed in an especially elegant seaside style; they overlook the garden or the ocean. You can enjoy a marvelous panorama from the salon-bar and the restaurant. Spacious bay windows give you the impression that the hotel is right on the beach: you definitely feel as if you're on vacation. The restaurant service is attentive and pleasant and the famous gastronomy of course gives a place of honor to seafood.

***How to get there*** *(Map 5): 17km northwest of Quimper.*

1998

## La Ferme de Porz-Kloz

Tredudon-Le-Moine 29690 Berrien (Finistère)
Tel. (0)2.98.99.61.65 - Fax (0)2.98.99.67.36
M. and Mme Berthou

**Rooms** 9 with telephone, bath or shower, WC, 3 with TV and minibar - 2 for disabled persons. **Price** Single and double 260-320F, 3 pers. 380F. **Meals** Breakfast 40F, served 9:00-11:00; half board 270-300F (per pers.). **Restaurant** Only for residents. Service 19:00-20:00; menu 100F. Specialties: Fricassée au cidre, épaule d'agneau aux poireaux, chevreau rôti. **Credit cards** Visa, Eurocard and MasterCard. **Pets** Dogs not allowed. **Facilities** Parking. **Nearby** Plougonven, Saint-Thegonnec, Guimiliau, Lampaul-Guimiliau - 18-hole Saint-Samson golf course in Plemeur-Bodou. **Open** Apr – Nov.

With sparse, broom-flecked vegetation, a checkerboard of stone-wall enclosures, their lakes mirroring the changing skies of Brittany, the Arrée Mountains seem to embody the very soul of the region's ancient Celtic legends. You will find the welcoming Ferme de Porz-Kloz in this strikingly beautiful site. Its group of buildings once belonged to the Relq Abbey, the oldest parts dating from the 13th century. Still a working farm, it supplies the hotel with meat and vegetables for the delectable evening meal, served in a pleasantly rustic room. Located in three houses, the bedrooms have a charming country air with their lovely fabrics, a few pieces of antique furniture, and cozy beds. Room 7 is very pretty; Numbers 8 and 9 are perfect for families, Room 4 has just been redecorated, and only Room 1 is a little less to our liking, but it has a new bathroom. The baths are pleasant despite a few elements that look rather amateurishly fitted. Picnic lunches can be prepared for hikers.

***How to get there*** *(Map 5): 20km south of Morlaix. In Morlaix, take D769 towards Huelgoat, then Abbaye de Releq, Tredudon; signs.*

## Les Grandes Roches

Route des Grandes-Roches
29910 Trégunc (Finistère)
Tel. (0)2.98.97.62.97 - Fax (0)2.98.50.29.19 - M. and Mme Henrich

**Category** ★★★ **Rooms** 22 with telephone, bath or shower and WC. **Price** Single and double 255F, 310F, 370F, 400F, suite 560F. **Meals** Breakfast 45F, served 8:00-9:30; half board 310-460F (per pers., 3 days min.). **Restaurant** Closed Nov 15 – Mar 15. Service 12:30-13:30 (only Saturday, Sunday and National Holidays), 19:15-21:30 (every night); menus 98-250F, also à la carte. Specialties: Seafood, saumon à la peau, poissons fumés à l'auberge, filets de canard, nougat glacé maison. **Credit cards** Visa, Eurocard and MasterCard. **Pets** Dogs not allowed. **Facilities** Parking. **Nearby** Pont-Aven, Nizon, Kérangosquer, Concarneau, Nevez – 18-hole l'Odet golf course in Bénodet and Queven. **Open** Jan 15 – Dec 15. Except Feb holidays.

This old farmhouse, which has been renovated and is very comfortable, stands in a large and well-shaded garden. There is a bar with a terrace, two dining rooms and a lounge with a television. The thatched cottages, an unusual and interesting feature, have been very well restored and turned into apartments furnished in traditional style. A *menhir* can be found in the grounds – evidence of prehistoric occupation – and in the countryside around there are more dolmens, menhirs and monoliths. A number of beaches are close by. The owner's husband is German, which makes this a popular spot for visitors from beyond the Rhine.

***How to get there*** *(Map 5): 28km southeast of Quimper via D783 to Trégunc via Concarneau; (the auberge is just outside the village).*

## Hôtel Richeux

35260 Cancale (Ille-et-Vilaine)
Tel. (0)2.99.89.25.25 - Fax (0)2.99.89.88.47
M. and Mme Roellinger

**Rooms** 11 and 2 suites with telephone, bath, WC, TV and minibar - Elevator - 1 for disabled persons. **Price** Double 750-1550F. **Meals** Breakfast 85F, served 8:00-10:00. **Restaurant** Closed Monday and Tuesday noon. Service 12:30-14:00, 19:30-21:30; menu shellfish from 110F, also à la carte. **Credit cards** All major. **Pets** Dogs allowed (+50F). **Facilities** Parking. **Nearby** Riding, Saint-Malo, Côte d'Emeraude, Mont Saint-Michel – 18-hole Dinard golf course in Saint-Briac. **Open** All year.

In this beautiful, spacious house, Olivier and Jeanne Roellinger have just opened a luxurious auberge on the seafront whose discreet charm, comfort and refinement will delight you. In each bedroom, with a view over the Bay of Mont Saint-Michel or the Breton countryside, you will find a different atmosphere, with beautiful old furniture and a bouquet of fresh flowers. All the bathrooms are bright and very pleasant. In the dining room, which opens onto the garden, you will savor the chef's fish specialties, along with fresh vegetables from the garden and fruit from the orchard. This is a very high-quality hotel which will surely satisfy the most demanding guests.

***How to get there*** *(Map 6): 12km east of Saint-Malo; in Cancale, turn towards of Mont Saint-Michel.*

## Hôtel Les Rimains

1, rue Duguesclin
35260 Cancale (Ille-et-Vilaine)
Tel. (0)2.99.89.64.76 - Fax (0)2.99.89.88.47 - M. and Mme Roellinger

**Rooms** 6 with telephone, bath, WC, TV and minibar. **Price** Double 650-850F. **Meals** Breakfast 85F, served 8:00-10:00. **Restaurant** "Olivier Roellinger" (600 m from hotel) Closed mid Dec - mid Mar. Tuesday and Wednesday in low season. Service 12:30-14:00, 19:30-21:00; menu, also à la carte. **Credit cards** All major. **Pets** Dogs allowed (+50F). **Facilities** Parking. **Nearby** Saint-Malo, Côte d'Emeraude, Mont Saint-Michel – 18-hole Dinard golf course in Saint-Briac. **Open** Mar 1 – Dec 31.

On the edge of a wild and unspoiled cliff overlooking the Bay of Mont Saint Michel, Les Rimains has six small, bright bedrooms which are tastefully decorated and have up-to-date amenities. From the ground floor and the upstairs rooms, the grandiose panoramic view dominates the hotel. There is no lounge here but the garden of this authentic Breton house is a lovely place in which to relax and enjoy the view of the beautiful countryside. You can also have a delicious breakfast in the garden. There is no restaurant but the owners will welcome you to their Relais Gourmand Olivier Roellinger and ply you with the tempting local specialties and the fresh products of the region. The welcome is charming and discreet.

***How to get there*** *(Map 6): 12km east of Saint-Malo; hotel signposted beginning at the church.*

# Hôtel Printania

5, avenue Georges V
35800 Dinard (Ille-et-Vilaine)
Tel. (0)2.99.46.13.07 - Fax (0)2.99.46.26.32 - Mme Caro

**Category** ★★ **Rooms** 59 (11 with telephone), bath or shower, WC, TV. **Price** Single and double 280-300F, 320-420F. **Meals** Breakfast 38F, served 7:00-10:30; half board 280-350F (per pers.). **Restaurant** Service 12:00-14:00, 19:00-21:30; menus 95-135F, also à la carte. Specialties: Fish, shellfish, soufflé Printania. **Credit cards** Amex, Visa, Eurocard and MasterCard. **Pets** Dogs allowed. **Nearby** Pointe du Moulinet, walk Clair de Lune, banks of the river Rance, Pointe du Décollé and Grottes des sirènes (cave of the sirens), pointe de la Garde-Guérin, castel and walled town of Saint-Malo, Cézembre island, Chausey island - 18-hole Dinard golf course in Saint-Briac. **Open** Mar 16 – Oct.

At the far end of Dinard going along the beautiful Promenade du Clair de Lune, the Hôtel Printania overlooks a small port and the embarcadero for boats to Saint Malo. A simple, very friendly, family atmosphere prevails here. We were immediately charmed by the rooms with Breton buffets, the region's typical enclosed beds, their fronts woodworked and copper-studded; old landscape paintings, Louis Philippe armchairs, chandeliers and objects, all forming a lovely Breton ensemble. The comfortable bedrooms--some delightfully old-fashioned, other more youthful--are all pleasant, especially those overlooking the sea. The others are somewhat small and the view of the street is less attractive. A special mention goes to Numbers 101, 102, 211 and 311, which have great character and charm. Breakfasts are served on a huge panoramic veranda which is used as a tea room and bar the rest of the day. The location and charm of the beautiful Printania compensate for the lack of a garden.

***How to get there*** *(Map ): 11km southeast of Saint Malo.*

## Château de la Motte Beaumanoir

35720 Pleugueneuc (Ille-et-Vilaine)
Tel. (0)2.99.69.46.01 - Fax (0)2.99.69.42.49
M. Bernard

**Category** ★★★ **Rooms** 6 and 2 suites with telephone, bath and WC, TV on request. **Price** Double 800-900F, suite 1000-1300F. **Meals** Breakfast incl., served 8:00-11:00. No restaurant. **Credit cards** Visa, Eurocard and MasterCard. **Pets** Dogs allowed. **Facilities** Heated swimming pool, tennis, boating, fishing, parking. **Nearby** Dinan, Léhon, Pleslin, château de la Hunaudaie – 18-hole Dinard golf course in Saint-Briac-sur-Mer. **Open** All year.

A landscape of forests, lakes and fields surrounds this tranquil 15th-century château. Most of the rooms are very spacious, furnished with antique or period furniture and have a superb view of the lake. These attractions and the beautiful swimming pool surrounded by a carefully tended garden, however, are not enough to make you forget the final bill. La Motte Beaumanoir thus is still a good place for a short visit, but we hesitate to recommend it for a longer stay.

***How to get there*** *(Map 6): 12km southeast of Dinan via N137; then north of Pleugeuneuc turn right at first crossroads from Dinan, towards Plesder.*

## Manoir de la Rance

Château de Jouvente
35730 Pleurtuit (Ille-et-Vilaine)
Tel. (0)2.99.88.53.76 - Fax (0)2.99.88.63.03 - Mme Jasselin

**Category** ★★★ **Rooms** 10 with telephone, bath, WC and TV. **Price** Single 400-450F, double 450-800F, suite 800-1200F (-20% Oct – Apr). **Meals** Breakfast 50F, served 7:00-11:00. No restaurant. **Credit cards** Visa, Eurocard and MasterCard. **Pets** Dogs allowed (+40F). **Facilities** Parking. **Nearby** Banks of the river Rance, castle and walled town of Saint-Malo, Cézembre island, Chausey island, côte d'Emeraude from Dinard to Le Val André – 27-hole Dinard golf course. **Open** Mar – Dec.

Facing the Rance and surrounded by trees and flowers, this 19th-century manor stands in large and lovely grounds. The big lounge is pleasantly furnished in a mixture of styles. The bar and the small living room, where tea is served, have a very homey atmosphere. Refreshments are served outside in the charming gardens and terraces, which have reclining chairs. Located on three floors, all the bedrooms are very comfortable and quiet, and all have a stunning view of the sea, the cliffs and the countryside. Mme Jasselin, the owner, is very friendly. For dining, you will find *Le Petit Robinson* in La Richardais (3km), and many restaurants in Saint-Malo.

***How to get there*** *(Map 6): 15km southeast of Saint-Malo via D168, then left after the Rance Dam on D114 to La Jouvente (via La Richardais). The manor is to the left on the way out of the village.*

## La Korrigane

39, rue Le Pomellec - Saint-Servan
35400 Saint-Malo (Ille-et-Vilaine)
Tel. (0)2.99.81.65.85 - Fax (0)2.99.82.23.89 - M. Marchon

**Category** ★★★ **Rooms** 10 with telephone, bath or shower, WC and TV. **Price** Single and double 400-800F. **Meals** Breakfast 55F, served 8:00-10:00. No restaurant. **Credit cards** All major. **Pets** Dogs allowed (+50F). **Facilities** Parking. **Nearby** Ramparts, castle and walled town of Saint-Malo, Chaussey islands, Cézembre island, Jersey, England, Saint-Samson cathedral in Dol-de-Bretagne. **Open** Feb 1 – Dec 31.

This is without doubt one of the most charming little hotels in France. It lies within a turn-of-the-century house which from the outside looks like an old holiday retreat turned into a family *pension.* The atmosphere is so comfortable that you feel quite at home, and the welcome is warm, discreet and courteous. Everything is restful, exquisitely tasteful and unpretentious. Each bedroom has its own color scheme, with perfectly harmonized colors and fabrics, and lovely furniture and paintings. Behind the house is a small garden where you can have breakfast or enjoy the sunshine. The large, book-lined living room is an invitation to relax as are the tea-room and bar. La Korrigane is better than a hotel: it is your own special *pied-à-terre* in Saint-Malo. *Le Saint Placide* is one of the best restaurants in this part of Saint Malo; note also the *Métairie de Beauregard, La Corderie* and *La Duchesse Anne* in the town.

***How to get there*** *(Map 6): In the center of town, on N137 take the Saint-Servan road.*

# L'Ascott Hôtel

35, rue du Chapitre - Saint-Servan
35400 Saint-Malo (Ille-et-Vilaine)
Tel. (0)2.99.81.89.93 - Fax (0)2.99.81.77.40 - M. and Mme Hardouin

**Category** ★★★ **Rooms** 10 with telephone, bath, WC and TV. **Price** Single 350-400F, double 400-600F. **Meals** Breakfast 50F, served all morning. No restaurant. **Credit cards** Visa, Eurocard and MasterCard. **Pets** Dogs allowed. **Facilities** Parking. **Nearby** Ramparts, castles and walled town of Saint-Malo, Chaussey and Cézembre islands, Jersey, England, Saint-Samson cathedral in Dol-de-Bretagne. **Open** All year.

In an elegantly renovated 19th-century mansion surrounded by a tiny garden, this small hotel is a charming new address in Saint Malo. The hospitality and atmosphere are very refined. No detail has been overlooked. The bedrooms, which are named after racetracks, are snug and quiet. The walls are covered with prettily colored fabrics, which are coordinated with the bedspreads and curtains. Some rooms have a small balcony where you can have breakfast. On the ground floor, there is the lounge, as appealing as the rest of the house, and which opens onto the small, lush garden where drinks are served. Near the hotel, you will find *Le Saint Placide,* one of the best restaurants in this part of Saint Malo; note also the *Métairie de Beauregard, La Corderie* and *La Duchesse Anne* in the town.

***How to get there*** *(Map 6): Via N137, take the towards Saint-Servan, then Boulevard Douville and the second street to the left (signposted).*

1998

## Hôtel Brocéliande

43, chaussée du Sillon
35400 Saint-Malo (Ille-et-Vilaine)
Tel. (0)2.99.20.62.62 - Fax (0)2.99.40.42.47 - M. and Mme Chombart

**Category** ★★★ **Rooms** 6 and 3 family-suites with telephone, bath, WC, TV and minibar. **Price** Single and double 300-550F, 4 pers. 500-750F. **Meals** Breakfast 50F, served until 10:30. No restaurant. Snack available. **Credit cards** All major. **Pets** Dogs allowed (+50F). **Facilities** Privat parking. **Nearby** castel and walled town of Saint-Malo, Cézembre island, Chausey island, Jersey, England; Saint-Samson cathedral in Dol-de-Bretagne. **Open** Dec 24 – Nov 17.

This freshly renovated hotel is on the Chaussée du Sillon running along the beach. Designed as a private home, it offers attractive bedrooms decorated with Laura Ashley wallpaper and fabrics, and pleasant baths. Small (except for the family suites) but bright and cheerful, most nevertheless give an impression of spaciousness with their view directly over the ocean; two rooms are on the courtyard. Upstairs on the *premier étage*, the rooms have balconies (the central room a huge terrace) offering a magnificent view of the ocean. Very hospitable, Anne-Marie and André-Guy serve good, varied breakfasts and it's not unusual for guests to be so taken with the friendly atmosphere that they have breakfast at the kitchen table. There is a lovely living/dining room with a huge bow-window against which the waves sometimes crash during an equinox. Just remember that a beach hotel holds great attraction for some, but it's not for those who prefer a desert island. For restaurants, we recommend: *Les Embrums, Le Chasse Marée* and *Le Borgne Fesse*.

***How to get there*** *(Map 6): On the Chaussée du Sillon*

## Hôtel Village La Désirade

56360 Belle-Ile-en-Mer (Morbihan)
Tel. (0)2.97.31.70.70 - Fax (0)2.97.31.89.63
Mme Mulon

**Category** ★★★ **Rooms** 24 with telephone, bath, WC and TV. **Price** Double 390-590F. **Meals** Breakfast 70F, served 8:00-11:00. No restaurant but evening meal Easter – Nov 10. **Credit cards** All major. **Pets** Dogs allowed (+30F). **Facilities** Heated swimming pool, parking. **Nearby** Vauban fortifications, les Aiguilles de Port-Coton – 18-hole Sauzon golf course in Belle-Ile-en-Mer. **Open** March 15 – Jan 6.

Facing the Côte Sauvage, 1500 meters from the sea in a hamlet typical of Belle-Ile-en-Mer where Monet painted "Les Aiguilles de Port-Coton," La Désirade is composed of five small houses built around a heated swimming pool. Each of these has four bedrooms, giving a family or group of friends a place entirely to themselves. The decor is simple but in good taste, with brightly colored chintzes creating a cheerful effect all year round. In the morning a breakfast buffet is set out by the swimming pool, allowing everybody to keep his own pace. This is a relaxed place where privacy is respected. There is a restaurant adjoining the hotel.

***How to get there*** *(Map 5): By car, take the Quiberon-Le Palais ferry; by air from Lorient by Finist-Air (20 min. flight); 7km southwest of Le Palais via D190 through Bangor; (the hotel is 2km from Bangor).*

## Petit Hôtel Les Pougnots

Rue du Chemin-Neuf - Le Sauzon
56360 Belle-Ile-en-Mer (Morbihan)
Tel. (0)2.97.31.61.03 - Mme Guillouët

**Rooms** 5 with telephone, shower and WC. **Price** Single 450F, double 550F. **Meals** Breakfast incl., served 8:30-12:00. No restaurant. **Credit cards** Not accepted. **Pets** Dogs not allowed. **Nearby** Vauban fortifications, cave of l'Apothicairerie, Port Donnan, les Aiguilles de Port-Coton – 18-hole Sauzon golf course in Belle-Ile-en-Mer. **Open** All year.

The Hôtel des Pougnots is in Sauzon, a little port surrounded by white-washed cottages with colored shutters. Built high up in the village with lots of stairways and now run by Madame Guilloët's son, the friendly hotel looks more like a chalet, offering only five bedrooms. Inside, the decoration is simple, even somewhat monastic in style, but tasteful and comfortable. Breakfast can be served on a small balcony overlooking the harbor. This delightful hotel, until recently known by word of mouth only, it is superbly located on wild, romantic Belle-Ile with its ocean-swept cliffs, gorse and heaths. In Le Sauzon, the friendly restaurant *Roz-Avel* serves delicious cuisine made with fresh ingredients; note also *Le Contre-Quai.*

***How to get there*** *(Map 5): By car, take the Quiberon-Le Palais ferry; by air from Lorient by Finist-Air (20 min. flight); 5km from Le Palais, at the port of Le Sauzon.*

## Domaine de Rochevilaine

Pointe de Pen Lan
56190 Billiers-Muzillac (Morbihan)
Tel. (0)2.97.41.61.61 - Fax (0)2.97.41.44.85 - M. Cotillard

**Category** ★★★★ **Rooms** 40 and 3 suites with telephone, bath, WC and TV - Wheelchair access. **Price** Double 495-1350F, suite 1400-2295F. **Meals** Breakfast 65F, served 7:15-10:30; half board 465-940F, (per pers., 3 days min.). **Restaurant** Service 12:15-13:30 and 19:15-21:30; menu 260-490F (with lobster), also à la carte. Specialties: Lobster and seafood. **Credit cards** All major. **Pets** Dogs allowed (+75F). **Facilities** Heated swimming pool, health center, parking. **Nearby** Rochefort-en-Terre, Morbihan gulf – 18-hole Kerver golf course. **Open** March 16 – end Jan.

Built on the majestic site of the Pointe de Pen Lan, a former lookout post, the Domaine de Rochevilaine looks like a small village. Its several buildings, dating from the 15th and 16th centuries, follow the geographic contours of the coast high above the Ocean, taking maximum advantage of the view over the Atlantic. This is a luxurious hotel whose bedrooms are well located and spacious, elegantly classic and comfortable. The most attractive are the ones with antique decoration; the more modern rooms are unremarkable. Note also the suites, each with a beautiful private terrace. The panoramic restaurant offers one of the finest cuisines of Brittany (try the lobster menu), but it is a shame that the tables are so close together. The Rochevilaine is a superb hotel for a very special weekend.

***How to get there*** *(Map 14): 20km southeast of Vannes via the express route (towards Nantes) to Muzillac; then to Billiers and Pointe de Pen Lan.*

## Les Chaumières de Kernavien

Route de Port-Louis
56700 Hennebont (Morbihan)
Tel. (0)2.97.76.29.04 - Fax (0)2.97.76.82.35 - M. de La Sablière

**Rooms** 11 with telephone, bath, minibar, WC and TV. **Price** Single and double 380-680F. **Meals** Breakfast 70F, served 7:30-10:30; half board 780F, full board 1030F (per pers., 3 days min.). **Restaurant** In the château of Locguénolé. **Credit cards** All major. **Pets** Dogs allowed (+50F). **Facilities** Swimming pool, sauna, tennis (4km), parking. **Nearby** La Cie des Indes museum in Port-Louis; haras nationaux d'Hennebont; Saint-Cado island; la Barre d'Etel; Groix island - 18-hole Val Queven golf course. **Open** Mar – Nov.

These two charming thatched-roof cottages are part of the Château of Locguénolé. They are located 3km away in the heart of the countryside but all enjoy the advantages of the hotel: a superb swimming-pool, sauna, tennis courts, and innumerable private paths along the seafront. You can alternate your stay between the luxurious atmosphere of the château and the calm countryside of your cottage. In the main *chaumière,* the bedrooms are vast and decorated in a style which is both rustic and elegant, with several pieces of smartly waxed antique furniture and exposed-stone walls. On the *premier étage,* the bedrooms have a mezzanine which families will enjoy, while on the ground floor, beautiful log fires crackle in imposing fireplaces (except for one, which we like somewhat less). In the other *chaumière,* the bedrooms are somewhat smaller, decorated in the same spirit and are a little less expensive. You can ask for your breakfast there, unless you prefer having it outdoors. Lunches and dinners are served in the château dining room, which has elegant yellow or blue tablecloths and an 18th-century Aubusson tapestry on one wall. You will enjoy famous cuisine and the especially friendly hospitality refutes the notion that luxury is always stuffy.

***How to get there** (Map 5): 5km of Hennebont, via Port-Louis.*

1998

## Auberge le Ratelier

4, chemin du Douet
56340 Carnac (Morbihan)
Tel. (0)2.97.52.05.04 - Fax (0)2.97.52.76.11 - M. Mobé

**Category** ★★ **Rooms** 9 with telephone, shower, WC and TV. **Price** Double 250-280F. **Meals** Breakfast 35F, served 8:00-10:00. **Restaurant** Service 12:00-14:00, 19:00-22:00; menus 95-225F. Specialties: Seasonal cuisine. **Credit cards** Visa, Eurocard and MasterCard. **Pets** Dogs allowed (+30F). **Nearby** Menhirs of Carnac and Erdeven, Etel, Plouhinec. **Open** Feb – Jan 15.

We are in the heart of the small town of Carnac, whose hustle and bustle invades the narrow streets surrounding the Auberge Le Ratelier. This is an old farmhouse, as you can see from the several rustic vestiges which remain in the interior. Decoration has added a more elegant note, particularly noticeable in the beautiful fabrics used in the living-room drapes and the bedroom wall-covers. The rooms are very small, comfortable, but they are quite simple and, with limited soundproofing, guests are obliged to be quiet so as not to disturb their neighbors. The cuisine deserves high praise for its quality and finesse, whether you order the least expensive menu or *à la carte*. This is a serious hotel, perhaps too much so: The staff could do with a few smiles.

***How to get there*** *(Map 5): 37km south of Lorient.*

# Logis Parc er Gréo

Mané-Guen-Le Gréo
56610 Arradon (Morbihan)
Tel. (0)2.97.44.73.03 - Fax (0)2.97.44.80.48 - M. and Mme Bermond

**Category** ★★★ **Rooms** 12 with telephone, bath or shower, WC and TV - Wheelchair access **Price** Single 266-448F, double 290-498F. **Meals** Breakfast 45F, served 8:00-11:00; half board 253-389F (per pers., 3 days min.). No restaurant but evening meal for residents only, by reservation in the morning; service from 20:00; menus 115F or seafood 220-320F. Specialties: Fish, seasonal cuisine. **Credit cards** All major. **Pets** Dogs allowed (+40F). **Facilities** Swimming pool, monutain bikes rentals. **Nearby** Morbihan Gulf, Ile de Gravinis, Ile aux Moines, Carnac – 18-hole Baden golf course. **Open** Feb 13 – Nov 14 and Nov 24 - Jan 3.

Even though the Logis Parc er Gréo has been built recently, this small hotel is indeed one of "character and charm," beginning with the welcome you receive. The decoration combines shapes and colors beautifully, with antique furniture here and there, a boat model, or a painting done by an artist friend. Finally, there is the beautiful island setting itself. From the terrace as well as the bedrooms, you have a lovely view of the swimming pool, the fields and trees and, just behind them, one of the small inlets that so charmingly dot the Morbihan Gulf. The bedrooms, which look due south, are a model of taste and comfort. On the ground floor, the living room is also a dining room where excellent breakfasts and dinners are served. When it's sunny, meals are served on the pretty flowery terrace. There is a small winter garden with luxuriant bougainvillia where you can enjoy a view of the countryside whether it rains or shines.

***How to get there*** *(Map 14): 10km southwest of Vannes via D101 to Le Moustoir, on left, then 6th turn on right.*

## Hôtel de la Marine

7, rue du Général-de-Gaulle
56590 Ile-de-Groix (Morbihan)
Tel. (0)2.97.86.80.05 - Fax (0)2.97.86.56.37 - Mme Hubert

**Category** ★★ **Rooms** 22 with telephone, bath or shower and WC. **Price** Single 200-237F, double 220-470F. **Meals** Breakfast 39F, served 8:00-10:00; half board 241-375F, full board 323-464F (per pers., 2 days min.). **Restaurant** Service 12:00-13:30, 19:30-21:30; menus 74-160F, also à la carte. Specialties: Feuilleté de Saint-Jacques, barbecue de poisson, marquise au chocolat. **Credit cards** Visa, Eurocard and MasterCard. **Pets** Dogs allowed (+22F). **Facilities** Parking. **Nearby** Museum in Groix, L'Enfer point, Saint-Nicolas seaport, Pen-Mer. **Open** Feb 1 – Dec 31.

The Hôtel de la Marine is located somewhat high up in the village, several hundred feet from the port. Lovingly decorated by Madame Hubert, a former stylist, it attracts a faithful, congenial clientele each summer. The hotel has just undergone beautiful renovation work, with a charming, boat-gangway decor in the communal rooms. The small lounge is delightfully furnished with antiques, and in the dining room, where you will enjoy good meals for very reasonable prices, the tables are set with attractive, colorful linens; on the fireplace and the shelves is a collection of pottery; in a corner, a shell-encrusted clock is the only reminder of the passage of time. The bedrooms are simple, painted white and brightened with colored curtains and bedspreads. Ask for those facing the sea (especially No. 1), but all are very pleasant and comfortable. Outside on the garden terrace, you can enjoy a drink in the shade of the oldest tree on the island.

***How to get there*** *(Map 5): Boat from Lorient (45 min., tel. 97.21.03.97).*

## Hôtel de la Jetée

1, quai Port Tudy
56590 Ile-de-Groix (Morbihan)
Tel. (0)2.97.86.80.82 - Fax (0)2.97.86.56.11 - Mme Tonnerre

**Category** ★★ **Rooms** 8 with telephone, bath or shower and WC. **Price** Single and double 200F, 250-380F. **Meals** Breakfast 35 F, served 8:00-10:30. No restaurant. In high season snack available on request. **Credit cards** Amex, Visa, Eurocard and MasterCard. **Pets** Dogs not allowed. **Nearby** Museum in Groix, L'Enfer point, Saint-Nicolas seaport, Pen-Men. **Open** Feb 16 – Jan 4.

A small hotel with one side on the port and the other beaten by the ocean spray, the Hôtel de la Jetée stands just at the beginning of the jetty, at the far side of the basin. The ground floor is divided between an attractive café with several pretty tables on the terrace (a meeting place for fishermen and sailors) and an Irish pub where you can enjoy oysters brought in by Monsieur and Madame Tonnerre's son, who has recently set up here as an oyster farmer. The bedrooms are absolutely irresistible. Totally renovated three years ago, they are decorated with handsome wallpaper trimmed with elegant friezes; smartly waxed antique furniture and English-style coordinated fabrics. They are perfectly beautiful, as are the cheerful, well-kept baths with modern amenities. You'll enjoy a picture-postcard view over the port or the sea, and a small terrace installed on a rock in the back which is reserved for hotel guests; looking out over the immense blue horizon and small creeks of fine sand not far away, one has the delicious feeling of utter peace and solitude.

***How to get there*** *(Map 5): Boat from Lorient (45 min.); tel. 02 97 21 03 97.*

## Le San Francisco

56780 Ile aux Moines (Morbihan)
Tel. (0)2.97.26.31.52 - Fax (0)2.97.26.35.59
M. Vérien

**Category** ★★ **Rooms** 8 with telephone, bath or shower, WC and TV. **Price** Double 370-535F. **Meals** Breakfast 45F, served 8:00-11:00; half board 315-390F (per pers.). **Restaurant** Service 12:00-14:00, 19:00-20:30; menu 110-240F, also à la carte. Specialties: Fish and shellfish, duo de sole lotte en brick sauce crustacés, gambas poêlées flambées sauce anisée. **Credit cards** Amex, Visa, Eurocard and MasterCard. **Pets** Dogs allowed (+30F). **Nearby** Morbihan Gulf – 18-hole La Bretesche golf course. **Open** Mar 25 – Nov 13.

The Franciscan sisters who used to come here to rest conveniently chose the most beautiful location on the island: facing the port, with the dramatic, jagged coast of the Gulf of Morbihan in the distance. Today a spot that tourists love, the small hotel nevertheless is beautifully quiet. The ambience is refined but not stiff, and the overall decoration is very pleasant. All the rooms are quiet, comfortable and brightened with elegant color schemes. Reserve in advance and ask for a room with a superb view over the sea. One has a small balcony facing the port. There is a pleasant reception area and a lovely dining room; but with the first rays of sunshine, the high points are the irresistible shady terraces where we loved to sit back and watch the sight of the small boats down below, constantly plying their way in and out of the gulf. Unfortunately, the cuisine is very mediocre. But Le San Francisco is a good island hotel where you'll always be pleasantly welcomed.

***How to get there*** *(Map 14): 14km south of Vannes; on highway E60, exit Vannes-Ouest; then follow signs for Ile aux Moines to boat landing. 5 min. crossing; in winter, 7:00 to 20:00; in summer, 7:00 to 22:00.*

## Moulin de Lesnehué

Lesnevé
56890 Saint-Avé (Morbihan)
Tel. (0)2.97.60.77.77 - Fax (0)2.97.60.78.39 - Mme Cheval

**Category** ★★ **Rooms** 12 with telephone, bath or shower and WC (5 with TV). **Price** Single and double 250-270F. **Meals** Breakfast 32F, served 8:00-10:00. No restaurant. **Credit cards** Amex, Visa, Eurocard, MasterCard. **Pets** Dogs allowed. **Facilities** Parking. **Nearby** Chapel of Notre-Dame-du-Loc in Saint-Avé, ramparts and Saint-Pierre cathedral in Vannes, Conleau peninsula, fortress of Largoët, château du Plessis-lossot – 18-hole Kcrver golf course in Saint-Gildas de Rhuys. **Open** Jan 15 – Dec 15.

This 15th-century stone mill has a lovely location in the middle of the countryside on the banks of a stream. The bedrooms are arranged in the two buildings which form the hotel. All of them are simple and modern, with contemporary furnishings, but charming and comfortable. Ferns, flowers, the sound of water and birdsong provide nature's backdrop to this lovely welcoming place.

***How to get there*** *(Map 14): 5km north of Vannes via D126; turn right on the way out of the village of Saint-Avé. Towards Monterblanc.*

1998

# Le Petit Hôtel des Hortensias

Place de la Mairie
56470 La Trinité-sur-Mer (Morbihan)
Tel. (0)2.97.30.10.30 - Fax (0)2.97.30.14.54 - P. le Gloahec - N. Gautier

**Rooms** 5 with telephone, bath, WC and satellite TV - 1 for disabled persons. **Price** Double 500-650F (low season), 750-850F (Apr – Oct). **Meals** Breakfast 55F, served 8:00-11:00. **Restaurant** "L'Arrosoir" by reservation (02.97.30.13.58). **Credit cards** Visa, Eurocard and MasterCard. **Pets** Dogs allowed (+40F). **Facilities** Parking. **Nearby** Morbihan Gulf, Baie de Quiberon (Belle Ile, Houat, Hoedic); 18-hole Saint Laurent and Baden golfs course. **Open** All year except Dec 1 – 21, Jan 8 – Feb 1.

In La Trinité-sur-Mer, we were quite familiar with the *L'Arrosoir* Restaurant, which two friendly young people have now converted into the charming Petit Hôtel des Hortensias. Both the restaurant and the hotel occupy an outstanding location on the port. Set somewhat back from the hustle and bustle of the quay, the hotel overlooks the entrance to the port. Regatta sailboats, old rigging, oyster-farm pontoons, fishing boats and ocean-racing trimarans provide a permanent spectacle, with yachts sailing in and out of the port in front of the hotel and the restaurant. The yachting crowd of La Trinité, the sailor's Mecca, love to meet there. In fact, it's not unusual to see crack skippers like Laurent Bourgnon, Loïc Peyron and Florence Arthaud at the Hortensias. The marine-inspired interior decoration, all in blue and white, is just what the sailor ordered.

***How to get there** (Map 5): 30km southwest of Vannes.*

# Château du Launay

Locuon 56160 Ploerdut (Morbihan)
Tel. (0)2.97.39.46.32 - Fax (0)2.97.39.46.31
Redolfi-Strizzot Family

**ooms** 10 with telephone, bath. **Price** Single and double 450-550F, 600-700F. **Meals** Breakfast (buf-et) 35F, served 8:30-10:30; half board 500F (per pers.). **Evening meals** Service 20:00; menus 125F. pecialties: Curry, brochet du lac. **Credit cards** Visa, Eurocard and MasterCard. **Pets** Dogs allowed. **acilities** Parking. Nearby Sainte-Noyale, Blavet Valley. **Open** Mar – Dec.

Surrounded by a 375-acre estate of forests, fields and a lake, this 18th-century chateau will delight those who enjoy quiet and privacy. You will be reeted by a young couple, Monsieur and Madame Redolfi-Strizzot, who are Nepalese and Danish, respectively. Their beautiful chateau has little in common with a traditional hotel. Deliberately stark, the tasteful decoration combines contemporary paintings and sculptures with a good amount of colonial urniture. In the same spirit, the bedrooms are spacious, with cream shades set off by colorful walls. They are furnished with armchairs in exotic wood or vrought iron; large, comfortable beds, beige throw-rugs, and small Oriental arpets; the baths are luxurious. For dinner, the hotel offers a single menu with ophisticated specialties, served at a communal table or at separate tables in a mall dining room. In low season, it's best to telephone for a reservation.

***low to get there** (Map 6): 30km from Pontivy*

# Hôtel de Kerlon

56680 Plouhinec (Morbihan)
Tel. 02 97.36.77.03 - Fax 02 97.85.81.14 - M. and Mme Coëffic
Web: http://www.oda.fr:aa/kerlon

**Category** ★★ **Rooms** 16 with telephone and WC, (15 with bath or shower and 15 with TV). **Price** Single and double 240-320F. **Meals** Breakfast 40F, served 8:00-10:00; half board 285-310F (per pers.) **Restaurant** Service 19:30-21:00; menus 82-160F, also à la carte. Specialties: Fish, seafood. **Credit cards** Visa, Eurocard and MasterCard. **Pets** Dogs not allowed. **Facilities** Parking. **Nearby** Quiberon, Morbihan Gulf, île de Groix, Port-Louis; 18-hole Queven golf course, 18-hole Ploemeur-Océan golf course in Saint-Jude. **Open** Mar 16 – Oct 31.

Standing in the heart of the countryside five kilometers from the sea and half-way between Lorient and Carnac, the Hôtel de Kerlon is beautifully kept and hospitably run by the owner, Madame Coëffic. It is a good, simple place where you can enjoy the quiet of the countryside while remaining near the beaches and famous resorts. The bedrooms and small baths are immaculate, the beds excellent, but you should ask for one of the renovated rooms as the decoration in the others is drab. The comfortable lounge-bar and especially the bright dining room are more attractive, the dining tables set with beautiful white linens and bouquets of fresh flowers. The cuisine is good and nutritious, based on fresh local products, with Breton fish and shellfish taking the gastronomic place of honor. You can enjoy a drink while you relax on the terrace facing the garden. Breakfasts are also excellent, differing each day of the week.

***How to get there*** *(Map 5): 30km southeast of Lorient. Leave N165 at Hennebont, "Carnac-Quiberon-Port-Louis" exit, then follow signs Carnac-Quiberon. D194, then D9.*

## Hostellerie Les Ajoncs d'Or

Kerbachique
56340 Plouharnel (Morbihan)
Tel. (0)2.97.52.32.02 - Fax (0)2.97.52.40.36 - Mme Le Maguer

**atcgory** ★★ **Rooms** 17 with telephone, bath or shower, WC and TV. **Price** Double 290-410F, suite 80F (4 pers.). **Meals** Breakfast 38F, served 8:00-10:00; half board 290-350F (per pers.). **Restaurant** ervice 19:00-21:30, menus 96 145F, also à la carte. Specialties: Regional cooking, seafood. **redit cards** Visa, Eurocard and MasterCard. **Pets** Small dogs allowed (+20F). **Facilities** Parking. **earby** Menhirs of Carnac and Erdeven, church in Plouhinec, Belle-Ile; 18-hole Saint-Laurent-loëmel golf course. **Open** Mar 15 – Nov 2.

Les Ajoncs d'Or is a pink granite Breton farmhouse made up of three adjoining buildings and situated outside the village. On the ground floor, a arge restaurant with a lovely fireplace happily combines beams, exposed tonework, flowered curtains and pictures. Next door is another very pleasant oom for breakfasts. Recently renovated, the bedrooms are often brightened vith lovely fabrics and beautiful carpets (some could almost be called suites, vith their small corner lounge.) All different, the rooms are comfortable and right. A special mention goes to those above the restaurant and on the ground loor in the adjacent building. You will enjoy good family-style cooking and a nost cheerful welcome from Madame Le Maguer, whose charming personal-y adds a big plus to this delightful place.

***ow to get there*** *(Map 5): 52km of Lorient via N165 to Auray, then D768 and )781 (between Carnac and Plouharnel).*

## Domaine de Bodeuc

Nivillac - 56130 La Roche-Bernard (Morbihan)
Tel. (0)2.99.90.89.63 - Fax (0)2.99.90.90.32
M. and Mme Grandpierre

**Category** ★★★ **Rooms** 8 with telephone, bath or shower, WC and TV - Elevator - Wheelchair access **Price** Double and simple 570F, 270F. **Meals** Breakfast 45F, served 8:00-12:30. **Restaurant** Closed Tuesday evening in Jul and Aug. Residents only, by reservation. Service 19:00-21:00; menu 170F **Credit cards** Amex, Visa, Eurocard and MasterCard. **Pets** Dogs allowed. **Facilities** Heated swimming pool, Parking. **Nearby** La Baule, tour of La Brière and the Guérande marshes, Morbihan Gulf; 18-hole La Bretesche golf course. **Open** All Year (except in Feb).

Nestling in the Breton countryside only twenty minutes from the beaches this charming hotel stands in a handsome 37-acre park. From the entrance, one feels that this is more like a house than a traditional hotel. Monsieur Grandpierre welcomes you on the doorstep as if you were an old friend of the family, his wife joining him in the friendly greeting. She has arranged the eight bedrooms of the hotel with great taste, adding a lovely touch to the comfortable amenities, the harmonious color schemes, the quality of the fabrics and the choice of antique furniture (a thoughtful finishing touch is the basket of fruit awaiting you in your room.) The bathrooms are equally attractive bright and well kept. On the ground floor, a comfortable lounge, classic and cheerful, is the venue at the apéritif or coffee hour. On reservation, Monsieu Grandpierre prepares dinners consisting of simple but savory dishes; he is also responsible for the homemade preserves served with the good breakfast.

***How to get there*** *(Map 14): 40km south of Vannes. A 4 way N 165, exit nea La Roche-bernard (exit Number 16), dir. Redon. Saint-Dolas, by D 34, during 5km then follow the signs.*

## Auberge du Moulin de Chaméron

18210 Bannegon (Cher)
Tel. (0)2.48.61.83.80 - Fax (0)2.48.61.84.92
M. Candore

**Category** ★★★ **Rooms** 13 with telephone, bath or shower, WC and TV. **Price** Single and double 350-515F, suite 680-705F. **Meals** Breakfast 51-85F, served 7:30-10:00. **Restaurant** Service 12:15-14:00, 19:30-21:00; menus 130-195F, ( children 58F) also à la carte. **Specialties:** Seasonal cooking. **Credit cards** Amex, Visa, Eurocard and MasterCard. **Pets** Dogs allowed (+30F). **Facilities** Swimming pool, parking. **Nearby** Basilica and château of Châteauneuf-sur-Cher, church of Saint-Amand-Montrond, abbey of Noirlac, châteaux of Meillant and Ainay-le-Vieil, Bourges – 18-hole Val-de-Cher golf course in Montluçon. **Open** Mar 1 – Nov 15. (closed Tuesday in low season).

This renovated 18th-century mill lies deep in the countryside. The old mill machinery has been kept intact in the middle of the building and a museum displays a collection of tools and objects used by millers in the past. The bedrooms, located in an annex, are attractive enough and vary in spaciousness; some have a small ground-floor terrace (where you can have breakfast). They still have their old flowery wallpaper and rustic furniture; all could do with refurbishing. In good weather, lunch and dinner are served in the garden near the millpond; otherwise, service takes place in a beautiful and intimate small room with fireplace in the old mill. The cuisine is excellent and the staff are very pleasant. The Auberge is particularly charming in good weather.

***How to get there*** *(Map 17): 42km southeast of Bourges via N76 towards Moulins, then D953 and D41.*

## La Solognote

18410 Brinon-sur-Sauldre (Cher)
Tel. (0)2.48.58.50.29 - Fax (0)2.48.58.56.00
M. and Mme Girard

**Category** ★★ **Rooms** 13 with telephone, bath or shower, WC and TV. **Price** Double 320-430F, suite (3-4 pers.) 550F. **Meals** Breakfast 60F; half board 840-940F (per 2 pers., 3 days min.). **Restaurant** Service 12:30-14:00, 19:30-20:30 (closed Tuesday lunchtime, Wednesday lunchtime except in July and Aug); menus 160-330F, also à la carte. Specialties: Gibier en saison. **Credit cards** Visa, Eurocard and MasterCard. **Pets** Dogs not allowed. **Facilities** Parking. **Nearby** Orléans Cathedral, La Source flower gardens in Olivet, châteaux on the Jacques-Coeur road, Aubigny-sur-Nère, the Berry from La Chapelle d'Angillon to Saint-Martin-d'Auxigny, Sancerre – 18-hole Sully golf course in Viglains. **Open** Mar 3 – May 11, May 19 – Sept 8, Sept 17 – Feb 12 (closed Tuesday and Wednesday in winter).

This pink brick inn, located in a small village in Sologne just fifteen minutes from the National Route 20, is famous for its excellent cuisine and beautiful rooms. The restaurant is warm, elegant, and very charming. The rooms are lovely, each one decorated in a different style, with one or two antique pieces, beautiful fabrics, and polished wooden floors. They are comfortable and very quiet, their bathrooms are well equipped, and many look out on a small flower garden. There are apartments available for families. Last but not least, a special mention should be made of Monsieur and Madame Girard's courteous management and commitment to quality.

***How to get there*** *(Map 17): 60km southeast of Orléans via N20 to Lamotte-Beuvron, then D923 towards Aubigny-sur-Nère.*

## Le Piet à Terre

21, rue du Château
18370 Châteaumeillant (Cher)
Tel. (0)2.48.61.41.74 - M. Finel and Mme Piet

**Category** ★★ **Rooms** 21 with telephone, bath or shower, WC and TV. **Price** Single and double 260-350F. **Meals** Breakfast 40-70F, served 8:00-10:30; half board 340-470F (per pers., 2-3 days min.). **Restaurant** Service 12:00-13:30, 19:30-21:00 (closed Sunday evening and Monday in low season); menus 98-270F, also à la carte. Specialties: œuf cocotte, foie gras de canard et jus de truffe, pigeon de ferme au foin, moelleux de chocolat mi-amer. **Credit cards** Visa, Eurocard and MasterCard. **Pets** Dogs allowed. **Nearby** Nohant-Vic (Festival of Nohant in June), La Châtre (museum of Geouge Sand), Abbey of Fontgombault - Dryades golf course in Pouligny-Notre-Dame. **Open** All year except in Feb. Closed Sunday evening and Monday in low season.

How we'd love to find more small village hotels like this one! Located in a quiet spot on a square, the Piet-è-Terre looks as prim as it is hospitable. With the talent of a skillful seamstress and great taste, Sylvie Piet has "dressed" each bedroom, skillfully concealing the small size of some. The comfortable beds of certain rooms have beautiful embroidered sheets, the bathrooms are impeccable, and all the rooms (except for two with small roof windows) enjoy a lovely view over the village. Served in two beautiful small dining rooms, the cuisine is the other strong point of the Piet-à-Terre. The specialties as well as the set-price meals, made with only the freshest products, are simply prepared so as to enhance the native tastes of ingredients, and yet the chef's original touches make for delicious gastronomic discoveries. The hotel has a promising future in this little-known but highly attractive region.

***How to get there*** *(Map 17): 25km southeast of Châteauroux.*

## Château de la Beuvrière

18100 Saint-Hilaire-de-Court (Cher)
Tel. (0)2.48.75.14.63 - Fax (0)2.48.75.47.62
M. and Mme de Brach

**Category** ★★ **Rooms** 15 with telephone, bath or shower and WC (4 with minibar). **Price** Single 300F, double 350-500F, duplex 460F, suite 600F. **Meals** Breakfast 40F, served 7:30-10:00. **Restaurant** Closed Sunday evening and Monday. Service 12:00-14:00, 19:30-21:00; menus 150-198F, gastronomic menu 250F, also à la carte. Specialties: Saumon fumé maison, foie gras frais maison, sandre braisé au beurre de truffes, ris de veau braisé à l'orange. **Credit cards** All major. **Pets** Dogs allowed. **Facilities** Swimming pool, tennis, parking. **Nearby** Saint-Etienne cathedral, hôtel Jacques-Coeur in Bourges, Aubigny-sur-Nère – 18-hole La Picardière golf course. **Open** Mar 16 – Dec 14 (closed Sunday evening).

The château has kept its 2,562-acre estate intact since the Middle Ages. Inherited by the present owners, it is a very charming hotel today. The family furniture is authentic and dates from the 15th to the 19th-century – the overall effect is one of excellent quality arranged with perfect taste. Lovely and very well-kept, the bedrooms overlook the grounds. Those on the *premier étage* are almost sumptuous, and if their bathrooms are a bit on the small side this allows room for the wood-panelled bed alcoves. The *deuxième étage* bedrooms have original beams and some have a mezzanine. You will dine sitting on Empire armchairs at a beautifully laid table. The food is as excellent as the decor, and the welcome is informal and cordial.

***How to get there*** *(Map 17): 39km northwest of Bourges via A71, Vierzon-Nord exit, then N20 towards Châteauroux.*

1998

## Le Grand Monarque

22, Place des Epars
28005 Chartres (Eure-et-Loir)
Tel. (0)2.37.21.00.72 - Fax (0)2.37.36.34.18 - M. Jallerat

**Category** ★★★ **Rooms** 49 and 5 apartments (2 with air-conditioning) with telephone, bath, WC, satellite TV and minibar - Elevator. **Price** Single and double 450-585F, 570-685F, apart. 985-1160F. **Meals** Breakfast (buffet) 55F, served 8:00-10:30. **Restaurant** Service 12:00-14:15, 19:30-22:00; menus 158-280F. **Credit cards** All major. **Pets** Dogs allowed. **Facilities** Parking and garage (41F). **Nearby** In Chartres: Notre-Dame cathedral, church of Saint-Pierre, maison Picassiette, Illiers, Combray (Proust Museum) - 18-hole maintenon golf course. **Open** All year.

This is the ideal spot for visiting famous Chartres Cathedral and the historic center of the town: Efficiently and professionally staffed, the Grand Monarque is a large hotel in a handsome building just at the beginning of Chartres' picturesque, small pedestrian streets. The sizeable lobby is discreetly quiet and decorated in classic good taste. The imposing dining room, where you will enjoy one of the best cuisines of the region, is lent distinction by well-spaced tables, comfortable armchairs, and a beautiful group of 18th- and 19th-century paintings. The large suites, very pleasant for families, as well as the rooms have comfortable amenities; the tasteful decoration--all the rooms are different--includes lovely fabrics, distinctive furniture, and interesting engravings. The rooms are bright and quiet, including the soundproofed rooms overlooking the square. The others are on an interior courtyard.

***How to get there*** *(Map 16): 90km from Paris via A 10 or A11, exit Chartres-Centre.*

## Hostellerie Saint-Jacques

Place du Marché-aux-Œufs
28220 Cloyes-sur-le-Loir (Eure-et-Loir)
Tel. (0)2.37.98.40.08 - Fax (0)2.37.98.32.63 - M. and Mme Thureau

**Category** ★★★ **Rooms** 22 with telephone, bath or shower, WC and TV. **Price** Single and double 360-590F. **Meals** Breakfast 55F, served 8:00-10:30; half board 470F, full board 610F (per pers.). **Restaurant** Service 12:00-14:00, 19:30-21:00; menus 98F. Specialties: Fricassée de poulet fermier à l'ail doux, poêlée de rascasse au romarin. **Credit cards** Visa, Eurocard and MasterCard. **Pets** Dogs allowed. **Facilities** Boats, table tennis, mountain bikes, parking. **Nearby** Chapel of Yrou at Châteaudun, Vendôme, valley of the Loir (Montoire-sur-le-Loir, Lavardin, Troo, manoir de la Possonnière) – 9-hole la Bosse golf course in Oucques. **Open** Mar 1 – Nov 20.

Located on the village square, l'Hostellerie Saint-Jacques is an old 16th-century coaching inn. Here you may go boating on the Loire, which crosses the shady 1 1/2-acre gardens. The bedrooms are comfortable and quite pretty, with printed cotton fabrics, period furniture (occasionally a beautiful antique wardrobe), and they are well-soundproofed, a detail so rare that it deserves mention. The tasteful and intimate dining room overlooks the garden. The Hostellerie is well known for its gastronomy and in good weather, when lunch is served on the flowery terrace, the pleasures of the table are enhanced by the charm of the site. Note also the *Petit Bistrot*, which serves excellent, reasonably priced meals.

***How to get there*** *(Map 16): 53km north of Blois via D957 to Vendôme, then N10 (going north) to Cloyes-sur-le-Loir.*

## Manoir de Boisvillers

11, rue du Moulin de Bord
36200 Argenton-sur-Creuse (Indre)
Tel. (0)2.54.24.13.88 - Fax (0)2.54.24.27.83 - M. and Mme Nowakowski

**Category** ★★ **Rooms** 14 with telephone, bath or shower, 13 with WC and TV. **Price** Single 200-280F, double 240-380F. **Meals** Breakfast 45F, served 7:30-10:00. No restaurant. **Credit cards** Amex, Visa, Eurocard and MasterCard. **Pets** Dogs allowed (+30F). **Facilities** Swimming pool, parking. **Nearby** Pont-Vieux and Saint-Benoît chapel in Argenton, château de Nohant-Vic, Georges Sand museum in La Châtre, abbey church of Fontgombault – 18-hole Dryades and Pouligny-Notre-Dame golf courses. **Open** Dec 31 - Dec 1.

This welcoming hotel in the center of town enjoys an excellent location with its large garden and the immediate proximity of the Creuse River. Taken over by Isabelle and Christophe Nowakowski, it has been rejuvenated with pleasant bedrooms, which are simply decorated in bright colors and located in the hotel and an outbuilding. (The bathrooms need some improvement but are still recommendable.) All the rooms are different, with some overlooking the river; others the garden or the courtyard. Room 5 is very beautiful with its wood paneling and vast proportions. On the ground floor, there is a small modern lounge and breakfast room. In good weather, you can enjoy a pleasant garden with swimming-pool and, if you prefer not to go out to dinner, you can have a meal platter brought to you here. The young owners are hospitable and very pleasant. A good restaurant is *Le Moulin des Eaux Vives* in Tendu.

***How to get there*** *(Map 16): 30km southwest of Châteauroux, Argenton-sur-Creuse exit.*

## Domaine de l'Etape

Route de Bélâbre
36300 Le Blanc (Indre)
Tel. (0)2.54.37.18.02 - Fax (0)2.54.37.75.59 - Mme Seiller

**Rooms** 35 with telephone, bath or shower and WC (20 with TV). **Price** Single 210-420F, double 22 460F. **Meals** Breakfast 48F, served 7:00-11:00. **Restaurant** Residents only. Service 12:30-13:30, 19:3 21:30; menus 130-300F, also à la carte. Specialties: Salade de homard à l'émulsion d'olives et corail, escalope de sandre au vinaigre de cidre, coq en barbouille. **Credit cards** Visa, Eurocard a MasterCard. **Pets** Dogs allowed. **Facilities** Riding, fishing, hunting, boating, parking. **Nearby** Museu of local history in Le Blanc, châteaux of Azay-le-Ferron, le Guillaume and le Bouchet, Benedictine abb of Fontgombault. **Open** All year.

We were immediately taken with the truly kind welcome we received at th Domaine de l'Etape, a 19th-century mansion standing on a 500-ac estate. The hotel is charming throughout, from the salon with its Louis-Philip furnishings (a lovely spot for reading or watching television) to the panelled di ing room which is often brightened by an open fire. The bedrooms in the ma building are the most delightful (notably Numbers 1, 6, and 15), even if som carpets and wallpapers are beginning to look a little frayed. However, Rooms 4, and 14 have just been renovated. In the modern house, the rooms are less pe sonalized though elegant and comfortable, and those on the ground level ope directly onto the garden. Finally, there are other bedrooms in a small farmhous they are much too simple for our taste but would certainly be cool in summe Adding to these fine qualities are the gourment meals served on the terrace summer; an immense lake for fishing and horses which you can ride through th beautiful countryside.

***How to get there*** *(Map 16): 59km west of Châteauroux via N20 and N151 to L Blanc, then D10 towards Bélâbre.*

## Château de Bouesse

36200 Bouesse (Indre)
Tel. (0)2.54.25.12.20 - Fax (0)2.54. 25.12.30 - M. and Mme Courtot-Atterton
E-mail: http://www.wsi.ca/prod/chateau

**Rooms** 11 with telephone, bath or shower and WC. **Price** Single and double 350-480F, suite 720F. **Meals** Breakfast 55F, served 8:00-10:00; half board 395-475F (per pers., 3 days min.). **Restaurant** Service 12:00-14:00, 19:30-21:30; menus 160F, also à la carte. Specialties: Fish, foie gras, rognons de veau à l'ancienne, saint jacques. **Credit cards** Amex, Visa, Eurocard and MasterCard. **Pets** Dogs not allowed. **Facilities** Parking. **Nearby** Pont-Vieux and Saint-Benoît chapel in Argenton, château de Nohant-Vic, Georges Sand museum in La Châtre, abbey church of Fontgombault – 18-hole Dryades and Pouligny-Notre-Dame golf courses. **Open** Feb 1 – Dec 31 (closed Monday in low season).

Monsieur and Mme Courtot-Atterton love history and have focused their enthusiasm on the restoration of this superb 13th- and 15th-century château. The bedrooms' names refer to the château's history: *Jeanne d'Arc, Raoul VI de Gaucourt,* etc. The bedrooms are all very large, and often have stone fireplaces bearing coats of arms. Some rooms have been redecorated recently in the style of the Middle Ages, using furniture specially made for the château. Others are in the romantic style of the English 19th century. The hotel is totally comfortable and peaceful. The view cannot have changed for centuries. We particularly admired the dining room, which has pale blue and grey panelling and a 17th-century painting on the ceiling. In summer an excellent breakfast is served outside on the terrace.

***How to get there*** *(Map 17): 33km south of Châteauroux, on D927 between Argenton-sur-Creuse and La Châtre.*

## Château de la Vallée Bleue

Saint-Chartier
36400 La Châtre (Indre)
Tel. (0)2.54.31.01.91 - Fax (0)2.54.31.04.48 - M. Gasquet

**Category** ★★★ **Rooms** 15 with telephone, bath or shower, WC, TV and minibar. **Price** Single 200-390F, double 350-590F. **Meals** Breakfast 47F; half board 425-520F, full board 500-600F (per pers., 3 days min.). **Restaurant** Service 12:00-13:30, 19:30-21:00; menus 100F lunch (except weekend) 140-195-250F, also à la carte. Specialties: Home-smoked produce, filet de sandre de Loire au beurre rouge, andouillette de canard, salade de lentilles vertes du berry et vinaigre de mures, croustillant aux poires épicées, crème vanillée. **Credit cards** Visa, Eurocard and MasterCard. **Pets** Dogs allowed (+50F). **Facilities** Swimming pool, health center, parking. **Nearby** Georges Sand museum in La Châtre, château des Maître-Sonneurs in Saint-Chartier, château de Nohant-Vic – 18-hole Dryades golf course. **Open** Mar – Jan (closed Sunday evening and Monday Oct – Mar).

The ghosts of George Sand and Chopin float over this small château, which was built by that couple's doctor in a 10-acre park. The entrance hall is lovely, and M. and Mme Gasquet are very welcoming. Everywhere there are pictures and memorabilia to do with the writer and the musician. The bedrooms are identified by small glass plaques with reproduction signatures of George Sand's artist friends. The bedrooms are comfortable, stylishly furnished and pleasantly decorated with Laura Ashley papers and fabrics, and they have lovely views over the park and the countryside. The English-style lounge is warm and a glass of old cognac or liqueur beside the fire is a pleasure. The list of *eaux-de-vie* is amazing. Off the lounge there are two very attractive dining rooms opening onto the park with its two-hundred-year-old oak tree. The cuisine is delicious.

***How to get there*** *(Map 17): 27km southeast of Châteauroux via D943 to Saint-Chartier. The hotel is outside the village on the Verneuil road.*

1998

## Le Fleuray

Route Dame Marie - Les Bois
37530 Cangey-Amboise (Indre-et-Loire)
Tel. (0)2.47.56.09.25 - Fax (0)2.47.56.93.97 - M. and Mme Newington

**Category** ★★ **Rooms** 11 with telephone, bath or shower and WC - 3 with wheelchair access - 1 for disabled persons. **Price** Double 315-475F. **Meals** Breakfast 58F, served 8:00-10:00; half board 325-360F (per pers.). **Restaurant** Service 19:30-21:30; menus 125-235F, also à la carte. **Credit cards** Visa, Eurocard and MasterCard. **Pets** Dogs allowed. **Facilities** Parking and garage. **Nearby** Château d'Amboise and Manoir du Clos-Lucé, Pagode de Chanteloup, forest of Amboise. **Open** Mar 1 – Dec 20 and Jan 5 – Feb 23 and Oct 24 - Nov 4 (national holidays).

After travels that took them around the world, Hazel and Peter chose the Tours region, and this beautiful farmhouse, as a place to settle down. With great initiative and taste, they've converted Le Fleuray into a delightful small hotel, ideally situated on the lush plain overlooking the Loire and the Vouvray vineyards. Each bedroom is decorated in a youthful, fresh style, with pink-striped wallpaper, floral fabrics, and white tulle bed canopies. Two rooms in the outbuildings have a private terrace on the garden; the others are in the main building (some have no bath.) With all the enthusiasm of the self-taught cook, Hazel turns out very copious meals, which Peter serves with a smile in the pretty dining room (with a fireplace) or on the shady terrace.

***How to get there** (Map 16): 11km northeast of Amboise via A 10, exit Château-Renault, then D31 to Autrèche (2km); turn left and follow signs for Dame Marie aux Bois; in the village turn right onto D74 towards Cangey.*

# Hôtel du Bon Laboureur et du Château

6, rue du Docteur Bretonneau
37150 Chenonceaux (Indre-et-Loire)
Tel. (0)2.47.23.90.02 - Fax (0)2.47.23.82.01 - M. Jeudi

**Category** ★★★ **Rooms** 33 with telephone, bath or shower, WC and satellite TV. **Price** Single 280-500F, double 320-600F, suite 900-1000F. **Meals** Breakfast 45F, served 7:30-10:30; half board 400-650F. **Restaurant** Service 12:00-14:00, 19:30-21:30; menus 160-300F, also à la carte. Specialties: Tartare de saumon, poêlée de saint-jacques, magret de canard au bourgueil, croustillant d'agneau, millefeuilles sablé aux fraises. **Credit cards** All major. **Pets** Dogs allowed. **Facilities** Swimming pool, parking. **Nearby** Château de Chenonceaux, Loire Valley (châteaux de la Loire), Montlouis-sur-Loire via the Cher Valley– 18-hole Touraine golf course in Ballan-Miré. **Open** Dec 16 –Jan 3 and Feb 16 – Nov 15.

Like a field regularly tended by a good laborer, this hotel, which has been in the same family for four generations, is constantly being improved. Located 200 meters from the Château de Chenonceaux, it consists of several buildings on either side of the street, gardens and a swimming pool. The bedrooms are all different, comfortable, prettily decorated and those which have just been renovated are, of course, the most attractive. Some are especially well-designed for families. You will also enjoy three pleasant, restful lounges. The first is English-style and has a bar; the two others are more modern, with their armchairs reflected in the beige lacquer of the ceilings. There is a bright, large dining room where guests greatly enjoy the owner's excellent regional cuisine. Note too that in summer several tables are set out on the terrace in the shade of a large tree. The staff are efficient and very friendly.

***How to get there*** *(Map 16): 35km southeast of Tours; on A10 Tours exit, then via D410, or N76 to Bléré, then D40 to Chenonceaux; (the hotel is in the center of the town).*

1998

# La Roseraie

7, rue de Docteur Bretonneau
37150 Chenonceaux (Indre-et-Loire)
Tel. (0)2.47.23.90.09 - Fax (0)2.47.23.91.59 - M. and Mme Fiorito

**Category** ★★★ **Rooms** 17 with telephone, 16 with bath or shower and WC, 15 with satellite TV. **Price** Double 440-480F. **Meals** Breakfast 38F, served 8:00-11:00; half board +150F (per pers.). **Restaurant** Service 12:00-14:30, 19:00-22:00; menus 98F (lunchtime) and 155F, also à la carte. Regional cooking. **Credit cards** All major. **Pets** Dogs allowed. **Facilities** Swimming pool, parking. **Nearby** Loire Valley (châteaux de la Loire), château de Chenonceaux, Montlouis-sur-Loire via the Cher Valley- 18-hole Touraine golf course in Ballan-Miré. **Open** Feb 16 –Nov 14.

This hotel has recently been taken over by a very hospitable family who have set their sights on restoring La Roseraie to its former distinction. The results are already visible: after vigorous cleaning, repainting and refurnishing (except in Room 12), the bedrooms are looking most inviting. It's true that the hotel overall is simple, but the decoration is tasteful, the baths well kept, and most of the bedrooms are quiet (those on the street side get some traffic noise in the morning.) In spring, the Roserie opens several bedrooms on a wing overlooking the garden and the terrace, which are connected by a broad exterior passageway on the *premier étage*. In good weather, several dining tables are set out there; otherwise, meals are served in the large, rustic dining room or in the Rôtisserie, which is often used for breakfast. The cuisine is copious and the prices reasonable.

***How to get there** (Map 16): 35km southeast of Tours; on A 10, take Tours exit, then via D140, or N76, to Bléré, and D40 to Chenonceaux. The hotel is in front of the* Poste.

# Hôtel Diderot

4, rue Buffon
37500 Chinon (Indre-et-Loire)
Tel. (0)2.47.93.18.87 - Fax (0)2.47.93.37.10 - M. Kazamias

**Category** ★★ **Rooms** 28 (4 in annex) with telephone, bath or shower and WC (TV on request). **Price** Single 250-320F, double 300-400F. **Meals** Breakfast 40F, served 7:30-10:00. No restaurant. **Credit cards** All major. **Pets** Dogs not allowed. **Facilities** Parking. **Nearby** Loire Château: Chinon, Ussé, Azay-le-Rideau, Richelieu, Rabelais country (La Devinière), château du Coudray-Montpensier, Lerné, château de la Roche-Clermanet – 18-hole Touraine golf course in Ballan-Miré. **Open** Jan 15 – Dec 15.

Its location close to the Place Jeanne D'Arc in the center of Chinon does not spoil the appeal or the tranquillity of this hotel. In the garden courtyard, Monsieur Kazamias has planted trees and herbs of his native Mediterranean: olive, fig, rosemary, and even banana trees, all uphold the region's much-vaunted reputation for its microclimate! On the ground floor, a corner bar has just been added; it could do with softer lighting and a few deep armchairs, but that will certainly come in time. Adjoining the bar is the breakfast room, where you will enjoy excellent homemade preserves (the proceeds go to aid Chad). There is often a log fire in the old fireplace, and the beamed ceiling and antique furniture all lend authentic charm to the room. For the time being, we recommend the bedrooms which have been renovated: numbers 1, 3, 5, 9, 10, 15, 22, 23, 24 and 25. For good restaurants, try the *L'Hostellerie Gargantua* and dine in a medieval setting; *Au Plaisir Gourmand*, offering delectable, delicate cuisine; and *L'Océanic.*

***How to get there** (Map 16): 48km southwest of Tours via D751. Go along the Vienne to the Place Jeanne-d'Arc; on the corner of the Rue Diderot.*

1998

## Agnès Sorel

4, quai Pasteur
37500 Chinon (Indre-et-Loire)
Tel. (0)2.47.93.04.37 - Fax (0)2.47.93.06.37

**Rooms** 6 with telephone, 3 with bath and WC, TV. **Price** 180-250F (with basin), 300-450F (with bath). **Meals** Breakfast 38F. Snacks avalaible by reservation. Menus from 70F. **Credit cards** All major. **Pets** Dogs allowed. **Facilities** Bicycle rentals. **Nearby** Loire Valley (châteaux de la Loire: Chinon, Ussé, Azay-le-rideau), Richelieu, Rabelais country (La Devinière), château Coudray-Montpensier, Lerné, Château de la Roche-Clermanet - 18-hole Touraine golf course in Ballan-Miré. **Open** All year.

The discreet small Hôtel Agnès Sorel, recently taken over by an enthusiastic, hospitable young couple, offers several bedrooms of varying attraction and amenities. Prices vary depending on whether the room has a bathroom or a simple washroom. We recommend the *Blue* and the *Rose* Rooms (overlooking the River Vienne and insulated from street noise by double glazing), as well as the *Verte* Room, which has a small terrace. On the ground floor, there is a dining area with charming old-fashioned furniture found in local *brocante* shops; excellent breakfasts are served there, as are afternoon tea and light meals in the evening, on reservation. Because of the small number of rooms, the staff can take special care of the guests: you'll be met at the station if you come by train, the chef will make you a picnic lunch, you can rent a bike....In short, the Agnès Sorel, named after the beautiful mistress of Charles VII, is a true hotel of character and charm. For restaurants, you can enjoy the gastronomic *Plaisir Gourmand* or the more folkloric *Hostellerie Gargantua*; good, too, are *Les Années 30* and *L'Océanic*.

***How to get there*** *(Map 16): 48km southwest of Tours via D751.*

1998

## Château de Beaulieu

67, rue de Beaulieu (D 207)
37300 Joué-lès-Tours (Indre-et-Loire)
Tel. (0)2.47.53.20.26 - Fax (0)2.47.53.84.20 - M. Lozay

**Category** ★★★ **Rooms** 19 with air-conditioning, telephone, bath, WC, TV and minibar. **Price** Single and double 380-750F. **Meals** Breakfast 50F, until 10:30; half board 780-1180F (2 pers., 2 days min.). **Restaurant** Service 12:00-14:15, 19:00-21:30 (closed Dec 24 evening); menus 195-480F, also à la carte. Specialties: Soupière de petits gris en lutée, mousseline de pigeonneau au foie gras, soupe de cerises glacée au vin d'épices et glace d'amandes amères. **Credit cards** Amex, Visa, Eurocard and MasterCard. **Divers** Dogs allowed. **Facilities** Tennis and parking. **Nearby** Tours: Palais de l'ancien archevêché, Museum of Fine Art, cathedral of Saint-Gatien, Prieuré de Saint-Côme, château de la Roche-racan, chateau-la-Vallière, Grange de Meslay, Vouvray wine cellars, Loire Valley (châteaux de la Loire) - 18-hole Touraine golf course in Ballan-Miré. **Open** All year.

Despite the immediate proximity of the center of Tours, the Château de Beaulieu enjoys a country setting, terraced gardens overflowing with flowers, and a panoramic view. Although this 15th-century château, redesigned in the 19th century, no longer has a great deal of antique furniture, it has been decorated so as to respect the original spirit of the structure: the period furniture gains in comfort what it loses in authenticity. The colors are luminous, the respect for detail can be seen throughout, and the staff is at your beck and call. Prices vary according to room size and the view from them; all have modern amenities. Some rooms are located in an independent building; our favorites there are Numbers 21 and 22 on the garden level and those on the *premier étage,* which are more spacious. The cuisine is truly *gastronomique,* cooked with precision for no-nonsense taste.

***How to get there*** *(Map 16): 5km southwest of Tours via A 10, exit number 24 bypass 585, Savonnieres-Villandry exit then then on the left.*

# Hôtel George Sand

39, rue Quintefol
37600 Loches (Indre-et-Loire)
Tel. (0)2.47.59.39.74 - Fax (0)2.47.91.55.75 - Mme and M. Fortin

**Rooms** 20 with telephone, bath or shower, WC and TV. **Price** Single and double 260-650F. **Meals** Breakfast 38F, served 7:00-9:30; half board 490-680F, full board 690-890F (per pers., 3 days min.). **Restaurant** Service 12:00-14:00, 19:30-21:30; menus 95-290F, also à la carte. Specialties: Géline de touraine, pavé de carpe au vin du Lochois, croustillant de pommes au vieux marc de Touraine et framboises. **Credit cards** Visa, Eurocard and MasterCard. **Pets** Dogs allowed (+25F). **Nearby** Château and keep of Loches, Carthusian monastery of Le Liget in the Loches forest, abbey church of Beaulieu-les-Loches, Montrésor, Indre valley, Cormery, Montbazon, Monts, Saché –18-hole Touraine golf course in Ballan-Miré. **Open** All year.

Standing at the foot of the impressive Château de Loches, this ancient 15th-century house once marked the boundary of the medieval town. M. Loiseau will welcome you with great kindness. Entering from the street you will be pleasantly surprised to find that the dining room and its large terrace are on the edge of the river Indre, which at this point forms a large waterfall. With access via an antique spiral staircase, many of the bedrooms still have their original beams and some a beautiful stone fireplace. All have just been fully renovated with new wallpaper, carpets, double-glazing windows and bathrooms. Some are especially convenient for families. The rustic furniture is nothing out of the ordinary but a few pieces of antique furniture are slowly being added. The delicate, traditional cuisine is excellent, perfectly prepared, culminating with delicious desserts. The staff is as friendly as always.

***How to get there*** *(Map 16): 42km southeast of Tours via N143.*

## Domaine de la Tortinière

Route de Ballan-Miré - Les Gués de Veigné
37250 Montbazon-en-Touraine (Indre-et-Loire)
Tel. (0)2.47.34.35.00 - Fax (0)2.47.65.95.70
Mme Olivereau-Capron and M. Olivereau

**Category** ★★★ **Rooms** 21 (3 with air-conditioning) with telephone, bath, WC and TV - 1 for disabled persons. **Price** Double 480-890F, suite 990-1250F. **Meals** Breakfast 75F, served 8:00-11:00; half board 580-955F (per pers.). **Restaurant** Service 12:15-13:45, 19:30-21:00; menus 220-360F, also à la carte. Specialties: Civet de homard et dorade au bourgueil et tagliatelles de légumes, pigeon de Touraine farci au Sainte-Maure et raisins, pêches pochées aux épices et granité au Montlouis. **Credit cards** Visa, Eurocard and MasterCard. **Pets** Dogs not allowed. **Facilities** Heated swimming pool, tennis, boat, mountain bikes on request, parking. **Nearby** Keep of Fouques Nerra in Montbazon, Indre valley, Cormery, Monts, Saché, Tours cathedral, château d'Azay-le-Rideau – 18-hole Touraine golf course in Ballan-Miré. **Open** Mar 1 – Dec 19.

A Renaissance-style château built in 1861, the Tortinière is set in a 37-acre park dominating the Indre valley, although it is only 10km from Tours. The two restaurants, the salon and most of the bedrooms are in the château. The bedrooms are all different, superbly decorated, and very comfortable; the ones in old pavillions outside are as beautiful and recommendable as those in the château. There is a beautiful restaurant with a terrace where meals are served in good weather. In autumn, the park is carpeted with cyclamen, and in good weather you can still enjoy the heated swimming pool.

***How to get there*** *(Map 16): 10km south of Tours via A10, Nr. 14 exit, then N10 towards Montbazon; via route of Ballan-Miré it's at Les Gués de Veigné.*

## Château de la Bourdaisière

25, rue de la Bourdaisière
37270 Montlouis-sur-Loire (Indre-et-Loire)
Tel. (0)2.47.45.16.31 - Fax (0)2.47.45.09.11 - M. de Broglie
Web: http://www.chateaux-france.com/bourdaisiere.htm.

**Rooms** 13 (2 suites) with bath or shower and WC (TV on request) - Elevator. **Price** Double 550-1100F, suite 750-1100F. **Meals** Breakfast 50F. No restaurant. **Credit cards** Visa, Eurocard and MasterCard. **Pets** Dogs allowed in kennel. **Facilities** Heated swimming pool, tennis, riding, parking. **Nearby** Tours, Vouvray wine cellars, Loire valley (châteaux de la Loire) – 18-hole Touraine golf course in Ballan-Miré. **Open** Feb 16 – Feb 1.

Built on the foundations of a 14th-century citadel by order of François I, the Château de la Bourdaisière was a gift from the king to his mistress, Marie Gaudin. The military edifice then was converted into a charming Renaissance château and, less than a century later, it was the birthplace of the beautiful Gabrielle d'Estrée, with whom Henri IV fell in love. It is no wonder, therefore, that the hotel's bedrooms and two suites are named after women who had an influence on French history. Beautiful, often large bedrooms are decorated with handsome copies of antiques. This room is dedicated to the Princesse de Broglie, whose young descendants will welcome you like old friends. The hotel has splendid and extensive grounds, with formal gardens, a kitchen garden, an arboretum, a rose garden and an animal park. For restaurants, we recommend: *Jean Bardet* (one of France's top chefs), *Le Canotier, Les Tuffeaux* in Tours; and *L'Oubliette* in Rochecorbon.

***How to get there*** *(Map 16): 11km east of Tours via D152.*

## Hostellerie Les Perce-Neige

37210 Vernou-sur-Brenne (Indre-et-Loire)
Tel. (0)2.47.52.10.04 - Fax (0)2.47.52.19.08
Mme Chemin

**Rooms** 15 with telephone, bath or shower (14 with WC) and TV. **Price** Double 200-295F. **Meals** Breakfast 32F, served 8:00-10:00; half board 400-515F, full board 580-695F (2 pers., 3 days min.). **Restaurant** Service 12:00-14:00, 19:30-22:00; menus 98-170F (children 55F), also à la carte. Specialties: Traditional cuisine. **Credit cards** Amex, Visa, Eurocard and MasterCard. **Pets** Dogs allowed. **Facilities** Parking. **Nearby** Tours, grange de Meslay, Vouvray wine cellars, Loire valley (châteaux de la Loire) – 18-hole Touraine golf course in Ballan-Miré. **Open** Dec 16 – Jan and Mar 15 - Nov 15.

The Perce-Neige ("Snow Drops") is a small, charming, simple hotel located in a lovely winegrowing village on the banks of the Loire just a few minutes from Tours. Decorated in cheerful color schemes, the ground floor contains an inviting bar and two lovely dining rooms where regional specialties are served, always made with fresh local products. Simple but very reasonably priced, the bedrooms are regularly renovated; many have retro furniture painted to match the room's predominant colors. When Room 28 is finished, ask for it even though it's on the *deuxiéme étage,* third floor: It's beautifully spacious and has immense windows overlooking the garden. On the caveat side, avoid Rooms 8 (unless it is redecorated), 22, 26, 32 and 34; otherwise, all the others can be recommended. In summer, you can have dinner in the park, which is shaded with beautiful trees: a veritable invitation to a romantic stroll before or after dinner. Last but not least, the hospitality is delightful.

***How to get there*** *(Map 16): 11km east of Tours, towards Amboise-Blois; in Vouvray, take towards Vernou.*

## La Croix Blanche de Sologne

41600 Chaumont-sur-Tharonne (Loir-et-Cher)
Tel. (0)2.54.88.55.12- Fax (0)2.54.88.60.40
M. and Mme Goacolou

**Category** ★★★ **Rooms** 18 with telephone, bath, WC, TV and minibar Wheelchair access. **Price** Single 250-400F, double 300-500F, suite 580-680F. **Meals** Breakfast 45F, served 7:30-12:00; half board 420-520F, full board 620-820F (per pers.). **Restaurant** Service 12:00-13:45, 19:30-21:30; menus 118-250F, also à la carte. Specialties: Sologne and Périgord cooking. **Credit cards** All major. **Pets** Dogs allowed. **Facilities** Bicycle, mountain bikes, parking. **Nearby** Saint-Viâtre, Marcilly, route des Etangs to La Ferté-Saint-Aubin (château), châteaux de la Loire (Chambord, Cheverny), Sologne aquarium – 27-hole Aisses golf course. **Open** All year.

The very old Croix Blanche auberge is located in a ravishing village in the Sologne forest. Since the 18th century, thirteen generations of women chefs have presided over the kitchen, gradually winning a solid gastronomic reputation. You walk through the old kitchen to get to the dining room, which is tastefully decorated with hunting trophies, antique country furniture, and the smartly laid tables of a good old-fashioned restaurant. In the summer, you can have dinner in the pretty flower garden. Service throughout is both friendly and efficient. The bedrooms are very comfortable and some have small sitting areas with rustic, warm decoration (though it is somewhat heavy on fabric and carpet motifs). In the annex, four duplex suites, with two bedrooms, a bathroom and a lounge in one, can accommodate four to six people.The breakfasts are especially pleasant. The Croix Blanche is a friendly, professionally run old inn, and a long-time favorite in the Loire Valley.

***How to get there*** *(Map 17): 34km south of Orléans via N20 to La Ferté-Saint-Aubin, then D922 to Chaumont. Via A71, exit Lamotte-Beuvron.*

## Château de Chissay

Montrichard
41400 Chissay-en-Touraine (Loir-et-Cher)
Tel. (0)2.54.32.32.01 - Fax (0)2.54.32.43.80 - M. Savry

**Category** ★★★★ **Rooms** 31 with telephone, bath and WC. **Price** Single 390F, double 550-910F, suite or apartment 950-1600F. **Meals** Breakfast 65F, served 7:30-10:30; half board 490-680F, full board 670-860F (per pers.). **Restaurant** Service 12:00-14:00, 19:30-21:30; menus 185-295F, also à la carte. Specialties: Marbré de sandre et langoustines, feuilleté de noix de Saint-Jacques, pigeonneau rôti au jus de truffes. **Credit cards** All major. **Pets Dogs** allowed (+45F). **Facilities** Swimming pool, parking. **Nearby** Tours, grange de Meslay, Vouvray wine cellars, Loire valley (châteaux de la Loire) – 18-hole Touraine golf course in Ballan-Miré. **Open** Mar 15 – Nov 15.

This ancient fortified château is full of historic memories: Charles VII, Louis XI and the Duke of Choiseul all stayed here. More recently, General de Gaulle spent several days here in June 1940 before going to England. This ancient fortress is steeped in history. Its guests have included Charles VI, Louis XI, the Duke of Choiseul and, more recently, General Charles de Gaulle, who stayed here in June 1940 before leaving for England. Arranged around a majestic interior courtyard, the reception rooms are decorated with pale oak period furniture, or in Louis XIII style; they are beautifully in keeping with the château. The bedrooms are luxurious, very comfortable, and some are immense. They are classically decorated, mixing styles to an often lovely effect. From the towering vantage point of the château, there is a sweeping view of the park and the swimming pool, and in the distance, the Tours plain traversed by the Cher River, just visible through the trees. The staff at the Château de Croissy is pleasant and professional.

***How to get there*** *(Map 16): 35km east of Tours via D40 to Chenonceaux, then D76; 4km before Montrichard.*

## Hôtel Les Charmilles

19, rue de la grande Sologne
41600 Nouan-le-Fuzelier (Loir-et-Cher)
Tel. (0)2.54.88.73.55 - Mme Madée

**Category** ★★ **Rooms** 13 with telephone, bath or shower, WC and TV. **Price** Single 140-260F, double 280-320F, suite 480F. **Meals** Breakfast 35F served 7:30-9:00. No restaurant. **Credit cards** Visa, Eurocard and MasterCard. **Pets** Dogs allowed in the ground-floor bedrooms (+30F). **Facilities** Parking. **Nearby** Church of Saint-Viâtre, château du Moulin, lake road from Saint-Viâtre to Romorantin via Selle Saint-Denis, La Source flower garden in Olivet. Châteaux Chambord, Cheverny 40km. **Open** Easter – Dec 1.

This big, comfortable family house, built at the beginning of the century, has been converted into a hotel. The decoration is old-fashioned, particularly the wallpapers and some pieces of furniture. However, the bedrooms and baths are comfortable and well-kept, and the surrounding countryside is delightful. Breakfast is served in the bedrooms – just hang your breakfast order on the doorknob the evening before. The grounds are delightful. The large garden has a lake, cool shady areas under very old trees, comfortable garden furniture, and a beautiful lawn. The owners are very hospitable. There is no restaurant, but you can picnic on the grounds. For meals, we recommend *Le Raboliot* and *Le Dahu* in Nouan; *Le Lion d'Or* in Pierrefitte, and *La Perdrix Rouge* in Souvigny.

***How to get there** (Map 17): 44km south of Orléans via N20 towards Vierzon; on the way out of the village D122.*

## Hôtel Château des Tertres

Route de Monteaux
41150 Onzain (Loir-et-Cher)
Tel. (0)2.54.20.83.88 - Fax (0)2.54.20.89.21 - M. Valois

**Category** ★★★ **Rooms** 14 with telephone, bath or shower and WC. **Price** Double 400-520F. **Meals** Breakfast 42F, served 8:00-10:00. No restaurant. **Credit cards** Amex, Visa, Eurocard and MasterCard. **Pets** Dogs not allowed. **Facilities** Bicycles, parking. **Nearby** Châteaux of Chaumont, Blois, Amboise, Chambord, Beauregard and Chenonceaux – 9-hole la Carte golf course in Onzain, 18-hole château de Cheverny golf course. **Open** Apr 5 – Nov 12.

This 19th-century château is a beautiful building and charmingly decorated. On the ground floor overlooking the garden and the countryside, the reception area adjoins a lounge with 19th-century furniture. To one side is a very attractive room where a delicious breakfast is served. The overall effect is that of a family house. The bedrooms are very comfortable and pretty. They are regularly redecorated with beautiful fabrics and the latest conveniences. Although in a popular tourist area, the château is quiet and reasonably priced. The welcome is very warm. The hotel does not serve meals but there are some good restaurants in the village, notably *Le Pont d'Ouchet* and *Le Domaine des Hauts de Loire,* which is more elegant and more expensive.

***How to get there** (Map 16): 198km of Paris via A 10, Blois exit; 17 km southwest of Blois via D58 towrads. Monteaux.*

# Relais des Landes

Ouchamps
41120 Les Montils (Loir-et-Cher)
Tel. (0)2.54.44.03.33 - Fax (0)2.54.44.03.89 - M. Badenier

**Category** ★★★ **Rooms** 28 with telephone, bath, WC, TV and minibar. **Price** Single and double 495-765F. **Meals** Breakfast 60F, served 7:30-10:00. **Restaurant** Service 12:30-13:30, 19:00-21:30; menus 180-280F, also à la carte. Specialties: Foie gras de canard des landes maison, folie de homard au pistou, filet de boeuf à la li de vin, blanc manger aux amandes douces et coulis de fruits rouges. **Credit cards** All major. **Pets** Dogs allowed (+40F). **Facilities** Bicycle rent, parking. **Nearby** Châteaux of Chaumont, Blois, Amboise, Chambord, Beauregard and Chenonceaux – 18-hole la Carte golf course in Onzain, 18-hole château de Cheverny golf course. **Open** Apr 1 – Nov 15.

Lying in the middle of the countryside in a 24-acre park, the Relais de Landes is a 17th-century house which has been restored and is well-kept. The lounge/reception area also houses the bar and offers corners for conversation or reading. The furniture is comfortable in these rooms and in the dining room, where a fire is lit in winter. Next to it there is a winter garden leading to the lawn where dining tables are also set. In summer, you can have meals in the flower garden beside its small streams. The bedrooms are very comfortable, prettily decorated and they have beautiful bathrooms. The staff is friendly and helpful.

***How to get there*** *(Map 16): 15km east of Blois towards Montrichard; follow the signs from Les Montils.*

1998

## Domaine de Valaudran

41300 Salbris (Loir-et-Cher)
Tel. (0)2.54.97.20.00 - Fax (0)2.54.97.12.22 - Debois-Frogé Family
E-mail: info@valaudran.com

**Category** ★★★ **Rooms** 31 with telephone, bath, WC, satellite TV and minibar - 2 for disabled persons. **Price** Single and double 390F, 465F, 595F, apart. 900F. **Meals** Breakfast 70-80F; half board 395-595F (per pers., 3 days min.). **Restaurant** Service 12:00-14:30, 19:30-22:00 (closed Sunday evening and Monday Dec – Mar); menus 120-350F, also à la carte. Specialties: Sandre en croûte de légumes au jus de fenouil, pigeonneauaux choux, moelleux chocolat praliné. **Credit cards** All major. **Pets** Dogs allowed (+60F). **Facilities** Heated swimming pool, mountain bike and parking. **Nearby** "Grand Meaulnes" Museum, Le Grenier Villâtre in Nançay, Bourges, Aubigny-sur-Nère, Sancerre, Chambord, Cheverny; 9-hole Meaulnes golf course. **Open** All year.

At the edge of Salbris, this hotel of brick and stone is typical of the hunting lodges which are part of the charm of the Sologne countryside. Less traditional, the living rooms are elegant and comfortable. In the reception salon, handsome wicker furniture sets the elegant, cheerful and contemporary decorative style. One side of the house extends into a long veranda where the restaurant tables are set. Formerly with the Côte d'Or restaurant (three Michelin stars) in Saulieu, the chef understandably has a fine hand with gourmet cuisine. The best bedrooms are those which have just been renovated. Located in the central building, they are of average size, discreetly contemporary, and the baths are beautiful. Several other rooms, less tastefully decorated, are nevertheless convenient for families.

***How to get there*** *(Map 17): 56km south of Orléans via A 71, exit Salbris; signs at traffic circle.*

# Château de la Voûte

Troo
41800 Montoire-sur-le-Loir (Loir-et-Cher)
Tel. (0)2.54.72.52.52 - Fax (0)2.54.72.52.52 - MM. Clays and Venon

**Rooms** 5 with bath or shower and WC. **Price** Double 380-480-600F. **Meals** Breakfast incl., served 8:00-10:00. No restaurant. **Credit cards** Not accepted. **Pets** Dogs not allowed. **Facilities** Parking. **Nearby** Benedictine abbey of la Trinité and church of Rhodon in Vendôme, valley of the Loir, chapel of Saint-Gilles in Montoire, Gué-du-Loir, Lavardin, Saint-Jacques-des-Guérets, manoir de la Possonière – 9-hole La Bosse golf course in Oucques. **Open** All year.

Here is a place for the discerning. The rooms in this old manor are full of beautiful things, reflecting the owners' passion for antiques. The bedrooms are furnished and decorated with some of their finds. Every room is different and has its own style and charm; even the smallest is lovely. Some are suites (named *Pompadour, Louis XIII* and *Empire*) and even apartments (*Les Tours*). The view is worthy of a 17th-century painting. This is an ideal place for exploring the Tours region and the valleys of the Loir and the Loire. This is a well managed hotel of great quality. For restaurants, we recommend *Le Cheval Blanc* in Troo, *Le Cheval Rouge* in Montoire and *Le Relais d'Antan* in Lavardin.

***How to get there*** *(Map 16): 48km north of Tours via D29 to La Chartre-sur-le-Loir, then right on D305 and D917 to Troo.*

# Manoir de la Forêt

Fort-Girard
41160 La Ville-aux-Clercs (Loir-et-Cher)
Tel. (0)2.54.80.62.83 - Fax (0)2.54.80.66.03
Mme Autebon - M. and Mme Redon

**Category** ★★ **Rooms** 19 with telephone, bath or shower, WC and TV. **Price** Double 295-355F, suite 420-480F. **Meals** Breakfast 45F, served 7:30-10:30; half board 450F, full board 580F. **Restaurant** Service 12:15-14:00, 19:30-21:00; menus 150-285F, also à la carte. Specialties: Foie gras frais au Muscat, grenadin de lotte et langoustines au sabayon de champagne, poêlée de ris de veau, spe-cialité de poisson. **Credit cards** Amex, Visa, Eurocard and MasterCard. **Pets** Dogs allowed. **Facilities** Fishing, parking. **Nearby** Benedictine abbey of la Trinité and church of Rhodon in Vendôme, Loire Valley (châteaux de la Loire), valley of Loir, chapel of Saint-Gilles in Montoire, Gué-du-Loir, Lavardin, Saint-Jacques-des-Guérets, manoir de la Possonnière – 9-hole la Bosse golf course in Oucques. **Open** All year (closed Sunday evening and Monday Oct – Mar).

The former hunting lodge of the Château de la Gaudinière, which dates from the 18th century, the Manoir de la Forêt stands in five acres of wooded grounds with a lake. The lounge/reception sets the scene with its restful atmosphere, fresh flowers and pleasant furniture. Two living rooms with deep armchairs and sofas are the ideal place for a drink, morning coffee or afternoon tea. Just next to it is a beautiful, very spacious dining room whose many windows overlook the garden (where meals are served in good weather). The cuisine is good, somewhat irregular in quality, but it can still be recommended. The bedrooms, combining modern amenities with harmonious, cheerful decoration, all enjoy a view over the park. The staff is most hospitable, offering attentive, professional service.

***How to get there*** *(Map 16): 72km northeast of Tours via N10 to 6km beyond Vendôme, then left on D141 to La Ville-aux-Clercs.*

## Hôtel de l'Abbaye

2, quai de l'Abbaye
45190 Beaugency (Loiret)
Tel. (0)2.38.44.67.35 - Fax (0)2.38.44.87.92 - M. Aupetit

**Category** ★★★ **Rooms** 18 with telephone, bath, WC and TV. **Price** Single 420-480F, double 510-560F, suite 560-700F. **Meals** Breakfast 45F, served 7:00-19:00. **Restaurant** Service 12:00-14:00, 19:00-21:30; menu 190F, also à la carte. Specialties: Traditional cooking. **Credit cards** All major. **Pet** Dogs allowed (+50F). **Facilities** Parking. **Nearby** Medieval and Renaissance quarters of Beaugency, château de Meung-sur-Loire, basilica and chapel of Saint-Jacques in Cléry-Saint-André – 18-hole Saint-Laurent-Nouan golf course. **Open** All year.

A discreet nameplate announces that this 17th-century former Augustine convent built on the banks of the Loire opposite the old bridge in Beaugency is a hotel. You will be charmingly welcomed in an immense but comfortable hall. Adjacent to it is a very inviting bar, which is next to the dining room. A tall fireplace, very tasteful rustic furnishings and windows overlooking the Loire all make it very pleasant, particularly as the cuisine is extremely good (the prices are somewhat high but the very reasonable wine list compensates for this when the bill comes). In the summer, several tables are set out on the extraordinary terrace, whose splendid austerity would not be out of place in an Italian palace. The bedrooms on the *premier étage* upstairs have a mezzanine, thus making good use of the high ceilings. They are comfortable, very elegant and the beautiful Louis XIII period furniture contributes to the authenticity of this truly exceptional hotel.

***How to get there*** *(Map 17): 25km southwest of Orléans via A10, Meung-sur-Loire exit, then N152.*

## Hôtel de la Sologne

Place Saint-Firmin
45190 Beaugency (Loiret)
Tel. (0)2.38.44.50.27 - Fax (0)2.38.44.90.19 - Mme Vinauger

**Category** ★★ **Rooms** 16 with telephone, bath or shower, WC and TV. **Price** Single and double 230-420F. **Meals** Breakfast 39F, served 7:00-9:30. No restaurant. **Credit cards** Visa, Eurocard and MasterCard. **Pets** Dogs not allowed. **Nearby** Medieval and Renaissance quarters of Beaugency, château de Chambord, basilica and chapel of Saint-Jacques in Cléry-Saint-André – 18-hole les Bordes golf course in Saint-Laurent-Nouan. **Open** All year except Christmas and New Year.

This charming hotel in the heart of old Beaugency is very courteously managed by Mme Rogue. The bedrooms are plain but comfortable, and she has equipped them with television sets with headphones (so as not to disturb the neighbors), wall lamps with pretty shades, hairdryers, and, in as many as possible, electric trouser presses. The living room is rustic and welcoming, with a fireplace, old beams and a huge selection of magazines. There is a pleasant verandah, which is also a lounge and winter garden. For restaurants, we recommend *Le Petit Bateau, Le Relais du Château* and *Le Vieux Fourneau* in Beaugency.

***How to get there*** *(Map 17): 29km southwest of Orléans via A 10, Meung-sur-Loire exit, then N152.*

## L'Auberge de Combreux

45530 Combreux (Loiret)
Tel. (0)2.38.46.89.89/02.38.59.47.63 - Fax 38.59.36.19
Christine and Dominique Gerardot

**Category** ★★ **Rooms** 20 with telephone, bath or shower, WC (2 with whirlpool and satellite TV ). **Price** 325-495F. **Meals** Breakfast 38F, served 8:00-10:00; half board 335-495F (per pers., 2 days min.). **Restaurant** Service 12:00-14:00, 19:15-21:15; menus 95-210F, also à la carte. Specialties: Mousseline de chèvre chaud au cresson, filet de brochet aux échalotes confites, tarte au citron. **Credit cards** Visa, Eurocard and MasterCard. **Pets** Dogs allowed. **Facilities** Heated swimming pool, tennis (30F), bicycles (50F half-hour), parking. **Nearby** Orléans, arboretum and museum in Châteauneuf-sur-Loire, La Source flower gardens in Olivet – 18-hole Orléans golf course. **Open** Jan 20 – Dec 20.

This is a lovely, simple inn with white walls, white beds, bunches of reeds, and wood everywhere: beams, rustic furniture, mantelpieces. Throughout there is a gentle harmony between the colors of the curtains, the lampshades and, to add brighter tones, bouquets of flowers. The bedrooms are all different, some quite small and others more spacious; they are like simple guest rooms, very much in the spirit of the inn. They are located in the main house and in *Les Loges*, a group of small houses buried in greenery on the other side of the street. In summer, the arbor is lovely for lingering over breakfast or refreshing cocktails in the evening. Meals (also served in the garden) are rustic and good: truly homemade cooking. We took special note of the charming region, which you can tour on bikes provided by the hotel.

***How to get there*** *(Map 17): 35km east of Orléans (Orléans nord exit) via N60, Châteauneuf-sur-Loire and Vitry-aux-Loges exit.*

1998

## Auberge la Clé des Champs

Route de Joigny
45320 Courtenay (Loiret)
Tel. (0)2.38.97.42.68 - Fax (0)2.38.97.38.10 - M. Marc Delion

**Rooms** 7 with telephone, bath, WC, TV and minibar - 1 for disabled persons. **Price** Single and double 395-580F, dupplex (2-4 pers.) 720-950F. **Meals** Breakfast 58F, served 7:30-10:30. **Restaurant** Service 12:00-14:00, 19:30-21:00 (closed Tuesday evening and Wednesday); menus 120-280F, also à la carte. Specialties: Escalope de ris de veau à la crème de vanille et à l'oseille, salade de homard sur brunoise de légumes, moelleux de chocolat, glace au pain d'épice. **Credit cards** Amex, Visa, Eurocard and MasterCard. **Pets** Dogs allowed. **Facilities** Parking. **Nearby** Sens, Ferrière-en-Gâtinais - 18-hole Savigny-sur-Clairis golf course. **Open** Feb 1 – Oct 14 and Nov 1 – Jan 7.

On the edge of Burgundy, don't miss "The Key to the Fields", a deliciously bucolic setting for a weekend of relaxation, gastronomy, and charming hospitality. For generations, the Délions had been farmers. Today, Brigitte and Marc have broken with tradition, converting the old family farmhouse, dating from the 17th century, into a ravishing auberge in the midst of colza and sunflower fields. The bedrooms have been very comfortably arranged in the former barn, which still has its beautiful, patinated old beams. The baths are modern and well equipped. In the dining room opening onto the garden, the table settings are beautiful: a complement to the hotel's excellent traditional cuisine, which has been crowned with a Michelin star.

***How to get there*** *(Map 18): On A 6 exit Courtenay, go 2km to Joigny via D32; between Montargis and Joigny.*

## Domaine de Chicamour

45530 Sury-aux-Bois (Loiret)
Tel. (0)2.38.55.85.42 - Fax (0)2.38.55.80.43
M. Merckx

**Category** ★★ **Rooms** 12 with telephone, bath or shower, and WC. **Price** Single and double 400-495F. **Meals** Breakfast incl., served 8:00-10:00; half board 430F, full board 530F. **Restaurant** Service 12:00-14:00, 19:30-21:00; menus 100-230F, also à la carte. Specialties: Foie gras, aumônière de chèvre chaud et son sorbet de tomates, noisettes d'agneau. **Credit cards** Visa, Eurocard and MasterCard. **Pets** Dogs allowed (+25F). **Facilities** Tennis, riding, bicycles, boules and parking. **Nearby** Orléans, arboretum and museum in Châteauneuf-sur-Loire, La Source flower gardens in Olivet – 18-hole Orléans golf course. **Open** Mar 16 – Nov 12.

Set in a 20-acre park in the heart of the Orléans National Forest, the small château of Chicamour has been turned into a hotel with the accent on simplicity and elegance. The result is remarkable. The lovely lounge has deep sofas surrounding the fireplace and beautifully chosen curtains and fabrics. The superb collection of paintings and decorative objects helps to make this a special place you will not want to leave. The bedrooms also are beautiful, with pale wood furniture and Laura Ashley fabrics matching the wallpapers and lampshades. They are all comfortable, overlook the park and have beautiful bathrooms. In the elegant dining room, you will enjoy refined cuisine based on regional produce. The cellar includes a great variety of Loire wines, which are available for purchase.

***How to get there*** *(Map 17): 39km west of Montargis on N60, between Bellegarde and Châteauneuf-sur-Loire.*

# Hôtel de l'Abbaye

8, rue des Tourelles
02600 Longpont (Aisne)
Tel. (0)3.23.96.02.44 - Fax (0)3.23.96.02.44 - M. Verdun

**Category** ★★ **Rooms** 12 with telephone, (8 with bath or shower and 9 with WC). **Price** Double 180-330F. **Meals** Breakfast "campagnard" 40F, served any time; half board 290-390F, full board 360-460F (per pers., 3 days min.). **Restaurant** Service 12:00-14:00, 19:30-21:00; menus 98-220F, also à la carte. Specialties: Wood grills, canard aux cerises, game and mushrooms in season. **Credit cards** All major. **Pets** Dogs allowed. **Facilities** Bicycle rent. **Nearby** Abbey and château of Longpont, château, Hôtel de Ville and Alexandre Dumas museum in Villers-Cotterêts, château de Vierzy, forest of Retz – 9-hole Valois golf course in Barbery. **Open** All year.

This fine old house is located in a village in the heart of the Forest of Retz. Its large, heavy dining tables and its fireplace are the scene of warm and friendly gatherings for walkers and sports enthusiasts. The delicious cooking owes a great deal to the proprietor, who does everything to make you feel at home. The few bedrooms vary in quality; five have full bathroom facilities, and all have a peaceful atmosphere and look out on the forest or the abbey. Their decoration is somewhat basic and old-fashioned but the overall effect is quite pleasant. Other amenities of the hotel are a reading room, a TV room, a delightful garden and a wealth of tourist information about the region.

***How to get there*** *(Map 10): 20km south of Soissons via N2 towards Villers-Cotterêts, then D2.*

## Hostellerie Le Château

Neuville-Saint-Amand
02100 Saint-Quentin (Aisne)
Tel. (0)3.23.68.41.82 - Fax (0)3.23.68.46.02 - M. Meiresonne

**Category** ★★★ **Rooms** 13 with telephone, bath, WC and TV (6 with minibar) - 2 for disabled persons. **Price** Single and double 330-390F. **Meals** Breakfast 45F, served from 7:30. **Restaurant** Service 12:00-13:30, 19:00-21:00; menus 125-350F, also à la carte. Specialties: Cassolette d'escargots crème d'ail et poivrons, mélange de ris et rognon au genièvre de Houlles, assiette gourmande. **Credit cards** All major. **Pets** Dogs not allowed. **Facilities** Parking. **Nearby** Antoine Lécuyer Museum (pastels by Quentin de la Tour), college and Hôtel de Ville of Saint-Quentin – 9-hole le Mesnil golf course. **Open** All year (closed Saturday noon and Sunday evening, 3 weeks in Aug).

This château lies in the heart of a beautiful wooded park. The ground floor rooms are occupied by its famous restaurant, while other pleasantly furnished rooms extend into a modern wing with bay windows and a view of the park. Viewed from the outside, however, the architectural effect is disappointing. The comfortable, pleasantly furnished bedrooms are very attractive, with pastel wall fabrics. The bathrooms are lovely. At the Hostellerie, you will enjoy a restful stay and welcoming hospitality.

***How to get there*** *(Map 2): 1km south of Saint-Quentin via A 26, exit number 11, to Lain via RN44. In Neuville-Saint-Amand-village, on right after the churche.*

## Château de Barive

Sainte-Preuve
02350 Liesse (Aisne)
Tel. (0)3.23.22.15.15 - Fax (0)3.23.22.08.39 - M. Bergman

**Category** ★★★★ **Rooms** 14 with telephone, bath or shower, WC and TV. **Price** Single 380F, double 480-880F. **Meals** Breakfast 55F, served from 7:30; half board from 400F (per pers.). **Restaurant** Service 12:00-14:00, 19:00-21:30; menus 150-330F, also à la carte. Specialties: Ravioles de crustacés servis dans leur nage, filet de Saint-Pierre aux truffes et poireaux. **Credit cards** All major. **Pets** Dogs not allowed. **Facilities** Heated swimming pool, sauna, tennis. **Nearby** Laon cathedral, abbey of Prémontrés, forest of Saint-Gobain, ruins of abbeys of Le Tortoir and Saint-Nicolas-aux-Bois. **Open** Mid Jan - mid Dec.

Surrounded by countryside, this 17th century château, first a hunting lodge, then a boarding house, has now been fully restored and opened as an impeccable hotel. The bedrooms are large and extremely comfortable, with thick eiderdowns and luxuriously fitted bathrooms. There is no period furniture, but some fine copies recreate something of the historic atmosphere of the château. The big breakfast room opens onto the surrounding greenery and is arranged rather like a winter garden. The lounge and dining room are still a little formal, but both rooms are comfortable, and the gourmet cuisine served in the latter certainly contributes much to the atmosphere. Hotel facilities include a large heated indoor swimming-pool, a sauna and a tennis court, so a stay here provides the perfect opportunity to get back into shape. The hospitality is friendly and attentive.

***How to get there*** *(Map 3 and 10): 18km east of Laon via D977.*

1998

## Le Champ des Oiseaux

20, rue Linard Gonthier
10000 Troyes (Aube)
Tel. (0)3.25.80.58.50 - Fax (0)3.25.80.98.34 - Mme Boisseau

**Category** ★★★ **Rooms** 12 with telephone, bath or shower, WC and TV - 1 for disabled persons. **Price** Single and double 420-690F, 450-700F. **Meals** Breakfast 55F, served from 7:30. No restaurant. **Credit cards** All major. **Pets** Dogs allowed (+40F). **Facilities** Parking (40F). **Nearby** In Troyes: Saint-Urbain Basilica, Saint-Pierre cathedral and Saint-Paul cathedral, Museum of contemporary Art; Lake and forest of Orient; 18-hole Troyes-La Cordelière golf course. **Open** All year.

This brand-new hotel is only "new" by virtue of its ultra-modern amenities: The half-timbered houses that make up "The Birds' Song" are among the oldest in Troyes, dating from the 16th and 17th centuries. Renovated at the request of the new owners by the Compagnons du Devoir--an exclusive guild of élite French workers--the houses are especially admirable for their elegant proportions. Around a small medieval inner courtyard, you will find twelve bedrooms with evocative names: The *Marinot, Bengali* and the *Bleue* Rooms are marvels, all very comfortably appointed and furnished with taste and elegance. Only *Les Perroquets* has a somewhat less desirable location. Excellent breakfasts are served in a beautiful dining room where an open fire burns in winter; in summer, there is a delicious small garden for the breakfast service. Amiable, attentive, and hospitable, Madame Boisseau has succeeded in her wish to make Le Chant des Oiseaux into a hotel like a home. For meals, we suggest the gastronomic *Le Clos Juillet; Les Matines* and *L'Auberge de Sainte-Maure.*

***How to get there*** *(Map 10): 158km southeast of Paris via A 5 exit Troyes-Centre, then dir. Centre-Ville, Cathédrale.*

1998

## Le Clos Raymi

3, rue Joseph de Venoge
51200 Epernay (Marne)
Tel. (0)3.26.51.00.58 - Fax (0)3.26.51.18.98 - Mme Woda

**Rooms** 7 with telephone, bath or shower, WC and satellite TV. **Price** Double 570-840F. **Meals** Breakfast 75F, served 8:00-11:00. No restaurant. **Credit cards** Visa, Eurocard and MasterCard. **Pets** Small dogs allowed (+40F). **Facilities** Parking. **Nearby** Wine Museum (Champagne) and cellar of Champagne visits (Moët et Chandon, Pol Roger, Mercier, de Castellane) in Epernay; Hautvillers (abbey where Dom Pérignon invented the Champagne); Verzy and in the fouêt: "les Faux de Verzy"; Reims - 18-hole golf course in Doumans. **Open** All year except 3 weeks in Feb.

The Champagne vineyards are one of the main tourist attractions of France, with Rheims and Epernay sharing the production of the festive wine. And so if you'd like to visit the cellars, taste various Champagnes, or buy them directly from the vineyard or the Champagne producer, you should not miss a new hotel called Le Clos Raymi. This beautiful house was built by the Chandon family of Champagne fame and has been converted into a beautiful small hotel which has conserved all the elegance and intimate atmosphere of the original house. Madame Woda has decorated it exquisitely, esentially with Art Déco furniture, beautiful Cubist paintings, and engravings by Jouve, a well-known painter of animals in the 1930s. The bedrooms also are lovely, with comfortably appointed bathrooms, a salon for enjoying a glass or two of champagne, and a garden where you will be served a delicious breakast in summer.

***How to get there*** *(Map 10): 26km south of Reims.*

## Château d'Etoges

51270 Etoges by Montmort (Marne)
Tel. (0)3.26.59.30.08 - Fax (0)3.26.59.35.57
Mme Filliette-Neuville

**Rooms** 20 with telephone, bath or shower and WC (TV on request). **Price** Double 600-800F, suite suites 1200F. **Meals** Breakfast 70F, served 7:00-11:00; half board 530-830F, full board 690-990F (per per pers., 2 days min.). **Restaurant** By reservation. Service 12:00-14:00, 19:30-21:30; menu 180F. Speciallies: Foie gras de canard maison, fricassée de lapin à la moutarde de violette, médaillon de lotte au coulis de poivrons rouges, granité au champagne et fruits d'été, moelleux de chocolat chaud. **Credit cards** All major. **Pets** Dogs allowed (+40F). **Facilities** Parking. **Nearby** Champagne Museum in Epernay, abbey of Hautvillers (where Dom Perignon invented champagne) – 18-hole La Vitarderie golf course in Dormans, 18-hole Val-Secret golf course in Château-Thierry. **Open** All year.

The splendid Château d'Etoges dates from the 17th century. It is set against a low hill beneath where springs emerge as elegant fountains. The interior of the château is equally enchanting; it has been refurbished with good taste to retain the building's character and provide modern amenities. (The bathrooms are beautiful). There is a grand staircase, as well as spacious lounges with decorative panels, delightful percale tablecloths in the dining room, and superb bedrooms. Some are big and sumptuous, others more intimate, but in each there is a delightful blend of antique furniture, pretty materials and romantic views over the moat. A warm, personal welcome at the Château d'Etoges evokes a way of life in a more graceful age. It is an ideal base for exploring the Champagne vineyards.

***How to get there*** *(Map 10): 40km west of Châlons-en-Champagne via D933.*

## Le Prieuré

Chevet de l'Eglise
60950 Ermenonville (Oise)
Tel. (0)3.44.54.00.44 - Fax (0)3.44.54.02.21 - M. and Mme Treillou

**Category** ★★★ **Rooms** 11 with telephone, bath or shower, WC, TV and minibar. **Price** Double 450-500F. **Meals** Breakfast 50F. No restaurant. **Credit cards** All major. **Pets** Small dogs allowed. **Nearby** Châalis abbey, Ermenonville forest, Astérix park, Eurodisneyland. **Open** All year except in Feb.

You will feel right at home at Le Prieuré, a true gem hidden in an English garden just next to the church. M. and Mme Treillou love polished antique furniture, paintings, knick-knacks, and rugs. The fabrics they have selected for the curtains and bedspreads reflect the atmosphere of each room. The bedrooms are very large and comfortable, and certain attic rooms have beautiful exposed beams. They are all quiet (the road to Ermenonville is not too far but is not busy on weekends). On the ground floor, the reception rooms open directly onto the garden. Each one has a fireplace, but when it's nice outside, the sun warms the polished tile floors all over the house and you can have breakfast in a charming country dining room. You can dine very pleasantly at *L'Ermitage,* about 100 yards from the hotel. Le Prieuré is enchanting.

***How to get there*** *(Map 9): 45km northeast of Paris via A1, exit Survilliers, towards Villepinte, then Ermenonville.*

# A l'Orée du Bois

Futeau - 55120 Clermont-en-Argonne (Meuse)
Tel. (0)3.29.88.28.41 - Fax (0)3.29.88.24.52
M. and Mme Aguesse

**Category** ★★ **Rooms** 7 with telephone, bath, WC and TV. **Price** Single 315F, double 360-380F. **Meals** Breakfast 50F, served 7:30-11.00; half board 430F, full board 530F (per pers., 3 days min.). **Restaurant** Closed Tuesday and Sunday evening in low season. Service 12:00-13:30, 19:00-20:30; menus 120F (in week), 165-360F, also à la carte. Specialties: Pigeonneau des Hauts de Chée, fricassée d'écrevisses, rognons de lapin aux champignons, bourgeon de sapin glaçé. **Credit cards** Visa, Eurocard and MasterCard. **Pets** Dogs allowed (+40F). **Facilities** Parking. **Nearby** Argonne Forest, Butte de Vauquois, Varennes-en-Argonne, Lachalade Abbey, Verdun, Rarécourt Museum, Les Islettes pottery factory (open July 1 – Aug 30). **Open** All year (closed Jan, Nov 1, school holidays, Sunday evening and Tuesday in low season).

With a beautiful forest at the back, the small Orée du Bois looks out over a beautiful, peaceful countryside. The interior decoration is pleasant and is lent character by traditional old furniture. Located in a recently built wing, the bedrooms are on the ground floor facing the lawn and all have a very beautiful view. They are large and decorated in a classically rustic style, but the pretty fabrics give the rooms warmth. The dining room with large bay windows has the most beautiful view. M. Aguesse turns out such regional specialties as fricassée of crayfish, while his wife, who oversees the dining room, will advise you very competently on wines. Both M. and Mme will see to it that your stay at "The Edge of the Woods" is memorable.

***How to get there*** *(Map 11): 40km west of Verdun via A 4, exit Sainte-Menehould. Then take N3 towards Verdun to Islettes, then D2 on the right, towards Futeau.*

# Auberge Le Fiacre

Rue des Pommiers
Routhiauville 80120 Quend (Somme)
Tel. (0)3.22.23.47.30 - Fax (0)3.22.27.19.80 - M. Masmonteil

**Category** ★★★ **Rooms** 11 with telephone, bath, WC and TV - Wheelchair access. **Price** Double 360-390F. **Meals** Breakfast 45F, served 8:00-10:00; half board 370-410F (per pers., 2 days min.). **Restaurant** Service 12:00-14:00, 19:00-21:30; menus 100-220F, also à la carte. Specialties: Poissons côtiens, agneau de pré salé de la baie de Somme, gibier an automne. **Credit cards** All major. **Pets** Dogs not allowed. **Facilities** Mountainbike rentals, parking. **Nearby** Beaches of Quend and Fort-Mahon (3km); parc ornithologique de Marquenterre; Le Crotoy; Le Touquet – 18-hole Belle Dune golf course. **Open** Feb 4 – Jan 14.

Standing in the midst of the Picardie countryside, this old auberge is located in a hamlet which is quiet day and night. The buildings, which have been very well restored, surround a charming dovecote and a beautifully tended garden. Well known in the region for their excellent restaurant, the owners have opened eleven bedrooms, half of them downstairs on the garden. All are comfortable, quite spacious, and decorated without ostentation; care is given to small details (like the high-quality water faucets and the excellent radio acoustics in the bathroom). The delicious homemade pastries and the good breakfast coffee, presented in pretty thermos bottles, are served in a new, much more attractive dining room; the restaurant has a beautiful old-farm decor, with a fireplace and period furniture. M. Masmonteil himself is the excellent chef and his elegant and discreet wife, a great wine connoisseur, will guide you in your choice of wines. In good weather, the owners plan to set up several tables outside as well as chaises-longues on the lawn.

***How to get there*** *(Map 1): 30 south of Le Touquet; in Quend-ville, take towards Fort-Mahon. Turn at the Routhiauville traffic circle.*

# Hôtel Dolce Vita

Route des Sanguinaires
20000 Ajaccio (Corse-du-Sud)
Tel. (0)4.95.52.42.42 - Fax (0)4.95.52.07.15 - M. Federici

**ategory** ★★★ **Rooms** 32 with telephone, bath, WC, TV and minibar. **Price** Single and double 435-70F. **Meals** Breakfast 60F, served 7:00-10:00; half board and full board (obligatory in July and Aug) 70-960F. **Restaurant** Service 12:30-13:45, 19:30-21:30; menu 200F, also à la carte. Specialties: aviolis au broccio, fricassée de langouste. **Credit cards** All major. **Pets** Dogs allowed (+60F). **Facilties** Swimming pool, water skiing, beach. **Nearby** Gulf of Ajaccio via the Route des Iles Sanguinaires, es Milelli, Château de la Punta, Bastelica. **Open** Easter – Nov 1.

The Dolce Vita is a modern hotel whose superb location compensates for the functional style of its architecture and its rather flashy interior decor. The erraces of the *premier étage* bedrooms all overlook luxuriant vegetation and arther on, the exotic panorama of the sea. They are located on two levels; the ower gives direct access to a small beach built on the rocks. The hotel is very omfortable and the bathrooms have all the usual facilities. There are flowers verywhere and it is a pleasure to stroll among the bougainvillea, oleanders nd palm trees. The dining area is composed of a large interior room, which is sed in winter, and a spacious terrace which overlooks the sea. The Dolce ita's famous, Michelin-starred restaurant is remarkable and if the maître d's uggestions sometimes seem to encourage spending, in the long run, it's all for good cause. At night, with the swimming pool floodlit, the twinkling lights n the trees and the glimmer of lights across the bay, the scene is reminiscent f Hollywood.

***low to get there*** *(Map 36): 8km west of Ajaccio via the Route des Sanuinaires. Ajaccio-Campo dell'Oro Airport 15km away, tel. (0)4.95.21.03.64.*

## Hôtel Genovese

Quartier de la Citadelle
20169 Bonifacio (Corse-du-Sud)
Tel. (0)4.95.73.12.34 - Fax (0)4.95.73.09.03
Web: http://www.oda.fr./aa/genovese.

**Category** ★★★ **Rooms** 14 with air-conditioning, telephone, bath, WC, TV and minibar. **Price** Double 700-1500F, suite 950-1700F. **Meals** Breakfast 70-80F, served 7:30-11:00. No restaurant. **Credit cards** All major. **Pets** Dogs allowed. **Facilities** Parking. **Nearby** Boat trip to marine grottoes, cave of Sdragonato and tour of the cliffs, gulf of Santa-Manza – 18-hole golf course in Sperone. **Open** All year

Set out along the walls of the Bonifacio ramparts, this hotel is in an old naval building and has a beautiful view of the sea, the town and the harbor. It is luxuriously and elegantly furnished. The rooms are set around a delightful courtyard and are decorated in pastel shades with flowered curtains. The bathrooms have comfortable amenities. Room 2 also has a balcony which overlooks the port. There is no restaurant but the ground floor has a breakfast area and a lounge where a handsome white settee blends delightfully with the stone walls. An additional asset is that the hotel is fully air conditioned. *La Caravelle* is the popular fish restaurant; *Le Voilier* and *Le Stella d'Oro* (upstairs), are favorites with the region's famous people; and *La Cantina Doria* serves the best authentic Corsican specialties.

***How to get there*** *(Map 36): In Bonifacio, turn right immediately on leaving the road to the Citadelle. Figari Airport 21km away, tel. (0)4.95.71.00.22.*

## Hôtel-Restaurant du Centre Nautique

Quai Nord
20169 Bonifacio (Corse-du-Sud)
Tel. (0)4.95.73.02.11 - Fax (0)4.95.73.17.47

**Rooms** 10 with air-conditioning, telephone, shower, WC, TV and minibar. **Price** Double 450-650F. **Meals** Breakfast 50-60F. No restaurant. Snacks available. **Restaurant** Service 12:00-15:00, 19:00-24:00. Specialties: Poissons et langoustines sur commande, specailites de pâtes. **Credit cards** All major. **Pets** Dogs allowed. **Facilities** Parking. **Nearby** Boat trip to the marine grottoes, Sdragonato Cave and tour of the cliffs, Santa-Manza Gulf – 18-hole golf course in Sperone. **Open** All year.

This hotel on Bonifacio harbor lies below the upper town and looks out over the moored boats. Despite its name it is a place that gives a cordial welcome to tourists as well as to sailing enthusiasts. The high ceilings have made it possible to convert the rooms into small duplexes. On the lower level there is a small living room and on the mezzanine the bedroom and bathroom. It is more like a studio than a conventional hotel bedroom and perfect for inviting your neighbors in for cocktails. Some units have a view over the garden and over the port (they're somewhat noisier, but how marvelous to lie in bed and watch the comings and goings of the boats and the seagulls careening above them!). You can have breakfast on the terrace overlooking the sailboats and yachts. For restaurants, note the several addresses given previously for the Hôtel Genovèse. There is also the outstanding *Chez Marco,* located by the water on Tonnara Beach, famous for its delicious, gargantuan shellfish platters, grilled fish, and bouillabaisse.

***How to get there*** *(Map 36): On the port. Figari Airport 21km away, tel. (0)4.95.71.00.22*

## Grand Hôtel Cala Rossa

Cala Rossa - 20137 Porto-Vecchio (Corse-du-Sud)
Tel. (0)4.95.71.61.51 - Fax (0)4.95.71.60.11
M. Canarelli and Mme Biancarelli

**Category** ★★★★ **Rooms** 50 with air-conditioning, telephone, bath, WC and TV. **Price** Single 600-2250F, double 800-2500F, suite 1500-2700F. **Meals** Breakfast incl., served 7:30-11:30; half-board obligatory in high season. **Restaurant** Service 12:30-14:30, 19:45-22:00; menus, also à la carte. Specialties: Mesclun de seiches à l'origan, craquant de loup aux aubergines fondantes, filet d'agneau à la choucroute de fenouil. **Credit cards** All major. **Pets** Animals not allowed. **Facilities** Private beach, water skiing, windsurfing, boat trips, parking. **Nearby** Palombaggia beach and Piccovaggia Peninsula, Ospedale Forest – 18-hole golf course in Sperone. **Open** Apr 15 – Nov 15.

The success of the Grand Hôtel Cala Rossa is due mainly to the enthusiasm of proprietor Toussaint Canarelli and his loyal and hard-working team. The hotel is very well located on the edge of the sea, and the restaurant, which is one of the best in Corsica, has become the summer haunt of famous politicians and actors from the Cala Rossa residential area. The bedrooms are all comfortable, but the suites decorated in Mediterranean style are especially luxurious as are the reception and the salon. The surroundings are magnificent: the garden with its shady pines, oleanders and plumbagos extends as far as the private beach. It is essential to reserve very early for this summer haunt of vacationers from the Cala Rossa residential development.

***How to get there*** *(Map 36): 10km northeast of Porto Vecchio via N198, D568 and D468. Figari Airport 33km away, tel. (0)4.95.71.00.22.*

# L'Aïtone

20126 Evisa (Corse-du-Sud)
Tel. (0)4.95.26.20.04 - Fax (0)4.95.26.24.18
M. Ceccaldi

**atcgory** ★★ **Rooms** 32 with telephone, bath or shower, WC and cable TV. **Price** Single 150-400F, ouble 200-550F. **Meals** Breakfast 35-38F, served 8:00-9:30; half board 250-450F, full board 380-50F (per pers, 3 days min.). **Restaurant** Service 12:00-14:00, 19:30-22:00; menus 85-160F, also à carte. Specialties: Terrine de sanglier aux châtaignes, omelette broccio et menthe, truites. **Credit ards** Amex, Visa, Eurocard and MasterCard. **Pets** Dogs allowed. **Facilities** Swimming pool, garage, arking. **Nearby** Waterfall and pool in the forest of Aïtone, riding, gorges of the Spelunca, forest of 'tone, calanques of Piana, villages of Ota and Vico, Girolata. **Open** Jan – Nov.

The Aïtone auberge is 2550 feet above sea level; in driving to it, you just may meet up with a horde of half-wild pigs roaming on the road (they fin-sh up in delicious Corsican *charcuterie.*). Toussaint Ceccaldi, the proprietor, as taken over from his parents and is constantly refurbishing and enlarging ie hotel. The building is not particularly attractive but it has a superb location, 'ith its large swimming pool overlooking the beautiful Spelunca Valley. All e bedrooms, large or small, are comfortably appointed and well kept; those ı the new part have a balcony each, with a beautiful view over the Gulf of orto. The good, family-style meals are served in the dining room or on the anoramic terrace; you can enjoy a very convivial bar with a warm open fire s soon as the weather cools off. This is a good place to stay in the mountains, 'here you are nevertheless near the Gulf of Porto.

***'ow to get there** (Map 36): 23km east of Porto via D84. Ajaccio-Campodel-Oro Airport 70km away, tel. (0)4.95.21.03.64.*

1998

## Capo Rosso

Route des Calanques
20115 Piana (Corse-du-Sud)
Tel. (0)4.95.27.82.40 - Fax (0)4.95.27.80.00 - M. Camilli-Ollivier

**Category** ★★★★ **Rooms** 57 with telephone, bath or shower, WC, minibar and satellite TV Wheelchair access. **Price** Double 350-450F. **Meals** Breakfast 45F, served 7:30-10:00; half board 450 565F (per pers., obligatory in sommer). **Restaurant** Service 12:00-13:30, 19:30-22:00; menus 100 380F, also à la carte. Specialties: Fish, spiny lobster, corsica products. **Credit cards** All major. **Pet** Dogs not allowed. **Facilities** Swimming pool, parking. **Nearby** Calanques of Piana, boat to Girolat (dep. Porto), villages of Ota, Evisa and Vico, Lava peak, route de Ficajola. **Open** Apr 2 – Oct 14.

Built in the 1970s, the "Red Cape" is surrounded by flowers and overlook one of Corsica's most sumptuous panoramas: the red rocks of Piana tumbling down to the sea and forming a succession of small gulfs, capes and mini peninsulas. The hotel's modern architecture is obviously not typically Corsican, but the site is used to optimum advantage: The swimming-pool area offer a superb viewpoint from which to admire the Gulf of Porto, and every bedroom has a small terrace. Well-kept and comfortable, they don't have a grea deal of personality but they're pleasant. A whole family helps run the establishment, some going fishing to supply the restaurant; others doing the cooking or handling the reception. Extending out onto a terrace, the panoramic dining room is decorated in pale pink, pearl grey and mother-of-pearl. Good, ver copious meals are served in an atmosphere of warmth and good humor. Ther are many sights to see in the area, including a beautiful drive to the fine sand of Arone Beach.

***How to get there*** *(Map 36): 71km north of Ajaccio via D 81. Ajaccio Airpor tel. (0)4.95.21.03.04. On the "Route des Calanques".*

## Le Maquis

20166 Porticcio (Corse-du-Sud)
Tel. (0)4.95.25.05.55 - Fax (0)4.95.25.11.70
Mme Salini

**Category** ★★★★ **Rooms** 19 with air-conditioning, telephone, bath, WC, TV and minibar. **Price** On request. **Meals** Breakfast served 8:00-10:30. **Restaurant** Service 12:30-14:00, 19:30-22:00; à la carte. **Credit cards** All major. **Pets** Dogs allowed (+60F). **Facilities** Heated swimming pool, tennis, gym, private beach, parking. **Nearby** Gulf of Ajaccio via the Route des Iles Sanguinaires, Les Milelli, Château de la Punta, Bastelica. **Open** All year.

The Maquis is one of the outstanding hotels in this guide. It is splendidly located on a small inlet off the Gulf of Ajaccio, two kilometers from Porticcio. Its pretty private beach, the elegant decor and the comfort of its communal rooms and bedrooms (ask for a room with a terrace facing the sea) make it ideal for a relaxing, comfortable vacation. The terrace, the covered swimming pool and the tennis court complete the picture. At noon, there is a delicious buffet lunch on the terrace and in the evenings an excellent menu, changed every day, is served. What more could we want? Mme Salini has made Le Maquis a veritable oasis on a coast that unfortunately has been rather spoiled. But if you do want to leave the hotel, you can explore the beautiful interior of Corsica. However, we hope that customers will be welcomed more courteously than we were when we asked for the new rates.

***How to get there*** *(Map 36): 18km southeast of Ajaccio via N196, D55 along the coast. Ajaccio-Campo dell'Oro Airport, tel. (0)4.95.21.03.64.*

1998

# La Villa Piana

Route de Propriano
20100 Sartène (Corse-du-Sud)
Tel. (0)4.95.77.07.04 - Fax (0)4.95.73.45.65 - Mme Abraini

**Category** ★★ **Rooms** 31 with telephone, bath or shower, WC - 2 for disabled persons. **Price** Single and double 250-380F. **Meals** Breakfast 36F, served 7:30-10:30. **Restaurant** Snack June – Aug. Service 12:00-21:00. Small carte. **Credit cards** All major. **Pets** Dogs not allowed. **Facilities** Swimming pool, tennis, parking. **Nearby** Museum of Prehistory in Sartène and Levie, belvédère-Campomoro, Filitosa, Olmeto, Sollocaro. **Open** Apr 1 – Oct 14.

Several minutes from the beaches of Propriano, the Villa Piana faces the very beautiful village of Sartène. It is a recent construction of ochre plaster, surrounded by Mediterranean vegetation covering the hillside. Pretty and comfortable, the bedrooms are pleasant, the baths beautiful. Some rooms have a private terrace brightened with pink oleander. Behind the hotel, a path leads up to a lovely overflow swimming pool surrounded by olive trees and lavender. Just next to it is a small stone bar which serves light meals for guests who prefer to stay by the pool rather than go out for lunch. Otherwise, there are plenty of restaurants, in both Sarthène and Propriano (note Le Lido, on the water.) A young, efficient staff adds a plus to the Villa Piana, which is recommendable for either a short visit or a longer holiday. Very near the hotel, you can enjoy good Corsican specialties at *L'Auberge Santa Barbara.*

***How to get there*** *(Map 36): Between Ajaccio and Portovecchio (about 70km). Ajaccio Airport, tel. 04 95 21 03 64; or Figari Airport.*

## Hôtel L'Aiglon

20147 Serriera (Corse-du-Sud)
Tel. (0)4.95.26.10.65 - Fax (0)4.95.26.14.77
M. Colonna-Ceccaldi

**Category** ★★ **Rooms** 18 with telephone, bath or shower (8 with WC). **Price** 210-360F **Meals** Breakfast 35F, served 8:00-9:30; half board 200-300F, full board 250-360F (per pers., 3 days min.). **Restaurant** Service 12:30-14:00, 20:00-21:30; menus 90-150F, also à la carte. Specialties: Omelette au broccio, daube de sanglier, cannellonis à la corse. **Credit cards** All major. **Pets** Dogs allowed. **Facilities** Parking. **Nearby** Waterfall and pool in the Forest of Aïtone, Gorges of the Spelunca, Forest of Aïtone, calanques of Piana, boat to Girolata, villages of Ota and Vico. **Open** May 1 – end Sept.

The Hôtel L'Aiglon, built about thirty years ago out of Porto stone, is a place for lovers of peace and tranquillity. It is set in the heart of the maquis. To reach the hotel, you take a winding road across hilly countryside; but it is not as isolated as this might suggest for the sea is only five kilometers away. Because it is patronized by a regular clientele, the bedrooms have not been updated. They are quite simple and the furniture is very 1950s. The bathrooms are behind rather thin partitions. To one side of the building there are six bedrooms, one bungalo, each enjoying a ground-floor terrace on the garden. The moderate rates are interesting if you wish to explore the interior of Corsica or want inexpensive proximity to the sea.

***How to get there*** *(Map 36): 5km north of Porto via D81; follow signs. Calvi - Sainte-Catherine Airport 80km, tel. (0)4.95.65.08.09.*

## Hôtel La Solenzara

20145 Solenzara (Corse-du-Sud)
Tel. (0)4.95.57.42.18 - Fax (0)4.95.57.46.84
M. Lucchini

**Category** ★★ **Rooms** 24 with telephone, bath or shower, WC (18 with TV) - 1 for disabled persons. **Price** Single and double 270-450F. **Meals** Breakfast 35F, served 6:45-11:00. No restaurant. **Credit cards** All major. **Pets** Dogs allowed. **Facilities** Swimming pool, parking. **Nearby** Aiguilles de Bavella, museum of Aléria, Gulf of Porto-Vecchio. **Open** All year. (by reservation in low season).

You'll find this small family-run hotel at the mouth of the Solenzara River very near fine sandy beaches. Built in the 18th century in the Genoese style by a wealthy man of the village, the hotel has conserved its original beautifully proportioned façade, its spacious, high ceilings and the 19th-century frescos in Room 11, on the street side. Located at the far side of the village, the Solenzara is in a limited-speed zone, which keeps traffic noise to a minimum. An elegant lobby furnished with several antiques gives access to the bedrooms. Often large (some are ideal for families), the rooms are simple, their Provençal-style drapes nicely contrasting with the white stucco walls. Our favorites overlook the sea: As they're no more expensive, it's best to reserve them in advance. Other smaller rooms are located in a neighboring house; less expensive, they nevertheless can be recommended. You can enjoy a flowery terrace around a charming overflow swimming-pool near a pleasant bar/tea room, and cheerful, informal service.

***How to get there*** *(Map 36): 38km north of Porto Vecchio. Figari Airport, tel. 04.95.71.00.22.*

## Hôtel Balanéa

6, rue Clémenceau
20260 Calvi (Haute-Corse)
Tel. (0)4.95.65.00.45 - Fax (0)4.95.65.29.71 - M. Ceccaldi

**Category** ★★★ **Rooms** 37 with air-conditioning, telephone, bath, WC and TV (31 with minibar). **Price** Double 300-1100F, suite 700-1200F. **Meals** Breakfast 60F, served 7:30-10:30. No restaurant. **Credit cards** All major. **Pets** Dogs allowed (+100F). **Nearby** Citadel of Calvi, tour of the villages of Balagne (Calenzana, Zilia, Montemaggiore, Sant'Antonino, church of the Trinity in Aregno, convent of Corbara), Scandola national park – 9-hole Lumio golf course. **Open** All year.

Located on the harbor in Calvi, the Balanéa is the most pleasant hotel in the center of town. The bedrooms, which are very comfortable, are spacious and well decorated; they have large bathrooms with all the amenities, including hair-dryers. Most have balconies and some have real terraces from which there are marvelous views of the fort and citadel. All the rooms are air-conditioned, making for pleasant sleeping in the hot summer. However, avoid the rooms overlooking the street, which are small and dark. Likewise, we advise you to have breakfast in your room, the dining room lacking similar appeal. The Balanéa is the only hotel open in Calvi during the winter. For an unforgettable evening, we recommend dinner on the marvelous terrace of *La Signoria* and the piano-bar of *Chez Tao*.

***How to get there*** *(Map 36): on the port in Calvi. Calvi-Sainte-Catherine Airport 7km, tel. (0)4.95.65.08.09*

## Auberge Relais de la Signoria

Route de forêt de Bonifato
20260 Calvi (Haute-Corse)
Tel. (0)4.95.65.93.00 - Fax (0)4.95.65.38.77 - MM. Ceccaldi

**Category** ★★★ **Rooms** 10 with telephone, bath, WC, TV and minibar. **Price** Single and double 500-1200F, suite 1200-1600F. **Meals** Breakfast 80F, served 8:00-11:00; half board 1150-1800F (per 2 pers., 2 days min.). **Restaurant** Service 12:00-13:30, 19:30-22:30 (at lunchtime in July and Aug grill until 14:00 in front of the swimming pool); menu 220F, 400F, also à la carte. Specialties: Carpaccio de saumon aigre doux, salade de pigeonneau, noisettes d'agneau à la croute d'herbes du maquis. **Credit cards** Amex, Visa, Eurocard and MasterCard. **Pets** Dogs allowed. **Facilities** Swimming pool, tennis, team bath, parking. **Nearby** Citadel of Calvi, tour of the villages of Balagne (Calenzana, Zilia, Montemaggiore, Sant'Antonino, church of the Trinity in Aregno, convent of Corbara), Scandola national park; 9-hole Lumio golf course. **Open** End Mar – Oct 15.

La Signoria is the kind of hotel that dreams are made of. It is in a beautiful old house on a large estate with eucalyptus and palm trees and a beautiful swimming pool in the garden. The owners have converted the house into a hotel, without spoiling any of its charm. The rooms in the main building are the most pleasant and comfortable ones, but you will not feel deprived if you have one in the annex. Dinner by candlelight under the canopy of palm trees on the terrace is one of the many lovely moments you will spend here. This beautiful hotel is perfectly quiet even in the middle of August.

***How to get there*** *(Map 36): 5km from Calvi on the airport road. Calvi-Sainte-Catherine Airport 2km, tel. (0)4.95.65.08.09.*

## Marina d'Argentella

L'Argentella
20260 Calvi (Haute-Corse)
Tel. (0)4.95.65.25.08 - Fax (0)4.95.65.25.12 - M. Grisoli

**Rooms** 25 with bath and WC. **Price** Double room with half board 350-450F (per pers.), reduced rate for children. **Meals** Breakfast incl. **Restaurant** Service 12:30-14:30, 20:00-22:00; menu 120F, also à la carte. Specialties: Fish and Corsican dishes. **Credit cards** Visa, Eurocard and MasterCard. **Pets** Dogs allowed. **Facilities** Parking. **Nearby** Citadel of Calvi, tour of the villages of Ballagne (Calenzana, Zilia, Montemaggiore, Sant 'Antonino, church of the Trinity in Aregno, convent of Corbara), Scandola regional park – 9-hole Lumio golf course. **Open** End May – Oct 3.

The Argentella is a very special place, not only because it is so beautifully located on the beach of Crovani Bay, but also because of Pierre and Dorine's friendly hospitality. The bedrooms, which are in small bungalows in a eucalyptus grove, are simple but charming, and all have comfortable bathrooms. Chef Dhair prepares new recipes regularly. At noon, meals are light and fresh, while in the evening the fare is more ambitious. Swimming, windsurfing, picnics and boat excursions are offered by the hotel. At seven in the evening, you can join in the traditional volleyball game and then enjoy a drink as you admire the wonderful sunset. The Argentella is ideal for a family vacation; note the special slimming week in June.

***How to get there*** *(Map 36): 22km south of Calvi towards Porto by coast road. Calvi-Sainte-Catherine Airport 25km away, tel. (0)4.95.65.08.09.*

1998

## Le Vieux Moulin

Le Port
20238 Centuri-Port (Haute-Corse)
Tel. (0)4.95.35.60.15 - Fax (0)4.95.35.60.24 - M. Alessandrini

**Rooms** 14 with telephone, bath or shower, WC and TV. **Price** Single and double 280F, 330F; half board 385F (per pers., obligatory in summer). **Meals** Breakfast 34F, served 8:30-11:00. **Restaurant** Service 12:00-15:00, 19:30-23:00; menus 115-290F, also à la carte. Specialties: Fish, shellfish, bouillabaisse. **Credit cards** All major. **Pets** Dogs allowed. **Facilities** Parking. **Nearby** Le Cap Corse from Bastia to Saint-Florent (Canari, Nonza, Saint-Florent...). **Open** Mar 16 – Oct 29.

The minuscule port of Centuri is an absolute must, a model of its kind that unfortunately is rarely found today on the continent. Local fishermen bring in lobsters, anchovy, crabs and an abundance of marvelous products which are served for very reasonable prices at the Vieux Moulin and other village restaurants. Fronting on a huge terrace beneath feathery old tamarisks, this beautiful house is located slightly above the port. Built in the 19th century by an uncle of the owner who had made a fortune in America, it has retained much of its original character and charm, especially in the lobby and the upstairs salon. The bedrooms in the house are the warmest in winter (Numbers 5 and 6 have a very beautiful view), while the rooms in the modern annex enjoy the use of a shady terrace, which is lovely in summer; all are simply furnished but well kept and pleasant. The garden is a delightful place for a drink or a meal surrounded by Mediterranean fragrances and the panorama of the fishing boats coming and going.

***How to get there*** *(Map 36): 50km north of Bastia. Bastia-Poretta Airport, tel. (0)4 95 54 54 54.*

## Hôtel Mare e Monti

20225 Feliceto (Haute-Corse)
Tel. (0)4.95.61.73.06 - Fax (0)4.95.61.78.67
M. Renucci

**Category** ★★ **Rooms** 18 with telephone, (10 with shower, 4 with bath and WC, and 2 suites with bath and WC). **Price** Single 260-280F, double 310-350F, suite 630F (4 pers.). **Meals** Breakfast 35F, served 8:00-10:00; half board 260-295F (per pers., 3 days min.). **Restaurant** Service 12:00-14:00, 19:30-22:00; menus 80-180F, also à la carte. Specialties: Truite à la Calamenti, agneau de lait à la mode corse. **Credit cards** All major. **Pets** Dogs allowed. **Facilities** Parking. **Nearby** Citadel of Calvi, tour of the villages of Ballagne (Calenzana, Zilia, Montemaggiore, Sant 'Antonino, church of the Trinity in Aregno, convent of Corbara). **Open** May 1 – Sept 30.

This lovely house, which lies between the sea and the mountains, was built in 1870 and is still lived in by the descendents of the same family. Behind the hotel there are steep rocky cliffs, and in the distance one can see the sea behind Ile Rousse. The lobby with its painted ceiling, the delightful Louis-Philippe lounge, the lovely Corsican lounge, and the large stairway have great character and charm. The bedrooms are appointed more simply but their amenities have been renovated. For the moment, ask for those with beautiful high ceilings on the *second étage,* third floor; however, the renovation planned for the *troisième étage* should soon improve those rooms. M. Renucci gives a cordial welcome to all his guests and the traditional, delicious cuisine provided by his chef is an attraction for people who want to know a more authentic Corsica than that found in its seaside resorts.

***How to get there*** *(Map 36): 26km northeast of Calvi via N197 to beyond Alcajola, then right on D13 to Feliceto via Santa Reparata. Calvi Sainte-Catherine Airport, Tel. (0)4.95.65.08.09.*

## La Bergerie

Route de Monticello
20220 L'Ile-Rousse (Haute-Corse)
Tel. (0)4.95.60.01.28 - Fax (0)4.95.60.06.36 - M. Caumer

**Category** ★★ **Rooms** 19 with telephone, bath or shower and WC. **Price** Single and double 260-420F. **Meals** Breakfast 35F, served 8:00-10:00; half board 320-400F (per pers., 5 days min.). **Restaurant** Service 12:00 and 19:30; also à la carte. Specialties: Brochettes de liche, araignées farcies, omelette aux oursins, sardines farcies, mérou à la juive. **Credit cards** Visa, Eurocard and MasterCard. **Pets** Dogs allowed. **Facilities** Swimming pool, parking. **Nearby** Citadel of Calvi, tour of the villages of Ballagne (Calenzana, Zilia, Montemaggiore, Sant 'Antonino, church of the Trinity in Aregno, convent of Corbara). **Open** Mar 15 – Dec 1 (closed Monday in low season).

La Bergerie is an old sheep farm converted into a small hotel 800 meters from Ile Rousse and the beach. Located in several buildings, the bedrooms have rough white walls and are plainly decorated. Each however has a small terrace. We recommend the rooms with a view over the sea, particularly as they're no more expensive. On the flip side, be sure to avoid Rooms 1 to 5, which are dark and bleak. In good weather, you can enjoy the lovely quiet swimming pool surrounded by flowers. The owner is an enthusiastic fisherman and delights his guests with dishes he creates using his catch of the day. These might include such refined dishes as sea-urchin omelette and sea-anemone fritters, and several Moroccan specialties. With the first rays of sunshine, meals are served outdoors on the shady terrace; otherwise, the dining room is in the small rustic shepherd's house. The atmosphere is relaxed and friendly.

***How to get there*** *(Map 36): 24km northeast of Calvi via N197 to L'Ile Rousse. Calvi-Sainte-Catherine Airport, tel. (0)4.95.65.08.09.*

## La Casa Musicale

20220 Pigna (Haute-Corse)
Tel. (0)4.95.61.77.31/81 - Fax (0)4.95.61.74.28
M. Jérome Casalonga

**Rooms** 7 with telephone, bath or shower and WC. **Price** Single and double 195-380F, triple 300-400F. **Meals** Breakfast 30F, served 8:00-11:00. **Restaurant** Service 20:00-22:30; also à la carte. Regional cooking. **Credit cards** Visa, Eurocard and MasterCard. **Pets** Dogs allowed. **Nearby** Citadel of Calvi, tour of the villages of Balagne (Calenzana, Zilia, Montemaggiore, Sant'Antonino, church of the Trinité in Aregno, convent of Corbara). **Open** Feb 16 – 31 Dec. Closed Monday.

Patiently renovated, the ravishing hillside village of Pigna invites you to wind through its cobblestone lanes and discover a few artisans' ateliers, a small panoramic square, and...La Casa Musicale, overlooking a magnificent countryside of trees and sea. The hotel was originally a venue for concerts and art courses; success was such that the owners decided to set dining tables out on the terrace and in the old olive- and grape-press for those who wished to stay for lunch or dinner. The traditional cooking was good, the atmosphere delightful, lots of guests would have enjoyed spending the night and, not wanting to disappoint them, Monsieur Casalonga soon opened several bedrooms. They are very simple but the magic of the place, the extraordinary view over the sea and hills, the colorful bedspreads, the wall frescos all make the rooms very pleasant. Two have a terrace (one of which is reached by a ladder.) Last but not least, the concerts still are given, once or twice a week depending on the season.

***How to get there*** *(Map 36): 8km southwest of Ile-Rousse. Calvi-Sainte-Catherine Airport, tel. (0)4.95.65.08.09.*

## U Sant' Agnellu

20247 Rogliano (Haute-Corse)
Tel. and Fax (0)4.95.35.40.59
M. and Mme Albertini

**Rooms** 9 with bath and WC. **Price** Double 240-320F. **Meals** Breakfast 30F; half board 250-300F (per pers.). **Restaurant** Service 12:00-15:00, 19:30-23:00; menu 90F, also à la carte. Specialties: Brandade, cabri, boulettes au broccio, cannelonis, tourte Sant Agnellu. **Credit cards** Visa, Eurocard and MasterCard. **Pets** Dogs allowed. **Nearby** Riding, Chemin des Douaniers, villages of Cap Corse from Bastia to Saint-Florent. **Open** Easter – Oct.

Young M. and Mme Albertini set up a restaurant in this old town hall in 1984 and three years later converted it into a hotel. They deserve encouragement for their delicious cuisine at unbeatable prices, as well as for the charming bedrooms. With white stucco walls and solid wooden furniture, the accomodations are simple but very comfortable and the tiled bathrooms are impeccable. Five bedrooms look out onto the sea and the others onto the mountains. In good weather, meals are served on the panoramic terrace: the spacious indoor dining room with its semicircle of large windows also has beautiful views. Visitors who enjoy old buildings will find much to interest them in this picturesque 12th-century village, which has two churches, a convent and the ruins of a château as well as various Genoese towers.

***How to get there*** *(Map 36): 42km north of Bastia via D80 towards Macinaggio (free bus from port of Macinaggio to the hotel). Bastia Airport, tel. (0)4.95.54.54.54.*

## Hôtel Castel Brando

20222 Erbalunga (Haute-Corse)
Tel. (0)4.95.30.10.30 - Fax (0)4.95.33.98.18
M. and Mme Piéri

**Category** ★★★ **Rooms** 10 and 6 apartments with air-conditioning, telephone, bath, WC and TV, kitchenette and safe - Wheelchair access. **Price** Double 380-580F, apart. 530-830F (per 3-4 pers). **Meals** Breakfast 30F, served 8:30-10:00. No restaurant. **Credit cards** All major. **Pets** Dogs allowed. **Facilities** Swimming pool, parking. **Nearby** Bastia, romanesque cathedral of La Canonica and San Parteo church, villages of Cap Corse from Bastia to Saint-Florent. **Open** Apr 1 – Oct 30.

Joëlle and Jean-Paul Piéri, who were born in this picturesque fishing village, have restored a beautiful and charming house here, lending it comfort and personality. You can live here at your own pace and the apartments with kitchenette are especially recommendable for long stays. The shady park has a swimming pool, but if you prefer the sea, the pebble beaches in Erbalunga or Piétracorba are nearby. Fairly new to the hotel business, M. and Mme Piéri have quickly become real professionals. They are very enthusiastic and will give you a warm welcome - as well as tips for discovering and enjoying the real Corsica. Erbalunga itself is classed as a preserved site and has inspired numerous painters and the Castel Brando, in our opinion, has become one of the most charming, if not *the* most charming hotel in Corsica.. For dinner, the owners will give you their special addresses. We recommend *La Citadelle* and *Le Romantique* in Bastia; and in Erbalunga, overlooking the sea, *Le Pirate*.

***How to get there*** *(Map 36): 9km north of Bastia. Bastia-Poretta Airport tel. (0)4.95.54.54.54.*

## Hôtel de la Corniche

San-Martino-di-Lota
20200 Bastia (Haute-Corse)
Tel. (0)4.95.31.40.98 - Fax (0)4.95.32.37.69 - Mme Anziani

**Category** ★★ **Rooms** 19 with telephone, bath or shower and WC (10 with TV). **Price** Single 250-300F, double 300-460F. **Meals** Breakfast 35-40F, served 7:30-10:00; half board 310-390F (per pers.). **Restaurant** Service 12:00-14:00, 19:30-21:30 (closed Sunday evening and Monday, Oct – end Mar); menus, also à la carte. Specialties: Raviolis au broccio et aux herbes, pageot du golf en étuvée de fenouil confit olives vertes, grenadins de veau sautés au gingembre et citron vert et ses canellonis de courgette au basilic, pastizzu du Cap Corse et son coulis d'orange caramélisé. **Credit cards** All major. **Pets** Dogs not allowed. **Facilities** Swimming pool. **Nearby** Romanesque cathedral of La Canonica and San Parteo church, villages of Cap Corse from Bastia to Saint-Florent. **Open** Feb 1 – Dec 20.

This hotel at San Martino-di-Lota lies along a winding road ten minutes drive from Bastia. It has been owned by the same family since 1935 and has incomparable views of the sea. The first thing you will notice is the beautiful terrace and its splendid plane trees. Meals are served here in beautiful weather and on clear days you can see as far as the Italian coast. Home cuisine and Corsican specialties are the keynotes of the menu. The bedrooms are excellent for their price range; they are tastefully and comfortably decorated with classic wooden furniture and attractive bathrooms, and all look out to the sea. You will find a cordial welcome here.

***How to get there*** *(Map 36): 6km north of Bastia via D80, then D131 at Pietranera. Bastia-Poretta Airport, tel. (0)4.95.54.54.54.*

1998

## Castan Relais

6, square Castan
25000 Besançon (Doubs)
Tel. (0)3.81.65.02.00 - Fax (0)3.81.83.01.02 - M. Dintroz

**Rooms** 8 with telephone, bath, WC, satellite TV and minibar - 1 for disabled persons. **Price** Single and double 580-980F. **Meals** Breakfast 60F, served 7:30-10:30. No restaurant. **Credit cards** Amex, Visa, Eurocard and MasterCard. **Pets** Dogs allowed. **Facilities** Parking. **Nearby** Citadel and Fine Art Museum in Besançon, Salines Royales of Arc and Senans, Arboi and the Maison Pasteur, Baume-les-Dames (la source bleue, caves of the Glacière), Museum of Courbet in Ornans - 18-hole Chevillotte golf course. **Open** All year except 1 week end Dec and 3 weeks in Aug.

Standing on a promontory far above a bend in the Doubs River, the old citadel of Besançon boasts a number of town houses, including that occupied by the Relais Castan. Well located in the historic quarter near the Porte Noire (a 2nd-century Roman arcade) and Saint Jean Cathedral, this beautiful 17th- and 18th-century house has been converted into a small luxury hotel. The eight bedrooms are named after a theme: the *Guillaume Tell* room pays homage to the local Franche-Comté culture; the *Trianon* and the *Régence* honor Louis XIV, who made the Franche-Comté part of France; and if you want to succumb to the pleasure of a Roman bath, ask for the *Olympe* or the *Pompéi* room. Many thoughtful details add to the pleasure of the Relais: a basket of fresh fruit in your room, and a delicious breakfast which you can enjoy in the trophy room. With all its positive qualities, the Relais does lack a touch of warmth. For restaurants, try *Mungo Park*, an excellent (one Michelin star) restaurant of the city and the region; *Le Vauban*, with a superb view over the citadel; and *Le Chaland*, on a boat.

***How to get there** (Map 20): In the center of town, follow signs for Citadelle and Conseil Régional.*

## Auberge Le Moulin du Plain

25470 Goumois (Doubs)
Tel. (0)3.81.44.41.99 - Fax (0)3.81.44.45.70
M. Choulet

**Category** ★★ **Rooms** 22 with telephone, bath or shower and WC. **Price** Single and double 208-310F. **Meals** Breakfast 38F, served 8:00-9:30; half board 240-280F, full board 310-340F (per pers., 3 days min.). **Restaurant** Service 12:00-13:30, 19:00-21:30; menus 110-195F, also à la carte. Specialties: Truite à l'échalote, feuilleté aux morilles, jambon du pays, coq au savagnin. **Credit cards** Visa, Eurocard and MasterCard. **Pets** Dogs allowed. **Facilities** Parking. **Nearby** Circuit from Maîche (D437) to Gière and Indevillers, Corniche of Goumois via the gorges of the Doubs to the Echelles de la Mort, art and clock making museums in Besançon; 18-hole Prunevelle golf course. **Open** Feb 25 – Nov 2.

This hotel is a great favorite with fishermen. It stands on the banks of the Doubs River with its sand and pebble beach, at the foot of the mountains facing Switzerland. The emphasis here is on calm and simplicity: the steep roof of the building is a typical feature of farmhouses in the Haut-Jura, and the bedrooms are attractively unpretentious. The Auberge du Moulin du Plain is ideal for those seeking a peaceful retreat. It has a small lounge, several fireplaces and a bar area. Its exceptional location has a lot to offer not only to fishermen but also to those in search of simple pleasures: bathing in crystal-clear waters, stunning walks and excursions (Switzerland is within easy reach). The cuisine is of the same calibre as the hotel.

***How to get there*** *(Map 20): 53km south of Montbéliard via D437 towards Maîche, at Maison Rouge D437b to Goumois; 4km before Goumois beside the River Doubs.*

# Hôtel Taillard

25470 Goumois (Doubs)
Tel. (0)3.81.44.20.75 - Fax (0)3.81.44.26.15
M. Taillard

**Category** ★★★ **Rooms** 24 with telephone, bath or shower, WC and TV (6 with minibar). **Price** Double 275-490F, apart. 580-740F. **Meals** Breakfast 54F, served 8:00-9:30; half board 360-500F (per pers., 3 days min.). **Restaurant** Service 12:00-14:00, 19:15-20:45; menus 135-370F, also à la carte. Specialties: Escalope de foie gras aux griottes de Fougerolles. **Credit cards** All major. **Pets** Dogs allowed (+40F). **Facilities** Swimming pool, parking. **Nearby** The Maîche road (D437) to Gière and Indevillers, Goumois (coastal road) via the Doubs gorges to Les Echelles de la Mort, art and clock making museums in Besançon; 18-hole Prunevelle golf course. **Open** Mar – mid Nov (closed Wednesday in Mar and Oct).

You will appreciate the innkeeping and gastronomic knowhow of four generations of Taillards in this hotel. It is in the middle of the Jura countryside on a hillside overlooking a small valley. You can see the blue foothills of the Swiss Alps on the horizon. The rooms are comfortable and most of them have a balcony facing the mountains. In the soft green pastures of the Haut-Doubs, you can still hear the tinkling of cow bells, and the Doubs River is great for trout fishing and kayaking. Everything is simple and quiet here. We especially liked M. Taillard's cuisine, which features regional specialties with a local flavor. The imaginative menu as well as the light dishes will satisfy many a gourmet. The service is also outstanding. Note the opening of La Résidence, offering apartments for two to four people, several bedrooms, a fitness room, sauna, and a whirlpool bath.

***How to get there*** *(Map 20): 53km south of Montbéliard via D437 towards Maîche, at Maison Rouge D437b to Goumois; near the church.*

# Hôtel Le Lac

"Au Village"
25160 Malbuisson (Doubs)
Tel. (0)3.81.69.34.80 - Fax (0)3.81.69.35.44 - M. Chauvin

**Category** ★★★ **Rooms** 54 with telephone, bath or shower, WC, TV, 2 with minibar - elevator. **Price** Single and double 250-380F, suite 700F. **Meals** Breakfast 40-50F, served 7:30-9:45; half board and full board 230-430F (obligatory in summer), 290-510F (per pers. 3 days min.). **Restaurant** Service 12:00-14:00, 19:00-21:00; menus 105-245F, also à la carte. Specialties: Fish, morilles. **Credit cards** Diners, Visa, Eurocard and MasterCard. **Pets** Dogs allowed (+35F). **Facilities** Parking. **Nearby** Château de Joux, Saline Royale of Arc and Senans; Le Saut du Doubs, Museum of Courbet in Ornans, Besançon. **Open** Dec 16 – Nov 14 except weekend.

Lying between a lake and a forest, this imposing turn--of-the-century building has retained its traditional *Vieille France* atmosphere. The cuisine and the reception are very much a family affair, with everyone lending a helping hand. Beginning with Grandfather Chauvin, who makes his rounds to see if everyone is happy in the dining room. Then there are the two chefs who man the stoves, their wives overseeing the service in the elegant, classic dining room. Highlighting the products of the region and fish from the lake, the chef duo turn out excellent meals. In the same building, the Restaurant du Fromage offers a 35-Franc chef's special in the beautiful wood-paneled decor of a Swiss chalet, while in the tea room, you can enjoy ice cream from the famous Paris *glacier,* Berthillon. The comfortable, cozy bedrooms do not all enjoy a view of Saint Point Lake which, if you wish, you should request. It's also possible to have a room with a balcony.

***How to get there*** *(Map 20): 75km south of Besançon.*

## Hôtel de France

39220 Les Rousses (Jura)
Tel. (0)3.84.60.01.45 - Fax (0)3.84.60.04.63
Mme Petit

**Category** ★★★ **Rooms** 31 with telephone, bath or shower and TV. **Price** Double 285-530F **Meals** Breakfast 48F; half board 330-445F, full board 425-550F (per pers., 2 days mim.). **Restaurant** Service 12:15-15:00, 19:15-21:30, menus 148-435F. Specialties: Marbré de queue de boeuf au foie gras, poëlée de lotte jurassiènne aux asperges, moelleux chocolat. **Credit cards** All major. **Pets** Dogs not allowed. **Nearby** Ski: 200m from the ski lift; 18-hole Rochat golf course, riding, hiking, lake. **Open** Dec 13 – Jun 8 and Jun 26 - Nov 18 .

The Petit family has been running this hotel for more than thirty years. It is a large chalet whose balconies overflow with flowers in summer. Once you're inside the front door, you will love the Hôtel de France; the large lounge with its wood paneling and beautiful exposed ceiling beams beckons you to take a seat by the large stone fireplace. On the left, the dining room is bright and welcoming. The chef, Jean-Pierre Durcrot, who was Roger Petit's apprentice and trained with famous Paris chefs, puts all his considerable talent in the service of the hotel's clientele. Meals are served on the large shady terrace in summer. All the bedrooms are simply and comfortably decorated and have a view of the forest. You can enjoy total relaxation here after a vigorous day of cross-country or downhill skiing. Mme Petit is very friendly and hospitable.

***How to get there*** *(Map 20): 85km southwest of Pontarlier via D72 to Chaffrois; D471 to Champagnole and N5 via Morez.*

## Les Rives de Notre-Dame

15, Quai Saint-Michel
75005 Paris
Tel. (0)1.43.54.81.16 - Fax (0)1.43.26.27.09 - M. Degravi

**Category** ★★★★ **Rooms** 10 with air-conditioning, telephone, bath or shower, TV, and minibar. **Price** Single and double 995F, 1200F, 1650F; suite 2500F. **Meals** Breakfast 85F. **Restaurants** Nearby: Balzar 49 rue des Ecoles (Tel. 01 43 54 13 57) - Les Bookinistes, 53 quai des Gands Augustins (Tel. 01 43 25 45 94) - L'Ecluse, 15 quai des Grands Augustins - Les Colonies, 10 rue Saint-Julien-le-Pauvre (Tel. 01 43 54 31 33) - Tea Caddy, square Saint-Julien-le-Pauvre (lunchtime) - Bistrot Notre Dame, 14 rue Cloître-Notre-Dame (Tel. 01 43 54 18 95). **Credit card** All major. **Pets** Small dogs allowed. **Parking** Square in front of Notre-Dame and 1, rue Lagrange. **Open** All year.

Your windows at Les Rives de Notre-Dame look out over a postcard setting between the Place Saint-Michel and Notre Dame. You can see the quays of the Seine with its bookstalls and the banks *(rives)* down below where lovers stroll and watch the *bateaux mouches* wending their way upstream. Excellent soundproofing means that you can enjoy this view from a quiet room, of which there are ten. No two are the same but all are handsomely decorated with a tasteful combination of motifs and colors. The rooms are large and include shaped sitting areas with a sofa-bed and pretty bathrooms. On the ground floor, there are three small bedrooms that are equally charming; they are usually for one person, but a couple could stay here if spaciousness is not important. The service is attentive.

***How to get there*** *(Map 37 and 38): Métro Cluny, RER Cluny-Saint-Michel, Bus 21, 24, 27, 47, 63, 67, 86, 87 and 96.*

## Hôtel des Deux Iles

59, rue Saint-Louis-en-l'Ile
75004 Paris
Tel. (0)1.43.26.13.35 - Fax (0)1.43.29.60.25 - M. Buffat

**Category** ★★★ **Rooms** 17 with air-conditioning, telephone, bath or shower, cable TV and hairdryer. **Price** Single 745F, double 857F. **Meals** Breakfast 48F, snacks available. **Restaurants** Nearby: Le Monde des Chimères, 69 rue Saint-Louis-en-l'Ile (Tel. 01 43 54 45 27) - Au Gourmet de l'Ile, au n° 42 (Tel. 01 43 26 79 27) - La Castafiore au n° 51 (Italien, Tel. 01 43 54 78 62) - Campagne et Provence, 25 quai de Tournelle (Tel. 01 43 29 74 93) - Le Pont Marie, 7 quai Bourbon (Tel. 01 43 54 94 62) - Bofinger, 5 rue Bastille (Tel. 01 42.72.87.82). **Credit cards** Amex, Visa, Eurocard and Mastercard. **Pets** Dogs not allowed. **Parking** At 2 rue Geoffroy-l'Asnier and square in front of Notre-Dame. **Open** All year.

M. and Mme Buffat have converted two buildings into charming hotels between a former Archbishop's Palace, the Church of Saint-Louis-en-l'Ile, and Bertillot, famous for its ice cream. We have chosen this one for its atmosphere – English with a tinge of exoticism: flowery fabrics and painted cane and bamboo furniture are the main features of the decor. The bedrooms are not very large, but they are delightful. Provençal fabrics replace the chintzes used in the lounge, and the bathrooms are lined with gleaming blue tiles. Everything here is comfortable, including the beautiful vaulted breakfast room. This hotel has a faithful following and often there are no vacancies. If this is the case, you might be able to reserve a room in the Buffat's Hôtel de Lutèce just next door, which is also very charming.

***How to get there*** *(Map 37 and 38): Métro Pont-Marie, Bus 24, 63, 67, 86 and 87.*

## Hôtel du Jeu de Paume

54, rue Saint-Louis-en-l'Ile
75004 Paris
Tel. (0)1.43.26.14.18 - Fax (0)1.40.46.02.76 - Mme Prache

**Category** ★★★★ **Rooms** 32 with bath, WC, telephone, cable TV, hairdryer and minibar. **Price** Double 895-1395F. **Meals** Breakfast 80F, snacks available. **Restaurants** Nearby: Le Monde des Chimères, 69 rue Saint-Louis-en-l'Ile (Tel. 01 43 54 45 27) - La Castafiore au n° 51 (Italien, Tel. 01 43 54 78 62) - Campagne et Provence, 25 quai de Tournelle (Tel. 01 43 29 74 93) - Le Pont Marie, 7 quai Bourbon (Tel. 01 43 54 94 62) - Brasserie Bofinger, 5 rue Bastille (Tel. 01 42.72.87.82). **Credit cards** All major. **Pets** Dogs allowed. **Facilities** Sauna, gym, patio and bar. **Parking** At 2 rue Geoffroy-l'Asnier and square in front of Notre-Dame. **Open** All year.

This hotel is an authentic old palm-tennis court. The spacious interior has been entirely and artfully restructured by creating a series of galleries and mezzanines to form a dynamic and very decorative architectural arrangement. Several areas have thus been created: On the ground-floor, there is an intimate lounge-bar and a warm, inviting breakfast room; on the mezzanine, you will find a reading room, and off the galleries are the elegant bedrooms with beautiful baths. The delicious breakfasts include excellent homemade preserves.

***How to get there*** *(Map 37 and 38): Métro Pont-Marie, Bus 24, 63, 67, 86 and 87.*

## Hôtel Relais Christine

3, rue Christine
75006 Paris
Tel. (0)1.40.51.60.80 - Fax (0)1.43.26.89.38 - M. Monnin

**Category** ★★★★ **Rooms** 34 and 17 duplex, with air-conditioning, bath, telephone, TV, hairdryer and minibar. **Price** Single and double 1750-1850F, suite 2700F, duplex 2700-3300F. **Meals** Breakfast 110F, snacks available. **Restaurants** Nearby: La Rôtisserie d'En Face, 2 rue Christine (Tel. 01 43 26 40 98) - Les Bookinistes, 53 quai des Grands Augustins (Tel. 01 43 25 45 94) - Jacques Cagna, 14 rue des Grands Augustins (gastronomic, Tel. 01 43 26 49 39) - Allard, 41 rue Saint-André-des-Arts (Tel. 01 43 26 48 23) - Le Petit Zinc, 11 rue Saint-Benoît (Tel. 01 47 34 01 13) - La Petite Cour, 8 rue Mabillon (Tel. 01 43 26 52 26). **Credit cards** All major. **Pets** Dogs allowed. **Parking** Free private parking. **Open** All year.

This hotel occupies a former Augustinian convent (entered through a paved courtyard/garden) but the interior has nothing monastic about it. On the contrary, it is decorated with a rainbow of warm colors, in both the panelled lounge - which has a handsome collection of portraits - and in the spacious, elegant bedrooms, some of which look onto the garden. Note also the duplexes, which are ideal for long stays. The breakfast room is in one of the most beautiful vaulted rooms of the cloister. The personnel is very attentive, discreet and efficient. Le Relais Christine has become a classic Paris *hôtel de charme.*

***How to get there*** *(Map 37 and 38): Métro Odéon, Saint-Michel, RER Cluny-Saint-Michel, Bus 24, 27, 58, 63, 70, 86, 87 and 96.*

## Hôtel Prince de Conti

8, rue Guénégaud
75006 Paris
Tel. (0)1.44.07.30.40 - Fax (0)1.44.07.36.34 - M. Roye

**Category** ★★★ **Rooms** 26 with air-conditioning, bath or shower and WC, telephone, satellite TV and minibar - elevator. **Price** Single 750-860F, double 920F, suite 1250F. **Meals** Breakfast 75F, served 7:00-10:30. **Restaurants** Nearby: Les Bookinistes, 53 quai des Gands Augustins (Tel. 01 43 25 45 94) - La Rôtisserie d'en Face, 2 rue Christine (Tel. 01 43 26 40 98) - Le Procope, 13 rue Ancienne-Comédie (Tel. 01 43 26 99 20) - Le Bourdonnais, 113 avenue de la Bourdonnais (gastronomic, Tel. 01 47 05 47 96). **Credit cards** All major. **Pets** Dogs allowed. **Parking** At 27 rue Mazarine. **Open** All year.

The Hôtel Prince de Conti is located in an 18th-Century building in the heart of artistic and literary Saint-Germain-des-Prés. The newly renovated hotel's bedrooms, we must note, are not large, but they are very beautiful. The choice of the various coordinated fabrics is superb and there are modern amenities like double windows, air-conditioning, and beautiful, well-equipped bathrooms. The duplex suites are also charming and are larger, with lounges and upstairs bedrooms. Note that there are two single rooms on the ground floor opening onto the courtyard. There is a refined, British atmosphere here, and the people are very friendly.

***How to get there*** *(Map 37 and 38): Métro Odéon,Saint-Michel, RER Saint-Michel, Bus 27, 58, 70, 96, 87 and 63.*

## Hôtel Le Régent

61, rue Dauphine
75006 Paris
Tel. (0)1.46.34.59.80 - Fax (0)1.40.51.05.07
Web: http://www.paris-hotel.com/leregent

**Category** ★★★ **Rooms** 25 with air-conditioning, bath or shower and WC, telephone, satellite TV, hairdryer and safe. **Price** Single and double 1000F. **Meals** Breakfast 55F. **Restaurants** Nearby: La Rôtisserie d'En Face, 2 rue Christine (Tel. 01 43 26 40 98) - La Petite Cour, 8 rue Mabillon (Tel. 01 43 26 52 26) - La Cafetière, 21 rue Mazarine (Tel. 01 46 33 76 90) - Lipp, 151 bld Saint-Germain (Brasserie, Tel. 01 45 48 53 91) - Yugaraj, 14 rue Dauphine (Indian, Tel. 01 43 26 44 91). **Credit cards** All major. **Pets** Dogs not allowed. **Parking** At 27, rue Mazarine. **Open** All year.

The Hôtel Le Régent has opened in a former 18th-century town house between the boulevard Saint-Germain and the Seine. In the lobby, a mirrored wall reflects the painted beams and old stones of the house. The lounge is classic, and the bedrooms, more fanciful, are light and very cheerful with their assorted printed fabrics. The harmonizing bathrooms have beautiful tiles. The owners of the hotel also own the legendary *Café des Deux Magots,* where you can conveniently have your meals.

***How to get there*** *(Map 37 and 38): Métro Odéon, RER Cluny-Saint-Michel, Bus 25, 27, 58, 63, 70, 86, 87 and 96.*

# Hôtel de Fleurie

32, rue Grégoire-de-Tours
75006 Paris
Tel. (0)1.43.29.59.81 - Fax (0)1.43.29.68.44 - Marolleau Family
E-mail: bonjour@hotel de fleurie.tm.fr - Web: http://www.hotel-de-fleurie.tm.fr

**Category** ★★★ **Rooms** 29 with air-conditioning, soundproofing, bath or shower and WC, telephone, satellite TV, hairdryer, safe and minibar. **Price** Single 680-880F, double 880-1200F. **Meals** Breakfast 50F (buffet), snacks available. **Restaurants** Nearby: La Rôtisserie d'En Face, 2 rue Christine (Tel. 01 43 26 40 98) - Le Bistrot d'à Côté, 10 bld Saint-Germain (Tel. 01 43 54 59 10) - La Bastide Odéon, 7 rue Corneille (Tel. 01 43 26 03 65) - L' Arrosée, 12 rue Guisarde (Tel. 01 43 54 66 59). **Credit cards** All major. **Pets** Dogs not allowed. **Parking** Opposite 21, rue de l'Ecole-de-Médecine. **Open** All year.

We were immediately attracted by the white façade of this hotel, which is highlighted on each level with a white niche and statue. There are the same light tones inside, with white stones or panelling and 18th-century-style caned chairs in the lounge and breakfast room. The bedrooms, which are not very spacious, are tastefully decorated in the same soft shades, and the bathrooms are comfortably equipped. (The rooms ending in 4 are the largest). The staff is efficient and welcoming.

***How to get there*** *(Map 37 and 38): Métro Odéon, RER Cluny-Saint-Michel and Luxembourg, Bus 58, 63, 70, 86, 87 and 96.*

# Hotel du Danube

58, rue Jacob
75006 Paris
Tel. (0)1.42.60.34.70 - Fax (0)1.42.60.81.18

**Category** ★★★ **Rooms** 40 with telephone, bath or shower, 30 with WC, hairdrayer and cable TV - elevator. **Price** Single and double 450-850F suite 1100F (2-4 pers.). **Meals** Breakfast 45F, served 7:00-10:30. **Restaurants** Nearby: Le Petit Zinc, 11 rue Saint-Benoît (Tel. 01 42 61 20 60) - Le Petit Saint-Benoît, 4 rue Saint Benoît (Tel. 01 42 60 27 92) - Lipp, 151 bld Saint-Germain (Brasserie, Tel. 01 45 48 53 91) - Marie et Fils, rue Mazarine (Tel. 01 43 26 69 49). **Credit cards** Amex, Visa, Eurocard and MasterCard. **Pets** Dogs allowed (+30F). **Facilities** Garden. **Parking** Saint-Germain-des-Prés. **Open** All year.

In the heart of Saint Germain des Prés, the Danube is one of our favorite hotels. It is a beautiful Napoléon III building with a discrete oak window behind which you can glimpse an inviting reception lounge with antique furniture, bronze lamps, and deep sofas, beautifully set off by the pink, green, and gray floral chintz wall fabrics and drapes. A charming patio with garden furniture and palm trees leads to the bedrooms, which overlook the courtyard or the street. On the courtyard, rooms are decorated with Japanese straw on the walls, antique and exotic furniture, decorative objects, and engravings. On the street side, the rooms are somewhat less quiet but they are more imaginatively decorated; huge, with light streaming in from two windows (except on the top floors), they are elegant and charming, with colorful wall fabrics, handsome mahogany pedestal tables, and lovely wing chairs forming a delightful corner sitting area. Breakfast is served in a room with pale, smooth, wood paneling on which small Chinese porcelains are displayed. The room opens onto a patio, where tables are set out in good weather. This is truly a hotel of great character and charm.

***How to get there*** *(Map 37 and 38): Métro: Châtelet, RER Châtelet-Les Halles - Bus: 21, 38, 47, 58, 67, 69, 70, 72, 75, 76, 81, 85.*

# Hôtel les Marronniers

21, rue Jacob
75006 Paris
Tel. (0)1.43.25.30.60 - Fax (0)1.40.46.83.56 - M. Henneveux

**Category** ★★★ **Rooms** 37 with air-conditioning, bath or shower, WC and TV. **Price** Single 540F, double 735-835F, suite 1060F. **Meals** Breakfast 45F, No restaurant. **Restaurants** Nearby: Le Chat Grippé, 87 rue Assas (Tel. 01 43 54 70 00) - Le Récamier , 4 rue Récamier (Tel. 01 45 48 86 58) - Le Rond de Serviette, 97 rue du Cherche-Midi (Tel. 01 45 44 01 02) - La Rôtisserie d'En Face, 2 rue Christine (Tel. 01 43 26 40 98) - La Petite Cour, 8 rue Mabillon (Tel. 01 43 26 52 26) - Le Petit Zinc, 11 rue Saint-Benoît (Tel. 01 47 34 01 13). **Credit cards** Visa, Eurocard and Mastercard. **Pets** Dogs not allowed. **Parking** Opposite 169, boulevard Saint-Germain and at place Saint-Sulpice. **Open** All year.

The Hôtel Les Marronniers is truly a delightful place, especially with its lovely garden. An ornate Napoleon III verandah houses the lounge and breakfast room. It is elegantly decorated with white cast-iron garden furniture, flowery carpets and graceful drapes in soft tones of pink and green. The bedrooms and bathrooms are more conventional. For a view of the garden, ask for a room on the *troisième étage* or higher, with a number ending in 1 or 2. The mansard rooms on the *cinquième* and *sixième étages* overlook the courtyard and have a pretty view of the rooftops. The staff is very pleasant.

***How to get there*** *(Map 37 and 38): Métro Saint-Germain-des-Prés, Bus 39, 48, 63, 68, 69, 86, 87 and 95.*

## Hôtel d'Angleterre

44, rue Jacob
75006 Paris
Tel. (0)1.42.60.34.72 -Fax (0)1.42.60.16.93 - Mme Blouin

**Category** ★★★ **Rooms** 23, 1 suite and 3 apartments with bath, WC, telephone and TV. **Price** Single and double 650-1200F, suite 1500, apart. 1500F. **Meals** Breakfast 52F with orange juice. **Restaurants** nearby: Le Muniche, 22 rue Guillaume Apollinaire (Tel. 01 47 34 01 06) - La Rôtisserie d'En Face, 2 rue Christine (Tel. 01 43 26 40 98) - Le Petit Zinc, 11 rue Saint-Benoît (Tel. 01 47 34 01 13) - La Bastide Odéon, 7 rue Corneille (Tel. 01 43 26 03 65). **Credit cards** All major. **Pets** Dogs not allowed. **Facilities** Patio. **Parking** Opposite 169, boulevard Saint-Germain. **Open** All year.

This beautiful house is historic, for it was here that the independence of the United States was recognized. It is now a marvelous hotel, with high-ceilinged rooms, ornate panelling, ancient beams and antique furniture. The bedrooms are all individually decorated. In one of the most remarkable rooms, a wall with exposed stonework provides a stunning backdrop for beautiful 17th-century furniture, including a canopy bed. Note that the largest rooms are those overlooking the garden. The service is excellent and the staff will make theatre and restaurant reservations and do everything to make your stay in Paris pleasant.

***How to get there*** *(Map 37 and 38): Métro Saint-Germain des Prés, Bus 39, 48, 63, 70, 86, 87, 95 and 96.*

## Hôtel Quartier Latin

9, rue des Ecoles
75005 Paris
Tel. (0)1.44.27.06.45 - Fax (0)1.43.25.36.70 - M. Roye

**Category** ★★★ **Rooms** 29 with air-conditioning, telephone, bath, WC, satellite TV and minibar; no smoking floor. **Price** Single and double 910F, 975F. **Meals** Breakfast (buffet) 75F. **Restaurants** Nearby: Moulin à vent-Chez Henri, 20 rue Fossés-Saint-Bernard (bistrot, Tel. 01 43 54 99 37) - Moissonnier, 28 rue Fossés-Saint-Bernard (bistrot, Tel. 01 43 29 87 65) - Mavrommatis, 42 rue Daubenton (Greece, Tel. 01 43 31 17 17) - La Timonerie, 35 quai de Tournelle (gastronomic, Tel. 01 43 25 44 42) - Chez Toutoune, 5 rue Pontoise (Tel. 0143.26.56.81). **Credit cards** All major. **Pets** Dogs not allowed. **Facilities** Secretariat. **Parking** Place Monge. **Open** All year.

Located in the Latin Quarter of university fame, Didier Gomez's hotel-library fits in logically with the quarter, offering a charming, intimate reception/living room in addition to the books. You will find shelves of them, which you can borrow, along with autographs, writers' correspondence, and an indispensable, pleasantly illuminated reading table for those who wish to browse through the books at the hotel. Dark, exotic woodwork highlights the garnet, brick, brown, and grey of the comfortable, velvet-upholstered sofas in the small lounge areas. In the breakfast room and on each floor as you leave the elevator, you will find a literary quotation. The bedrooms and baths are simple, elegant, and comfortable, with interesting furniture designed especially for the hotel. The staff is especially courteous, making the Quartier Latin a beautiful place to relive the time when Jean-Paul Sartre, Louis Aragon, Boris Vian, and Simone de Beauvoir made Saint-Germain-des-Prés known around the world.

***How to get there*** *(Map 37 and 38): Métro Cardinal Lemoine.*

1998

## Hôtel Duc de Saint-Simon

14, rue Saint-Simon
75007 Paris
Tel. (0)1.44.39.20.20 - Fax (0)1.45.48.68.25 - M. Lindquist

**Category** ★★★ **Rooms** 29 and 5 suites (some with air-conditioning) with telephone, bath or shower, WC, TV on request, safe - Elevator. **Price** Single and double 1050-1450F, suite 1825-1875F. **Meals** Breakfast 70F, served from 7:30. Snack available. **Restaurants** Nearby: La Ferme Saint-Simon, 6 rue Saint-Simon (Tel. 01 45 48 35 74) - Arpège, 84 rue de Varenne (gastronomic, Tel.01 45 51 47 33) - L'Œillade, 10 rue Saint-Simon (Tel. 01 42 22 01 60) Goyo, 44 rue du Bac (Tel. 01 45 44 73 73). **Credit cards** Amex, Visa, Eurocard and MasterCard. **Pets** Dogs not allowed. **Facilities** Bar, patio. **Parking** Garage de l'Abbaye: 30 boulevard Raspail. **Open** All year.

The Duc de Saint Simon is undoubtedly one of the most beautiful hotels in Paris. You enter through a handsome porch leading into a lovely paved courtyard with brilliant wisteria and garden tables. You will find an inviting interior, with the atmosphere of a magnificent old home. The cheerful colors of the patinated woodwork and the fabrics are set off by paintings and decorative objects throughout the hotel. The lounges, bedrooms, and suites (some of which have a terrace) are furnished with very tastefully chosen antiques. Whatever their size, the bedrooms are comfortable, and the gorgeous bathrooms are covered in gleaming Salernes tiles. The barrel-vaulted cellars are occupied by the breakfast room, the bar, and small, very pleasant lounges. This elegant hotel is amazingly quiet, when you consider that the busy Boulevard Saint Germain is just down the street.

***How to get there*** *(Map 37 and 38): Métro: rue du Bac - Bus: 63, 83, 84, 84, 68, 69, 94.*

## Hôtel des Saints-Pères

65, rue des Saints-Pères
75006 Paris
Tel. (0)1.45.44.50.00 - Fax (0)1.45.44.90.83 - Mme Samon
E-mail: espfran@micronet.fr

**Category** ★★★ **Rooms** and suites 39 with air-conditioning, soundproofing, bath or shower and WC, telephone, satellite TV, safe and minbar. **Price** Single and double 550-1650F, suite 1650F. **Meals** Breakfast 55F, snacks available. **Restaurants** Nearby: La Petite Chaise, 36 rue de Grenelle (Tel. 01 42 22 13 35) - Le Récamier, 4 rue Récamier (Tel. 01 45 48 86 58) - La Petite Cour, 8 rue Mabillon (Tel. 01 43 26 52 26) - Brasserie (of the hotel) Lutetia, 45 bd Raspail, (Tel. 01 49 54 46 76). **Credit cards** Amex, Visa, Eurocard and MasterCard. **Pets** Dogs not allowed. **Parking** Opposite 169, boulevard Saint-Germain. **Facilities** Bar. **Open** All year.

An atmosphere of elegance and comfort prevails in this lovely hotel. The spacious bedrooms and bathrooms have been tastefully decorated with simplicity and refinement. Worthy of special note is the *chambre à la fresque,* which has retained its lovely period ceiling. Most of the rooms overlook the hotel patio, and the ground-floor reception rooms lead out into this delightful courtyard full of flowers, where comfortable cane chairs are set in the shade in summer. The service is extremely efficient and professional.

***How to get there** (Map 37 and 38): Métro Saint-Germain-des-Prés, Bus 39, 48, 63, 70, 84, 86, 87 and 95.*

## Hôtel Montalembert

3, rue de Montalembert
75007 Paris
Tel. (0)1.45.49.68.68. - Fax (0)1.45.49.69.49
M. Bonnier

**Category** ★★★★ **Rooms** 51 and 5 suites with soundproofing, air-conditioning, bath and WC, telephone, TV, video, hairdryer, safe and minibar. **Price** Single 1695F, double 1960-2200F, suite 2750-3800F. **Meals** Breakfast 100F, served 6:30-10:30. **Restaurant** Service 12:00-22:30; à la carte. **Credit cards** All major. **Pets** Dogs allowed on request. **Parking** Montalembert opposite to the hotel. **Facilities** Bar. **Open** All year.

The new "grand hotels" have changed in style and the Montalembert is one of the most beautiful examples of them. There is no nostalgic reference to the past; instead, modernity is employed to beautiful advantage: Clients of the grand hotels will surely enjoy the Montalembert's discreet luxury. The sobriety of the lobby enhances the interior architecture. The decoration of the lounge, which is both chic and warm, is centered around a fireplace-library at guests' disposal. The bedrooms and their refined baths have every amenity, and the service and welcome are on a par with the hotel's class.

***How to get there*** *(Map 37 and 38): Métro rue-du-Bac, RER Gare d'Orsay, Bus 24, 63, 68, 69, 83, 84 and 95.*

## Hôtel Raspail-Montparnasse

203, boulevard Raspail
75014 Paris
Tel. (0)1.43.20.62.86 - Fax (0)1.43.20.50.79
M. and Mme Branche

**Category** ★★★ **Rooms** 36 and 2 suites with soundproofing, air-conditioning, bath or shower and WC, telephone, cable TV, minibar and safe. **Price** Single and double 520F, 740-890F, suite 1160F. **Meals** Breakfast 50F. **Restaurants** Nearby: Le Bistrot du Dôme, 1 rue Delambre (Fish and shellfish, Tel. 01 43 35 32 00) - Le Caméléon, 6 rue Chevreuse (Tel. 01 43 20 63 43) - Bouchon de la Grille, 6 rue L. Robert (Tel. 01 43 21 69 49) - L'Auberge de Venise, 10 rue Delambre (Fish and shellfish, Tel. 01 43 35 43 09) - Il Barone, 5 rue L. Robert (Italien, Tel. 01 43 20 87 14). **Credit cards** All major. **Pets** Dogs not allowed. **Parking** At 116, boulevard du Montparnasse. **Open** All year.

Shortly before he died, the famous decorator Serge Pons became fond of this Art Deco hotel. In 1992, he restored the noble, vast and light-filled lobby with its large rounded bay windows and its ceilings outlined with beautiful geometric moldings. He opened up the monumental stairway, brought back the lounge-bar, and restored the superb canopy of the façade. The bedrooms are tastefully decorated with grey tones enhanced with brighter fabrics on the walls. Each bedroom bears the name of, and is decorated with, a fine reproduction of a painting by an artist who lived in Montparnasse. Pierre Branche and his wife are always here, personally ensuring that guests are well taken care of.

***How to get there*** *(Map 37 and 38): Métro Porte Vavin, Raspail, RER Port-Royal. Bus 68, 82, 83 and 91.*

# Hôtel Sainte-Beuve

9, rue Sainte-Beuve
75006 Paris
Tel. (0)1.45.48.20.07 - Fax (0)1.45.48.67.52
Mme Compagnon

**Category** ★★★ **Rooms** 23 with air-conditioning, bath and WC, telephone, TV, safe and minibar. **Price** Single and double 700-1300F, suite 1500F, apart. 1700F. **Meals** Breakfast 80F, snacks available. **Restaurants** Nearby: Le Parc aux Cerfs, 50 rue Vavin (Tel. 01 43 54 87 83) - Dominique, 19 rue Bréa (russe, Tel. 01 43 27 08 80) - Valértie Tortu, 11 rue Grande-Chaumière (Tel. 01 46 34 07 58) - La Coupole, 102 bld Montparnasse (Brasserie, Tel. 01 43 20 14 20) - Le Dôme, 108 bld Montparnasse (Brasserie, Tel. 01 43 35 25 81) - Le Bistrot du Dôme, 1 rue Delambre (Fish and shellfish, Tel. 01 43 35 32 00) - Le Caméléon 6 rue Chevreuse (Tel. 01 43 20 63 43) - Le Chat Grippé, 87 rue d'Assas (Tel. 01 43 54 70 00). **Credit cards** Amex, Visa, Eurocard and MasterCard. **Pets** Dogs not allowed. **Facilities** Bar. **Parking** At 116, boulevard du Montparnasse. **Open** All year.

The Sainte-Beuve is the model of a charming hotel. For the decoration, David Hicks's Paris ateliers were called in and the spirit of the master is seen in the hotel's comfortable, simple luxury. A great refinement, created by the subtle harmony of colors and materials, distinguishes the neo-Gothic architecture of the lounge. Decoration apart, the amenities are modern and the bedrooms spacious and bright with delicate colors which are well coordinated with the print wall-fabrics and antique furniture. The breakfasts are delicious and the service impeccable in this beautiful hotel.

***How to get there*** *(Map 37 and 38): Métro Vavin and Notre-Dame-des-Champs, RER Port-Royal, Bus 68, 82, 83 and 91.*

## Hôtel le Saint Grégoire

43, rue de l'Abbé-Grégoire
75006 Paris
Tel. (0)1.45.48.23.23 - Fax (0)1.45.48.33.95 - Mme Agaud and M. Bouvier
Web: http://www.paris-hotel.com/saint-gregoire - E-mail: www.paris-hotel.com/saint-gregoire

**Category** ★★★ **Rooms** 20 with soundproofing, air-conditioning, bath or shower and WC, telephone, satellite TV and hairdryer. **Price** Double 690-990F, suites and rooms with terrasse 1390F. **Meals** Breakfast 60F, snacks available. **Restaurants** Nearby: La Marlotte, 55 rue du Cherche-Midi (Tel. 01 45 48 86 79) - Joséphine "Chez Dumonnet", 117 rue du Cherche-Midi (Tel. 01 45 48 52 40) - L'Epi Dupin, 11 rue Dupin (Tel. 01 42 22 64 56) - Petit Lutetia, 107 rue de Sèvres (Tel. 01 45 48 33 53) - La Cigale, 11 bis rue Chomel (Tel. 01 45 48 87 87). **Credit cards** All major. **Pets** Small dogs allowed. **Parking** At rue de l'Abbé-Grégoire, rue Boucicaut and rue de Rennes. **Open** All year.

The Saint Grégoire is located halfway between Montparnasse and Saint Germain in a small 18th-century building. The intimate decor beautifully blends a range of colors, subtly mixing shades of orange and mauve in the lounge, and pink and brown in the bedrooms. The rooms are well appointed with period furniture and very functional bathrooms. Some have terraces. You can have breakfast in a beautiful room with a vaulted ceiling, and you will enjoy a warm and pleasant welcome.

***How to get there*** *(Map 37 and 38): Métro Saint-Placide, Bus 48, 89, 94, 95 and 96.*

# L'Abbaye Saint-Germain

10, rue Cassette
75006 Paris
Tel. (0)1.45.44.38.11 - Fax (0)1.45.48.07.86 - M. Lafortune

**Category** ★★★ **Rooms** 42 and 4 suites (duplex with balcony) with air-conditioning, bath, WC, telephone and TV. **Price** Standard room 930-1000F, large room 1500-1600F, duplex or apartment 1860-1950F. **Meals** Breakfast incl., snacks available. **Restaurants** Nearby: La Petite Cour, 8 rue Mabillon (Tel. 01 43 26 52 26) - Le Chat Grippé, 87 rue Assas (Tel. 01 43 54 70 00) Brasserie (of the hotel) Lutetia, 45 bd Raspail (Tel. 01 49 54 46 76) - Le Bamboche, 15 rue de Babylone ( Tel. 01 45 49 14 40) - L'Epi Dupin, 11 rue Dupin (Tel. 01 42 22 64 56). **Credit cards** Amex, Visa, Eurocard and MasterCard. **Pets** Dogs not allowed. **Parking** At place Saint-Sulpice. **Facilities** Patio, bar. **Open** All year.

Recent renovations have made the Hotel de L'Abbaye even more charming. The ground floor now has a broader view onto the flowering patio, where breakfast is served and bar service is provided in good weather. The plush couches around the fireplace in the lounge are ideal for relaxing in cooler weather. All the rooms are very comfortable, refined, and homey; some are air-conditioned. Among the most recently renovated rooms are the largest ones, which are lovely garden-level duplexes with balconies.

***How to get there*** *(Map 37 and 38): Métro Saint-Sulpice and Sèvres-Babylone, Bus 48, 63, 70, 84, 87, 95 and 96.*

## Hôtel de l'Odéon

13, rue Saint-Sulpice
75006 Paris
Tel. (0)1.43.25.70.11 - Fax (0)1.43.29.97.34 - M. and Mme Pilfert

**Category** ★★★ **Rooms** 30 with soundproofing on the street, air-conditioning, bath or shower and WC, telephone, cable TV, hairdryer and safe - Elevator. **Price** Single 680F, double 780-970F, suite 1180-1250F. **Meals** Breakfast 55F, orange juice 20F, snacks available. **Restaurants** Nearby: L'Arrosée, 12 rue Guisarde (Tel. 01 43 54 66 59) - Au Grilladin, 13 rue de Mézières (Tel. 01 45 48 30 38) - La Bastide Odéon, 7 rue Corneille (Tel. 01 43 26 03 65). **Credit cards** All major. **Pets** Dogs allowed. **Parking** At place Saint-Sulpice and opposite 21, rue de l'Ecole-de-Médecine. **Facilities** Patio and bar. **Open** All year.

This handsome 16th-century building incorporates a skilful blend of decorative styles. Thus, in the ground-floor lounges, you find Louis-Philippe armchairs and pedestal tables beside a large church pew, and Persian rugs with a flowery English fitted carpet all creating a warm, intimate atmosphere. The bedrooms are individually decorated: Haute Epoque rooms with canopied beds and romantic rooms with large brass beds or Sicilian painted-iron twin beds. All have small writing or sitting areas. As this is the center of Paris, the rooms overlooking the street are well soundproofed, and the more exposed ones have air-conditioning for the summer. Lavish amounts of care and attention have been devoted to creating a stunning decor.

***How to get there*** *(Map 37 and 38): Métro Odéon, Saint-Sulpice and Saint-Germain-des-Prés, RER Cluny-Saint-Michel, Bus 58, 63, 70, 86, 87 and 96.*

# Le Clos Médicis

56, rue Monsieur-le-Prince
75006 Paris
Tel. (0)1.43.29.10.80 - Fax (0)1.43.54.26.90 - M. Beherec

**Category** ★★★ **Rooms** 38 with soundproofing, air-conditioning, bath, WC, telephone, cable TV, hairdryer, safe and minibar - 1 room for disabled persons - Elevator. **Price** Single 790F, double 890-990F, duplex 1206F. **Meals** Breakfast 60F, served 7:00-11:00. **Restaurants** nearby: Chez Maître Paul, 12 rue Monsieur-le-Prince (Tel. 01 43 54 74 59) - Chez Marie, 25 rue Servandoni (Tel. 01 46 33 12 00) - Au Bon Saint-Pourçain, 10 bis rue Servandoni (Tel. 01 43 54 93 63) - Caves Bailly, 174 rue Saint-Jacques (lunchtime). **Credit cards** All major. **Pets** Dogs allowed (+60F). **Parking** At rue Soufflet. **Open** All year.

The Clos Médicis, like many hotels in this quarter, is named after the Medici Palace which was built in the Luxembourg Gardens for Marie de Medicis. At Number 54 next door, Blaise Pascal wrote a large part of *Les Provinciales* and *Les Pensées.* It has just been entirely renovated, with a beautiful and inviting reception area brightened by a cheerful fireplace in winter. With the first fine days of spring, breakfasts are served in the leafy courtyard which is just off the breakfast room. The bedrooms are generally spacious, and very comfortable, with modern conveniences and well-designed bathrooms; double windows and air-conditioning ensure that they are quiet. The walls are a pretty yellow, and the draperies and bedspreads are coordinated with lovely prints. The staff is very courteous.

***How to get there*** *(Map 37 and 38): Métro Odéon, RER Luxembourg, Bus 21, 27, 38, 58, 82, 84, 85 and 89.*

## Hôtel Saint-Dominique

62, rue Saint-Dominique
75007 Paris
Tel. (0)1.47.05.51.44 - Fax (0)1.47.05.81.28 - Mme Petit and M. Tible

**Category** ★★ **Rooms** 34 with bath or shower and WC, telephone, TV, hairdryer, safe and minibar. **Price** Single and double 400-520F, executive 610-710F. **Meals** Breakfast 40F with orange juice and cheese. **Restaurants** Nearby: Thoumieux, 79 rue Saint-Dominique (Tel. 01 47 05 49 75) - La Fontaine de Mars, 129 rue Saint-Dominique (Tel. 01 47 05 46 44) - Du Côté 7eme, 29 rue Surcouf (Tel. 01 47 05 81 65) - Beato, 8 rue Malar (Italien, Tel. 01 47 05 94 27). **Credit cards** All major. **Pets** Dogs allowed. **Parking** At Esplanade des Invalides. **Open** All year.

Its convenient location and reasonable prices make the Saint-Dominique a very popular hotel. There is English-style decor in the lobby, where the pale pine furniture blends with the soft colors of the walls and the pink-beige fabrics. A charming country style has been chosen for the bedrooms, which have well equipped bathrooms. Some rooms are larger, with sitting areas, and most overlook patios full of flowers in summer. Those on the street are soundproofed. This is a lovely place to stay.

***How to get there*** *(Map 37 and 38): Métro Latour-Maubourg and Invalides, RER Pont de l'Alma. Terminal Invalides, Bus 28, 42, 49, 69, 80 and 92.*

## Hôtel de Tourville

16, av. de Tourville
75007 Paris
Tel. (0)1.47.05.62.62 - Fax (0)1.47.05.43.90
M. Bouvier - Mme Agaud - Mlle Piel

**Category** ★★★★ **Rooms** 30 with air-conditioning, bath or shower and WC, telephone, satellite TV, hairdryer and minibar. **Price** Single and double 590-1090F, suite 1390-1690F. **Meals** Breakfast 60F. **Restaurants** Nearby: Paul Minchelli, 54 bd La Tour Maubourg (Fish, shellfish and gastronomic, Tel. 01 47 05 89 96) - Le Divellec, 107 rue de l'Université (Fish, shellfish and gastronomic, Tel. 01 45 51 91 96) - Auberge Bressane, 16 avenue La Motte-Piquet (Tel. 01 47 05 98 37) - Le Maupertu, 94 bd La Tour Maubourg (Tel. 01 45 51 37 96) - D'Chez Eux, 2 av. Lowendal (Tel. 01 47 05 52 55) - Le P'tit Troquet, 28 rue Exposition (Tel. 01 47 05 80 39) - Gildo, 153 rue de grenelle (Italien, Tel. 01 45 51 54 12). **Credit cards** All major. **Pets** Dogs allowed (+70F). **Parking** At place de l'Ecole Militaire. **Open** All year.

The Hôtel de Tourville was very recently opened in a beautiful building between the dome of the Invalides and the Rodin Museum. There is an intimate atmosphere in the elegant lounge which was decorated by the David Hicks Atelier. The muted lighting and colors lend softness also to the bedrooms, which are personalized with antique furniture and paintings. The bathrooms are immaculate, with beautiful tiles and veined grey marble, and some open onto pleasant private terraces. This is also a hotel where you will enjoy the charm and quiet of this part of the Left Bank, not to mention the very attractive prices.

***How to get there*** *(Map 37 and 38): Métro Ecole-Militaire. Terminal Invalides, Bus 28, 82, 92 and 95.*

# Hotel Le Parc

55/57, rue Raymond Poincaré
75016 Paris
Tel. (0)1.44.05.66.66 - Fax (0)1.44.05.66 00 - M. Delahaye

**Category** ★★★★ **Rooms** 113, 14 suites and 3 duplex with air-conditioning, telephone, bath (1 with whirlpool), hairdryer, WC, satellite TV, safe - Elevator -4 for disabled persons. **Price** Standards 1990F, supérieures 2350F, junior-suite 2950F. **Meals** Breakfast 135F, served at any time. **Restaurant** "Le Relais du Parc" - Service 12:30-14:30, 19:30-22:15. **Credit cards** All major. **Pets** Dogs allowed. **Facilities** Laundry service, room-service, bar and fitness center. **Parking** Rue Raymond Poincaré (125F). **Open** All year.

Composed of five Anglo-Norman-style buildings (one of which was the atelier of Bagues, the decorator of the *Normandie* ocean liner), Le Parc is truly a grand hôtel. It was designed in the style of an English manor house by the famous English decorator Nina Campbell. The beautiful Edwardian decor includes figured carpets, quilted chintzes, four-poster beds, antique engravings, and paintings. The only exception is a handsome modern sculpture by Arman at the reception desk, who also designed the tables and sconces at the bar. The bedrooms are all magnificent and very comfortable. Alain Ducasse, the master himself, supervises the hotel's restaurant, Le Relais du Parc. Meals are served either on the Indo-English colonial-style veranda or on the terrace in a beautiful courtyard with trees. The delicious breakfast is also supervised by Alain Ducasse. The hotel is run by a distinguished, efficient manager, who is assisted by a charming and attentive staff–another plus for the hotel. Don't forget that only a door separates you from what is considered the temple of French cuisine. But be quick: Ducasse says he's retiring soon.

***How to get there*** *(Map 37 and 38): Métro: Vavin and Notre-Dame-des-Champs, RER Port-Royal - Bus: 68, 82, 83 et 91.*

1998

## Hôtel d'Argentine

1/3, rue d'Argentine
75016 Paris
Tel. (0)1.45.02.76.76 - Fax (0)1.45.02.76.00 - M. Courtade

**Category** ★★★★ **Rooms** 40 with soundproofed, telephone, bath or shower, WC, hairdryer, cable TV - Elevator - 1 for disabled persons. **Price** 870F, 930F. **Meals** Breakfast (buffet) 75F, served 7:00-10:30. **Restaurants** Nearby: Stella, 133 av. V. Hugo (Tel. 01 47 27 60 54) - Prunier, 16 av. V. Hugo (Fish, Tel.01 441735 85) - Relais du Parc, 55 av. R. Poincaré (Tel.01 44 05 66 10) - Conti, 72 rue Lauriston (Tel.01 47 27 74 67). **Credit cards** Amex, Visa, Eurocard and MasterCard. **Pets** Dogs allowed. **Facilities** Laundry service, room-service, bar. **Parking** Foch: avenue Foch. **Open** All year.

The Hôtel d'Argentine is on a small, quiet street near the Etoile. It were named after the country whose fashionable set traditionally frequented this neighborhood in the 19th century. The hotel was completely renovated by the architect Frédéric Méchiche, who designed it in the manner of a private home. The lobby is neoclassical-style, with fluted columns, Greek staff, faux marble, and Empire mahogany furniture upholstered with Jouy fabric. In the adjacent bar, where the original rotunda ceiling and cornices have been retained, you will 19th-century chairs, allegorical engravings, a thick carpet, and complimentary tea makings. The bedrooms are charming, with finely striped wall fabrics, coordinated checked bedspreads, and calico curtains. The lovely, comfortable bathrooms are done in dark-gray and putty-colored marble. It's pleasant to enjoy a leisurely breakfast in a room (with areas for smokers and non-smokers) that is decorated in Consulate style: walls elegantly painted with large, Wedgewood-blue stripes; antique-style, with white pilasters, and marble medallions. The service is four-star.

***How to get there*** *(Map 37 and 38): Métro: Argentine, Etoile-Charles de Gaulle, RER Etoile-Charles de Gaulle - Bus: 22, 30, 31, 42, 52, 73, 92.*

# Hôtel de Banville

166, boulevard Berthier
75017 Paris
Tel. (0)1.42.67.70.16 - Fax (0)1.44.40.42.77 - Mlle Lambert

**Category** ★★★ **Rooms** 39 with air-conditioning, telephone, bath or shower, WC, hairdayer, satellite TV and safe - Elevator. **Price** Single and double 635F, 760F. **Meals** Breakfast 50-80F, served unti 6:00. Snacks available. **Restaurants** Nearby: Pétrus, 12 place Maréchal Juin (fish and shellfish, Tel.01 43 80 15 95) - Caves Petrissans, 30 bis avenue Niel (bistrot, Tel. 01 42 27 83 84) - La Table de Pierre 116 boulevard Péreire (Tel. 01 43 80 88 68). **Credit cards** Amex, Visa, Eurocard and MasterCard. **Pets** Dogs allowed. **Facilities** Room-service - Bar (Piano-bar Wednesday evening). **Parking** 210 rue de Courcelles. **Open** All year.

The Banville is an excellent hotel located in the dynamic quarter of the Porte Maillot centering around the Palais des Congrès convention center near the Etoile. It occupies a small 1930s building in the quiet, shady Boulevard Berthier. An elegant hotel, the Banville is very smoothly run by its charming owner who wouldn't receive her own friends with greater hospitality. In the lounge, a hushed ambiance is created by lovely furniture, old paintings, and beautiful Rubelli fabrics. The bedrooms, spacious and bright, are decorated with similar taste and offer all modern comforts. The breakfast also is special, offering a choice of continental, dietetic, or copious fare, served in the romantic veranda-dining room.

***How to get there*** *(Map 37 and 38): Métro: Péreire and Porte-de-Champerret - RER C: Péreire - Bus: 84, 92, 93, PC and Bus for Roissy: Porte-Maillot.*

## Hôtel Square

3, rue de Boulainvilliers
75016 Paris
Tel. (0)1.44.14.91.90 - Fax (0)1.44.14.91.99 - M. Derderian

**Category** ★★★★ **Rooms** 22 with air conditioning, telephone and fax, bath, cable TV, minibar and safe - Elevator - 1 for disabled persons. **Price** Standard 1350F, 1550F, 1700F; luxe 1950F; suite 2250-2500F. **Meals** Breakfast 60-90 F, served 7:00-11:00. **Restaurant** Zebra Square; menus 125-300F, also à la carte. **Credit cards** All major. **Pets** Dogs not allowed. **Facilities** Lounge. **Garage** In the hotel. **Open** All year.

Patrick Derderian is not someone to limit himself to a single project but it took seven years to complete the most ambitious undertaking of his career: building a hotel from scratch. The inauguration of the Zébra Square Restaurant preceded that of the hotel, and we're betting that his hotel will enjoy the same success. As we went inside, we felt we were entering an ocean liner, with gangways on three floors leading to the bedrooms. Paintings by Vialat are colorful complements to the large carpets by Hilton McConnico. The bedrooms are similarly modern with ethnic touches, the bedcovers by Pierre Bonnefille harmonizing with the grey, brick, and anisette-green striped wall fabrics and the dark-wood end tables. The bathrooms are also magnificent, with Carrara marble washbasins and showers. Several details say much of the hotel's elegance and comfortable amenities: mohair blankets from Scotland, private telephone and fax numbers, the accent on spaciousness in all the rooms and the rotunda-shaped suites, which are larger still and overlook the trees on the square or the Seine, in the case of those on the upper floors. The hotel has been beautifully designed in the latest fashion, as is each new project of its dynamic owner.

***How to get there*** *(Map 37 and 38): Métro: Passy (10 minutes), RER Radio France - Bus: 22, 52, 70, 72.*

## Hôtel Galileo

54, rue Galilée
75008 Paris
Tel. (0)1.47.20.66.06. - Fax (0)1.47.20.67.17 - M. Buffat

**Category** ★★★ **Rooms** 27 with air-conditioning, bath and WC, telephone, safe, hairdryer, cable TV and minibar - Elevator - 2 rooms for disabled persons. **Price** Single and double 800-950F. **Meals** Breakfast 50F. **Restaurants** Nearby: Marius et Jeanette, 4 av. Georges-V (Fish, shellfish, Tel. 01 47 23 41 88) - Bistro de Marius, 6 av. George-V (Fish, shellfish, Tel. 01 40 70 11 76) - Brasserie de l'Alma, 5 place de l'Alma (Tel. 01 47 23 47 61) - Chez André, 12 rue Marbeuf (Tel. 01 47 20 59 27) - La Maison du Caviar, 21 rue Q.-Beauchard (Tel. 01 47 23 53 43) - Le Fouquets, 99 av. des Champs-Elysées (Tel. 01 47 23 70 60). **Credit cards** Amex, Visa, Eurocard and MasterCard. **Pets** Dogs not allowed. **Parking** Georges V (70-80F). **Open** All year.

Well located between the Champs Elysées and the Avenue Georges V, the Galiléo is truly a *hôtel de charme.* Refinement and modernity are in evidence throughout, from the elegant lounge with its 18th-century fireplace and Aubusson tapestry to the breakfast room with its lovely soft colors and lighting. The elegant bedrooms also have very modern amenities with air-conditioning, good reading lamps, an office area with fax plug and extremely comfortable bathrooms with a radio. The most spacious are the two ground-floor rooms and the two on the *cinquième étage* with a lovely verandah, which are our favorites.

***How to get there*** *(Map 37 and 38): Métro and RER Charles-de-Gaulle-Etoile and Georges V, Bus 22, 30, 31, 52 and 73.*

1998

## Hôtel Elysées Mermoz

30, rue Jean-Mermoz
75008 Paris
Tel. (0)1.42.25.75.30 - Fax (0)1.45.62.87.10 - M. Breuil

**Category** ★★★ **Rooms** 26 with soundproofed, air-conditioning, telephone, bath, WC, hairdryer, TV, safe - Elevator - 1 for disabled persons. **Price** Single and double 720F, 780-890F, suite (1-4 pers.) 1190F. **Meals** Breakfast 47F, served 7:00-10:30. **Restaurants** Nearby: Le Meurisier, 8 rue Rabelais - Bœuf sur le Toit, 34 rue du Colisée (Brasserie, Tel. 01 43 59 83 80) - Yvan, 1 bis rue Jean-Mermoz (Tel. 01 43 59 18 40) - L'Avenue, 41 avenue Montaigne (Tel. 01 40 70 14 91). **Credit cards** All major. **Pets** Small dogs allowed. **Facilities** Laundry service. **Parking** Rond-Point des-Champs-Elysées, rue Rabelais. **Open** All year.

The Hôtel Elysées Mermoz, which has just been entirely redone, is between the Rond Point des Champs-Elysées and the Rue du Faubourg Saint-Honoré, on a lively street lined with ministries, corporate headquarters, restaurants, and the famous Arcurial art gallery and bookshop. The entrance and veranda are very charming, with a skylight, rattan furniture, and a colorful patchwork quilt in the reception area. The bedrooms are decorated in bright, sunny colors, with a predominance of yellow and blue, or yellow and red; rooms on the courtyard are brightened with lovely, Provençal-yellow walls: a ray of sunshine in a gray Paris day. There are handsome modern amenities, and the bathrooms, some of which are paneled, have beautiful white tiles with blue borders, and even heated towel racks. The bedrooms are fairly large, and the suites can accommodate four people. Noise is no problem, regardless of the season: All the bedrooms are soundproofed and air-conditioned.

***How to get there*** *(Map 37 and 38): Métro: Franklin-Rossvelt, Saint-Philippe-du-Roule - Bus: 28, 32, 49, 43, 46, 49, 52, 73, 83, 93.*

## Hôtel Queen Mary

9, rue Greffulhe
75008 Paris
Tel. (0)1.42.66.40.50 - Fax (0)1.42.66.94.92 - M. Byrne - M. Tarron

**Category** ★★★ **Rooms** 36 with soundproofing, air-conditioning, bath and WC, telephone, cable TV, hairdryer, safe (extra charge) and minibar. **Price** Single 755F, double 875-935F, suite 1300F. **Meals** Breakfast 75F. **Restaurants** Nearby: Caviar-kaspia, 17 place de la Madeleine (Tel. 01 42 65 33 32) - Brasserie Mollard, 6 rue Isly (Tel. 01 45 22 38 66) - Pub Saint-Lazare, 10 rue Rome (Tel. 01 42 93 15 27) - Chez Tante Louise, 41 rue Boissy-d'Anglas (Tel. 01 42 65 06 85). **Credit cards** Amex, Visa, Eurocard and MasterCard. **Pets** Dogs allowed. **Parking** At place de la Madeleine. **Open** All year.

Sheltered from the traffic in this busy quarter of large department stores, the Queen Mary has opened following a successful renovation. The light-filled lounge is handsomely decorated with 18th-century French furniture. The colors chosen for the bedrooms are well coordinated with the mahogany furniture, and beautiful striped fabrics are used for the walls, the chairs and the bedspreads. There are, of course, the usual modern conveniences and very thoughtful details like the trouser press and the carafe of sherry awaiting your arrival. The efficient staff will help you make the most of your vacation or business trip.

***How to get there*** *(Map 37 and 38): Métro Madeleine and Havre-Caumartin, Opéra, RER Auber, Bus 22, 24, 28, 32, 48, 80, 84 and 94.*

## Hôtel Beau Manoir

6, rue de l'Arcade
75008 Paris
Tel. (0)1.42.66.03.07 - Fax (0)1.42.68.03.00
Mme Teil and Mme Duhommet

**Category** ★★★★ **Rooms** 32 with soundproofing, air-conditioning, bath and WC, telephone, cable TV, hairdryer, safe and minibar. **Price** Single and double 1100-1300F, suite 1600F. **Meals** Breakfast (buffet) incl. **Restaurants** Nearby: Chez Tante Louise, 41 rue Boissy-d'Anglas (Tel. 01 42 65 06 85) - Lucas Carton, 9 place de la Madeleine (Tel. 01 42 65 22 90), Le Soufflé, 36 rue du Mont Thabor (Tel. 01 42 60 27 19). **Credit cards** All major. **Pets** Dogs allowed. **Parking** At place de la Madeleine, rue Chauveau-Lagarde. **Open** All year.

The owners have put their knowhow to good use here and created a lovely small *hôtel de prestige*. In the lounge, antique-style panelling is a beautiful complement to an 18th-century Aubusson tapestry. Damask-covered sofas and armchairs also contribute to the atmosphere, which is both luxurious and intimate. The decoration in the bedrooms includes a tasteful combination of coordinated prints. The rooms are spacious and most have corner sitting areas. (We prefer the rooms ending in 1). Note that the family Teil manage also the *Hôtel du Lido* (Tel. 01.42.66.27.37), near the *Beau Manoir*; on the *Rive Gauche* the *Left Bank Hôtel Saint-Germain* (Tel. 01.43.54.01.70) and the *Manoir Saint-Germain-des-Prés* (Tel. 01.42.22.21.65).

***How to get there*** *(Map 37 and 38): Métro Madeleine, RER Auber, Bus 24, 42, 43, 52, 84 and 94.*

# Hôtel de l'Arcade

9, rue de l'Arcade
75008 Paris
Tel. (0)1.53.30.60.00 - Fax (0)1.40.07.03.07

**Category** ★★★ **Rooms** 41 with soundproofed, air-conditioning, telephone, bath, WC, hairdryer, satellite TV, minibar, safe - Elevator. **Price** Single and double 780-880F, 960F, 3 pers. and duplex 1150F. **Meals** Breakfast (buffet) 55F, served 7:00-10:30. **Restaurants** Nearby: Hôtel Bedford, 17 de la rue de l'Arcade (same street) - Chez Tante Louise, 41 rue Boissy-d'Anglas (Tel.01 42650685) - Bistrot du Sommelier, 97 bld.Haussmann (Tel. 01 42 65 24 85) - Ag. Le Poête, 27 rue Pasquier (Tel.01 47 42 00 64). **Credit cards** All major. **Pets** Small dogs allowed. **Facilities** Laundry service. **Parking** Place de la Madeleine. **Open** All year.

Following a long closure and complete renovation, the Hôtel de l'Arcade has just reopened, and it is very beautiful. The reception area is an open, airy space, where benches, period armchairs, and small sofas create pleasant places to relax. The soft colors–pink-beige armchairs, pale green carpet, blue-gray cerused wall paneling–contribute to the serene atmosphere. The adjacent breakfast room is similarly decorated, and the bedrooms are just as elegant, differing only in size. The pleasant rooms for two and three people are the most spacious, and the duplexes, with the bed in a loft, are lovely. The marble bathrooms are comfortable and very well equipped: They even have a telephone, and in some rooms, there is a small window between the bath and the bedroom. This restful hotel is just a few steps off the Place de la Madeleine.

***How to get there*** *(Map 37 and 38): Métro Madeleine, RER Auber - Bus: 24, 42, 43, 52, 84 and 94.*

# Hôtel Mansart

5, rue des Capucines
75001 Paris
Tel. (0)1.42.61.50.28 - Fax (0)1.49.27.97.44 - M. Dupain
E-mail: espfran@micronet.fr

**Category** ★★★ **Rooms** 57 (air-conditioning in some rooms) with bath and WC, telephone, satellite TV, safe and minibar - Elevator. **Price** Single 550-980F, double 700-980F, suite 1250-1600F. **Meals** Breakfast 55F, snacks available. **Restaurants** Nearby: Carré des Feuillants, 14 rue de Castiglione (gastronomic, Tel. 01 42 86 82 82) - Le Soufflé, 36 rue du Mont-Thabor (Tel. 01 42 60 27 19) - L'Escure 7 rue Mondovi (Tel. 01 42 60 18 91) - La Bonne Fourchette, 320 rue Saint-Honoré (Tel. 01 42 60 45 27) - A la Grille saint-Honoré, 15 place du Marché-Saint-Honoré (Tel. 01 42 61 00 93) - Gaya Rive Droirte, 17 rue Duphot (Fish, shellfisc, Tel. 01 42 60 04 03). **Credit cards** Amex, Visa, Eurocard and MasterCard. **Pets** Dogs not allowed. **Parking** At place Vendôme. **Open** All year.

On the corner of the Place Vendôme and the Rue des Capucines, the Hôtel Mansart has an idyllic location. The refurbishment was conceived in homage to Louis XIV's architect, Jules Mansart. Thus, you will find a tastefully baroque décor in the lobby, with mauve damask-covered 18th-century-style furniture and large paintings inspired by the famous formal gardens of Le Nôtre, Mansart's contemporary. The bold decorative scheme has been carried out tastefully. The spacious bedrooms are marvelously comfortable and decorated in pretty shades of coordinated colors. If you would like to be a neighbor of the Ritz and look out over the Place Vendôme, ask for the Mansart Room, which is superb.

***How to get there*** *(Map 37 and 38): Métro Opéra, Madeleine, Concorde, Tuileries, RER Auber-Opéra, Bus 21, 27, 52, 68, 72, 81 and 95.*

1998

## Hôtel Costes

239, rue Saint-Honoré
75001 Paris
Tel. (0)1.42.44.50.00 - Fax (0)1.42.44.50.01 - M. Costes

**Category** ★★★★ **Rooms** 85 with air-conditioning, telephone and fax, bath, WC, TV, minibar, safe - Elevator - 3 for disabled persons. **Price** Single and double 1750F, 2000-2250F, suite 2750-3750F. **Meals** Breakfast 130F. **Restaurant** Open all year. Carte. **Credit cards** All major. **Pets** Dogs allowed. **Facilities** Sauna, swimming pool, health center and bar. **Parking** Place Vendôme. **Open** All year.

On the Rue Saint Honoré near the Place Vendôme, you'll notice only the name Costes over a plain façade and a discreet entrance. Once inside, you'll find a totally different atmosphere. A corridor leads to the reception and the lounges, opening onto a large Italianate courtyard and terraces decorated with antique-style statues. Such luminosity is in great contrast with the intimate, theatrical ambiance of the small lounges surrounding the patio. It's a veritable *La Traviata* decor: fringed and braided armchairs in black pearwood arranged around floor lamps heavy with pearls and pendants, an imposing ceramic fireplace, all creating intimate corners for conversation or reading. The turn-of-the-century decor is carried through to the jewelbox bedrooms of red brocade. The details are highly elegant: a subtle combination of colors in the quilted bedspreads, beautiful monogrammed bath towels, bits and pieces of old furniture put to charming use. The suites are even more luxurious and more baroque still. Following the Costes brothers' Café Beaubourg and Café Marly, decorated by Christian de Portzamparc and Philippe Starck respectively, the Hôtel Costes, designed by Jacques Garcia, is the latest artistic happening in Paris created by the enterprising partners.

***How to get there*** *(Map 38): Métro Opéra, Madeleine, Concorde, Tuileries, RER Auber-Opéra. Bus 21, 27 52, 68, 81, 95.*

## Hôtel Lafayette

49/51, Rue Lafayette
75009 Paris
Tel. (0)1.42.85.05.44 - Fax (0)1.49.95.06.60 - Mme Dessors

**Category** ★★★ **Rooms** 103, (*premier étage* no-smoking, 28 with air-conditioning) with telephone, bath or shower, WC, hairdryer, satellite TV, minibar, safe - Elevator - 2 for disabled persons. **Price** Single and double 875F, 940F, suite 1650F. Snack available. **Meals** Breakfast (buffet) 75F, served 6:30-10:30. **Restaurants** Nearby: Bistro de Gala, 45 rue du Fg.Montmartre (Tel.01 40 22 90 50) - Au Petit Riche, 25 rue Le Peletier (Tel. 01 47 70 68 68) - La table d'Anvers, 2 place d'Anvers (gastronomic, Tel. 01 48 78 35 21) - Grand Café Capucines, 4 bld. des Capucines (Brasserie, Tel. 01 40 07 30 20) - Table de Linh, 3 rue de Châteaudun (Chinese). **Credit cards** All major. **Pets** Small dogs allowed. **Facilities** Laundry service. **Parking** Rue Buffault. **Open** All year.

Near the Opera, the *grands boulevards*, many theaters, music halls, and large department stores, the Libertel Lafayette has just been entirely transformed into a hotel of character and charm. The renovation carried out by Anne-Marie de Ganay was aimed at recreating the elegance and comfort that characterize many large, English country houses. On the façade, two windows with cobalt-blue lacquered molding frame the entrance with its large copper lanterns. The elegant reception area, which extends into the bar and a lounge/smoking room beneath a skylight in clever *trompe-l'oeil,* is light, airy, and further brightened by a beige stone floor, cerused furniture, walls in medallion-print linen fabric, beige-and-white checked chairs, and mahogany furniture. The bedrooms are tastefully done in blue, green, or beige Jouy fabric, which lends them a soft, country feel. Many thoughtful details, including coffee and tea makings furilities in the rooms, add to the pleasure of staying here.

***How to get there** (Map 37 and 38): Métro Peletier-Cadet - Bus: 26, 42, 49, 74.*

## Hôtel de la Place du Louvre

21, rue des Prêtres Saint-Germain-l'Auxerrois
75001 Paris
Tel. (0)1.42.33.78.68 - Fax (0)1.42.33.09.95 - M. Chevalier
E-mail: espfran@micronet.fr

**Category** ★★★ **Rooms** 20 with bath and WC, telephone, satellite TV, safe and hairdryer - Elevator. **Price** Single 510-700F, double 700-790F, duplex 830F. **Meals** Breakfast 40-50F. **Restaurants** Nearby: Café Marly, parvis du musée du Louvre (Tel. 01 49 26 066 60) - Aux Bons Crus, 7 rue des Petits-Champs (lunchtime) - A Priori Thé, 35 galerie Vivienne (lunchtime) - Juvénile's, 47 rue Richelieu (Tel. 01 42 97 46 49) - Willi's, 13 rue des Petits-Champs (Tel. 01 42 61 05 09 - L'Epi d'or, 27 rue Jean-Jacques Rousseau - Brin de Zinc et Madame, 50 rue Montorgueil (Tel. 01 42 21 10 80) - Chez Pierrot, 18 rue E.-Marcel (Tel. 01 45 08 17 64) - Rendez-Vous-des-Camionneurs, 72 quai des Orfèvres (Tel. 01 43 54 88 74) - Taverne Henri IV, 13 rue du Pont-Neuf (lunchtime). **Credit cards** All major. **Pets** Dogs allowed. **Parking** At Place du Louvre, Saint-Germain-l'Auxerrois. **Facilities** Bar. **Open** All year.

A room with a view awaits you at this hotel. And what a view! You will look out over the famous Louvre itself. A few beautiful vestiges of this ancient building have been preserved and successfully incorporated with modern decorative elements. The lounge and bar are located beneath a glass roof, while breakfast is served in a beautiful vaulted cellar called the *Salle des Mousquetaires,* which once communicated with the Louvre. The bright, sunny bedrooms have up-to-date amenities, and each is named after a painter. The service is efficient.

***How to get there** (Map 37 and 38): Métro Louvre-Rivoli and Pont-Neuf, RER Châtelet-les-Halles, Bus 21, 24, 27, 67, 69, 74, 76, 81 and 85.*

# Hôtel Britannique

20, avenue Victoria
75001 Paris
Tel. (0)1.42.33.74.59 - Fax (0)1.42.33.82.65 - M.Danjou
E-mail: mailbox@hotel-britannique.fr - Web: http://www.hotel-britannique.fr

**Category** ★★★ **Rooms** 40 with soundproofed, telephone, bath or shower, WC, hairdryer, satellite TV, minibar, safe - Elevator. **Price** Single and double 527-659F, 631-898F. **Meals** Breakfast (buffet) 55F, served 7:00-10:30. **Restaurants** Nearby: Le Grizzli, 7 rue Saint-Martin (Tel.01 48 87 77 56) - Le Vieux Bistro, 14 rue du Cloître Notre-Dame (Tel. 01 43 54 18 95) - Le Coude Fou, 12 rue du Bourg-Tibourg (Tel. 01 42 77 15 16) - La Poule au Pot, 9 rue Vauvilliers (Tel.01 42 36 32 96). **Credit cards** All major. **Pets** Dogs not allowed. **Facilities** Laundry service and bar. **Parking** Hôtel de Ville and quai de Gesvres. **Open** All year.

A plaque at the entrance to the Hotel Britannique informs us that it was built in 1840 and has been run to this day by a family of English origin: It has always been a favorite hotel with Anglo-Saxon tourists. The lounge downstairs is faithful to this British influence, with leather chesterfields and Turner reproductions. The cozy, elegant ambience is heightened by figured carpets in the corridors, and bouquets of fresh flowers throughout the hotel. The bedrooms are of varying sizes, from singles and small doubles to more spacious rooms on the courtyard. But all are pleasant, comfortable, bright, and well decorated. The Hôtel Britannique is next door to the *Cèdre Rouge,* one of the most famous garden stores in Paris, and near many other flower and horticultural shops off the Place du Châtelet and the Quai de la Messagerie. Scattered among the flower shops on the quay are other shops selling billy goats, roosters, rabbits, turtles, rods and reels–you name it. Tourists and Parisians alike love it.

***How to get there** (Map 37 and 38): Metro Chatelet, RER Châtelet-Les Halle -*

## Hôtel Saint-Merry

14, rue de la Verrerie
75004 Paris
Tel. (0)1.42.78.14.15 - Fax (0)1.40.29.06.82 - M. Crabbe

**Category** ★★★ **Rooms** 11 and 1 suite with telephone, bath or shower, 9 with WC. **Price** 400-1100F, suite 1800F (2 pers.), 2200F (4 pers.). **Meals** Breakfast 50F, served 7:30-11:00. **Restaurants** Nearby: Au Chien qui Fume (Tel. 01 42 36 07 42) - Benoît, 20 rue Saint-Martin (Tel. 01 42 72 25 76) - Table des Gourmets, 14 rue des Lombards (Tel. 01 40 27 00 87). **Credit cards** Amex, Visa, Eurocard and MasterCard. **Pets** Dogs allowed. **Parking** Saint-Martin/Rivoli, rue Saint-Bon. **Open** All year.

This hotel is named after the Saint-Merry Church, which was built in the Renaissance in the flamboyant Gothic style. The hotel occupies the building adjoining the church, once the residence of the nuns of Saint-Merry. The owner, Monsieur Crabbe, has restored the hotel to its original splendor. (Room 9 is traversed from one side to the other by a magnificent flying buttress, which you should see even if you're not staying in this room.) He spent years gathering period pieces from the Drouot Auction Rooms, like furniture and old panels, which were reconstructed as headboards and closet doors. Ironwork, another major Gothic art form, is also well represented in the chandeliers and large candelabras that have been transformed into beautiful lamps. The bathrooms are decorated with small panes of stained glass. The result is one of great taste and proportion. A suite on the top floor is hailed by the owner as the "apotheosis of the Saint-Merry". Note that the Rue de la Verrerie, on the edge of Les Halles, is one of the most colorful streets in Paris, with old shops, jazz clubs, and bistrots: At the *Vieux Paris,* you can drink and sing to accordion accompaniment.

***How to get there*** *(Map 37 and 38): Métro Châtelet, Hôtel de Ville, RER Châtelet-Les Halles - Bus: 58, 70, 72, 74, 76.*

## Grand Hôtel Jeanne d'Arc

3, rue de Jarente
75004 Paris
Tel. (0)1.48.87.62 11 - Fax (0)1.48.87.37.31

**Category** ★★ **Rooms** 36 with telephone, bath or shower, WC, cable TV - Elevator. **Price** Single and double 300-400F, 3-4 pers. 490-570F. **Meals** Breakfast (buffet) 35F, served 7:00-11:00. **Restaurants** Nearby: L'Auberge de Jarente (Tel. 01 42 77 49 39) - Le Marais-Sainte-Catherine (Tel. 01 42 72 39 34) - Bourguignon du Marais, 52 rue F.-Miron (Tel. 01 48 87 15 40). **Credit cards** Visa, Eurocard and MasterCard. **Pets** Dogs allowed. **Parking** Rue Saint-Antoine. **Open** All year.

The Marais is famous for its historic Place des Vosges, prestigious town houses, and the Picasso and Carnavalet Museums, but it's less known for the small "village" just off the noble square: the Place du Marché Sainte-Catherine and the Rue de Jarente, where you'll find the small Hôtel Jeanne d'Arc. Named after the Jeanne d'Arc Convent, which was demolished in the 18th century to make way for a market, the hotel reflects the simple charm of the neighborhood, which abounds with picturesque cafés and outdoor restaurants on tree-lined sidewalks. The hotel's reception area/lounge and the breakfast room with white crocheted tablecloths give it the feel of a family home. There are four small bedrooms, but they are reasonably priced, especially if there are two of you. Other rooms are larger, and some are very large, like Room 63, which is on the top floor and can accommodate four people; it has an immense bathroom and mansard roof. Most rooms are decorated in blue, which you'll find repeated in the *trompe-l'œil* bathroom tiles. And from most of the rooms, you will have a view over the flower-filled inner courtyards or the rooftops of this enchanting neighborhood.

***How to get there*** *(Map 37 and 38): Métro Saint-Paul - RER Châtelet-Les Halles - Bus: 29, 69, 76, 96.*

## Hôtel Caron de Beaumarchais

12, rue Vieille-du-Temple
75004 Paris
Tel. (0)1.42.72.34.12 - Fax (0)1.42.72.34.63 - M. Bigeard

**Category** ★★★ **Rooms** 19 with soundproofing, air-conditioning, bath or shower and WC, telephone, satellite TV, hairdryer, safe and minibar - Elevator. **Price** Double 690-770F. **Meals** Breakfast 54F, brunch:78F, served until 12:00. **Restaurants** nearby: Miravile, 72 quai de l'Hôtel-de-Ville (Tel. 42 74 72 22) - Le Grizzli, 7 rue Saint-Martin (Tel. 01 48 87 77 56) - Benoît, 20 rue Saint-Martin (Tel. 01 42 72 25 76) - Amadeo, rue François Mirou - Brasserie Bofinger, 5 rue Bastille (Tel. 01 42.72.87.82). **Credit cards** All major. **Pets** Dogs not allowed. **Parking** Rue Baudoyer. **Open** All year.

The Marais quarter now has a new hotel in keeping with its history. This comfortable 18th-century house has been restored in homage to the famous author of *The Marriage of Figaro,* who lived on this street. The decoration was carried out by Alain Bigeard, who researched and took inspiration from documents of the time. Thus, in the lobby, the walls are covered with embroidered fabric reproduced from the original designs, and there are Burgundian stone floors with period furniture. The same elegance is found in the beautifully comfortable bedrooms and the bathrooms, whose tiles are modeled on those of Rouen and Nevers. In addition, the prices are very reasonable.

***How to get there** (Map 37 and 38): Métro Hôtel-de-Ville, Saint-Paul-le-Marais, Bus 54, 68, 74, 80, 81 and 95.*

1998

# Hôtel de France

2, place du Marché
91670 Angerville (Essonne)
Tel. (0)1.69.95.11.30 - Fax (0)1.64.95.39.59 - Mme Tarrene

**Rooms** 17 with telephone, bath or shower, WC and TV - Elevator. **Price** Single and double 310F, 420F; 3 pers. 520F. **Meals** Breakfast 45F; half board 420F (per pers.). **Restaurant** Service 12:00-14:30, 19:30-21:30; menus 140F. **Credit cards** Amex, Visa, Eurocard and MasterCard. **Pets** Dogs allowed. **Facilities** Parking. **Nearby** Juine Valley and château de Méréville, Chalouette Valley and Chalou-Moulineu Valley, Château de Farcheville, Dourdan (Place of Marché-aux-grains). **Open** All year.

There is a big family of "Hôtels de France" with their opulent façades occupying the main square of provincial towns. In Angerville, the comparison stops there as the interior decoration of this hotel is much more tasteful than that generally found in this kind of establishment. The hotel in fact is made up of five small, very old houses, joined together around a leafy courtyard with several tables in summer. Charmingly decorated and insulated from street noise by double-glazing, the bedrooms are all different, with a small 18th-century wardrobe in one, a Louis-Philippe chest-of-drawers in another, a scattering of engravings, and famous-name fabrics, all creating an intimate, tasteful atmosphere. On the ground floor, excellent cuisine is served in an elegant dining room. Depending on the hour, you can enjoy breakfast and drinks in a charming room with a sofa and armchairs, a stone fireplace, and a warm log fire in winter.

***How to get there*** *(Map 9): 40km south of Paris via N20 to Etampes, 15km south of Etampes.*

# Auberge de l'Ile du Saussay

Route de Ballancourt
91760 Itteville (Essonne)
Tel. (0)1.64.93.20.12 - Fax (0)1.64.93.39.88 - M. Lebrun

**Category** ★★★ **Rooms** 7, 2 apartments (4 pers.), 13 suites with telephone, bath or shower, WC, TV minibar and safe. **Price** Double 350F, apart. 900F, suite 450F. **Meals** Breakfast 45F, served 7:00-10:30. **Restaurant** Service 12:00-14:30, 19:00-22:00 (closed Monday); menus 145-195F, also à la carte. **Credit cards** All major. **Pets** Dogs allowed. **Facilities** Parking. **Nearby** Dourdan, Arpajon and Renarde Valley, château of Farcheville. **Open** All year except in Aug (closed Monday).

Monsieur Lebrun was immediately captivated by the beautiful setting of the Auberge de l'Ile de Saussay. Although the Auberge is very contemporary in design, the surrounding lakes and trees make it perfectly charming. Three different categories of accommodations are proposed, but all enjoy modern amenities, tasteful decoration, and large bay windows opening onto a terrace with a view of the lake or, in the back, trees and a small inlet. You have a choice of bedrooms; suites with a small living room and bedroom on the mezzanine; or apartments with two bedrooms and a living room. The overall effect is lovely. The entire inn is lovely, restful, and the excellent dinners served overlooking the large illuminated trees reflected in the lake are a pleasure for the eye as well as the palate.

***How to get there*** *(Map 9): 40km south of Paris via N20 to Etampes; then, after Arpajon, towards La Fertais-Alais.*

## Hostellerie Les Pléiades

21, Grande-Rue
77630 Barbizon (Seine-et-Marne)
Tel. (0)1.60.66.40.25 - Fax (0)1.60.66.41.68 - M. Karampournis

**Category** ★★★ **Rooms** 23 with telephone, bath (1 with shower), WC and TV. **Price** Double 320-550F. **Meals** Breakfast 45F; half board 390-490F, full board 650F. **Restaurant** Service 12:30-14:30, 19:30-21:30; menus 185-280F, also à la carte. Specialties: Fresh local produce. **Credit cards** All major. **Pets** Dogs allowed. **Facilities** Parking. **Nearby** Museum of Théodore Rousseau, Museum of Auverge Ganne; Milly-la-forêt; forest and palace of Fontainebleau – 18-hole Fontainebleau golf course. **Open** All year.

Located in the large street lined with old houses which leads directly into Fontainebleau Forest, the Hostellerie Les Pléiades was frequented between the two wars by illustrious representatives of politics, the arts and literature. But it is above all the memory of Millet, Théodore Rousseau, Ziem and their landscape-artist friends which lingers in this ravishing village. (Note that the auberge-museum of Père Ganne has reopened after seven years of closure). At the Pléiades, the comfortable bedrooms still retain their charm of the past even though they are regularly repainted and repapered. That does make them seem rather old-fashioned but the rooms and baths are nevertheless well kept. (In *La Villa*, the rooms are more modern but also more impersonal.) The large dining room, which opens onto the shady terrace in summer, the inventive cuisine and the friendly, generous hospitality all contribute to making this an excellent hostelry.

***How to get there*** *(Map 9): 57km southeast of Paris via A6 to Fontainebleau exit, then N37 and D64 to Barbizon.*

## Château des Bondons

47/49, rue des Bondons
77260 La Ferté-sous-Jouarre (Seine-et-Marne)
Tel. (0)1.60.22.00.98 - Fax (0)1.60.22.97.01 - M. Busconi

**Category** ★★★ **Rooms** 14 with telephone, bath, WC, satellite TV and minibar. **Price** Double 450-550F, suite 800-1000F, apart. 550-800F. **Meals** Breakfast 60F. No restaurant. **Credit cards** All major. **Pets** Dogs allowed (+30F). **Facilities** Parking. **Nearby** Jouarre, Eurodisneyland. **Open** All year.

Set in a vast park, this small 19th-century château was sinking into oblivion before the Busconis thoroughly renovated and resuscitated it. The reception rooms on the ground floor look out onto the surrounding gardens. The entrance hall has an elaborate marble mosaic floor and the same geometrical patterns can be seen in the ivory inlay of the paneling. In the dining-room there is delightful paneling inlaid with small landscape pictures. You will find a wealth of 18th-century-style furniture – modern copies, but elegant. The lounge is vast and light, but the tiled floor could do with a few rugs. A beautiful wooden staircase leads up to the bedrooms which are extremely warm and cozy, with thick carpets and lovely flowered fabrics. The bedrooms are individually decorated and have luxuriously equipped bathrooms. Rooms 4 and 8 are particularly noteworthy (albeit more expensive). You will enjoy an friendly welcome and excellent, hearty breakfasts. *L'Auberge de Condé* is the best restaurant in the city; another good choice is *L'Auberge du Petit Morin* in Mourette.

***How to get there*** *(Map 10): 65km east of Paris via A4, Ferté-sous-Jouarre exit, then N3; in the village Châlons-sur-Marne and Montménard towards.*

## Au Moulin

2, rue du Moulin
77940 Flagy (Seine-et-Marne)
Tel. (0)1.60.96.67.89 - Fax (0)1.60.96.69.51 - M. and Mme Scheidecker

**Category** ★★★ **Rooms** 10 with telephone, bath and WC. **Price** Single 260-320F, double 330-500F. **Meals** Breakfast 52F, served 7:45-11:00; half board 392-464F, full board 552-624F (per 2 pers., 4 days min.). **Restaurant** Service 12:15-14:15, 19:15-21:15; menus 160-250F, also à la carte. **Credit cards** All major. **Pets** Dogs allowed. **Facilities** Parking. **Nearby** Palace and forest of Fontainebleau, Barbizon, Moret-sur-Loing – 18-hole La Forteresse golf course. **Open** Jan 24 – Sep 12 and Sep 25 – Dec 20. (closed Sunday evenings and Monday except Easter, Mai 31, June 1 evening and June 2).

This 13th-century flour mill has been well restored. Beneath the stucco façade the ancient masonry was discovered in a remarkable state of preservation. The original half-timbering, the cob walls, the ground-floor stonework and the beautiful vaulted gable have all been stripped bare and greatly contribute to the strong period atmosphere of the building. The hotel accommodates guests in ten fully equipped and carefully decorated bedrooms. The dining-room looks out onto the river, and there is also a terrace and a garden. Dinner is served by candlelight in the evening and log fires are lit in winter. You are assured of a comfortable stay in this hotel where a quiet rural setting and beautiful architecture combine to create an ambience of warmth and well-being only an hour away from Paris.

***How to get there*** *(Map 9): 88km southeast of Paris via A6, Fontainebleau exit, then N6 for 18km; at the traffic lights turn right onto D403 and immediatly on your left D120.*

## Hostellerie Aux Vieux Remparts

3, rue Couverte - Ville Haute
77160 Provins (Seine-et-Marne)
Tel. (0)1.64.08.94.00 - Fax (0)1.60.67.77.22 - M. Roy

**Category** ★★★ **Rooms** 25 with telephone, bath or shower, WC, TV and minibar. **Price** Single 340-470F, double 395-650F. **Meals** Breakfast 50F, served 7:00-11:00; half board 420-590F, full board 570-800F (per pers.). **Restaurant** Service 12:00-14:30, 19:30-21:30; menus 170-350F, also à la carte. Specialties: Petite salade de langouste tiède en crudité, gapacho de tomates, lasagnes de homard breton et ragoût de coquillages, pomme de ris de veau piquée de foie gras braisée au beurre mousseux, confiture de vieux garçon. **Credit cards** All major. **Pets** Dogs allowed (+60F). **Facilities** Parking. **Nearby** Ramparts, tower of César, church of Saint-Quiriace in Provins, spectacle de fauconnerie, tournoi de chevalerie, church of Saint-Loup-de-Naud – 18-hole Fontenaille golf course. **Open** All year.

Located in the most beautiful part of medieval Provins, the Hostellerie Aux Vieux Remparts has twenty-five bedrooms in an adjoining modern building. It successfully blends in with the town's splendid medieval architecture. In the comfortable, quiet bedrooms, the modern decor includes quilted bedcovers, carpets, and many white-lead pieces of furniture. In the restaurant, you will have the choice between a highly reputed gastronomic menu or the bistrot fare, which is served in a beautiful half-timbered 16th-century house, or on the terrace in summer. The decoration is in strict keeping with the traditional character of the village and tables are also set up in a very charming small courtyard in good weather. The Hostellerie is very lovely and you will be warmly welcomed.

***How to get there*** *(Map 10): 86km southeast of Paris via A4, then D231 to Provins.*

## Hostellerie Le Gonfalon

2, rue de l'Eglise
77910 Germigny-L'Evêque (Seine-et-Marne)
Tel. (0)1.64.33.16.05 - Fax (0)1.64.33.25.59 - Mme Colubi

**Rooms** 10 with telephone, bath, WC, TV and minibar. **Price** Single and double 280-380F. **Meals** Breakfast 45F, served 7:30-10:30. **Restaurant** Service 12:00-13:30, 19:30-21:00; menus 198-260-330F, also à la carte. **Credit cards** All major. **Pets** Dogs allowed. **Facilities** Parking. **Nearby** Forest of Montceaux, boat on the Marne from Meaux. **Open** All year except in Jan (closed Sunday evening and Monday).

In the heart of Brie country and right on the Marne River, an unremarkable village auberge in 1977 was transformed into a beautiful country inn by Mme Line Colubi, already a reputable Cordon Bleu chef. Behind the plain façade of the Gonfalon, you discover a cool terrace out of a summer's dream, shaded by enormous century-old linden trees and surrounded by luxuriant vegetation overlooking the banks of the Marne. Bons vivants come here especially for Mme Colubi's delicately sauced specialties, which are served either on the delicious terrace or in the elegant Louis XIII dining room with its warm woodwork and beautiful log fires in winter. There are ten comfortable, very quiet bedrooms upstairs and on the *second étage*; ask for those with a large private terrace-conservatory overlooking the trees and the river (especially number 2). For a more youthful, brighter decoration, request the mansard rooms on the second floor. The delicious breakfasts, with hot homemade brioches and fruit juice, are served either in your room, the dining room or on the terrace in good weather. The friendly waitresses are discreet and professional. Less than an hour from Paris, this is a beautiful place for your gastronomic weekends.

***How to get there*** *(Map 9): 60km east of Paris via A4 to Meaux, then N3 to Trilport and D97.*

1998

## Domaine du Verbois

38, avenue de la République
78640 Neauphle-le-Château (Yvelines)
Tel. (0)1.34.89.11.78 - Fax (0)1.34.89.57.33 - M. and Mme Boone

**Category** ★★★ **Rooms** 20 with telephone, bath, WC, satellite TV, 10 with minibar - 1 for disabled persons. **Price** Single and double 490F, 590F, suite 860F. **Meals** Breakfast 68F, served 7:15-13:00. **Restaurant** Service 12:00-14:00, 19:30-21:30 (closed Sunday evening); menu 155F, also à la carte. Specialties: Poularde Houdan, barbue au jus de viande, Neauphleen. **Credit cards** Amex, Visa, Eurocard and MasterCard. **Pets** Dogs allowed (+60F). **Facilities** Parking and garage (60F). **Nearby** visit of the Grand-Marnier cellars, Versailles, Giverny, Auvers - 18-hole Isabella golf course, 18-hole Saint-Nom golf course. **Open** Dec 28 – Aug 9 and Aug 27 – Dec 18.

A luxurious hotel in a region not lacking in points of touristic interest, this 19th-century house stands in a beautiful 7 1/2-acre park in the plain of Neauphle-le-Château. The ground floor offers a series of salons and dining rooms of different sizes. In good weather, meals are served on the terrace where you can see Rambouillet Forest in the distance. Named after mythological Greek goddesses, the bedrooms are comfortable, those upstairs offering more space. Lovely floral fabrics, antique or period furniture harmoniously complement the Chinese rugs. An unusual detail: old magazines from the owner's collection are placed in your bedroom for your midnight reading. This is a good hotel on the doorstep of Paris, even if you might encounter a group attending a congress, and despite the cool reception at the desk. This, however, is quickly compensated for by the owner's friendliness.

***How to get there*** *(Map 9): 29km west of Paris, via A13 to Dreux, A12 to Saint-Quentin-en-Yvelines, N12 Neauphles-le Château exit and Verbois (2km).*

1998

## Château de Cavanac

11570 Cavanac (Aude)
Tel. (0)4.68.79.61.04 - Fax (0)4.68.79.79.67
M. and Mme Gobin

**Category** ★★★ **Rooms** 15 with telephone, bath or shower, WC, safe and TV - Elevator - 1 for disabled persons. **Price** Single and double 320-525F. **Meals** Breakfast (buffet) 45F. **Restaurant** Service 20:00-22:00; menu 198F (wine incl.), also à la carte. Specialties: Foie gras maison, baron d'agneau au four à bois - Fromages de pays à l'huile et au miel - Pain maison. **Credit cards** Visa, Eurocard and MasterCard. **Pets** Dogs not allowed. **Facilities** Swimming pool, tennis, sauna, fitness center, parking. **Nearby** La Cité, church of Saint-Vincent and church of Saint-Nazaire in Carcassonne, Château de Pennautier - 9-hole Auriac golf course in Carcassonne. **Open** Mid. Feb – mid. Jan.

A winegrowing family's château for generations, this splendid 17th-century edifice has now been converted into a magnificent hotel by its young owner. The bedrooms are huge, with a scattering of antique furniture and beautiful fabrics to conserve their original charm; most rooms overlook the vineyard or the surrounding countryside. They are equipped with gleaming, modern bathrooms. Installed in the former stables, the immense dining room, with its fireplace, antique copper objects and a superb butcher's block, creates a lovely, inviting atmosphere in which to enjoy elaborate regional specialties and wines from the property. Intimate and charming, the breakfast room with its pedestal tables still looks like an old kitchen. On your way to the tennis court or the swimming pool, don't miss a visit to the wine cellars. Just five minutes from the historic city of Carcasonne, what a beautiful place to stay.

***How to get there*** *(Map 31): 7km south of Carcassonne. From Toulouse Carcassonne-ouest exit; depuis Narbonne, Carcassonne-est exit, towards hospital "hôpital",Saint-Hilaire and Cavanac road.*

## Clos des Souquets

11200 Fabrezan (Aude)
Tel. 04.68.43.52.61 - Fax 04.68.43.56.76
M. Julien

**Rooms** 4 and 1 studio with bath, WC and TV on request - Wheelchair access. **Price** Double 280-380F, studio 480F. **Meals** Breakfast 40F; half board 330-380F (per pers.). **Restaurant** Service 12:15-14:15, 19:30-21:30 (closed Sunday evening except for residents); menus 95-185F, also à la carte. Specialties: Fish and regional cooking. **Credit cards** Visa, Eurocard and MasterCard. **Pets** Dogs allowed. **Facilities** Swimming pool, bicycle and parking. **Nearby** Saint-Just Cathedral in Narbonne, mountain of la Clape, African reserve of Sigean, abbey of Fontfroide, Lagrasse, Corbières Wine Route, Carcassonne - 9-hole Auriac golf course in Carcassonne. **Open** Apr 1 - Nov 1.

Nestling in the heart of the tranquil village of Fabrezan, this is a small auberge unlike any other. It is composed of a group of buildings centered around the dining room, which opens out onto a patio and a swimming pool. You will find two bedrooms on the ground floor, giving onto a courtyard with olive trees; a large, all-white studio, reminiscent of a Greek house, which is located upstairs in a converted barn; and two other bedrooms opening onto small shady terraces and another swimming pool reserved for guests in those two rooms. Monsieur Julien's inventive cuisine makes abundant use of fish and shellfish, a delicious plus adding to the feeling of relaxation and vacation created by his and Madame Julien's warm hospitality. It's a place you won't want to leave.

***How to get there*** *(Map 31): 25km north of Carcassonnne and Narbonne. On A 61 take exit Lezignan-Corbières, dir. Fabrezan. In Fabrezan, dir. Lagrasse.*

# Hostellerie du Grand Duc

2, route de Boucheville
11140 Gincla (Aude)
Tel. (0)4.68.20.55.02 - Fax (0)4.68.20.61.22 - M. and Mme Bruchet

**Category** ★★ **Rooms** 10 with telephone, bath or shower, WC, TV and hairdryer. **Price** Single 250-270F, double 280-330F. **Meals** Breakfast 40F, served 8:00-11:00; half board 300-325F, full board 420-445F (per pers., 3 days min.). **Restaurant** Service 12:15-14:00, 19:30-21:00 (Closed Wednesdays lunchtime except July and Aug); à la carte. Specialties: Baignades de sépiole au Fitou, cailles au muscal, faux-filet au foie gras et aux griottes, duo de lotte et saumon sur fondue de poivrons. **Credit cards** Visa, Eurocard and MasterCard. **Pets** Dogs allowed. **Facilities** Parking. **Nearby** Forest of Fanges, Saint-Paul-de-Fenouillet, Belvianes, Saint-Paul-de-Fenouillet, gorges of Galamus. **Open** Mar 25 – Nov 15.

This hotel of great charm – a carefully restored family mansion – is set in a small village. Their guests' well-being is the friendly owners' chief concern and they pride themselves on their warm hospitality. The bedrooms are all individually designed and decorated in a wide range of styles. Whitewashed walls, exposed stonework and beamed ceilings highlight the rustic character of the pleasant dining room. The lounge and the bar area are particularly cozy. In summer, breakfast and dinner can be served in the garden, with candles on the tables in the evening.

***How to get there*** *(Map 31): 63km northwest of Perpignan via D117 to Lapradelle, then D22 to Gincla.*

## La Buissonnière

Hameau de Foussargues
30700 Aigaliers (Gard)
Tel. (0)4.66.03.01.71 - Fax 01.66.03.19.21 - Mme Hanotin and G. Zandstra

**Rooms** 6 and 2 apartments (2-4 pers.) with kitchen, telephone, bath or shower, WC, minibar and TV on request. **Price** Double 380-700F, apart. 500-800F. **Meals** Breakfast incl., served 8:30-10:00. **Credit cards** Visa, Eurocard and MasterCard. **Pets** Dogs not allowed. **Facilities** Swimming pool and parking. **Nearby** Le Duché, Church of Saint-Etienne and Saint-Théodorit in Uzès; pont du Gard; Nîmes; Avignon – 9-hole golf course in Uzès, 18-hole glof course (20km). **Open** All year (by reservation in winter, 2 days min.).

A Franco-Dutch couple have put great enthusiasm into restoring this old *mas* a few kilometers from Uzès. While authenticity was their major concern, comfort and decoration have not been overlooked. The bedrooms are spacious, some with a fireplace and others with a mezzanine. The apartments have a small kitchen. Mediterranean decoration lends a personal touch to each room, but all have a small terrace where breakfast is served, unless you prefer to enjoy it in the cool of the courtyard. Lavender, pink oleander and olive trees all create a lovely decor in the garden and an inviting place to relax.

***How to get there*** *(Map 32): 7km from Uzès, towards Arles; in 6km towards Aigaliers, go 800m, turn right at the intersection, then left immediately, and follow signs.*

## Hôtel Les Arcades

23, boulevard Gambetta
30220 Aigues-Mortes (Gard)
Tel. (0)4.66.53.81.13 - Fax (0)4.66.53.75.46

**Rooms** 6 with air-conditioning, telephone, bath, WC and TV. **Price** Double 480-550F. **Meals** Breakfast incl. **Restaurant** Closed Monday and Tuesday lunchtime in low season. Menus 128-200F, also à la carte. Specialties: Gardiane de taureau à l'ancienne, huîtres chaudes, filet de taureau grillé, croustillant aux fruits. **Credit cards** All major. **Pets** Small dogs allowed. **Nearby** The Camargue, Arles, Saintes-Maries-de-la-Mer (gypsies' pilgrimage May 24 – 25), Tarascon, Nîmes, Montpellier. **Open** All year except Feb 13 – 28 and Nov 12 – 28.

We loved this 16th-century house set in a quiet street in the old town. Inside, everything is neat and charming. A lovely aged and patinated paint effect, in colors ranging from lime green to brown, enhances the corridors and the bedrooms, where curtains, bedspreads and antique furniture are in perfect harmony. The bedrooms are vast, with high, elaborate ceilings and tall mullioned windows, and fully equipped bathrooms provide all the modern comforts. Breakfast and dinner – which are excellent – are served in a pleasant dining-room with an ancient terra-cotta tiled floor. It opens on one side into a little garden, and on the other into an arcade where a few tables are set up. A warm, family atmosphere prevails.

***How to get there*** *(Map 32): 48km west of Arles towards Saintes-Maries-de-la-Mer, then D58.*

## Hôtel Les Templiers

23, rue de la République
30220 Aigues-Mortes (Gard)
Tel. (0)4.66.53.66.56 - Fax (0)4.66.53.69.61 - M. Duval

**Category** ★★★ **Rooms** 11 with air-conditioning, telephone, bath or shower, WC and satellite TV - Wheelchair access. **Price** Double 450-770F, suite 600-800F. **Meals** Breakfast 50F, served from 7:30. No restaurant. **Credit cards** All major. **Pets** Dogs allowed. **Facilities** Garage. **Nearby** La Camargue, Arles, Les Sainte-Marie-de-la-Mer (gypsies' pilgrimage May 24 – 25), Tarascon, Nîmes, Montpellier. **Open** Mar 1 – Oct 31.

Over the last four years, the present owners have made an elegant hotel in the center of Aigues-Mortes out of what was once a dilapidated 17th-century merchants' house. They are in love with the region, the city, the hotel, and their work - which is a very recent discovery for them - and they are anxious to share their enthusiasm in every way with their guests. After their tasteful restoration of the house, the couple searched the region for Provençal furniture, which lends each bedroom a personal touch, as do the family portraits on the walls. Some rooms look out onto the street but are nevertheless very quiet except on holidays: Aigues-Mortes is a pedestrian town. We liked other rooms for their view onto the interior courtyard and a cool fountain. There is no restaurant but the hotel serves pleasant snacks and will provided list of good restaurants. Our own favorites are *Le Minos* in front of the hotel, and *Le Maguelone.*

***How to get there*** *(Map 32): 48km west of Arles, towards Saintes-Maries-de-la-Mer, then D58.*

## Hostellerie Le Castellas

Grand' Rue
30210 Collias (Gard)
Tel. (0)4.66.22.88.88 - Fax (0)4.66.22.84.28 - M. and Mme Aparis

**Category** ★★★ **Rooms** 15 and 2 suites with air-conditioning, telephone, bath or shower, WC, TV and minibar. **Price** Single 400-440F, double 500-590F, suite 800-1000F. **Meals** Breakfast 60F, served 7:30-11:00; half board 495-750F. **Restaurant** Service 12:00-14:00, 19:00-21:15; menus 160-300F, also à la carte. Specialties: Foie gras poêlé et gâteau de pommes de terre à la truffe, suprême de pigeon rôti à la provençale, champignons et jus de ses abats. **Credit cards** All major. **Pets** Dogs allowed (+50F). **Facilities** Swimming pool, parking. **Nearby** Pont du Gard, Uzès, Nîmes – 9-hole golf course in Uzès. **Open** Mar 10 – Jan 6.

In a little street in the center of Collias, two venerable 17th-century dwellings house the Hostellerie Le Castellas. Making admirable use of the arrangement of the houses, Madame Aparis has succeeded in transforming the enclosed courtyard into an oasis of greenery and flowers, hiding a small swimming pool farther down, with space for four or five chaise-longues. A favorite haunt of artists and sculptors, the second house offers bedrooms with outstanding interior decoration, some with fabulous bathrooms (one even enjoys the use of a terrace-solarium on the roof with a bathtub in the center!) More classic, the bedrooms in the main house are also lovely and have all the amenities. Excellent dinners, refined and inventive, are served on the terrace in summer, in the shade of large parasols or an arbor.

***How to get there*** *(Map 33): 26km northeast of Nîmes via A9, Remoulins exit; at Remoulins D981 then D112 to Collias.*

## La Bégude Saint-Pierre

D 981
30210 Vers - Pont du Gard (Gard)
Tel. (0)4.66.22.10.10 - Fax (0)4.66.22.73.73 - M. Griffoul
E-mail: bruno.griffoul@enprovence.com - Web: http://www.enprovence.com/welcome/begude

**Rooms** 28 with air-conditioning, telephone, bath, WC, TV, hairdryer, safe and minibar - Wheelchair access. **Price** Double 415-680F, suite 800-1300F. **Meals** Breakfast 60F, served 7:00-10:30; half board +210F, full board +360F (per pers., 3 days min.). **Restaurant** Service 12:00-14:00, 19:30-22:00; menus 150-360F, also à la carte. Specialties: Symphonie gardoise à l'emulsion de tapenade et huile d'olive, saumon fumé par nos soins, crème brûlée à la vanille. **Credit cards** All major. **Pets** Dogs allowed (+40F). **Facilities** Swimming pool, parking. **Nearby** Pont du Gard, Uzès, Nîmes, Avignon. **Open** All year except in Nov.

A *bégude* used to be a postal relay station with a twin farmhouse next door. The owner of an auberge in a village near Uzès, M. Griffoul has extensively restored this pretty Provençal *bégude,* creating a comfortable, luxurious hotel with a swimming pool, bedrooms with large terraces, a bar, a restaurant and a grill for the summer. We especially liked room 31 for its unusual spaciousness, and number 15 for its charming mezzanine. All are decorated with the simplicity which is appropriate to Provençal houses, including Souleïado fabrics and regional furniture. The lounges and dining rooms are decorated with similar traditional charm, conferring homogeneity to the style of this recently inaugurated hotel. Special attention is given to the cuisine because M. Griffoul is first and foremost a chef! He even smokes his own salmon on the premises.

***How to get there*** *(Map 33): 25km northeast of Nîmes via A9, exit Remoulins, then D981 towards Uzès.*

## La Vieille Fontaine

30630 Cornillon (Gard)
Tel. (0)4.66.82.20.56 - Fax (0)4.66.82.33.64
M. Audibert

**Category** ★★★ **Rooms** 8 (4 with air-conditioning) with bath, WC, TV and minibar. **Price** Double 550-850F. **Meals** Breakfast 55F, served 8:00-10:00; half board 550-700F (per pers., 3 night min.). **Restaurant** Service 12:00-13:30, 19:30-21:30; menus from 195F, also à la carte. Specialties: Moules farçies à la Diable, soupe au pistou in season, gratiné de langoustines, civet de porcelet. **Credit cards** Amex, Visa, Eurocard and MasterCard. **Pets** Dogs allowed (+50F). **Facilities** Swimming pool. **Nearby** Avignon, Orange, Modern Art Museum in Bagnols-sur-Cèze, village of Roque-sur-Cèze, Goudargues Abbey Church, gorges of the Cèze. **Open** Mar 1 – Dec 31.

Restaurant owners for more than twenty years, M. and Mme Audibert have discovered a new calling as hotel keepers. Within the walls of the former medieval castle of Cornillon, they have integrated a very modern structure with eight bedrooms decorated by Mme Audibert. There are two bedrooms per floor. Upstairs, the original small medieval apertures have been kept, providing lovely cool air in the summer. Your climb up to the last floor is rewarded with the view from pleasant balconies, which look out over the château walls and the valley. To reach the swimming pool, you must climb up a terraced garden which is not advisable for people who have difficulty walking. Those who do stroll through the beautiful, carefully arranged garden, however, do not regret it!

***How to get there*** *(Map 33): 45km northwest of Avignon via A9, exit Tavel to Bagnols-sur-Cèze; then D980 towards Barjac. On A7, take Bollène exit.*

## L'Hacienda

30320 Marguerittes - Mas de Brignon (Gard)
Tel. (0)4.66.75.02.25 - Fax (0)4.66.75.45.58
M. and Mme Chauvin

**Category** ★★★ **Rooms** 12 with telephone, bath or shower, WC, satellite TV, hairdryer, safe and minibar. **Price** Single and double 350-600F. **Meals** Breakfast 65-85F, served 8:00-10:00; half board 420-620F (per pers.). **Restaurant** Service 12:00-13:30, 19:30-21:30; menus 105-340F, also à la carte. Specialties: Feuillantine de bravadade de Nîmes aux arômes de provence, pigeonneau désossé rôti à l'ail confit, fondant au chocolat chaud et glace au lait d'amande. **Credit cards** Visa, Eurocard and MasterCard. **Pets** Dogs allowed (+50F). **Facilities** Swimming pool, pétanque, bicycles, sauna (70F), parking and garage. **Nearby** Nîmes, Maison Carrée, Art Museum in Nîmes, Pont du Gard, château de Villevieille in Sommières, chapel of Saint-Julien-de-Salinelles – 18-hole Hauts-de-Nîmes and Nîmes Campagne golf course. **Open** All year.

The Hacienda is set in a quiet park enclosed by walls. In the center of the house, we were pleasantly surprised to find a beautiful patio with a few tables where drinks and dinner are served around a magnificent swimming pool. Next to the patio is the dining room, where you will be served by candlelight and enjoy delicious cuisine, which M. Chauvin and his young assistant prepare with the freshest farm products. The bedrooms are comfortable and furnished in rustic English style. Some are lighted by large, half-moon windows and others, on the ground floor, have a terrace on the garden. Not far away, you will find a *pétanque* court set among pink oleanders and roses, and a small Scandinavian chalet which houses a sauna. This is a friendly, lovely place to stay.

***How to get there*** *(Map 33): 6km east of Nîmes via A9, Nîmes-Est exit; then N86 and D135; go through Marguerittes and follow red signs.*

# Hôtel Imperator Concorde

Quai de la Fontaine
30900 Nîmes (Gard)
Tel. (0)4.66 21 90 30 - Fax (0)4.66 67 70 25 - M. Creac'h

**Category** ★★★★ **Rooms** 62 with air-conditioning, telephone, bath or shower, WC, TV, minibar - Elevator. **Price** Single and double 680-850F, suite 1800F. **Meals** Breakfast 65F, served 7.00-11.00. **Restaurant** Service 12:30-13:45, 19:30-21:45; menu and also à la carte. **Credit cards** All major. **Pets** Dogs allowed (+60F). **Nearby** Arènes, Maison Carrée, art museum and Carré d'Art in Nîmes, Pont du Gard, château de Villevieille in Sommiéres, chapel of Saint-Julien-de-Salinelles – 18-hole Haut-de-Nîmes golf course. **Open** All year.

Well located in the town center very near the beautiful Jardin de la Fontaine gardens, the Impérator is an institution in Nîmes: It is here that the most famous toreros and bullfight aficionados stay during the *féria.* The hotel, which has undergone renovation, has lost some of its sparkle, but the bedrooms, especially those on the *troisième étage*, are more spacious and more comfortable. It is preferable to have a room on the garden side, even if the air-conditioning insulates the other rooms from the noise of the quay. The pleasantly decorated bar and restaurant overlook the walled garden behind the hotel. Meals are served either on the modern veranda or the large shady terrace. The cuisine is inventive and subtly seasoned, and the set menu at lunch offers a large number of specialities. The staff is very courteous.

***How to get there*** *(Map 32): In the town center, between the Jardin de la Fontaine and the Maison Carrée.*

# Royal Hôtel

3, boulevard Alphonse-Daudet
30000 Nîmes (Gard)
Tel. (0)4.66.67.28.36 - Fax (0)4.66.21.68.97 - Mmes Riera and Morel

**Category** ★★★ **Rooms** 23 with telephone, bath or shower, WC and TV. **Price** Single and double 250-480F. **Meals** Breakfast 40F, served 7:00-12:00. **Restaurant** "La Bodeguita". Service 12:00-15:00, 19:30-23:30; menu and à la carte. Specialties: Spain cooking. **Credit cards** Amex, Visa, Eurocard and MasterCard. **Pets** Dogs allowed (+40F). **Nearby** Maison Carrée, art museum in Nîmes, Pont du Gard, château de Villevieille in Sommiéres, chapel of Saint-Julien-de-Salinelles – 18-hole Haut-de-Nîmes golf course. **Open** All year.

This small hotel is located close to the Quai de la Fontaine and the Maison Carrée, and looks out onto the Place d'Assas renovated by Martial Raysse. The hotel has a clientele of artists and designers and the atmosphere is relaxed and informal. The hotel has been entirely renovated, with white walls and sparse decoration including several 1950s and '60s pieces of furniture; it is quite unusual but attractive. A tempting restaurant serves salads and brunches; in summer tables are set up outside in the square. It is better to take a room at the back of the hotel to avoid hearing the clattering of forks deep into the night. During the *férias* the atmosphere is animated and festive, with the *tapas* bar staying open late. Jazz and flamenco concerts are held every Thursday evening.

***How to get there** (Map 32): In the town center.*

## Le Mas d'Oléandre

Saint-Médiers
30700 Uzès (Gard)
Tel. (0)4.66.22.63.43 - Eva and Carl-Heinz Törschen

**Rooms** 3, 2 apartments and 1 studio, with bath or shower and WC. **Price** Single 180F, double 280F, apart. 380-420F(per 2 pers.) 500-600F (per 4-5 pers.). **Meals** Breakfast 45F, served 9:00-10:00. No restaurant. **Credit cards** Not accepted. **Pets** Dogs not allowed. **Facilities** Swimming pool, parking. **Nearby** le Duché, churches of Saint-Etienne and Saint-Théodorit in Uzès, Pont du Gard, Nîmes, Avignon – 9-hole golf course in Uzès. **Open** Mar 16 – Oct 31.

A secluded location and a stunning view are the main features of this hotel tucked away at the end of a peaceful little village. All around it cypresses, vineyards and hills combine to create a beautifully harmonious landscape and that may be what kept the owners from returning to their native Germany once they had set eyes on it. This doesn't feel like a hotel at all. The farmhouse has been carefully restored to make your stay as pleasant as possible. The bedrooms are comfortable and welcoming, two practical small apartments enable you to accommodate relatives and children, and there is a studio with a small kitchen. The hotel is an ideal base for exploring the beautiful Uzès area, and the swimming pool proves an irresistible invitation to laze in the sun. In the evening your hosts will gladly indicate the best local restaurants, including *L'Auberge de Cruvier,* or *Le Fou du Roi* in Pougnadoresse, and dinner *L'Auberge Saint-Maximin* in Saint-Maximin.

***How to get there*** *(Map 33): 40km west of Avignon via N100 and D981 to Montaren, then D337 to Saint-Médiers; (the Mas is on the edge of the hamlet).*

## Auberge du Pont Romain

2, rue Emile-Jamais
30250 Sommières (Gard)
Tel. (0)4.66.80.00.58 - Fax (0)4.66.80.31.52 - Michel Family

**Category** ★★★ **Rooms** 19 with telephone, bath or shower and WC. **Price** Single 265-445F, double 265-450F. **Meals** Breakfast 50F, served 7:45-10:00; half board 360-430F. **Restaurant** Service 12:00-13:30, 20:00-21:30; menus 170-250F (children 98F), also à la carte. Specialties: Petit gris des garrigues au roquefort, foie gras maison. **Credit cards** All major. **Pets** Dogs allowed. **Facilities** Swimming pool, parking. **Nearby** Château de Villevieille, chapel of Saint-Julien-de-Salinelles, church of Notre-Dame-des-Pommiers in Beaucaire, Pont du Gard, Nîmes – 18-hole Nîmes-campagne golf course, 18-hole Massane-Montpellier golf course. **Open** Mar 15 – Jan 15. Closed Wednesday in winter.

The façade that looks out onto the street is austere and barracks-like, betraying something of the history of the building. It was a carpet factory in the 19th-century, then a laundry, then, until 1968, a distillery. But as soon as you walk through the porch you enter a different world. A garden full of trees and flowers (all the more marvelous for its unlikely location) provides a pleasant setting for a terrace and a swimming-pool, and leads down to the Vidourle River. The vastness of the bedrooms can prompt memories of dormitories; the best rooms are those on the garden. The cuisine is traditional and generous, but the service can be a bit casual. This is the only hotel in France which is surmounted by a factory chimney.

***How to get there*** *(Map 32): 28km southwest of Nîmes via D40.*

## Hostellerie du Seigneur

Place du Seigneur
30126 Tavel (Gard)
Tel. (0)4.66.50.04.26 - Mme Bodo

**Rooms** 7 with basin. **Price** Double 180F. **Meals** Breakfast 35F, served 8:00-9:30; half board 240F. **Restaurant** Service 12:15-14:00, 19:15-20:30 (closed evening Oct – March); menus 98-140F. Specialties: Cuisse de canard au vin de pays, langue de porcelet au poivre vert, charlotte maison. **Credit cards** Visa, Eurocard and MasterCard. **Pets** Dogs allowed. **Nearby** Avignon; Villeneuve-lez-Avignon; le Lubéron. **Open** Mid Jan – mid Dec (closed Thusday).

The Hostellerie du Seigneur was installed more than thirty years ago in the former town hall of the village, which lends it a special charm. Dating from the 18th-century, the hostelry has cool, tastefully appointed rooms and the beautiful stone of the stairway bears witness to the generations who have come through here. M. Bodo is mainly known for his good regional cooking but you will also enjoy the hotel even if the bathrooms and toilets are separate from the bedrooms, as in a private house. The seven rooms are quiet and decorated *à l'ancienne.* This is an excellent, friendly hostelry, located off the main roads in the small village of Tavel, which has given its name to one of the heady, beautifully colored rosés of the Côtes du Rhône vineyards.

***How to get there*** *(Map 32): 12km north of Avignon. On A9, Roquemaure exit, towards Tavel.*

## Demeures du Ranquet

Tornac
30140 Anduze (Gard)
Tel. (0)4.66.77.51.63 - Fax (0)4.66.77.55.62 - M. and Mme Majourel

**Rooms** 10 (air-conditioning in some rooms), telephone, bath, WC, TV and minibar - Wheelchair access. **Price** Single 500-720F, double 640-900F. **Meals** Breakfast 80F, served from 7:30; half board 600-720F (per pers., 3 days min.). **Restaurant** Service 12:00-13:30, 19:30-21:30; menus 180-380F, also à la carte. Specialties: Daurade rose en croûte de sel, fenouille braisé à l'huile d'olive, épaule d'agneau au four, gratin de pommes de terre à l'ancienne, beignets d'aubergines sucrées avec glace au miel. **Credit cards** Visa, Eurocard and MasterCard. **Pets** Dogs allowed (except in the restaurant). **Facilities** Swimming pool, golf practice green, cooking lessons, parking. **Nearby** Prafance, Bamboo Grove, Générargues, Luziers, Mas-Soubeyran (Desert Museum), Trabuc Cave, Saint-Jean-du-Gard. **Open** Mar 11 – Nov 10.

The distinguished people who have long been coming here are still faithfully returning. If you're not immediately charmed by the bungalows scattered in the woods, you will soon fall under the spell of the original ambiance of the Ranquet. The beautiful cuisine adds a great deal to the appeal of the place. The breakfasts are fabulous, the lunch and dinner menus are varied, and new recipes (eggplant fritters with honey ice cream) are often created. Everything is made on the premises and wine lovers will also be enchanted. Then too, you will sense the Majourels' love of a difficult job, which they handle with skill. If you enjoy painting and gardening, you will want to discuss both with them.

***How to get there*** *(Map 32): 47km northwest of Nîmes, towards Alès; 6km south of Anduze on D982, on the road to Sainte-Hippolyte-du-Fort.*

## Hôtel Marie d'Agoult

Château d'Arpaillargues
30700 Uzès (Gard)
Tel. (0)4.66.22.14.48 - Fax (0)4.66.22.56.10 - Mme and M. Savry

**Category** ★★★ **Rooms** 29 (23 with air-conditioning) with telephone, bath, WC, TV and minibar. **Price** Single and double 400-850F, suite 900-1150F. **Meals** Breakfast 55F, served 7:30-10:30; half board 460-810F (per pers.). **Restaurant** Service 12:30-14:00, 19:30-21:30; menus 145-230F, also à la carte. Specialties: Filets de rougets au basilic. **Credit cards** All major. **Pets** Dogs allowed (+60F). **Facilities** Swimming pool, tennis, parking. **Nearby** Le Duché, churches of Saint-Etienne and Saint-Théodorit in Uzès, Pont du Gard, Nîmes, Avignon – 9-hole golf course in Uzès, 18-hole golf course at 20km. **Open** Apr 1 – Nov 2.

This hotel is in the beautiful 18th-century Château d'Arpaillargues, once the home of Marie de Flavigny, Franz Liszt's companion. The bedrooms are comfortably furnished and tastefully decorated. Eleven bedrooms have a terrace, either at ground level on the garden, or on the rooftop. A small duplex in the annex enjoys a covered terrace. Elegance and professional service are also among the star qualities of this hotel. The extremely high standards of everything here make up for the somewhat formal atmosphere that prevails. A pleasant bar area, lunch by the swimming-pool, and breakfast and dinner in the garden in summer make a stay here a delightful prospect. The cuisine is light and refined.

***How to get there*** *(Map 33): 40km west of Avignon via N100 to Remoulins (on A9, Remoulins exit), then D981 to Uzès and D982 (westward) to Arpaillargues (4km).*

## Hôtel de l'Atelier

5, rue de la Foire
30400 Villeneuve-lès-Avignon (Gard)
Tel. (0)4.90.25.01.84 - Fax (0)4.90.25.80.06 - M. and Mme Gounaud

**Category** ★★ **Rooms** 19 with telephone, bath or shower and WC (17 with TV). **Price** Double 240-430F. **Meals** Breakfast 36-40F, served 7:00-10:00. No restaurant. **Credit cards** All major. **Pets** Dogs allowed. **Nearby** "The Crowning of the Virgin" by Enguerand Quarton in the Musée Municipal in Villeneuve, Carthusain monastery of the Val-de-Bénédiction, fort Saint-André in Villeneuve, chapel of Notre-Dame-de-Belvezet, Avignon – 18-hole Châteaublanc-les-Plans golf course in Avignon. **Open** Beg. Dec – beg. Nov.

The Hôtel de l'Atelier is in Villeneuve-lès-Avignon, a small town at the foot of the Fort Saint-André which faces Avignon across the Rhône river. Avignon was once the City of the Popes; Villeneuve was home to the cardinals. Outwardly a quiet village house, the building has many hidden charms: a sequence of flower-filled patios where fig-trees provide welcome shade, a roof terrace – the perfect setting for a cup of tea or an evening drink – and delightful bedrooms. The latter have all been carefully and individually designed, and their shape and size vary, as do the pieces of period furniture they contain. Our favorite is room 42 on the top floor: it has all the character of an attic roos ( but with air-conditioning!), and if you stand on the little platform you can see Avignon through the high window. The hotel doesn't have a restaurant of its own but Avignon is just on the doorstep and in Villeneuve itself there are some very good restaurants. Try *La Magnaneraie* or *Le Saint-André* (less expensive).

***How to get there*** *(Map 33): 2km west of Avignon via N100; if on A6, Avignon-Nord exit.*

## Château de Madières

Madières
34190 Ganges (Hérault)
Tel. (0)4.67.73.84.03 - Fax (0)4.67.73.55.71 - M. and Mme Brucy
E-mail: madieres@mnet.fr

**Category** ★★★★ **Rooms** 10 with telephone, bath or shower, WC, TV and minibar. **Price** Double 600-1200F, suite 960-1390F. **Meals** Breakfast 80F, served 8:30-10:30; half board 615-925F (per pers., 3 days min.). **Restaurant** Service 12:30-14:00, 19:30-21:00; menus 195-395F, also à la carte. Specialties: Foie gras chaud au banyuls, minute de saint-jacques, pigeon et pintade rotis, soufflé de rougets. **Credit cards** All major. **Pets** Dogs allowed (extra charge). **Facilities** Heated swimming pool, fitness room, parking. **Nearby** Gorges of the river Vis, cirque de Navacelles, La Couvertoirade, cave of the Demoiselles, church of Saint-Guilhem-le-Désert. **Open** Apr 3 – Nov 2.

Set on the southern slopes of the Cévennes among the gorges of the River Vis, this 14th-century fortified house juts out like a balcony on the side of the mountain, only 40 minutes away from the Cirque de Navacelles. The Château has been carefully restored to become a hotel of great character. The bedrooms are luxuriously equipped and look out onto a patio. They are extremely comfortable and pleasant, and their individual decoration shows great attention to detail. The elegant lounge still has a Renaissance fireplace and leads out onto a terrace overlooking the river and the village. There are two dining-rooms (one with panoramic views) in which to enjoy Mme Brucy's excellent cooking. In summer, meals can be served by the swimming-pool which has just been completed on a terrace below the hotel.

***How to get there*** *(Map 32): 60km northwest of Montpellier via D986 towards Le Vigan to Ganges, then D25 towards the Cirque de Navacelles, Lodève (18km from Ganges).*

## Relais Chantovent

34210 Minerve (Hérault)
Tel. (0)4.68.91.14.18 - Fax (0)4.68.91.81.99
Mme Evenou

**Rooms** 7 with shower (1 with bath) and WC. **Price** Single and double 200-260F. **Meals** Breakfast 30F, served 8:00-10:00; half board 320F (per pers., 3 days min.). **Restaurant** Service 12:30-14:00, 19:30-21:00; menus 100-230F. Specialties: Croustillant aux deux saumons sur coulis de poivrons doux. **Credit cards** Visa, Eurocard and MasterCard. **Pets** Dogs allowed. **Nearby** Minerve, châteaux cathares de Lastours, Carcassonne, abbey of Lagrasse, abbey of Fontfroide, African reserve of Sigean, Minervois vineyard. **Open** Mar 15 – Dec 31 (closed Monday in July and Aug).

Minerve is a village high up between the gorges of the rivers Cesse and Briand, and the hotel buildings are scattered in its narrow alleys. The annex is a tastefully restored old village house next to the "post-office library" and the rooms are as charming as the ones in the main building. Two of them share a terrace, and the one in the attic has kept its original layout, with the bathroom more or less in the room; all have charm and character. The rooms facing the restaurant have been redecorated and renovated, with fabrics and contemporary lithographs brightening the decor. The restaurant, with a view over the limestone Briand Valley, serves good regional cuisine (on the terrace in good weather.) The village and its surroundings are splendid and the welcome is very friendly.

***How to get there*** *(Map 31): 45km northwest of Carcassonne via N113 and D160 to Homps, then D910 to Olonzac and D10 to Minerve (northward).*

# Bastide Les Aliberts

Les Aliberts 34210 Minerve (Hérault)
Tel. (0)4.68.91.81.72 - Fax (0)4.68.91.22.95
Mme Bourgogne

**Rooms** 5 cottages (4-8 pers.) with kitchen, lounge, bath, WC. **Price** Cottage 3500-9000F (8-9 pers., 1 week), 2500-6200F (4-5 pers., 1 week), 3000-6700F (6 pers., 1 week) - if possible: 400F (2 pers./day), 600F (3-4 pers./day). **Meals** Breakfast incl. **Evening meals** By reservation. Menu 100F. **Credit cards** Not accepted. **Pets** Dogs not allowed. **Facilities** Swimming pool Apr – Oct and parking. **Nearby** Minerve, châteaux cathares in Lastours, Carcassonne, abbey of Lagrasse, abbey of Fontfroide, African reserve of Sigean, Minervois vineyard. **Open** All year.

Les Aliberts is composed of a group of farmhouses which have been converted into five small individual houses accommodating four to nine people. Very comfortable, well equipped and prettily decorated, they're a perfect vacation home for a week or more. A large barrel-vaulted room in the *bastide* serves as a living room, and what a lovely place in which to curl up in front of the fire in winter, or to take refuge within its cool walls in summer. The charm of Les Aliberts owes much to its friendly, hospitable owners and to the village of Minerve itself, which has been described as "a prow of burnt rock washed up in the blue of heaven like an arc from the deluge; a village...which reigns over a desert of scrub and stones, indented with gorges, punctured with grottos, scattered with dolmens and remote farmhouses."

***How to get there*** *(Map 31): 45km northwest of Carcassonne via N113 and D610 to Homps, then D910 to Olonzac and D10 to Minerve (towards the north).*

## Domaine de Rieumégé

Route de Saint-Pons
34390 Olargues (Hérault)
Tel. (0)4.67.97.73.99 - Fax (0)4.67.97.78.52 - M. Sylva

**Category** ★★★ **Rooms** 14 with telephone, bath or shower and WC. **Price** Single 395-490F, double 490-545F, suite (4 pers.) 925F. **Meals** Breakfast (buffet) 55F, served 8:30-10:00; half board 445-520F, full board 545-620F (per pers., 2 days min. + 160F per pers. with private swimming pool). **Restaurant** Service 12:00-14:00, 19:00-21:30; menus 100F (lunchtime) - 160-210F, also à la carte. **Credit cards** Amex, Visa, Eurocard and MasterCard. **Pets** Dogs allowed (+40F). **Facilities** 2 swimming pools, tennis, parking. **Nearby** Abbey of Fontcaude, mountains of l'Espinouse, cave of la Devèze. **Open** Apr – Oct.

The mountains of the Haut-Languedoc provide an impressive backdrop for the Domaine de Rieumégé, a pleasant place to stay in an area where good hotels are few and far between. This is an old 17th-century house which has been restored by the owners with great taste and a feeling for comfort. The terraces, lounges and kitchen have been improved this year. The interior decoration skillfully combines country-style antiques with more modern pieces of furniture, exposed stonework, and well-chosen colors on the walls. Despite the nearby road the hotel is quiet. A luxury accommodation is also possible, offering a bedroom and a suite giving onto a private swimming pool with a tropical garden, which is reserved exclusively for the occupants. The price is 160F extra per person.

***How to get there*** *(Map 31): 50km northwest of Béziers via D14, then D908 towards Olargues; 3km from Olargues in the Saint-Pons-de-Thomières towards.*

# La Villa d'Eléis

Avenue du Château
34210 Siran (Hérault)
Tel. (0)4.68.91.55.98 - Fax (0)4.68.91.48.34 - M. Lafuente - Mme rodriguez

**Category** ★★★ **Rooms** 12 with telephone, bath or shower, WC, 6 with TV and minibar - Elevator - 1 for disabled persons. **Price** Single and double 300-600F, 350-700F. **Meals** Breakfast 60F, served 8:00-11:00. **Restaurant** Service 12:00-14:30, 19:30-22:00 (closed Sunday evening and Monday Oct – Apr); also à la carte. Specialties: Morue safranée à la languedocienne, fondue de tomate au basilic et huile d'olive, tarte tiède de lisette. **Credit cards** Visa, Eurocard and MasterCard. **Pets** Dogs allowed (+40F). **Facilities** Tennis and parking. **Nearby** Abbey of Fontfroide, Naturel Park of Haut-Languedoc, gorges of the Cesse and the Brian, Minerve, Lastours. **Open** All year except 1 week in Feb.

Set in the heart of the Minervois vineyards, one of the most beautiful regions of Languedoc, Siran is a quiet village of pale stone houses. The Villa d'Eléis was originally a farmhouse built by wealthy winegrowers on the site of the ramparts which once surrounded the village. The Villa has now been transformed into a beautiful country inn by Bernard Lafuente and Marie-Hélène Rodriguez, who are well-known for their restoration of famous hotels. Here, modern accommodations combine harmoniously with the old charm and character of the place. Whether the bedrooms overlook the vines or the village, each has its special personality and predominant color. All have lovely bathrooms and are beautifully restful. Bernard Lafuentes' elegant meals are served in a large, thick-walled dining room, or in the garden shaded by large trees. Small concerts or readings are occasionally given in the interior courtyard. An atmosphere of well-being and relaxation reigns at the Villa, a welcome respite after a day of visiting the splendid sites of the region.

***How to get there*** *(Map 31): 20km northwest of Lezignan; A1 Lézignan-Corbières exit to Olonzac, Pépieux, Siran.*

## Hôtel Chantoiseau

48220 Vialas (Lozère)
Tel. (0)4.66.41.00.02 - Fax (0)4.66.41.04.34
M. Patrick Pagès

**Category** ★★★ **Rooms** 15 with bath or shower, WC, TV and minibar. **Price** Single and double 400-480F. **Meals** Breakfast 50F, served 8:00-10:00; half board 520F (per pers., 3 days min.). **Restaurant** Service 12:00-13:30, 19:00-20:30; menus 100-800F, also à la carte. Specialties: Ravioles au pélardon, carré d'agneau, suprême au chocolat. **Credit cards** All major. **Pets** Dogs not allowed. **Facilities** Swimming pool, parking. **Nearby** Ridgeway to Alès via Portes; La Garde de Guérin, Florac. **Open** Apr 16 – Oct 14 (closed Tuesday evenings and Wednesday).

With one of the outstanding gastronomic restaurants (one Michelin star) of the region, Chantoiseau is a converted 17th-century postal relay station lying at an altitude of 1800 feet in a region of steep escarpments that already evoke the Mediterranean: a sunny place to stay on the doorstep of the Cévennes National Park. Overlooking the valleys and mountains, the bedrooms are comfortable but dark and small, the architecture obliging. The dining room retains the austere character of houses in the area: walls built from large slabs of granite, deep embrasures, the warm presence of wood. It commands beautiful views over the valley. The menu features specialties of the Cévennes only, prepared by the owner whose talent has earned wide recognition, and who has chosen the finest wines to accompany them. The wine list is outstanding, ranging from modest but charming *vins de pays* to great wines.

***How to get there*** *(Map 32): Northwest of Alès via D906, towards Genolhac; in Belle-Poèle, D998 to Vialas.*

## La Terrasse au Soleil

Route de Fontfrède
66400 Céret (Pyrénées-Orientales)
Tel. (0)4.68.87.01.94 - Fax (0)4.68.87.39.24 - B. and P. Leveillé-Nizerolle

**Category** ★★★★ **Rooms** 27 with air-conditioning, telephone, bath, WC, hairdryer, TV, minibar and safe. **Price** Single and double 595-795F. **Meals** Breakfast 80F, served 7:00-12:00; half board 498-698F, full board +150F (per pers.). **Restaurant** Service 12:00-14:00, 19:30-21:30; menus 160-380F (gastronimic menu). Specialties: Rosée des Pyrénées poêlés, étuvée de girolles à la catalane, pigeon fermier rôti et son jus fin aux tagliatelles fraîches. **Credit cards** Diners, Visa, Eurocard and MasterCard. **Pets** Dogs allowed. **Facilities** Heated swimming pool, tennis, par-3 golf course, parking, helicopter pad. **Nearby** Museum of modern art and church of Saint-Pierre in Céret, Cabestany, Prats-de-Mollo, château de Quéribus, Arles-sur-Tech, Quilhac and the château de Peyrepertuse, Perpignan – 27-hole Saint-Cyprien golf course, 18-hole Falgos golf course. **Open** Mar 1 – Oct 31.

La Terrasse au Soleil is an old farmhouse which has been completely restored. It occupies an enviable position crowning the village among cherry trees. If offers several comfortable, spacious apartments and bedrooms with a lounge area and a terrace overlooking the mountains. We still prefer the rooms on the *premier étage* rather than those at ground level on the garden. The La Cerisaie restaurant will delight you with its excellent cuisine; for lunch, it also proposes a simpler *brasserie* menu, in addition to the dessert menu: don't miss the superb *mille-feuille* pastry. In good weather meals can be served in the garden. A heated swimming-pool, tennis court, and the golf course (without supplement) will add further to your enjoyment of the hotel, a charming and informal place to stay.

***How to get there*** *(Map 31): 31km southwest of Perpignan via A9, Le Boulou exit, then D115 towards Céret; it's 2km from the center of the village via D13f on the Fontfrède towards.*

## Le Mas Trilles

66400 Céret-Reynès (Pyrénées-Orientales)
Tel. (0)4.68.87.38.37 - Fax (0)4.68.87.42.62
M. and Mme Bukk

**Category** ★★★ **Rooms** 10 with telephone, bath, WC and TV - 1 room for disabled persons. **Pric** Double and suite 480-990F. **Meals** Breakfast 65F, served 8:30-10:30; half board 480-740F (per pers.) **Restaurant** Service 20:00; menus 180-220F. Specialties: Seasonal cooking. **Credit cards** Visa, Euro card and MasterCard. **Pets** Dogs allowed (extra charge). **Facilities** Heated swimming pool, parking **Nearby** Museum of modern art and church of Saint-Pierre in Céret, Cabestany, Prats-de-Mollo château de Quéribus, Quilhac and the château de Peyrepertuse, Perpignan – 27-hole Saint-Cyprie golf course, 7-hole Amélie-les-Bains golf course, 18-hole Falgos golf course. **Open** Easter – Oct 14.

The Mas Trilles is an old house surrounded by a garden with fruit trees From the swimming-pool, when there is a lot of traffic and the wind i blowing in the wrong direction, the rumble of cars on the road above the hote can sometimes be heard. The bedrooms, however, are quiet at all times. Inside the house has been fully refurbished and decorated with exquisite taste: ther are terra-cotta floors, the walls in some rooms have been sponge painted an in others whitewashed, and each fabric has been carefully chosen by Mm Bukk to blend in with, and round off, the decor. The bedrooms have lovel bathrooms and many of them also have a private terrace where breakfas (which always includes fresh fruit) can be served. Dinner (for residents only is in a charming dining-room or on the terrace. Friendly hospitality adds to th pleasant homey atmosphere that prevails. This is a beautiful, comfortabl hotel.

***How to get there*** *(Map 31): 31km southwest of Perpignan via A9, Le Boulo exit, then D115 towards Céret; 2km from the center, in Amélie-les-Bain towards.*

## Hôtel Casa Païral

Impasse des Palmiers
66190 Collioure (Pyrénées-Orientales)
Tel. (0)4.68.82.05.81 - Fax (0)4.68.82.52.10 - Mmes De Bon and Lormand

**Category** ★★★ **Rooms** 28 with air-conditioning, telephone, bath or shower, WC, satellite TV and minibar. **Price** Single 320-630F, double 350-750F, suite 790-950F. **Meals** Breakfast (buffet) 55-60F. No restaurant. **Credit cards** Amex, Visa, Eurocard and MasterCard. **Pets** Dogs allowed (+30F). **Facilities** Swimming pool, parking (+40F). **Nearby** The Vermeille coast between Argelès-sur-Mer and Cerbère, Balcon de Madeloc, mountain road between Collioure and Banyuls, Château de Salses, museum of modern art in Céret – 27-hole Saint-Cyprien golf course. **Open** Apr – Oct.

A real gem, Casa Païral is hidden in a small *cul-de-sac,* right in the center of Coullioure, just a few minutes from the beach, restaurants, and cafés. It is perfectly quiet. This luxurious 19th-century town house was built in a Moorish style with wrought ironwork, marble, and ceramic tilework. On the patio, lush vegetation grows in the shade of a stately palm tree and a hundred-year-old magnolia tree. All the rooms are comfortable, but ask for the ones in the main house, which are nicer. The very pleasant breakfast room and lounges open onto the walled garden and swimming pool. This hotel is very much in demand, so you will need a reservation. For dinner, try the fish at *Pa i Trago* or at *La Nouvelle Vague* in the old town, or at *La Marinade*, for its pretty terrace on the town square.

***How to get there*** *(Map 31): 26km southeast of Perpignan via N114.*

## Auberge L'Atalaya

Llo - 66800 Saillagouse (Pyrénées-Orientales)
Tel. (0)4.68.04.70.04 - Fax (0)4.68.04.01.29
M. and Mme Toussaint

**Category** ★★★ **Rooms** 12 and 1 suite with telephone, bath or shower, WC, satellite TV, safe and minibar. **Price** Single and double 490-650F, suite 750F. **Meals** Breakfast 60F, served 7:30-10:30; half board 470-600F, full board 620-740F (per pers., 3 days min.). **Restaurant** Service 12:30-14:30, 19:30-21:30 (closed Mondays and Tuesday lunchtime in low season); menus 165-390F, also à la carte. **Credit cards** Visa, Eurocard and MasterCard. **Pets** Dogs allowed in the bedrooms. **Facilities** Swimming pool, solarium, parking. **Nearby** Ski in Eyne, Odeillo solar furnace, lake of Les Buoillouses north of Mont-Louis, gorges of the river Aude, château de Quérigut – 18-hole Real Club de Cerdana golf course, 9-hole golf course in Font-Romeu, 18-hole Fontanals golf course (15km). **Open** Dec 21 – Nov 4.

Llo is the most typical pastoral village of the Cerdagne region on the border between Andorra and Spain, which can be seen from some of the bedrooms. Clustered around its watchtower – called an *atalaya* in old Castilian – and the ruins of its 11th-century castle, the village stands above the gorges of the River Sègre. Needless to say, its location is one of the memorable features of the Auberge. But the building itself is well worth the stay. The magnificent house has been tastefully decorated throughout and the bedrooms are comfortable and attractive. In summer, meals are served outside on a terrace among geraniums and hollyhocks, and there is now also a swimming-pool. In winter, there are eight ski resorts nearby.

***How to get there*** *(Map 31): 90km west of Perpignan via N116 to Saillagouse, then D33.*

## Lou Rouballou

66210 Mont-Louis (Pyrénées-Orientales)
Tel. (0)4.68.04.23.26 - Fax (0)4.68.04.14.09
M. and Mme Duval

**Rooms** 14 with bath or shower and 8 with WC. **Price** Double 160-350F. **Meals** Breakfast 35F; half board 230-280F, full board 270-320F (per pers., 3 days min. in high season). **Restaurant** Service 12:30-13:30, 19:30-20:30; menus 125-195F, also à la carte. Specialties: Catalan and gastronomic cooking. **Credit cards** Visa, Eurocard and MasterCard. **Pets** Dogs not allowed. **Nearby** Romanesque church of Planès, lake of Les Bouillouses, gorges of the river Aude, château de Quérigut, pass of Saint-Georges, Font-Romeu-Odeillo-Via station. **Open** All year except in mid Apr, Nov and Dec (closed Wednesday in low season).

You will find this auberge among the village houses. Its façade is inconspicuous, but as soon as you walk through the door you will feel at ease. Inside, the decor is rustic, cozy and genuine. Some of the bedrooms are more comfortable than others: we recommend rooms 3, 18, 19, 20, 21, which Christiane Duval has lovingly arranged with antique furniture, extremely comfortable beds and pleasant bathrooms. But Lou Raballou is also renowned for the gourmet cuisine turned out by Pierre Duval. The menu features excellent traditional dishes, prepared with only the freshest products. In the autumn, Pierre will take you hunting for mushrooms, and then prepare the mushrooms in a delicious dish for dinner. This is a charming, friendly, unpretentious inn.

***How to get there*** *(Map 31): 10km east of Font-Romeu via N116 (in the old part of the town).*

# Château de Camon

09500 Camon (Ariège)
Tel. (0)5.61.68.28.28 - Fax (0)5.61.68.81.56
M. du Pont

**Rooms** 7 with bath or shower and WC. **Price** Single and double 600-1000F, suite 1500F. **Meals** Breakfast incl. **Restaurant** Evening meals on reservation; menu 350F. **Credit cards** All major. **Pets** Dogs not allowed. **Facilities** Swimming pool, parking. **Nearby** Mirepoix, châteaux of Lagarde and of Caudeval, Montségur and Foix. **Open** Easter – Oct.

At the château Camon, in the beautiful region of Ariège on the wooded road into Spain, you will be treated more like a guest than a customer. The château has been in the family of M. du Pont for two centuries: "Only two hundred years," he says as if to apologize for so recent an acquisition. The château is closed to the public unless, of course, you are a guest, but there is an abbey next to it which can be visited; they both overlook the village below. A colorful terraced garden descends to a lawn with a swimming pool. The bedrooms have been admirably decorated by the owner, (who is an interior decorator) with antique furniture. You will be delighted with every aspect of this château which feels like a private home.

***How to get there*** *(Map 31): 59km southwest of Carcassonne via D119 to Mirepoix, then D7 towards Chalabre. If on A61, Castelnaudary exit.*

# La Maison des Consuls

09500 Mirepoix (Ariège)
Tel. (0)5.61.68.81.81/83.84 - Fax (0)5.61.68.81.00/81.15
M. Garcia

**Category** ★★★ **Rooms** 7 and 1 suite (1 with air-conditioning) with telephone, bath, WC, TV and minibar. **Price** Double 420-680F, 680 F with terrasse. **Meals** Breakfast 40-60F, served 7:15-12:00. No restaurant. **Credit cards** Visa, Eurocard and MasterCard. **Pets** Dogs allowed (+40F). **Nearby** Cathedral of Mirepoix; tour Sainte-Foy; châteaux of Lagarde and of Caudeval, Montségur and Foix; caves of mas d'Azil. **Open** All year.

La Maison des Consuls is a historic residence located on the medieval square for which Mirepoix is famous. The hotel's letterhead reads "Panoramic view of the 18th century;" this is a figurative way of saying that four of the seven bedrooms recently decorated with antique furniture look out over the magnificently preserved square. All the bedrooms are very comfortable and have beautiful bathrooms. Breakfast is served in a small salon upstairs. For dinner, try *La Flambée*, just next door, or other small restaurants in the village during the summer season. M. Garcia is a jovial host.

***How to get there*** *(Map 31): 59km southwest of Carcassonne via D119.*

## Hôtel Eychenne

8, avenue Paul Laffont
09200 Saint-Girons (Ariège)
Tel. (0)5.61.66.20.55 - Fax (0)5.61.96.07.20 - M. and Mme Bordeau

**Category** ★★★ **Rooms** 42 with telephone, bath or shower, WC, cable TV and 35 with minibar. **Price** Single and double 290-565F. **Meals** Breakfast 48F, served 7:00-11:00; half board 380-443F, full board 505-565F (per pers., 3 days min.). **Restaurant** Service 12:15-13:30, 19:45-21:30 (closed Sunday evening and Monday Nov – Mar); menus 135-320F, also à la carte. Specialties: Foie de canard frais aux raisins, pigeonneau au fitou, gigot de lotte safrané, soufflé au grand marnier. **Credit cards** All major. **Pets** Dogs allowed. **Facilities** Swimming pool, parking. **Nearby** Saint-Lizier, Montjoie, Romanesques churches at the valley of Couserans in Oust and Cominac, Ercé Chapel in Garbet Valley, Castillon, Audressein, Sentein, Ayet, Ourtjou-les Bordes. **Open** Beg. Apr – Oct. Closed Sunday evening and Monday except National Holidays.

Managed by the Bordeau family for generations, the Eychenne has preserved its atmosphere of the past while offering the latest in modern amenities. In the two lounges, small bar, and dining room, the furniture, family objects and pictures create a friendly atmosphere. Most of the comfortable bedrooms, which are not very large, are furnished with antiques. Some have a beautiful view out over the Pyrénées. The cuisine – savory specialties of the Southwest – warrants a visit here. In summer, meals are served in the dining room which looks onto a garden, or lighter fare is available by the swimming pool. Breakfasts are generous. The staff is friendly and attentive.

***How to get there** (Map 30): In Saint-Girons, head towards Foix and follow the signs.*

## Château de Seignan

Montjoie
09200 Saint-Girons (Ariège)
Tel. (0)5.61.96.08.80 - Fax (0)5.61. 96.08.20 - M. de Bardies

**Category** ★★★ **Rooms** 9 with telephone, bath or shower, WC, TV and minibar. **Price** Double 320-850F. **Meals** Breakfast 45F, served 7:00-11:00, half board 395-580F (per pers., 3 days min.). **Restaurant** Service 12:00-14:30, 19:30-22:00; menus 150-380F, also à la carte. Specialties: Ravioles de homard, petit bar grillé, moelleux au chocolat chaud. **Credit cards** All major. **Pets** Dogs allowed. **Facilities** Swimming pool, tennis, parking. **Nearby** Saint-Lizier, Montjoie, Romanesque churches in the Couserans Valleys in Oust and Cominac, Ercé Chapel in the Garbet Valley, Castillon, Audressein, Sentein, Ayet, Ourtjou-les Bordes. **Open** Dec 1 – Oct 31.

At the foot of the Pyrénées, on the edge of the mysterious valleys of the Couserans and scarcely 1km from Saint-Girons, this family château was opened to guests several years ago by M. de Bardies. There are nine large, comfortable bedrooms furnished with antiques, while the bathrooms are very modern. The dining room is welcoming, as is the small lounge, where a pianist plays during cocktail hour. In summer, meals are served in the garden, which is shaded by century-old chestnut trees along the edge of the River Baup. A tennis court and swimming pool lend further appeal to the site. The staff is kind and courteous.

***How to get there*** *(Map 30): 1km east of Saint-Girons. In Saint-Girons, take D117 in the towards of Foix, on the right.*

## Hôtel Longcol

La Fouillade
12270 Najac (Aveyron)
Tel. (0)5.65.29.63.36 - Fax (0)5.65.29.64.28 - Luyckx Family - F. Cardaillac

**Category** ★★★ **Rooms** 17 with telephone, bath or shower, WC, TV and minibar. **Price** Double 600-850F. **Meals** Breakfast 70F, served 7:30-10:30; half board 575-760F (per pers., 2 days min.). **Restaurant** Service 19:45-21:30 (closed Tuesday in low season); menus 145-250F. **Credit cards** Amex, Visa, Eurocard and MasterCard. **Pets** Dogs allowed. **Facilities** Swimming pool, tennis, fishing, helicopter pad, parking. **Nearby** Château of Najac, Gorges of the Aveyron, Carthusian Monastery, Pénitents Noirs chapel and Place of Notre-Dame in Villefranche-de-Rouergue. **Open** Easter – Nov 11.

This old Rouergue country house is like a miniature village sitting on a wild mountain pass with the Aveyron flowing below. Recently restored and decorated beautifully, each room is furnished with Oriental objects, antique rugs and furniture and old studded doors – all elegantly arranged and comfortable. The lounge and billiards rooms are particularly gracious, a corner fireplace and large leather armchairs creating a convivial atmosphere. The bedrooms are all individually decorated, bright and cheerful. All have views of either the swimming pool or the valley. In summer you can fish in the river that runs through the property and can enjoy lunch by the pool, looking out over the beautiful countryside. The staff is courteous in keeping with the beauty of this hotel.

***How to get there*** *(Map 31): 19km south of Villefranche-de-Rouergue towards Monteils D47. After the bridge, towards La Fouillade D638 during 2,5km.*

# L'Oustal del Barry

Place du Bourg
12270 Najac (Aveyron)
Tel. (0)5.65.29.74.32 - Fax (0)5.65.29.75.32 - Mme Miquel

**Category** ★★ **Rooms** 20 with telephone, bath or shower, WC and TV - Elevator. **Price** Single 220-320F, double 325-450F. **Meals** Breakfast 48F, served 8:00-10:30; half board 320-360F, full board 390-430F (per pers., 2 days min.). **Restaurant** Service 12:30-14:00, 19:30-21:30; menus 130-250F, also à la carte. **Credit cards** Amex, Visa, Eurocard and MasterCard. **Pets** Dogs allowed. **Facilities** Parking. **Nearby** Château of Najac, Gorges of the Aveyron, carthusian Monastery, Pénitents Noirs chapel and Place of Notre-Dame in Villefranche-de-Rouergue. **Open** Apr – Oct (closed Monday, except public holidays, from Apr – June and Oct).

Five generations of the same family have presided over the Oustal del Barry, which has all the charms of a traditional French hotel. On the whole the bedrooms are rustic but with a curious mixture of other styles, principally Art Deco. The dining room has a panoramic view of the flowers and greenery of the 15-acre grounds. A vegetable garden cultivated by Mme Miguel grows several types of herbs used in the excellent cuisine, which also incorporates other local produce. The kindness of your hosts will make you regret leaving this simple and charming hotel. Hotel rates include free admission to the swimming pool at Najac, one hour of tennis a day and the use of bicycles.

***How to get there*** *(Map 31): 24km south of Villefranche-de-Rouergue via D922, then D239.*

## Grand Hôtel de la Muse et du Rozier

La Muse
12720 Peyreleau-le-Rozier (Aveyron)
Tel. (0)5.65.62.60.01 - Fax (0)5.65.62.63.88 - Mme Rigail

**Category** ★★★ **Rooms** 35, 3 apartments, with telephone, bath or shower, WC and TV - Elevator. **Price** Single 350-430F, double 410-650F, apart. 710-810F (per 2 pers.), 795-880F (per 3 pers). **Meals** Breakfast 65F, served from 8:00; half board 555-635F (obligatory in high season), full board 720-800F (per pers., 2 nights min.). **Restaurant** Service 12:30-14:15, 19:30-21:30; menus 160-220F, also à la carte. Specialties: Truite farcie au bleu des Causses, ravioles de Roquefort aux trompettes des bois, côtes d'agneau et son tripoux aux blettes et noix, gratin de chocolat et son jus d'orange au safran. **Credit cards** All major. **Pets** Dogs allowed (+50F). **Facilities** Swimming pool, parking, canoeing, garage (50F). **Nearby** Gorges of Tarn; gorges of the Jonte; gorges of the Dourbie; Montpelier-le-Vieux; the Aven Armand; caves of Dargilan; Batelier de la Malène; caves de Roquefort. **Open** Mar 16 – Nov 5.

Located at the entrance to the gorges of the Tarn, this large hotel, decorated in a resolutely modern and somewhat flashy style, is like a great ocean liner docked at the river's edge. Thirty-five bedrooms, all different and equipped with beautiful bathrooms, look out over the river. Several lounges and a large terrace where meals are served in summer enable you also to enjoy the superbly unspoiled site. At the hotel, you can swim in the pool, canoe or fish, and there are innumerable sports and touristic activities nearby. The Muse et Rozier is ideal for a stopover or a restful vacation, but it must be said that the charm of the hotel truly resides in its spectacular location.

***How to get there*** *(Maps 31 and 32): 19km northeast of Millau, take towards Clermont-Ferrand to Aguessac, then road to Florac, CD907. Then go about 13km.*

# Hostellerie Les Magnolias

12550 Plaisance (Aveyron)
Tel. (0)5.65.99.77.34 - Fax (0)5.65.99.70.57
Mme Roussel

**Rooms** 6 with telephone, bath, WC and TV. **Price** Single and double 250-350F. **Meals** Breakfast 48F (buffet); half board 250-300F (per pers.). **Restaurant** Service 12:15-14:00, 20:00-21:30; menus 68-295F, also à la carte. Specialties: Cuisine based on traditional local products. **Credit cards** All major. **Pets** Dogs allowed (+25F). **Nearby** Churches in Plaisance, Abbey of Sylvanes, Château du Bosc, Toulouse-Lautrec Museum in Albi – 18-hole golf course in Albi. **Open** Apr – Dec.

This is one of the outstanding hotels in this guide. A beautiful 14th-century dwelling once owned by Paul Valéry's brother, the property will enchant you at first glance. Carefully chosen, delicate decor has transformed this village house into a hotel of charming intimacy and character. Tremendous enthusiasm went into restoring and decorating the Magnolias with beautiful old stones, furniture, and the region's traditional *lauze* volcanic tiles. A new chef has arrived, offering regional dishes inspired by the outstanding cuisine of the hotel's founder, Monsieur Roussel. It is with the same enthusiasm that he has collected the materials and furnishings to decorate and restore his hotel. The already beautiful bedrooms at the top of a lovely staircase are to be renovated to further enhance the charm and comfort of this superb hotel. The Hostellerie is a place where the staff goes to great pains to ensure that you are content.

***How to get there*** *(Map 31): 42km east of Albi via D999 to Alban, then after 4km take D127.*

## Hôtel du Midi-Papillon

12230 Saint-Jean-du-Bruel (Aveyron)
Tel. (0)5.65.62.26.04 - Fax (0)5.65.62.12.97
M. and Mme Papillon

**Category** ★★ **Rooms** 18 and 1 suite with telephone, 13 with bath, 3 with shower and 18 with WC. **Price** Single 82F, double 131-203F, suite 335F. **Meals** Breakfast 24F, served 8:00-10:00; half board 193-294F, full board 228-264F (per pers. in double, 3 days min.). **Restaurant** Service 12:30-14:00, 19:30-21:30; menus 74-208F, also à la carte. Specialties: Galettes croustillantes aux écrevisses, mousse de tomates et crème aux fines herbes, tarte tatin d'escargots petits gris au ragoût de blettes et champignons, timbale de lapin aux courgettespanequet d'aubergines, nougatine et marbré aux 2 chocolats mousseline de marrons caramel à la crème. **Credit cards** Visa, Eurocard and MasterCard. **Pets** Dogs allowed. **Facilities** Heated swimming pool, whirlpool. **Nearby** Millau Belfry, Montpellier-le-Vieux, Gorges of the Tarn. **Open** Palm Sunday – Nov 11.

On the road to Mont Aigoual, the highest point in the Cévennes, Saint-Jean-du-Bruel is a good stopping place in the gorges of the Dourbie. The hotel is an old coach inn and has been run by the same family for four generations. Well situated on an outcrop above the river, it offers an outstanding picture-postcard view of the old village houses and a stone bridge. You'll find a friendly atmosphere and good cuisine prepared with homemade ingredients (poultry, *confits, foie gras, charcuteries*). Our favorite rooms are those which have just been renovated and have terraces overlooking the river. The breakfasts are excellent. The prices are surprisingly reasonable.

***How to get there*** *(Map 32): 99km northwest of Montpellier via N109 and N9 in the towards of Le Caylar to La Cavalerie, then D999 (as you enter the village).*

## Le Sénéchal

12800 Sauveterre-de-Rouergue (Aveyron)
Tel. (0)5.65.71.29.00 - Fax (0)5.65.71.29.09
M. Truchon

**Category** ★★★ **Rooms** 11 with air-conditioning, telephone, bath, WC, TV and minibar - Elevator – 1 for disabled persons. **Price** 450-550F, duplex 650-750F, suite 850-950F. **Meals** Breakfast 70F; half board 450-550F (per pers., 3 days min.). **Restaurant** Service 12:00-14:00, 19:30-21:30 (closed Monday and Tuesday lunchtime except public holidays, July and Aug); menus 130-400F, also à la carte. Specialties: Terrine de queues de bœuf en gelée à l'orange, tournedos de pied de porc en écailles de truffes, mousse de verveine fraîche et son sorbet. **Credit cards** All major. **Pets** Dogs allowed. **Facilities** Heated and covered swimming pool. **Nearby** Rodez, Plateau Le Ségala, lakes of Levézou and villages of Saint-Beauzély, Combéroumal, Castelnau-Prégayrols, Montjaux, Chestnut Festival on Nov 1, Saint-Christophe's Feast Day in July, Light Festival in Aug. **Open** All year except Feb.

In a former royal fortified village in the heart of the lovely Avéyron countryside, the big, brand-new Sénéchal is a haven of refinement and hospitality. The bedrooms, decorated in pale lemon colors, are very spacious, and look out over gentle hillsides. Spacious, too, are the bathrooms, the lounge and the dining room. Decor is modern and comfortable, with some antique furniture. The cuisine is delicious, inventive, and subtly spiced: a true feast. Don't miss a visit to the medieval village, which has beautifully conserved its chessboard layout, its arcades, fortifications, and church-dungeon. A small museum retraces the history of Sauveterre.

***How to get there*** *(Map 31): 32km southwest of Rodez.*

## Hôtel des Trois Lys

38, rue Gambetta
32100 Condom (Gers)
Tel. (0)5.62.28.33.33 - Fax (0)5.62.28.41.85 - Mme Manet

**Category** ★★★ **Rooms** 10 with telephone, bath or shower, WC and TV. **Price** Single 260F, double 380-560F. **Meals** Breakfast 42F, served 7:30-10:00. **Restaurant** Service 12:00-14:00, 19:30-22:00 (closed in Feb, Sunday evening and Monday except July and Aug); menus 80-140F, Chef's special (lunchtime) 48F, also à la carte. Specialties: Fish, confit de canard, magret. **Credit cards** Visa, Eurocard and MasterCard. **Pets** Dogs allowed. **Facilities** Swimming pool, garage. **Nearby** Armagnac Museum in Condom, châteaux, churches and bastides of Armagnac; Flaran, Larresingle, Fourcès, Tillac, Bassoues, Lavarders, Collegiate Church of La Romieu, Jazz festival in Marciac (August) – 18-hole Guinlet golf course in Eauze. **Open** All year except in Feb.

When they converted this 18th-century manor house into a hotel, the Manets decorated it with their own fine taste. The ten rooms are done in coordinated colors and furnished with antiques or excellent reproductions finished in splendid fabrics. The rooms are big – some very big – and some retain their wood paneling and Louis XV alcoves; double doors, thick carpeting and double windows ensure absolute silence. The bathrooms are also beautiful, with gleaming taps, colored tiles and soft lighting. A monumental stone staircase leads from the bedrooms to the ground floor. Pleasingly decorated in pastel tones, the dining room and the lounge wind to the back of the house where a swimming pool tempts you to plunge into its refreshing depths, especially in the height of summer. Needless to say the hospitality stems from Mme Manet's kindness. You can have your meals at the restaurant of the Hôtel *Le Dauphin* next door, where chef Philippe Hollard prepares good regional recipes and fish specialties.

***How to get there*** *(Map 30): 40km south of Agen.*

## Château de Fourcès

32250 Fourcès (Gers)
Tel. (0)5.62.29.49.53 - Fax (0)5.62.29.50.59
Mme Barsan

**Category** ★★★ **Rooms** 15 with telephone, bath or shower, WC and TV. **Price** Single and double 320-660F, 420-710F, suite 760-930F. **Meals** Breakfast 60F, served 8:00-10:00; half board 380-600F (per pers.). **Restaurant** Service 12:00-14:00, 20:00-22:00; menus 140-280F, also à la carte. Specialties: Foie gras en terrine, magret, games in season, mushrooms, pigeon. **Credit cards** All major. **Pets** Dogs allowed. **Facilities** Swimming pool, billiard, parking. **Nearby** Museum of Armagnac in Condom, châteaux, chruchs and bastide town in Armagnac: Flaran, Larressingle, Fourcès, Tillac, Bassoues, Lavardens, collégiale de La Romieu; boat trip on the Baïse in Condom- 18-hole Guinlet golf course in Eauze. **Open** Mid. Feb – mid. Jan.

On the route through the old fortified villages called *bastides* that dot the Armagnac region, Fourcès, built in the 11th century, is one of the smallest. Nevertheless, it boasts all the charm of traditional *bastide* architecture, including the half-timbered houses encircling its square, its arcades, and the castle that today is the beautiful Château de Fourcès hotel. The noble, austere edifice stands in a gentle site surrounded by happy fields sloping to the riverside. The castle is very restful inside as well, an atmosphere created by the elegance and refinement of the decor and by light filtering through the mullioned windows. The bedroom walls are made of the region's traditional blond stone, or decorated in pastel shades; the rooms are furnished with antiques and offer all the amenities, even though some have only a shower room. In a matter of months, the hotel's restaurant, presided over by the young chef Jean-Marc Rougier, has made a name for itself in the Gers, honoring specialties of this gastronomic region, and breakfast has the same delicious accent. So that you can enjoy the unique location of the village square, lunch is served in the *Auberge de Fourcès.*

***How to get there*** *(Map 30): 50km south of Agen, towards Condom. 12km west of Condom.*

## Hôtel de Bastard

Rue Lagrange
32700 Lectoure (Gers)
Tel. (0)5.62.68.82.44 - Fax (0)5.62.68.76.81 - M. Arnaud

**Category** ★★ **Rooms** 27 and 2 suite with telephone, bath or shower, WC and TV. **Price** Single 195-300F, double 230-360F. **Meals** Breakfast 40F; half board 265-360F, 460F for the suite (per pers., 3 days min.). **Restaurant** Service 12:15-13:30, 19:30-21:30; menus 85-240F, also à la carte. Specialties: Foie frais, carpaccio de magret. **Credit cards** All major. **Pets** Dogs allowed (+15F). **Facilities** Swimming pool, parking. **Nearby** Château de Gramont; châteaux, churches and bastides of Armagnac; Flaran, Larresingle, Fourcès, Tillac, Bassoues, Lavarders; Collegiate Church of La Romieu; jazz festival in Marciac (August) – 9-hole Fleurance golf course. **Open** Feb 16 – Jan 5.

Lectoure is a magnificent small fortified town overlooking the undulating countryside of the Gers. Setting out to explore the narrow streets lined with old houses, you will come across a large carved stone gateway which is the entrance to this 18th-century house. A large paved terrace with a swimming pool overlooks the village rooftops and open countryside. This view can be seen from the reception rooms, which are beautifully decorated, with pretty fabrics, high ceilings and handsome 18th-century style furniture. The bedrooms are small but comfortable; choose a room on the *premier étage* and make sure that the hotel is not giving a wedding party if it is a weekend! The Hôtel de Bastard is a charming place to stay.

***How to get there*** *(Map 30): 35km north of Auch via N21.*

## Château de Projan

32400 Projan (Gers)
Tel. (0)5.62.09.46.21 - Fax (0)5.62.09.44.08
Bernard Vichet

**Rooms** 10, 2 with shower, 1 with bath and WC. **Price** 200-500F. **Meals** Breakfast 40F, served 8:00-12:00; half board 340F (per pers., 3 days min.). **Restaurant** Only by reservation. Service from 13:00, 20:00 (closed Sunday in high season, Sunday and Monday in low season); menu 95F. Specialties: Melon au floc de gascogne, pintade du gers sauce cèpes, croustade aux pommes et à l'armagnac. **Credit cards** Visa, Eurocard and MasterCard. **Pets** Dogs allowed on request (+40F). **Nearby** Landes and Gascony Regional Parks; bastides; Lourdes (1hr); Château of Mascaraas, Museum of Vic-Bilh, the ocean 1 1/2 hr., jazz festival in Marciac (August). **Open** Easter – end Nov.

The beautiful, ancient Château de Projan is located in a 7-1/2-acre park on a rocky spur overlooking the two Valleys of the Lees. The present owners, who are veritable patrons of the arts, have gathered an impressive collection of contemporary art, which is exhibited throughout the château; combined with several imposing 17th- and 18th-century pieces of furniture, the overall effect is warm and inviting. The bedrooms, impeccably renovated and tastefully decorated, vary from vast to tiny. Some ultra-modern designer baths were cleverly integrated into the château, where space was available. Don't be horrified if you have to use the communal showers: the owners have transformed the ancient thermal baths into modern and beautiful facilities. Come here with an open mind, curious to discover a chateau that truly deserves a detour.

***How to get there*** *(Map 29): A 64, exit Pau. 40km north of Pau via N134 to Sarron, and D646 in the towards of Riscles.*

## Auberge du Bergeraye

32110 Saint-Martin d'Armagnac (Gers)
Tel. (0)5.62.09.08.72 - Fax (0)5.62.09.09.74
Mme Sarran

**Category** ★ **Rooms** 13 with telephone, bath or shower, WC, 7 with TV. **Price** 300-425F. **Meals** Breakfast 35F; half board 255-310F (obligatory in july and Aug), full board 335-400F (per pers.). **Restaurant** Service 12:00-14:30, 19:30-21:00 (closed Wednesday); menus 80-200F, also à la carte. Specialties: Foie gras de canard sur le grill, magret fourré de foie sur lit de cèpes et pommes de terre, pastis gascon. **Credit cards** Diner's, Visa, Eurocard and MasterCard. **Pets** Dogs allowed. **Facilities** Parking. **Nearby** Landes and Gascony Regional Parks; bastides; Lourdes (1hr); Château of Mascaraas, Museum of Vic-Bilh, jazz festival in Marciac (Aug) – 18-hole Quintet golf course, 18-hole Bigone golf course. **Open** All year.

The Auberge du Bergeraye is a typical house of the Gers *département:* simple, solid, and planted in the midst of vineyards and fields. At the foot of the auberge is a lake, and in the distance the Pyrénées appear, splendid and mysterious. You will find fourteen bedrooms here, some in the old auberge, others around the swimming pool, and the most recent in another building which has just been renovated. Each decorated individually, the rooms are quiet and comfortable. A discreet garden shades a large swimming pool, which the guests love. Pierrette Sarran, who is a cooking teacher from November to April, turns out a generous *cuisine de terroir,* employing products from neighboring farms and confering on this delicious auberge the charm of the past.

***How to get there*** *(Map 29): 35km southeast of Mont-de-Marsan towards Aire-sur-l'Adour, then N134; at the traffic circle, take towards Nogaro/Riscle and follow signs.*

## Domaine de Bassibé

32400 Ségos(Gers)
Tel. (0)5.62.09.46.71 - Fax (0)5.62.08.40.15
M. and Mme Lacroix

**Category** ★★★★ **Rooms** 11, 7 suites with telephone, bath, WC and TV. **Price** Double 650F, suite 980F. **Meals** Breakfast 75F, half board 640-805F, full board 850-1015F (per pers.). **Restaurant** Service 12:00-14:00, 19:30-22:00 (closed Tuesday and Wednesday lunchtime in low season); menus 160-240F, also à la carte. Specialties: Salade de joue de bœuf aux deux pommes et ciboulette, foie chaud petites pommes aux épices, bonne poule au pot d'autrefois, craquant de noisette. **Credit cards** All major. **Pets** Dogs allowed. **Facilities** Swimming pool, bicycle, parking. **Nearby** Landes and Gascony Regional Parks; bastides; jazz festival in Marciac (August) – 18-hole Mont-de Marsan golf course, 18-hole golf course in Pau, Tursan golf course (8km). **Open** Mid-Mar – Dec (closed Tuesday and Wednesday lunchtime in low season).

The Domaine de Bassibé was built in the old family mansion of a large farming estate. The ancient trees in the park and the carefully tended garden confer it with the reassuring atmosphere of tradition. Modern conveniences and elegance are also the key words in the bedrooms and bathrooms in the *Maison Vieille* as well as in the more recent *Maison des Champs* facing it. The rooms overlook the fragrant honeysuckle garden or, as far as the eye can see, the gentle hills of the Gers. There is no set time for breakfast, which you can enjoy in the flower garden in summer. Elegant meals accompanied by well-chosen wines are served around the large swimming pool shaded by great oak trees or in the pleasant dining room installed in the old wine press. The hospitality is friendly and attentive, too, making the Domaine de Bassibé, without reservation, a very charming hotel.

***How to get there*** *(Map 29): 35km southeast of Mont-de-Marsan towards Aire-sur-l'Adour, then N134. Airport and TGV (train) in Pau, 40km.*

# Auberge du Poids Public

31540 Saint-Félix-Lauragais (Haute-Garonne)
Tel. (0)5.61.83.00.20 - Fax (0)5.61.83.86.21
M. and Mme Taffarello

**Category** ★★★ **Rooms** 10 with telephone, bath or shower, WC, TV and minibar. **Price** Double 260-320F. **Meals** Breakfast 45F, served 8:00-10:00; half board 570-630F (per 2 pers.). **Restaurant** Service 12:00-13:30, 19:30-21:15 (closed Sunday evening Oct – Apr); menus 140-310F, also à la carte. Specialties: Terrine de foie gras cuit au torchon, gigotin d'agneau de lait des Pyrénées, croustillant aux fruits rouges. **Credit cards** Amex, Visa, Eurocard and MasterCard. **Pets** Dogs allowed. **Facilities** Parking. **Nearby** Cathedral of Saint-Papoul, Toulouse-Lautrec museum in Albi, Toulouse, Pastel road, Midi Canal road – 9 and 18-hole golf courses in Toulouse. **Open** Feb – Dec.

Located on the outskirts of the village, this old inn makes a pleasant stopping place. The bedrooms are fairly large and simply furnished with some antique pieces; six of them enjoy a beautiful view. Most are quiet; the few that look onto the street are only used if the others are full. There is a private bar-lounge. Depending on the time of year lunches and dinners are served either in the large, bright and prettily decorated dining room or in the shade of wide umbrellas on the lovely terrace. In either case the marvelous view is enhanced by outstanding cuisine, some of the best in the region.

***How to get there*** *(Map 31): 40km southeast of Toulouse; on the bypass of Toulouse via Revel towards Saint-Orens, exit number 18.*

# Hostellerie des 7 Molles

31510 Sauveterre-de-Comminges (Haute-Garonne)
Tel. (0)5.61.88.30.87 - Fax (0)5.61.88.36.42
M. Ferran

**Category** ★★★ **Rooms** 19 with telephone, bath, WC, TV and minibar. **Price** Single and double 420-780F, suite 900-1100F. **Meals** Breakfast 75F, served 8:00-11:00; half board 470-650F, full board 645-825F (per pers., 3 days min.). **Restaurant** Service 12:00-13:30, 19:30-21:30; menus 195-300F, also à la carte. Specialties: Pastis gersois de foie gras à la pomme reinette, agneau de lait des Pyrénées, cèpes. **Credit cards** All major. **Pets** Dogs allowed. **Facilities** Swimming pool, tennis, parking. **Nearby** Saint-Bertrand-de-Comminges, Montréjeau, Gallo-Roman villa of Montmaurin – 18-hole Lannemezan golf course, 9-hole golf course in Luchon. **Open** Mai – Oct.

The seven watermills have disappeared but the millstones remain and lend their name to the hotel. The immediate surroundings are superb: meadows, vines and groves of trees surround the house. The spacious, luminous bedrooms are furnished in traditional style. There is a warm ambience in the dining room and reception rooms. The cuisine, both traditional and modern, is made largely from homemade products, including sausages from the hotel's own pig farm, trout from the fish tank, *foie gras* and pastries. The staff is welcoming and friendly.

***How to get there*** *(Map 30): 74km southeast of Tarbes via A64, N117 to Saint-Gaudens, then D8 to Valentine and D9 (follow signs).*

1998

## Hôtel des Beaux-Arts

1, place du Pont-Neuf
31000 Toulouse (Haute-Garonne)
Tel. (0)5.61.23.40.50 - Fax (0)5.61.22.02.27 - M. Courtois de Viçose

**Category** ★★★ **Rooms** 20 with air-conditioning, telephone, bath or shower, WC, TV and minibar - Elevator. **Price** Single and double 450-800F, suite 900F. **Meals** Breakfast 65-75F, served 7:00-10:00. Snack available. **Credit cards** All major. **Pets** Dogs not allowed. **Facilities** Parking: Esquirol. **Nearby** In Toulouse: Fondation Bemberg, basilica of Saint-Cernin, Jacobins church, Museum of Saint-Raymond and Museum of Augustins, Le Capitole (Hôtel de ville), bastide of Grenade, cathedral of Lombez - 9-18-hole golf course in Toulouse. **Open** All year.

Of the original 17th-century building, this simple but elegant hotel still retains the façade and the bedrooms' unique view out over the Garonne River, the Hôtel Dieu and the Pont Neuf, especially magnificent at sunset. Twenty bedrooms with ultra-modern amenities, discreetly and tastefully decorated, have been designed to make the Beaux Arts a place of relaxation in the center of the city: Double windows and air-conditioning make for rest and relaxation in all seasons. The most delightful room is like a cozy loft, opening onto the sky and the river. If you don't want to go out for meals, the Brasserie Flo in the same building will serve you in your room. The breakfast-buffet is set out in a small vaulted room in the basement--a typical Toulouse cellar. For restaurants, try the gastronomic *Les Jardins de l'Opéra; La Frégate, La Brasserie des Beaux-Arts,* or *La Bascule.*

***How to get there** (Maps 30 and 31): Near the Pont Neuf.*

## Chez Marcel

Rue du 11 mai 1944
46100 Cardaillac (Lot)
Tel. (0)5.65.40.11.16 - M. Marcel Bernard

**Rooms** 5. **Price** Double 150F. **Meals** Breakfast 30F, served all morning, half board 200F, full board 250F (per pers., 3 days min.). **Restaurant** Service 12:00-13:30, 19:00-20:30 (closed Monday except in July and Aug); menus 80-180F, also à la carte. Specialties: Foie gras, omelette aux cèpes ou aux truffes, tripoux, truite aux croûtons, agneau du causse, fromage de Rocamadour, gâteau aux noix, clafoutis, profiterolles à la menthe et à la crème. **Credit cards** Visa, Eurocard and MasterCard. **Pets** Dogs allowed in restaurant. **Facilities** Parking on the Place du Fort. **Nearby** "Musée Eclaté" in Cardaillac, Valleys of the Lot and the Célé (Figeac-Cahors-Figeac). **Open** All year (closed Monday in low season).

In tiny Cardaillac, the grocery store is also the tobacco shop and the picturesque village restaurant Chez Marcel has several rooms for visitors. You'll enjoy delicious regional dishes and delightful hospitality. Although the traditionally furnished bedrooms are not very large, they are charming. But there's only one shower room on the floor for the five bedrooms. Still, at 150 F, we can't complain. And then there is the beautiful village of Cardaillac, which still has many vestiges of the Middle Ages and the time when it was a Protestant refuge. Today, the community takes pride in what is voted "one of the most beautiful villages of France."

***How to get there*** *(Map 24): 9km northwest of Figeac via N140, then D15 on the right.*

## Château de la Treyne

La Treyne
Lacave 46200 Souillac (Lot)
Tel. (0)5.65.27.60.60 - Fax (0)5.65.27.60.70 - Mme Gombert

**Category** ★★★★ **Rooms** 12, 2 apartments, with air-conditioning, telephone, bath, WC and TV. **Price** Double 700-1600F, apart. from 1600F. **Meals** Breakfast 80F, served all the morning; half board and full board 850-1260F (per pers., obligatory in summer). **Restaurant** Service 12:30-14:00, 19:30-22:00, menus 220F (lunchtime, wine and coffee incl.) 290-390F; à la carte. Specialties: Superposition de cabécou, agneau du quercy, pastis aux pommes. **Credit cards** All major. **Pets** Dogs allowed. **Facilities** Swimming pool, tennis, canoeing/kayaking, parking. **Nearby** Quercy region of the Dordogne from Souillac to Saint-Céré, Rocamadour, Padirac – 9-hole Rochebois golf course in Vitrac. **Open** Easter – mid-Nov.

The Château de la Treyne enjoys an exceptional location. Surrounded by a 297-acre forest, it has a formal garden and a park with age-old trees in which a crystalline swimming pool and tennis courts are nestled. This is a château on a human scale. The owner has elegant taste and has skillfully combined the respect for authenticity with the most modern conveniences. All the bedrooms are different and attractive in their own way. With names like *Soleil Levant, Prison Dorée, Enfant Modèle* and *Turenne,* each has an individual atmosphere. Here, luxury and charm blend marvelously, making this a very special and delightful place to stay.

***How to get there** (Map 23): 37km south of Brive-la-Gaillarde via N20 to Souillac, then D43 for 5km to La Treyne. Toulouse-Blagnac Airport.*

# Le Pont de L'Ouysse

46200 Lacave (Lot)
Tel. (0)5.65.37.87.04 - Fax (0)5.65.32.77.41
M. and Mme Chambon

**Category** ★★★ **Rooms** 13 with air-conditioning, telephone, bath, WC, TV and minibar. **Price** Single and double 600-650F, suite 800F. **Meals** Breakfast 65F, served 8:00-10:00; half board 650-700F (per pers.). **Restaurant** Service 12:30-14:00, 19:30-21:00; à la carte. Specialties: Ecrevisses, foie gras, pigeon aux cèpes, poulette rôtie aux truffes. **Credit cards** All major. **Pets** Dogs allowed. **Facilities** Swimming pool, parking. **Nearby** Quercy region of the Dordogne from Souillac to Saint-Céré, Rocamadour, Padirac – 9-hole Rochebois golf course in Vitrac. **Open** Mar 1 – Dec (closed Monday in low season).

The same family has always run this hotel, which is perched on the side of a rock surrounded by lush vegetation. The large, light bedrooms are very comfortable, with an attractive decor based on English wallpapers and coordinated fabrics. The bathrooms are equally pleasant. The road which goes over the river and up to the hotel is a dead end, ensuring peace and quiet. The charm of this place is enhanced by its lovely terrace, which is shaded by a horse chestnut and a linden tree, and provides outdoor dining in summer. The menu is not extensive but changes often, and the excellent cooking is a result of the imagination and skill of M. Chambon. Mme Chambon will give you a very friendly welcome.

***How to get there*** *(Map 23): 37km south of Brive-le-Gaillarde via N20 to Souillac, then D43.*

## La Petite Auberge

Domaine de Saint-Géry
46800 Lascabanes (Lot)
Tel. (0)5.65.31.82.51 - Fax (0)5.65.22.92.89 - M. and Mme Duler

**Rooms** 4 and 1 apartment with telephone, bath, WC. **Price** Double from 400F, apart. 680F. **Meals** Breakfast 60F, served 8:30-10:00; half board 380-620F (per pers., 3 days min., the night, obligatory in July and Aug). **Restaurant** Service 20:00-21:00 (closed Monday and Tuesday except in July and Aug), menus 125-350F. Specialties: Marcassin à la broche, salaisons de porc noir gascon maison, pain à l'ancienne cuit au fou à bois, carpaccio de magret de canard aux truffes, marquise au chocolat. **Credit cards** Visa, Eurocard and MasterCard. **Pets** Dogs allowed (+35F). **Facilities** Swimming pool, parking. **Nearby** Cathedral of Saint-Etienne in Cahors, Cahors wine route (château de Bonaguil), valley of the Lot and the Célé (Saint-Cirq-Lapopie). **Open** Mar 16 – Jan 9 (closed Monday and Tuesday in low season).

This is an auberge but it is above all Patrick and Pascale Duler's home where you will share with them the atmosphere of the past. The beautiful farm buildings surrounding the auberge are used for the farm. Acres of grain, a wild-boar farm, several black Gascon pigs, ducks and a vegetable garden provide the basis for hearty meals prepared and served with discreet charm by Pascale. The dinners served at a communal table, in the lounge or on the adjoining terrace in summer, are moments of great pleasure. (For proof, you only need to see the smiles when guests gather around the dessert buffet.) Five guest rooms with country furniture have been tastefully arranged, offering you space, quiet and comfort. At the Petite Auberge, you know what hospitality means.

***How to get there*** *(Map 30): 18 km southwest of Cahors via N20, towards Toulouse, then on right towards Montcuq on 500 meters, then* La bastide Marnhac *via D7 on 15km and follow signs.*

# Hostellerie Le Vert

Le Vert
46700 Mauroux (Lot)
Tel. (0)5.65.36.51.36 - Fax (0)5.65.36.56.84- M. and Mme Philippe

**Category** ★★ **Rooms** 7 with telephone, bath or shower, WC and TV. **Price** Single 240F, double 290-390F. **Meals** Breakfast 38F, served 7:30-10:30; half board 315-365F, full board 405-455F (per pers. 3 days min.). **Restaurant** Service 12:00-13:15, 19:30-20:30 (closed Thursday and Friday lunchtime); menus 100-165F, also à la carte. Specialties: Foie gras frais aux fruits frais, agneau du Quercy, poêlée de cèpes aux petits gris. **Credit cards** Amex, Visa, Eurocard and MasterCard. **Pets** Dogs allowed (+25F). **Facilities** Swimming pool, parking. **Nearby** Cathedral of Saint-Etienne in Cahors, Cahors wine route (château de Bonaguil), valley of the Lot. **Open** Feb 14 – Nov 11.

The Hostellerie Le Vert is an old converted farmhouse. Its windows shed a soft and gentle light on the spacious, comfortable and refined interior. A lovely terrace looks out over the surrounding countryside – a pleasant spot for a summer breakfast. The cuisine is very good. In summer, ask for the bedroom that has been made in the old vaulted cellar (No. 6), which is cool and unusual. Above it a large, bright new bedroom has just been added, with a beamed ceiling, stone floor, a beautiful fireplace and a piano. The bedrooms in the main hotel are not so original but are no less inviting and comfortable.

***How to get there*** *(Map 30): 37km west of Cahors via D911 to Puy-l'Evêque, then D5 in the towards of Mauroux.*

## Relais Sainte-Anne

Rue du Pourtanel
46600 Martel (Lot)
Tel. (0)5.65.37.40.56 - Fax (0)5.65.37.42.82 - Mme Lachèze

**Category** ★★★ **Rooms** 13 with telephone, bath or shower, WC, TV and 8 with minibar - 1 for disabled persons. **Price** Single and double 220-780F. **Meals** Breakfast 55F, served 8:00-12:00. No restaurant. **Credit cards** All major. **Pets** Dogs allowed (+50F). **Facilities** Heated swimming pool, parking. **Nearby** Rocamadour, Padirac, caves of Lacave, Dordogne Valley, Collonges-la-Rouge, abbey of Aubazines - Music festival in summer. **Open** Easter – Nov 14.

Don't be surprised to find a chapel here: The Relais Sainte-Anne was once a boarding house for nuns. There are ten lovely bedrooms located in several recently renovated buildings. All have very modern conveniences but each room is individually decorated in sober, elegant fabrics and colors. The largest room has a fireplace and a large terrace. All around the Relais, there is a walled-in, old garden with a lovely terrace, small paths and a beautiful swimming pool surrounded by a lawn. Breakfast can be served in your room, in the breakfast room which has a fireplace or, in good weather, on the terrace. In summer, classical music concerts are performed in the chapel. The Relais Sainte-Anne radiates with turn-of-the-century charm.

***How to get there*** *(Map 23): 30km south of Brive.*

## Claude Marco

Lamagdelaine 46090 Cahors (Lot)
Tel. (0)5.65.35.30.64 - Fax (0)5.65.30.31.40
Mme and M. Marco

**Rooms** 4 with telephone, bath with whirlpool bath, WC, satellite TV and minibar. **Prices** Double 480F, 550F, 580F; suite 680F. **Meals** Breakfast 50F, served 8:00-11:00; half board 450-680F (per pers.). **Restaurant** Service 12:00-14:00, 19:30-21:30 (closed Sunday evening and Monday except June 15 – Sep 15), menus 130F (lunchtime) 200-295F; also à la carte. Specialties: Foie gras au sel, tatin de foie gras, pot-au-feu de canard, filet de bœuf aux morilles. **Credit cards** Amex, Visa, Eurocard and MasterCard. **Pets** Dogs allowed. **Facilities** Swimming pool, parking. **Nearby** Cahors; Cahors Wine Route from Mercues to Montcabrier; Lot and Célé valley. **Open** Mar 6 –Jan 4 (closed Sunday evening and Monday in low season).

Claude Marco is well known and highly rated in all the French gastronomic guides. The addition of several bedrooms now gives us the opportunity to include his address in our guide and to suggest, a true gourmet's stay in an inn of character and charm. This beautiful old Quercy building and balcony are covered in greenery; inside, the lounges and dining room are located in superb barrel-vaulted rooms of pale-yellow stone, while the bedrooms have been installed in the garden, around the swimming pool. They are fresh, cheerful, elegant, and very comfortable, as are the the bathrooms with whirlpool bathtubs. In the restaurant, you may choose between the Menu Quercynois if you wish to discover the regional specialties; the Menu Surprise, which is made up depending on the best products from the market that day, and the chef's inspiration; and finally the Carte des Saisons, for seasonal specialties. The delicious cuisine aside, remember that you are in a very beautiful region, which has many natural and touristic sites of interest.

***How to get there*** *(Map 3): 7km from Cahors via D653 towards Figeac.*

1998

## Hôtel Beau Site

46500 Rocamadour (Lot)
Tel. (0)5.65.33.63.08 - Fax (0)5.65.33.65.23
M. Martial Menot

**Category** ★★★ **Rooms** 43 (20 with air-conditioning) with telephone, bath or shower, WC, TV - Elevator. **Price** Single and double 300-400F, 350-480F, suite 650F. **Meals** Breakfast 49F, served 7:00-9:30/10:30; half board 295-380F (per pers.). **Restaurant** Service 12:00-14:00, 19:00-21:00 (19:30-22:00 in summer); menus 98-250F, also à la carte. Specialties: Foie gras de canard à croque sel, agneau fermier des Causses. **Credit cards** All major. **Pets** Dogs allowed. **Facilities** Garage. **Nearby** Rocamadour, Padirac, caves of Lascaux - 9-hole Saint-Céré golf course. **Open** Feb 6 – Dec 31.

Rocamadour is world famous not only because pilgrims have been coming here since the Middle Ages, but also because of its extraordinary location on the flanks of a gigantic outcrop overlooking the cliffs rising above the causse limestone plateaux. The well-named "Beautiful Site" hotel stands in the very heart of the medieval city where, once the throngs have emptied the tiny pedestrian streets about 7 P.M., you will be one of the rare and privileged people to whom Rocamadour offers its most beautiful visage. A witness to the ancient age of the Beau Site, the lobby has a distinctly medieval, Haute Epoque style with, hidden behind the central stairway, two small vaulted lounges which are much appreciated in the heat of summer. The bedrooms are pleasant and all enjoy a beautiful view, our preference going to the room in the main house; the others are in front, above the restaurant. They have been renovated in a discreetly modern style, with attractive color schemes. Good regional cuisine is served in the panoramic restaurant, in the dining room or on the terrace.

***How to get there*** *(Map 24): 53km south of Brive-la-Gaillarde via N20 to Cressensac, then N140 and D673; 3km from Rocamadour, towards Payrac/Gourdon.*

## Hôtel Les Vieilles Tours

Lafage
46500 Rocamadour (Lot)
Tel. (0)5.65.33.68.01 - Fax (0)5.65.33.68.59 - M. and Mme Zozzoli

**Category** ★★ **Rooms** 18 with telephone, bath or shower and WC. **Price** Double 215-460F. **Meals** Breakfast 42-63F, served 8:00-11:00; half board 305-430F. **Restaurant** Lunch Sunday and National Holiday, 19:30-21:00; menus 118-320F, children 56F, also à la carte. Specialties: foie gras au vin de cahors, confit aux deux cuissons, escalope de foie gras, dos d'esturgeon, truite farcie au confit. **Credit cards** Visa, Eurocard and MasterCard. **Pets** Dogs allowed (+30F). **Facilities** Swimming pool, parking. **Nearby** Old town, Francis Poulenc museum in Rocamadour, Padirac chasm, Lascaux caves – 9-hole Saint-Céré golf course. **Open** Apr 4 – Nov 11.

This hotel is only 2 kilometers from Rocamadour. It has been well restored using beautiful local stone and enjoys exceptional views and tranquillity. The reception and dining room have their original stone walls and the tables are tastefully laid. There are bedrooms in both the old building and its modern annex, which was built in the local style. Pleasantly furnished, with some 19th-century pieces, the bedrooms are all different and have comfortable amenities, as do the bathrooms. M. Zozzoli is a painter, engraver and lithographer and you will find frequent examples of his work, which is inspired by the region. The menu offers delicious regional dishes, which change according to the season and Mme Zozzoli's inspiration.

***How to get there*** *(Map 24): 53km south of Brive-la-Gaillarde via N20 to Cressensac, then N140 and D673; 3km from Rocamadour, in the towards of Payrac/Gourdon.*

## Domaine de la Rhue

La Rhue
46500 Rocamadour (Lot)
Tel. (0)5.65.33.71.50 - Fax (0)5.65.33.72.48 - M. and Mme Jooris

**Category** ★★★ **Rooms** 12 with telephone, bath or shower, WC and 4 with TV. **Price** Single 370F, double 370-570F, apart. (4 pers.) 680F. **Meals** Breakfast 45-65F, served 8:00-10:00. No restaurant. **Credit cards** Visa, Eurocard and MasterCard. **Pets** Dogs allowed (+30F). **Facilities** Swimming pool, parking. **Nearby** Old town, Francis Poulenc museum in Rocamadour, Dordogne valley, Lascaux caves, Padirac chasm – 9-hole Montal golf course in Saint-Céré. **Open** Easter – Oct 17.

This hotel is located in the splendid stables of a château which is surrounded by beautiful rolling countryside. The Domaine is tastefully and comfortably furnished throughout. The vast entrance hall still has its original paving and traces of the stalls. Pleasantly furnished in a rustic style, the bedrooms are named after horse breeds, and are all spacious, quiet and attractive, with some antique furniture, elegant fabrics and many original beams. Some of the rooms on the ground floor are like small houses with a private terrace. The Domaine has all the modern amenities, mixed with the charm of the past. For excellent cuisine try the *Sainte-Marie* Restaurant.

***How to get there*** *(Map 24): 55km south of Brive-la-Gaillarde via N20 towards Cressensac, then N140; 1km before junction with D673, take the road on the right.*

## Hôtel Ric

Route de Leyme
46400 Saint-Céré (Lot)
Tel. (0)5.65.38.04.08 - Fax (0)5.65.38.00.14 - M. Ric

**Category** ★★★ **Rooms** 6 with telephone, bath, WC and TV. **Price** Double 300-400F **Meals** Breakfast 45F, served until 10:00; half board 350-400F (per pers.). **Restaurant** Service 12:00-14:00, 20:00-21:30 (closed Monday in low season except national holidays); menus 110-250F, also à la carte. Specialties: Parmentier de foie gras aux oignons frits, fleurs de courgettes farcies aux écrevisses, taboulé de langoustines, fondant au chocolat aux framboises et fraises des bois. **Credit cards** Visa, Eurocard and MasterCard. **Pets** Dogs allowed. **Facilities** Swimming pool, parking. **Nearby** Quercy region of the Dordogne from Souillac to Saint-Céré – 9-hole Saint-Céré golf course. **Open** All year except in Feb (closed Monday in low season except national holidays).

Surrounded by beautiful foliage, this small hotel has a magnificent view over the hills of Saint-Céré. The accommodations are modern, as is the decor. All the bedrooms are comfortable, but we prefer those on the front. In the pale-green dining room or on the terrace in summer, you will enjoy the inventive cuisine of the owner, M. Ric, who serves such specialties as fresh squash blossoms stuffed with crayfish. The staff is young and friendly.

***How to get there*** *(Map 24): 55km south of Brive-la-Gaillarde via D702, in the towards of Saint-Céré. At 2.5km from Saint-Céré, Leymé road by D48.*

# Auberge du Sombral

46330 Saint-Cirq-Lapopie (Lot)
Tel. (0)5.65.31.26.08 - Fax (0)5.65.30.26.37
M. and Mme Hardeveld

**Category** ★★ **Rooms** 8 with telephone, 5 with bath, 5 with shower. **Price** Single 300F, double 400F. **Meals** Breakfast 48F, served until 9:30. **Restaurant** Service 12:00-14:00, 19:30-21:00; menus 100-280F, also à la carte. Specialties: Truite au vieux Cahors, feuilleté d'asperges aux morilles, escalope de foie chaud aux pommes, terrine de foie de canard confit. **Credit cards** Visa, Eurocard and MasterCard. **Pets** Dogs allowed. **Nearby** Saint-Etienne Cathedral, Cahors Wine Route from Cahors to Bonaguil by the Lot Valley, valleys of the Lot and the Célé. **Open** Apr – Nov 11 (closed Tuesday evening and Wednesday).

This auberge is in an old house which has been perfectly restored. It faces the town square in the heart of this village, now classed as a historic monument. The village is on an escarpment overlooking the Lot Valley. The atmosphere is calm, the surroundings exceptional. The bedrooms are pleasant and comfortable. You can explore the village with its alleys and picturesque houses, as well as the auberge itself, which has its own museum with a permanent display of paintings by local artists. The restaurant offers excellent cuisine and emphasizes regional specialties.

***How to get there*** *(Map 31): 33km east of Cahors via D653 towards Saint-Géry, then D662.*

# Hostellerie La Source Bleue

Touzac
46700 Puy-l'Evêque (Lot)
Tel. (0)5.65.36.52.01 - Fax (0)5.65.24.65.69 - M. and Mme Bouyou

**Category** ★★★ **Rooms** 16 with telephone, bath, WC and TV - 1 for disabled persons. **Price** Single 280-320F, double 335-460F, suite 450-495F. **Meals** Breakfast 35F, served all the morning; half board from 290F, full board from 400F (per pers. in double, 2 days min.). **Restaurant** Service 12:00-13:30, 19:30-21:15 (closed in Jan and Feb, Wednesday lunchtime); menus 100, 140, 220F, also à la carte. Specialties: Saint-Jacques au safran, feuilleté de foie gras, agneau du Quercy, nougat glacé. **Credit cards** Amex, Visa, Eurocard and MasterCard. **Pets** Dogs allowed (+20-30F). **Facilities** Swimming pool, sauna (100F), health center, boat, bicycles rentals, parking. **Nearby** Marguerite-Moréno museum, Cahors wine route (château de Bonaguil) – 18-hole La Chapelle golf course in Auzac, 18-hole Castelnaud-de-Gratecambe golf course, Roucous golf course (18km). **Open** Mar 26 – Dec 31.

La Source Bleue, in a converted 14th-century paper mill on the left bank of the Lot, has been tastefully restored by its owners. The bedrooms, some with modern furniture, are comfortable, and the bathrooms are impeccable. Four new bedrooms have been added in the tower and decorated with antique furniture. The restaurant, located at the entrance to the park, is separate from the hotel. The cooking is refined and served in a beautiful dining room. The service is attentive but discreet, and there is soft background music. The gardens and park of "The Blue Spring" are beautiful with their many species of trees, including an impressive bamboo forest.

***How to get there*** *(Map 30): 39km west of Cahors via D911 towards Fumel/Villeneuve-sur-Lot; at Touzac, cross the Lot.*

## Hostellerie Saint-Antoine

17, rue Saint-Antoine
81000 Albi (Tarn)
Tel. (0)5.63.54.04.04 - Fax (0)5.63.47.10.47 - MM. Rieux and son

**Category** ★★★★ **Rooms** 48 with air-conditioning, telephone, bath, WC, TV and minibar. **Price** Single 360-450F, double 450-750F, suite 850-950F. **Meals** Breakfast 60F; half board 420-720F (per pers.). **Restaurant** Service 19:00-21:30 (closed Sunday); menu 140F, also à la carte. Specialties: Foie gras, salade d'écrevisses, daube de bœuf à l'albigeoise, tournedos Périgueux, tarte à l'ancienne, glace aux noix. **Credit cards** All major. **Pets** Dogs allowed (+30F). **Facilities** Tennis in "La Réserve", parking. **Nearby** Cathedral of Sainte-Cécile, Toulouse-Lautrec museum in Albi, Viaur viaduct, Ambialet, Gaillac, Cordes – 18-hole golf course in Albi. **Open** All year.

Founded in the 18th-century and run by the same family for five generations, this inn was restored in 1960. Elegantly modernized, each room is enhanced by antique furniture – including Directoire and Louis-Phillippe pieces, and bright fabrics. The bedrooms are extremely comfortable, quiet, well-designed and many have a view of the flower garden. Some of the larger ones have a lounge area. On the ground floor the dining room opens onto the garden. You will enjoy good traditional cooking, attentive service and warm hospitality.

***How to get there*** *(Map 31): In the town center.*

## Cuq-en-Terrasse

Cuq-le-Château - 81470 Cuq-Toulza (Tarn)
Tel (0)5.63.82.54.00 - Fax (0)5.63.82.54.11
M. and Mme Whitmore

**Rooms** 7 and 1 apartment (duplex) with tel., bath or shower, WC and TV. **Price** 400-500F, suite 700F, apart. 900F. **Meals** Breakfast 55F, served 8:30-10:00. **Restaurant** By reservation. Service 12:00-14:30, 19:30-21:30; menus 130F (lunch), 150F (dinner). Specialties: Vichyssoise, gazpacho, mousse de saumon fumé, filet mignon de veau à l'estragon et aux baies roses, noisettes d'agneau aux deux poivrons. **Credit cards** Diner's, Visa, Eurocard and MasterCard. **Pets** Dogs allowed. **Facilities** Swimming pool. **Nearby** Albi, Carcassonne, Castres market in Revel – 18-hole Fiac Golf Course. **Open** Feb 7 – Jan 5.

This ancient house spreads out over an enchanting terraced hillside. From the terraces and the garden swimming pool, you will have a superb view over the patchwork of rich valleys the locals call *Le Pays de Cocagne*, the land of abundance. Le Cuq en Terrasse has been magnificently restored and decorated by an English architect and his wife. Tasteful decoration in the bright bedrooms and baths make this a very beautiful hotel, in which traditional decor has been skillfully combined with the most modern amenities. You will enjoy the sheer serenity of the place, from the terrace to the shady nooks around the swimming pool. Breakfasts are generous and elegant and Zara Whitmore serves delicious regional cuisine. There is an excellent choice of wines, and the owners are friendly and considerate.

***How to get there*** *(Map 31): 35km east of Toulouse, towards Castres. In Cuq, take towards Revel for 2km. On A61, exit number 17.*

## Demeure de Flore

106, Grande rue
81240 Lacabarède (Tarn)
Tel. (0)5.63.98.32.32. - Fax (0)5.63.98.47.56 - Mme Tronc

**Category** ★★★ **Rooms** 10 and 1 suite with telephone, bath, WC and TV - Wheelchair access **Price** Single 370F, double 480F, suite 780F. **Meals** Breakfast 56F. **Restaurant** Service 19:30-21:00 menus 100-130F, also à la carte. **Credit cards** Visa, Eurocard and MasterCard. **Pets** Small dogs allowed (+70F). **Facilities** Swimming pool, parking. **Nearby** Goya museum in Castres, le Sidobre and the Monts Lacaune de Castres in Mazamet – 18-hole La Barouge golf course in Pont-de-l'Arn. **Open** All year except in Dec.

This small hotel is hidden from the road by lush vegetation. Indoors, the decor is elegant; antique furniture, paintings and curios combine to create a warm and cozy atmosphere. The comfortable bedrooms are all individually decorated with colorful designer fabrics and antiques bought locally. The bathrooms are modern and luxuriously equipped. Our favorite rooms are those with a small terrace and access to the garden and swimming pool. Evening meals, based on fresh local produce, are served in the lovely dining room. This is a marvelous place to stay.

***How to get there*** *(Map 31): 15km east of Mazamet via N112.*

## Château de Montlédier

Route d'Anglès
81660 Pont-de-L'Arn (Tarn)
Tel. (0)5.63.61.20.54 - Fax (0)5.63.98.22.51 - Mme Thiercelin

**Category** ★★★ **Rooms** 12 with telephone, bath, WC, TV and minibar. **Price** Single 370F, double 450-600F. **Meals** Breakfast 50F; half board 360-440F, full board 480-560F (per pers., 3 days min.). **Restaurant** Service 12:00-13:30, 19:30-21:30 (closed Sunday evening and Monday except July – Aug); menus 130-200F, also à la carte. Specialties: Foie gras maison, carré d'agneau, magret de canard, soufflé léger à la poire. **Credit cards** All major. **Pets** Dogs allowed. **Facilities** Swimming pool, parking. **Nearby** Goya museum in Castres, le Sidobre and the Monts Lacaune de Castres in Mazamet; 18-hole La Barouge golf course in Pont-de-l'Arn. **Open** Feb 1 – Dec 31.

From one side, the Château de Montlédier seems to be quietly poised on the hilltop, while from the other, it overlooks a dizzying precipice. You enter the château through the main courtyard. Inside, the bedrooms are spacious and beautifully decorated, and each is extremely comfortable. The smallest and least expensive rooms *(Victoria* and *Alexandra)* are as charming as the others, and the *Raymond IV* bedroom has a particularly charming bathroom – it is huge and from it you can see through the trees into the ravine. Four new, recently opened bedrooms are quiet and comfortable, but they lack the distinction of the others. Meals are served in a large, barrel-vaulted dining room—once the kitchen of the château—or on the terrace. Madame Thiercelin manages the hotel with great cordiality.

***How to get there*** *(Map 31): 19km southeast of Castres via N112 towards Mazamet, then at Pont-de-l'Arn D54.*

# Le Métairie Neuve

81660 Pont-de-L'Arn (Tarn)
Tel. (0)5.63.97.73.50 - Fax (0)5.63.61.94.75
Mme Tournier

**Category** ★★★ **Rooms** 14 with telephone, bath, WC, TV and minibar. **Price** Single 320-440F, double 390-480F. **Meals** Half board 300-550F, full board 450-680F (per pers., 3 days min.). **Restaurant** Service 19:30-21:00 (closed Saturday and Sunday Oct 1 – Mar 30); menus 95-120F, also à la carte. Specialties: Regional cooking. **Credit cards** Diner's, Visa, Eurocard and MasterCard. **Pets** Dogs allowed. **Facilities** Swimming pool, parking. **Nearby** Goya museum in Castres, le Sidobre and the Monts Lacaune de Castres in Mazamet – 18-hole La Barouge golf course in Pont-de-l'Arn. **Open** Jan 20 – Dec 13.

This lovely old farmhouse is on the outskirts of a village which is expanding with commercial developments, but the hotel remains in a leafy, quiet area. The bedrooms are all well equipped and elegantly furnished; the colors are harmonious and the old furniture blends perfectly with the more modern pieces. The hotel has a beautiful courtyard, a large garden with a terrace, and a swimming pool. One of the restaurant's two rooms is reserved for non-smokers. But the cuisine itself needs improvement.

***How to get there*** *(Map 31): 19km southeast of Castres via N112 towards Mazamet.*

# Domaine de Rasigous

81290 Saint-Affrique-les-Montagnes (Tarn)
Tel. (0)5.63.73.30.50 - Fax (0)5.63.73.30.51
M. Fons Pessers

**Rooms** 4 and 1 suite with telephone, bath or shower, WC and TV. **Price** Single and double 225F, 400-500F, suite 600F. **Meals** Breakfast 50F, served from 8:00. **Restaurant** By reservation, for residents, from 19:00; menus 135F. Seasonal cuisine. **Credit cards** Not accepted. **Pets** Dogs allowed. **Facilities** Swimming pool, parking and garage. **Nearby** Goya Museum in Castres, Le Sidobre, mounts of Lacaune and Castres in Mazamet - 18-hole Mazamet golf course. **Open** Jan 2 – Dec 14.

Set in the beautiful green countryside of the southern Tarn, this large 19th-century house has been skillfully renovated by its new owners, who have a fine appreciation for the comfort and charm of the past. With hospitality and efficiency, they have created the warm atmosphere of a vacation house here, offering quiet and relaxation. You will find five bedrooms where no detail has been overlooked. Beautiful antique furniture and paintings make them seem like guests' rooms in a home, and all have ultra-modern baths. The marriage of past and present is achieved with special flair in the garden full of flowers and in the park with its century-old shade trees. Dinners, reserved for residents, feature generous, light cuisine with an abundance of fresh seasonal vegetables.

***How to get there*** *(Map 31): 18km west of Mazamet, dir. Toulouse, La Bruiguière. Go 12km, then towards Dourgne. In 2km from Sainte-Affrique, on the left.*

# Château de l'Hoste

Saint-Beauzeuil
82150 Montaigu-de-Quercy (Tarn-et-Garonne)
Tel. (0)5.63.95.25.61 - Fax (0)5.63.95.25.50 - M. Poumeyrau

**Category** ★★ **Rooms** 32 with telephone, bath and WC. **Price** Single and double 210-260F. **Meals** Breakfast 40F, served 8:00-10:00; half board 280F, full board 380F (per pers., 3 days min.). **Restaurant** Service 12:00, 19:45 (closed Sunday evening and Monday in low season); menus 115-220F, also à la carte. Specialties: Lamproie bordelaise, trilogie de bœuf, cassoulet d'antan. **Credit cards** Visa, Eurocard and MasterCard. **Pets** Dogs allowed (+20F). **Facilities** Swimming pool, parking. **Nearby** Agen museum, Port-Sainte-Marie, Villeneuve-sur-Lot, Beauville – 18-hole Castelneau golf course. **Open** All year.

We were charmed by the country setting of this 18th-century *gentilhommière,* its pale walls of exposed stone, the beautiful courtyard designed on a human scale, and the proximity of the swimming pool. The decoration has been less successful in the bedrooms where the antique-style furniture is disappointing. They are nevertheless large, well kept rooms with comfortable beds and impeccable bathrooms. We recommend rooms 204 and 210, which are smaller but charming. In summer avoid the rooms that overlook the terrace where dinner is served; the enthusiasm of the diners enjoying the chef's excellent cooking (especially the *lamproie à la bordelaise*) may disturb you if you want to retire early.

***How to get there*** *(Map 30): 30km northeast of Agen via D656 (at the level of Roquecor); towards Agen and Tournon d'Agenais.*

1998

## Le Lys Bleu

29, place de la Halle
82140 Saint-Antonin-Noble-Val (Tarn-et-Garonne)
Tel. (0)5.63.30.65.06 - Fax (0)5.63.30.62.27 - M. Risi-Charlot

**Category** ★★★ **Rooms** 11 with telephone, bath or shower, WC, TV and minibar. **Price** Single and double 360-490F. **Meals** Breakfast 50F; half board 340-405F (per pers., 3 days min.). **Restaurant** Service 12:30-14:30, 19:30-23:00; menus 100F (lunchtime), 160-250F, also à la carte. Specialties: Foie gras, magret, fish, tarte aux noix. **Credit cards** Visa, Eurocard and MasterCard. **Pets** Dogs allowed. **Facilities** Parking. **Nearby** In Saint-Antonin-Noble-Val: Prehistory Museum, Varen, Abbey of Beaulieu, villages in Bonette Valley (Caylus, Chapelle-Livron), Montauban (Ingres Museum), Moissac, Lauzerte, Montpezat-de-Quercy, Caussade. **Open** All year.

The former prosperity of Saint-Antonin-Noble-Val is still reflected in the town's elegant terrace on the edge of the Aveyron River, and in its beautiful houses, one of which is the Lys Bleu. Offering the tranquillity of the town as it must have been in the past, eleven simple bedrooms are discreetly appointed and have small baths. Downstairs, you can relax in several corner lounges and on a small, cool patio where breakfast is served in summer. The hotel's restaurant, located two houses farther on, is truly delightful, offering delicious cuisine complemented by a large, somewhat baroque dining room where an open fire crackles in winter; in summer, you can enjoy dinner until 11 P.M. in the tropical garden. It all makes for a rare and welcoming atmosphere.

***How to get there*** *(Map 30): 45km northeast of Montauban, towards. Gorges de l'Aveyron and Saint-Antonin.*

# Auberge du Bon Fermier

64-66, rue de Famars
59300 Valenciennes (Nord)
Tel. (0)3.27.46.68.25 - Fax (0)3.27.33.75.01 - M. Beine

**Category** ★★★★ **Rooms** 16 with telephone, bath, WC, TV and minibar. **Price** Single 400-600F, double 480-700F. **Meals** Breakfast 45F, all the morning. **Restaurant** Service 12:00-14:30, 19:00-22:30; menus 120-200F, also à la carte. Specialties: Langue Lucullus, cochon de lait à la broche, tarte au maroilles (goyère). **Credit cards** All major. **Pets** Dogs allowed. **Facilities** Parking (+50F). **Nearby** Remains of the ancient abbey in Saint-Amand-les-Eaux, fortifications of Le Quesnoy, the Helpe valley; Watteau museum in Valence – 9-hole golf course in Valenciennes. **Open** All year.

Stop off at the Auberge du Bon Fermier for a comfortable evening in what used to be a royal carriage house in the17th-century, on the road from the Tuileries to Brussels. It has been an inn since 1840, and is now registered a historic monument, scrupulously restored by its present owners. The red bricks of the outer walls and many inner ones, the exposed beams, and the oak floors all help recreate the atmosphere of that era. The rooms are all spacious and enchanting, and each has a sitting area. The quietest ones are on the park. Modern conveniences have been carefully blended into the decor. The restaurant serves regional specialties but also features fresh lobster and a wide range of spit-roasted meats. The atmosphere is somewhat theatrical, but this is nonetheless a place not to be missed.

***How to get there*** *(Map 3): In the town center, between the "Place du Canada" and the town hall.*

## Chartreuse du Val Saint-Esprit

1, rue de Fouquières
62199 Gosnay (Pas-de-Calais)
Tel. (0)3.21.62.80.00 - Fax (0)3.21.62.42.50 - M. and Mme Constant

**Category** ★★★★ **Rooms** 56 with telephone, bath, WC, TV and minibar. **Price** Single 340-610F, double 420-910F, suite 1500F (1-2 pers.). **Meals** Breakfast 60F, served 6:30-10:00. **Restaurant** Service 12:00-14:30, 19:00-22:00; menus 265F (lunchtime in week, wine incl.); 285-365F, also à la carte. Specialties: Médaillons de homard et ravioles de Royans dans un bouillon à la tomate au basilic, foie gras rôti et caramélisé au miel, filet d'esturgeon grillé, vinaigrette de lentilles et beurre battu. **Credit cards** All major. **Pets** Dogs allowed (+45F). **Facilities** Parking. **Nearby** Golf course at Aa. **Open** All year.

At first sight this splendid brick and stone edifice, with its great courtyard and large park, may seem rather austere. This first impression is, however, immediately dispelled by a warm and friendly welcome and the refinement of the interior decoration. Most of the rooms are vast, and the *premier étage* bedrooms with impressive high-ceilings are extremely comfortable, with beautiful bathrooms. Lavish amounts of attention have been devoted to features such as bedspreads, curtains and wallpapers, which all blend to perfection. The *deuxième étage* rooms tend to be less bright, but this makes them more cozy and intimate. The breakfast room is delightful, with a row of arched windows overlooking the gardens. The hotel has added new bedrooms which match the charm of the older ones. A recent *brasserie* service has been added for simple meals.

***How to get there*** *(Map 2): 5km south of Béthune via A26, number 6 exit, in the towards of Chartreuses.*

## Château de Cocove

62890 Recques-sur-Hem (Pas-de-Calais)
Tel. (0)3.21.82.68.29 - Fax (0)3.21.82.72.59
M. Cyril Maupin

**Category** ★★★ **Rooms** 22 with telephone, bath or shower, WC and TV. **Price** Single and double 455-735F. **Meals** Breakfast 45F, served 7:30-10:30; "weekend gastronomic" 2250F (2 pers.). **Restaurant** Service 12:00-14:00, 19:30-21:30; menus 135-350F, also à la carte. Specialties: Fricassée de soles et langoustines, foie gras maison. **Credit cards** All major. **Pets** Dogs allowed (+45F). **Facilities** Sauna (25F), parking. **Nearby** Basilica of Notre-Dame and Sandelin museum in Valenciennes, blockhouse in Eperlecques, church of Saint-Eloi and museum in Hazebrouck, the 'Bourgeois de Calais', art and lace museum in Calais – 27-hole Saint-Omer golf course in Lumbres. **Open** All year (closed Dec 25).

Only a few minutes from Calais, this 18th-century château is deep in the countryside surrounded by an extensive English-style park. You will enjoy youthful and charming hospitality here. The interior has been beautifully restored in keeping with the age of the building. In the same spirit the dining room has been converted from the old stables, its wide doors replaced by bay windows; pale subdued decor adds to the elegance of the room. The cuisine is good, attractively presented and offers excellent value for money. The bedrooms are bright and quiet and some are very large; there are occasional antiques. Renovation of the rooms is being completed and we are already very satisfied with the result as regards the cheerful, elegant decoration as well as the modern amenities. Before leaving, wine lovers can visit the cellars and buy from a large selection of excellent wines at reasonable prices.

***How to get there*** *(Map 2): 17km southeast of Calais: from Calais by A26, number 2 Ardres-Licques exit. Or via N43 towards Saint-Omer.*

# Hôtel Cléry

62360 Hesdin-l'Abbé (Pas-de-Calais)
Tel. (0)3.21.83.19.83 - Fax (0)3.21.87.52.59
M. and Mme Legros

**Category** ★★★ **Rooms** 17 and 5 suites with telephone, bath or shower, WC and satellite TV. **Prices** Single and double 330-585F, 745F, pavillon 1100F (5 pers.). **Meals** Breakfast 55F, served 7.00-10:30. **Restaurant** For residents only. Service 19:00-21:00; menus 135-165F, also à la carte. **Credit cards** All major. **Pets** No dogs allowed. **Facilities** Tennis, mountain bike rentals, parking. **Nearby** Castle-museum and national marine center in Boulogne-sur-Mer, pottery museum in Desvres, Opal coast, Cap Gris-Nez, Cap Blanc-Nez – 18-hole golf course in Hardelot. **Open** Feb 1 – Dec 10.

Legend has it that Napoleon stayed at this small château. There are three rooms on the ground floor: a large, light room where breakfast is served, a bar and a beautiful room where you can sit in deep leather armchairs by an open fire. An elegant staircase with a Louis XV style wrought iron banister leads to the premier étage. The bedrooms are comfortable and the decor simple. The rooms on the deuxième étage have gently sloping mansard roofs, but whether they look out on the chestnut trees in the park or on the drive, all the bedrooms are quiet. Behind a beautiful paved courtyard filled with flowers, seven bedrooms are located in the former stables. Room 8 is on the ground floor, and those on the *premier étage* include two small rooms which are lovely. Finally, there is a pavilion containing two bedrooms with a small lounge and an open fire if you wish. A short distance from the national highway, the hotel is conveniently located on the road to England. For restaurants, *La Matelote* in Boulogne is very good; simpler fare is served at *l'Huitrière* and *Chez Jules*; and at the Centre National de la Mer, you can enjoy delicious shellfish at the *Grand Pavois*.

***How to get there*** *(Map 1): 9km southeast of Boulogne via N1.*

## Hostellerie du Moulin du Pré

14860 Bavent (Calvados)
Tel. (0)2.31.78.83.68 - Fax (0)2.31.78.21.05
Hamchin-Holtz Family

**Category** ★★ **Rooms** 10 with telephone, bath or shower and 5 with WC. **Price** Double 225-350F. **Meals** Breakfast 40F, served 8:00-10:00. **Restaurant** Service 12:30-13:30, 19:30-21:00; menus 189F, 255-300F, also à la carte. Specialties: Pommes de terre en millefeuille au saumon fumé, panaché de poissons fins à l'oseille, filet de rouget-barbet rôti sauce bouillabaisse, assiette normande. **Credit cards** All major. **Pets** Dogs not allowed. **Facilities** Parking. **Nearby** Deauville, Caen, Normandy landing beaches, Houlgate – 18-hole Le Home Varaville golf course in Cabourg. **Open** All year except Mar 1-15 and Oct (closed Sunday evening and Monday except July, Aug and national holidays).

Surrounded by fields but not far from the Caen-Cabourg road (the sea is 5 kilometers away in Franceville), this old renovated farmhouse is a good, simple hotel with a very pleasant staff. The interior decoration is quite typical of a rustic country inn. Located upstairs, the bedrooms are modest, quite small, and somewhat old-fashioned, but they are reasonably priced for the region. They are equipped with hip baths or showers and some do not have private toilets. Rooms 1 and 2 share a bathroom. Soundproofing depends greatly on the room. Good, copious meals are served in a lovely dining room with a big fireplace and beamed ceilings, which is pleasantly illuminated in the evening. Next to the reception desk is a lounge corner which is somewhat dark and charmless, but the garden, the lake and the wooded surroundings make a lovely spot to walk in the fresh country air.

***How to get there*** *(Map 7): 14km northeast of Caen via D513 towards Cabourg, then left onto D95A (after the Bavent nursery) towards Gonneville-en-Auge.*

## Hostellerie du Château de Goville

14330 Le-Breuil-en-Bessin (Calvados)
Tel. (0)2.31.22.19.28 - Fax (0)2.31.22.68.74 - M. Vallée

**Category** ★★★ **Rooms** 12 with telephone, bath or shower, WC and minibar. **Price** Double 495-695F, suite 695F. **Meals** Breakfast 60F, served 8:30-11:30; half board 475-585F (per pers., 2 days min.). **Restaurant** "Le Baromètre". Service 12:30-14.00, 19:30-21:30 (closed Tuesday in low season except by reservation); menus 140-245F, also à la carte. **Credit cards** All major. **Pets** Dogs allowed (+75F). **Facilities** Parking. **Nearby** Bayeux tapestry and cathedral, châteaux of Vaulaville and of Fontaine-Henry, beach of debarquement, church of Saint-Loup-Hors, abbey of Mondaye – 27-hole Omaha Beach golf course. **Open** All year.

The Château de Goville has retained all the character and charm of a private home. It has belonged to Monsieur Vallée's family since 1813 and the owner is greatly attached to the setting, the furniture and the objects which have been left by the generations preceding him. The interior decoration is outstandingly elegant: there is not a single piece of furniture, an object, or a picture which is not an original antique. The bedrooms are especially charming and decorated with great taste and thought; each has its special personality. Our favorites are those on the premier étage, but all are attractive. On the upper floors, you will find collections of dolls which are either antiques or Monsieur Vallée's own creations. The salon, Napoléon III in style, is very inviting and comfortable for afternoon relaxation or cocktails. The dinners, illuminated by real candles in an immense crystal chandelier, are simply...enchanting. The produce and bread are homemade, and all the recipes are made with fresh ingredients. Monsieur Vallée's hospitality puts a lovely finishing touch on the Château de Goville, making it one of the most charming hotels in Normandy.

***How to get there*** *(Map 7): 38km northwest of Caen via N13 to Bayeux, then D5 towards Molay-Littry, singposted before Molay.*

## Ferme Hôtel La Rançonnière

Route d'Arromanches
Crépon 14480 Creully (Calvados)
Tel. (0)2.31.22.21.73 - Fax (0)2.31.22.98.39 - Mmes Vereecke and Sileghem

**Category** ★★ **Rooms** 35 with telephone, bath or shower, WC and TV. **Price** Single and double 295-380F, in "La Ferme de Mathan" 380-480F. **Meals** Breakfast 45F, served 7:45-10:00; half board 310-410F (per pers.). **Restaurant** Service 12:00-14:00, 19:00-21:30; menus 98-280F, also à la carte. Specialties: Homard frais flambé, salade champêtre. **Credit cards** All major. **Pets** Dogs allowed. **Facilities** Parking. **Nearby** Bayeux tapestry and cathedral, châteaux of Creullet and of Creully, church of Saint-Loup-Hors, abbey of Mondaye – 27-hole Omaha Beach golf course. **Open** All year.

The Bessin region is full of old manor houses and Crépon has more than its share in terms of both numbers and quality. You enter this old farm through a crenellated carriage gate into a vast courtyard around which are the reception, restaurant and the bedrooms of the hotel. The interior is decidedly rustic with wooden furniture and exposed timbers everywhere. Comfortable bedrooms have small windows and old furniture whose dark tones are at times a little heavy. We particularly like rooms 2, 3, 5, 6, 7, 9, 18, 24, 28, 29 and for families we like rooms 8, 23, 25, 31 and 32. Note also the Ferme de Mathan, 300 feet away, where several bedrooms have just been opened, the largest being also the most attractive. The excellent restaurant is very popular in the region. The Rançonnière seems to get better and better, and you couldn't ask for a warmer welcome.

***How to get there*** *(Map 7): 21km northwest of Caen (exit number 6) via D22 towards Creully/Arromanches. In Creully onright of the church and 3km.*

1998

## L'Augeval

15, avenue Hocquart de Turtot
14800 Deauville (Calvados)
Tel. (0)2.31.81.13.18 - Fax (0)2.31.81.00.40 - Mme Guilbert

**Category** ★★★ **Rooms** 32 (8 with air-conditioning) with telephone, bath (26 with whirlpool), WC, satellite TV and minibar - 2 for disabled persons. **Price** Double 380-820F; suite 820-1400F. **Meals** Breakfast 60F; half board +200F (per pers.). **Restaurant** with air-conditioning. Service 12:00-14:30, 19:00-22:30; menus 128-280F, also à la carte : Fricassée de pintade, filets de sole noumande, crêpes flambées. **Credit cards** All major. **Pets** Dogs allowed on request (+40-80F). **Facilities** Heated swimming pool, small fitness center and garage (5 places) in the hotel (+50F). **Nearby** Deauville: architecture (le casino, les Bains Pompéiens, le Noumandy, le Royal), Promenade des planches (walk); Honfleur: Vieux Bassin, Greniers à sel, church of Sainte-Catherine, museum of Eugène-Boudin; Trouville; Houlgate; Cabourg - 27 hole New-Golf golf course and 9-18-hole Saint-Gatien golf course in Deauville. **Open** All year.

A ten-minute walk from the center of Deauville, L'Augeval is a typical turn-of-the-century villa which has been enlarged and renovated by the present owners. The comfortably appointed bedrooms are arranged with classic contemporary furniture harmoniously set off by a sober, tasteful décor. Five rooms have direct access to the small garden and to the swimming pool located on the side near the road to the racetrack, which is unfortunately very busy in summer. Guests who enjoy a quiet, equestrian setting should ask for the bedrooms at the back with a view of the Hippodrome stables (Numbers 107, 108, 207, 208). The most spacious rooms are those with a lounge and a balcony. Monsieur Moutier turns out elaborate gastronomic cuisine based on regional recipes, served outside in good weather. You will enjoy friendly, efficient service at this traditional hotel.

*How to get there (Map 8): 211km of Paris via A 13, Pont-Levêque exit to Deauville. Beside the racecourse.*

# La Chenevière

Escures-Commes
14520 Port-en-Bessin (Calvados)
Tel. (0)2.31.51.25.25 - Fax (0)2.31.51.25.20 - M. Esprabens

**Category** ★★★★ **Rooms** 19 with telephone, bath, WC, TV and minibar - Elevator - Wheelchair access. **Price** Double 780-1580F. **Meals** Breakfast incl. **Restaurant** Menus 150-380F, also à la carte. Specialties: Fricassée de langoustines aux girolles, agneau de prés-salé au jus de truffes, feuillantine de pommes au caramel de cidre. **Credit cards** Amex, Visa, Eurocard and MasterCard. **Pets** Dogs allowed (+150F). **Facilities** Parking. **Nearby** Epaves museum in Commes, Port-en-Bessin, cathedral of Bayeux – 27-hole Omaha Beach golf course. **Open** Feb 29 – Nov 30.

Very near Port-en-Bessin, Arromanches and Omaha Beaches, this is an elegant mansion surrounded by a beautifully kept park. The interior resembles a private home which has been furnished to please the eye as well as to provide the comfort you crave after a tiring drive. You will find a succession of very pretty, bright rooms which are generously decorated with light fabrics, collections of paintings (old seals, architectural drawings) and handsome objects. The bedrooms, with efficient soundproofing, are furnished in the same tasteful style; bathrooms are luxurious. All the windows look out on the lawn and flowers.

***How to get there*** *(Map 7): 8km north of Bayeux via D6, in the towards of Port-en-Bessin.*

1998

## Le Manoir de Butin

Phare du Butin
14600 Honfleur (Calvados)
Tel. (0)2.31.81.63.00 - Fax (0)2.31.89.59.23 - Mme Jacquet

**Category** ★★★★ **Rooms** 9 with telephone, bath, WC, TV and minibar. **Price** Double 640-1970F. **Meals** Breakfast 65F, served 7:30-11:00; half board 565-1230F (per pers., menu imposed). **Restaurant** Service 12:30-14:00, 19:30-21:30 (closed Monday and Tuesday lunchtime); menus 128-265F, also à la carte. **Credit cards** Amex, Visa, Eurocard and MasterCard. **Pets** Dogs allowed (+80F). **Facilities** Parking. **Nearby** Old dock, church of Sainte-Catherine, Eugène-Boudin Museum in Honfleur, Deauville, Trouville - 27- hole New-Golf golf course, 18-hole Saint-Gatien golf course and 9-hole golf course in Deauville. **Open** All year.

The owners of Normandy's luxurious Chaumière have now opened Le Manoir de Butin, a hotel in the same spirit very near the sea. Set in a beautiful park full of trees and flowers, the house is a handsome residence with traditional Norman half-timbering. The interior is somewhat enclosed, creating an atmosphere of intimacy and tranquil comfort, antique furniture, and tastefully chosen fabrics further the feeling of comfort. The passage of time will doubtless confer the hotel with the charm of La Chaumière. The beautiful bedrooms open onto the countryside or the sea. Meals are served on the terrace in summer, making the Manoir de Butin another lovely place to stay in Honfleur.

***How to get there*** *(Map 8): 97km west of Rouen via A 13, exit 28, then exit Honfleur, towards Deauville via the coast.*

## L'Absinthe

1, rue de la Ville
14602 Honfleur (Calvados)
Tel. (0)2.31.89.39.00 - Fax (0)2.31.89.53.60 - M. and Mme Ceffrey

**Category** ★★★ Rooms 6 and 1 suite with telephone, bath (whirl pool), WC and satellite TV - 1 for disabled persons. **Price** Double 500 (just 1)-700F; suite 1200F. **Meals** Breakfast 55F, served 8:00-11:00. **Restaurant** Service 12:15-14:30, 19:15-21:30 (closed mid. Nov – mid. Dec); menus 165-330F. Specialties: Fish. **Credit cards** Diners, Visa, Eurocard and MasterCard. **Pets** Dogs allowed (+40F). **Facilities** Garage in the hotel (+30F). **Nearby** Vieux bassin, Greniers à sel, church of Sainte-Catherine, museum of Eugène-Boudin in Honfleur; Deauville; Trouville - 27 hole New-Golf golf course and 9-18-hole Saint-Gatien golf course in Deauville. **Open** Mid. Dec – mid. Nov.

This small hotel is just off the Place Eugène Boudin, not an area of peace and quiet but all the bedrooms are well soundproofed. The quietest rooms are in the back or on the side (Numbers 4, 5 and 6). From the reception area and lounge, with its imposing stone fireplace, and the bar, you can admire the elegant decoration, worthy of a magazine cover. Throughout the hotel, handsomely patinated antique materials have been used in the restoration of this former 16th-century rectory. Beautiful and comfortably appointed, the bedrooms are rather small, except for the suite beneath the eaves. The rooms are decorated with Nobilis fabrics in discreet colors, and furniture, objects and rugs found in local antique shops. The breakfast room, illuminated by a veranda, is more simply decorated with rattan furniture. You will be warmly greeted by the owners, who have long welcomed guests to their fish restaurant just in front.

***How to get there*** *(Map 8): 97km west of Rouen via A 13 Beuzeville exit, then towards Honfleur. Opposite at the harbour (parking near the hotel).*

## Hôtel l'Ecrin

19, rue Eugène-Boudin
14602 Honfleur (Calvados)
Tel. (0)2.31.14.43.45 - Fax (0)2.31.89.24.41 - Mme Blais

**Category** ★★★ **Rooms** 22 with telephone, bath or shower, WC, TV and minibar. **Price** Double 390-950F, suite 990F. **Meals** Breakfast 50F, served 8:00-11:00. No restaurant. **Credit cards** All major. **Pets** Dogs not allowed. **Facilities** Sauna (65F), parking. **Nearby** Old dock, church of Sainte-Catherine, Eugène Boudin museum in Honfleur, Deauville, Trouville – 27-hole New-Golf, 18- and 9-hole Saint-Gatien golf courses in Deauville. **Open** All year.

This elegant Napoléon III house and its garden make a restful place to stay in the center of the charming fishing port of Honfleur. The ground-floor rooms have retained their late-19th-century design and much of the style of the epoch. The reception office with its large fireplace is stunning. The lounge, where the gilt woodwork echoes that of the armchairs, is filled with pictures, drapes, and carpets. Breakfast is served on the veranda overlooking the garden, which is filled with flowers in summer, though somewhat forlorn in low season. Ask for a room in the house on the garden side; on the courtyard side, Number 5, with a four-poster bed, is also lovely. On the *premier étage*, families will enjoy the suite with two bedrooms. On the top floor, the rooms have mansard roofs; Numbers 11 and 12 are delightful, while Numbers 7 and 9 are waiting to be renovated. Simple or more comfortable (but somewhat garish), the rooms in the outbuildings overlook the courtyard and the cars parked just in front. The hotel staff is extremely pleasant. For dinner, try *L'Hostellerie Lechat, La Taverne de la Mer,* or *L'Assiette Gourmande,* Honfleur's gourmet restaurant.

***How to get there*** *(Map 8): 97km west of Rouen via A13, Beuzeville exit, then D22 (in the town center).*

1998

## Au Repos des Chineurs

Chemin de l'Eglise
14340 Notre-Dame-d'Estrées (Calvados)
Tel. (0)2.31.63.72.51 - Fax (0)2.31.63.62.38 - Mme Steffen

**Category** ★★ **Rooms** 10 with telephone, bath (2 with whirlpool) or shower and WC. **Price** Double 350F, 500-650F; suite (4 pers.) 900F. **Meals** Breakfast 55F, served 7:00-11:30; half board and full board 300F, 380F. **Restaurant** and Tea-salon. Service 10:00-19:30; menus 65-120F. Specialties: Assiette du chineur, du pêcheur, du fromage, bouquets de saveurs salées or sucrées. **Credit cards** Diners, Visa, Eurocard and MasterCard. **Pets** Dogs allowed. **Meals** Parking. **Nearby** Bernay (museum), Château de Broglie, Le Pays d'Auge de Lisieux in Deauville and Le Pays de Lisieux in Cabourg by Vimoutiers and Le Pays du camembert. **Open** All year.

On the edge of a street but quiet at night, this postal relay station from the 17th and 18th centuries, dominated by a beautiful 16th- and 18th-century church, has been resuscitated thanks to Mrs. Stephen's hard work and sure taste. Lying in the heart of the Pays d'Auge region, the country inn is an attractive and pleasant place to stay, offering a tea room, lovely bedrooms, and a *brocante*, a shop selling old furniture and objects, in this case from the 18th and 19th centuries. The chests-of-drawers, tables, wardrobes, and objects which furnish the inn are all for sale at the "Antique-Hunter's Rest", but they remain as décor until they find a new owner. The reception area includes a pleasant lounge, and the tea room is totally charming with its exposed beams and big fireplace, its small tables set with pretty dishes for your breakfast and your Norman brunch. Comfortable, simple but very tasteful, the bedrooms named after flowers are cheerful, their floors stained to match the carpets, the wallpaper friezes and the fabrics (the beds are queen, not king, size.) Dressing growns await you in the pretty bathrooms.

***How to get there*** *(Map 7): 15km east of Lisieux.*

## Auberge Saint-Christophe

14690 Pont-d'Ouilly (Calvados)
Tel. (0)2.31.69.81.23 - Fax (0)2.31.69.26.58
M. Lecoeur

**Category** ★★ **Rooms** 7 with telephone, bath or shower, WC and TV. **Price** Double 280F. **Meals** Breakfast 40F, served 8:00-9:30; half board 295F, full board 400F (per pers., 2 days min.). **Restaurant** Service 12:00-13:30, 19:30-21:00; menus 95-250F, also à la carte. Specialties: Bœuf ficelle à la crème de camenbert, salade tiède de queues de langoustines, crème brûlée. **Credit cards** Amex, Visa, Eurocard and MasterCard. **Pets** Dogs allowed (+25F). **Facilities** Parking. **Nearby** Castle of Falaise, 'La Suisse Normande', Thury-Harcourt, Clécy (châteaux of La Pommeraye and Placy), Oëtre rock, gorges of Saint-Aubert, château de Pontécoulant – 18-hole Clécy-Cantelou golf course. **Open** Nov 4 – Jan 25, Feb 20 – Oct 18. Closed Sunday evening and Monday.

This hotel is in an elegant house in the Suisse Normande. Its interior has been carefully designed to provide every comfort. Plants and flowers adorn every corner. There is a small lounge, a breakfast room which becomes a bar in the evening, and many places to sit, talk and read. The bedrooms are small but charming and have recently been renovated in a modern style. They look out over peaceful gardens, but the soundproofing in the hotel could be better. During the summer, lunch can be enjoyed on the terrace. The cuisine is excellent and the young owners will make you feel at home.

***How to get there*** *(Map 7): 26km south of Caen via D562 towards Flers, or N158 towards Falaise, then D1;1.5km from Pont-d'Ouilly via D23 towards Thury-Harcourt.*

# Hôtel Victoria

Tracy-sur-Mer 14117 Arromanches (Calvados)
Tel. (0)2.31.22.35.37 - Fax (0)2.31.21.41.66
M. and Mme Selmi

**Category** ★★ **Rooms** 14 with telephone, bath or shower, WC and TV. **Price** Double 300-560F. **Meals** Breakfast 40F, served 7:30-10:00. No restaurant. **Credit cards** Visa, Eurocard and MasterCard. **Pets** Small dogs allowed. **Facilities** Parking. **Nearby** Port-en-Bessin, beach of debarquement, Bayeux, cathedral and tapestry of the Queen Mathilde - 27-hole Bayeux golf course (10 km). **Open** Apr – Sept.

Two kilometers from the sea and from the modest town of Arromanches, today famous as a D-Day landing site on June 6, 1944, the Victoria is a small country hotel, pretty and well kept. The bedrooms are in the two wings and in the central building, where you will find the largest and most pleasant accommodations (except for the Verte room, which is best for families.) Furnishings include some antiques, and all rooms have a lovely view over the countryside or the garden full of flowers. Don't neglect the rooms on the *second étage,* which have low ceilings and are often illuminated only by a small roof window, but whose decoration is especially warm and inviting. The rooms in the wings, however, are more ordinary, except for the smallest ones beneath the eaves, which are more intimate and reasonably priced. The traditionally decorated lounge is Regency in style, with gilt wood, bric-a-brac, crystal chandeliers....Breakfasts are served outdoors in good weather.

***How to get there*** *(Map 7): 10km north of Bayeux; before Arromanches, signs on D516.*

## La Chaîne d'Or

27, rue Grande
27700 Petit Andelys (Eure)
Tel. (0)2.32.54.00.31 - Fax (0)2.32.54.05.68 - Mme Foucault

**Category** ★★★ **Rooms** 10 with telephone, bath or shower, WC and TV. **Price** Single and double 400-740F. **Meals** Breakfast 70F, served 8:00-9:30. **Restaurant** Service 12:00-14:00, 19:30-21:30 (closed Sunday evening and Monday); menus 140-298F, also à la carte. Specialties: Miroir d'huîtres normandes au raifort, salade de homard breton à l'estragon vinaigrette de pamplemousse, sorbet à l'estragon, plaisir au chocolat chaud et sirop de jasmin. **Credit cards** Amex, Visa, Eurocard and MasterCard. **Pets** Dogs not allowed. **Facilities** Parking. **Nearby** Church of Notre-Dame and Château Gaillard in Les Andelys, Giverny – 18-hole Vaudreuil golf course. **Open** Feb 1 – Dec 31.

This friendly hostelry was founded in 1751. From the wing in the inner courtyard there is a stunning view of the Seine. Most of the bedrooms are large and light. The ones overlooking the river have just been entirely refurbished; very elegant and refined, they have gained in comfort what they have lost in traditional style. The rooms looking out over the church or the courtyard have period furniture, rugs and engravings; foreign guests prefer them for their "old France" atmosphere. The breakfast room has a high ceiling with polished beams, and is sometimes used in the evening as a lounge. In the dining room, half timbering, paintings and flowers combine to create a warm and cozy ambience, while the pink tablecloths compliment the silvery green of the Seine. The traditional cuisine is delicious.

***How to get there*** *(Map 8): 92km northwest of Paris via A13, Gaillon exit, then D316.*

## Relais Moulin de Balisne

Baline
27130 Verneuil-sur-Avre (Eure)
Tel. (0)2.32.32.03.48 - Fax (0)2.32.60.11.22 - M. Gastaldi

**Category** ★★ **Rooms** 10 and 2 suites with telephone, bath, WC, 10 with TV and minibar. **Price** Double 350-450F. **Meals** Breakfast 50F, served 8:00-11:00; half board 380-400F, full board 500-550F (per pers., 2 days min.). **Restaurant** Service 12:00-15:00, 19:30-22:00 (closed Monday noon in winter); menus 150-300F, also à la carte. Specialties: Duo de sole et langouste, cassolette d'escargots et gambas aux petits lardons, œuf d'autruche farci. **Credit cards** All major. **Pets** Dogs allowed. **Facilities** Lake and river fishing, parking. **Nearby** Senonches forest, châteaux de Beauménil and d'Anet – 9-hole golf course in Coulonges. **Open** All year.

When you first see this hotel you may worry about its proximity to the road, but as soon as you enter, you will be reassured by the beautifully quiet surroundings. The only sound is that of the waters converging here from the Rivers Avre and Iton. The Moulin is surrounded by 25-acres of land with a small lake; boats are available for fishing enthusiasts. The bar dining room is furnished with antiques, Persian tablecloths and a splendid fireplace. The bedrooms are just as appealing. Some of them in the attic seem to be "perched in the trees." You will be warmly welcomed at the Relais and its proximity to Paris makes it an appealing place to stay.

***How to get there*** *(Map 8): 75km west of Paris via Autoroute-Ouest (in the towards of Dreux), Bois d'Arcy exit, then N12 to Dreux, Alençon. 45km southwest of Evreux via N154 to Nonancourt, then N12 toward Verneuil-sur-Avre.*

## La Ferme de Cocherel

Route de la vallée d'Eure D836
Cocherel 27120 Paçy-sur-Eure (Eure)
Tel. (0)2.32.36.68.27 - Fax (0)2.32.26.28.18 - M. and Mme Delton

**Rooms** 3, 1 with bath, 2 with shower and WC. **Price** Double 350-400F **Meals** Breakfast incl. **Restaurant** Service 12:00-14:00, 19:30-21:15 (closed Tuesday and Wednesday except National Holidays); menu 195F, also à la carte. Specialties: craquelin de queue de bœuf aux navets confits, la marmite gourmande, civet de homard aux haricots rouges. **Credit cards** All major. **Pets** Dogs allowed. **Facilities** Parking. **Nearby** Historique village of Cocherel, château of Bizy, Monet museum in Giverny, château of Anet – 18-hole Vaudreuil golf course. **Open** All year except in 3 weeks in Jan, 1 week in Sept (closed Tuesday and Wednesday except National Holidays).

There is only a small country road between the Ferme de Cocherel and the peaceful Eure River. The Ferme consists of several picturesque Norman houses with old tile roofs. The largest is reserved for the acclaimed gastronomic restaurant, where the tables are set in a room decorated like an elegant winter garden. You will enjoy succulent meals made with fresh products bought in the local market or from nearby farms. The three bedrooms, opening onto a carefully tended flower garden, are on the ground floor in separate houses; they are decorated with several pieces of rustic or lacquered cane furniture, floral fabrics and a few engravings. The breakfasts are excellent. This is truly a beautiful country inn, located in the peaceful hamlet where Bertrand Du Guesclin won a historic victory over Anglo-Navarre troops in 1364.

***How to get there*** *(Map 8): 7km northwest of Pacy-sur-Eure via D836, towards Louviers. On A13, number 16 exit towards Vernon, then on left to Cocherel.*

## Le Moulin de Connelles

40, route d'Amfreville-sur-les-Monts
27430 Connelles (Eure)
Tel. (0)2.32.59.53.33 - Fax (0)2.32. 59 21 83 - M. and Mme Petiteau

**Category** ★★★★ **Rooms** 7 and 6 suites with telephone, bath, WC, TV and minibar. **Price** Single and double 600-800F, suite 800-950F. **Meals** Breakfast 70F, served 7:30-10:30. **Restaurant** Service 12:00-14:30, 19:30-21:00 (closed Sunday evening and Monday); menus 140-295F (child 70F), also à la carte. Specialties: Foie de canard au vieux calvados, saumon soufflé en portefeuille, bar en croûte de sel, rognons de veau sauce Meaux, délice noix de coco et chocolat chaud. **Credit cards** All major. **Pets** Dogs allowed. **Facilities** Heated swimming pool, tennis, Mountain bikes, boad, parking. **Nearby** Centre de loisirs Lery Poses (water skiing, golf, sailing...), church of Notre-Dame in Louviers; cathedral of Rouen; Monet museum in Giverny – 18-hole Vaudreuil golf course. **Open** All year except Jan (closed Sunday evening and Monday Oct 1 – May 15).

A beautiful lawn and flower gardens on the banks of the Seine surround the Moulin de Connelles, an old mill which was converted into a lovely home and, then, into a luxurious hotel. The Moulin is extremely comfortable, with thick carpets, a handsome decor of soft green and gold-yellow tones, coordinated fabrics, and superb bathrooms. Many bedrooms and the restaurant look out on an enchanting river scene, where the Seine winds in and out of its course and finally forms several lush green islands. It's a lovely place for strolling or having a drink before dinner, and the hotel will happily lend you a boat to explore it all up close, including the resident moorhens.

***How to get there*** *(Map 1 and 8): 100km of Paris via A13, Louviers exit, towards N15, Saint-Pierre-du-Vauvray, Andé, Connelles.*

## Château de Brécourt

Route de Vermon to Pacy
27120 Pacy-sur-Eure (Eure)
Tel. (0)2.32.52.40.50 - Fax (0)2.32.52.69.65 - M. Savry and Mme Langlais

**Category** ★★★★ **Rooms** 30 with telephone, bath, shower and WC. **Price** Single and double 410-1680F. **Meals** Breakfast 73F, served 7:00-12:00; half board 490-960F, full board 710-1300F. **Restaurant** Service 12:00-14:00, 19:30-21:30; menus 190F (lunchtime except public and national holidays), 235-360F, also à la carte. Specialties: Minestrone de langoustines et vieuxparmesan en copeaux, côte de veau fermier coulis de persil pomme cocotte, filet de bœuf en coque de sel de Guérande pomme au lard jus de veau. **Credit cards** All major. **Pets** Dogs allowed (+55F). **Facilities** Swimming pool, whirlpool, tennis, parking. **Nearby** A.G. Poulain museum and church of Notre-Dame in Vernon, château de Gaillon, Monet museum and American Art museum in Giverny – 9-hole golf course in Gaillon. **Open** All year.

On the threshold of Normandy and only sixty kilometers from Paris, this magnificent Louis XIII chateau with its symmetrical wings stands on the edge of a 55-acre park. The interior still charms with its original distinctive character highlighted by ravishing 17th-century floor tiles in the corridors and in many bedrooms. The rooms offer comfortable amenities as well as handsome antique furniture in most, painted ceilings, and tall windows overlooking the lush expanse of the immense park. (The bedrooms could do with a little smartening up.) Served in two highly elegant dining rooms, the delicious cuisine, of course, gives a place of honor to Norman specialties. You will be warmly welcomed, without the stuffiness one might expect in a chateau.

***How to get there*** *(Map 8): 21km east of Evreux via N13, Pacy-sur-Eure exit, then D181 and D533. 70km west of Paris via A13, number 16 Vernon exit.*

1998

## La Licorne

27, place Benserade
27480 Lyons-la-Forêt (Eure)
Tel. (0)2.32.49.62.02 - Fax (0)2.32.49.80.09 - M. and Mme Brun

**Category** ★★★ **Rooms** 19 with telephone, bath or shower, WC and satellite TV. **Price** Double and apart. 420-850F. **Meals** Breakfast 55F, served 8:00-11:00; half board and full board 390-555F, 555-720F (per pers.). **Restaurant** Service 12:30-14:00, 19:30-21:00 (closed Sunday evening and Monday Oct – Apr); menus 185F. Specialties: Tartare de thon et saumon fumé, sauté de lotte au noilly, fondant au chocolat. **Credit cards** All major. **Pets** Dogs not allowed. **Facilities** Parking. **Nearby** Lyons forest, Château of Bonnemare, Château of Mortainville, Abbey of Fontaine-Guerard, filature Levasseur. **Open** Jan 21 – Dec 19.

On the square of this charming village, a popular spot on the weekends, you can't miss the pink half-timbered façade and blue shutters of La Licorne, a former postal relay station that has been welcoming travelers since 1610. The interior decoration combines antique with rustic contemporary styles: The stairway leading to the bedrooms is itself an antique. The bedrooms are comfortable and plainly decorated, with carpets and well-equipped, tiled bathrooms. Our favorites are those overlooking the interior courtyard and those with bathtubs. You should avoid the smallest rooms (Numbers 2, 3 and 9) and enjoy the apartments with a lounge. Depending on the number of guests, you will have the choice of two dining rooms: one small and charming to the left of the entrance; the other installed in a rustic outbuilding. The cuisine is traditional and the chef's specialties are fine regional recipes. The Licorne is a pleasant inn from which to discover the region and take lovely walks in the forest. Best to reserve ahead for the weekend.

***How to get there*** *(Map 8): 21km east of Evreux. A13 Gaillon-les-Andelys exit then D316, to Les Andelys.*

## Auberge du Vieux Puits

6, rue Notre-Dame-du-Pré
27500 Pont-Audemer (Eure)
Tel. (0)2.32.41.01.48 - Fax (0)2.32.42.37.28 - M. and Mme Foltz

**Category** ★★ **Rooms** 12 with telephone, bath or shower, 10 with WC and 6 with TV - 2 for disabled persons. **Price** Single 170-380F, double 280-430F. **Meals** Breakfast 46F, served 8:00-9:30. **Restaurant** Service 12:00-14:00, 19:30-21:00; menus 198F (weekday lunch only)-310F, also à la carte. Specialties: Canard aux griottes, truite 'Bovary'. **Credit cards** Visa, Eurocard and MasterCard. **Pets** Dogs not allowed. **Facilities** Parking. **Nearby** Insect collection in the Canel museum in Pont-Audemer, Risle valley, bridge of Normandie, abbey of Le Bec-Hollouin – 18-hole Champ-de-Bataille golf course in Neubourg. **Open** Feb 1 – Dec 20 (closed Monday and Tuesday in low season).

This inn in Pont-Audemer is easily accessible by the highway and is perfect for travelers who want to get aquainted with Normandy. The buildings, in typical 17th-century Norman timbered style, surround a flower garden, with an old well and two impressive willows, where you can have cocktails, coffee, and excellent afternoon snacks in summer. Inside, there are several cozy little lounges where you can have tea or read by the fireplace. The dining room is slightly larger and is decorated with antique china and gleaming copper. The savory cuisine is innovative yet based on traditional Norman recipes. You can choose between the simple, rustic, charming bedrooms in the old houses, or the modern comfort of those in another building, which is built in the same style.

***How to get there*** *(Map 1 and 8): 52km west of Rouen via A13, Pont-Audemer exit, then D139 and N182 (300m from the town center).*

## Le Manoir des Saules

2, place Saint-Martin
27370 La Saussaye (Eure)
Tel. (0)2.35.87 25 65 - Fax (0)2.35 87 49 39 - M. Monnaie-Metot

**Rooms** 6, 3 apartments with telephone, bath or shower, WC and TV - 1 for disabled persons. **Price** Double 550-690F, apart. 850-1150F. **Meals** Breakfast 75F. **Restaurant** Service 12:00-14:00, 20:00-21:30 (closed Sunday evening and Monday except National Holidays); menus 185-365F, also à la carte. Specialties: Foie gras, ragoût de homard frais, fish. **Credit cards** Amex, Visa, Eurocard and MasterCard. **Pets** Dogs allowed. **Meals** Parking. **Nearby** Château of Champ-de-Bataille, château and arboretum of Harcourt, collégiale de La Saussaye, Abbey of Bec-Hellouin – 18-hole Champ-de-Bataille golf course. **Open** All year, except Feb 4 – 18 and beg Oct.

With its half-timbering, turrets and recessed walls, the Manoir is as Norman as they come. The decoration is highly colorful and cheerful. The bedrooms are delightfully appointed with a mixture of antiques and Louis XV copies, amusing old objects and heavy drapes which are coordinated with silky bedspreads. All the rooms are beautifully kept, including the bathrooms. A lovely lounge in blue and cream colors is an intimte, cozy place for a drink. Adjacent to it, the dining room with its smartly set tables serves excellent cuisine which is based on fresh, seasonal products. In charming weather, you can of course have meals outside on the terrace amidst the flowers. You will always receive very friendly and attentive service.

***How to get there** (Map 8): South of Rouen, 4km from Elbeuf via D840, towards Le Neubourg. On A13, Pont-de-l'Arche exit.*

# Hôtel du Golf

Golf du Vaudreuil
27100 Le Vaudreuil (Eure)
Tel. (0)2.32.59.02.94 - Fax (0)2.32.59.67.39 - Mme Launay

**Category** ★★ **Rooms** 20 with telephone, bath or shower, 17 with WC and TV, 10 with minibar. **Price** Single 160-225F, double 225-350F. **Meals** Breakfast 30-45F, served 7:00-11:00. No restaurant. **Credit cards** Amex, Visa, Eurocard and MasterCard. **Pets** Dogs allowed (+25F). **Facilities** Parking, 18-hole golf course. **Nearby** Rouen, Château Gaillard. **Open** All year.

The Château de Vaudreuil was destroyed during the Revolution and all that remains of it are two buildings beside an avenue that leads nowhere. The château's large park is now a golf course and one of the buildings is a hotel. It is quiet here, and you can enjoy views over the greens from the breakfast room and the living room. The bedrooms, with big windows and almond-green wallpaper, are simply furnished but pleasant. The rooms on the *premier étage* are small but those on the second are considerably larger. The decor is modern but elegant. There is no restaurant at the hotel but golfers can eat at the golf club.

***How to get there*** *(Map 8): 15km southeast of Rouen via A13, exit 18 or 19; then D77 to the entrance of Le Vaudreuil.*

## Hôtel du Château d'Agneaux

Avenue Sainte-Marie
50180 Saint-Lô - Agneaux (Manche)
Tel. (0)2.33.57.65.88 - Fax (0)2.33.56.59.21 - M. and Mme Groult

**Category** ★★★ **Rooms** 12 with shower, WC, TV and 10 with minibar. **Price** Double 370-585F, "nuptiala" 720F, suite 870F. **Meals** Breakfast 57-67F. **Restaurant** Service 19:30-21:00; menus 133-282F, 326F, also à la carte. Specialties: Fish and the chef's desserts. **Pets** Dogs allowed (+50F). **Facilities** Tennis (30F), sauna (80F), parking. **Nearby** Church and museum in Saint-Lô, château de Torigni-sur-Vire – 9-hole golf course in Courtainville. **Open** All year.

Leaving the ugly suburbs of Saint-Lô, you'll find that the Château d'Agneaux has escaped the town planners. A narrow gravel lane leads away from the main road to the old chapel, the château and the watchtower which look out over the unspoiled and peaceful valley, with nothing in view but trees and the River Vire flowing gently through the green countryside. M. and Mme Groult owned a farmhouse inn for many years, and now Agneaux is their dream come true; they have refurbished it with love. The bedrooms are very comfortable and prettily though not overwhelmingly decorated, with some four-poster beds and lovely parquet floors. Room 4, with it's five windows, is well-lit all day.

***How to get there*** *(Map 7): 1.5km west of Saint-Lô via D900.*

## Hôtel Le Conquérant

16/18, rue Saint-Thomas-Becket
50760 Barfleur (Manche)
Tel. (0)2.33.54.00.82 - Fax (0)2.33. 54 65 25 - Mme Delomenède

**Category** ★★ **Rooms** 13 with telephone, 10 with bath or shower, 3 with basin, 8 with WC and TV. **Price** Double 200-370F. **Meals** Breakfast 27-50F (4 menus), served 8:00-10:00. **Crêperie** Only for residents, by reservation. Service 19:00-21:00; menus 80-130F, also à la carte. Specialties: Galette camembert sur beurre d'escargot, galette manchotte, crêpe Le Conquérant. **Credit cards** Visa, Eurocard and MasterCard. **Pets** Dogs not allowed. **Facilities** Parking (30F). **Nearby** Ile Tatihon, Valognes, Thomas-Henry museum in Cherbourg – 9-hole golf course in Fontenay-en-Cotentin. **Open** Feb 16 – Nov 14.

Just off the port of Barfleur, you will find a charming garden hidden behind the granite walls of this 17th-century manor house. The bedrooms, all differently furnished, are improved year in and year out, varying in size, modern amenities and soundproofing (some rooms still share a shower and toilet on the same floor). The renovated rooms have been tastefully redone with Jouy-motif wallpaper and a scattering of antiques. We like the green room, which overlooks both the street and the garden and has a large bathroom. On the *second étage*, the bedrooms are simpler and unfortunately are not soundproofed. Rooms 1, 2, 3, 9, 16 and 17 overlook the garden, while the others give onto the street in the back. For a long stay, you will enjoy the bedroom with a terrace in the small house in the garden. In the evening, on reservation, you can make a meal of the hotel's special traditional crêpes. For breakfast, depending on your appetite, you can order a classic French petit déjeuner or one of four more copious menus. Finally, for a modest price, Monsieur Delomenède will take you deep-sea fishing. Or you can rent bikes in the village. The Conquerant is, of course, named after William the Conqueror.

***How to get there*** *(Map 7): 30km east of Cherbourg via D901.*

1998

## Hôtel de la Marine

11, rue de Paris
50270 Barneville-Carteret (Manche)
Tel. (0)2.33.53.83.31 - Fax (0)2.33.53.39.60 - M. Cesne-Emmanuel

**Category** ★★ **Rooms** 31 with telephone, bath or shower, WC, TV and minibar. **Price** Double 398-560F. **Meals** Breakfast 50F, served 7:30-10:00; half board 410-495F (per pers., 3 days min.). **Restaurant** Service 12:30-13:30, 19:30-21:30; menus 138-400F, also à la carte. Specialties: Fish and shellfish. **Credit cards** All major. **Pets** Dogs not allowed. **Facilities** Parking. **Nearby** Island of Jersey, Valognes, museum of Thomas-Henry in Cherbourg, Cotentin Tour between Le cap de la hague, Barfleur and Le cap de Carteret - 9-hole golf course in Saint-Jean-de-rivière. **Open** Feb 16 – Nov 2.

The Hôtel de la Marine is right on the water in the delightful seaside resort of Carteret. Although the building itself is of no particular interest, its outstanding panoramic location makes you feel as if you're on an ocean liner. Towering high above the sea, the hotel offers the permanent spectacle of the tides and the boats as they come and go. You will enjoy the view from the two dining rooms, the rotunda-shaped lounge, and from most of the bedrooms, notably those with a terrace or a balcony. The very bright bedrooms are different but classical in decor, with antique-style furniture and pale fabrics. In a second building of the Marine, the rooms are pleasant although they have no balcony and the toilet is equipped with a mechanical flush. The least attractive rooms are those overlooking only the street in the back (Numbers 6, 9, 16, 20, 32, 34, 37). For five generations, the owners have proven that professionalism and the talent for hospitality can be inherited, and the Michelin Guide has awarded one star to their young son and chef for such delicate, inventive specialties as rack of Norman lamb in puff pastry. The breakfasts are delicious, too.

***How to get there*** *(Map 7): 28km south of Cherbourg; A13, Barneville-Carteret exit. The hotel is in Carteret.*

## La Beaumonderie

1998

20, route de Coutances
50290 Bréville-sur-Mer (Manche)
Tel. (0)2.33.50.36.36 - Fax (0)2.33.50.36.45 - Mme Denèfle

**Category** ★★★ **Rooms** 12 with telephone, bath or shower, WC, TV, 8 with minibar - 1 for disabled persons. **Price** Single and double 280-330F, 570-870F. **Meals** Breakfast 50F, served 7:30-11:00; half board +175F (per pers., 3 days min.). **Restaurant** Service 12:00-14:00, 19:30-22:00 (closed Sunday evening and Monday lunchtime); menus 110-230F. Specialties: Fish and lobster. **Credit cards** All major. **Pets** Dogs allowed (+35F). **Facilities** Covered swimming pool, squash, tennis and parking. **Nearby** Thalasso center and casino in Granville; Mont Saint-Michel, îles anglo-normandes, Avranches, abbey of La Lucerne, cathedral of Coutances - 27-hole Granville golf course. **Open** All year. Closed Sunday evening in low season.

Don't be discouraged by the road that runs along the east side of this elegant, turn-of-the-century house. Efficiently double-glazed windows keep out the noise, and the traffic all but stops at night. We were immediately impressed with the emphasis on decor, both youthful and classical; the beauty of the materials used and the attention to detail, all confering the hotel with a charming, home-like ambiance. Ask for a room on the west side, which overlooks a lush countryside near the sand dunes. You will see a small race track, a golf course and, above all, the sea and its promise of unforgettable sunsets. Wide, comfortable beds, harmonious color schemes and pleasant baths combine to make the rooms truly lovely. On the ground floor, you will enjoy the same panoramic view, an English-style bar, and in the dining room, delicate, finely sauced cuisine: fresh Chausey lobster is a specialty.

***How to get there*** *(Map 6): 25km north of Avranches via D973 to Granville, then dir. Coutances (3km from Granville).*

## Manoir de Roche Torin

50220 Courtils (Manche)
Tel. (0)2.33.70.96.55 - Fax (0)2.33.48.35.20
Mme Barraux

**Category** ★★★ **Rooms** 13 with telephone, bath (1 with whirlpool bath) or shower, WC, TV and 3 with minibar. **Price** Single and double 450-800F, suite 850F. **Meals** Breakfast (buffet) 59F, served 8:00-10:00. **Restaurant** Service 12:00-13:00, 19:15-21:00 (closed Monday and Tuesday noon), menus 100-250F, also à la carte. Specialties: Agneau de pré salé, homard de Chaussey grillé. **Credit cards** All major. **Pets** Dogs allowed (+42F). **Facilities** Parking. **Nearby** "Jardin des Plantes" in Avranches, Mont Saint-Michel. **Open** Feb 16 – Nov 14 and Dec 16 – Jan 4.

A happy compromise between the old and the new best describes the decoration of this turn-of-the-century family mansion. Floral fabrics have been selected for the salon. The bedrooms, like the rest of the house, are appointed with a combination of modern, rattan, and period furniture. Three rooms enjoy a view over Mont Saint Michel, while those on the *second étage* beneath the eaves are beautifully bright and also have a lovely view. All the bedrooms are attractive, our favorites being those with cheerful striped or checked cotton fabrics. Only three bedrooms are still awaiting renovation. Smokers can dine in the small rustic room with a large fireplace where salt-marsh lamb and lobsters are grilled. Just next to it is the dining room for non-smokers, which is surrounded by panoramic picture windows overlooking the sunset. Although the cuisine is irregular, the staff is friendly and efficient. All around, the countryside and the polder where Normandy's famous sheep graze offer a quiet setting and an unrestricted view as far as Mont Saint Michel.

***How to get there*** *(Map 7): 12km southwest of Avranches via N175, then towards Mont Saint-Michel via D43.*

## Hôtel des Bains

50400 Granville (Manche)
Tel. (0)2.33.50.17.31. - Fax (0)2.33 50 89 22
M. Cillandre

**Category** ★★★ **Rooms** 47 with telephone, 32 with bath, 6 whirlpool bath, 15 with shower, WC and TV. **Price** Single and double 220-580F, suite 850F. **Meals** Breakfast 35F, served 7:00-10:00; half board from 395F (per pers., 3 days min.). **Restaurant** Service 19:30-22:00; menu 98-170F. **Credit cards** Amex, Visa, Eurocard and MasterCard. **Pets** Dogs allowed (extra charge). **Nearby** Mont Saint-Michel, îles anglo-normandes, Avranches, La Lucerne abbey, cathedral of Coutances – 9-hole and 18-hole Bréhal golf course. **Open** Mar – Oct.

This town hotel dramatically overlooks the English Channel, very near a long quay where you can take a lovely walk and watch the waves crash onto the shore.The interior has been very elegantly and imaginatively appointed. The bedrooms are bright and cheerful and decorated with contemporary furniture and fabrics. On the ground floor, there is a small tea room next to the dining room, which also has a corner lounge. The traditionally Norman cuisine, featuring lots of fresh fish and local cheeses, is succulent and the service is efficient and courteous. The tables are well spaced, and here too, the decoration is attractive. Ask for a room facing the sea, for a view of spectacular sunsets. Service with a smile adds a final positive note to this excellent hotel.

***How to get there*** *(Map 6): 25km north of Avranches via D973.*

## Château de la Roque

50180 Hébécrevon (Manche)
Tel. (0)2.33.57.33.20 - Fax (0)2.33.57.51.20
M. and Mme Delisle

**Rooms** 15 with telephone, bath or shower, WC and TV - Wheelchair access - 1 for disabled persons. **Price** Single 260F, double 360F, suite 530F. **Meals** Breakfast incl. **Restaurant** Evening meals. Service 20:00; menus 100F (wine incl.). Specialties: Regional cuisine. **Credit cards** All major. **Pets** Dogs allowed. **Facilities** Bicycle, fishing, hunting, tennis, parking. **Nearby** Church and museum (Tenture des Amours de Gombault and Macé) in Saint-Lô, château of Torigni-sur-Vire – 9-hole golf course in Couttainville. **Open** All year.

In the midst of the gentle Norman countryside, this very pretty château has been opened to guests by Raymond Delisle of cycle racing fame. It's a great success: All the rooms are comfortable and beautiful, with special attention paid to the choice of fabrics, which are complemented by antique furniture. The rooms in the chateau itself as well as in the outbuildings are all marvelously attractive and well kept (Number 4, somewhat small, is best for one person.) Bread is made every day in an old oven here; it is served at the breakfasts which guests enjoy at a large communal table in the charming dining room. If you reserve ahead, you can enjoy the excellent *table d'hôtes* dinner presided over by Madame Delisle with charm and vivacity. The dinner is served in a huge, beautiful room located in the converted barn and adjacent to an attractive lounge. The Château de la Roque is one of our outstanding addresses in Normandy.

***How to get there*** *(Map 7): 6km northwest of Saint-Lô. Before Saint-Lô, take D972, towards Coutances, to Saint-Gilles, then towards Pont Hébert (D77) for 3km.*

1998

# Relais du Busard

Ferme des Mares
50550 Saint-Germain-sur-Ay (Manche)
Tel. (0)2.33.07.56.47 - Fax (0)2.33.07.56.49 - M. and Mme Berlot dos Santos

**Category** ★★ **Rooms** 7 with telephone, shower and WC - 1 for disabled persons. **Price** Double 350-480F. **Meals** Breakfast 45F; half board 350-420F (per pers., 3 days min.). **Restaurant** By reservation. Service 12:30-14:30, 19:30-21:30; menus 120-280F, also à la carte. Specialties: Poulet au cidre, crustacés, homard sauvage, savours du terroir, saveurs de la mer, agneau de pré salé, canard rouennais. **Credit cards** All major. **Pets** Dogs not allowed. **Facilities** Parking. **Nearby** Coutances (cathedral), beach of Coutainville and Hauteville-Plage, Lessay (abbey church), abbey of Hambye. **Open** All year except in Feb.

Lying in the heart of a marsh, this hotel has recently been opened in a U-shaped farmhouse. Guests enjoy total peace and quiet, disturbed only by birds chattering or horses neighing in the equestrian center located in one wing of the buildings. The owners have created a pleasant inn, decorated in contemporary country style with tastefully appointed bedrooms: antique or hand-painted furniture, kilims, wrought iron sconces, frieze-trimmed wallpaper. For a long stay, ask for the big bedroom with a double exposition. With a real sense of hospitality while leaving guests to enjoy their privacy, Monsieur and Madame Berlos dos Santos enjoy chatting with them at breakfast time around the communal table. You can relax in a pleasant lounge after enjoying the Relais' inventive cuisine--a mixture of regional tastes and exotic seasonings. Meals are served in the dining room, a more intimate setting. Some may find fault with the somewhat cold tiles on the ground floor or the proximity of a picnic ground, but we quickly forgot them because we felt so happy here.

***How to get there*** *(Map 6): 21km north of Coutances, to Lessay par D2 then*

1998

## Le Gué du Holme

14, rue des Estuaires
Saint-Quentin sur-le-Homme 50220 Ducey (Manche)
Tel. (0)2.33.60.63.76 - Fax (0)2.33.60.06.77 - M. Leroux

**Category** ★★★ **Rooms** 10 with telephone, bath and WC - 1 for disabled persons. **Price** Double 400-490F. **Meals** Breakfast 50F; half board 480-500F (per pers., 3 days min.). **Restaurant** By reservation. Service 12:00-14:00, 19:00-21:00; menus 145-380F, also à la carte. Specialties: Foie gras aux pommes, aumonière de homard, poissons. **Credit cards** Amex, Visa, Eurocard and MasterCard. **Pets** Dogs allowed (+40F). **Facilities** Parking. **Nearby** Poilley-Ducey-Museum; garden and Museum of the Palais des Evêques (manuscripts of Mont Saint-Michel) in Avranches; villedieu-les-Poêles-Museum; Mont Saint-Michel. **Open** All year except Jan 2 – 24; Saturday morning and Sunday evening Oct 1 – Easter.

Not too close to Mont Saint Michel nor too far away, this small village inn is ideally located for discovering the regional marvels without being too disturbed by the hordes of tourists who come to this part of Normandy. Charming and very tasteful, the interior decoration contrasts with a somewhat dull façade, making the surprise inside even greater. We were particularly impressed with the small details throughout, even in the corridors with their thick green carpet and pale antique furniture. Pleasant and very comfortable, the bedrooms are handsomely modern and perfectly kept. Most overlook a small garden where you can enjoy breakfast in good weather. Other meals are served in the very elegant dining room where the lithographs and brass sconces are highlighted by the orange walls. The chef makes talented use of the excellent local produce, scoring another strong point, not to mention the friendly, efficient staff, for the beautiful Gué du Holme.

***How to get there*** *(Map 7): 40km southwest of granville. A 11 number 175 exit.*

## Hôtel de France et des Fuchsias

20, rue du Maréchal-Foch
50550 Saint-Vaast-la-Hougue (Manche)
Tel. (0)2.33.54.42.26 - Fax (0)2.33.43.46.79 - M. and Mme Brix

**Category** ★★ **Rooms** 33 and 1 suite with telephone, 29 with bath or shower, WC and TV. **Price** 280-450F **Meals** Breakfast 43F, served 8:00-10:00; half board 305-365F, full board 385-435F (per pers., 3 days min.). **Restaurant** Service 12:00-14:00, 19:00-21:15 (closed Tuesday lunchtime Nov – Mar and Monday Sept 15 – Apr); menus 85-275F, also à la carte. Specialties: Choucroute de la mer au beurre blanc, feuilleté de pommes tièdes à la crème de calvados, salade tiède de queues de langoustines. **Credit cards** All major. **Pets** Dogs allowed (+30F). **Facilities** Bicycle rental. **Nearby** Ile Tatihon, Valognes, Barfleur, Thomas Henry museum in Cherbourg – 9-hole golf course in Fontenay-en-Cotentin. **Open** Feb 22 – Jan 2 (closed Tuesday lunchtime Nov – Mar and Monday Sept 15 – Apr).

At Saint Vaast-la-Hougue on the eastern side of the Cotentin Peninsula the climate is so mild that mimosas flourish. The bedrooms in this old coachman's inn are simple but elegant, with muted colors and handsome furniture (Room 14 is a bit small, however). Those at the back of the garden, in the *Les Feuillantines* house, are decorated in the same spirit and most are more spacious. The last two weeks of August, chamber-music concerts are given in the pleasant small lounge (and the garden). They are very popular with guests, who attend them at no charge. Meals are served on a veranda opening onto the garden and feature seafood along with produce from the nearby farm at Quettehou. In addition, this beautiful hotel is in a part of Normandy where the climate is especially clement more, near a small fishing port, a sandy beach, and hedgerows and woods.

***How to get there*** *(Map 7): 37km southeast of Cherbourg via N13 to Valognes, then D902 and D1 to Saint-Vaast-la-Hougue (it's in the town center).*

## Moulin de Villeray

61110 Condeau (Orne)
Tel. (0)2.33.73.30.22 - Fax (0)2.33.73.38.28
M. Eelsen

**Category** ★★★ **Rooms** 16 and 2 apartments with telephone, bath or shower, WC, TV and minibar. **Price** Single and double 390-950F, apart. 8950-1200F. **Meals** Breakfast 70F; half board 495-925F (obligatory in high season). **Restaurant** Service 12:00-14:00, 19:00-22:00; menus 145-330F, also à la carte. Specialties: Regional cuisine. **Credit cards** All major. **Pets** Dogs allowed (+50F). **Facilities** Swimming pool, parking. **Nearby** Hills of the Perche (about 150km), museum of the philosopher Alain in Mortagne-au-Perche – 18-hole Perche golf course. **Open** All year.

The River Huisne flows peacefully at the foot of a lovely hamlet in the Perche region. The river branches out to form an arm of water which is quiet upstream and turbulent downstream, at the level of the "Mill of Villeray". All around it, a carefully tended park full of flowers follows the watercourse. Dispersed among the two floors of the main building and two beautiful small houses, the bedrooms are very prettily redecorated with harmonious, charmingly colored fabrics, and antique or pine furniture. Located in the small houses, the most recent rooms are also the most attractive. Upstairs, some rooms have a balcony. Avoid the two or three bedrooms which are waiting to be redecorated. The bathrooms also are being progressively renovated. Forming an angle on the terrace are the lounge and the dining room, the mill's large paddle wheel lending it a charmingly rustic atmosphere. While the prices are somewhat high, the light, beautifully seasoned cuisine is excellent, the staff pleasant and helpful, the setting restful and enchanting.

***How to get there*** *(Map 8): 9km north of Nogent-le-Rotrou; on A11, Chartes-Est exit, Luigny or La Ferté-Bernard.*

# Manoir du Lys

La Croix Gauthier
61140 Bagnoles-de-l'Orne (Orne)
Tel. (0)2.33.37.80.69 - Fax (0)2.33.30.05.80 - M. and Mme Quinton

**Category** ★★★ **Rooms** 23 with telephone, bath or shower, WC, TV and minibar - Elevator - Wheelchair access. **Price** Single and double 300-780F, suite 780-1000F. **Meals** Breakfast 60F; half board 385-630F, full board 565-810F (per pers., 3 days min.). **Restaurant** Service 12:30-14:30, 19:30-21:30; menus 130-350F, also à la carte. **Credit cards** All major. **Pets** Dogs allowed (+35F). **Facilities** Covered swimming pool, tennis, golf (3 greens), parking. **Nearby** Andaine forest, Bonvouloir lighthouse, château de Carrouges, Sées cathedral – 9-hole golf course in Bagnoles-de-l'Orne. **Open** Feb 13 – Jan 6 (closed Sunday evening and Monday Feb 14 – Easter and Nov 1 – Jan 5).

Lying in the midst of the Andaine Forest very near the Bagnoles-de-l'Orne spa, the Manoir du Lys is beautifully quiet. The bedrooms, many large, are bright and very well equipped, their decoration varying from classic to discreetly modern, with antiqued or lacquered furniture. Cheerful colors, beautiful baths in the recent part and effective soundproofing combine to make them extremely pleasant. Some rooms have terraces and those with mansard ceilings overlook the orchard, where deer can often be seen in search of the fruit. The lounge and the bar are lovely, rather like those in a private home. Adjacent to them is the panoramic dining room, the alliance of yellow and pale green there seeming like an extension of the greenery in the garden (where you can have meals in summer.) Monsieur Quinton and his son Frank preside over the excellent cuisine, which combines traditional Norman recipes with the finesse of original creations. Warm hospitality is extended by the whole family, who love their job as much as their region.

***How to get there*** *(Map 7): 53km west of Alençon via N12 to Pré-au-Pail, then N176 and D916.*

1998

# Hôtel du Tribunal

4, Place du Palais
61400 Mortagne-au-Perche (Orne)
Tel. (0)2.33.25.04.77 - Fax (0)2.33.83.60.83 - M. le Boucher

**Category** ★★ **Rooms** 11 with telephone, bath or shower, WC and satellite TV. **Price** Single and double 220-320F. **Meals** Breakfast 40F, served 7:30-10:30; half board 290F (per pers. in double room). **Restaurant** Service 12:00-14:00, 19:00-21:00; menus 85-170F, also à la carte. Specialties: Croustillant de boudin moutagnais, confit de canard au cidre, tarte fine aux pommes flambée au calvados. **Credit cards** Visa, Eurocard and MasterCard. **Pets** Dogs allowed (+20F). **Nearby** Museum Alain, cloister of Bellême, church of Notre-Dame in Moutagne-au-Perche; forest and hills of Perche (150 km) - 18-hole Bellême-Saint-Martin golf course. **Open** All year.

In the heart of a magnificent region and the pretty village of Mortagne with its historic architectural riches, the Hôtel du Tribunal is located in a landmarked building constructed in the 13th and 18th centuries. Set on a small square shaded with linden trees, the hotel appeals immediately with its warm, family atmosphere and its interior decoration, at once simple and elegant. The bedrooms are papered in different colors and decorated with a mixture of antique, period, or rattan furniture; the bathrooms offer comfortable amenities. Illuminated by three windows, the pink and blue family bedroom is especially lovely with its large farm table and its lounge area. Three bedrooms directly overlook the small interior courtyard, where several tables are set out in summer. In the charming dining room, its tables smartly laid with white cloths, you can enjoy good regional cuisine. In place of lounge, there is a pleasant room at the entrance with several tables and a fireplace.

***How to get there*** *(Map 8): 38km west of Alençon via N12.*

1998

# Hôtel du Mouton Gras

2, rue de l'Abbé Dauchy
76390 Aumale (Seine-Maritime)
Tel. (0)2.35.93.41.32 - M. and Mme Gauthier

**Rooms** 6 with telephone, bath or shower, and TV, (3 with WC). **Price** Single and double 280-440F. **Meals** Breakfast 35F, served from 7:00; half board (except in weekend) 350F (per pers.). **Restaurant** Service 12:00-14:00, 19:30-21:00 (closed Monday evening and Tuesday); menus 100-170F, also à la carte. Specialties: Shellfish, tête de veau, tarte aux pommes flambée au calvados. **Credit cards** All major. **Pets** Dogs allowed on request. **Facilities** Parking (30F). **Nearby** Le Pays de Bray: Fouges-les-eaux, Saint-Léger-aux-Bois, Rezancourt, Château de Mesnières-en-Bray, Saint-Saëns starting-point of the Varenne-Valley and the forest of Eawy. **Open** All year except 15 days in Sep, for Christmas day and New Year's day.

It doesn't take much imagination to hear the bells and the snorts of the horses as they once arrived at this old postal relay station. Today, people come to the "Fat Sheep" mainly for its excellent restaurant. The dining room opens directly onto the enclosed courtyard, its brick walls hung with brightly shining antique copper pots and its red checkered tablecloths creating a warm and inviting atmosphere, as does the large fireplace stocked with wines awaiting a taker. To prolong the pleasure of a meal with good traditional regional dishes, there are several very simple bedrooms upstairs and in a small adjacent out-building. In summer, the Norman weather willing, meals are served in the flowery courtyard.

***How to get there*** *(Map 1): 62km southeast of Dieppe towards Neuchâtel-en-Bray then Aumale.*

1998

## Le Saint-Pierre

Place du Bateau
76530 La Bouille (Seine-Maritime)
Tel. (0)2.35.18.01.01 - Fax (0)2.35.18.12.76

**Rooms** 6 with telephone, bath or shower, WC and TV. **Price** Single and double 280-350F. **Meals** Breakfast 40F, served 8:00-11:00. **Restaurant** Service 12:00-14:00, 19:30-21:00 (closed Sunday and Monday); menus 190-260F, also à la carte. **Credit cards** All major. **Pets** Dogs allowed on request. **Facilities** Parking (30F). **Nearby** Rouen; Elbeuf (GR2 for the Roches d'ouival, 4 km) ; church in Yvetot; the oak millenaire in Allouville-Bellefosse, museum of the nature. **Open** Apr – Aug. Closed Sunday evening and Monday.

An hour's drive from Paris takes you to this small 18th-century village on the banks of the Seine and the Saint-Pierre hotel, whose terrace offers a panoramic view of the river and the large trawlers that regularly pass by. Partly demolished during World War II, the building unfortunately no longer has its old charm, but the large bay windows in the dining room (and in the conference room upstairs) afford light and a beautiful view. Popular with the region's business people, the cuisine is delicate and refined. The interior decoration is classic throughout. The six bedrooms on the *second étage* are decorated in the contemporary Roche Bobois style, with bamboo furniture and dark Pierre Frey drapes. The bathrooms are well equipped and comfortable. Ask for Rooms 1, 2, or 7 on the Seine side. Only Room 3 overlooks the village road in the back but it is spacious and can accommodate a child in a sofa bed. The staff is courteous and professional, and the Saint-Pierre is a pleasant place to stay on the way to Normandy. But avoid the weekend traffic.

***How to get there*** *(Map 8): 20km northwest of Rouen via A15, to Yvetot, then D5 (3km) towards Duclair.*

## Auberge du Val au Cesne

Le Val au Cesne
76190 Croix-Mare (Seine-Maritime)
Tel. (0)2.35.56.63.06 - Fax (0)2.35.56.92.78 - M. Carel

**Rooms** 5 with telephone, bath, WC and TV. **Price** Double 400F. **Meals** Breakfast 50F, served 8:00 11:00; half board and full board 400-700F (per pers.). **Restaurant** Service 12:00-14:00, 19:00-21:00; menu 150F, also à la carte. Specialties: Terrine de raie, tête et fraise de veau, sole farcie à la mousse de langoustines, escalope de dinde 'Vieille Henriette', feuilleté aux pommes. **Credit cards** Visa, Eurocard and MasterCard. **Pets** Dogs allowed. **Facilities** Parking. **Nearby** Rouen cathedral, church and museum in Yvetot, abbey of Saint-Wandrille – 18-hole golf course in Etretat. **Open** All year.

The Auberge was initially a restaurant with an excellent reputation, consisting of two charmingly furnished rooms separated by a fireplace. At his customers' request, M. Carel opened five comfortable bedrooms in a house very near the Auberge. In a charming small valley, it has an elegant, welcoming atmosphere which is created by a very tasteful decoration, faithful to the regional style, as well as by the basic architecture which makes you feel very much at home. Part of the garden is home to various animals: you can admire a family of parrots, rare species of hens and doves... The five bedrooms are pleasant, but we like the Rose Room less. The small country road nearby will not disturb you as it happily is quiet before nightfall in the heart of the *Pays de Caux*.

***How to get there** (Map 1 and 8): 30km northwest of Rouen via A15 towards Yvetot, then D5 for 3km in the towards of Duclair.*

# Les Hêtres

Le Bourg 76460 Ingouville-sur-Mer (Seine-Maritime)
Tel. (0)2.35.57.09.30 - Fax (0)2.35.57.09.31
M. Liberge

**Rooms** 4 with telephone, bath, WC and TV - Wheelchair access. **Price** Double 480-680F. **Meals** Breakfast 75F, served 7:30-12:00. **Restaurant** Service 12:00-14:00, 19:30-22:00; menus 160-350F, also à la carte. Specialties: Fish and local products. **Credit cards** Visa, Eurocard and MasterCard. **Pets** Dogs allowed (+50F). **Facilities** Parking. **Nearby** Beach (3 km), château and museum in Dieppe, church and cemetery in Varengeville, villages in Caux Country (Luneray, Blosseville...), Fécamp, château de Bailleul, Etretat. **Open** All year except 3 weeks between Jan and Feb. Closed Monday evening and Tuesday end Sept – end Mar.

In a small hamlet not far from the chalk cliffs of the seashore, this small, welcoming hotel is lovely, even if you can see the nuclear power plant in the distance. You should reserve early, because Les Hêtres has only four bedrooms, but what rooms they are! Each is a model of good taste and ultra-modern amenities, with fabrics by Patrick Frey or Braquenier, a few pieces of handsome, smartly waxed antique furniture, and an elegant series of engravings. Their price varies with the size of the room (the most expensive has a private terrace on the garden;) the baths are simply luxurious. Excellent breakfasts are served beneath the half-timbered eaves. On the ground floor, the long dining room is just as beautiful, with a lovely fireplace in one corner. Bertrand Warin's celebrated cuisine puts a delicious finishing touch on this special place.

***How to get there*** *(Map 1): 30km south of Dieppe via D925, to Saint-Valéry-en-Caux, then to Cany-Barville. After the trafic circle towards aero club and 2nd on right.*

## Auberge du Clos Normand

22, rue Henri IV
76370 Martin-Eglise (Seine-Maritime)
Tel. (0)2.35.04.40.34 - Fax (0)2.35.04.48.49 - M. and Mme Hauchecorne

**Category** ★★ **Rooms** 7 with telephone, bath or shower, WC and cable TV. **Price** Double 280-390F, suite 480F. **Meals** Breakfast 40F, served 8:00-10:00; half board 360-410F (per pers., 3 days min.). **Restaurant** Service 12:15-14:00, 19:30-21:00; menu 160F, à la carte. Specialties: Tarte aux moules, filets de sole dieppoise, turbotin sauce crème estragon, tarte aux pommes chaude. **Credit cards** All major. **Pets** Dogs allowed (+50F). **Nearby** Castle and museum in Dieppe, church and graveyard in Varengeville, château de Mesnières-en-Bray, Saint-Säens, valley of the Varenne and Eawy forest – 18-hole golf course. **Open** Dec 18 – Nov 18 (closed Monday evening and Tuesday).

This is a beautiful little hotel dating back to the 15th century; it is on the edge of the Forest of Arques a few kilometers from the sea. From the pretty, rustic dining room you can watch the chef at work. You can have lunch in the garden that borders the river. There are seven bedrooms in the annex at the bottom of the garden, all of them individually decorated, with floral wallpaper, and views over the green landscape. They are very quiet (ask for those with bathrooms). Their overall decoration is unremarkable and somewhat dull and so their main attraction is the view over the river. In this part of the auberge, there is also a lounge which is entirely at guests' disposal. As is often the case with overnight stops, you will be asked to dine in the hotel.

***How to get there*** *(Map 1): 5km southeast of Dieppe via D1 towards Neufchâtel-en-Bray.*

# Le Fort de l'Océan

La Pointe du Croisic
44490 Le Croisic (Loire-Atlantique)
Tel. (0)2.40.15.77.77 - Fax (0)2.40.15.77.80

**Rooms** 9 with air-conditioning, telephone, bath, WC, satellite TV and minibar - 1 for disabled persons. **Price** Single and double 800-1200F; suite 1500F. **Meals** Breakfast 80F, served 7:30-11:00; half board 730-1080F (per pers., 3 days min.). **Restaurant** Service 12:00-14:00, 19:30-21:30 (closed Monday evening and Tuesday); menus 240F (Chef's special), 480F (tasting), also à la carte. **Credit cards** Amex, Visa, Eurocard and MasterCard. **Pets** Dogs allowed (+80F). **Facilities** Swimming pool, parking and garage. **Nearby** La Baule, La Brière and La Guérande marshes - 18-hole La Baule golf course in Saint-Denac. **Open** Feb 7 – Nov 16 and Dec 13 – Jan 4.

A fort often occupies a strategic position meaning that, once converted into a hotel, it enjoys an exceptional location. Such is the case of the Fort de l'Océan, which stands right on the rocks of Croisic Point, long abandoned but still a favorite hiking destination for summer vacationers. Built by Vauban, Louis XIV's Commissioner of Fortificatons, the hotel has become one of character and charm thanks to the combined efforts of good local builders, the owners Monsieur and Madame Louis, and talented Catherine Painvin, who has done a marvelous decorating job. The bedrooms are lovely and luxuriously comfortable, with beautiful fabrics coordinated with antique furniture, including some painted pieces, and elegant handicrafts created by Everwood. The "luxury-hotel white" style was chosen for the bathrooms and their soft, thick, numbered towels. We would have enjoyed tarrying in the elegant, refined public rooms, but we couldn't resist the comfortable chaises-longues in the garden and the sight of the sea: it was the next best thing to being on a boat.

***How to get there*** *(Map 14): 15km east of la Baule.*

1998

## Hôtel Maris Stella

1, Avenue Becquerel - Plage Pout-Lin
44490 Le Croisic (Loire-Atlantique)
Tel. (0)2.40.23.21.45 - Fax (0)2.40.23.22.63 - M. and Mme Garnier

**Category** ★★★ **Rooms** 10 with telephone, bath, WC, TV and minibar. **Price** Single and double 495-795F; suite 695-895F. **Meals** Breakfast 53F, served 7:30-10:30. **Restaurant** Service 12:00, 19:30 (closed Monday); menus 145F, 185F, 245F; also à la carte. Specialties: Lobster, fish. **Credit cards** Visa, Eurocard and MasterCard. **Pets** Dogs not allowed. **Facilities** Swimming pool and parking. **Nearby** La Baule, La Brière and La Guérande marshes - 18-hole La Baule golf course in Saint-Denac. **Open** Dec 21 – Nov 14. Closed Jan and Monday.

Facing the sea, the Maris Stella was one of the first resort hotels built in Le Croisic at the turn of the century. Behind its austere granite façade is hidden a marvelously comfortable interior, which has made the most of its magnificent view. The communal rooms are decorated identically, from their attractive, sand colored modern furniture to the matching thick carpets and drapes. The bedrooms have a very restful atmosphere and you won'tbe disturbed by the small road (for local traffic only) which separates the building from the beach and the sea. Two small dining rooms are at your disposal, serving good breakfasts and refined cuisine. For families or groups of friends, we heartily recommend the duplexes located in the former outbuildings on the other side of the garden. Each is tastefully decorated, has a large lounge area, and note that the price is lower for a group of people. Reasonable prices throughout the hotel are offered in low season and during week days following a long weekend.

***How to get there*** *(Map 14): 15km esat of la Baule.*

## Hôtel Sud-Bretagne

42, boulevard de la République
44380 Pornichet (Loire-Atlantique)
Tel. (0)2.40.11.65.00 - Fax (0)2.40.61.73.70 - M. Bardouil

**Category** ★★★★ **Rooms** 30 with telephone, bath, WC and TV. **Price** Single 450F, double 600-800F, suite 1000-1500F. **Meals** Breakfast 60F; half board 500-850F, full board 750-1050F. **Restaurant** Service 12:00-15:00, 19:00-22:00; menus 130-270F, also à la carte. **Credit cards** All major. **Pets** Dogs allowed. **Facilities** Swimming pool, parking. **Nearby** La Baule, La Brière and La Guérande marshes – 18-hole La Baule golf course in Saint-Denac. **Open** All year.

Ideally located not far from the beaches at La Baule, the Hôtel Sud-Bretagne has been in the same family since 1912, and to this day every member of the family joins in running and improving the hotel. Their contributions range from interior decoration to the organization of excursions aboard *La Orana,* a 17-meter teak-and-mahogany ketch. You will feel at home here. And a magnificent home it is, where each room has its own style. There is a lounge with a cozy fireplace, a billiard room, and several dining rooms over looking an indoor swimming pool. Outside, garden furniture invites you to relax in the sun. Each bedroom has a different theme reflected in the choice of fabrics, furniture and objects. There are some small apartments, with a lounge, a terrace, and typical Breton box beds for children. The Sud-Bretagne is one of a few luxury hotels which has retained all its charm and character.

***How to get there*** *(Map 14): 5km east of La Baule.*

1998

# Hôtel Villa Flornoy

7, avenue Flornoy
44380 Pornichet (Loire-Atlantique)
Tel. (0)2.40.11.60.00 - Fax (0)2.40.61.86.47 - M. Rouault

**Category** ★★ **Rooms** 21 with telephone, bath or shower, WC and TV - Wheelchair access. **Price** Single and double 320-410F, 350-510F. **Meals** Breakfast 40F, served from 7:30; half board and full board 335-410F, 435-510F. **Restaurant** Service 12:30-14:00, 19:30-21:00; menus 105-130F, also à la carte. Specialties: Escalopée de Saint-Jacques, filet mignon de pouc au gingembre et courgettes. **Credit cards** Visa, Eurocard and MasterCard. **Pets** Dogs allowed (+35F). **Nearby** La Baule, La Brière and La Guérande marshes - 18-hole La Baule golf course in Saint-Denac. **Open** Mar – Oct.

Guests at the Villa Flornoy are not disturbed by the summer hustle and bustle of the beaches at Pornichet and La Baule because the hotel is located in a quiet residential quarter 900 feet away. Its façade is very much in the "Norman Coast" turn-of-the-century style. Today completely refurbished in contemporary taste, the hotel offers lovely bedrooms with cheerful, classic, comfortable furnishings. All overlook the street and the neighboring villas, or the pleasant garden behind the hotel. On the ground floor, an elegant reception lounge with antique furniture, engravings, and carefully chosen objects could be those of a private house; from the lounge, glass doors lead into the garden, and on the other side by a beautiful dining room in shades of orange. This particularly harmonious and comfortable arrangement is a fine example of a new generation of charming hotels, hospitable, simple, colorful, and reasonably priced.

***How to get there*** *(Map 14): 5km east of la Baule. Opposite the Town hall of Pornichet.*

# Auberge du Parc - La Mare aux Oiseaux

162, Ile de Fédrun
44720 Saint-Joachim (Loire-Atlantique)
Tel. (0)2.40.88.53.01 - Fax (0)2.40.91.67.44 - M. Guérin

**Rooms** 5 with telephone, bath or shower and WC. **Price** Single and double 300F. **Meals** Breakfast 35F. **Restaurant** Service 12:00-14:00, 19:00-21:00 (closed Sunday evening and Monday in low season); menus 150-195F, also à la carte. Specialties: Croquant de grenouilles aux algues bretonnes, gingembre confit et beurre d'agrumes, anguilles rôties aux pommes acidulées. **Credit cards** Not accepted. **Pets** Dogs allowed (+30F). **Facilities** Parking. **Nearby** Guérande, Marais Salants, Regional Park of Brière, aquarium of Croisic - 18-hole Bretesche golf course, 18-hole La Baule golf course in Saint-Denac. **Open** Mar 2 – Dec 31. Closed Sunday evening and Monday in low season.

Fédrun is an island village lost in the midst of the immense marshes of the Brière region. Eric Guérin, the young owner of the Auberge du Parc and a great admirer of the island's small thatched-roof cottages and the wild countryside he knows so well, interrupted a promising career in Paris to transfer his abilities here: he had been maître d' at the Tour d'Argent and head chef at the Jules Verne. It is in fact difficult to imagine a more charming combination of magnificent surroundings, fine and inventive gastronomy which completely captivated us, and ravishing bedrooms, deliciously decorated: natural shades, sober and beautiful furniture, amusing Eskimo lithographs.... The atmosphere throughout is artistic, elegant, amiable. Stéphanie Guérin oversees the restaurant with passion and competence. She will also advise you on finding a guide to explain the history and wildlife of the marshes. Or you can go there in the hotel's boat and see them for yourself. A young and magic place, and a must.

***How to get there*** *(Map 14): 16km northwest of Saint-Nazaire via D47.*

## Abbaye de Villeneuve

Route des Sables-d'Olonne
44840 Les Sorinières (Loire-Atlantique)
Tel. (0)2.40.04.40.25 - Fax (0)2.40.31.28.45 - M. Brevet

**Category** ★★★★ **Rooms** 20 with telephone, bath and WC (15 with TV). **Price** Single and double 390-935F, suite 1150-1245F. **Meals** Breakfast 70F, served 7:00-10:30; half board 430-970F, full board 645-1190F. **Restaurant** Service 12:00-14:00, 19:00-21:30; menus 140-315F, also à la carte. Specialties: Maraîchère de homard et sa vinaigrette parfumée, saumon fumé de l'abbye, dos de sandre poché au beurre blanc primeurs nantais, canard challandais au sang, charlotte moelleuse au chocolat amer. **Credit cards** All major. **Pets** Dogs allowed. **Facilities** Swimming pool, parking. **Nearby** Art museum and Jules Verne museum in Nantes, valley of the Erdre, Clisson – 18-hole golf course in Nantes. **Open** All year.

This former cistercian abbey, founded in 1201 by Constance of Brittany, was partially destroyed during the French Revolution and then restored in 1977 as a hotel only ten minutes from the center of Nantes. The great hall of the monastery is now the restaurant and the bedrooms retain the magnificent timbers of the building's frame. In the lounges, plaster ceilings and stone fireplaces give the room a grand air, but they are comfortable spots to relax – surely less forbidding then the austerity of the original abbey. The cuisine is classic and you will be looked after in grand style.

***How to get there*** *(Map 14): 10km south of Nantes via A83 towards Bordeaux, then La-Roche-sur-Yon.*

1998

# Hôtel du Mail

8, rue des Ursules
49100 Angers (Maine-et-Loire)
Tel. (0)2.41.25.05.25 - Fax (0)2.41.86.91.20 - M. Dupuis

**Category** ★★ **Rooms** 27 with telephone, bath, shower, 3 with basin, TV and minibar. **Price** Single and double 150-245F, 185-320F. **Meals** Breakfast (buffet) 34F, served 7:00-10:00. No restaurant. **Credit cards** All major. **Pets** Dogs allowed (+20F). **Facilities** Parking (17F). **Nearby** Abbey of Solesmes, abbey of Fontevrault, tapestry of the château d'Angers, Loire Valley - 18-hole Anjou country club golf course. **Open** All year. Closed Sunday lunchtime and National Holidays between 12:00-18:30.

Efficiently and charmingly run by Monsieur and Madame Dupuis, the Hôtel du Mail brings off the *tour de force* of being quiet and yet in the heart of a bustling city. Installed in a 17th-century town house, it is located on a street with very little traffic. In addition, the stairways and corridors inside are covered with thick carpets, thus muffling the sounds of footsteps. A further advantage is the hotel's wide range of bedrooms, varying from modest rooms with wash basins at very reasonable prices, to the most spacious and luminous, offering excellent value for the price; in mid-range, you will find three bedrooms on the ground floor, which open directly onto the courtyard, where a few tables are set out in summer. All together, a dozen rooms have had a face lift, offering a fresh decor and renovated baths with modern amenities. The large dining room, furnished with several antiques, is the venue for a hearty breakfast buffet. Good restaurants in town include *L'Auberge d'Eventard* and *Le Provence Caffé*--our favorites--as well as *Le Toussaint, Les Templiers* and *Lucullus.*

***How to get there** (Map 15): Behind the "Hôtel de Ville" (town hall).*

## Château des Briottières

49330 Champigné (Maine-et-Loire)
Tel. (0)2.41.42.00.02 - Fax (0)2.41.42.01.55
M. and Mme de Valbray

**Category** ★★★★ **Rooms** 10 with telephone, bath. **Price** Double 650-750F, suite 900-1200F. **Meals** Breakfast 50F; half board 1450-1800F (per 2 pers.). **Restaurant** Evening meals at 20:00 (on reservation); menu 300F (all incl.). Specialties: Regional cooking. **Credit cards** All major. **Pets** Dogs allowed (+50F). **Facilities** Heated swimming pool, bicycle, billiard, parking. **Nearby** Abbey of Solesmes, abbey of Fontevrault, château of Angers (tapisserie), Loire Valley (châteaux de la Loire) – 18-hole Anjou country club golf course. **Open** All year (by reservation in winter).

Off the beaten path and surrounded by an immense English-style garden, the Château des Briottières is a private château which hosts guests. It alone is worthy of a trip to the Loire. The young owners are warm and friendly. On the ground floor, a vast gallery leads to the reception areas. The lounges are furnished in 18th-century style, and the large dining room is brightened by pearl-grey woodwork and pink drapes. The owners join you for the excellent, friendly dinners, which are served on a magnificently set dining table. There is a library with a French billiard table. Upstairs, the comfortable bedrooms are all tastefully decorated with lovely fabrics and very beautiful antique furniture. Some rooms are intimate, while others are vast. The bathrooms are luxurious, and all have a view of the park. The swimming pool is located in a beautiful garden. And if you stay on, the sixth night is free!

***How to get there*** *(Map 15): From Paris A11 Durtal exit. 32km north of Angers towards Laval and take immediately towards Sablé in Montreuil-Juigné.*

# Le Prieuré

49350 Chenehutte-les-Tuffeaux (Maine-et-Loire)
Tel. (0)2.41.67.90.14 - Fax - (0)2.41.67.92.24
M. Doumerc

**Category** ★★★★ **Rooms** 35 with telephone, bath or shower, WC and TV - Wheelchair access. **Price** Single and double 500-1600F; suite 1250-1600F. **Meals** Breakfast 85F, served 7:30-10:30; half board and full board 715-1120F, 945-1350F (per pers.) **Restaurant** Service 12:30-14:00, 19:30-21:00 (closed in Jan and Feb); menus 235F and 400F; also à la carte. Specialties: Saint-pierre à la vanille Bourbon, pigeonneau cuit en cocotte à la purée d'échalotes. **Credit cards** Amex, Visa, Eurocard and MasterCard. **Pets** Dogs allowed (+60F). **Facilities** Swimming pool and tennis **Nearby** in Saumur: church of Notre-Dame de Nantilly, château de Saumur (museum of horse); Château de Montgeoffroy, abbey of Fontevrault, Montreuil-Bellay (château), museum of mushroom in Saint-Hilaire-Saint-Flouent, Château de Brissac. **Open** Mar 9 – Jan 7.

Clinging to a cliffside far above the Loire, this Renaissance priory affords an absolutely splendid view. The bedrooms on the manor house side, the huge salon, the dining room, and the terraces all enjoy a sweeping view of this panorama, and that is only one of the hotel's strong points. We also loved the classic, cheerful decoration, the antique and period furniture, the way the hotel is kept, and the professional, efficient service. The tasteful bedrooms all offer modern amenities, their price varying with their size and their view. Somewhat farther away, ensconced in greenery (the park spreads over 62 acres), fifteen bedrooms are located in outbuildings constructed some twenty years ago. They are simpler but less expensive and each has a private terrace. It all adds up to a beautiful, luxurious place--with professional service to match.

***How to get there*** *(Map 15): 7km of Saumur, via A85, Saumur exit.*

## Hôtel Anne d'Ajou

32, quai Mayaud
49400 Saumur (Maine- et-Loire)
Tel. (0)2.41.67.30.30 - Fax (0)2.41.67.51.00 - M. and Mme Touzé

**Category** ★★★ **Rooms** 50 with telephone, bath or shower, WC and TV - 1 for disabled persons. **Price** Single 280F, double 450F, suite 650F. **Meals** Breakfast 48F, served 7:00-10:00; half board 425-475F. **Restaurant** "Les Ménestrels". Service 12:15-13:30, 19:30-21:30 (closed Sunday and Monday noon in low season), also à la carte. **Credit card** All major. **Pets** Dogs not allowed. **Facilities** Parking. **Nearby** Notre-Dame church of Nantilly, Horse Museum in Saumur, Château of Montsoreau, abbey of Fontevraud, Montreuil-Bellay (château), Mushroom Museum in Saint-Hilaire-Saint-Florent, Château of Boumois. **Open** All year except Dec 23 – Jan 3.

The Anne d'Anjou is a beautiful 18th-century mansion which is ideally located between the Loire and the imposing medieval Château of Saumur. A magnificent Louis XVI stairway surmounted by a stunning *trompe l'oeil* ceiling leads to the bedrooms. Those on the *premier étage* still have much of their original charm, particularly the room with Empire *bas-reliefs* covered with gold leaf. The rooms are beautifully decorated with elegant fabrics, many with antique furniture or rugs. The price of the rooms varies according to their size and the floor they are on. (We are less enthusiastic about those on the *troisième étage*). Some rooms have a view on the garden and the château rising in the immediate background; others look out over the immense span of the Loire (guests here are somewhat disturbed by the noise of the road). With the first warm days of spring, tables are set out in the beautiful garden for breakfast. The restaurant is excellent and the overall atmosphere of the hotel owes much to Madame Touzé, a friendly and attentive manager.

***How to get there*** *(Map 15): 66km west of Tours. A85 Saumur exit.*

## Relais Cicéro

18, boulevard d'Alger
72200 La Flèche (Sarthe)
Tel. (0)2.43.94.14.14 - Fax (0)2.43.45.98.96 - Mme Cherel

**Category** ★★★ **Rooms** 21 with telephone, bath or shower, WC and TV. **Price** Single 395-425F, double 525-675F. **Meals** Breakfast 45F, served from 7:00. No restaurant. **Credit cards** Amex, Visa, Eurocard and MasterCard. **Pets** Small dogs allowed. **Nearby** Chapel of Notre Dame-des-Vertus, Tertre Rouge zoological park, château de Lude, Solesmes abbey. **Open** Jan 7 – Dec 19.

This hotel isn't really a country hotel since it is in the small, pretty town of La Flèche, yet the Relais Cicéro has various advantages that make it a first-class place to stay. It is on a peaceful tree-lined street away from the bustle and noise of the town. Its large garden is tranquil and the beautiful 16th- and 18th-century building is both comfortably and elegantly furnished. There is a bar, a reading room. In the dining room a very good breakfast is served – in winter to the warmth of a blazing fire in the fireplace. The bedrooms are comfortable and tastefully furnished. Our favorite rooms are those in the main building. Try the traditional *Fesse d'Ange*, *Le Vert Galant* and *Le Moulin des Quatres Saisons*, three restaurants in the village.

***How to get there*** *(Map 15): 52km northwest of Angers via A11, Durtal exit, then N23 to La Flèche.*

## Auberge du Port-des-Roches

72800 Luché-Pringé (Sarthe)
Tel. (0)2.43.45.44.48 - Fax (0)2.43.45.39.61
Mme and M. Lesiourd

**Category** ★★ **Rooms** 12 with telephone, bath or shower, WC and 4 with TV. **Price** Double 240-300F, 3 pers. 360F. **Meals** Breakfast 32F, served 8:00-9:30; half board 250-290F, full board 310-360F (per pers., 3 days min.). **Restaurant** Service 12:00-13:30, 19:30-20:30; menus 115-190F, also à la carte. Specialties: Blanquette de sandre aux noix et jasnières, ris de veau braisé aux oreilles de cochon, crème caramélisée au cidre en coque de pomme. **Credit cards** Visa, Eurocard and MasterCard. **Pets** Dogs allowed on request. **Facilities** Parking. **Nearby** Châteaux of Montmirail, Courtanvaux and Saint-Calais, château of Lude, château of Bazouges – 18-hole Le Mans golf course in Mulsanne. **Open** All year except in Feb (closed Sunday evening and Monday).

Recently taken over by a young couple, this small inn is reflected in the calm waters of the Loire, which is just across a small road. The inn is in the process of extensive interior renovation, which Thierry and Valérie Lesiourd spend their winters doing. The small bedrooms are attractive and tastefully decorated in cool, cheerful colors. Six rooms overlook the river, the others occupying a side wing. The lounge and dining room are decorated in a rustic style which is pleasant enough, but it too should be discreetly retouched. You will find a beautiful terrace full of flowers, right on the river bank. Real progress is being made at this delightful inn, its prices are reasonable, and the region is full of attractions.

***How to get there*** *(Map 16): 40km southwest of Le Mans in the towards of La Flèche, then D13 to Luché-Pringé and D214 to "Le Port-des-Roches".*

## Haras de la Potardière

La Portardière
72200 Crosmières (Sarthe)
Tel. (0)2.43.45.83.47 - Fax (0)2.43.45.81.06 - François et Marie Benoist

**Rooms** 17 with telephone, 16 with bath, 1 with shower, WC, TV, 16 with minibar - Wheelchair access. **Price** Single 450F, double 550F. **Meals** Breakfast 40F. No restaurant but snacks available in winter. **Credit cards** Visa, Eurocard and MasterCard. **Pets** Dogs allowed. **Facilities** Heated swimming pool, billiards, 3-hole compact golf, tennis, horseback trips by reservation. **Nearby** Notre-Dame-des-Vertus chapel, Malicorne pottery, Rairies terra cotta, Tertre Rouge zoological park, château de Lude, abbey of Solesmes – 27-hole Sablé-Solesmes golf course. **Open** All year (by reservation Nov – March).

A countryside of forests and green valleys surrounds this horse farm, a large part of which has been transformed into a hotel. *Haras* means "stud farm," so it is not surprising that the architecture of the stables is as handsome as that of the château. Located in the two buildings, the lovely bedrooms are well appointed, softly illuminated, and some have antique furniture. The attractive bathrooms are supplied with an assortment of toiletries. And if you are a family or a group of friends, the suites offer good value for the money. One reserve, however: the paint and materials in certain places of the much frequented hotel are beginning to show wear and tear. For restaurants, we highly recommend *La Petite Auberge* in Malicorne, *La Fesse d'Ange, Le Vert Galant,* and *Le Moulin des Quatre Saisons* in La Flèche.

***How to get there*** *(Map 15): 10km northwest of La Flèche. On A11, exit La Flèche/Sablé, Crosmières, then towards Bazouges to La Potardière (2nd castel on right).*

## Château de Saint Paterne

Saint-Paterne - 72610 (Sarthe)
Tel. (0)2.33.27.54.71. - Fax (0)2.33.29.16.71 - M. de Valbray
Web: http://www.chateaux-france.com/rsaintpaterne

**Rooms** 7 with telephone, bath and WC. **Price** Double 450-650F, suite 800F. **Meals** Breakfast 45F, served 7:30-12:00. **Restaurant** Evening meals. Service 20:00; menu 250F (all incl.). **Credit cards** Amex, Visa, Eurocard and MasterCard. **Pets** Dogs allowed. **Facilities** Parking. **Nearby** Châteaux of Montmirail, Courtanvaux and Saint-Calais; Carrouges, Bazouges, Ludes; haras du Pin; Alençon; Perche – 18-hole Mans golf course in Luisanne. **Open** Mar 1 – Jan 14.

Alençon is on the doorstep of the village of Saint Paterne but this château remains sheltered in its vast walled-in park. With all the enthusiasm of youth, the owner has restored it throughout and will greet you very warmly. On the ground floor, there is a superb salon with extremely elegant antique furniture, a beautiful dining room and a bedroom. There are other bedrooms upstairs, each with its own special style, including the *Henri IV* with its superb French polychrome ceilings. Enhanced by lovely pieces of family furniture, all the rooms are beautifully appointed and have faultless baths. For dinner, the hotel has opened a charming small auberge in one wing; decorated in Mediterranean colors, it serves cuisine that's spiced with sunshine and made with excellent fresh products, including the vegetables grown in the chateau's extraordinary vegetable garden. This is a superb place to stay with the charm of a private home and the amenities of a luxurious hotel.

***How to get there*** *(Map 8): 3km east of Alençon, towards Chartres-Mamers.*

## Hôtel du Martinet

Place de la Croix-Blanche
85230 Bouin (Vendée)
Tel. (0)2.51.49.08.94 - Fax (0)2.51.49.83.08 - Mme Huchet

**Category** ★★ **Rooms** 21 with telephone, bath or shower, WC and TV. **Price** Single 200-240F, double 270-350F. **Meals** Breakfast 36F; half board 270-305F (per pers.). **Restaurant** Service 12:30-13:30, 19:30-21:30 (closed Oct – Mar), menus 110-160F (60F child), also à la carte. Specialties: Fish and shellfish. **Credit cards** All major. **Pets** Dogs allowed (+20F). **Facilities** Bicycles, swimming pool, parking. **Nearby** Church of St-Philbert-de-Grand-Lieu, Machecoul, oyster beds, Ile d'Yeu – 18-hole golf courses in Saint-Jean-de-Monts and in Pornic. **Open** All year.

You will be enchanted by this late 18th-century residence where the smell of wax mingles with that of bowls of cut flowers. The furniture in the bedrooms on the ground floor and *premier étage* is plain but very comfortable. There are two other bedrooms under the eaves which are ideal for families of four. In a small wing of the hotel, five beautiful bedrooms have just been added.They are cheerful and very pretty, their bathrooms are immaculate and all are at ground level, opening onto a large flower garden and the swimming pool. Beyond the swimming pool in the distance, you will have a beautiful view over the countryside and the Vendée marshes. In the restaurant, the owner's oyster-farmer husband will be delighted to serve you oysters from his beds and other seafood. The Hôtel du Martinet is a delightful place to stay, perfect for visiting the Vendée marshes. Madame Huchet is an extremely kind manager, and the prices are truly reasonable.

***How to get there*** *(Map 14): 51km southwest of Nantes via D751 and D758 in the towards of Noirmoutier.*

## Château de la Vérie

Route de Saint-Gilles-Croix-de-Vie
85300 Challans (Vendée)
Tel. (0)2.51.35.33.44 - Fax (0)2.51.35.14.84 - M. Martin

**Category** ★★★ **Rooms** 23 with telephone, bath, WC, TV and minibar. **Price** Single and double 300 880F. **Meals** Breakfast 60F, served 7:30-10:30. **Restaurant** Service 12:00-14:00, 19:30-21:30; menus 100-290F, also à la carte. Specialties: Pommes de terre de Noirmoutier farcies aux langoustines, canard de Challans aux sang en deux services, brioche vendéenne dorée aux framboise. **Credit cards** All major. **Pets** Dogs allowed (+50F). **Facilities** Swimming pool, tennis, parking. **Nearby** Le Puy du Fou, Château of Apremont, church of Sallertaine, château and market in Clisson, church of Saint-Philbert-de-Grand-Lieu, Machecoul, Saint-Gilles-Croix-de-Vie, la Fromentine (boats for Ile d'Yeu), Les Sables d'Olonne, beach (15km). **Open** All year.

Converted into a hotel, the Château de la Vérie offers beautiful, comfortable bedrooms. Japanese wickerwork, vivid colors, charming little engravings and antique furniture – nothing is lacking: even the mirrors in the bathrooms have china frames. The dining room and lounge have been decorated in the same spirit; they are welcoming rooms, feel very much like a private house, and look out onto a large terrace where breakfast is served and you can look out over the verdant park. Not far away is the swimming pool, a welcome attraction in the second-sunniest *département* of France. Delicious, nourishing meals are pleasantly served, but with a touch of amateurism. This is a beautiful place to stay, just ten minutes from the beaches.

***How to get there*** *(Map 14): 60km south of Nantes via D65 to Saint-Philibert, then D117 to Machecoul, then D32 to Challans; it's 2.5km from the town hall in the towards of Saint-Gilles-Croix-de-Vie on D69.*

# Hôtel L'Escale

Port Joinville
85350 Ile-d'Yeu (Vendée)
Tel. (0)2.51.58.50.28 - Fax (0)2.51.5933.55 - M. and Mme Taraud

**Category** ★★ **Rooms** 26 and 2 suites (15 with air-conditioning) with telephone, bath or shower and WC. **Price** Single and double 190-300F, suite 400F. **Meals** Breakfast 32F. No restaurant. **Credit cards** Visa, Eurocard and MasterCard. **Pets** Dogs allowed (+30F). **Facilities** Parking. **Nearby** Beach of Ker-Chalon, the large lighthouse, church of Saint-Sauveur, ruins of the old château. **Open** All year except Jan 3 – 14.

This is exactly the kind of small seaside hotel we love. Just five minutes from the port, it is an old establishment to which a new wing with fifteen bedrooms has just been added. Comfortable and perfectly kept, the recent part is the only one we can recommend as the old part is no particular interest. The new lobby has an elegant seaside atmosphere with its film-director armchairs, matching teak tables, and a corner fireplace. The beautifully decorated bedrooms combine sober, modern brown-red furniture with thick bedspreads in eggshell Mayenne cloth, and lovely curtains with broad stripes or colorful motifs matching the headboards; the small bathrooms are very pleasant. The Escale is as hospitable as they come and an ideal stopover, escale, for walking or biking around the Island of Yeu. For lunch or dinner, we suggest the Flux Hôtel, very nearby, with its panoramic dining room overlooking the sea; and the restaurant on the port at La Meule.

***How to get there*** *(Map 14): Steamer connections with Port-Joinville (tel. 02.51.58.36.66) and Fromentine (tel. 02.51.68.52.32); on the harbour towards Saint-Sauveur.*

## Fleur de Sel

85330 Noirmoutier-en-L'Ile (Vendée)
Tel. (0)2.51.39.21.59 - Fax (0)2.51.39.75.66 - M. and Mme Wattecamps
E-mail: fleurdesel@aol.com - Web: http://www.oda.fr/aa/fleurdesel

**Category** ★★★ **Rooms** 35 with telephone, bath, WC, TV, 22 with minibar - Wheelchair access. **Price** Single 380-480F, double 530-630F. **Meals** Breakfast 50F, served 8:00-9:30 in lounge, 10:30 in room; half board 380-535F (per pers., 2 days min.). **Restaurant** Service 12:00-14:00, 19:00-22:00; menus 125-170F, also à la carte. Specialties: Seafood, shellfish and fish, lobster. **Credit cards** Amex, Visa, Eurocard and MasterCard. **Pets** Dogs allowed (+40F). **Facilities** Swimming pool, tennis (30-50F in hight season), sauna (60F), uva (50F) golf practice green, mountain beach bikes. **Nearby** Château and museum of Noirmoutier, passage du Gois and the woods of la Chaize, Saint-Phibert church, salt marshes, oyster beds; 18-hole Golf Course in Saint-Jean-de-Monts, 18-hole golf course in Pornic. **Open** Mid. Feb – Nov 1.

Fleur de Sel is a large white house built around a turquoise swimming pool and a pretty garden. It is located somewhat outside the lovely island village of Noirmoutier. The bedrooms are bright and very pleasant. (Those on the ground floor have small private terraces). The furniture is of English pine, mahogany, and colored rattan, which is complemented by matching fabrics and attractive watercolors on the walls. The large dining room is bright and opens onto the sea in summer. Two small lounges decorated in blue and white lend a warm touch to the hotel. This is a beautiful, friendly hotel and the cuisine is excellent.

***How to get there*** *(Map 14): 82km southwest of Nantes via D751 and D758. Road bridge as you leave Fromentine, the hotel is 1/2 km behind the church.*

## Hôtel Les Prateaux

Bois de la Chaize
85330 Noirmoutier-en-l'Ile (Vendée)
Tel. (0)2.51.39.12.52 - Fax (0)2.51.39.46.28 - M. Blouard

**Category** ★★★ **Rooms** 22 with telephone, bath or shower, WC and TV. **Price** Single and double 360-780F. **Meals** Breakfast 55-65F; half board 355-620F, full board 430-710F (per pers.). **Restaurant** Service 12:30-13:30, 19:30-20:30; à la carte. Specialties: Fish and shellfish. **Credit cards** All major. **Pets** Dogs not allowed. **Facilities** Parking. **Nearby** Church of Saint-Philbert-de-Grand-Lieu, Machecoul, oyster beds, Ile d'Yeu – 18-hole golf courses in Saint-Jean-de-Monts and Pornic. **Open** Feb 15 – Nov 11.

Les Prateaux has been entirely renovated and nothing has been spared to make the new and old bedrooms beautifully comfortable. The newest rooms are larger, and one even has a private 144-square-foot terrace over looking the park. The other rooms have balconies. The principal building is composed of the dining rooms (which open onto a vast terrace) the lounge and some of the bedrooms. The other rooms are located nearby in the garden. The hotel is very attractively located; built in 1939 on the end of the Ile du Noirmoutier in the middle of the forest of La Chaize, it is very quiet. The sea is only about 300 meters away and a walk through the woods will bring you to a pretty beach. The atmosphere is very summery and there is a scent of the pines and mimosas is reminiscent of the Côte d'Azur.

***How to get there*** *(Map 14): 82km southwest of Nantes by D751 and D758. Access by road bridge from Fromentine, 1.5km from Noirmoutier to Bois de la Chaize, then follow signs.*

# Logis de la Couperie

85000 La Roche-sur-Yon (Vendée)
Tel. (0)2.51.37.21.19 - Fax (0)2.51.47.71.08
Mme Oliveau

**Category** ★★★ **Rooms** 7 with telephone, bath or shower, WC and TV. **Price** Single 268-420F, double 295-480F, suite 420-480F. **Meals** Breakfast 40F, served 7:30-10:00. No restaurant. **Credit cards** Amex, Visa, Eurocard and MasterCard. **Pets** Dogs not allowed. **Facilities** Lake, bike, parking. **Nearby** History museum and château of Chabotterie, Saint-Sulpice-le-Verdon, Tiffauges, military Vendée. **Open** All year.

The Logis de la Couperie is a former manor house which was rebuilt at the end of the 18th-century. It is located in open countryside, five minutes from the center of town, and surrounded by a 5-acre park with a small lake. Nature lovers will find peace here. In the large entrance hall there is a magnificent staircase which leads to the upper floors. The bedrooms are all comfortable and tastefully furnished with antiques and regional furniture. There is a well-stocked lounge/library, where a cheerful log fire burns in winter. The excellent breakfast, which can include homemade apple juice and the local brioche, is served in the dining room or your room. *L'Halbran* and *Le Rivol* are among the very good restaurants in La Roche-sur-Yon.

***How to get there** (Map 14): On D80 towards Château-Fromage, five minutes from the town center, via the Route Nationale from Cholet.*

## Hôtel La Barbacane

2, place de l'Eglise
85130 Tiffauges (Vendée)
Tel. (0)2.51.65.75.59 - Fax (0)2.51.65.71.91 - Mme Bidan

**Category** ★★ **Rooms** 16 with telephone, bath or shower, WC and TV. **Price** Double 299-469F. **Meals** Breakfast 31-45F. No restaurant. **Credit cards** All major. **Pets** Dogs allowed. **Facilities** Heated swimming pool, billiards, garage. **Nearby** Ruins of château of Gilles de Retz ('Blue Beard'), spectacle of Puy-du-Fou, military Vendée – 18-hole golf course in Cholet. **Open** All year.

This charming little hotel is in a village the mention of whose name made the entire surrounding region tremble in the 15th-century. The fortress of Gilles de Retz, alias Blue Beard, is located here. You will go past its imposing ruins to get to La Barbacane, where you'll find the friendly welcome of Mme Bidan. The hotel is also her home, which is why each room has travel souvenirs and family furniture. On the ground floor there is a billiards room and a dining room where you can have generous breakfasts. The bedrooms are on several floors and in a ground-floor wing which opens onto the main garden; they are charming, often with exotic wicker furniture and pretty bathrooms (terracotta and blond wood), and are reasonably priced. Behind the hotel, there is another garden, with a beautiful terrace around a swimming pool. For dinner, the village restaurant, *L'Auberge du Donjon*, is right next door. If you don't mind going a little further, visit the castle at Clisson and the market before having dinner at *La Bonne Auberge*.

***How to get there*** *(Map 15): 20km west of Cholet via D753 towards Montaigu.*

## Auberge de la Rivière

85770 Velluire (Vendée)
Tel. (0)2.51.52.32.15 - Fax (0)2.51.52.37.42
M. and Mme Pajot

**Category** ★★ **Rooms** 11 with telephone, bath and WC (6 with TV). **Price** Single and double 380-450F. **Meals** Breakfast 60F, served 8:00-10:30; half board 405-440F, full board 490-525F (per pers., 3 days min.). **Restaurant** Service 12:15-14:00, 20:00-21:30 (closed Sunday evening and Monday in low season); menus 110-230F, also à la carte. Specialties: Feuilleté de langoustines, bar aux artichauts, pigeonneau sauce morilles. **Credit cards** Visa, Eurocard and MasterCard. **Pets** Dogs allowed (+30F). **Nearby** Church of Notre-Dame and museum of the Vendée in Fontenay-le-Comte, Poitou marshes – 9-hole golf course in Niort. **Open** Feb 21 – Jan 9 (closed Monday in low season).

This hotel is in the little village of Velluire on the banks of the Vendée and is only a few kilometers from Fontenay-le-Comte. The place is very peaceful and there are various types of bedrooms. All are very pleasant; those in the main building are decorated with several beautiful pieces of antique furniture, while those in the house next door are more functional, elegant, bright and very comfortable. All except one look out on the river. In the large, beautiful dining room, Mme Pajot serves excellent seafood and regional specialities. This is a pleasant and unpretentious place to stay, far from the tourist hordes. It is near the Ile de Ré, famous for is salt marshes and network of canals called "Venise Verte," Green Venice.

***How to get there*** *(Map 15): 45km northwest of Niort via N148 towards Fontenay-le-Comte, then D938 on 10km and D68 to Velluire.*

## Les Pigeons Blancs

110, rue Jules Brisson
16100 Cognac (Charente)
Tel. (0)5.45.82.16.36 - Fax (0)5.45.82.29.29 - Tachet Family

**Rooms** 7 with telephone, bath or shower, WC and TV. **Price** Single 290-450F, double 350-500F. **Meals** Breakfast 50F, served 8:00-10:00. **Restaurant** Service 12:00-14:00, 19:30-21:00; menus 138-250F, also à la carte. Specialties: Poêlée de petits gris aux pleurotes, fricassée de morue charentaise, ris de veau au foie gras frais, voiture de gourmandises. **Credit cards** All major. **Pets** Dogs not allowed. **Nearby** In Cognac: museum of Cognac, Chais of Cognac, festival du film policier; Romanesque churches of Cherves and Saint-Hérie in Matha, Le Marestay, Châtres, châteaux of Saint-Sauvan, Richemont and Garde-Epée; Randonnées en roulotte à partir de Matha; Road along the banks of the Charente de Jarnac in Angoulême, cruises on the Charente from June to Sept. **Open** All year.

In the same family since the 18th century, the Pigeons Blancs is a former postal relay station which is set in a quiet private park. The hotel is renowned for its restaurant, which is considered one of the finest in the region and is where merchants from the famous cognac houses often come for business lunches. But the Pigeons Blancs can also be proud of its lovely, comfortable bedrooms. They are decorated with elegant antique furniture, pretty coordinated fabrics and wallpaper. And they are kept immaculate, as are the bathrooms. There is a small, comfortable lounge with deep sofas, books and games which provide pleasant relaxation as you enjoy one of the region's famous brandies. Next to the lounge are two warmly decorated dining rooms with handsome family furniture.

***How to get there*** *(Map 22): 40km west of Angoulême via N141; road to Saint-Jean-d'Angély, Matha.*

1998

## Hostellerie Château Sainte-Catherine

Route de Marthon
16220 Montbron (Charente)
Tel. (0)5.45.23.60.03 - Fax (0)5.45.70.72.00 - Mme Crocquet

**Category** ★★★ **Rooms** 10 and 4 suites with telephone, bath or shower, WC and TV. **Price** Double 350-550F, suite (2 rooms, 2 bath) 600-800F. **Meals** Breakfast 49F, served 8.00-10:30; half board 350-450F (per pers., 3 days min.). **Restaurant** Service 12:00-14:00, 19:30-21:00 (closed in Feb); menus-carte 120F (lunchtime) 250F. Specialties: Foies gras, confits, magret, mousses, tarte tatin. **Credit cards** All major. **Pets** Dogs allowed. **Facilities** Swimming pool, mountain bikes and parking. **Nearby** Angoulême, forest of Braconne, La Rochefoucauld, source de la Tiouvre, caves and château of Rancogne, Romanesque church of Angoumois (Celletrouin, Lichères, Diran, Dignac, Villebois-Lavalette, Mouthiers-sur-Boëme, Saint-Michel, Saint-Amand-de-Boixe). **Open** All year except Feb.

Lying in the midst of a beautifully tended 20-acre park far from the beaten path, this handsome manor house was built for Joséphine de Beauharnais by Napoleon. Ten bedrooms and four suites (twelve give onto the park) have been discreetly arranged in light colors, offering recently renovated baths with all modern amenities. The two dining rooms, which have conserved their original character and charm, also overlook the park. The room in which breakfast is served is brightened with painted wood panels depicting country scenes, while the woodwork in the other dining room lends it the warm atmosphere of the past. The surrounding park is a haven of tranquillity in summer: a place you want to linger in. The cuisine, based on specialties of the neighboring Périgord, is excellent.

***How to get there*** *(Map 22): 17km east of Angoulême via D699.*

## Château de Nieuil

16270 Nieuil (Charente)
Tel. (0)5 45.71.36.38 - Fax (0)5 45.71.46.45 - Mme and M. Bodinaud

**Category** ★ **Rooms** 11 (6 with air-conditioning) with telephone, bath, WC, TV and minibar - Wheelchair access. **Price** Singles 630-900F, double 700-1500F, suite 1500-2300F. **Meals** Breakfast 80F, served 8:00-11:00; half board 760-1135F, full board 925-1300F (per pers., 3 days min.). **Restaurant** Service 12:00-14:00, 20:00-21:30; menus 195F (lunch), 250-340F, also à la carte. Specialties: Fish and meat with fresh vegetables. **Credit cards** All major. **Pets** Dogs allowed. **Facilities** Swimming pool, tennis, art galery, parking. **Nearby** Forest of Braconn, château of Rochebrune and Peyras, romanesque churches in Angoumois country. **Open** Apr 26 – Nov 2.

In the 14th century, the Château de Nieul was a fortress; and in the 16th century, turrets, crenalations, balusters and watchtowers were added to keep in step with the fashion. In 1937, the present owner's grandparents transformed it into a hotel. The château today is a romantic ensemble lying behind the volutes of a formal garden surrounded by semi-circular moats and an immense park with a lake. *Haute Epoque* interior decoration is predominant in the reception rooms. Each bedroom has its special style, recreated by means of precise and often superb decoration. Throughout, the antique furniture and paintings are of fine quality. But for us, more important still is M. Bodineau's hospitality and that of his staff. Warm and very attentive, it is very far from the stuffy "château" atmosphere we often find. Last but not least, Luce Bodineau's excellent cuisine and the many sports and leisure activities available (you can even rent equipment) make the Château de Nieul a luxurious hotel in which to stay and relax. Note that in winter the country restaurant of the château, the *Grange aux Oies*, offers a more rustic but equally savory version of the château's cuisine (180 F).

***How to get there** (Map 23): 40km northwest of Angoulême via N141 toward Chasseneuil, Fontafie and Nieul on D739.*

## Hôtel l'Ecailler

65, rue du Port
Ile d'Oléron - 17310 La Cotinière (Charente-Maritime)
Tel. (0)5.46.47.10.31 - Fax (0)5.46.47.10.23 - M. Rochard

**Category** ★★★ **Rooms** 8 with air-conditioning, telephone, bath, WC, TV and minibar. **Price** Single and double 350-430F. **Meals** Breakfast 43F, served 8:00-9:30, until 11:30 in room; half board 380-440F, full board 460-560F (per pers.). **Restaurant** Service 12:00-14:00, 19:00-22:00. Specialties: Boudin de Saint-Jacques, escargots charentais, huîtres chaudes printanières au vieux Pineau. **Credit cards** All major. **Pets** Dogs allowed (+35F). **Facilities** Parking (22F). **Nearby** Beachs of Le Coureau and La Giraudière, Aliénor d'Aquitaine Museum in Saint-Pierre-d'Oléron; from Boyardville, boat for Islands of Aix and Fouras; beach of Les Saumonards facing Fort Boyard - 9-hole Oléron golf course. **Open** Feb 1 – Nov 14.

L'Ecaillier is an ideal place from which to enjoy this delightful island fishing village. There is only a small street between the hotel and the picturesque fishing boats, and half the bedrooms have a view over this scene. The other rooms look out on a small garden and have the advantage of being quieter. All are well equipped. On the ground floor, you can enjoy a winter garden where there are a few tables covered with pretty floral cloths. In the adjacent large restaurant, there is a permanent exhibit of bright paintings and watercolors by local artists. The delicious fish on your plate (the *boudin* of scallops is special) is caught each morning. The atmosphere is relaxed and friendly at the Ecaillier, which means "oyster merchant".

***How to get there*** *(Map 22): 10km west of Marennes via the viaduct bridge. 3km west of Saint-Pierre-d'Oléron.*

## Hôtel Le Chat Botté

Ile de Ré
17590 Saint-Clément-des-Baleines (Charente-Maritime)
Tel. (0)5.46.29.21.93 - Fax (0)5.46.29.29.97- Mmes Massé-Chantreau

**Category** ★★ **Rooms** 19 with telephone, bath or shower and WC - Wheelchair access. **Price** Single 320F, double 370-600F. **Meals** Breakfast 44-62F, served 8:15-10:30. No restaurant. **Credit cards** Visa, Eurocard and MasterCard. **Pets** Dogs allowed (+40F). **Facilities** Small health center, parking. **Nearby** Museum and citadel of Saint-Martin-de-Ré, Baleines Lighthouse – 9-hole Trousse golf course. **Open** All year except Dec 1 – 15 and Jan 5 – Fev 6.

The Chat Botté ("puss in boots") is an adorable village house with a patio and a large flower garden on the delightful Ile de Ré. Bright wood paneling harmonizes with elegant terra cotta floors and fabrics. Everything is impeccably kept and decorated,including the bedrooms. We noted that they were quiet even in the summer vacation season: Saint-Clément is still spared the hordes of tourists who invade the Island of Ré in July and August. Not only is the Chat Botté quiet, it is also relaxing, given the fitness and beauty-care facilities offered. Breakfast is served in a very pretty room overlooking the garden. There is no restaurant in the hotel but the excellent seafood restaurant *Le Chat Botté* is just next door; *L'Auberge de la Rivière* in Les Portes-en-Ré, and *L'Ecailler,* one of the best fish restaurants of the Charentes and Vendée Coast.

***How to get there*** *(Map 22): 28km west of La Rochelle via the Pallice Bridge.*

1998

# Hôtel de l'Océan

172, rue Saint-Martin
Ile de Ré 17580 Le Bois-Plage-en-Ré (Charente-Maritime)
Tel. (0)5.46.09.23.07 - Fax (0)5.46.09.05.40 - M. and Mme Bourdet

**Category** ★★ **Rooms** 24 with telephone, bath or shower, WC, TV - Wheelchair access. **Price** Single and double 350-450F. **Meals** Breakfast 45F, served 7:45-10:45; half board 340-400F (per pers.). **Restaurant** Service 12:15-14:30, 19:15 22:30; menus 130F, 180F, also à la carte. Specialties: Chaurchée charentaise, douade grillée au romarin. **Credit cards** Visa, Eurocard and MasterCard. **Pets** Dogs allowed. **Facilities** Parking privated (150 m.). **Nearby** Museum and citadelle of Saint-Martin de-Ré, lighthouse of Baleines - 9-hole Trousse Chemise golf course. **Open** Feb 6 – Jan 4.

Bois-Plage is a town that so far has been not been affected by the fashions that are progressively overtaking the Island of Ré. Along a small street, the pretty white and green façade of the Hôtel de l'Océan is a good indication of the charm you'll find inside. The dining room and fireplace, its colonial-style furniture painted pearl-grey, its white panelled walls hung with beautiful ocean-liner lithographs, is an invitation to tarry over the excellent meals served there. To the right of the entrance, two small lounges in eggshell colors reminded us that the owner used to be an antiques dealer. Across a terrace dining room outside, you'll find a long garden which several bedrooms overlook. Bulrush-covered floors, thick piqué bedspreads, beautiful drapes, natural plaster on the walls and antique furniture here and there are several sound decorative qualities that are sure to please. (If you reserve in time, ask for the bedrooms located above the restaurant: they are the largest and our favorites; avoid the rare rooms that have not yet been renovated.) Good breakfasts with delicious homemade preserves are served with a smile.

***How to get there*** *(Map 22): 28km west of la Rochelle, via La Pallice bridge.*

## Hôtel de Bordeaux

1, rue Gambetta
17800 Pons (Charente-Maritime)
Tel. (0)5.46.91.31.12 - Fax (0)5.46.91.22.25- M. Jaubert and Mlle Muller

**Category** ★★ **Rooms** 16 with telephone, bath, WC, TV. **Price** Single 220F, double 260F. **Meals** Breakfast 35F, served 7:30-10:30; half board 230F, full board 315F (per pers., 3 days min.). **Restaurant** Service 12:00-14:00, 19:30-21:30, menus 85-230F, also à la carte. Specialties: Fumage minute de langoustines, turbot rôti, minestrone de homard, hachis de basilic, barigoule d'artichauts et langoustines. **Credit cards** Amex, Visa, Eurocard and MasterCard. **Pets** Dogs allowed. **Facilities** Parking. **Nearby** Dungeon of Pons, château of Usson; romanesque churches of Saintonges; Aulnay; château of Damierre; Saintes – 18-hole Saintes golf course. **Open** All year (closed Sunday in low season).

From the street, this hotel is like many other establishments in the center of town, but inside, pleasant surprises abound. First, there is a small, quite British bar (reserved for hotel guests except on Saturday morning); a lounge decorated with true elegance; and finally the patio, which is the very charming prolongation of the two dining rooms. Sheltered from the wind, bordered by shrubs and hollyhocks, it is a perfect setting for dinner and relaxation in the gentle climate of the southern Charente-Maritime. In the kitchen, young M. Jaubert turns out masterful specialties and the prices are right. After having apprenticed with the greatest chefs, he has returned to his native town to open his own business, and his reputation is growing still. As for the bedrooms, the conveniences and decoration are very ordinary but not unpleasant. Four look out onto the patio and the others onto a quiet street at night; all are perfectly maintained. Let us add that the atmosphere is very welcoming, youthful and informal, and you will understand why the Hôtel de Bordeaux is the delight of all who stay there.

***How to get there*** *(Map 22): 22km south of Saintes.*

## Hôtel France et Angleterre et Champlain

20, rue Rambaud
17000 La Rochelle (Charente-Maritime)
Tel. (0)5.46.41.23.99 - Fax (0)5.46.41.15.19 - Mme Jouineau

**Category** ★★★ **Rooms** 36 with telephone, bath or shower, WC, cable TV, 4 with air-conditioning and 28 with minibar - Elevator. **Price** Single and double 315-520F, suite 680F. **Meals** Breakfast 50F, served 7:15-11.30. No restaurant. **Credit cards** All major. **Pets** Dogs allowed (+30F). **Facilities** Garage (35-48F). **Nearby** New World museum, Lafaille museum, Protestant and arts museum in La Rochelle, Ile de Ré, Esnandes, church portal and dungeon in Vouvant, Poitou marshes – 18-hole La Prée golf course in La Rochelle. **Open** All year.

This 17th-century former convent hides a beautiful garden behind its walls, which is a good place for breakfast. To get to the garden you cross a large hall and some lovely reception rooms. Period woodwork, antique statues and lovely old furniture create a warm and elegant ambience. The bedrooms, reached by elevator or by the splendid stone staircase, offer you the choice of a comfortable modern style or the charm and elegance of an earlier era. They are different in decor but all are comfortable, though you will probably prefer those with a view overlooking the garden; the rooms on the street have double glazing and all will soon be air-conditioned. There is no restaurant but the hotel has a *demi-pension* arrangement with the adjacent restaurant. The staff is very pleasant, adding further to the hotel's many attractive features. For the best seafood in La Rochelle, try *La Marmite*, or the bustling bistrot *La Marée*, for its giant platters of shellfish.

***How to get there*** *(Map 22): In the center of La Rochelle.*

## Résidence de Rohan

Parc des Fées - Route de Saint-Palais
17640 Vaux-sur-Mer (Charente-Maritime)
Tel. (0)5.46.39.00.75 - Fax (0)5.46.38.29.99 - M. and Mme Seguin

**Category** ★★★ **Rooms** 41 with telephone, bath or shower, WC and TV. **Price** Single and double 300-700F. **Meals** Breakfast 54F, served 7:30-13:00. No restaurant. **Credit cards** Amex, Visa, Eurocard and MasterCard. **Pets** Dogs allowed. **Facilities** Heated swimming pool, tennis (+50F), parking. **Nearby** Lighthouse of Cordouan, La Rochelle, Sablonceaux abbey, Talmont-sur-Gironde, zoo of La Palmyre – 18-hole Côte de la Beauté golf course in Royan. **Open** Mar 26 – Nov 10.

The elegant Résidence de Rohan stands in the Parc des Fées, a lovely small wood on the edge of the beach at Nauzan. The trees surrounding the house, the lawn gently sloping towards the sea and several chaise-longues scattered among the parasol pines create the whole charm of this pink-and-white 19th-century villa. Inside, the decor is quite different from what you might expect to find in a seaside house; the velvet-covered armchairs in the lounge, the mahogany Charles X-style furniture in the bar, the carpets and rugs create a rather opulent ambience. All the bedrooms have their own style and beautiful fabrics; many are furnished with antique furniture. Some rooms, notably those in the annex, are very spacious, while others open onto the garden. You can enjoy an excellent breakfast on the terrace overlooking the panorama of the ocean and its changing lights. The hosts are friendly and hospitable. A swimming pool with snack bar on the seaside offer further enjoyment of the water. Good restaurants nearby include *Le Chalet, Les Trois Marmites, Les Filets Bleus* and *La Jabotière*.

***How to get there*** *(Map 22): 3km northwest of Royan via D25, which follows the coast in the towards of Saint-Palais-sur-Mer.*

## Au Marais

46-48, quai Louis-Tardy
79510 Coulon (Deux-Sèvres)
Tel. (0)5.49.35.90.43 - Fax (0)5.49.35.81.98 - M. and Mme Nerrière

**Category** ★★★ **Rooms** 18 with telephone, bath, WC and TV. **Price** Double 250-600F. **Meals** Breakfast (buffet) 40F, served 7:30-10:00 No restaurant. **Credit cards** Visa, Eurocard and MasterCard. **Pets** Dogs allowed (+30F). **Nearby** Poitou marshes, museums and church of Notre-Dame in Niort – 18-hole golf course in Niort. **Open** All year except in Jan.

All the magic of the Poitou marshland is here in front of the hotel: the Sèvre River is directly in front of the hotel and the cruise boats are nearby. The hotel is built in classic Poitou style and has been totally restored without being spoiled. The interior decoration is very tasteful. In the bedrooms, there is a beautiful assortment of fresh colors and handsome furniture and fabrics. They are all remarkably well kept and the bathrooms are immaculate. The hotel is quiet despite the numbers of tourists in July and August. This is an excellent small hotel which is ideal for visiting "Green Venice" and where you will find a young, very friendly staff. There is no restaurant in the hotel but the owners will give you good addresses. Our favorites are *Le Central*, on the Place de l'Eglise in Coulon, if you wish to remain in the village; and in Niort, we recommend the gourmet *Relais Saint Antoine* and the delightful *Belle Etoile*.

***How to get there*** *(Map 15): 10km west of Niort via D9 and and D1 (on the edge of the Sèvre).*

## Le Logis Saint-Martin

Chemin de Pissot
79400 Saint-Maixent-l'Ecole (Deux-Sèvres)
Tel. (0)5.49.05.58.68 - Fax (0)5.49.76.19.93 - Mme and M. Heintz

**Category** ★★★ **Rooms** 10 with telephone, bath or shower, WC and TV. **Price** Single and double 390-530F. **Meals** Breakfast 62F, served 8:00-10:00; half board 440-480F (per pers., 3 days min.). **Restaurant** Service 12:15-14:00, 19:30-21:30; menus 95F (lunch), 160-290F, also à la carte. Specialties: Foie gras poelé au pain d'épices jus court à la réglisse, pigeonneau roti en cocotte, julienne de citron confit sauce aux agrumes et cardamome. **Credit cards** All major. **Pets** Dogs not allowed. **Facilities** Parking. **Nearby** Local history museum, arts museum, Notre-Dame church in Niort, church in Melle, Tumulus of Bougon museum, Futuroscope in Poitiers – 9-hole golf courses in Mazières-en-Gatine, Sainte-Maxire and Les Forges. **Open** All year except in Jan.

This large, 17th-century stone house, so cool when it is hot outside, and so warm in the winter, is a great place to spend a weekend. From here you can walk along the Sèvre River which runs in front of the hotel, and through the countryside described by René Bazin in *L'église Verte*. You can also enjoy the local architecture in this region rich in Romanesque art and buildings. The comfortable rooms look out on the river. They are all light, quiet, and very pleasant. The cuisine is very good and the hosts are warm and welcoming.

***How to get there*** *(Map 15): 24km northeast of Niort via N11.*

## Auberge Charembeau

Route de Niozelles
04300 Forcalquier (Alpes-de-Haute-Provence)
Tel. (0)4.92.70.91.70 - Fax (0)4.91.70.91.83 - M. Berger

**Category** ★★ **Rooms** 14 with telephone, bath or shower and WC. **Price** Single 290F, double 470F. Rooms with kitchenette 1850-3000F per week. **Meals** Breakfast 44F, served 8:00-9:30. No restaurant. **Credit cards** All major. **Pets** Dogs allowed (+20F). **Facilities** Swimming pool, tennis, bicycles rentals, parking. **Nearby** Lure mountain, Salagon priory, Ganagobie priory, château de Sauvan, Saint-Michel-l'Observatoire. **Open** Feb 1 – Nov 30.

This little hotel in the middle of the lovely countryside of the Forcalquier region is run by a friendly couple who have given the old restored house a charming family atmosphere. You have a choice of the traditional bedrooms, smartly furnished and fresh, or the suites with a small kitchen, which are just as charming. In front of the inn, you can enjoy relaxing around the swimming pool surrounded by the Provençal countryside. On request, the Charembeau rents bikes, including those with a baby-carrier, for exploring the region on marked bicycle trails. For restaurants, we recommend that you try the Provençal country cooking at the *Hostellerie des Deux Lions* in Forcalquier; the *Pie Margot* in Dauphin, or the *Café de la Lavande* in Lardier.

***How to get there** (Map 34): 39km south of Sisteron via N96 (or A51, exit La Brillanne), then N100 towards Forcalquier. It's 4km from Forcalquier via N100 towards Niozelles.*

# La Fare

Pierrerue 04300 Forcalquier (Alpes-de-Haute-Provence)
Tel. (0)4.92.70.48.10 - Fax (0)4.92.72.71.02
M. Baussan

**Category** ★ **Rooms** 3 with air-conditioning, telephone, bath or shower, WC, satellite TV and minibar. **Price** Single and double 800-950F, suite 950F. **Meals** Breakfast incl., served from 8:00; half board 550F (per pers.). **Restaurant** Evening meals only for residents. Service 20:00, menu 160F. Specialties: Regional cooking. **Credit cards** All major. **Pets** Dogs not allowed. **Facilities** Heated swimming pool, whirlpool, hammam, mountain bikes, parking. **Nearby** Lure mountain, Salagon priory, Ganagobie priory, château of Sauvan, Saint-Michel-l'Observatoire. **Open** All year.

We are happy to be able to suggest a new hotel in the Haute Provence beloved of Jean Giono, which is so beautiful and yet less known than southern Provence. Dating from 1789, this house has just been entirely restored and the owners have taken advantage of the occasion to create two guest bedrooms and a suite with salon in one part of the building. The services available are half-way between those of an auberge and those of a bed-and-breakfast. In addition to exceptionally comfortable modern amenities, the decoration of the reception rooms and the bedrooms is truly magnificent, contemporary combining with exotic, wrought iron with terra cotta, woven wicker with natural wood. A hammam, fitness facilities, mountain bikes, and a big, beautiful swimming pool for the less energetic are good illustrations of the attention that has been given to making your stay enjoyable. La Fare is a warmly welcoming inn of great distinction—so much so that you won't see any signs for it on the roads. So it's a good idea to phone ahead for directions.

***How to get there** (Map 34): 39km south of Sisteron via N85 (or A51, La Brillanne exit); then D12 towards Forcalquier; 3km from Forcalquier.*

# Hostellerie de la Fuste

La Fuste 04210 Manosque (Alpes-de-Haute-Provence)
Tel. (0)4.92.72.05.95 - Fax (0)4.92.72.92.93
Jourdan-Bucaille Family

**Category** ★★★★ **Rooms** 14 (4 with air conditioning) with telephone, bath, shower, WC, TV and minibar - 1 for disabled persons. **Price** Single and double 500-1000F, suite 1100F. **Meals** Breakfast 90F, served at any time; half board and full board 750-1050F (per pers.). **Restaurant** Service 12:00-14:00, 19:30-21:30 (22:30 in summer); menus 250-350F. Specialties: Agneau de pays, truffes and games in season. **Credit cards** All major. **Pets** Dogs allowed. **Facilities** heated swimming pool and covered in winter, parking. **Nearby** Le plateau de Valensole, Manosque: Carzou fondation, museum of Jean Giono, Moustiers, Gorges of Verdon. **Open** Feb 21 – Jan 14. Closed Sunday evening and Monday Oct 1 – June 15 except National Holidays.

In the country of Jean Giono and this marvelous region of Haute Provence covered with olive trees and lavender, this old bastide has become a gourmet's haven. Served in the garden with the first buds of spring or around the fireplace, Dominique Bucaille's inspired cuisine, crowned with a Michelin star, is a harmonious marriage of creation and tradition. The spacious, classically decorated bedrooms offer comfortable amenities and overlook an orchard surrounded by aromatic plants. The breakfast is excellent, the service professional. When you visit Manosque, you can discover authentic Provençal specialties also at *La Rôtisserie*, run by the same family and served in the convivial ambiance of an old spinning mill.

***How to get there*** *(Map 34): On A51 (Aix-en-Provence/Manosque), take Manosque exit; 6km from Manosque via D4.*

# Bastide de Moustiers

04360 Moustiers-Sainte-Marie (Alpes-de-Haute-Provence)
Tel. (0)4.92.70.47.47 - Fax (0)4.92.70.47.48 - M. Ducasse
Web: http://www.bastide-moustiers.i2m.fr - E-mail: bastide@i2m.fr

**Category** ★★★★ **Rooms** 7 with air-conditioning, telephone, fax, bath, WC, TV, safe and minibar. **Price** Double 800-1300F. **Meals** Breakfast 75F. **Restaurant** Service 12:00-14:00, 19:30-21:45 (closed Nov 17 – Mar 12); menus 195-260F. Specialties: Regional cooking. **Credit cards** Amex, Eurocard and MasterCard. **Pets** Dogs allowed only in the restaurant. **Facilities** Heated swimming pool, mountain bikes, parking. **Nearby** Church and Pottery Museum in Moustiers, the Grand Canyon of the Gorges of the Verdon via the road or GR4; Lake of Sainte-Croix. **Open** Beg. Feb – Nov 15.

Great names in French gastonomy are regularly mentioned in this guide. Far from changing our criteria for selection, we have included the great chefs who have opened a charming hotel or inn along with their prestigious restaurant. Three-star chef Alain Ducasse's Bastide de Moustiers, whose chef is trained by the master, reflects the loveliest tradition of this region. It is a tradition of hospitality, and you will be received as friends. The kitchen is open to you; you can have dinner at the same table or enjoy a romantic *tête à tête* in one of the dining rooms; and you can browse quietly through the books in the library. You will also find tradition in the decor, with its elegant furnishings and antique Provençal furniture; and in the natural surroundings, where cypresses intermingle with poplars, oaks with olive, chestnut, and almond trees, not to mention the indispensable country vegetable garden. Nor have animals been overlooked: horses, fawns and even the neighbor's donkey find Ducasse's grass tastier. At the Bastide de Moustiers, simplicity and charm are what you see; efficiency and the Ducasse quality are what you experience.

***How to get there*** *(Map 34): On A51, Cadarache/Vinon-sur-Verdon exit, towards Gréoux-les-Bains, Riez, Moustier. On A8 Le Muy exit, towards Draguignan, Aups, Moustiers.*

# La Ferme Rose

04360 Moustiers-Sainte-Marie (Alpes-de-Haute-Provence)
Tel. (0)4.92.74.69.47 - Fax (0)4.92.74.60.76
M. Kako Vagh

**Category** ★★ **Rooms** 7 with telephone, shower and WC, TV on request. **Price** Double 390-430F. **Meals** Breakfast 48F or brunch à la carte. No restaurant. **Credit cards** Amex, Visa, Eurocard and MasterCard. **Pets** Dogs allowed. **Facilities** Mountain bikes. **Nearby** Church and Pottery Museum in Moustiers, the Grand Canyon of the Gorges of the Verdon via the road or GR4; Lake of Sainte-Croix. **Open** Mar 16 – Nov 14.

From the terrace of "The Pink Farm," you will have a beautiful view over the lovely village of Moustiers, which seems suspended between two cliffs. The hotel is charming. The owner has decorated it in a very personal style, combining his collection of 1950s objects, paintings done by his grandfather - a well-known Provençal painter - and amusing pieces of furniture. Note the tables, chairs and bar banquettes which came from the old Brasserie Noailles in Marseilles. The bedrooms are very pleasant, bright and cheerful, with shower rooms decorated in pretty Salernes tiles from the region. The very helpful owner, Kako, will reserve a mattress for you on a private beach on Sainte Croix Lake, rent you an electric boat to ascend the Verdon Falls, or give you tips insider's for visiting this endearing village in the spectacular Alps of Haute Provence. Several good restaurants: *Les Santons* in the village; *La Bastide de Moustiers* nearby.

***How to get there*** *(Map 34): On A51, Cadarache/Vinon-sur-Verdon exit, towards Gréoux-les-Bains, Riez, Moustier. On A8 Le Luc exit, towards Aups, Moustiers. In Moustiers take towards the village of Sainte-Croix on 1km.*

## Auberge du Clos Sorel

Les Molanès
04400 Pra-Loup (Alpes-de-Haute-Provence)
Tel. (0)4.92.84.10.74 - Mme Mercier

**Category** ★★★ **Rooms** 11 with telephone, bath, WC and TV. **Price** Single 400F, double 520-850F. **Meals** Breakfast 50F, served 8:00-10:30; half board 400-600F (per pers., 3 days min.). **Restaurant** Service 12:30-14:30; menu 150F, also à la carte. Specialties: Morilles, ravioles, gigots. **Credit cards** Visa, Eurocard and MasterCard. **Pets** Dogs allowed (+35F). **Facilities** Swimming pool. **Nearby** Skiing from hotel, Colmars, route de la Bonette. **Open** Dec 11 – Sept 1 and June 21 – Apr 11.

Well located on a hillside in a hamlet that seems not to have changed for centuries, the Auberge du Clos Sorel occupies the oldest farmhouse of the region, in immediate proximity of the ski slopes. The building has lovely stone walls and an entranceway built of logs, and blends in perfectly with the surrounding chalets. Inside, original features such as beams, an impressive fireplace and sloping ceilings have been retained, and these combine with the polished furniture to create the kind of warm and cozy atmosphere one looks forward to after a long day spent skiing or walking. In the evening, dinner is served by candlelight in what used to be the main room of the farmhouse. The tables are pretty and the cuisine is refined. In summer, a swimming pool and tennis courts facing a magnificent panorama make the inn a lovely place to stay. The ambiance is a happy mixture of informality and sophistication.

***How to get there*** *(Map 34): 70km southwest of Gap via D900B and D900 to Barcelonnette, then D902 and D109 to Pra-Loup. (Les Molanès is just before the resort.)*

## Auberge de Reillanne

04110 Reillanne (Alpes-de-Haute-Provence)
Tel. (0)4.92.76.45.95
M. Bellaiche

**Rooms** 7 with telephone, bath, WC and minibar. **Price** Single 280F, double 380F. **Meals** Breakfast 45F; half board 380F (per pers.). **Restaurant** Service 19:30-21:00 (closed Wednesday except for residents); menu 180F, also à la carte. Specialties: Piccata de fois gras aux navets confits, solimane d'agneau à la menthe et au miel, home-smoked fish, pintade à la crème d'ail et de sauge. **Credit cards** Visa, Eurocard and MasterCard. **Pets** Dogs allowed. **Facilities** Parking. **Nearby** Manosque, priories of Salagon and Ganagobie, château de Sauvan. **Open** All year.

Located in a part of the Luberon which has remained unspoiled, this hotel is surrounded by greenery. The few bedrooms are large, plainly furnished, but warm and comfortable, with an emphasis on natural materials: light-colored wood or cane, unbleached wool and flowery fabrics. All the bedrooms have pleasant views and lovely bathrooms with terracotta floor tiles. There is no charge to use the minibars in the rooms, guests decide how much they want to pay for the drinks – obviously trust is the keyword here. Maurice Bellaiche chose the hotel business because he enjoys it, and has created a peaceful and above all friendly atmosphere. He does the cooking himself, and his good seasonal cuisine is based on fresh local produce, with a touch of exoticism. You will find it all the more delectable in the charming dining room where meals are served. The Auberge de Reillanne is an unpretentious place to stay, but somewhat lacking in gaiety.

***How to get there*** *(Map 33): 15km northwest of Manosque towards Apt, then N100 and D214 towards Reillanne.*

## Le Pyjama

04400 Super-Sauze (Alpes-de-Haute-Provence)
Tel. (0)4.92.81.12.00 - Fax (0)4.92.81.03.16
Mme Merle

**Category** ★★★ **Rooms** 10 with telephone, bath, WC, TV and minibar. **Price** Single 260-330F, double 340-440F, suite 480-620F. **Meals** Breakfast 20-45F. No restaurant. **Credit cards** All major. **Pets** Dogs allowed. **Nearby** Skiing from the hotel, village of Colmars, Beauvezer, gorges of Saint-Pierre, Guillaumes via the col des Champs, route de la Bonette. **Open** June 26 – Sept 4 and Dec 16 – Apr 19.

Having spent twenty years running another hotel in the resort, Geneviève Merle (ski champion Carole Merle's mother) had this hotel designed to integrate harmoniously with the surroundings. Eight of the ten bedrooms face south, their terraces overlooking a field of larch trees. They are tastefully decorated, with very pleasant bathrooms. M. Merle owns an antique shop nearby, and it has provided the hotel furniture. Four rooms have a mezzanine which can accommodate two extra people. In the annex there are four studios complete with kitchen areas which are very convenient for families. This is a comfortable, informal hotel at the foot of the ski slopes, with outstanding breakfasts, good value for the money, and a very friendly staff. Le Pyjama has no restaurant but there are many in the village and *L'Optraken,* run by Madame Merle's children, is not far. This is an extremely comfortable establishment, at the foot of the slopes, offering a friendly and informal atmosphere.

***How to get there*** *(Map 34): 79km southeast of Gap via D900B and D900 towards Barcelonnette, then D9 and D209 to Super-Sauze.*

## La Boule de Neige

15, rue du Centre
05330 Serre-Chevalier - Chantemerle (Hautes-Alpes)
Tel. (0)4.92.24.00.16 - Fax (0)4.92.24.00.25 - Sandrine et Bruno Chauveteau

**Category** ★★ **Rooms** 10 with telephone, bath or shower and WC. **Price** Double 350-450F, 330-680F in winter. **Meals** Breakfast 50F served 8:00-10:45; half board 320-365F, 330-495F in winter (per pers.). **Restaurant** Service 12:00-14:00, 19:00-21:00; menus 97-160F, also à la carte. Specialties: Foie gras en gelée de Sauterne, ballotine de langoustines en habit vert, croquant de chocolat aux framboises. **Credit cards** Visa, Eurocard and MasterCard. **Pets** Dogs allowed. **Nearby** Ski, clinbing, mountain bikes – 9-hole Montgenèvre Golf Course (18km), 9-hole Clavière Golf Course (21km). **Open** Nov – May 14 and June 16 – Sept 14.

This village house has just been entirely renovated with great taste and good practical sense. On the ground floor, a small curved bar stands next to a room tiled in Burgundian stones and prettily decorated with elegant wooden tables, an imposing piece of Indian furniture and several sprays of dried flowers on the walls. The room extends into a charming barrel-vaulted dining room and, three steps down, there is a pleasant small lounge with fireplace. The bedrooms, comfortable and impeccably kept, have been designed in a modern style, making them less charming than the rest of the hotel. Except for the two bedrooms located on the street side of the *premier étage,* all are very bright. Four rooms have a balcony and look out over the old rooftops of the village and a bumpy field beyond, where skiers can get a final bit of practice before heading out for the slopes.

***How to get there*** *(Map 27): 5km northwest of Briançon via N91.*

## Hôtel de Paris

34, boulevard d'Alsace
06400 Cannes (Alpes-Maritimes)
Tel. (0)4.93.38.30.89 - Fax (0)4.93.39.04.61 - M. Lazzari
Web: http://www.hotel-de-paris.com - E-mail: reception@hotel-de-paris.com

**Category** ★★★ **Rooms** 45 and 5 suites, with air-conditioning, sounproofing, telephone, bath or shower, WC and satellite TV - Elevator. **Price** Single 500-650F, double 550-750F, suite 900-1600F. **Meals** Breakfast 50F, served 7:00-11:00. No restaurant. **Credit cards** All major. **Pets** Dogs not allowed. **Facilities** Swimming pool, private beach, whirlpool, steam bath, bar, garage (90F). **Nearby** Massif du Tanneron, Auribeau-sur-Siagne, Mougins, Vallauris, îles de Lérins – 27-hole Cannes golf course in Mandelieu. **Open** Dec 27 – Nov 19.

This hotel is in a large white house near the highway. Its facade is decorated with columns and pediments in typical turn of the century Côte d'Azur style. Although the hotel is in the center of Cannes it has a garden (a bit noisy) with palms and cypresses around a very pleasant swimming pool. The interior is very smart. The bedrooms are decorated with prints. The suites are luxurious and have a private lounge. All the rooms are air-conditioned and soundproofed and some have a balcony on which you can have breakfast. For restaurants, try *Gaston et Gastounette* for bourride or bouillabaisse; *Côté Jardin, Au Bec Fin* or *La Brouette de Grand-mère* for fresh cuisine and good chef's-special menu; and a interesting menu; *Chez Franco* for Italian cooking; *Le Café Carlton* on the beach of the *Carlton Hotel*, for an informal and chic buffet lunch; and *Le Rado-Plage* under the parasols on the Croisette.

***How to get there*** *(Map 34): In the town center.*

## Auberge du Soleil

Quartier Porta-Savel
06390 Coaraze (Alpes-Maritimes)
Tel. (0)4.93.79.08.11 - Fax (0)4.93.79.37.79 - M. and Mme Jacquet

**Category** ★ **Rooms** 8 and 2 suites with telephone, bath or shower, WC and TV on request. **Price** Single 330-390F, double 350-495F, suite 495-940F. **Meals** Breakfast 45F, served 8:00-12:00; half board 360-440F, (per pers., 3 days min.). **Restaurant** Service 12:00-14:00, 19:30-21:00; menu 142F, also à la carte. Specialties: Tourte maison, gibelotte de lapin, caille aux raisins. **Credit cards** Amex, Visa, Eurocard and MasterCard. **Pets** Dogs allowed (+35F). **Facilities** Swimming pool, boules, table tennis. **Nearby** Mercantour reserve, valley of the Merveilles, Turini forest, villages of Lucéram, Peille and Peillon – 18-hole Agel golf course in La Turbie. **Open** Mar 15 – Nov 15.

This hotel is only half an hour from Nice and not far from the magnificent nature reserve of Mercantour. It is splendidly located in a medieval village 640 meters up on a rocky outcrop. The maze of narrow village streets ensures total peace and calm: you may need to call on the hotel to help with your luggage up the steep slopes. You will find an informal, almost bohemian atmosphere in the hotel but it is all in elegant taste. There is a summer lounge located in a cool vaulted cellar and an attractive dining room which extends out over a covered terrace with panoramic views of the valley. The cuisine is simple and good. The garden slopes down in steps to the swimming pool and orchard, where you can pick the fruit without feeling guilty.

***How to get there*** *(Map 35): 2km north of Nice via A8 exit Nice-Est, then "voie rapide" (highway) towards Drap-Sospel. At the Pointe des Contes, left towards Contes-Coaraze.*

# La Tour de l'Esquillon

Miramar
06590 Théoule-sur-Mer (Alpes-Maritimes)
Tel. (0)4.93.75.41.51 - Fax (0)4.93.75.49.99 - M. and Mme Dérobert
Web: http://www.cannes-hotels.com/esquillon - E-mail: esquillon@compuserve.com

**Category** ★★★ **Rooms** 25 with telephone, bath, WC, TV and minibar. **Price** Single and double 400-800F. **Meals** Breakfast 65F, served 8:00-10:00; half board 520-720F. **Restaurant** Service 12:00-14:00, 19:00-21:00; menus 165-215F, also à la carte. Specialties: Fish, bouride, aïoli. **Credit cards** All major. **Pets** Dogs allowed. **Facilities** Private beach, parking. **Nearby** Château of Napoule, Estérel Mountains, point of l'Esquillon, bight of Napoule – 18-hole Cannes-Mandelieu golf course. **Open** Feb 1 – Oct 14.

At the edge of the winding road overlooking the deep-red Esterel Mountains, The Tour de l'Esquillon is perched like a bird's nest overlooking the Estérel Massif, its deep-red rocks forming a beautiful, jagged coastline between Cannes and Saint-Raphaël. Brilliant yellow broom, pink oleander, hydrangeas and fruit trees covering the terraced garden lie between the hotel and its private beach which you can reach by minibus, and where you can enjoy light meals. The Esquillon has a kind of old-fashioned charm, which is accented by its 1950s furniture and its discreet, friendly service. The 25 bedrooms are large and cool, and they face the Mediterranean. Some more expensive rooms have a balcony, which is a pleasant place to have breakfast. In the restaurant, you will enjoy the savory, spicy specialties of Provence. From the dining room, you will have a panoramic view over Cannes. Note that there is noise from the road on days of peak traffic.

***How to get there*** *(Map 34): Between Saint-Raphael and Cannes, on A7, exit Mandelieu, then in the towards of Théole Miramar.*

## Le Manoir de l'Etang

66, allée du Manoir
06250 Mougins (Alpes-Maritimes)
Tel. (0)4.93.90.01.07 - Fax (0)4.92.92.20.70 - Gridaine-Labro Family

**Category** ★★★ **Rooms** 15 with telephone, bath or shower, WC, TV and minibar. **Price** Double 660-1000F, suite 1300-1500F. **Meals** Breakfast 55F, served 8:00-10:30. **Restaurant** Service 12:00-14:00, 20:00-22:00; menus 150F (lunchtime, wine incl.) and 190F, also à la carte. Specialties: Canelloni de homard au jus de favouilles, lapereau mijoté à la niçoise, millefeuille de framboise et chocolat, nougat glacé au miel du manoir. **Credit cards** Amex, Visa ,Eurocard and MasterCard. **Pets** Small dogs allowed on request. **Facilities** Swimming pool, parking. **Nearby** The Riviera and her villages – 5 golf courses nearby. **Open** All year except Nov and Jan.

This superb 19th-century house, surrounded by cypresses and oleander, overlooks a lake in a rolling 17-acre park. On the ground floor there is a warmly decorated lounge with a terra-cotta floor and a bright dining room overlooking the pool; which is framed by olive trees. Beyond the pool there are extensive views over the Provençal landscape. The comfortable bedrooms are brightened by cheerful materials printed with flowers and fruits. You will enjoy delicious regional cuisine which is light and inventive. Enjoy the tranquil atmosphere and the good humor of the owners, who will give you a real family welcome. This is a delightful and charming place to stay.

***How to get there*** *(Map 34): 5km north of Cannes via "voie rapide" (highway).*

1998

## Hôtel L'Aiglon

7, avenue de la Madone
06500 Menton (Alpes-Maritimes)
Tel. (0)4.93.57.55.55 - Fax (0)4.93.35.92.39 - M. and Mme Caravelli

**Category** ★★★ **Rooms** 28, 1 apartment and 2 suites (24 with air-conditioning) with telephone, bath or shower, WC, satellite TV, safe and minibar - Elevator. **Price** Single and double 350-620F, 430-770F, suite and apart. 780F, 1050F. **Meals** Breakfast incl.; half board 395-565F, 673F in suite (per pers.). **Restaurant** Service 12:30-13:30, 20:00-22:00 (closed Wednesday lunchtime); menus 100F (lunchtime in week) and 180-300F, also à la carte: Foie gras de canard maison, bar à la tapenade, chausson aux fruits frais. **Credit cards** All major. **Pets** Dogs allowed. **Facilities** Heated swimming pool and parking. **Nearby** in Menton: Museum of J.Cocteau, fronts of the Casino, Palais de l'Europe, exotical garden; village of Goubio; Roya Valley; the french Riviéra; garden of Villa Hambury - 18-hole Cannes-Mougins golf course. **Open** Dec 23 – Nov 4.

This former mansion is one of our happiest discoveries this year. Its spacious reception rooms with their rococo gilt, the many corner lounges with 1930s furniture, the daily papers attached to wooden poles: it all brings back the atmosphere of the great luxury hotels in the days when elderly English people came to winter on the Riviera. Decorated in old-fashioned sepia tones, the bedrooms with their comfortable beds and immaculate bathrooms (well soundproofed) are nevertheless as appealing as anything modern. Their reasonable prices vary depending on their size and the season; some even have a view of the sea as the hotel is separated from the Mediterranean only by a row of small buildings. Served on the veranda or in the shady arbor, lunches and dinners offer simple, delicious specialties. Not far away, the luxuriant garden conceals a heated (86°F) outdoor swimming pool.

***How to get there*** *(Map 34): 29km of Nice, 15km of Monaco.*

# Hôtel La Pérouse

11, quai Rauba-Capeu
06300 Nice (Alpes-Maritimes)
Tel. (0)4.93.62.34.63 - Fax (0)4.93.62.59.41 - Mme Giometti
Web: http://www.hroy.com/la-perouse - E-mail: lp@hroy.com

**Category** ★★★★ **Rooms** 64 with air-conditioning, telephone, bath or shower, WC, TV and minibar. **Price** Single 415-1380F, double 695-1380F, suite 1700-2290F. **Meals** Breakfast 90F, served 7:00-11:00. **Restaurant** Service 12:00-15:00, 19:30-22:00 (closed Sept 15 – May 15); à la carte. Specialties: Grills in the hotel gardens. **Credit cards** All major. **Pets** Dogs allowed. **Facilities** Swimming pool, sauna, whirlpool, solarium. **Nearby** Turini forest, valley of La Tinée (Roure, Roubron), valley of La Vésubie, villages of Utelle, Belvédère, le Boréon, Venanson – 18-hole Opio golf course in Valbonne, 18-hole Bastide-du-Roy golf course in Biot. **Open** All year.

La Pérouse is in a large Mediterranean-style mansion at the foot of the château that dominates old Nice and the Baie des Anges. It is surrounded by aloe plants and lemon trees; to reach it you have to take one of the two elevators from the quayside. The bedrooms are spacious and quiet, and prices vary according to whether you have a view of the garden or the sea; some have a terrace with deck chairs. In summer you might take advantage of the barbecue, swimming pool, and solarium, and enjoy a drink on the terrace.

***How to get there*** *(Map 35): In the town center.*

## Hôtel Windsor

11, rue Dalpozzo
06300 Nice (Alpes-Maritimes)
Tel (0)4.93.88.59.35 - Fax (0)4.93.88.9457 - M. Redolfi-Strizzot

**Category** ★★★ **Rooms** 60 with telephone, bath or shower, WC, TV and minibar - Elevator. **Price** Single 300-525F, double 400-670F. **Meals** Breakfast 40F, served 7:00-10:30; half board 390-495F (per pers.). **Restaurant** Service 12:00-14:00, 19:00-22:30 (closed Saturday noon and Sunday); also à la carte. **Credit cards** All major. **Pets** Dogs allowed. **Facilities** Swimming pool, sauna (70F), parking (60F). **Nearby** Turini forest, valley of La Tinée (Roure, Roubron), valley of La Vésubie, villages of Utelle, Belvédère, le Boréon, Venanson – 18-hole Opio golf course in Valbonne, 18-hole Bastide-du-Roy golf course in Biot. **Open** All year.

From the street, the Windsor seems like a classic mid-town hotel. Once you step inside, however, this impression soon fades. In the modern reception area, there is an ornate Oriental bed encrusted with mother-of-pearl and an ancient gilt shrine with a seated Buddha in the center. Just outside, you will also discover a luxuriant exotic garden with an aviary in the hollow of an old tree; here, a few tables are hidden away not far from a small swimming pool. In the bedrooms, the furniture is deliberately 1950s-60s hotel style. Many are large and all are comfortable. But the personality of the Windsor is that of its owner, who offers sixteen contemporary "artists' bedrooms" *(Ben, Pete, Fend, Honegger, Panchounette...)*. It's best to let Monsieur Redolfi-Strizzot explain why: "An artist is related to an inherent reality. That's what attracts me. In the hotel business, we have gotten to a limit as regards material competition. We can always add an iron, a hair dryer, of course; but it's best to enrich the human fabric...".

***How to get there** (Map 35): In the center of town.*

## Auberge de la Madone

06440 Peillon (Alpes-Maritimes)
Tel. (0)4.93.79.91.17 - Fax (0)4.93.79.99.36
Millo Family

**Category** ★★★ **Rooms** 20 with telephone, bath, shower and WC. **Price** Double 450-780F, suite 850-1100F. **Meals** Breakfast 60F, served 8:00-10:00; half board 460-700F (per pers.). **Restaurant** By reservation. Service 12:30-14:00, 19:30-20:30; menus 140-280F, also à la carte. Specialties: Bouillabaisse froide, carré d'agneau aux petits légumes fondants. **Credit cards** Visa, Eurocard and MasterCard. **Pets** Dogs not allowed. **Facilities** Tennis, parking. **Nearby** Nice, valleys of La Tinée and La Vésubie – 18-hole Mont-Agel golf course. **Open** All year except 20 Oct – 20 Dec and 7 Jan – 24 Jan (closed Wednesday).

The Auberge is a good place for those with a taste for adventure. All around it are deep ravines and rocky summits which you would hardly suspect existed only twenty minutes from Nice. From the hotel's sunny terraces you will have all the time in the world to look out on Peillon, one of the most spectacular villages in the Niçois hinterland, perched on a steep crag and with superb views all around. You can explore it on foot, up the steep stairways which lead up to the Chapel of the Pénitents Blancs. The hotel has an attractive decor with all the refinements for a comfortable stay. The excellent regional cooking is reasonably priced and encourages visitors who prefer the tranquillity of Peillon to the tourist frenzy of the Nice coast. A small village house offering less luxurious but more affordable accommodations serves as an annex to the Auberge de la Madonne.

***How to get there*** *(Map 35): 19km north of Nice via D2204 towards L'Escarène, then on the Peille bridge D21 towards Peillon. On the left as you enter in the village.*

# Hôtel Les Deux Frères

Place des Deux-Frères
Roquebrune Village, 06190 Cap-Martin (Alpes-Maritimes)
Tel. (0)4.93.28.99.00 - Fax (0)4.93.28.99.10 - M. Bonestroo

**Category** ★★ **Rooms** 10 with telephone, bath or shower, WC and TV. **Price** Single 385F, double 495F. **Meals** Breakfast 45F. **Restaurant** Service 12:00-14:00, 19:30-22:00; à la carte. Specialties: Fish, duck, foie gras. **Credit cards** Amex, Visa, Eurocard and MasterCard. **Pets** Dogs allowed (+40F). **Nearby** Rue Moncolet in Roquebrune, La Turbie church, footpath to Cap Martin – 18-hole Monte-Carlo Golf Course in La Turbie. **Open** Dec 21 – Nov 11 (closed Thursday).

The two brothers of the hotel's name are actually the two rocks that gave their name to the village of Roquebrune. The square named for them is one of the best sites in the medieval village, protected by its Carolingian castle. Here a school was built; 15 years after its closing a Dutch architect transformed it into a hotel. The classrooms were turned into pretty white-walled bedrooms, and the courtyard into a restaurant. Around the great fireplace comfortable leather covered sofas are grouped, creating a place that most guests find difficult to tear themselves away from in the evenings. The decor is delightful, there are always plenty of flowers, and you will receive a warm welcome.

***How to get there*** *(Map 35): 5km south of Menton via A8 or N98.*

## Auberge du Colombier

06330 Roquefort-les-Pins (Alpes-Maritimes)
Tel. (0)4.92.60.33.00 - Fax (0)4.93.77.07.03
M. Wolff

**Category** ★★★ **Rooms** 18, 2 suites with telephone, bath, shower, WC and TV. **Price** Single 200-350F, double 350-550F, suite 450-800F. **Meals** Breakfast 50F; half board +170F, full board +340F. **Restaurant** Service 12:00-14:30, 19:30-22:00 (closed Tuesday in low season); menus 135-190F, also à la carte. Specialties: Ravioles de homard en nage de pistou, carré d'agneau en croûte d'herbes. **Credit cards** All major. **Pets** Dogs allowed (+40F). **Facilities** Swimming pool, tennis (+50F), parking. **Nearby** Nice, Grasse, gorges of Le Loup and Gourdon, Saint-Paul-de-Vence (Fondation Maeght) – 18-hole Opio golf course in Valbonne. **Open** All year except Jan 10 – Feb 10.

This old stagecoach stop on the route from Nice to Grasse (once a two-day journey) still makes a good overnight halt or a pleasant base from which to explore the many attractions of the French Riviera. The auberge was modernized in 1980 but preserves its old charm. Today it has a beautiful swimming pool, a tennis court and some more recently built bedrooms in which, however, some of the atmosphere has been lost. You will find a pleasant welcome here and a restaurant which is renowned for its cuisine and its *spécialités de la maison*.

***How to get there*** *(Map 34): 25km west of Nice via A8, exit Villeneuve-Loubet, then D2085 towards Grasse. From Cannes, Cagnes-sur-Mer exit, towards Grasse.*

## Hôtel Brise Marine

58, avenue Jean-Mermoz
06230 Saint-Jean-Cap-Ferrat (Alpes-Maritimes)
Tel. (0)4.93.76.04.36 - Fax (0)4.93.76.11.49 - M. Maîtrehenry

**Category** ★★★ **Rooms** 16 with air-conditioning, telephone, bath or shower, WC, TV and safe. **Price** Double 670-730F. **Meals** Breakfast 57F, served 8:00-10:00. No restaurant. **Credit cards** Visa, Eurocard and MasterCard. **Pets** Dogs allowed. **Nearby** Saint-Pierre chapel (Cocteau) in Villefranche, Villa Ephrussi-de-Rothschild in Saint-Jean-Cap-Ferrat, Villa Kerylos in Beaulieu – 18-hole La Bastide-du-Roy golf course in Biot. **Open** Feb 1 – Oct 31.

Located among the luxurious villas, grand hotels and noble residences in Saint-Jean-Cap-Ferrat, this is a little Italian house built in the 19th century. The Hôtel Brise Marine has a delightful garden with flowers, palm trees, espaliers, stone balustrades, fountains and terraces. The owner has personally looked after the hotel and its sixteen elegant and comfortable little bedrooms for forty-five years. Many of them overlook the garden of an inaccessible chateau and the sea. Regularly redecorated, they invariably retain their touch of seaside charm (several rooms only, on ground level with a lovely small courtyard, are still somewhat old-fashioned). The staff is very friendly and excellent breakfasts are served overlooking the most beautiful view imaginable: the luxuriant vegetation of the garden, the sea slightly below, and Monte Carlo Bay in the distance. *La Voile d'Or* and *Le Provençal* are among the chic, expensive restaurants of Saint Jean. *Le Sloop* is a simpler, reasonably priced fish restaurant.

***How to get there*** *(Map 35): 15km east of Nice via N98.*

## Hôtel Le Hameau

528, route de La Colle
06570 Saint-Paul-de-Vence (Alpes-Maritimes)
Tel. (0)4.93.32.80.24 - Fax (0)4.93.32.55.75 - M. Huvelin

**Category** ★★★ **Rooms** 14 and 3 apartments with air-conditioning, telephone, bath or shower, WC, safe and minibar. **Price** Single and double 410-640F, suite 740F. **Meals** Breakfast 55F, served 8:00-10:00. No restaurant. **Credit cards** Visa, Eurocard and MasterCard. **Pets** Dogs allowed. **Facilities** Swimming pool, garage (35F), parking. **Nearby** Chapel of Le Rosaire (Matisse), perfume museum, Maeght Foundation, church of Saint-Charles-Borromée in Saint-Paul-de-Vence, les Clues de Haute-Provence – 18-hole Opio golf course in Valbonne. **Open** All year except Jan 8 – Feb 15 and Nov 15 – Dec 22.

This white 1920s house looks over the valley and the village of Saint-Paul-de-Vence, and is up a path bordered by lemon trees in a flowering garden. The hotel has terraces and arcades and is almost hidden by honeysuckle, fig trees and climbing vines. The bedrooms are large and prettily decorated, and the furniture is traditionally Provençal. Numbers 1, 2 and 3 have a loggia and an impressive view of Saint-Paul. The old iridescent green tiles of some of the bathrooms are superb. In the adjoining 18th-century farmhouse there are other smaller attic rooms but they all have a lovely view. The friendly welcome you will find here will explain why so many guests return. There is no restaurant but apart from a gastronomic pilgrimage to the famous *Colombe d'Or,* you can enjoy delicious Provençal cuisine at *La Brouette*.

***How to get there*** *(Map 34): 20km west of Nice via A8, exit Cagnes-sur-Mer, then D7 towards Vence via La Colle-sur-Loup; it's 1km before Saint-Paul-de-Vence.*

## Auberge des Seigneurs et du Lion d'Or

Place du Frêne
06140 Vence (Alpes-Maritimes)
Tel. (0)4.93.58.04.24 - Fax (0)4.93.24.08.01 - M. and Mme Rodi

**Category** ★★ **Rooms** 10 with telephone, shower and WC. **Price** Single 290F, double 354-374F. **Meals** Breakfast 55F, served 7:30-10:00. **Restaurant** Service from 12:30 and 19:30; menus 170-240F (closed Sunday evening and Monday); also à la carte. Specialties: Carré d'agneau à la broche, tian vençois. **Credit cards** All major. **Pets** Dogs allowed. **Nearby** Chapel of Le Rosaire (Matisse), perfume museum, Carzou museum in Vence, Maeght Foundation, church of St-Charles-Borromée in Saint-Paul-de-Vence, les Clues de Haute Provence – 18-hole Opio golf course in Valbonne. **Open** Mar 16 – 14 Nov.

This is a lovely, almost timeless auberge. Some parts of it date from the 14th century and some from the 17th century. In its day it has welcomed many famous guests such as King Francis I and, more recently, Renoir, Modigliani, Dufy, and Soutine. Mme Rodi knows the exact dates of their visits and will enjoy telling you about them. The hotel is situated in a wing of the Château des Villeneuve de Vence. It is on the square where the ash tree planted by Francis I still flourishes. The reception rooms contain an eclectic collection of objects (a 16th-century washstand, an olive oil press, modern lithographs, etc.) all of which have a history. The bedrooms are large, furnished plainly but appropriately for the building, and there is always a basket of fruit and flowers awaiting every guest. The most attractive rooms look out on the square, the quietest over the rooftops. The whole Auberge is full of character and is very welcoming.

***How to get there*** *(Map 34): 10km north of Cagnes-sur-Mer via D36.*

## Hôtel Villa Roseraie

Avenue Henri-Giraud
06140 Vence (Alpes-Maritimes)
Tel. (0)4.93.58.02.20 - Fax (0)4.93.58.99.31 - M. and Mme Ganier

**Category** ★★ **Rooms** 12 with telephone, bath or shower, WC, TV and minibar. **Price** Single and double 395-630F. **Meals** Breakfast 60F, served 8:30-12:00. No restaurant. **Credit cards** Amex, Visa, Eurocard and MasterCard. **Pets** Dogs allowed. **Facilities** Swimming pool, bike (50F/day), parking. **Nearby** Chapelle du Rosaire (Matisse), fondation Maeght, Saint-Charles church, Borromée in Saint-Paul-de-Vence, les Clues de Haute-Provence – 18 hole Opio golf course in Valbonne. **Open** All year.

Dating from the turn of the century, the "Rose Garden" is a beautiful old Mediterranean-style residence in the heart of picturesque Vence. Graceful palm trees, magnolias, yucca, eucalyptus, banana trees, and roses, combined with a spectacular view over Vence and Baou Hill, create a veritable oasis of beauty and charm here. There are only twelve bedrooms, all decorated in the loveliest Provençal style; although all have a beautiful view, the best is to be enjoyed from rooms 4, 5, 8 (which have balconies), and from number 12, which has a terrace. The bathrooms are comfortable and prettily decorated with the famous Provençal tiles from nearby Salernes. The breakfasts are carefully prepared, with homemade croissants and traditional preserves. M. and Mme Ganier make every effort to please you. For restaurants, try *Le Vieux Couvent*, whose chef has two well-deserved Gault-Millau toques, and *L'Auberge des Seigneurs*: try the succulent rack of lamb grilled in the fireplace.

***How to get there** (Map 34): 10km north of Cagnes-sur-Mer via D36.*

# Hôtel Welcome

1, quai Courbet
06230 Villefranche-sur-Mer (Alpes-Maritimes)
Tel. (0)4.93.76.27.62 - Fax (0)4.93.76.27.66 - M. and Mme Galbois
Web: http://www.riviera.fr/hotels/welcome.htm - E-mail: welcome@riviera.fr

**Category** ★★★ **Rooms** 32 with air-conditioning, telephone, bath or shower, WC, TV and minibar. **Price** Single and double 400-950F. **Meals** Breakfast 40F, served 7:15-10:00; half board 425-625F (per pers.). **Restaurant** Service 12:30-14:00, 19:30-22:30; menus 160-200F, also à la carte. Specialties: Fish. **Credit cards** All major. **Pets** Dogs allowed (+25F). **Nearby** The Lower Corniche, St-Jean-Cap-Ferrat (Villa Ephrussi de Rothschild), Beaulieu (Villa Kerylos) – 18-hole Opio golf course in Valbonne. **Open** Dec 19 – Nov 17.

On the quayside of the old port of Villefranche you will find colorful fishing boats, a chapel decorated by Jean Cocteau and a hotel in the pedestrian area which is built on the site of a 17th-century monastery. The hotel is modern with many balconies and large, comfortable, sunny rooms, all of them air-conditioned. The balconies have *chaise longues* and small tables on which you can enjoy your breakfast. On the top story the rooms are outfitted in a nautical style with copper fittings and exotic woodwork. They are smaller than the other rooms but still lovely and warm.

***How to get there*** *(Map 35): 6km from Nice via N559.*

## Villa Gallici

Avenue de la Violette
13100 Aix-en-Provence (Bouches-du-Rhône)
Tel. (0)4.42.23.29.23 - Fax (0)4.42.96.30.45 - M. Gil Dez

**Category** ★★★★ **Rooms** 19 with air-conditioning, telephone, bath, WC, satellite TV, safe and minibar. **Price** 950-3000F. **Meals** Breakfast 70-100F. **Restaurant** Only for residents. Service 12:30-14:30, 19:30-21:30; also à la carte. Specialties: Regional cooking. **Credit cards** All major. **Pets** Dogs allowed (+100F). **Facilities** Swimming pool, parking. **Nearby** Place d'Albertas, Hôtel de Ville, Saint-Sauveur Cathedral (burning bush triptych by N. Froment) in Aix-en-Provence, Roquefavour aqueduct – 18-hole Club des Milles golf course, 18-hole Fuveau Golf Course. **Open** All year.

In the Villa Gallici, Gil Dez found a bastide in which to exercise his talents as an interior decorator and create an elegant *hôtel de charme*. The villa has been decorated with exquisite style, and designed like a home rather than a hotel. The bedrooms are spacious, comfortable and individually decorated. *Toile de Jouy* and gingham have been used in one, while another boasts a flowery cotton canopied bed along with boldly striped fabrics. In each room styles, colors and materials have been subtly and successfully combined. In the immaculate bathrooms, earthenware tiles, Carrara marble and glossy white wood panelling create an elegant decor. Breakfast beneath the plane trees is a delight. In an annex, new bedrooms have been added: veritable apartments which are even more luxurious. *Villa Gallici* is nearby *Le Clos de la Violette*, one of the best restaurant in Provence.

***How to get there*** *(Map 33): Near the Archbishop's Palace.*

1998

# Hôtel Le Pigonnet

5, avenue du Pigonnet
13090 Aix-en-Provence (Bouches-du-Rhône)
Tel. (0)4.42.59.02.90 - Fax (0)4.42.59.47.77 - MM. Swellen

**Category** ★★★★ **Rooms** 52 with telephone, bath or shower, WC, satellite TV and minibar - Elevator. **Price** Single and double 630-880F, 630-1500F, suite 1900F. **Meals** Breakfast 70-100F, served 7:00-11:00; half board and full board +250F, +500F (per pers., 3 days min.). **Restaurant** Service 12:15-13:30, 19:15-21:30 (closed Satuday lunchtime and Sunday lunchtime except July); menus 250-320F, also à la carte. Specialties: Baudroie du golf à la nîmoise, carré d'agneau rôti. **Credit cards** All major. **Pets** Dogs allowed. **Facilities** Swimming pool, parking. **Nearby** Place d'Albertas, Hôtel de Ville, Saint-Sauveur Cathedral (burning bush triptych by N. Froment), Pavillon Vendôme in Aix-en-Provence; Roquefavour aqueduct - 18-hole Club des Milles golf course, 18-hole Fuveau golf course. **Open** All year.

Le Pigonnet has regained its intimate, familial atmosphere thanks to the two charming Swellen sons who have recently taken over and revitlized the hotel, profiting from their parents' long experience. Standing in the middle of a large park with a formal garden offering guests the historic view of the Montagne Sainte-Victoire immortalized by Cézanne, the hotel is only some ten minutes from the center of Aix. In the lounges, a beautiful collection of paintings by Provençal artists and an elegant decor create an atmosphere of great comfort. The bedrooms have not yet all been redecorated. Our favorites are those in the old house (some have a private terrace) and the independent villa, just next to the swimming pool, which has two bedrooms, two bathrooms and a lounge. For meals, guests may choose between the gastronomic cuisine served in the beautiful *Riviera* room overlooking the park, or lighter meals around the swimming pool or on the shady terrace.

***How to get there*** *(Map 33): A8 or A51, Aix/Pont-de-l'Arc exit, then in the town center and 3th traffic light on left (avenue Pigonnet).*

## Hôtel des Quatre-Dauphins

54, rue Roux-Alphéran
13100 Aix-en-Provence (Bouches-du-Rhône)
Tel. (0)4.42.38.16.39 - Fax (0)4.42.38.60.19- MM. Darricau and Juster

**Category** ★★ **Rooms** 12 with telephone, bath or shower, WC, TV and minibar. **Price** Single 290-330F, double 330-400F, suite 490F (3 pers.). **Meals** Breakfast 39F, served 7:00-10:00. No restaurant. **Credit cards** Visa, Eurocard and MasterCard. **Pets** Dogs allowed. **Nearby** Place d'Albertas, Hôtel de Ville, Saint-Sauveur Cathedral (burning bush triptych by N. Froment) in Aix-en-Provence, Roquefavour aqueduct – 18-hole Club des Milles golf course, 18-hole Fuveau golf course. **Open** All year.

This three-story family house in a quiet side street near the famous Place des Quatre Dauphins in Aix has recently been converted into a hotel. On the ground floor there is a small reception area and a lounge which also serves as a breakfast room. The bedrooms are tiny and the closets basic but functional enough so as not to make space a problem. Everything has been done with simplicity and much taste, and the baths are well equipped. For restaurants try: *Maxime, Côté Cour* on the Cours Mirabeau; *Le Petit Bistro Latin, Chez Gu,* and don't forget to have a drink at the *Deux Garçons*. A charming restaurant, *Le Garde*, takes you to Vauvenargues for dinner in the heart of the country.

***How to get there*** *(Map 33): In the center of the town.*

## Hôtel d'Arlatan

26, rue du Sauvage
13200 Arles (Bouches-du-Rhône)
Tel. (0)4.90.93.56.66 - Fax (0)4.90.49.68.45 - M. Desjardin

**Category** ★★★ **Rooms** 41 with air-conditioning, telephone, bath, WC, satellite TV and minibar. **Price** Double 455-695F, suite 795-1350F. **Meals** Breakfast 62F, served 7:00-11:00. No restaurant. **Credit cards** All major. **Pets** Dogs allowed. **Facilities** Garage (+60F). **Nearby** Saint-Trophime church, les Aliscamps, Réattu museum in Arles, abbey of Montmajour, the Camargue – 18-hole Servanes golf course in Mouriès. **Open** All year.

Arles the museum city has an archaeological counterpart in the Hôtel d'Arlatan, where vestiges of the past span the centuries. Built on the Basilica and the Baths of Constantine, the entire building is a veritable architectural patchwork. The unique hotel, owned by the same family for three generations, is regularly restored and renovated. It would indeed take a book to describe the Arlatan's bedrooms. Wall fragments from the fourth century and beams from the eighteenth can be seen in Suite 43, and a monumental 17th-century fireplace in Suite 41. Ask for the rooms which have just been (very well) redone and overlook the Rhône: Numbers 23 and 27 among others; Room 34, with very beautiful stone walls and one of the least expensive; or one of the suites, large or small. Nestling in a small street overlooking gardens, the Arlatan is a hotel of singular character and charm. The most popular restaurants in Arles are *L'Olivier* and *Le Vaccarès*. For a very fashionable spot, try the restaurant or bar of the famous Hôtel Nord-Pinus.

***How to get there*** *(Map 33): In the center of the town, signposted.*

# Grand Hôtel Nord-Pinus

Place du Forum
13200 Arles (Bouches-du-Rhône)
Tel. (0)4.90.93.44.44 - Fax (0)4.90.93.34.00 - Mme Igou

**Category** ★★★★ **Rooms** 23 with air-conditioning, telephone, bath, WC, TV and minibar. **Price** Single and double 770-990F, suite 1700F. **Meals** Breakfast 65F, served 7:00-11:00. **Restaurant** Service 12:00-14:00, 19:30-22:00, menus 120-180F, also à la carte. Specialties: Provençal cooking. **Credit cards** All major. **Pets** Dogs allowed. **Nearby** Saint-Trophime church, les Aliscamps, Réattu Museum in Arles, abbey of Montmajour, the Camargue – 18-hole Servanes golf course in Mouriès. **Open** All year.

Like Giono, you might wonder; "Why Pinus? Nord, I understand, but Pinus? It was simply the name of the founder. Nothing is more logical. I now realize that I have entered the land of the imagination and fantasy." Picasso, Cocteau, Dominguez are just some of the famous names in the visitors' book. The hotel was run for some time by Germaine, a chanteuse, and Nello, a famous clown, both of whom were well-known characters in Arles. When they died the hotel lost its soul. It has returned under the care of Anne Igou, whose love for the place has brought back the magic and atmosphere, aided by a skillful restoration combining sensitivity and good taste. The bedrooms are large, with pretty furniture and Provençal fabrics, and the bathrooms have every facility. It is worth remembering to ask for suite 10 or the bedrooms looking onto the courtyard; these are recommended for people who are concerned about the noise on the Place du Forum in summer. This is truly a charming hotel.

***How to get there*** *(Map 33): In the town center.*

1998

# Hôtel Calendal

22, place Pomme
13200 Arles (Bouches-du-Rhône)
Tel. (0)4.90.96.11.89 - Fax (0)4.90.96.05.84 - Mme Lespinasse-Jacquemin

**Category** ★★ **Rooms** 27 with air-conditioning, telephone, bath, WC, satellite TV - 1 for disabled persons. **Price** Single and double 250-320F, 250-420F, suite 450F. **Meals** Breakfast 36F, served 7:00-10:30 (buffet), 7:00-12:00 (continental). **Tea-Salon** Salades, omelettes, pâtisseries anglaises. **Credit cards** All major. **Facilities** Parking. **Pets** Dogs allowed. **Nearby** Saint-Trophime church, arena, les Alyscamps, Réattu museum in Arles, abbey of Montmajour, the Camargue - 18-hole Servanes golf course in Mouriès. **Open** All year.

If you're a bullfight aficionado, you'll be delighted with the Calendal, where some rooms have a direct view of the ring: you can't, however, actually see the fight from your room. Recently renovated in traditional Provençal colors, the bedrooms are all spacious, fresh and spruce, and there are modern amenities in the bathrooms. The old-fashioned tea room, decorated with beautiful bullfight posters, serves light meals and delicious homemade pastries; in good weather, you will be served on the terrace or in a lovely garden shaded by palm trees and a two-century-old Provençal *micoucoulier* tree. The hotel is well located for enjoying the historic center of charming Arles. To help you with parking, the hotel supplies a card enabling you to use the parking lots on the *Boulevards Extérieurs.*

***How to get there*** *(Map 33): Near the Arènes.*

## Hôtel Castel-Mouisson

Quartier Castel Mouisson
13570 Barbentane (Bouches-du-Rhône)
Tel. (0)4.90.95.51.17 - Fax (0)4.90.95.67.63 - Mme Mourgue

**Category** ★★ **Rooms** 17 with telephone, bath and WC. **Price** Double 280-350F, suite 400F. **Meals** Breakfast 40F, served 8:00-10:30. No restaurant. **Credit cards** Not accepted. **Pets** Dogs not allowed. **Facilities** Swimming pool, tennis, parking. **Nearby** Barbentane, Avignon, Villeneuve-lès-Avignon, abbey of Saint-Michel-de-Frigolet – 18-hole Châteaublanc golf course, 18-hole Vedène golf course in Grand Avignon, 4-hole Lou Compact golf course in Barbentane. **Open** Mar 15 – Oct 15.

This peaceful and reasonably priced hotel is at the foot of the Montagnette Mountain not far from Avignon. It was built twenty years ago in the style of a Provençal farmhouse and is surrounded by tranquil countryside. There are cypresses and fruit trees growing beneath the grey cliffs of the Montagnette, which overlooks the valley. Brightened with Provençal fabrics, the bedrooms are simple but reasonably comfortable. In hot weather you will enjoy cooling off in the pretty swimming pool. In Avignon, there are numerous good small restaurants such as *La Fourchette, L'Entrée des Artistes,* as well as charming places for lunch such as the *Les Félibres* tearoom and bookshop, *Le Bain Marie* and *Simple Simon.* For a lovely dinner, try the restaurant in the *Mirande Hotel* or *La Vieille Fontaine* in the Hôtel d'Europe.

***How to get there** (Map 33): 8km southwest of Avignon via N570, then D35 towards Tarascon along the Rhône.*

# Hôtel Le Benvengudo

Route d'Arles D78
13520 Les Baux-de-Provence (Bouches-du-Rhône)
Tel. (0)4.90.54.32.54 - Fax (0)4.90.54.42.58 - Beaupied Family
E-mail: Benvengudo@aol.com

**Category** ★★★ **Rooms** 17 with air-conditioning, telephone, bath or shower, WC and TV. **Price** Double 600-700F, suite 930F. **Meals** Breakfast 62F, served 7:30-11:05; half board 1164-1494F (per 2 pers., 3 days min.). **Restaurant** Service 19:30-21:30 (closed Sunday); menu 240F. Specialties: Croustade de ris d'agneau au coulis de tomate fraîches, pavé de mérou de méditerranée grillé au basilic rouge, soufflé glacé au marc de Châteauneuf du Pape. **Credit cards** Amex, Visa, Eurocard and MasterCard. **Pets** Dogs allowed (+50F). **Facilities** Swimming pool, tennis, boule, parking. **Nearby** Contemporary art museum at the Hôtel des Porcelets in Les Baux, Queen Jeanne's pavilion, Alphonse Daudet's windmill in Fontvieille, the Val d'enfer – 9-hole golf course in Les Baux, 18-hole Servanes golf course in Mouriès. **Open** Feb 1 – Nov 1.

The Benvengudo nestles at the foot of the strange and beautiful Alpilles, whose jagged outline is reminiscent of some of the highest mountain peaks in the world, while their white rocks and vegetation lend an air of Greece to this part of Provence. Built twenty-one years ago, the *mas* seems to have been here forever. The bedrooms, some air-conditioned, are very comfortable, each with its style and its color scheme, and some with small private terraces. The lounge and dining room are decorated in lovely Provençal style. The son of the family is the chef, preparing dinners of savory regional recipes; for lunch in summer, there is a small menu of fresh salads.

***How to get there*** *(Map 33): 30km south of Avignon via A7, Cavaillon exit, then D99 to Saint-Rémy and D5.*

# Les Roches Blanches

Route des calanques
13260 Cassis (Bouches-du-Rhône)
Tel. (0)4.42.01.09.30 - Fax (0)4.42.01.94.23 - M. Dellacase

**Category** ★★★★ **Rooms** 25 with telephone, bath or shower, WC, TV and minibar - Elevator. **Price** Single 450F, double 900F, suite 1150F. **Meals** Breakfast 75F, served 7:15-11:00. **Restaurant** Service 12:30-14:00, 19:30-21:30; menus 170-240F, also à la carte. Specialties: Provençal cooking. **Credit cards** All major. **Pets** Dogs allowed. **Facilities** Swimming pool, parking. **Nearby** The Calanques: Port-Miou, Port-Pin and Envau – 18-hole Frégate Golf Course, 18-hole Salette golf course in La Penne-sur-Huveaune. **Open** Feb 15 – Nov 15.

Les Roches Blanches is a former town house built in 1885 and then transformed into a hotel in 1930. Built on the rocks next to the rocky inlets *(calanques)* of Cassis, this large house combines the charm of a beach hotel–the terraced garden slopes down directly to the water, where you can swim–with the charm of a family house whose large dining-room windows overlook the sea. The bedrooms are all comfortable, and some have terraces looking out over pine trees and either the sea or Cape Canaille. In their concern for preserving the old charm of the house, the owners have kept several pieces of 1930s furniture, the door and the vast stairway in Art Déco wrought iron, and the pretty *faïence* mosaic tables of the garden. There is a very beautiful overflow swimming pool with a view of the sea.

***How to get there*** *(Map 33): 23km east of Marseille via A50 towards Toulon, Cassis exit. In summer you can cross the village, so take the Calanques road and Le Bestouan beach.*

1998

## Le Jardin d'Emile

Plage du Bestouan
13260 Cassis (Bouches-du-Rhône)
Tel. (0)4.42.01.80.55 - Fax (0)4.42.01.80.70 - M. Morand

**Rooms** 6 with air-conditioning, telephone, bath or shower, WC, TV and minibar. **Price** Double 300-600F. **Meals** Breakfast 50F, served 7:00-10:30. **Restaurant** Service 12:00-14:30, 19:30-22:30; menus 98-250F, also à la carte. Specialties: Bouillabaisse, pieds-paquets, raviolis ouverts de moules. **Credit cards** Amex, Visa, Eurocard and MasterCard. **Pets** Dogs allowed. **Facilities** Parking. **Nearby** The Calanques: Port-Miou, Port-Pin and Envau - 18-hole Frégate golf course, 18-hole Salette golf course in La Penne-sur-Huveaune. **Open** All year.

The last beach on the road along Cassis' famous *calanques,* deep coves, the Bestouan has always been popular with Marseilles families in summer. You can get to the beach by a direct subterranean passageway if you stay at the Jardin d'Emile, a charming small hotel that has just been opened in an old residence and redecorated with taste and a sense of comfort. The colors of Cape Canaille inspired the decor, with warm terra cotta tiles on the floors and ochre-yellow striped fabrics bringing Provençal sunshine into the dining room, which spills over onto a veranda. The excellent cuisine has the same spicey Mediterranean accent. Two bedrooms with terraces overlook the sea and enjoy an exceptional view. All are air-conditioned, but for a quieter room, ask for one on the garden (one room also has a private terrace.) The hotel is ideal for those who love the sun, the sea, the accent of Provence, and this small beach, famous for its cool water and its pebbles.

***How to get there*** *(Map 33): 23km east of Marseilles via A50, towards. Toulon, exit Cassis. In summer, you cannot go through the village: take the Route des Calanques, Plage du Bestouan.*

## Le Clos des Arômes

10, rue Paul-Mouton - Rue Agostini
13260 Cassis (Bouches-du-Rhône)
Tel. (0)4.42.01.71.84 - Fax (0)4.42.01.31.76 - Mme and M. Bonnet

**Category** ★★ **Rooms** 8 with telephone, soundproofing, bath or shower and WC. **Price** Double 295-570F. **Meals** Breakfast 45F, served 8:00-12:00. **Restaurant** Service 12:00-14:00, 19:30-22:30; menus 98-145F, also à la carte. Specialties: Provençal cooking. **Credit cards** Amex, Visa, Euracard and MasterCard. **Pets** Dogs allowed (+35F). **Facilities** Garage (+50F). **Nearby** The Calanques: Port-Miou, Port-Pin and Envau – 18-hole La Salette Golf Course in Marseille-La Valentine. **Open** May 1 – Oct 3.

Though located in a little street in the village, this dollhouse of a hotel is brightened by a garden that is a riot of blue and white with lavender, peonies, arum lilies and marguerites. In beautiful weather this makes a fragrant setting for breakfast and for dinners of delicious Provençal dishes. Indoors the ambience is just as delightful, with lavender-painted furniture, flowered tablecloths and a large fireplace. The bedrooms, with blue and yellow Provençal fabrics, are very small (especially Room 1), and four overlook the garden. Located in the center of the village near the old port, the hotel is quiet, its bedrooms soundproofed with double glazed windows. The hotel is very quiet though in the middle of the village and only a few meters from the old port.

***How to get there*** *(Map 33): 23km east of Marseille via A50 towards Toulon, Cassis exit.*

## Auberge Provençale

Place de la Mairie
13810 Eygalières (Bouches-du-Rhône)
Tel. (0)4.90.95.91.00 Fax (0)4.90.90.60.92 - M. Pézevil

**Category** ★★★ **Rooms** 7 with telephone, bath or shower and WC. **Price** Double 285-500F. **Meals** Breakfast 40F, served 8:30-10:30; half board 350-450F (per pers., 2 days min.). **Restaurant** Service 12:00-13:30, 19:30-21:30; menus 125F (lunchtime)-175F, also à la carte. Specialties: Cabillaud rôti aux 15 épices douces, filet d'agneau et concassé de tomates, jambonette de lapin en tapenade confit de souris d'agneau, tarte aux figues et amandes. **Credit cards** Visa, Eurocard and MasterCard. **Pets** Dogs allowed. **Facilities** Parking. **Nearby** Les Baux, Saint-Rémy-de-Provence, Fontvieille – 18-hole Servanes golf course in Mouriès. **Open** Feb 16 – Jan 4. Closed Wednesday.

The auberge is in the center of a beautifully preserved village of the Alpilles. Formerly a restaurant in an 18th-century postal relay station, it has recently become a small, seven-bedroom establishment. The three most comfortable rooms open onto a charming courtyard with trees, where meals are served in summer (our favorites are numbers 4 and 5, and 1 and 3, which have recently been renovated); the two smaller rooms look out over the Place de la Mairie. A bistro area also serves as a lounge for hotel guests. The young owner doubles as the chef. Meals are served on the terrace in good weather or in the restaurant, which has a beautiful fireplace. The excellent cuisine is based on seasonal market produce, and the menu changes often. The hospitality is generous.

***How to get there*** *(Map 33): 13km southeast of Cavaillon via A7, Cavaillon exit, then D99 and D74a.*

## Mas doù Pastré

Quartier Saint-Sixte, 13810 Eygalières (Bouches-du-Rhône)
Tel. (0)4.90.95.92.61 - Fax (0)4.90.90.61.75
M. and Mme Roumanille

**Rooms** 11 and 1 suite (5 pers.) with telephone, bath or shower, WC, TV and 5 with minibar. **Price** Double 350-690F, suite 1100F. **Meals** Breakfast 50F, served 8:00-10:30. No restaurant. **Credit cards** All major. **Pets** Dogs not allowed. **Facilities** Heated swimming pool, whirpool, winter's garden, parking. **Nearby** Les Baux, Saint-Rémy-de-Provence, Fontvieille – 18-hole Servanes golf course in Mouriès. **Open** All year.

Mme Roumanille, who has just renovated this old farmhouse as she would have her own home, is a friendly and hospitable hostess. Throughout the house, the ceilings and walls are decked out in Provençal colors, and there is a wealth of antique furniture, paintings, engravings, prints, and local curios–enough to make you feel even better than you would at home. The evocatively named bedrooms are all different; their decor owes much to carefully chosen furnishings, and to the owners' boundless imagination in adding a touch of exuberance and humor. You can also sleep in an authentic, elaborately carved wooden trailer, which is very old but equipped with air-conditioning and every modern comfort. Breakfast is delicious (there are always fresh fruit juices), whether you have it outside or in the charming dining room. This is an excellent and very Provençal hotel. *L'Auberge Provençale* is the famous restaurant in Eygalières, and the fashionable spot is *Sous les Micocouliers.*

***How to get there*** *(Map 33): 13km southeast of Cavaillon via A7, Cavaillon exit, then D99 and D74a.*

## Le Relais de la Magdelaine

Route d'Aix-en-Provence
13420 Gémenos (Bouches-du-Rhône)
Tel. (0)4.42.32.20.16 - Fax (0)4.42.32.02.26 - M. and Mme Marignane

**Category** ★★★★ **Rooms** 24 with telephone, bath or shower, WC and TV. **Price** Single 470-580F, double 580-790F, suite 1100F. **Meals** Breakfast 75F, served from 7:15; half board 650-750F, full board 850-950F (per pers., 3 days min.). **Restaurant** Service 12:00-14:00, 20:00-21:30; menu 250F, also à la carte. Specialties: Galettes de grenouilles à la provençale, pavé de canard au miel de lavande, griottes au chocolat sauce pistache. **Credit cards** Visa, Eurocard andMasterCard. **Pets** Dogs allowed (+30F) but not in the swimming pool. **Facilities** Swimming pool, parking. **Nearby** Marseille, Aix-en-Provence, Cassis and the Calanques – 18-hole La Salette golf course in Marseille-La Valentine. **Open** Mar 15 – Nov 30.

To find this beautiful 18th-century country house covered in ivy and roses, you leave the highway, drive along an avenue of century-old plane trees and cross a formal garden designed by Le Nôtre. Here you will find M. and Mme Marignane, who have been welcoming an international clientele for thirty years. Their dedication and good taste in creating a very special holiday hotel is evident in the bedrooms. These have superb old furniture; those that look out on the terrace are the largest. Their son is the chef and turns out refined Provençal food. The garden and swimming pool are very pleasant; you will be delighted by the cordial welcome.

***How to get there*** *(Map 33): 23km from Marseille via A50 towards Toulon, Aubagne-Est or Aubagne-Sud exit, then D2 to Gémenos.*

## L'Oustaloun

Place de l'Église
13520 Maussane-les-Alpilles (Bouches-du-Rhône)
Tel. (0)4.90.54.32.19 - Fax (0)4.90.54.45.57 - M. Fabrégoul

**Category** ★★ **Rooms** 10 with telephone, bath or shower, WC and 8 with TV. **Price** Double 290-400F. **Meals** Breakfast 35F, served 7:30-9:30. **Restaurant** Service 12:15-13:45, 19:15-21:30; menu 70-130F, also à la carte. Specialties: Provençal and italian cooking. **Credit cards** Amex, Visa, Eurocard and MasterCard. **Pets** Dogs allowed. **Facilities** Garage. **Nearby** Avignon, Arles, St-Rémy-de-Provence, Les Baux and le Val d'enfer, Alphonse Daudet's windmill in Fontvieille – 9-hole golf course in les Baux, 18-hole Servanes golf course in Mouriès. **Open** All year except Jan 8 – Feb 15.

In 1792, this was the first town hall of the village, then the gendarmerie (and the prison). Today, L'Oustaloun is a typical small Provençal auberge looking out on - what else? - a square shaded with towering plane trees and a tinkling fountain. The bedrooms are lovely and comfortable; all are decorated with Provençal fabrics and antique furniture. Most of the bathrooms are old-fashioned and have not yet been renovated as planned. One of the two rustic dining rooms is in the former "chapel", as the room were olives were crushed was called. With the first good weather, the Oustaloun spills out to the center of the square, where a bar-terrace is set up, shaded by large parasols. This is a charming spot just several minutes out of spectacular (and gastronomically acclained) town of Les Baux. The prices are reasonable and you will be welcomed with a very warm Provençal smile.

***How to get there*** *(Map 33): 40km south of Avignon via A7, exit Cavaillon, then D99 to Saint-Rémy and D5.*

# Le Berger des Abeilles

13670 Saint-Andiol (Bouches-du-Rhône)
Tel. (0)4.90.95.01.91 - Fax (0)4.90.95.48.26
Mme Grenier

**Category** ★★ **Rooms** 6 with telephone, bath or shower, WC and TV. **Price** 320-370F. **Meals** Breakfast 60F, served 8:00-10:00; half board 480F (per 1 pers.), 740F (per 2 pers., 3 days min.). **Restaurant** Service 12:30-13:30, 20:00-21:30 (closed Monday lunchtime except for residents); menus 140-250F, also à la carte. Specialties: Provençale cooking, mousse au miel de lavande, vieux marc de Provence. **Credit cards** Amex, Visa, Eurocard and MasterCard. **Pets** Dogs allowed (50F). **Facilities** Parking. **Nearby** Les Baux, Saint-Rémy-de-Provence, Avignon. **Open** Feb 11 – Dec 31.

Le Berger des Abeilles is as welcoming as a hotel could possibly be. There are only six bedrooms and so the owners provide a personal style of service. All the rooms are perfectly comfortable, but you should choose our favorites if they're available, *Alexia or Caroline*. (The rooms are named after the women in the family.) A few items of period furniture set the trend for the cheerful, intimate decor. Mme Grenier does the cooking herself and her cuisine has an excellent reputation. Dinner is served in a beautiful, rustic dining-room or outside in the shade of a gigantic plane tree. The noise of traffic on the main road, muffled by luxuriant vegetation, can hardly be heard in the hotel garden, and not at all indoors (thanks to the thick walls). This is a lovely place to stay.

***How to get there*** *(Map 33): 13km south of Avignon via N7 (2km from north of Saint-Andiol). On A7, Avignon-Sud exit, towards Cabannes, 5km south, towards Salon, Marseille.*

## Hostellerie de Cacharel

Route de Cacharel
13460 Les Saintes-Maries-de-la-Mer (Bouches-du-Rhône)
Tel. (0)4.90.97.95.44 - Fax (0)4.90.97.87.97 - M. Colomb de Daunant

**Category** ★★★ **Rooms** 11 with telephone, bath or shower and WC. **Price** Single and double 540F. **Meals** Breakfast 45F, served 8:00-10:00. Snacks available: 80F "assiette campagnarde". **Credit cards** Visa, Eurocard and MasterCard. **Pets** Dogs allowed. **Facilities** Swimming pool, horse trekking, parking. **Nearby** Church of Saintes-Maries-de-la-Mer, gypsy pilgrimage (May 24 and 25), sea wall (30km), Arles – 18-hole Servanes golf course in Mouriès. **Open** All year.

The Hostellerie is an old farmhouse on the borders of the Camargue, a land of nature reserves, placid lakes and white horses. The ground-floor bedrooms are furnished charmingly and look out either on a flower-filled inner courtyard or on the lakes and salt marshes. As the hotel is part of the farm, guests can walk or ride horses on the property. There is no restaurant but snacks can be provided. You will receive a good welcome at this tranquil and genuine Camargue house in its popular tourist region.

***How to get there*** *(Map 33): 38km southwest of Arles. 4km north of Saintes-Maries-de-la-Mer by D85a, called the Route de Cacharel.*

## Mas du Clarousset

Route de Cacharel
13460 Les Saintes-Maries-de-la-Mer (Bouches-du-Rhône)
Tel. (0)4.90.97.81.66 - Fax (0)4.90.97.88.59 - Mme Eyssette

**Category** ★★★ **Rooms** 10 with telephone, bath, WC, TV and minibar. **Price** Single 730F, double 750F, 3 pers. 850F. **Meals** Breakfast 50F, served 7:00-11:00; half board 980F (1 pers.), 1250F (2 pers.). Extra bed for children under 12 (free). **Restaurant** Service 12:00-14:00, 20:00-22:00 (closed Sunday evening and Monday in low season); menus 250-350F, also à la carte. Specialties: Terrine de canard colvert, loup en croûte, terrines à la provençale, Aïgue Saoü. **Credit cards** All major. **Pets** Dogs allowed (+50F). **Facilities** Swimming pool, gypsy evenings (on request), parking. **Nearby** Church of Saintes-Maries-de-la-Mer, gypsy pilgrimage (May 24 and 25), sea wall (30km), Arles – 18-hole La Grande Motte golf course. **Open** Dec 17 – Nov 14.

The very pleasant Mas du Clarousset is an ideal place to absorb the spirit of Provence. Here, Henriette gives a special welcome to lovers of the Camargue and likes to introduce them to the local way of life with gypsy evenings, walks on little-known beaches, and a midnight Christmas mass to which everyone rides on horseback. She can also reserve a horse or a boat for you. The pretty and comfortable bedrooms all have private terraces and views over the Carmargue. Each room has a separate private entrance with a parking space right in front of the door. After a day's excursion in the area you can relax and cool off in the swimming pool in the garden. Afterwards, you can enjoy the very good restaurant at the Mas, where Henriette offers traditional cuisine, featuring many regional specialties.

***How to get there*** *(Map 33): 38km southwest of Arles, then D85a (7km from Saintes-Maries).*

## Château des Alpilles

Ancienne route des Baux
13210 Saint-Rémy-de-Provence (Bouches-du-Rhône)
Tel. (0)4.90.92.03.33 - Fax (0)4.90.92.45.17 - Mmes Bon

**Category** ★★★★ **Rooms** 19 with air-conditioning, telephone, bath, WC, TV, and minibar. **Price** Single 900-1130F, suite 1320-1690F. **Meals** Breakfast 80F, served 7:30-11:30. Snacks available with reservation, also à la carte 190-220F. **Credit cards** All major. **Pets** Dogs allowed (+50F). **Facilities** Swimming pool, tennis, sauna, parking. **Nearby** Frédéric Mistral museum in Maillane, Eygalières, Les Baux, Avignon, Arles – 9-hole golf course in Les Baux, 18-hole Servanes golf course in Mouriès. **Open** All year except Nov 13 – Dec 19 and Jan 6 – Feb 17.

The château was built at the beginning of the 19th-century by one of the oldest families of Arles and became the meeting place of politicians and writers staying in the region. The lounge the bar, and the dining room, richly decorated with plasterwork and mirrors, are all very pleasant rooms and open out onto the garden. Their contemporary furniture (sofas and armchairs upholstered in deep-red leather) harmonize well with this decor; the impressive white ensemble in the dining room will delight those who like the Knoll style but will perhaps shock others less sensitive to 1970s design. The bedrooms are much more classic with their antique or period furniture, charming, tasteful decoration, and large, functional bathrooms. If you wish to stay at the hotel for dinner, you can enjoy simple but refined cuisine. The large park, with a swimming pool and tennis courts, is planted with many trees, some a century old and others of rare species.

***How to get there*** *(Map 33): 14km west of Cavaillon via A7, exit Cavaillon, then D99; 1km from Saint-Rémy-de-Provence.*

## Château de Roussan

13210 Saint-Rémy-de-Provence (Bouches-du-Rhône)
Tel. (0)4.90.92.11.63 - Fax (0)4.90.92.50.59
Mme McHugo

**Rooms** 21 with telephone, bath or shower and WC - Wheelchair access. **Price** Double 430-750F. **Meals** Breakfast 60-80F in room, served 8:00-11:00; half board 415-575F (per pers., 3 days min.). **Restaurant** Service 12:00-14:00, 19:30-21:30; also à la carte. **Credit cards** Amex, Visa, Eurocard and MasterCard. **Pets** Dogs allowed. **Facilities** Parking. **Nearby** Museum Frédéric-Mistral in Maillane, Eygalières, les Baux, Avignon, Arles – 9-hole golf course in Baux, 18-hole Servanes golf course in Mouriès. **Open** All year.

An avenue of superb, century-old plane trees leads up to this fanciful and splendid house which was built at the beginning of the 18th-century by the Marquis of Ganges. A hotel since 1951, the château has nevertheless retained all its original character. The salons, the dining room, the library, and many bedrooms are still furnished with beautiful antiques; and the floors still have beautiful old parquet and terra-cotta tiles. Also furnished with antiques, many of the bedrooms have charming storage niches and alcove beds. But the interior decoration might not be to everyone's taste because there is an old-fashioned atmosphere behind these old walls, a neglected and even dilapidated surrounding that will appeal only to those who love discovering the charms of history and old places. They will certainly enjoy the magic of the chateau and the beauty that lurks there. However, avoid the *Laurier Rose* and *Lila* bedrooms, and don't expect much of the bathrooms. The chateau is surrounded by a 15-acre park, an orange grove, a basin, and a lake with a small island. It is said that the elegant Marquis used to give sumptuous suppers here.

***How to get there*** *(Map 33): 14km west of Cavaillon via A7, exit Cavaillon, then D99; 2km from Saint-Rémy, take road to Tarascon.*

## Le Mas des Carassins

1, chemin Gaulois
13210 Saint-Rémy-de-Provence (Bouches-du-Rhône)
Tel. (0)4.90.92.15.48 - Fax (0)4.90.92.63.47 - M. and Mme Ripert

**Category** ★★★ **Rooms** 10 with telephone, bath and WC - Wheelchair access. **Price** Single 370-520F, double 400-570F. **Meals** Breakfast 52F, served 8:00-9:30. No restaurant. **Credit cards** Visa, Eurocard and MasterCard. **Pets** Dogs not allowed. **Facilities** Parking. **Nearby** Frédéric Mistral museum in Maillane, Eygalières, Les Baux, Avignon, Arles – 9-hole golf course in Les Baux, 18-hole Servanes golf course in Mouriès. **Open** Apr – Oct.

This 19th-century farm is now a small family hotel. It is just outside the center of Saint Rémy-de-Provence in what has become the residential quarter. In its pretty garden, however, you can imagine yourself in the middle of the country. The bedrooms are all different. In *Magnaneraie,* for example, there is a rustic ambience with stone walls, while the Jassé room is the only one with a terrace. There is a pretty dining room and a small, pleasant lounge with cane furniture. There is no restaurant, but if you are staying in the hotel, the helpful Mme Ripert will prepare a snack for you. The restaurants we recommend are: *Bistrot des Alpilles, Café des Arts, Jardin de Frédéric* in the village, or *L'Oustalet Maïenen* in Maillane.

***How to get there** (Map 33): 14km west of Cavaillon via A7, Cavaillon exit, then D99.*

# Le Mas de Peint

Le Sambuc
13200 Arles (Bouches-du-Rhône)
Tel. (0)4.90.97.20.62 - Fax (0)4.90.97.22.20 - Mme and M. Bon
E-mail: peint@avignon.pacwan.net

**Rooms** 8 and 2 suites with air-conditioning, telephone, bath, WC, minibar, safe, and satellite TV. **Price** Double 1050-1500F, suite 1750-1980F. **Meals** Breakfast 85F, served 8:00-10:00; half board on request. **Restaurant** Service 12:00-13:30, 20:00-21:30; menus 185F (lunch), 230F (dinner). Specialties: Produits de la ferme, taureau de notre élevage, riz du marais. **Credit cards** All major. **Pets** Dogs allowed (+50F). **Facilities** Swimming pool, mountain bikes rentals, horseback trips, parking. **Nearby** Saintes-Maries-de-la-Mer (gypsy pilgrimage, May 24 and 25), sea wall (30km), Arles (féria for easter) – 18-hole La Grande Motte golf course. **Open** Mar 20 – Jan 4.

The Mas de Peint is a formidable compromise between the friendliness of a Camargue guest house and the modern accommodations of a luxurious hotel of character and charm. The owner of a famous herd of horses and bulls, Jacques Bon, is always proud to discuss (and show) his 1235 acres devoted to growing rice and breeding horses and bulls. Mme Bon has contributed her art as a talented architect and interior decorator to the Mas de Peint, which feels like a house for entertaining friends. There is a large table with a bouquet of fresh flowers in the entrance, and a comfortable sofa surrounded by bookshelves. You will find a small reading room and a larger room with a fireplace. In the kitchen, guests gather for an informal meal offering regional specialties. The bedrooms are extraordinarily large, some have bathrooms on a mezzanine, and every room has its personal charm.

***How to get there** (Map 33): 20km south of Arles via D36, towards Salin de Giraud; at the exit from Sambuc, 3km to the left.*

# Logis du Guetteur

Place du Château
83460 Les Arcs-sur-Argens (Var)
Tel. (0)4.94.73.30.82 - Fax (0)4.94.73.39.95 - M. Callegari

**Category** ★★★ **Rooms** 10 with telephone, bath or shower, WC, TV and minibar. **Price** Double 450-520F. **Meals** Breakfast 48F, served 8:00-10:30; half board 430F, full board 550F (per pers., 2 days min.). **Restaurant** Service 12:00 and 19:15; menus 130-330F, also à la carte. Specialties; Saumon fourré à l'écrevisse, Saint-Jacques au beurre de muscat, pigeon de ferme aux truffes, ris de veau aux oranges, bourride. **Credit cards** All major. **Pets** Dogs allowed (+30F). **Facilities** Swimming pool, parking. **Nearby** Sainte Rosaline chapel (4km from Arcs), Château d'Entrecasteaux, Thoronet abbey, Seillans, Simon Segal museum in Aups – Saint-Andiol golf course. **Open** All year (closed Jan 15 – Feb 15).

The old 11th-century Château du Villeneuve, which houses the Logis. However, was restored in 1970 its rough stone medieval walls have been preserved. In your comfortable, pleasantly furnished bedroom, you can be assured that no enemies will scale the castle walls. On the contrary, you can relax and take in the magnificent, panoramic views. The dining room, which is in the old cellars, has a covered terrace that looks out over the charming belltower and rooftops below. There is a lovely swimming pool, delicious cuisine, and a very kind welcome.

***How to get there*** *(Map 34): 12km south of Draguignan via N555 and D555; in the medieval village.*

# Hostellerie de la Reine Jeanne

83230 Bormes-les-Mimosas (Var)
Tel. (0)4.94.15.00.83 - Fax (0)4.94.64.77.89
M. Roux - Mme Héry

**Category** ★★★ **Rooms** 8 with telephone, bath or shower, WC, TV and minibar - 1 for disabled persons. **Price** Single and double 500F, 600 and 700F. **Meals** Breakfast 65F; half board 525F (per pers., 3 days min.). **Restaurant** Service 12:00 and 19:30 (closed Sunday evening and Monday lunchtime in low season); menus 150F, 220F, 280F; also à la carte. **Credit cards** Visa, Eurocard and MasterCard. **Pets** Dogs allowed. **Facilities** Swimming pool, parking and helicopter pad. **Nearby** Chartreuse de la Verne, forest of Dom, Gulf of Saint-Tropez. **Open** All year except in Jan.

Lying in the heart of the Dom Forest along the road to Saint Tropez, this inn offers bedrooms that have been intelligently arranged: you won't be disturbed by the traffic. Spacious and comfortably designed, all overlook a wood of pines and oaks. Three ground-level rooms open directly onto the garden and the others have a terrace. The group of buildings is arranged around a spacious patio and a canopy facing an immense barbecue pit that is very popular in good weather. Chef Christophe Petra religiously respects the innate taste of regional produce, turning out truly excellent cuisine. Each morning, depending on what is best in the market, he decides on the single menu for the day and we were delighted to let him choose for us. (There is always a substitute dish for those who wish it; likewise, you can order among his many specialties with a 48-hour advance notice.) The service is pleasant and the waiter is especially competent in giving advice on wines.

***How to get there*** *(Map 34): 12km south of Draguignan via N555 and D555; in the old town.*

# Hostellerie Bérard

Rue Gabriel-Péri
83740 La Cadière-d'Azur (Var)
Tel. (0)4.94.90.11.43 - Fax (0)4.94.90.01.94 - Mme Bérard
Web: http://ww.mm.soft.fr/raw/berard - E-mail: berard@aol.com

**Category** ★★★ **Rooms** 40 (15 with air-conditioning) with telephone, bath or shower, WC, TV and minibar. **Price** Single and double 440-760F, suite 900-1200F. Meals Breakfast 70F, served 7:30-9:30. **Restaurant** Service 12:30-13:30, 19:30-21:30 (closed Sunday evening and Monday in low season); menus 160-450F, menu lunchtime in the garden 75-120F, also à la carte. Specialties: capuccino de homard, agneau de lait rôti à la broche, saint-pierre rôti à la peau aux endives sauce xérès, saint-honoré "pomme-passion". **Credit cards** Amex, Visa, Eurocard and MasterCard. **Pets** Dogs allowed (+40F). **Facilities** Swimming pool, sauna, fitness center, cooking school, parking. **Nearby** Sanary exotic garden, Bandol, village of Le Castellet, beach (3km) – 18-hole La Frégate golf course in Saint-Cyr-sur-Mer. **Open** All year except Jan 10 – Feb 20.

You will enjoy the festive atmosphere of the Thursday market and don't worry about being disturbed by it: the hotel has a quiet garden behind medieval walls. The bedrooms in the former convent are large, cool in summer, and decorated in shades of brown matching those of the baths, which are covered with Salernes tiles. In the *bastide*, the bedrooms are more classic but also more colorfully appointed with beautiful Provençal fabrics. All are comfortable and well furnished. You can have a view of the rooftops, the garden, the ramparts, the village itself, or the countryside with the medieval village of Le Castellet in the distance. Monsieur Bérard's cuisine, which pays homage to regional products, is one of the outstanding restaurants of Provence. We were charmed by the friendly hospitality extended by Madame Bérard and her daughter.

***How to get there*** *(Map 34): 20km west of Toulon via A50, La Cadière d'Azur exit.*

# Hostellerie Les Gorges de Pennafort

83830 Callas (Var)
Tel. (0)4.94.76.66.51 - Fax (0)4.94.76.67.23

**Category** ★★★ **Rooms** 16 with telephone, bath, WC, TV and minibar. **Price** Single and double 500-650F, suite 800-1450F. **Meals** Breakfast 65F, served 8:00-11:00; half board 560-720F (per pers., 2 days min.). **Restaurant** Service 12:00-14:00, 19:30-22:00 (closed Sunday evening and Monday in low season); menus 225-295F, also à la carte. Specialties: Fricassée de petits gris et pied de porc aux asperges, filet de rougets au Sauterne et curry, lapereau rôti aux petits oignons et artichauts, ananas et pruneaux au gingembre glace à l'armagnac. **Credit cards** Amex, Visa, Eurocard and MasterCard. **Pets** Dogs allowed (+50F). **Facilities** Parking. **Nearby** Le Malmont, villages of Bargemon, Seillans, Salernes, Tourtour, Aups (Simon-Segal museum), Les Arcs (Sainte-Roseline chapel), château of Entrecasteaux, Thoronet Abbey. **Open** Mar 15 – Jan 15 (closed Sunday evening and Monday in low season).

This pretty, ochre-colored Provençal hotel lies in the heart of dramatic mountain gorges. At night, the trees, the craggy cliffs, and the nearby lake are beautifully illuminated by invisible projectors. Decorated with colorful fabric wall coverings, the bedrooms are prim and modern, impeccably kept, and very comfortable; all have gleaming bathrooms. The lounges, the bar, and the dining room (where you will enjoy excellent Provençal specialties) are decorated in the same charming style. There is a ravishing shady terrace, and the service is attentive.

***How to get there*** *(Map 34): 20km northeast of Draguignan via D56 and D25. On A8, exit Le Muy and then D25.*

## Château de Valmer

Route de Gigaro
83420 La Croix Valmer
Tel. (0)4.94.79.60.10 - Fax (0)4.94.54.22.68 - Mme Jovanny

**Category** ★★★ **Rooms** 42 (32 with air-conditioning) with telephone, bath or shower, WC and TV - Elevator - Wheelchair access. **Price** Double 770-1400F. **Meals** Breakfast 90F, served 8:00-10:30. **Restaurant** "Le Coin pique-nique" snack available, service 12:30-15:00 – "La Pinède-plage", grill on the beach, service 12:30-15:00, gastronomic dinner 19:30-21:00. **Credit cards** All major. **Pets** Dogs allowed (+50F). **Facilities** Swimming pool, private beach, tennis, parking. **Nearby** Saint-Tropez gulf, Les Maures, islands of Porquerolles and Port-Cros. **Open** Apr 1 – Sept 30.

A luxurious hotel, elegant and comfortable, the Château de Valmer stands on a rise surrounded by a 12-acre park with a century-old palm grove leading down to a private beach; the adjoining hotel's La Pinède Plage Restaurant is right on the beach, offering lunch at the grill or more gastronomic fare in the evening. At noon, you can also enjoy a light lunch at the Château Valmer, whose interior decoration has been magnificently renovated. In the lounges, there are antiques and deep sofas which are elegantly covered with printed fabrics coordinated with those of the drapes. The decor matches the handsome paintings. The bedrooms are beautiful and impeccably kept, and they have very luxurious bathrooms. Prices vary according to the size of the room and the view. Lovely terraces with stone colonnades lend charm to the façade of the château– and there are also tables here where you can have breakfast.

***How to get there*** *(Map 34): A8, Le Luc exit, towards La Garde-Freinet, Gassin and La Croix-Valmer.*

## Moulin de la Camandoule

Chemin Notre-Dame-des-Cyprès
83440 Fayence (Var)
Tel. (0)4.94.76.00.84 - Fax (0)4.94.76.10.40 - M. Raybaud - Mme and M. Rilla

**Category** ★★★ **Rooms** 11 with telephone, bath, shower, WC and TV. **Price** Single and double 500-675F, suite 750-950F. **Meals** Breakfast 65F, served 8:00-10:00; half board 530-700F (per pers., obligatory March 15 – Oct 31). **Restaurant** Service 12:00-14:00, 19:30-22:00 (closed Wednesday noon); menus 160-265F, also à la carte. Grill on the swimming pool June – Sept. **Credit cards** Visa, Eurocard and MasterCard. **Pets** Dogs allowed (+35F). **Facilities** Swimming pool, parking. **Nearby** Seillans, Bargenon, Sainte-Roseline chapel (4km from Arcs), château d'Entrecasteaux, abbey of Le Thoronet, Saint-Gassien Lake – 18-hole golf course in Roquebrune-sur-Argens. **Open** All year.

This old olive oil mill has been well preserved and today belongs to an English couple who run it like an old-fashioned English guest house. You will enjoy a warm, friendly welcome and all the services and comforts of a good hotel. The interior decoration is in excellent taste. The bedrooms are furnished in an attractive Provençal style, although the attention to detail is uneven. In the unusual lounge the old machinery of the oil press has been cleverly incorporated into the decor. Around the hotel are large grounds through which the River Camandre flows. A look at the menus on the walls of the swimming pool bar will tell you much about the care given to the cooking. Mme Rilla, who has worked on many radio and TV food programs, has made La Camandoule a favorite destination for travelers with a passion for good food.

***How to get there*** *(Map 34): 31km north of Fréjus via D4, then D19.*

## La Grillade au feu de bois

Flassans-sur-Issole
83340 Le Luc (Var)
Tel. (0)4.94.69.71.20 - Fax (0)4.94.59.66.11 - Mme Babb

**Category** ★★ **Rooms** 16 with telephone, bath or shower, WC and TV. **Price** Single and double 400-600F, suite (with whirlpool) 900F. **Meals** Breakfast 50F, served 8:00-10:30. **Restaurant** Service 12:00-14:00, 19:30-21:00; menu 180F, also à la carte. Specialties: Traditional Provençal cooking. **Credit cards** Amex, Visa, Eurocard and MasterCard. **Pets** Dogs allowed. **Facilities** Heated swimming pool, parking. **Nearby** Abbey of Thoronet, tour of Luc, abbey of La Celle, La Loube mountain – 18-hole Barbaroux golf course in Brignoles. **Open** All year.

This very well restored 18th-century Provençal *mas* is surrounded by lush vegetation and has a terrace shaded by beautiful trees, the oldest of which is a 100-year-old mulberry. Inside, the various living areas and the long vaulted dining room, with a fireplace at one end, are remarkably furnished. (Mme Babb, who is also an antiques dealer, has personalized the decor with numerous lovely objects, paintings, and pieces of furniture.) The bedrooms are superb, large, and comfortable, in fact immense; they are very quiet despite the proximity of the N7 highway (500m away). We can heartily recommend them. The bathrooms are also lovely. You will enjoy good Provençal cuisine and, as you would expect, there are delicious grills.

***How to get there*** *(Map 34): 13km east of Brignoles via N7 between Flassans-sur-Issolle and Le Luc.*

## Auberge du Vieux Fox

Place de l'Eglise
83670 Fox-Amphoux (Var)
Tel. (0)4.94.80.71.69 - Fax (0)4.94.80.78.38 - M. Martha

**Category** ★★★ **Rooms** 8 with telephone, bath or shower, WC and 4 with TV. **Price** Double 350-480F. **Meals** Breakfast 40F, served 8:00-12:00; half board 660F (1 pers.), 700-800F (2 pers.). **Restaurant** Service 12:30 and 19:305; menus 135-250F, also à la carte. Specialties: Agneau de Haute-Provence, galette du berger. **Credit cards** Amex, Visa, Eurocard and MasterCard. **Pets** Dogs allowed (+35F). **Facilities** Parking. **Nearby** Abbeys of Thoronet and La Celle, Verdon lake and gorges – 18-hole Barbaroux golf course in Brignoles. **Open** All year.

The old village of Fox-Amphoux, perched on its wooded crag, was first a Roman camp and then became a headquarters of Knights Templars. The hotel is in the old presbytery adjoining the church in the center of the village. The interior will instantly charm you: there is a delightful dining room with prettily set tables alongside lovely old furniture. In summer you can also have dinner on the enchanting little terrace in the shade of a large fig tree. The bedrooms and bathrooms have been recently renovated. They are comfortable and look out on the massifs of Sainte-Victoire and Sainte-Baume. In addition to the comfort and charm of this small hotel (where *demi-pension* is recommended), you will enjoy very good cuisine and reasonable prices.

***How to get there*** *(Map 34): 32km north of Brignoles via A8, Saint-Maximin-la-Sainte-Baume exit, then D560 to Tavernes, D71 and D32.*

# L'Arena

145, rue du Général de Gaulle
83600 Fréjus (Var)
Tel. (0)4.94.17.09.40 - Fax (0)4.94.52.01.52 - Mme Bouchot - M. Bluntzer

**Category** ★★★ **Rooms** 25 with air conditioning, telephone, bath or shower, WC, satellite TV, and minibar - 2 for disabled persons. **Price** Single and double 350-480F, 400-650F; suite 500-1200F. **Meals** Breakfast 45F, served 7:30-10:30. **Restaurant** Service 12:00-14:00, 19:00-22:30 (closed Monday lunchtime and Saturday lunchtime); menus 120-210F, also à la carte. Regional cooking. **Credit cards** Amex, Visa, Eurocard and MasterCard. **Pets** Dogs allowed (+40F). **Facilities** Swimming pool and parking (+45F). **Nearby** Fréjus: cathedral and cloister; Massif de l'Estérel between Saint-Raphaël and La Napoule, Saint-Tropez, Cannes - 18-hole Beauvallon golf course in Sainte-Maxime **Open** All year except 15 days in Nov.

Standing in the heart of the city, this small hotel has made admirable use of its garden so that apart from a little noise from the outside, we quickly forgot the Arena's urban location (which is even an advantage if you want to visit the Roman ruins of the old city.) Inside, an elegant tiled floor, painted-wood furniture, and Provençal fabrics are a perfect expression of the Mediterranean bonhomie and carefree way of life. Refined and simple, the bedrooms are pleasant and well kept, and the soundproofing is totally effective. All the rooms are somewhat small except for the one (our favorite) located on ground level near the swimming pool and those which have just been opened in an independent building. Delicate and delicious meals are served on the terrace or in a lovely dining room.

***How to get there*** *(Map 34):40 km west of Cannes; A7, Fréjus-Saint-Raphaël exit.*

## La Boulangerie

Route de Collobrières
83310 Grimaud (Var)
Tel. (0)4.94 43.23.16 - Fax (0)4.94.43.38.27 - Mme Piget

**Category** ★★★ **Rooms** 11 (6 with air-conditioning) with telephone, bath, WC, 4 with TV and 1 with minibar. **Price** Single 560F, double 660-690F, suite 780-1520F. **Meals** Breakfast 60F, served 7:45-11:00. **Restaurant** Service 12:00-13:30, 20:00-21:15. Specialties: Aïoli de poissons, poulet fermier aux truffes, filet de loup aux fruits de provence, moeleux au chocolat. **Credit cards** Amex, Visa, Eurocard and MasterCard. **Pets** Dogs allowed (+60F). **Facilities** Swimming pool, tennis, table tennis, parking. **Nearby** La Garde-Freinet, ridgeway to the Notre-Dame-des-Anges hermitage, Collobrières, Carthusian monastery of La Verne, Saint-Tropez – 9-hole Beauvallon golf course in Sainte-Maxime. **Open** Apr 1 – Oct 10.

This place has nothing to do with bakeries as its name would suggest–it is named after a small village–and additionally, it has a very different atmosphere from a traditional hotel. Far from the crowds in a tranquil spot in the Massif des Maures, it is more like a holiday house in the interior of Provence. Everything conspires to produce this impression: both the terrace where you can have meals, and the dining room, which is part of the lounge. There is a happy informality that makes you feel instantly at ease. The bedrooms have the same homey atmosphere and are more like guest rooms in a friend's house. This is a beautiful hotel where you will be warmly received.

***How to get there*** *(Map 34): 10km west of Saint-Tropez via D14; 1km from the village.*

# Le Verger

Route de Collobrières
83310 Grimaud (Var)
Tel. (0)4.94.43.25.93 - Fax (0)4.94.43.33.92 - Mme Zachary

**Rooms** 9 (first floor with air-conditioning) with telephone, bath or shower, WC, TV and 3 with air conditioning. **Price** Double 550-850F. **Meals** Breakfast 60F, served 8:30-11:30. **Restaurant** Service 12:00-14:30, 19:30-23:30; à la carte. Specialties: Salade de foie gras aux truffes, médaillon de lotte au curry, carré d'agneau au miel, sabayon chaud aux framboises, bourride. **Credit cards** Visa, Eurocard and MasterCard. **Pets** Dogs allowed. **Facilities** Swimming pool, parking. **Nearby** La Garde-Freinet, ridgeway to the Notre-Dame-des-Anges hermitage, Collobrières, Carthusian monastery of La Verne, Saint-Tropez – 9-hole Beauvallon golf course in Sainte-Maxime. **Open** Apr – Oct.

This pretty house looks like a private dwelling. The bedrooms have French windows which open onto a terrace or a lawn with fruit trees. The tasteful Provençal decor is enhanced with lovely fabrics and beautiful bathrooms. You will find your bed turned down every evening, and bouquets of flowers add a pleasant touch. Every day, the restaurant is filled with customers who come back regularly for Monsieur Zachary's fine cuisine, and newcomers delighted to have discovered his outstanding specialties made with aromatic herbs and vegetables from the kitchen garden. Shielded by a bamboo grove on the small river in back, the Verger is very quiet. And the hospitality is charming.

***How to get there*** *(Map 34): 9km west of Saint-Tropez. From A8, exit Le Luc, then D558 towards Saint-Tropez; In Grimaud take D14 for 1km towards Collobrières and follow signs.*

## Le Manoir

Ile de Port-Cros
83400 Hyères (Var)
Tel. (0)4.94.05.90.52 - Fax (0)4.94.05.90.89 - M. Buffet

**Category** ★★★ **Rooms** 23 with telephone, bath or shower and WC. **Price** Double with half board 750-1050F (per pers.). **Meals** Breakfast 60F, served 7:45-10:00. **Restaurant** Service from 13:00 and 20:00; menus 250-300F, also à la carte. Specialties: Bourride provençale, baron d'agneau à la broche, fricassée de gambas au whisky. **Credit cards** Visa, Eurocard and MasterCard. **Pets** Dogs not allowed. **Facilities** Heated swimming pool. **Nearby** Nature trails in the Port-Cros national park, Porquerolles. **Open** Mid. Apr – beg. Oct.

The eucalyptus, palm trees, white walls, and graceful columns of the Manoir evoke an exotic dream, a lost island. And yet Toulon is so close. The island of Pont-Cros is a nature reserve and no vehicles are allowed. The hotel was opened just after the war in this private house and it still preserves a family atmosphere, blending conviviality with elegance. There is a large lounge and several small ones, which card players frequent towards the end of the summer season. The bedrooms are cool and charming and some have little loggias; from Room 4 you can see the sea through the trees. A beautiful, quiet 30-acre park adds to the considerable charm of this lovely hotel.

***How to get there*** *(Map 34): Ferry connection from Le Lavandou and Cavalaire - tel. (0)4.94.71.01.02, from Hyères - tel. (0)4.94.58.21.81. Cars not allowed on the island. Airport Toulon-Hyères.*

# Les Glycines

Place d'Armes - Ile de Porquerolles
83400 Hyères (Var)
Tel. (0)4.94.58.30.36 - Fax (0)4.94.58.35.22

**Category** ★★ **Rooms** 12 with air-conditioning, telephone, bath or shower, WC and TV. **Price** Double with half board 550-850F (per pers.). **Meals** Breakfast (buffet) 50F, served from 8:30. **Restaurant** Service 19:30-22:30: menu 99-140F, also à la carte. Specialties: Fish. **Credit cards** Amex, Visa, Eurocard and MasterCard. **Pets** Dogs not allowed. **Nearby** Bike rides along island paths, beaches, boat rental. **Open** All year.

Located on the village square, Les Glycines ("wisteria") nestles behind a garden in the shade of a century-old fig tree, its whitewashed walls and blue shutters evoking the quiet charm of Provençal homes of yesteryear. In the bedrooms, all air-conditioned and comfortable, some overlooking the square and others the garden, the same soft atmosphere is created by Provençal fabrics, sandstone floor tiles, and walls in pastel colors. The baths also are comfortable and well equipped. Breakfast and dinner are served in the cool shade of the garden on tables set with crimson linens. So before the first hordes of "day trippers" descend from the boats, it's best to enjoy your coffee on the terrace of *L'Escale,* and in the evening go to the Plage d'Argent, the Silver Beach, for dinner (the return trip by bike at night is unforgettable): Voil^: the recipe for being an authentic *"Porquerollais"*.

***How to get there*** *(Map 34): Ferry connection from Hyères or La Tour Fondue -tel. (0)4.94.58.21.81) or boat-taxi (tel. (0)4.94.58.31.19 - at any time. Cars not allowed on the island. Airport Toulon-Hyères (7km).*

1998

# L'Oustaou

Place d'Armes
Ile de Porquerolles - 83400 Hyères (Var)
Tel. (0)4.94.58.30.13 - Fax (0)4.94.58.34.93 - M. and Mme Garbit

**Category** ★★★ **Rooms** 5 with air-conditioning, telephone, shower, WC and TV. **Price** Double 450-800F. **Meals** Breakfast incl., served from 8:00. **Restaurant** Service 11:30-15:30, 19:30-22:30; Chef's special 69F, menu 100F, also à la carte. Specialties: Marmite du pêcheur, poissons, petits légumes farcis. **Credit cards** Amex, Visa, Eurocard and MasterCard. **Pets** Dogs allowed. **Nearby** A lot of promenades by bicycle inthe island, beach, boat rentals. **Open** Mar 2 – Jan 1.

Standing on the port with its façade on the village square, the Oustaou on Porquerolles Island features charmingly simple bedrooms with modern amenities. Two overlook the Mediterranen, and three look out over the square. On the ground floor, the terrace restaurant offers a quiet view of the sea on one side, and on the other, you can follow the spectacle of village life from your dining table, while enjoying good fish specialties. Note that it's indispensable to rent bikes to get to the beaches and creeks on the south shore of the island, or to discover the eighty kilometers of paths criss-crossing Porquerolles' 3125-acre national park.

***How to get there*** *(Map 34): Ferry connection from Hyères or La Tour Fondue - tel. 04.95.58.21.81) or boat-taxi (tel. 04.94.58.31.19 - at any time. Airport Toulon-Hyères, 7km. Cars forbidden on the island.*

# La Maurette

83520 Roquebrune-sur-Argens (Var)
Tel. (0)4.94.45.46.81 - Fax (0)4.94.45.46.81
M. and Mme Rapin

**Rooms** 11 with telephone, bath or shower and WC (7 with kitchenette) **Price** Double 350-450F. **Meals** Breakfast 45F, served 8:00-10:00. No restaurant. **Credit cards** Visa, Eurocard and MasterCard. **Pets** Dogs not allowed. **Facilities** Swimming pool, parking. **Nearby** Roquebrune, Fréjus cathedral, massif de l'Estérel – 18-hole Saint-Endréongolf course in La Motte. **Open** Easter – mid. Oct.

M. Rapin may well owe his vocation as a hotelier to a grandfather who owned a hotel in Cannes. But is "hotelier" the right word in his case? For La Maurette is really more like a guest house. It is the kind of place where you will almost feel you have been invited. And anyway, would a hotel really choose such a secluded location, so removed from the crowds? This could be the setting for a monastery, facing the rock of Roquebrune and the foothills of the Massif des Maures. And in the back, there are the Estérel, the Mediterranean, and the valley. The bedrooms are bright, cheerful, and very comfortable, with charming, carefully chosen furniture, curios, and paintings. Who could ask for more? Well, perhaps a good restaurant for dinner in the village, like *La Sainte Candie* or *Les Templiers* for aromatic Provençal dishes and fresh vegetables. Note that La Maurette cannot accommodate small children.

***How to get there*** *(Map 34): 10km west of Fréjus via N7 and D7;then after the Pont de l'Argens follow signs; from A8, Le Muy or Puget-sur-Argens exit.*

1998

# Grand Hôtel

24, avenue du Port
Les Lecques 83270 Saint-Cyr-sur-Mer (Var)
Tel. (0)4.94.26.23.01 - Fax (0)4.94.26.10.22 - Mme Vitré

**Category** ★★★ **Rooms** 58 with telephone, bath or shower, WC and TV - Elevator. **Price** Single and double 415-835F. **Meals** Breakfast 65F, served 7:30-10:00. **Restaurant** Service 12:30-14:00, 19:00-21:00; menus 85-165F, also à la carte. Specialties: Regional cooking. **Credit cards** Amex, Visa, Eurocard and MasterCard. **Pets** Dogs allowed. **Facilities** Swimming pool, tennis and parking. **Nearby** Exotic Garden in Sanary, Bandol, La Cadière, Le Castellet - 18-hole Frégate golf course in Saint-Cyr-sur-Mer. **Open** Mar 30 – Oct 19.

Le Grand Hôtel was once summer home to wealthy Provençal families who came here to enjoy the beach and its dunes. Today, the long, dune-less ribbon of sand attracts families and August vacationers from all over. Set back slightly from the main street along the sea, the recently renovated hotel has conserved the essential part of its original park and garden so as to offer a quiet oasis of trees and flowers. The big white building is charming and the skillful renovations have created a fresh, cheerful ambiance in the lounges and the dining room. The newly renovated bedrooms on the upper floors in the front, with a view over the sea, are the most beautiful. You simply cross the street and you're on the beach, unless you prefer the hotel's swimming pool; snacks are served there, and the restaurant offers aromatic Provençal specialties. This is a good hotel for a vacation on the sea, in Provence, and in Saint-Cyr-sur-Mer itself, where a reproduction of the Statue of Liberty stands on the Place de l'Eglise. It's a traditional village where local farmers still come to animate the big open market on Sunday morning.

***How to get there*** *(Map 34): 20km west of Toulon via A 50, exit Saint-Cyr-sur-Mer, then to Les Lecques.*

## Hôtel Le Pré de la Mer

Route des Salins
83990 Saint-Tropez (Var)
Tel. (0)4.94.97.12.23 - Fax (0)4.94.97.43.91 - Mme Blum

**Category** ★★★ **Rooms** 3, 1 suite and 8 studios (with kitchenette) with telephone, bath, shower, WC, TV, safe and minibar. **Price** Single and double 510-695F, studio 660-950F, suite 1050-1375F. **Meals** Breakfast 60F, served 8:30-12:00. No restaurant. **Credit cards** Amex, Visa, Eurocard and MasterCard. **Pets** Dogs allowed (+50F). **Facilities** Parking. **Nearby** L'Annonciade museum in Saint-Tropez, Ramatuelle festival in July and Aug, La Nioulargue in October, la Garde-Freinet, ridgeway to Notre-Dame-des-Anges hermitage, Collobrières, Carthusian monastery of La Verne – 9-hole Beauvallon golf course in Sainte-Maxime. **Open** Easter – Sept 30.

This is a low-roofed white house built in Saint-Tropez–Mexican style. The bedrooms are large and comfortable, cooled by large fans. Some have a kitchen (which helps you forget the prices of the restaurants in Saint-Tropez) and all have a private terrace with white wooden table and chairs, perfect for breakfast and meals. The terraces lead out into a pleasant garden where lemon and pomegranate trees and oleanders bloom. But to get into this peaceful haven just minutes from Saint-Tropez, you will have to charm Joséphine Blum, the owner, who likes to choose her clientele. Restaurant fashions come and go here, but there are always *Le Gorille* and *Le Sénequier* on the port; *Le Bistrot des Lices* and *Le Café des Arts* on the Place des Lices; *Chez Fuchs* and *La Table du Marché*; and on the beaches, *Le Club 55, Le Nioulargo* for his Thai cuisine. Or try *Les Jumeaux.*

***How to get there** (Map 34): 3km east of Saint-Tropez on the Salins road.*

## La Ferme d'Augustin

83350 Ramatuelle - Saint-Tropez (Var)
Tel. (0)4.94.97.23.83 or (0)4.94.97.23.83 - Fax (0)4.94.97.40.30
Mme Vallet

**Category** ★★★ **Rooms** 46 with telephone, bath (5 with shower), WC, TV, safe and minibar, 30 with air-conditioning - Elevator. **Price** Double 580-1600F, suite 1800F. **Meals** Breakfast 75F, served 6:00-14:00. No restaurant but snacks available for residents only. **Credit cards** Amex, Visa, Eurocard and MasterCard. **Pets** Dogs allowed (+70F). **Facilities** Heated swimming pool, parking. **Nearby** L'Annonciade museum in Saint-Tropez, Ramatuelle festival in July and Aug, La Nioulargue in October, la Garde-Freinet, ridgeway to the Notre-Dame-des-Anges hermitage, Collobrières, Carthusian monastery of La Verne – 9-hole Beauvallon golf course in Sainte-Maxime. **Open** Mar 25 – Oct 15.

This former family farmhouse has now been completely renovated. As soon as you arrive, you will be captivated by the pine grove and the garden full of wisteria, bougainvillea, rambling roses, and the great parasol-shaped mulberry trees. In the lounges, antique country-style furniture is tastefully combined with modern sofas. The bedrooms have pretty bathrooms with wall tiles from Salernes. They all overlook the garden and have a balcony or terrace commanding sea views. The hotel occupies a truly enviable position, just off Tahiti Beach, 200 meters from hiking paths and mountainbiking trails. If you want to stay on the beach all day, ask for a box lunches; the bar serves light meals and provides 24-hour room service. Ask your hotel for restaurant recommendations; or see ours on page 486.

***How to get there*** *(Map 34): 5km from Saint-Tropez on the Tahiti Beach road.*

## Hôtel Les Bouis

Route des Plages-Pampelonne
83350 Ramatuelle - Saint-Tropez (Var)
Tel. (0)4.94.79.87.61 - Fax (0)4.94.79.85.20

**Category** ★★★ **Rooms** 14 and 4 duplex with air-conditioning, telephone, bath, WC, TV, safe and minibar. **Price** Double 750-1200F. **Meals** Breakfast 70F, served 8:00-12:00. No restaurant, but grill and Chef's special by the swimming pool at lunchtime. **Credit cards** Visa, Eurocard and MasterCard. **Pets** Dogs allowed (+50F). **Facilities** Swimming pool, parking. **Nearby** L'Annonciade museum in Saint-Tropez, Ramatuelle festival in July and Aug, La Nioulargue in October, la Garde-Freinet, ridgeway to the Notre-Dame-des-Anges hermitage, Collobrières, Carthusian monastery of La Verne – 9-hole Beauvallon golf course in Sainte-Maxime. **Open** Mar 22 – Oct 25.

Les Bouis' special attraction in this town of many charming hotels is its exceptional location, high in the hills yet only a kilometer from the sea, commanding an impressive view out over Pampelonne and Camarat Beaches, and one of the most beautiful gulfs of the Côte d'Azur. Recently constructed, the hotel has only a few bedrooms; some open directly onto the garden and have a private terrace with a panorama of the swimming pool and the coast. All the rooms are very comfortable. Breakfast, which is special, can be served in your room or around the swimming pool until noon. Here also, a grill is set up in the summer. The atmosphere is relaxed and the service is charming. The owner will give you good restaurant recommendations; our own are given on page 486.

***How to get there** (Map 34): 5km from Saint-Tropez, on the road to Pampelonne Beach.*

## La Ferme d'Hermès

Route de l'Escalet - Val de Pons
83350 Ramatuelle - Saint-Tropez (Var)
Tel. (0)4.94.79.27.80 - Fax (0)4.94.79.26.86 - Mme Verrier

**Category** ★★ **Rooms** 8 and 1 suite with telephone, bath, WC, TV, minibar and kitchenette. **Price** Double 600-880F, suite 1100F. **Meals** Breakfast 80F, served 9:00-12:00. No restaurant. **Credit cards** Visa, Eurocard and MasterCard. **Pets** Dogs allowed (+50F). **Facilities** Swimming pool, parking. **Nearby** L'Annonciade museum in Saint-Tropez, Ramatuelle festival in July and Aug, La Nioulargue in Oct, Grimaud. **Open** Apr 1 – Oct 31 and Dec 27 – Jan 10.

A dirt path through the vineyards, a fragrant garden full of rosemary bushes and olive trees, a pink house: this is the address in the Midi you have always dreamed of, a place where you want to welcome your friends. Madame Verrier, the owner, has thought of every detail. The fireplace, homemade preserves and pastries for breakfast, bouquets of flowers–all make this house thoroughly charming. The rooms are lovely, and some have a small terrace right on the vineyard. Most have a pleasant kitchenette. Madame Verrier can advise you on restaurants; otherwise, see our note on page 486.

***How to get there*** *(Map34): 2km south of Ramatuelle on L'Escalet Road.*

## La Figuière

Route de Tahiti - 83350 Ramatuelle - Saint-Tropez (Var)
Tel. (0)4.94.97.18.21 - Fax (0)4.94.97.68.48
Mme Chaix

**Category** ★★★ **Rooms** 42 with air-conditioning, telephone, bath (3 with shower) and WC, 31 with TV, 42 with safe and minibar. **Price** Double 500-950F, duplex (4 pers.) 1300-1400F. **Meals** Breakfast 65F, served 8:00-11:00. **Restaurant** Service 12:00-15:00, 20:00-23:00; also à la carte. Specialties: Grills. **Credit cards** Amex, Visa, Eurocard and MasterCard. **Pets** Dogs allowed (+50F). **Facilities** Swimming pool, tennis, parking. **Nearby** L'Annonciade museum in Saint-Tropez, Ramatuelle festival in July, La Nioulargue in Oct, La Garde-Freinet, ridgeway to the Notre-Dame-des-Anges hermitage, Collobrières, Carthusian monastery of La Verne, Saint-Tropez – 9-hole Beauvallon golf course in Sainte-Maxime. **Open** Apr 4 – Oct 8.

In the morning, opening the shutters to a vista of sunny vineyards is one of the many charms of this hotel in the countryside a few kilometers from Saint-Tropez. La Figuière is composed of five small typical Provençal buildings in a garden full of fig trees. Overlooking a small private terrace (except for the rooms in the former villa), the bedrooms are spacious and quiet. The regional decoration is sober and the bathrooms are comfortable–some have a double washbasin, shower, and bath. Our favorites have numbers ending in 30 and 40 and enjoy pretty, private terraces surrounded by lavender and lantanas; they have a panoramic view over the vineyards and hills covered with parasol pines. Good breakfasts are served with the morning newspaper. Grills are served at lunchtime around the swimming pool bordered with pink oleander and japonica. A tennis court is hidden behind the hotel, and the staff is very friendly.

***How to get there*** *(Map 34): 2.5km south of Saint-Tropez.*

## Hôtel des Deux Rocs

Place Font d'Amont
83440 Seillans (Var)
Tel. (0)4.94.76.87.32 - Fax (0)4.94.76.88.68 - Mme Hirsch

**Category** ★★★ **Rooms** 15 with telephone, bath or shower, WC and minibar. **Price** Double 280-550F. **Meals** Breakfast 45F, served 8:00-10:00; half board 330-470F, full board 420-550F (per pers., 3 days min.). **Restaurant** Service 12:00-14:00, 19:30-21:00 (closed Tuesday and Thursday lunchtime); menus 90F (lunchtime in week)-140-220F, also à la carte. Specialties: Saint-jacques à l'ail et aux amandes, foie gras poelé aux poires, filet de bœuf aux morilles. **Credit cards** Visa, Eurocard and MasterCard. **Pets** Dogs allowed. **Nearby** Chapel of Saint-André in Comps-sur-Artuby, Fayence, les Arcs and the Sainte-Roseline chapel (4km), château d'Entrecasteaux, abbey of Le Thoronet – 18-hole golf course in Roquebrune-sur-Argens. **Open** Apr 1 – end Oct.

Standing at the top of the splendid village of Seillans, close to the city walls and the old castle, is the Hôtel des Deux Rocs, a large Provençal house which is a modest, rustic replica of certain Italian residences. Variety is the keynote of the decor, which is exquisite. You will feel at home and relaxed in the small lounge with a fireplace. The bedrooms are all individually designed: period furniture, wall fabrics, curtains, and bathroom towelsare unique to each one of them. Breakfast can be served at tables set up in the pleasant little square not far from Max Ernst's *Génie de la Bastille*; homemade preserves are just one of the many delicious details which make a stay here memorable. You will love this hotel, and prices are very reasonable.

***How to get there*** *(Map 34): 34km north of Fréjus via A8, Les Adrets exit, then D562 towards Fayence and D19.*

## Les Bastidières

2371, avenue de la Résistance
83100 Toulon Cap Brun (Var)
Tel. (0)4.94.36.14.73 - Fax (0)4.94.42.49.75 - Mme Lagriffoul

**Rooms** 5 with telephone, bath or shower, WC, TV and minibar. **Price** Double 450-800F. **Meals** Breakfast 60-70F, served 8:00-10:00. No restaurant. **Credit cards** Not accepted. **Pets** Dogs allowed. **Facilities** Swimming pool, parking. **Nearby** Mont Faron; gorges of Ollioules and Evenos; villages of the Castellet and The Cadière d'Azur; cap Sicié; Porquerolles; Port-Cros; Saint-Tropez. **Open** All year.

This beautiful villa stands on the lush heights of Cape Brun in Toulon and is surrounded by a garden where exoticism and the air of Provence mingle harmoniously. Palm trees, yuccas, and ancient pine trees cast shade over large earthenware jars overflowing with impatiens and geraniums. The owners live in the main house. Just next door, there is an annex with five spacious bedrooms that are comfortably equipped with very functional bathrooms. Each room opens onto a small flowery terrace where it is pleasant to have breakfast. The food is excellent and is presented on beautiful silver service. The quietest and most intimate rooms are near the swimming pool, which is beautifully large and surrounded by trees, exotic plants, and Mediterranean flowers. It is midway between the hotel and the guest house–"guest" in the sense that you live very independently of the main house, and that all the services of a hotel are not provided (the lounge is in the owners' house). But Les Bastidières is a beautiful place to stay.

***How to get there*** *(Map 34): On A8, Toulon exit; towards Mourillon beaches, Cap Brun, Pradet.*

# Château de Trigance

83840 Trigance (Var)
Tel. (0)4.94.76.91.18 - Fax (0)4.94.85.68.99
M. Thomas

**Category** ★★★ **Rooms** 10 with telephone, bath, WC and TV. **Price** Double 600-700F, suite 900F. **Meals** Breakfast 68F, served 7:30-10:00; half board 550-720F (per pers.). **Restaurant** Service 12:00-14:00, 19:30-21:00 (closed Wednesday lunchtime in low season); menus 210-360F, also à la carte. Specialties: Terrine marbré de foie gras et ris de veau sur une fine gelée au vin d'orange, croustillant d'agneau des Alpilles aux senteurs de garigue et ail confit, trigançois aux infusions de miel de thym et d'Hypocras. **Credit cards** All major. **Pets** Dogs allowed. **Facilities** Parking. **Nearby** Verdon canyon, ridgeway from La-Palud-sur-Verdon, Moustiers-Sainte-Marie – 9-hole château de Toulane golf course in La Martie. **Open** Mar 23 – Nov 1.

Originally a fortress built in the 9th-century by the monks of the Abbey of Saint-Victor, the château de Trigance became a castle of the Counts of Provence two hundred years later. A massive structure perched like an eagle's nest on the top of a hill, it has been restored with local stones. The salon and the barrel-vaulted dining room have retained their medieval character, including the ancient music. The bedrooms are arranged around an enormous, magnificent terrace, making them quieter and more intimate. They are very comfortable. Excellent regional cuisine is served inside only, but you can enjoy drinks at the bar on the terrace facing this fantastic panorama. In summer plays are performed on the esplanade by the ramparts. The owners extend a warm welcome.

***How to get there** (Map 34): 44km north of Draguignan via D995 to Comps-sur-Artuby; then D905 to Trigance.*

# Hôtel de la Mirande

Place de la Mirande
84000 Avignon (Vaucluse)
Tel. (0)4.90.85.93.93 - Fax (0)4.90.86.26.85 - M. Stein

**Category** ★★★★ **Rooms** 20 with air-conditioning, telephone, bath, shower, WC, TV and minibar. **Price** Double 1050-2400F, suite 2800F. **Meals** Breakfast 95F, served until 11:00. **Restaurant** Service 19:00-21:45; menus 135F (lunchtime in week), 210-380F, also à la carte. Specialties: Piperade de langoustines, émincé de carré de veau à la provençal. **Credit cards** Visa, Eurocard and MasterCard. **Pets** Dogs allowed (+80F). **Facilities** Cooking lessons 500-1600F, parking (+80F). **Nearby** Palace of the Popes, Notre-Dame des Doms, Campana collection at the Petit-Palais, Calvet museum, theater festival at Avignon in July, Villeneuve-Lès-Avignon, la Provence romaine and les Alpilles, le Lubéron – 18-hole Châteaublanc golf course in Avignon. **Open** All year.

This marvelous hotel in Avignon is charming, to say the least. The inner courtyard has been turned into a delightful conservatory, where the wicker armchairs in delicate caramel colors set the tone. Off the courtyard there is a stunning sequence of rooms richly decorated with beautiful antiques, Provençal style fabrics, and chintzes. The bedrooms are spacious, elegant and comfortable, and all have a lounge or anteroom. Those on the *premier étage* are more spacious, while those on the mezzanine and *deuxième étage* are more intimate. Some rooms on the last floor have a lovely terrace which is very pleasant at lunchtime. The ancient–and baroque–music evening concerts in the autumn or the cooking workshops directed by leading chefs will perhaps give you the opportunity to discover this hotel, which is both exquisite and sumptuous. If you are simply passing through Avignon, the tea room and the piano bar are also very pleasant places to spend a lovely afternoon. Last, but not least, the people are very charming.

***How to get there*** *(Map 33): In the town center, at the foot of the Palais des Papes.*

## Hôtel d'Europe

12, place Crillon
84000 Avignon (Vaucluse)
Tel. (0)4.90.82.66.92- Fax (0)4.90.85.43.66 - M. Daire

**Category** ★★★★ **Rooms** 47 with air-conditioning, telephone, bath, WC, TV and minibar. **Price** Single and double 630-1750F, suite 2150-2500F. **Meals** Breakfast 90F, served 6:30-11:00. **Restaurant** Service 12:00-14:00, 19:30-22:00 (closed Monday noon and Sunday); brunch 11:30-15:00, menu, also à la carte. **Credit cards** All major. **Pets** Dogs allowed (+50F). **Facilities** Private garage (50F). **Nearby** Palace of the Popes, Notre-Dame des Doms, Campana collection at the Petit-Palais, Calvet museum, theater festival at Avignon in July, Villeneuve-Lès-Avignon, la Provence romaine and les Alpilles, le Lubéron – 18-hole Châteaublanc golf course in Avignon. **Open** All year.

The seigneurial 17th-century Hôtel d'Europe was once the mansion of the Marquis de Graveson. The refinement of the hotel has been carefully preserved: handsome antique furniture and paintings along with brilliant Aubusson tapestries decorate the salons and the very beautiful dining room. The bedrooms, which are of varying size, are all furnished with antiques and have very comfortable accommodations. Three suites have been opened and from their private terrace in the evening, you will enjoy a unique view the illuminated Palace of the Popes and the medieval ramparts surrounding the town. In summer, you can dine in the pretty patio, shaded by plane and palm trees, which are planted in huge traditional pots made in the nearby village of Anduze. The cuisine is excellent, and there is a very good wine cellar. Note the private garage, which solves the thorny problem of parking in the old town.

***How to get there*** *(Map 33): Inside the ramparts.*

1998

# Hôtel du Palais des Papes

1, rue Gérard-Philippe
84000 Avignon (Vaucluse)
Tel. (0)4.90.86.04.13 - Fax (0)4.90.27.91.17 - M. Gayte

**Category** ★★ **Rooms** 23 (3 with air-conditioning) with telephone, bath or shower, WC and TV - Elevator. **Price** Single and double 280-620F. **Meals** Breakfast 40-42F, served 7:00-10:00. **Restaurant** "Le Lutrin". Service 12:30-14:30, 19:00-22:00; menus 110F (Lunchtime)-170F, also à la carte. Specialties: Escargots à l'aïoli, aubergines confites à la provençale, bourride, râble de lapin rôti au romarin. **Credit cards** Amex, Visa, Eurocard and MasterCard. **Pets** Dogs allowed (+40F). **Facilities** Public parking opposite at the hotel (45F). **Nearby** In Avignon: Palace of the Popes, Notre-Dame-des-Doms, Campana collection at the Petit-Palais, Calvet museum, theater festival at Avignon in July; Villeneuve-lès-Avignon, Romanesque Provence and Les Alpilles, Le Lubéron - 18-hole Châteaublanc golf course in Avignon. **Open** All year.

This is a small hotel well located in the center of Avignon. On one side, the windows overlook the Popes' Palace; on the other, the Place de l'Horloge with its innumerable restaurant terraces--and the disadvantage of noise in the summer. The bedrooms, many of which are small, have good modern amenities. Nine have recently been redecorated in more contemporary Provençal taste: wrought-iron furniture, tastefully chosen fabrics; some baths have been redone. The other rooms are still somewhat old-fashioned but can be recommended, except for Room 12, which needs a touch-up. In summer, ask for a room on the courtyard: these are cooler and also quieter. The most beautiful (and most expensive) room of all is Number 25, on the courtyard. There is a small lounge/bar/breakfast room with medieval decor, where a fire crackles in the winter.

***How to get there*** *(Map 33): In front of the Palais des Papes*

## L'Anastasy

Ile de la Barthelasse
84000 Avignon (Vaucluse)
Tel. (0)4.90.85.55.94 - Fax (0)4.90.82.59.40 - Mme Manguin

**Rooms** 4 with bath or shower. **Price** Single and double 300-400F. **Meals** Breakfast incl. **Restaurant** For residents only. Service from 13:00 and 20:30; menu 150F. Specialties: Provençal and Italian cooking. **Credit cards** Not accepted. **Pets** Dogs allowed. **Facilities** Swimming pool, parking. **Nearby** Palace of the Popes, Notre-Dame des Doms, Campana collection at the Petit-Palais, Calvet museum, Villeneuve-lès-Avignon – 18-hole Châteaublanc golf course. **Open** All year.

L'Anastasy used to be a farm typical of the area surrounding Avignon, where animals and harvests were the sole concern. Now the barns and stables have been converted to make a large family house where friends and guests can be welcomed. On the ground floor there is now a spacious lounge and kitchen-dining room which is the very heart of the house, for the warm and friendly hostess, Olga Manguin, enjoys nothing more than cooking for her guests; indeed, the Provençal and Italian specialties she excels at are delicious. The bedrooms are pretty. The attractions of the house are many, including the terrace leading into the garden planted with lavender and rosemary, hollyhocks and acanthus. Although the atmosphere is convivial, you nevertheless can be left on your own, but it would be a shame not to join in the activities here. Olga's friends, including journalists, directors, stage designers and actors, wouldn't dream of staying anywhere else during the Avignon Festival.

***How to get there*** *(Map 33): From Avignon towards île de la Barthelasse on D228 over the Daladier bridge (towards Nimes, Villeneuve-les-Avignons). Then towards church and 2nd on left after the church.*

## Les Géraniums

Place de la Croix
84330 Le Barroux (Vaucluse)
Tel. (0)4.90.62.41.08 - Fax (0)4.90.62.56.48 - M. and Mme Roux

**Category** ★★ **Rooms** 22 with telephone, bath or shower and WC. **Price** Single and double 240-270F. **Meals** Breakfast 38F, served 8:00-10:00; half board 240-260F, full board 320-340F (per pers., 3 days min.). **Restaurant** Service 12:00-14:00, 19:00-21:00; menus 90-250F, also à la carte. Specialties: Terrine de lapin à la sauge, foie gras au Muscat de Beame de Venise, lapin à la sarriette, parfait à la lavande. **Credit cards** All major. **Pets** Dogs allowed (+30F). **Facilities** Parking. **Nearby** Château de Barroux, Sainte-Madeleine Monastery, pharmacy museum at the Hôtel-Dieu in Carpentras, Mazan Gallo-Roman cemetery, dentelles de Montmirail – 18-hole Le Grand Avignon golf course. **Open** Mar – Dec.

Le Barroux is a village set high on a hill between the Ventoux and the jagged peaks of Montmirail, commanding stunning views of the whole Avignon area. The place has a charm of its own, and this small hotel provides pleasantly comfortable accommodation. It also serves as that typical French institution, the *café de la place*, thus offering first-hand insight into local village life. The bedrooms are simple but pleasant and have recently been improved. The nicest have a small terrace. The menu features good local dishes based on fresh products and is likely to include game in season. Meals can be served on the terrace or in the dining room.

***How to get there*** *(Map 33): 9km from Carpentras via D938; between Carpentras and Malaucène.*

# Château de Rocher-La Belle Ecluse

42, rue Emile Lachaux
84500 Bollène (Vaucluse)
Tel. (0)4.90.40.09.09 - Fax (0)4.90.40.09.30 - M. Carloni

**Category** ★★★ **Rooms** 19 with telephone, bath or shower, WC and TV. **Price** Single and double 220-370F. **Meals** Breakfast 45-55F, served 7:30-10:00; half board and full board 280-400F, 360-480F (per pers., 3 days min.). **Restaurant** Service from 12:00 and 19:00; menus 100F (lunchtime)-150-250F; also à la carte. Specialties: Duo de foie gras mi cuit et poëllé, filet de bœuf aux truffes, nougat glacé au miel de lavande. **Credit cards** All major. **Pets** Dogs allowed (+30F). **Facilities** Parking. **Nearby** Arc de triomphe and old theatre in Orange, Henri Fabre museum in Sérignan – 18-hole Grand Avignon golf course. **Open** All year.

Built in 1826 for Count Joseph Maurice de Rocher, this beautiful aristocratic mansion was decorated by Florentine artists. It stands on the edge of a large 10-acre park inhabited by domestic animals and some wild species, and culminates in a magnificent semi-circle of trees in front of the entrance. The bedrooms, many large, are bright and comfortable. Their decoration combines classic with retro styles, and some original touches such as Room 8, which is located in a chapel illuminated by stained-glass windows. The elegant cuisine can be served outside on the terrace, in summer, or in the Richelieu dining room, which has a painted wooden ceiling, a beautiful carved stone chimney and a portrait of the famous Cardinal above the mantel.

***How to get there*** *(Map 33): 25km from Orange via A9, Bollène exit, towards town center then towards Gap, Nyons road.*

# Bastide de Capelongue

84480 Bonnieux (Vaucluse)
Tel. (0)4.90.75.89.78 - Fax (0)4.90.75.93.03
Mme Loubet

**Rooms** 17 with telephone, bath, WC, satellite TV and minibar. **Price** Single and double 500-700F, 700-1400F; suite 1200-1800F. **Meals** Breakfast 85F, served 7:30-11:00; half board and full board 700-1000F, 950-1250F (per pers., 2 days min.). **Restaurant** Service 12:15-14:00, 19:00-22:00; menus 180-250F, also à la carte. **Credit cards** All major. **Pets** Dogs allowed (+90 F). **Facilities** Swimming pool, parking and garage. **Nearby** Avignon, Aix-en-Provence, Les Alpilles, villages of the Luberon - 18-hole Pont Royal golf course. **Open** Mid. Mar – mid. Nov.

From its hilltop scattered with shrubs and lavender, the Bastide enjoys a magnificent view over the old village of Bonnieux. Recently opened to the public, it is a mansion belonging to the Loubet family, who also own the Moulin de Lourmarin, one of the great restaurants of the region. The interior decoration highlights half-tones of pale grey, pastel blue, terra-cotta ochre, while beautifully patinated Provençal furniture--lovely remakes of 18th-century wardrobes, tables, and chairs--can be admired throughout the hotel. The overall effect is one of soft, serene refinement. Each bedroom is named after a character from the novels of Daudet or Giono; we loved their contemporary comfort and, here too, their delicate shades and materials. Served in a luminous dining room or on the terrace, the menus change daily depending on the vegetables from the hotel's 2 1/2-acre garden, and the meat, fish, and poultry on offer in the market. The Bastide is luxurious but worth it.

***How to get there*** *(Map 33): A7 Cavaillon exit; towards Apt, then D36 Bonnieux.*

## Hostellerie du Prieuré

84480 Bonnieux (Vaucluse)
Tel. (0)4.90.75.80.78 - Fax (0)4.90.75.96.00
Mme Coutaz and M. Chapotin

**Category** ★★★ **Rooms** 10 with telephone, bath, WC and TV. **Price** Single 350F, double 498-640F. **Meals** Breakfast 48F, served 8:00-10:00. **Restaurant** Service 12:30-14:00, 19:30-21:00 (closed Wednesday and Thursday noon and Tuesday noon in summer); menu 198F, also à la carte 120F. Specialties: Fleurs de cougette farci à la mousse de saint-jacques, chartreuse d'agneau aux aubergines, fondant au chocolat. **Credit cards** Visa, Eurocard and MasterCard. **Pets** Dogs allowed (extra charge). **Facilities** Parking, garage (40F). **Nearby** Avignon, Aix-en-Provence, Lubéron villages – 18-hole Saumane golf course. **Open** Mar 1 – Nov 4.

Spared the gentrification that is slowly taking over the hotels of the Luberon, the Hostellerie du Prieuré has retained the charm of the old residences of the past. The grand stairway and its wrought-iron railing, the traditional red floor tiles, and the heavy oak doors evoke memories of the past which will delight those who love beautiful old architecture. We also like the comfortable bedrooms, many with antique furnishings, and their warm colors. The sizes of the rooms, their expositions (the darkest rooms are marvelously cool in summer, yet more somber in winter), and their furnishings are all different. In the spring and summer, the bar service and the dining tables are transported to the leafy garden but we are just as fond of the interior bar and dining room (the bar, in particular, has a highly interesting showcase with old layouts of the main Paris theatres). If you decide one evening to go out for dinner, *Le Fournil* serves delicate cuisine on the terrace; and *Le Berger* in Sivergues attracts the fashionable Luberon crowd in an informal setting.

***How to get there** (Map 33): On A7, exit Cavaillon, go towards Apt, then D36 to Bonnieux.*

## Relais de la Rivière

RD 943 - 84480 Bonnieux (Vaucluse)
Tel. (0)4.90.04.47.00 - Fax (0)4.90.04.47.01
M. and Mme Clavert

**Category** ★★★ **Rooms** 12 with telephone, bath, 9 with WC, TV on request. **Price** Single and double 600-660F, suite (3-4 pers.) 800-920F **Meals** Breakfast 55F, served 8:00-11:30; half board and full board 475-720F, 500-550F (per pers., 3 days min.). **Restaurant** Service 12:00-14:00, 19:30-22:00 (closed Tuesday except in summer); menu-carte 170F. Specialties : Truffe and regional cooking. **Credit cards** Visa, Eurocard and MasterCard. **Pets** Dogs allowed (in some rooms). **Facilities** Swimming pool and parking. **Nearby** Le pont Coquille in the domain, Luberon, Avignon, Aix-en-Provence; La Roque-d'Antéron Festival, market in Apt (Satuday) - 18-hole Saumane golf course. **Open** Mar 2 – Jan 14.

Lined with a few poplars, the lovely road leading to the Relais de la Rivière runs through several small villages in Lourmarin's narrow valley, the only breach cutting through the Luberon Massif. A few church spires tell you that you're getting close as you descend to the edge of the Aigue Brun River and this magnificent site. The Relais has been redesigned by Agnès Varda, whose more open layout has emphasized the presence of the river, its cool water and its peaceful murmur. The lounge walls are covered in Napoléon III-style red fabric, the bedrooms are comfortable without excessive decor, with home-like appointments such as big, old-fashioned wardrobes, Anglo-Indian furniture, and attractive rattan pieces. If you're a family, ask for the pretty cottage. The restaurant offers *à la carte* and fixed-price menus, with gourmet specialties and homemade pastries, also served in the afternoon in the tea room.

***How to get there*** *(Map 33): On A7, exit Cavaillon; take to. Apt, then D36, to Bonnieux. 6km from Bonnieux towards Lourmarin.*

# Hostellerie de Crillon-le-Brave

Place de l'église
84410 Crillon-le-Brave (Vaucluse)
Tel. (0)4.90.65.61.61 - Fax (0)4.90.65.62.86 - M. Chittick

**Category** ★★★★ **Rooms** 19 and 4 suites (2 suites and 1 room with air-conditioning) with telephone, bath or shower, WC and TV on request. **Price** Single and double 890-1650F, suite 1450-2500F. **Meals** Breakfast 80F, served 7:30-11:00; half board +295F (per pers., 3 days min.). **Restaurant** Open just for the weekend lunchtime. Service 12:00-14:30 (grills on the swimming pool in summer with service 19:30-21:30); menus 250-340F, also à la carte. **Credit cards** Amex, Visa, Eurocard and MasterCard. **Pets** Dogs allowed (+80F). **Facilities** Swimming pool, bike, garage. **Nearby** Bédoin, dentelles de Montmirail, chapel of Le Grozeau, château du Barroux, pharmacy museum at Hôtel-Dieu in Carpentras – 18-hole Grand Avignon golf course. **Open** Apr – Dec.

Just next to the church stands this beautiful hotel: formerly a large family house, its bedrooms are still named after the former occupants. The building still has its worn flagstone floors and is tastefully decorated with terracotta objects and Provençal antiques found at nearby Isle-sur-la-Sorgue. The bedrooms are extremely comfortable and cozy, and their yellow-ochre walls evoke the Midi sun. The two lounges contain shelves loaded with old books, comfortable sofas and windows looking over the pink rooftops of the village. A terraced garden, with pretty wrought-iron furniture in its many shady corners, leads down from a waterlily pond to the swimming-pool, where a grill has been set up.

***How to get there*** *(Map 33): 15km north of Carpentras via D974 and D138.*

## Hostellerie La Manescale

Route de Faucon
Les Essareaux - 84340 Entrechaux (Vaucluse)
Tel. (0)4.90.46.03.80 - Fax (0)4.90.46.03.89 - Mme Warland

**Rooms** 5 with telephone, bath or shower, WC, TV and minibar. **Price** Double 450-650F, suite 950F **Meals** Breakfast 75F, served 8:30-10:00; half board 450-690F (per pers., 2 days min). **Restaurant** For residents only. Service at 19:30 (closed Monday and Thursday evening). Specialties: Cooking with fresh local produce. **Credit cards** All major. **Pets** Dogs allowed (+60F). **Facilities** Swimming pool, parking. **Nearby** Cathedral of Notre-Dame-de-Nazareth in Vaison-la-Romaine, dentelles de Montmirail, Séguret – 18-hole Grand Avignon golf course. **Open** Easter – Oct.

Formerly a shepherd's house and now carefully rebuilt and restored, this pleasant inn stands among vineyards and olive trees between the Drôme and the Vaucluse, facing Mont Ventoux. The bedrooms are luxuriously equipped and tastefully decorated, providing every thoughtful detail. Some of them are small suites (the Provence room, for instance). The pleasure of a hearty breakfast on the terrace is enhanced by the magical scenery: a peaceful valley, crowned by the Ventoux, displaying a subtle and ever-changing palette of colors and light. Hotel facilities also include a superb swimming pool. This is a place one would like to keep to oneself, but enthusiastic readers' letters have made sharing the secret a pleasure. In the evening, you can enjoy a good cold dinner, or you can go out to the *Saint-Hubert* or *Chez Anaïs* in Entrechaux. Note that only children over seven can stay in the hotel.

***How to get there*** *(Map 33): 8km east of Vaison-la-Romaine via D205. From A7, take Bollène exit.*

## Les Florets

Route des Dentelles
84190 Gigondas (Vaucluse)
Tel. (0)4.90.65.85.01 - Fax (0)4.90.65.83.80 - Mme Bernard

**Category** ★★ **Rooms** 13 with telephone, bath or shower, WC and TV. **Price** Double 350-410F. **Meals** Breakfast 52F, served 8:00-10:00; half board 800F (2 pers., 3 days min.). **Restaurant** Service 12:00-14:00, 19:30-21:00; menus 95-220F, also à la carte. Specialties: Méli mélo de lot et de saumon à l'oseille, filet de rougets sur gateau de brandade provençale, crème brûlée aux senteurs de puneau. **Credit cards** All major. **Pets** Dogs allowed (+40F). **Facilities** Parking. **Nearby** Chapel of Notre-Dame-d'Aubune, Séguret, dentelles de Montmirail, cathedral and Roman bridge in Vaison-la-Romaine – 18-hole Grand Avignon golf course. **Open** Mar – Dec (closed Wednesday).

Les Florets occupies an enviable position in the middle of the countryside at an altitude of 1200 feet facing the peaks of Montmirail and overlooking the Gigondas vineyards. This is a simple country hotel, traditional in style, with a pleasant family atmosphere. The jagged peaks above can be viewed from the terrace, where an arbor provides welcome shade. The bedrooms are simple and unpretentious, but comfortable enough and have a view of the trees. We recommend the new and very charming bedrooms in the annex. Each opens directly onto the garden. The furniture is tasteful and the rooms and baths have modern conveniences. The restaurant serves regional specialties accompanied by local Gigondas wines. The staff are very friendly and the owner will be happy to show you his cellars and have you taste his wines.

***How to get there*** *(Map 33): 25km east of Orange via D975 towards Vaison-la-Romaine, then D8 and D80; on the Dentelles de Montmirail road.*

1998

## Hostellerie Le Phébus

Route de Murs
Joucas 84220 Gordes (Vaucluse)
Tel. (0)4.90.05.78.83 - Fax (0)4.90.05.73.61 - M. Mathieu

**Category** ★★★★ **Rooms** 17 (and 5 apartments with privated swimming pool) with air-conditioning, telephone, bath, shower, WC, TV and minibar 3 for disabled persons. **Price** Single and double 605F, 890F, 1080F, apart. 1395F. **Meals** Breakfast 85F, served 8:00-11:00; half board 680-795F (per pers.). **Restaurant** Service 12:00-13:30, 19:30-21:30; menus 160-290F, also à la carte. Specialties: Escabèche de caille, salade tiède au homard, jus de carottes au miel, parmentier d'agneau aux aubergines, turbot rôti aux épices. **Credit cards** Amex, Visa, Eurocard and MasterCard. **Pets** Dogs allowed (extra charge). **Facilities** Swimming pool, parking. **Nearby** Les Bories, abbey of Sénanque, Roussillon, Isle-sur-la-Sorgue, Fontaine de Vaucluse - 18-hole Saumane golf course. **Open** Mid. Mar – mid. Oct.

A location in the heart of the garrigue, beautifully decorated bedrooms with cheerful, typically Provençal furniture in the height of taste, private terraces (some have a small swimming pool for you alone!), a sure eye for comfort and detail: It all has a price, of course, but some things are just worth it. Let's not overlook the elegant lounge with antique furniture, the magnificent summer dining room whose colonnaded loggia with balustrades overlooks the blue water of the big swimming pool, the view over the Luberon....You can see why this luxurious establishment has been added to this Guide, although many of our other choices are quite simple. The cuisine is mouthwatering, the least expensive set-price meal offering excellent dishes.

***How to get there*** *(Map 33): 25km northeast of Cavaillon via D2, then to Joucas.*

1998

## Le Mas du Loriot

Route de Joucas
Murs 84220 Gordes (Vaucluse)
Tel. (0)4.90.72.62.62 - Fax (0)4.90.72.62.54 - Mme Thillard

**Rooms** 6 with telephone, bath or shower, WC, TV and minibar - Wheelchair access. **Price** Single and double 500-550F, 1 room 270F. **Meals** Breakfast 70F, served 8:30-10:30; half board 498F (per pers., in double, obligatory in summer). **Restaurant** Service from 20:00; menu 180F. Specialties: Filet de bœuf à l'anchoïade, lotte aux petits légumes, pavé de cabillaud à l'huile d'olive et tapenade, grenadins de veau aux amandes. **Credit cards** Visa, Eurocard and MasterCard. **Pets** Dogs allowed (+50F). **Facilities** Swimming pool and parking. **Nearby** Les Bories, abbey of Sénanque, Roussillon, Isle-sur-la-Sorgue, Fontaine de Vaucluse - 18-hole Saumane golf course. **Open** Mar 6 – 18 Dec and Dec 27 – Feb 7.

The small road winds around Joucas, begins to climb the slope and a few hundred feet farther up, a lane leads into the garrigue and to this minuscule hotel surrounded by lavender, pine trees, and green oaks. Six recently installed bedrooms offer modern amenities, a private terrace for each, charming decoration in cool colors, and a magnificent view: perfect for those who love an intimate, quiet place to stay. The restaurant has a single menu, different every evening. Lovingly prepared by Madame Thillard, it's good family cooking, made with fresh farm products; you will be served in a dining room with elegant wrought-iron furniture, or on the terrace overlooking the Luberon. The welcome extended by Monsieur and Madame Thillard and their young children, Julien and Sophie-Charlotte, made us want to return. Soon.

***How to get there*** *(Map 33): 25km northeast of Cavaillon via D2, then towards Joucas, then Murs.*

## Ferme de la Huppe

Route D 156
Les Pourquiers - 84220 Gordes (Vaucluse)
Tel. (0)4.90.72.12.25 - Fax (0)4.90.72.01.83 - Mme Konings

**Rooms** 8 (4 with air-conditioning) with telephone, bath, shower, WC, TV and minibar. **Price** Single 400F, double 700F **Meals** Breakfast incl., served 8:30-10:00. **Restaurant** Open the night and Saturday noon, closed Thusday. Service 12:00-13:30, 19:30-21:00; menus 150-200F, also à la carte. Specialties: Seasonal cooking. **Credit cards** Visa, Eurocard and MasterCard. **Pets** Dogs not allowed. **Facilities** Swimming pool, parking. **Nearby** Les Bories, Sénanque abbey, Roussillon, l'Isle-sur-la-Sorgue, Fontaine de Vaucluse – 18-hole Saumane golf course. **Open** Apr 1 – Nov 7.

The small road winding across the Luberon plain gradually turns into a track, leading to this beautifully restored, extremely secluded old farmhouse. Everything revolves around the fig tree, the olive trees and the well in the middle of a small inner courtyard. It gives access to the six delightful bedrooms named after the old parts of the building: *La cuisine, L'écurie, La cuve...* the kitchen, the stables, and the wine vat. Their terracotta floors, thick walls and typically small windows ensure both privacy and coolness. They are decorated with old objects and elegant fabrics, and all are very comfortable. A covered patio adjoining the dining room looks onto a beautiful swimming pool screened by flowers and lavender. Young chef Gérald Konings' inspired cuisine is fast gaining him a reputation. The Ferme offers an excellent reputation in this region of high gastronomic standards. Last but not least, the hospitality is charming and the prices are still very reasonable.

***How to get there*** *(Map 33): 25km northeast of Cavaillon to Gordes via D2; then toward Joucas for 2.5km, then right toward Goult for 500 meters.*

## Hôtel Les Romarins

Route de Sénanque
84220 Gordes (Vaucluse)
Tel. (0)4.90.72.12.13 - Fax (0)4.90.72.13.13 - Mme Charles

**Category** ★★★ **Rooms** 10 with telephone, bath or shower, WC, TV (8 with minibar). **Price** Single and double 450-750F. **Meals** Breakfast 53F, served 8:00-10:00. No restaurant. **Credit cards** Amex, Visa, Eurocard and MasterCard. **Pets** Dogs not allowed. **Facilities** Swimming pool, parking. **Nearby** Les Bories, Sénanque abbey, Roussillon, l'Isle-sur-la-Sorgue, Fontaine de Vaucluse – 18-hole Saumane golf course. **Open** Feb 16 – Jan 14.

This 200-year-old house has just been fully refurbished and turned into a hotel; it is the only establishment in Gordes commanding a view of the old village more houses. That is a beautiful asset indeed if you delight, as we do, in that breathtaking assemblage of ancient walls, terraced gardens and cypresses. Most of the bedrooms have this view, but make sure when you reserve. They are neat and comfortable, and simply and elegantly decorated in either Directoire or contemporary style. The delicious breakfast – with the view of Gordes – can be served in a small, bright dining-room, or outside in the shade of an ancient mulberry tree. The atmosphere is friendly and informal (all the more so because of the a talking parrot on the staff!). The bird, however, is not in sole charge, and M. and Mme Charles extend an urbane and congenial welcome. There is no restaurant but those previously mentioned for Gordes will delight you. Don't forget *Le Mas Tourteron* on the Imberts road.

***How to get there*** *(Map 33): 25km northeast of Cavaillon via D2.*

# Mas de Cure Bourse

Carrefour de Velorgues
84800 Isle-sur-la-Sorgue (Vaucluse)
Tel. (0)4.90.38.16.58 - Fax (0)4.90.38.52.31 - M. and Mme Donzé

**Category** ★★★ **Rooms** 13 with telephone, bath, WC and TV. **Price** Single 290-500F, double 320-550F **Meals** Breakfast 45F; half board 400-470F **Restaurant** Service 12:00-13:30, 20:00-21:30 (closed 3 weeks in Oct and 2 weeks in Jan, Monday and Tuesday noon); menu 165-260F, also à la carte. Specialties: Fleurs de courgettes farcies aux champignons, barigoule de lapin, croustillant de rougets à l'huile d'olive, petits chèvres pané aux noisettes, gâteau aux poires et caramel. **Credit cards** Visa, Eurocard and MasterCard. **Pets** Dogs allowed (+30F). **Facilities** Swimming pool, parking. **Nearby** l'Isle-sur-Sorgue, flea market and Provençal market on Sunday, Fontaine de Vaucluse, Gordes, les Bories, abbey of Sénanque – 18-hole Saumane golf course. **Open** All year.

The Mas de Cure Bourse is a former postal relay station which was built in 1754 in the plain of Isle-sur-la-Sorgue and you'll probably have the impression of getting lost in a labyrinth of tiny roads before reaching the *mas*. It is in this very charming old Provençal *mas*, surrounded by orchards and a 5-acre park, that M. and Mme Donzé receive their visitors. Françoise Donzé is a renowned chef and will make outstanding meals of succulent regional specialties. You will be served in the pretty dining room in front of a large fireplace or on the shady terrace. Through the large glassed-in opening between the reception area and the kitchen, you can even watch the chef and her helpers at work. The decoration and the modern amenities in the bedrooms are impeccable. We prefer *La Chambre du Bout,* the Room at the End, with its small balcony and view over the swimming pool.

***How to get there*** *(Map 33): On A7, exit Avignon-sud or Cavaillon. 3km from Isle-sur-la-Sorgue, on D938, road from Carpentras to Cavaillon, Velorgues cross road.*

1998

# Domaine de la Fontaine

920, chemin du Bosquet
84800 Isle-sur-la-Sorgue (Vaucluse)
Tel. (0)4.90.38.01.44 - Fax (0)4.90.38.53.42 - M. and Mme Sundheimer

**Rooms** 3 and 2 suites with telephone, shower, WC and TV. **Price** Single and double 410-450F, 450-490F; suite 680F. **Meals** Breakfast incl. **Restaurant** For resident only by reservation. service 20:00; menu 130F. Specialties: Lotte à la provençale, lapin aux pruneaux, magret de canette. **Credit cards** Not accepted. **Pets** Dogs not allowed. **Facilities** Swimming pool and parking. **Nearby** l'Isle-sur-Sorgue, flea market and Provençal market on Sunday, Fontaine de Vaucluse, Gordes, les Bories, abbey of Sénanque; Avignon; Le Luberon - 18-hole Saumane golf course. **Open** All year except in Jan and Feb.

Once directors of two restaurants in Munich, Irmy and Dominique Sundheimer fell in love with this old Provençal *mas* and the surrounding countryside. Just minutes from Isle-sur-la-Sorgue, the Domaine de la Fontaine is surrounded by an immense cultivated plain criss-crossed by hedgerows for protection from the strong *mistral* wind. As the Domaine has few rooms and is so quiet and intimate, it's like a cross between a small hotel and a bed and breakfast. The bedrooms have been entirely renovated, each with its predominant color, simple, pleasant furnishings, lovely beds and bedding, and huge bathrooms. Dinners consist of a single menu, which varies with the market and Irmy's inspiration. The dining tables are set up in the spacious dining room (its decoration still lacks warmth and patina) or on the terrace beneath the shade of three century-old plane trees. Breakfast is also served there, and we enjoyed lingering over our coffee while listening to the murmur of the fountain for which the Domaine is named.

***How to get there*** *(Map 33): A7, Avignon-sud or Cavaillon exit. In the town, take the road N100 to Apt, after "Citroën/Total" garage on the right and first on the left.*

## Le Mas des Grès

Route d'Apt
84800 Lagnes (Vaucluse)
Tel. (0)4.90.20.32.85 - Fax (0)4.90.20.21.45 - M. and Mme Crovara

**Category** ★★ **Rooms** 14 with telephone, bath, WC and 6 with TV. **Price** Single and double 390-600F, suite (4 pers.) 1000F. **Meals** Breakfast 60F, served 8:00-11:00; half board +200F (per pers.). **Restaurant** Residents only. Menu 140F. Specialties: Provençal cooking. **Credit cards** Visa, Eurocard and MasterCard. **Pets** Dogs not allowed. **Facilities** Swimming pool, parking. **Nearby** Isle-sur-la-Sorgue, Fontaine de Vaucluse, Gordes, les Bories, Sénanque abbey – 18-hole Saumane golf course. **Open** Mar 15 – Nov 15, except on reservation.

Habitués of the Mas des Grès will regret the departure of Jacques and Doune Lhermitte, but let them be reassured. Extremely anxious to preserve the charm and spirit of the hotel beloved by so many of their guests, the Lhermittes were very careful in choosing new owners. Under the Crovaras' management, the hotel is still beautiful, everything cheerful and in good taste. It's a lovely place, a hotel that is the contrary of a hotel, more like a vacation home filled with laughter and *joie de vivre*. The lounge and the bedrooms are elegantly simple, as charming as the guest room you'd find in a friend's house; and some also have a most practical advantage: Room 8 and two adjoining rooms can accommodate an entire family, and Room 6 is perfect for children. In the evening, the restaurant, reserved for residents, offers seasonal Provençal cuisine, which you can enjoy outside beneath an arbor; in July and August, a small buffet is served at lunch. Surrounded by orchards, the Mas des Grès is your home away from home in the Luberon.

***How to get there*** *(Map 33): On A7, take Avignon exit toward l'Isle-sur-la-Sorgue, then toward Apt via N100 for 5km.*

## Auberge La Fenière

Route de Cadenet
84160 Lourmarin (Vaucluse)
Tel. (0)4.90.68.11.79 - Fax (0)4.90.68.18.60 - Mme Reine Sammut

**Rooms** 7 (6 with air-conditioning) with telephone, bath or shower, WC and TV - 1 for disabled persons. **Price** Single and double 500-700F, 550-750F; suite 950F. **Meals** Breakfast 80F, served at any time. **Restaurant** Service 12:30-13:30, 19:00-21:30 (closed Monday lunchtime in high season, Monday in low season); menus 190-490F. Specialties: Saint-pierre à la vanille et huile d'olive de Cucuron, loup rôti à la peau au pistou de légumes verts et moelle panée. **Credit cards** All major. **Pets** Dogs allowed (+40F). **Facilities** Swimming pool and parking. **Nearby** Le Luberon, Aix-en-Provence, La Roque d'Anthéron (Piano Festival in Aug), Marcket in Apt (Saturday) - 18-hole Pont Royal golf course in Mallemout. **Open** All year except in Jan.

Reine Sammut needs no introduction in France: She is famed as one of the country's leading women chefs and the name "La Fenière" will surely bring back mouth-watering memories for many a gourmet. Today, the restaurant has moved from the center of Lourmarin and opened very nearby in the heart of the countryside. Taking advantage of the move and greater space, Madame Sammmut has opened seven bedrooms with all the amenities, each dedicated to an art or a craft. Designed to reflect their name, the rooms are fashionable, warm, and original in décor. Five rooms also have a pleasant terrace: they're our favorites. On the ground floor, the reception lounge has a somewhat colonial atmosphere with its tables and small armchairs in exotic wood, while the large, more modern dining room adjacent to it is the soul of Provençal *joie de vivre* with its high, bright-red chairs and its stunning, rainbow-colored plates. The newly planted gardens outside are as carefully tended as Reine Sammut's *grande cuisine.*

***How to get there*** *(Map 33): 30km northeast of Aix-en-Provence; A7, Sénas exit, sur A51 Pertuis exit.*

## Auberge Les Engarouines

Quartier Engarouines
84570 Malemort-du-Comtat (Vaucluse)
Tel. (0)4.90.69.92.25 - M. Cuyt

**Category** ★★ **Rooms** 4 with bath or shower and WC. **Price** Double 375-435F. **Meals** Breakfast 55F, served 8:00-9:30; half board 360-405F, obligatory in summer, (per pers., 3 days min.). **Restaurant** By reservation only. Service 19:30-20:30 (closed Thusday evening); menu 150F. Specialties: Market products. **Credit cards** Not accepted (Eurochèque and Traveller chek). **Pets** Dogs not allowed. **Facilities** Swimming pool and parking. **Nearby** Venasque, Mazan Gallo-Roman cemetery, Pernes-les-Fontaines, Carpentras, Mont Ventoux, laces of Montmirail, Gordes, Fontaine du Vaucluse - 18-hole Saumane golf course, 18-hole Pont-Royal golf course. **Open** Apr – mid. Nov Closed Tuesday afternoon and evening in July and Aug.

It's true that this minuscule hotel is of recent construction and it could do with the patina of years, but how could we resist this garden overflowing with flowers, surrounded by vineyards and Mediterranean vegetation? Four small bedrooms, no more and no less, await you at Les Engarouines. They are smartly kept, discreetly decorated and each has its own terrace, separated from its neighbor by a hedge of pink oleander. We also loved the small dining room, charmingly decorated *à la Provençale,* sunny and cheerful, where you will be served the chef's delicious daily menu, finely seasoned and washed down with regional wines. There are several tables outside where you can enjoy breakfast or a drink near an adorable swimming pool surrounded by lavender and aromatic cypress. The prices are reasonable for a region where they are sometimes exaggerated.

***How to get there*** *(Map 33): On A7, exit Avignon-Nord, to Carpentras, then D5 towards Methamis.*

## Mas des Capelans

84580 Oppède (Vaucluse)
Tel. (0)4.90.76.99.04 - Fax (0)4.90.76.90.29
Poiri Family

**Rooms** 8 with telephone, bath, WC and TV. **Price** Double 400-900F, suite 600-1000F. **Meals** Breakfast 55F, served 8:30-10:30; half board 400-650F (per pers., 3 days min.). **Restaurant** Evening meals. Service at 20:00 (closed Sunday and Monday); menu 155F. Specialties: Lapereau au romarin, navarin aux petits légumes, pintade aux cerises. **Credit cards** All major. **Pets** Dogs allowed on request (+70F). **Facilities** Heated swimming pool, billiards, parking. **Nearby** The north of Luberon (Ménerbes, Lacoste, Bonnieux, Saint-Symphorien priory, Buoux, Saignon, Apt) – 18-hole Saumane golf course. **Open** Feb 15 – Nov 15.

The Mas des Capelans once belonged to the monks of the abbey of Sénanque, who used the building to breed silkworms. The guest bedrooms are large and very comfortable, and have been carefully decorated. Each one is named after the view it commands – *Roussillon, Gordes* – or simply after the vineyard it overlooks, like some of the ground-floor rooms (which have private entrances). The living room, dominated by high roof beams, is decorated with comfortable furniture. The surroundings are pleasant, and dinner in the courtyard beneath the mulberry-trees and acacias is one of the highlights of a stay.

***How to get there*** *(Map 33): 10km east of Cavaillon. Via A7, exit Avignon-Sud, toward Apt, N100 between Coustellet and Beaumette, then follow signs.*

# Hôtel Arène

Place de Langes
84100 Orange (Vaucluse)
Tel. (0)4.90.34.10.95 - Fax (0)4.90.34.91.62 - M. and Mme Coutel

**Category** ★★★ **Rooms** 30 with air-conditioning, telephone, bath or shower, WC, minibar, safe and TV. **Price** Single and double 340-500F. **Meals** Breakfast 44F, served 7:00-12:00. No restaurant. **Credit cards** All major. **Pets** Dogs allowed. **Facilities** Garage. **Nearby** Old theater and Arc de Triomphe in Orange, Mornas, Henri Fabre museum in Sérignan, gorges of Ardèche, Vaison-la-Romaine – 18-hole Grand Avignon golf course. **Open** Dec 1 – Nov 7.

Ideally located close to the Roman Theatre in a small pedestrian square shaded by hundred-year old plane trees, the Arène is the most sought-after hotel in town. M. and Mme Coutel devote lavish amounts of care to their guests' well-being and are constantly refurbishing the hotel. The bedrooms, all different, very comfortable and cheerful, though some are a little dark. There is no restaurant, but there is a pleasant lounge with a large fireplace and period furniture. Guests very much enjoy the hospitality of the hotel, where it is necessary to reserve well ahead, especially during the Festival.*Le Parvis* and *Au Goût du Jour* are good restaurants in Orange.

***How to get there*** *(Map 33): In the old town center.*

# Auberge de L'Orangerie

4, rue de L'Ormeau
84420 Piolenc (Vaucluse)
Tel. (0)4.90.29.59.88 - Fax (0)4.90.29.67.74 - Mme de la Rocque

**Rooms** 5 with bath or shower and WC. **Price** Single 190-300F, double 190-380F. **Meals** Breakfast 45F, served from 8:30; half board 285-485F (obligatory in summer), full board 355F. **Restaurant** Service 12:00-14:00, 19:30-21:30; menus 90-200F. Specialties: Foie gras, crabe farci, ossobuco de langouste, zarzuela, magret aux airelles. **Credit cards** Visa, Eurocard and MasterCard. **Pets** Dogs allowed (+40F). **Facilities** Parking. **Nearby** Henri Fabre museum in Sérignan, old theatre and Arc de Triomphe of Orange, Chorégies of Orange in July and August, Mornas – 18-hole Moulin golf course. **Open** All year.

Vegetation has overrun the inner courtyard of this hotel, where everything is decidedly entangled (in the best sense of the word.) Set back on a small road in Piolenc just six kilometers from Orange, L'Orangerie is a quiet hotel which was originally just a restaurant. Meals are served in a beautiful barrel-vaulted dining room with huge French windows, the tables spilling over outside and making for lovely cool summer dinners beneath a canopy of flowers and climbing plants. The entire hotel has been decorated as if it were a private home. An amateur artist, Monsieur de la Rocque executes strikingly faithful reproductions of chiaroscuro paintings by Georges de la Tour, which you can see hanging in the hotel. The bedrooms, with antique objects and some with Louis-Philippe furniture, have an endearing provincial charm; one even has a terrace-solarium. The cuisine is delicious, the wine list—especially the Bordeaux selections—extraordinary, the hospitality friendly, and the prices are very reasonable.

***How to get there*** *(Map 33): 6km north of Orange. Via A7, exit Orange (or Bollène if you're coming from Lyon); N7 dir. Bollène.*

## Auberge de Cassagne

450, allée de Cassagne
84130 Le Pontet - Avignon (Vaucluse)
Tel. (0)4.90.31.04.18 - Fax (0)4.90.32.25.09 - MM. Gallon, Boucher, Trestour
Web: http://www.hotels.fr/cassagne - E-mail: cassagne@adi.fr

**Category** ★★★★ **Rooms** 25 and 5 apartments with air-conditioning, telephone, bath, WC, satellite TV, safe and minibar. **Price** Single 420-490F, double 490-1380F, suite 1380-1780F. **Meals** Breakfast 95F, served 7:30-10:30; half board 710-1155F, full board 900-1345F (per pers.). **Restaurant** Service 12:00-13:30, 19:30-21:30; menus 230-460F, also à la carte. Specialties: Terrine provençale au coeur de foie gras, filets de rouget au citron vert, émincé d'agneau et côtelettes de lapereau panées aux petits légumes farcis. **Credit cards** All major. **Pets** Dogs allowed (+60F). **Facilities** Tennis, parking (+20F). **Nearby** Palace of the Popes, Campana collection at the Petit Palais and Calvet museum in Avignon, Avignon festival in July, Villeneuve-les-Avignon – 18-hole Grand Avignon golf course, 18-hole Châteaublanc golf course in Avignon. **Open** All year.

You will find the beautiful Auberge de Cassagne nestling in an oasis of greenery where there isn't a trace of the outskirts of Avignon. The reception and service are perfectly complemented by the staff's professionalism and human touch. Most of the bedrooms are located in a group of Provençal-style buildings around or near the swimming pool, buried in vegetation and flowers. They enjoy extensive modern amenities, attractive interior decoration, and immaculate bathrooms. Philippe Boucher, who trained with Paul Bocuse and Georges Blanc, prepares renowned cuisine (one Michelin star), and the beautiful wine cellar is in the hands of André Trestour. Lunch and dinner are thus special moments, made even more enjoyable in summer by service in the shade of a gigantic plane tree.

***How to get there*** *(Map 33): 5km east of Avignon via A7, Avignon-Nord exit, then 5 mins. and left on small road before the traffic lights.*

## Mas de Garrigon

Route de Saint-Saturnin
84220 Roussillon (Vaucluse)
Tel. (0)4.90.05.63.22 - Fax (0)4.90.05.70.01 - Mme Christiane Druart

**Category** ★★★ **Rooms** 9 with telephone, bath, shower, WC, TV and minibar. **Price** Single and double 650-820F, suite1080F. **Meals** Breakfast 90F, served 7:30-10:30; half board 600-850F, full board 850-1050F (per pers.). **Restaurant** Service 12:00-14:00 (closed Monday and Tuesday noon); menus 145F (lunchtime, 190-340F, also à la carte. Specialties: Souris d'agneau à la rabasse, loup en barigoule d'artichauts, chocolat en folie. **Credit cards** All major. **Pets** Dogs not allowed. **Facilities** Swimming pool, parking. **Nearby** Gordes, les Bories, Sénanque abbey, Isle-sur-la-Sorgue, Luberon – 18-hole Saumane golf course. **Open** All year.

An attractive place to stay in all seasons, the Mas de Garrigon is a Provençal-style house built in 1978 and surrounded by luxuriant vegetation with the marvelous smell of Provence. Around the swimming pool, reserved exclusively for residents of the hotel, the chaises-longues are a veritable invitation to sit back and relax; you can also have lunch there. The comfortable lounge-library has the appeal of a private room with its objects, paintings, and its beautiful fireplace. All the bedrooms have been decorated with similar care, and we felt very much at home in them (each room has a private terrace facing due south, with a superb view over the ochre soil of Roussillon). Light cuisine is made with fresh produce from the local markets and prepared so as to enhance the innate taste of the ingredients. Roussillon is truly a jewel in the crown of the Luberon.

***How to get there*** *(Map 33): 48km east of Avignon via N100 towards Apt, then D2 towards Gordes and D102.*

## Auberge du Presbytère

Place de la Fontaine
Saignon - 84400 Apt (Vaucluse)
Tel. (0)4.90.74.11.50 - Fax (0)4.90.04.68.51 - M. and Mme Bernardi
Web: http://www.provence-luberon.com - E-mail: auberge.presbytere@provence-luberon.com

**Rooms** 10, 8 with bath and WC. **Price** Double 240-450F. **Meals** Breakfast 50F, served 8:30-10:00. **Restaurant** Service 12:30-13:30, 20:00-21:00; menu 160F. Specialties: Provençal cooking. **Credit cards** Amex, Visa, Eurocard and MasterCard. **Pets** Small dogs allowed on request. **Nearby** Saignon church, Luberon, Buoux, Saint-Symphorien priory, Bonnieux, Lacoste, Ménerbes, Oppède, Maubec, Robion – 18-hole Saumane golf course. **Open** All year except Nov 15 – 30 and 15 days in Jan (closed Wednesday).

When Monsieur and Madame Bernardi left Saint-Tropez, their idea was to open a bed-and-breakfast here in the heart of the Luberon. Things turned out differently, but the idea is the same: welcoming guests at their Auberge du Presbytère as if they were friends. The auberge is made up of three village houses which have been combined, creating a complex of rooms on charmingly different levels. The interior is furnished with antiques, as in a country house. The bedrooms are delightful. Two, which share a bathroom in the corridor, will interest travelers on a small budget. The restaurant offers two menus daily, with appetizing traditional and regional Provençal recipes.

***How to get there** (Map 33): 35km southeast of Apt; in the village.*

# Hostellerie du Val de Sault

Route de Saint-Trinit
84390 Sault (Vaucluse)
Tel. (0)4.90.64.01.41 - Fax (0)4.90.64.12.74

**Rooms** 11 with telephone, bath, WC, TV and minibar - 1 for disabled persons. **Price** Double 420-640F. **Meals** Breakfast 59F, served 8:15-10:00; half board 420-560F (per pers.). **Restaurant** Service 12:30-14:00, 19:30-21:00; menu-carte 123F (lunchtime)-217F, 480F (menu with truffles). Specialties: Agneau de Sault au vin de lavande et cassis. **Credit cards** Amex, Visa, Eurocard and MasterCard. **Pets** Dogs allowed. **Facilities** Swimming pool, tennis, fitness center and parking. **Nearby** Mazan, Venasque, Pernes-les-Fontaines, Comtat Venaissin: Carpentras, Crillon le-Brave, Bédoin, Chalet Reynard and Le Ventoux, Malaucène, Le Barroux, Caromb; Gordes, abbey of Sénanque, Vaison-la-Romaine. **Open** Mar 28 – Nov 6.

As you head up the mountain, you might find it hard to imagine that there is a hotel up there, lost in the midst of oak trees at an altitude of 2400 feet, and just above a superb valley speckled with blue as soon as the first lavender blossoms. Recently constructed, the buildings blend in perfectly with the spectacular site. One houses the spacious restaurant with a high, beamed ceiling, which opens out onto a beautiful terrace. Its reputed cuisine looks fine and creative: unfortunately, we were not able to taste it during our visit, but we are told that the *demi-pension,* half-board, is excellent. The bedrooms are located somewhat higher up, in the other building. They are very comfortable, with a lounge on a veranda extending onto a large private terrace with a view of the trees and the sunset; the decoration is simple and cheerful, somewhat reminiscent of that of a chalet (natural or streaked pine, carpets, colorful fabrics...). You will enjoy total quiet at the Val de Sault, and a most friendly welcome.

***How to get there*** *(Map 33): 50km east of Carpentras via D1, to Mazan and Sault.*

## Hostellerie du Vieux Château

Route de Sainte-Cécile
84830 Sérignan (Vaucluse)
Tel. (0)4.90.70.05.58 - Fax (0)4.90.70.05.62 - M. and Mme Truchot

**Rooms** 7 with telephone, bath, WC, TV and minibar - Wheelchair access. **Price** Double 300-800F. **Meals** Breakfast 50F, served 8:00-10:00 **Restaurant** Service 12:30-13:30, 19:30-21:00 (closed Sunday evening and Monday in low season); menus 150-190F, also à la carte. Specialties: Jambon persillé, foie gras au Beaume de Venise, canard aux cassis, agneau de la Drôme, truffé chocolat aux raisins au marc. **Credit cards** Amex, Visa, Eurocard and MasterCard. **Pets** Dogs allowed (+50F). **Facilities** Swimming pool, parking. **Nearby** Arc de triomphe and old theater in Orange, Chorégies of Orange in July and Augut, Mornas, Henri Fabre museum in Sérignan. **Open** All year except Dec 19 – 30, 1 week in Nov (closed Sunday evening and Monday in low season).

This was originally a farmhouse with a mill in the back whose only remaining trace is a canal which flows by the house. Today, the hotel is a large village house flanked by a small vegetable garden and a pleasant flower garden filled with fragrant lavender around the swimming pool. The owners run a very traditional hotel, with M. Truchot in the kitchen and his wife at the reception. The atmosphere is that of a quiet, family-style provincial auberge. The bedrooms are all individually decorated, with the decor occasionally overdone. Our favorite is number 6, with the poppies. In summer, meals are served in the shade of the beautiful plane trees in the garden, making for a very Provençal setting.

***How to get there*** *(Map 33): 7km northeast of Orange. Via A7, Orange-centre exit, (or Bollène if you are coming from Lyon), in the toward of Bollène and D976 in the toward of Sérignan.*

## Hostellerie Le Beffroi

Haute Ville - Rue de l'Evêché
84110 Vaison-la-Romaine (Vaucluse)
Tel. (0)4.90.36.04.71 - Fax (0)4.90.36.24.78 - M. Christiansen

**Category** ★★★ **Rooms** 22 with telephone, bath or shower, WC, TV and minibar. **Price** Single 330-460F, double 450-655F. **Meals** Breakfast 50F, served 7:30-9:45; half board 405-495F, full board 555-645F (per pers., 3 days min.). **Restaurant** Service 12:00-13:45 (except in weekday), 19:15-21:30 (closed Nov 1 – Apr 1); menus 98F (lunchtime), 195F, also à la carte. Specialties: Aïgo boulido, tourte au vert, gigot d'aubergine, daube d'agneau à l'Avignonnaise. **Credit cards** All major. **Pets** Dogs allowed (+35F). **Facilities** Swimming pool, minigolf, games, garage (40F). **Nearby** Arc de Triomphe and old theatre in Orange, Mornas, Henri Fabre museum in Sérignan. **Open** Dec 21 – Nov 9.

This hotel high up in the medieval part of Vaison consists of several mansions joined together. The buildings' character has been preserved with tiled floors, polished paneling, spiral staircases and beautiful antiques, paintings and curios. The bedrooms are all different; antique lovers will be especially taken by the quality of the period furniture. The lounges are also pleasantly furnished and have open fireplaces. A superb terrace garden offers a lovely view over the rooftops of Vaison. If you crave a heartier meal at lunch, Robert Bardot's *Le Moulin à Huile* is a delicious address.

***How to get there*** *(Map 33): 30km northeast of Orange via D975; at the top of the town.*

## Hostellerie La Grangette

Chemin Cambuisson
84740 Velleron (Vaucluse)
Tel. (0)4.90.20.00.77 - Fax (0)4.90.20.07.06 - Mme and M. Blanc-Brude

**Category** ★★★ **Rooms** 16 telephone, bath or shower, WC, TV on request. **Price** Double 550-950F, suite 1050F. **Meals** Breakfast 70F, served 8:00-10:00; half board +200F (per pers.). **Restaurant** Service 12:00-14:00, from 20:00; menu 165-230F, also à la carte. Specialties: Pigeon de Tartarin, délice des calanques, gratin des charmettes. **Credit cards** Amex, Visa, Eurocard and MasterCard. **Pets** Dogs allowed (+140F). **Facilities** Swimming pool, parking. **Nearby** Isle sur Sorgue; Fontaine de Vaucluse; Gordes; les Bories; abbey of Sénanque; Avignon; Le Lubéron– 18-hole Saumane golf course. **Open** All year.

La Grangette occupies a beautiful old farmhouse surrounded by nature. Sixteen beautiful bedrooms, all different, are decorated in Provençal colors and offer you comfort and silence. There are *La Mistrale, La Mule du Pape, La Mireillo* and the lovely *L'Arlesienne* room, with a terrace and two windows facing the evening light. Brightly waxed antique furniture throughout is combined with a gaily regional decor. There is an immense swimming pool, a shady terrace for meals and a large garden with trees which can be the starting point for pleasant walks. Add the friendly hospitality and you have a very pleasant hostelry.

***How to get there*** *(Map 33): 20km from Avignon. On A7, take Avignon exit toward L'Isle-sur-la-Sorgue; in L'Isle, take toward Pernes-les-Fontaines via D938 for 4km, then signs on right.*

## Auberge de la Fontaine

Place de la Fontaine
84210 Venasque (Vaucluse)
Tel. (0)4.90.66.02.96 - Fax (0)4.90.66.13.14 - M. and Mme Soehlke

**Rooms** 5 suites with air-conditioning, telephone, bath, WC, TV, minibar, kitchen, fireplace and terrasse. **Price** Suite 800F. **Meals** Breakfast 50F. **Restaurant** Service every evening 20:00-22:00 (closed Wednesday and from mid-Nov to mid-Dec); menu 220F, also à la carte. Specialties: Assiette du pêcheur, choucroute au foie gras, gibier frais en saison, pigeonneau aux airelles. "Bistro": menu 80-150F, also à la carte (closed Sunday evening and Monday). **Credit cards** Visa, Eurocard and MasterCard. **Pets** Dogs allowed. **Facilities** Mountain bikes, parking in the village. **Nearby** Venasque church, Gallo-Roman cemetery in Mazan, Pernes-les-Fontaines, Carpentras – 18-hole Saumane golf course. **Open** All year.

The Auberge de la Fontaine is a beautiful old village house which Ingrid and Christian Soehlke have completely restructured inside, creating an amusing maze of mezzanines, terraces and stairways. While conserving the structure's noble appearance, they particularly sought to create the informal atmosphere of a house for friends. And it would be difficult not to feel at ease: each suite includes a bedroom and a lounge with a fireplace, tastefully decorated and furnished in very Provençal style and equipped with a direct-dial phone, television, and cassette, CD players, fax and minitel. Each has a secluded terrace and a kitchenette, but the charming dining room and the Soehlkes' succulent cuisine should not be missed. There is a dinner concert each month, and in the low season, the hotel proposes a 5-day package with cooking lessons.

***How to get there*** *(Map 33): 11km south of Carpentras via D9.*

## Auberge Les Bichonnières

Route de Savigneux
01330 Ambérieux-en-Dombes (Ain)
Tel. (0)4.74.00.82.07 - Fax (0)4.74.00.89.61 - M. Sauvage

**Category** ★★ **Rooms** 9 with telephone, bath or shower and WC. **Price** Single 220F, double 250-380F. **Meals** Breakfast 40F, served 8:00-10:00; half board 290F (per pers., 3 days min.). **Restaurant** Service 12:15-13:45, 19:30-20:45 (closed Monday in July and Aug); menus 98-250F, also à la carte. Specialties: Grenouilles fraîches, volaille de Bresse. **Credit cards** Amex, Visa, Eurocard and MasterCard. **Pets** Dogs allowed. **Facilities** Parking. **Nearby** Trévoux, bird reserve in Villard-les-Dombes, Montluel, Pérouges – 18-hole Le Clou golf course in Villard-les-Dombes. **Open** All year except Christmas holiday (closed Sunday evening and Monday in low season).

The Dombes is a lush, green region of lakes and birds, yet it has few good hotels. Some thirty kilometers from Lyon on the edge of a roadside, yet in a quiet setting, the Bichonnières, an old farmhouse with country charm, is one of those few. In the comfortable small bedrooms, the light-brown shades of the plaster and beams are brightened with bucolic fabrics, and the bathrooms are quite presentable. On each floor, you will find a small corner lounge. For meals, depending on the season, the dining tables are set in an attractive dining room, on a covered terrace, or beneath the large parasols on a flowery interior courtyard. Chef Marc Sauvage prepares excellent regional specialties, including the region's famous Bresse chicken. As the hotel-restaurant business is a demanding one, the owners close for several days during the year. It's best to reserve in advance.

***How to get there*** *(Map 26): 30km north of Lyon via A6, Villefranche exit, then D904 towards Bourg-en-Bresse, then Villars-les-Dombes.*

## Auberge des Chasseurs

Naz-Dessus - 01170 Echenevex (Ain)
Tel. (0)4.50.41.54.07 - Fax (0)4.50.41.90.61
M. and Mme Lamy

**Category** ★★★ **Rooms** 15 with telephone, bath or shower, WC and TV. **Price** Single 400-530F, double 450-650F. **Meals** Breakfast 55F, served 8:00-10:00; half board 530 (per pers. in double room) 650F (per pers.). **Restaurant** Service 12:00-13:30, 19:00-21:30; menus (75-100F lunchtime except Saturday and Sunday), 185F and 280F also à la carte. Specialties: Salade de langoustines tiedes, vinaigrette durry, aiguillette de fera du lac rotie au vin d'arbois, fricassée de volaille au cidre. **Credit cards** All major. **Pets** Dogs allowed (+40F). **Facilities** Swimming pool, tennis, parking. **Nearby** Le Pailly and col de la Faucille, château of Fernet-Voltaire – 27-hole Maison Blanche golf course in Echenevex. **Open** March 10 – Nov 15.

Standing on the slopes of the Jura, amidst fields and woods, and yet just 15 minutes from Geneva, the Auberge des Chasseurs is an old farmhouse which has been very well restored. The homey atmosphere inside is very charming. The beamed ceillings, chairs and bedroom doors are decorated with floral frescos recently done by a Swedish artist. In the restaurant, there is a magnificent series of photographs by Cartier-Bresson. Upstairs, you will find a very inviting lounge and bar. The bedrooms are beautifully decorated with Laura Ashley fabrics and wallpapers, English-pine furniture and their charming bathrooms are as lovely. Outside, the oak garden furniture was designed by an artist, as was the mosaic of the terrace floor. The garden is full of flowers and shady spots, and the view is splendid. The cuisine is excellent, the service attentive and Dominique Lamy is a very hospitable owner.

***How to get there*** *(Map 20): 17km northwest of Genève via D984 towards St-Genis-Pouilly, then D978c towards Gex. Echeneves 2km before Gex on left.*

## Hostellerie du Vieux Pérouges

Place du Tilleul
01800 Pérouges (Ain)
Tel. (0)4.74.61.00.88 - Fax (0)4.74.34.77.90 - M. Thibaut

**Category** ★★★★ **Rooms** 28 with telephone, bath, shower, WC and TV. **Price** Single 450-750F, double 550-980F, suites 1050F. **Meals** Breakfast 60F, served 8:00-12:00. **Restaurant** Service 12:00-14:00, 19:00-21:00; menus 195-450F, also à la carte. Specialties: Filet de carpe farci à l'ancienne, volaille de Bresse, panaché pérougien, galette de l'hostellerie. **Credit cards** Visa, Eurocard and MasterCard. **Pets** Dogs allowed. **Facilities** Parking. **Nearby** Trévoux, bird reserve in Villard-les-Dombes, Montluel – 18-hole Le Clou golf course in Villard-les-Dombes. **Open** All year.

Pérouge is an exceptional small medieval town that you should be sure to visit and to plunge yourself into the atmosphere, what more appropriate than this inn which is made up of several very old houses. Stone stairways, stained glass windows, French ceilings, fireplaces... nothing is amiss. The most luxurious bedrooms are resplendent with Haute Epoque furniture and marble baths. The other, simpler rooms are also well furnished and offer excellent modern amenities. Each house borders on a small paved lane with, here and there, a small garden or open ruins overgrown with vegetation. The house opens onto the main square where the restaurant is located. Here too, the medieval atmosphere is prevalent; a wide-board floor, a baker's kneading trough, china cupboards, a large fireplace in which several large logs are often burning, all combine to whet the appetite for the Ostellerie's regional cuisine which is served by waiters in traditional dress.

***How to get there*** *(Map 26): 35km northeast of Lyon via A42, Pérouges exit.*

1998

## La Huchette

01750 Replonges (Ain)
Tel. (0)3.85.31.03.55 - Fax (0)3.85.31.10.24
Mme Gualdieri

**Rooms** 12 with telephone, bath, WC, TV and minibar - Wheelchair access. **Price** Single and double 400-500F, 500-600F, suite 1000-1200F. **Meals** Breakfast 60F, served from 7:00. **Restaurant** Service 12:00, 19:30 (closed Monday and Tuesday lunchtime): menus 160-230F, also à la carte. Specialties: Gâteau de foie bressan, suprême de poulet de Bresse aux morilles, nougatine au coulis de fraises. **Credit cards** All major. **Pets** Dogs allowed. Facilities Swimming pool and parking. **Nearby** Mâcon, church of Saint-André-de-Bagé, Lamartine tour (65 km): Roche de Solutré, Pouilly, Fuissé, Chasselas, col du grand Vert and lake of Saint-Point, Berzé-le-Châtel and chapel of Berzé-la-Ville, Milly-Lamartine and Château of Pierre-Clos, château of Monceau. **Open** Mid. Dec – mid. Nov. Closed Monday.

Although it is legally in the Rhône-Alpes region, Replonges nevertheless lies in the heart of Burgundy and Bresse, only four kilometers from Mâcon. Bordering on the Route Nationale through the village, this old Bresse hotel, renovated and enlarged, faces a spacious park and gardens. The bedrooms are accordingly quiet, spacious and comfortable, with a view over the century-old trees on the property. The lounges are pleasantly hushed, and the dining room, with its beamed ceiling and a large mural evoking country scenes, all create an appealing decor in which to enjoy the excellent cuisine made with local produce. The Huchette is somewhat expensive but it's delightful, as is the region.

***How to get there** (Map 26): 4km from Mâcon.*

## Hôtel de la Santoline

07460 Beaulieu (Ardèche)
Tel. (0)4.75.39.01.91 - Fax (0)4.75.39.38.79
M. and Mme Espenel

**Category** ★★★ **Rooms** 7 with telephone, bath, WC and minibar (some with air-conditioning). **Price** Double 340-480F, suite 580F. **Meals** Breakfast 45F, served 8:30-10:00; half board 340-405F (per pers., 3 days min.). **Restaurant** Service 19:30-20:30; menus 165F, also à la carte. Specialties: Market cooking. **Credit cards** Visa, Eurocard and MasterCard. **Pets** Dogs allowed (+30F). **Facilities** Swimming pool, parking. **Nearby** La Cocalière cave, bois de Païolive, corniche du Vivarais, Les Vans to la Bastide-Puylaurent. **Open** March – Nov.

Standing right in the middle of Provençal Ardèche, la Santoline is a converted stone hunting lodge. It is a haven of peace and commands views as far as the Cévennes. A beautiful vaulted cellar has been turned into a dining-room, and the simple decor of the bedrooms, all of which have pretty bathrooms, is perfectly in tune with the unadorned style of the building. Our favorites are Room 5 and especially Room 4, under the eaves; both have marvelous view of the surrounding country side and are equipped with air conditioning. The swimming pool is much appreciated in summer, as is the pleasant flowery terrace where breakfast and dinner can be served. Pierre and Marie-Danièle Espenel are friendly hosts, and prices are very reasonable.

***How to get there*** *(Map 32): 84km north of Nîmes via N106 to Alès, then D904 and D104 to La Croisée de Jalès, then D225.*

# Château d'Urbilhac

07270 Lamastre (Ardèche)
Tel. (0)4.75.06.42.11 - Fax (0)4.75.06.52.75
Mme Xompero

**Category** ★★★ **Rooms** 12 with telephone, bath or shower and WC. **Price** Single 500F, double 550-700F. **Meals** Breakfast 65F, served 8:00-10:30; half board 550-625F (per pers.). **Restaurant** Closed lunchtime except weekends. Service at 12:30 and 19:30; menus 230F. **Credit cards** All major. **Pets** Dogs allowed. **Facilities** Heated swimming pool, tennis, parking. **Nearby** Tournon, Vivarais steam train between Tournon and Lamastre – 18-hole golf course in Chambon-sur-Lignon. **Open** May 1 – Sep 30.

The Château d'Urbilhac, built in the last century in Renaissance style over the cellars of a 16th-century fortified house, is set in 148-acres of parkland. In the reception rooms, 19th-century style is predominant. The bedrooms, each with its own style, are equally beautiful. Restful and comfortable, they are further enhanced with superb bathrooms and often look out on a sublime panorama. In the spring, the dining room is moved out onto a vast veranda. You will enjoy outstanding cuisine, which is intelligently original and which reflects great respect for the proper use of farm products. (The prices are expensive at first but the reasonable demi-pension price is applicable beginning with the first night.) Mme Xompero is especially attentive, going from table to table, ensuring that everyone is pleased and generally contributing to the excellent atmosphere here. Finally, you should not leave Urbillac without first stepping onto the immense terrace and looking out over the valley where distant Ardèche farms are scattered between pastures and chestnut groves.

***How to get there*** *(Map 26): 36km west of Valence via D533.*

## Domaine de Rilhac

07320 Saint-Agrève (Ardèche)
Tel. (0)4.75.30.20.20 - Fax (0)4.75.30.20.00
Mme and M. Sinz

**Category** ★ **Rooms** 8 with telephone, bath or shower, WC and TV. **Price** Single and double 360-460F, apart. 720F. **Meals** Breakfast 65F, served 8:00-10:30; half board 420F, full board 470F (per pers., 2 days min.). **Restaurant** Service 12:30-13:30, 20:00-21:30, menus 115-320F (70F child), also à la carte. Specialties: Ecrevisses, saumon de Fontaines, bœuf salers, chataignes, myrtilles. **Credit cards** Visa, Eurocard and MasterCard. **Pets** Dogs allowed (+40F). **Facilities** Parking. **Nearby** Mont-Gerbier-des-Joncs; gorges de l'Eyrieux – 18-hole Chambon-sur-Lignon golf course. **Open** All year except Feb (closed Monday evening and Tuesday except July and Aug.).

Behind Saint-Agrève, an immense plateau lies at an altitude of 1000 meters facing Mounts Gerbier de Jonc and Mézenc. The air is pure, brown cows lead a peaceful existence there and several trout streams wind through the valley hollows. Ludovic Sinz, hôtel de charme shows that not only is he a talented young chef but also, with his wife Florence, he knows how to restore charming places. A stairway with a beautiful wrought-iron railing crafted by a local artisan leads to the comfortable bedrooms. They are named after flowers and each has a framed alphabet. The colors of the embroideries are repeated in the coordinated bedcover fabrics, drapes and table skirts, all contributing to a fresh and tasteful decor. The view is magnificent throughout, with large bay windows affording fine panoramas. The yellow plaster in the entrance, the small lounge and the dining room creates a joyful, almost Provençal atmosphere in all seasons. You will find the same refinements in the shady garden outside, which is protected by an old wall and is very carefully tended.

***How to get there** (Map 26): 56km west of Valence via D533.*

# Grangeon

07800 Saint-Cierge-la-Serre (Ardèche)
Tel. (0)4 75.65.73.86
Mme Valette

**Rooms** 1 double room, 1 duplex of which 4, 1 with shower, firepalce, bath and WC. **Price** Double 310-510F, duplex 850F. **Meals** Breakfast 39F, served 8:00-9:00; half board in July and Aug (2 days min.). **Restaurant** Evening meals for residents only. Service 19:30; menu 140F in half board or 180F. Specialties: Agneau au miel, papillotes de lapin à l'aneth et au pastis. **Credit cards** Not accepted. **Pets** Dogs not allowed. **Facilities** Parking. **Nearby** Valence museum, villages romanesque church and châteaux of the Ardèche – 18-hole Valence golf course in Saint-Didier-de-Charpey. **Open** By reservation Apr 1 – Nov 15 by reservation only.

Grangeon is the ideal place for those seeking a peaceful retreat and for nature lovers. It is an estate of 155-acres of parkland and forests, 4km away from the nearest village, and is reached by a small road winding through hills and woods. The house itself was built at the beginning of the 18th century and has seven bedrooms. The decoration combines wood and stone to create a warm country atmosphere. (Guests can play the piano.) All kinds of vegetables grow in Mme Valette's lovely terraced garden, and as she bakes her own bread and raises sheep, she is almost self-sufficient. Set in the heart of the Ardèche region and yet only 15km from the motorway, Grangeon provides an opportunity to relax in the countryside.

***How to get there*** *(Map 26): 35km south of Valence via A7, Loriol exit, then N104 towards Privas-Aubenas; at Les Fonts-du-Pouzin D265 towards Saint-Cierge (follow signs).*

1998

## La Châtaigneraie

07130 Soyons (Ardèche)
Tel. (0)4.75.60.83.55 - Fax (0)4. 75.60.85.21
M. Philippe Michelot

**Rooms** 18 with air-conditioning, telephone, bath, WC, TV and minibar - 1 for disabled persons. **Price** Single and double 390-490F, 420-650F, 3 pers. 750-1000F. **Meals** Breakfast 55-90F, served 8:00-10:00; half board from 450F (per pers.). **Restaurant** Service 12:00-14:00, 19:00-22:00; menus 120F (lunchtime)-280F. Regional and Provançal cooking. **Credit cards** All major. **Pets** Dogs allowed (+50F). **Facilities** Swimming pool, tennis (1 covered), sauna, whirlpool and parking. **Nearby** Museum of Soyons, Château of Crussol, tasting in château de Saint-Peray and Cornas, Valence (museum of H. Robert), villages, Romanesque church - 18-hole golf course in Saint-Didier-de-Charpey. **Open** All year.

As the Rhône Valley is one of the most frequented thoroughfares in the world, this hotel could seem just a useful place to stay on the roadside. Which it is, but in addition every effort has been made to make us forget the proximity of the autoroute: perfect soundproofing, air-conditioning, many leisure activities, not to mention the lovely decoration and hospitality of the staff. The Chataigneraie is made up of two houses: La Musardière, a four-star hotel with all amenities, smart decoration and prices to match; and our favorite, the three-star La Châtaigneraie itself, with comfortable amenities and a more youthful decor hinting of Provence. Several bedrooms designed for families or groups have a kitchenette, and some an extra bed on a loggia. For couples, we highly recommend Rooms 701, 702, 703 and 704, which are lovely. Delicious cuisine is served in an intimate dining room or on the veranda. The charming lounge at the entrance is elegantly furnished with antiques.

***How to get there*** *(Map 26): 10km south of Valence.*

## La Treille Muscate

26270 Cliousclat (Drôme)
Tel. (0)4.75.63.13.10 - Fax (0)4.75.63.10.79
Mme Delaitre

**Category** ★★★ **Rooms** 12 with telephone, bath, WC and TV. **Price** Double 280-500F. **Meals** Breakfast 45F, served 8:00-10:00. **Restaurant** Closed Wednesday. Service 12:00-13:30, 20:00-21:30; menus 89-135F, also à la carte. Specialties: Beignets d'aubergines, croustillant de pigeon laqué au miel d'épices, crème de potiron aux moules et coriandre fraîche. **Credit cards** Visa, Eurocard and MasterCard. **Pets** Dogs allowed. **Facilities** Swimming pool, parking. **Nearby** Mirmande, Poët-Laval; le quartier des Forts in Nyons – 18-hole Valdaine golf course. **Open** All year except Jan and Feb.

La Treille Muscate is exactly the kind of small hotel you hope to find in a Provençal village. Beautiful sunny yellow walls brighten the on the ground floor rooms; here you will find the dining room with its bright Provençal table linens, the corner bar and the small TV room. There are several pieces of handsome regional furniture, large watercolors, varnished jugs and splendid dinnerware crafted by a skilled potter, a neighbor and friend; all create a decor that makes you feel truly at home. Upstairs, pretty bedrooms have recently been installed and beautifully decorated. They have a lovely view out over the quiet village or the countryside.The excellent cuisine is enhanced with aromatic herbs and local products. In good weather, a few tables are set out on the village side or in a small garden, bordered with terraced walls and overlooking the countryside. The hospitality and service at "The Muscat Arbor" are informal.

***How to get there*** *(Map 26): 16km north of Montélimar via A7, Loriol exit, then 5km. On N7 Loriol-Montélimard toward*

## Manoir de la Roseraie

26230 Grignan (Drôme Provençale)
Tel. (0)4.75.46.58.15 - Fax (0)4.75.46.91.55 - M. and Mme Alberts
E-mail: roseraie.hotel@wanadoo.fr - Web: http://www.ila-chateau.com

**Category** ★★★★ **Rooms** 13 and 2 suites with telephone, bath or shower, WC and TV - Wheelchair access. **Price** Single and double 690-1100F, suite 1580-1680F. **Meals** Breakfast 90F, served 8:00-10:00; half board 670-865F (per pers., 3 days min.). Restaurant Service 12:00-13:30, 20:00-21:15; menus 195-250F. Specialties: Carré d'agneau de l'Adret, jus au basilic et bayaldi de légumes provançaux, filet de bar grillé au lait de badiane et sa compotée de fnouil, très belle cave de côte du Rhône. **Credit cards** All major. **Pets** Dogs allowed (+60F). **Facilities** Heated swimming pool, tennis, parking. **Nearby** Château and museum of Mme de Sévigné in Grignan, Poët-Laval, Dieulefit – 9-hole Valaurie golf course. **Open** All year except Jan 5 – Feb 14 (closed Monday in low season).

In this beautiful private mansion built in 1850 by the mayor of Grignan, Michèle Alberts and her husband have tastefully refurbished and decorated the bedrooms and the suite. With comfortable amenities, they are classic and cheerful in decor. Depending on the floor, they are spacious or smaller and more intimate. The bathrooms are bright with colors and some are quite original, like that in the *Baccara* room, whose circular bathtub opens directly onto the bedroom. Tables in the new dining room, its skylight in a rontunda shape, are elegantly set facing a panoramic view over the ravishing park, which is planted with some 400 rose bushes, bougainvillea, lindens, cedars, and perennials. The heated swimming pool, beautifully integrated into the park, is perhaps the ideal spot for enjoying the lovely setting.

***How to get there*** *(Map 33): 90km north of Avignon via A7, Montélimar-Sud exit, then N7 and D133.*

# Domaine du Colombier

Route de Donzère
Malataverne - 26780 Montélimar (Drôme)
Tel. (0)4.75.90.86.86 - Fax (0)4.75.90.79.40 - M. and Mme Barette

**Category** ★★★ **Rooms** 19 and 5 suites with telephone, bath, WC and TV. **Price** Single and double 450-860F, triple 780-960F, 4 pers. 880-1060F, suite 860-1200F. **Meals** Breakfast 70F, served 7:30-11:00. **Restaurant** Service 12:15-14:30, 19:15-21:30; menus 150F all incl. (lunchtime except Sunday 195F Wine not incl.), 90-230-360F, also à la carte. Specialties: Gougeonettes de sole à la crème de morilles, omelette aux truffes du Tricastin, carré d'agneau de pays au romarin, charriot de desserts. **Credit cards** All major. **Pets** Dogs allowed (+50F). **Facilities** Swimming pool, bowling alley, bicycles, parking. **Nearby** Poët-Laval, Nyons, château and museum of Mme de Sévigné in Grignan, villages of the Drôme between Montélimar and Orange. **Open** All year.

Formerly a 14th-Century abbey, the Domaine du Colombier maintains its tradition of hospitality to travelers to this day, as it is now a pleasant hotel conveniently located on the road south. Although only minutes off the highway, it seems to be in the middle of the countryside. When you walk through the door be prepared to find furniture and fabrics piled up in the entrance hall, for it is also a shop. The bedrooms are bright, colorful and comfortably decorated; three of them have a small mezzanine. In the garden, the swimming pool, surrounded by chaises longues, is a lovely place to relax. The lavender-blue furniture in the dining room is Provençal in style, and dinner or an evening drink can also be served on the patio.

***How to get there*** *(Map 33): 9km south of Montélimar via N7 and D144a (2km after Malataverne dir. Donzere). A7 Montélimarsouth exit dir. Malataverne.*

# Auberge de la Gloriette

26170 Mérindol-les-Oliviers (Drôme)
Tel. (0)4.75.28.71.08
M. and Mme Mina

**Rooms** 4 with bath or shower and WC. **Price** Single and double 250-300F. **Meals** Breakfast 30-50F, served 8:30-11:00. **Restaurant** Only by reservation. Service 12:00-14:00, 19:30-21:00 (closed Thusday (except in summer) and Sunday evening); menu 100F, also à la carte. Specialties: Provençale cooking. **Credit cards** Visa, Eurocard and MasterCard. **Pets** Dogs allowed. Facilities Swimming pool and parking. **Nearby** Orange, Mornas, Museum of Henri Fabre in Sérignan. **Open** All year.

The son of a baker, Jacques Mina grew up watching his father rolling out dough and removing hot, aromatic batches of golden pastries from the oven. In 1988, the bakery in Mérindol was up for sale and, with his companion Michèle, Jacques left Paris, bought the bakery, and opened a small restaurant with several bedrooms next door: the Auberge de la Gloriette. The Minas' savory experience and their natural friendliness quickly made the inn a success. And it's not surprising. The Provençal specialties fresh from the baker's oven and served in generous portions are irresistible; the lovely dining room and the shady terrace overlooking vineyards and olive trees, and the charming little bedrooms all play their part in making the Gloriette a special play to stay (not to mention the swimming pool, a godsend when the summer heat wave sets in.) It's a hotel right out of Marcel Pagnol, tailor-made for guests who enjoy friendly people and the simple pleasures of life.

***How to get there*** *(Map 33): 9km east of Vaison-la-Romaine, dir. Buis-les-Baronies, Puymerols, Mérindol.*

## La Capitelle

Rue du Rempart
26270 Mirmande (Drôme)
Tel. (0)4.75.63.02.72 - Fax (0)4.75.63.02.50 - M. and Mme Melki

**Category** ★★ **Rooms** 19 and 2 apartments with telephone, bath or shower, WC and satellite TV. **Price** Double in half board 355-450F per pers., apart. (3-4 pers.) 400-335F per pers. **Meals** Breakfast incl. served 8:00-11:00. **Restaurant** Service 12:00-13:45, 19:30-21:30; menu 140-260F, also à la carte. Specialties: Terrine de foie gras aux pommes, pissaladière de rougets au basilic, rosace d'agneau à la crème d'aïl, surprise de melon au vin épicé, nougat glacé. **Credit cards** Amex, Visa, Eurocard and MasterCard. **Pets** dogs allowed (+35F). **Facilities** Garage (+50F). **Nearby** Mirmande church, Pöet-Laval, Nyons – 18-hole Valdaine golf course. **Open** Mar - end Nov.

La Capitelle is a tall Renaissance building with mullioned windows. The lounge and dining-room have vaulted ceilings and handsome stone fireplaces. Items of period furniture combine well with more simple contemporary furnishings to create an elegant and yet warm atmosphere. A sober and sure taste is also in evidence in the bedrooms, most of which have a beautiful antique wardrobe with a bouquet of dried flowers. All the rooms are different and most enjoy a magnificent view over the plain below. Breakfast and drinks can be served on the ramparts, while meals are served in the dining room or on the shady terrace in summer: the regional cuisine is excellent. To enjoy optimum service as well as the beauty of the site, guests are kindly requested to arrive by 8:30 P.M. at the latest. The staff is hospitable and very friendly.

***How to get there*** *(Map 26): 35km south of Valence; A7 Montélimar-north exit, RN7 until saulce then D204.*

## La Ferme Saint-Michel

26130 Solérieux (Drôme)
Tel. (0)4.75.98.10.66 - Fax (0)4.75.98.19.09
M. Laurent

**Category** ★★ Rooms 14 (5 with air-conditioning) with telephone, bath, WC and TV. **Price** Single 300-330F, double 310-350F. **Meals** Breakfast 38F, served 7:00-10:00. **Restaurant** Service 12:30-14:00, 19:30-21:15 (closed Dec 23 – Jan 24, Sunday evening and Monday and Tuesday lunchtime); menus 130-180F, also à la carte. Specialties: Menu-truffe. **Credit cards** Visa, Eurocard and MasterCard. **Pets** Dogs not allowed. **Facilities** Swimming pool, parking. **Nearby** Vercors High Plateaux Natural Reserve; Choranche Caverns; skiing; Corrençon Golf Course, 18 holes. **Open** All year.

Partially renovated and under new ownership, the Ferme Saint-Michel is a traditional old Provençal *mas*, isolated from the road by thick vegetation, whose origins go back to the 16th century. The Ferme opens onto an inviting terrace where, in summer, a few tables are set for dinner. You will savor excellent local products such as the truffles harvested on the property, and game in season. Large trees afford lovely shade over the terrace, while a few steps away, there is the swimming pool. Quiet, well kept, and attractive, all the bedrooms have been renovated. Their decor remains simple but comfortable, and the local Souleïado fabrics go well with the Provençal painted furniture. On the ground floor, there is a cool dining room, a small bar and inviting lounges with fireplaces.

***How to get there*** *(Map 33): North of Bollène. On A7, Bollène or Montélimar-Sud exit, toward Saint-Paul-Trois-Châteaux. On D341.*

## Auberge de la Rochette

La Rochette
26400 Vauvaneys-la-Rochette (Drôme)
Tel. (0)4.75.25.79.30 - Fax (0)4.75.25.79.25 - A. Cordonier and P. Danis

**Rooms** 5 with telephone, bath or shower, WC, TV, safe and minibar. **Price** Double 400-450F, duplex 600F (4 pers.). **Meals** Breakfast-brunch 60F, served 8:30-10:00; half board 390-420F (per pers., 3 days min.). **Restaurant** Service 12:00-13:15, 19:30-21:00 (on reservation); menus 165-200F. Specialties: Foie gras de canard maison, agneau de la Drôme à la crème d'aïl doux, pavé de turbot à l'huile d'olive parfumée, crème brûlée à la lavande. **Credit cards** Visa, Eurocard and MasterCard. **Pets** Dogs not allowed. **Facilities** Swimming pool, parking. **Nearby** Shoe Museum in Romans, Facteur Cheval's Palace in Hauterives, Massif du Vercors, villages of the Drôme. **Open** All year except 15 days in Oct, 15 days in Feb and Wednesday in low season.

Located in the stunningly beautiful setting of Provençal Drôme, the Auberge is an old barn which has been restored in the regional style. The small size allows the owners to receive guests informally, like friends. The beautiful rooms have been carefully designed down to the last detail. (A room with a mezzanine and high ceilings was designed with families or groups of friends in mind). The decor includes warm sand-colored walls, Provençal quilted bedspreads and matching drapes, terra cotta floors and painted furniture. An elegant small dining room opens onto a flower-filled terrace where regional specialties are served. This is a charming, very friendly inn.

***How to get there*** *(Map 26): 20km south of Valence, on A7 exit Loriol or Valence-Sud, toward Crest; before Crest, take road for Vauvaneys, then La Rochette on D538 coming from Valence.*

# Château de Passières

38930 Chichilianne (Isère)
Tel. (0)4.76.34.45.48 - Fax (0)4.76.34.46.25
M. Perli

**Category** A A **Rooms** 23 with telephone, bath, shower and 20 with WC. **Price** Single 280F, double 280-450F. **Meals** Breakfast 40F, served 7:30-9:30; half board from 310F on request (per pers., 3 days min.). **Restaurant** Closed Monday in low season and Nov – Jan. Service 12:15-13:30, 19:15-21:00; menus 95-200F, also à la carte. Specialties: Fricassée de cèpes et escargots, escalope de saumon au miel de pissenlit, crêpes d'agneau, truffes. **Credit cards** Visa, Eurocard and MasterCard. **Pets** Dogs allowed (+20F). **Facilities** Swimming pool, tennis, sauna, parking. **Nearby** Mont Aiguille, Vercors plateau, Grenoble. **Open** Feb 1 – Nov 30 (closed Sunday evening and Monday in low season).

Restored by a very friendly family, this 15th-century château occupies a truly exceptional position at the foot of Mont Aiguille, a magnificent rock wall which creates a somewhat unreal atmosphere throughout the region. We particularly recommend the three bedrooms with dark-brown antique wood paneling and red carpets; they have great character and are very warm and inviting. The other rooms are more modern and impersonal. On the ground floor there is an irresistible salon, with almond-green, figured paneling, antique furniture and, above all, a superb collection of paintings. In good weather, dining tables are set out on the terrace and in winter, the good regional cuisine is served in the large dining room. On the walls, several paintings by Edith Berger remind art lovers that a small museum dedicated to her works is located on the top floor. This very hospitable château is a must in a region which is not to be missed.

***How to get there*** *(Map 26): 50km south of Grenoble via N75 towards Sisteron until Clelles, then D7.*

1998

## Hôtel du Golf

Les Ritons
38250 Corrençon-en-Vercors (Isère)
Tel. (0)4.76.95.84.84 - Fax (0)4.76.95.82.85 - M. Sauvajon

**Category** ★★★ **Rooms** 8 and 4 duplex with telephone, bath, WC, satellite TV and minibar. **Price** Single and double 360-630F, 450-750F; duplex (4 pers.) 650-960F. **Meals** Breakfast 60F, served 7:30-11:00; half board and full board 440-615F, 520-620F (per pers.). **Restaurant** Service 12:30-13:30/15:00, 19:30-20:30/21:00 (closed Sunday evening and Monday in low season); menus 100-180F; also à la carte. Specialties: Foie gras de canard farci au homard, truite de rivière au beurre de noix confites au vinaigre de Malte et ravioles. **Credit cards** All major. Pets Dogs allowed. **Facilities** Swimming pool, sauna and parking. **Nearby** Skiing in Courençon and in Villard de Lans (5 km), caves of Chouanche - 18-hole Courençon golf course. **Open** Mid. Dec – end March and beg. May – beg. Oct.

Especially well located at the entrance to the immense Vercors Natural Park, the Hôtel du Golf is in the immediate proximity of all the sports activities of this resort: golf, hang gliding, mountain biking, and others. The Sauvajon family is outstandingly hospitable and does its utmost to make your visit enjoyable. The bedrooms, some with lofts, are comfortably appointed and well kept (Number 2 is somewhat small). They are very quiet and pleasant although their decoration could do with a bit more personality. On the ground floor, an inviting lounge-bar with comfortable, beige-leather armchairs is a lovely spot to relax over a drink before dinner. Under the direction of a former head chef at Paul Bocuse, the cuisine is the hotel's other great attraction. Delicate, inventive, occasionally daring, it's a major factor (with the copious brunches) in the favorable quality-price ratio of the *demi-pension.*

***How to get there*** *(Map 26): 40km southwest of Grenoble, Villard de Lans exit.*

# Chalet Mounier

38860 Les Deux-Alpes (Isère)
Tel. (0)4.76.80.56.90 - Fax (0)4.76.79.56.51
M. and Mme Mounier

**Category** ★★★ **Rooms** 48 with telephone, bath or shower, TV (44 with WC). **Price** Single 320-680F, double 420-905F. **Meals** Breakfast incl., served 7:30-9:30; half board 380-640F, full board 470-730F (per pers., 3 days min.). **Restaurant** Service 12:30-14:00, 19:30-21:00; menus 125-290F, also à la carte. **Credit cards** Visa, Eurocard and MasterCard. **Pets** Dogs allowed (extra charge). **Facilities** Heated swimming pool, covered swimming pool, sauna, hamman, health center, tennis half court (summer). **Nearby** Ski lifts (100m), village of Venosc, Bézardé valley, Ecrins park, massif of La Meije. **Open** Dec 15 – May 1, June 29 – Sep 1.

This chalet was originally a mountain refuge and farm but since 1933 has grown into a large and modern hotel while retaining its charm. The welcoming entrance hall immediately establishes the atmosphere of the hotel. You will be charmed by the decor of the lounge and the restaurant, whose large windows open onto the garden and the swimming pool and onto the snow-clad slopes in winter. The bedrooms are all comfortable and have balconies with unrestricted views of the mountains. Chef Robert Mounier prides himself on his hearty, succulent cuisine, which is very professionally served. There is also a newly opened small restaurant for gourmet fare. The hotel is very quiet and the people are very friendly.

***How to get there*** *(Map 27): 74km southeast of Grenoble (detour from Grenoble via Pont-de-Claix) via N85 to Vizille; then N91 to the barrage (dam) on the Chambon via Bourg-d'Oisans, then D213 to Les Deux-Alpes.*

## Château de la Commanderie

17, avenue d'Echirolles
Eybens- 38320 Grenoble (Isère)
Tel. (0)4.76.25.34.58 - Fax (0)4.76.24.07.31 - M. de Beaumont

**Category** ★★★ **Rooms** 25 with telephone, bath or shower, WC, satellite TV and minibar. **Price** Single 425-693F, double 465-733F. **Meals** Breakfast 57F, served 7:00-10:00. **Restaurant** Closed Saturday lunchtime, Sunday evening and Monday. Service 12:00-13:00, 20:00-21:45; menu 142-225F, also à la carte. **Credit cards** All major. **Pets** Dogs allowed (+50F). **Facilities** Swimming pool, parking. **Nearby** Grenoble museum, massifs of Vercors, Chartreuse and Oisans – 18-hole Bresson-Eybens golf course. **Open** All year.

Formerly a hospice of the Knights of Malta, the Château de la Commanderie is ideally located just 5km from the center of Grenoble and half an hour from the Olympic ski slopes. A large, lovely walled garden planted with centuries-old trees gives it an air of space and tranquillity rare in a town hotel. The bedrooms combine modern comforts and facilities with period furniture, old engravings and carefully chosen fabrics. Breakfast is a substantial affair served on the terrace in summer, or in vast 18th-century rooms decorated with family portraits. Next to it is a large dining room decorated with pastoral Aubusson tapestries. The superb cuisine is intelligently innovative and respect ful of its ingredients. A friendly, family atmosphere prevails.

***How to get there*** *(Map 26): 4km east of Grenoble via the bypass (south), exit Eybens (Route Napoléon); 500m from the town center.*

## Le Lièvre Amoureux

38840 Saint-Lattier (Isère)
Tel. (0)4.76.64.50.67 - Fax (0)4.76.64.31.21
M. Breda

**Category** ★★★ **Rooms** 14 with telephone (12 with bath and 5 with TV) **Price** Double 320-470F, suite 380F. **Meals** Breakfast 65F, served 8:30-10:30. **Restaurant** Menus 179-199F, also à la carte. Specialties: Game, hare on the spit. **Credit cards** All major. **Pets** Dogs allowed (+40F). **Facilities** Swimming pool, parking. **Nearby** Saint-Bernard college in Romans, Facteur Cheval palace, Saint-Antoine abbey. **Open** Mar 16 – Oct 1 (closed Sunday evening and Monday in low season).

Overlooking the foothills of the Vercors, "The Hare in Love" is the kind of establishment which has upheld fine French hotel traditions for many years. The main building houses the lobby and the beautiful dining room with wall paneling in cerused oak surmounted by shades of pale blue and white, adding a refined touch to the overall rustic decor. The bedrooms occupy several buildings, our preferences definitely going to those around the swimming pool. Huge, modern, with comfortable amenities, they are illuminated by glass doors opening out onto a small private terrace with walnut trees. The cuisine is copious—we prefer the meat specialties to the fish dishes—and the service is highly professional.

***How to get there*** *(Map 26): 15km north of Romans via N92 or N532; via A49, exit number 8.*

1998

# Hôtel des Skieurs

38700 Le Sappey-en-Chartreuse (Isère)
Tel. (0)4.76.88.82.76 - Fax (0)4.76.88.85.76
M. Jail

**Category** ★★★ **Rooms** 18 with telephone (04.76.88.80.15), bath or showerand TV. **Price** Single and double 310F; chalet 400F. **Meals** Breakfast 35F, served 7:00-9:30; half board and full board 345F, 395F (per pers., 3 days min.). **Restaurant** Service 12:15-13:30, 19:30-21:30 (closed Sunday evening and Monday); menus 120-250F, also à la carte. Specialties: Ragout de noix de saint-jacques aux ravioles du Dauphiné. **Credit cards** Visa, Eurocard and MasterCard. **Pets** Dogs allowed (+30F). **Facilities** Swimming pool, parking and garage. **Nearby** Skiig, Mountain of Chartreuse: belvédère des Sangles, convent of the Grande Chartreuse, gorges of the Guiers-Vif; museum of Fine Art in Grenoble. **Open** All year except in Apr, Nov and Dec. Closed Sunday evening and Monday.

From Grenoble, the road bravely climbs the flank of the Chartreuse Mountains before arriving in this small mid-mountain (3000 feet) village and the Hôtel des Skieurs. Run by a hard-working young couple, the big chalet has just undergone extensive renovation during which the small lounge-bar, the stairway, and the bedrooms were entirely paneled in larch. Today, they they exude a warm, cheerful, mountain atmosphere, with a delicate aroma of pine in the air. On the ground floor, a spacious dining room opens wide onto an equally spacious terrace where meals are served with the first rays of sun: the excellent cuisine, nutritious and traditional, is prepared by the owner and served by his wife. The hotel is simple, comfortable, and professionally run: great for those who love walking and the fresh mountain air.

***How to get there*** *(Map 26): 12km north of Grenoble, to Saint-Pierre-de-Chartreuse.*

# Hôtel Le Christiania

38250 Villars-de-Lans (Isère)
Tel. (0)4.76.95.12.51 - Fax (0)4.76.95.00.75
Mme Buisson

**Category** ★★★ **Rooms** 24 with telephone, bath or shower, WC and TV; 5 with lounge - Elevator. **Price** Single 320-420F, double 420-680F. **Meals** Breakfast 52F, served 7:30-10:00; half board 395-550F, full board 495-650F (per pers., 4 days min.). **Restaurant** Service 12:30-14:00, 19:30-21:00, menus 130-235F, also à la carte. Specialties: Truite d'eau vive, terrine de foie gras au vin de noix, carré d'agneau, croustillant aux poires, tarte au chocolat. **Credit cards** All major. **Pets** Dogs allowed (+40F). **Nearby** Mountain of Vercors, caves of Choranche; skiing, Corrençon de Golf 18-hole. **Open** Dec 15 –Apr 20, May 15 – Sept 20.

From the outside, the Christiania is architecturally classic, as are many mountain hotels, and its location on the edge of the road is not a plus. But you will be pleasantly surprised once you have gone inside and seen how charming it is. The very friendly owners have in fact decorated the hotel like their own home. Paintings, family furniture and objects lend special touches to the small lounge on the left. And a corner of the elegant dining room is bright with a collection of shining antique carafes. Mme Buisson herself is the artist behind the small floral motifs on each door. In the same spirit, the green and red tartan fabrics, the drapes and the checked eiderdowns have been tastefully selected, all creating a lovely effect (although the bedrooms are somewhat small). The owner's son is the chef, while his wife presides over the dining room. They maintain a reputation for excellent meals, which are served outdoors with the first good weather.

***How to get there*** *(Map 26): 35km southwest of Grenoble, highway Villar-de-Lans exit.*

# Hôtel des Artistes

8, rue Gaspard-André / Place des Célestins
69002 Lyon (Rhône)
Tel. (0)4.78.42.04.88 - Fax (0)4.78.42.93.76 - Mme Durand

**Category** ★★★ **Rooms** 45 with telephone, bath or shower, WC, TV and 36 with minibar. **Price** Single 355-435F, double 395-475F. **Meals** Breakfast 48F, served 7:00-11:30. No restaurant. **Credit cards** All major. **Pets** Dogs not allowed. **Facilities** Parking. **Nearby** Town hall, art museum in Lyon, Yzeron, Mont d'Or Lyonnais, Trévoux, Pérouges – 18-hole Lyon Verger golf course, 9-hole Lyon Chassieux golf course. **Open** All year.

The Hôtel des Artistes (a favorite haunt of artists, as its name and many autographs indicate) is in that old quarter of Lyon, which lies between the embankments of the Rhône and Saône, close to the Place Bellecour and the Célestins Theatre. The bedrooms are decorated with very simple, modern furniture, differing only in the cheerful colors of the fabrics. Effectively soundproofed, comfortable, and equipped with lovely small baths, they overlook either the back of the hotel, the side façade of the Théâtre des Célestins, or the elegant Place des Célestins. (Some rooms are air-conditioned.). Breakfast is very good, and there is a friendly atmosphere. Special weekend rates are available. As Lyons has a number of world-famous restaurants, here are several simpler traditional bistros, which also are famous in Lyon: *Le Bistrot de Lyon, Le Bouchon aux Vins, Le Garet*, the *Brasserie Brotteaux,* the *Café Comptoir Abel,* the *Café des Fédérations,* and the *Café des Négociants, Assiette et Marée.*

***How to get there** (Map 26): In the town center near "Place des Célestins".*

1998

## Château de Candie

Rue du Bois de Candie
73000 Chambéry-le-Vieux (Savoie)
Tel. (0)4.79.96.63.00 - Fax (0)4.79.96.63.10 - M. Lhostis

**Category** ★★★ **Rooms** 19 with telephone, bath, WC and satellite TV - 1 for disabled persons - Elevator. **Price** Single and double 400F, 500-950F; suite 900 -1200F. **Meals** Breakfast 65F; half board and full board 465-645F, 605-790F (per pers., 3 days min.). **Restaurant** Service 11:30-14:00, 19:00-22:00 (closed Sunday evening); menus 145-290F, also à la carte. Specialties: Ravioles de champignons aux truffes, filets de lavaret à la grenobloise, tarte aux agrumes et soubet. **Credit cards** Amex, Visa, Eurocard and MasterCard. **Pets** Dogs allowed. **Facilities** Parking. **Nearby** Château de Miolans, Les Charmettes (Rousseau's house), Gorges du Guiers-Vif, Bourget Lake; Aiguebelette Lake. **Open** All year.

Built as a fortress more than four centuries ago to keep watch over the valley, the typically Savoyard Château de Candie proudly towers over Chambéry. Eight years ago, it had the good luck to catch the eye of a château lover, who devoted himself to beautifying the fortress and sharing his passion with guests passing through. Everywhere, in the bedrooms, the salons, and even the corridors, the result is magnificent: without ever betraying the search for a "decorative effect", it the height of modern comfort with the nobility of beautiful antique furniture, paintings, objects, chandeliers, fabrics....Not surprisingly, the bedrooms are as lovely as they can be, and well exposed. (Five are less than 600 F.) Meals are served in a recently built part, decorated on the outside in the regional *trompe-l'oeil,* and on the inside with white or waxed antique woodwork. The talented chef Gilles Hérard skillfully exploits Savoie's wealth of delicious regional products.

***How to get there*** *(Map 27): 5km of Chambery*

## La Sivolière

Quartier des Chenus
73120 Courchevel (Savoie)
Tel. (0)4.79.08.08.33 - Fax (0)4.79.08.15.73 - Mme Cattelin
Web: http://www.oda.fr/aa/sivoliere

**Category** ★★★ **Rooms** 30 with telephone, bath, WC and TV. **Price** Double 870-2250F. **Meals** Breakfast 78F, served at any time; half board on request. **Restaurant** Service 12:00-14:30, 19:00-23:00; menus 180-280F. Specialties: Savoyard dishes, côte de bœuf à la cheminée, tartiflette, raclettes, gratin de potiron. **Credit cards** Amex, Visa, Eurocard and MasterCard. **Pets** Dogs not allowed. **Facilities** Sauna, jacuzzi, hammam. **Nearby** Skiing, cable car to La Saulire – 9-hole Courchevel golf course, 18-hole Méribel golf course. **Open** Dec 1 – May 1.

Lying sheltered by trees at the foot of the ski runs is Courchevel's hôtel de charme. Although quiet and tranquil, it is within walking distance of the village center. The hotel's friendly atmosphere reflects the personality of Mme Cattelin, who looks after her guests personally and has spent twenty years creating what some would call a little paradise. Everything in the chalet is in good taste: the decor, the food, the hospitality. Its success is due to a thousand small touches such as potpourris, fresh flowers and pretty tablecloths, the delicious plats du jour and homemade tarts. The same care and attention to detail is found in the ski room and living rooms. This is the kind of place that visitors tend to keep secret.

***How to get there*** *(Map 27): 50km southeast of Albertville via N90 to Moûtiers, then D915 and D91.*

## Lodge Nogentil Hôtel

73123 Courchevel 1850 (Savoie)
Tel. (0)4.79 08 32 32 - Fax (0)4.79 08 03 15
M. Manuel

**Category** ★★★ **Rooms** 10 with telephone, bath, WC, TV and minibar. **Price** Double in half board 600-800F (per pers.), 680-980F (per pers. in double room), duplex (4 pers) 880-1080F (per pers.). **Meals** Breakfast incl., served 8:00-11:00. **Restaurant** Residents only. Service 19:30-21:30, menu. **Credit cards** Visa, Eurocard and MasterCard. **Pets** Dogs not allowed. **Facilities** Parking. **Nearby** Skiing from hotel – 9-hole Courchevel golf course, 18-hole Méribel golf course. **Open** Nov - end Apr and Jul - Sep.

The new architectural policy of Courchevel is designed to encourage the construction of hotels in the traditional Savoyard style, and the Lodge Nogentil is one of the latest of its new charming chalet-hôtels. Well located at the edge of the Bellecôte ski run, the Nogentil offers only a few rooms, all very pretty indeed. They are bright with luminous wood paneling. The pleasant decor includes rustic furniture, which complements the handsome armoires from Afghanistan. There is the same exotic touch in the lounge. And you're sure of after-ski relaxation, what with the sauna and gym at your disposal.

***How to get there*** *(Map 27): 50km southeast of Albertville via N90 to Moûtiers, then D915 and D91 to Courchevel 1850.*

## La Tour de Pacoret

Montailleur
73460 Grésy-sur-Isère (Savoie)
Tel. (0)4.79.37.91.59 - Fax (0)4.79.37.93.84 - M. Chardonnet

**Category** ★★ **Rooms** 9 with telephone, bath or shower, WC and TV. **Price** Single and double 280-450F. **Meals** Breakfast 50F, served 8:00-10:00; half board 300-400F, full board 390-490F (per pers., 3 days min.). **Restaurant** Service 12:00-13:30, 19:30-21:00; menus 90-220F, also à la carte. Specialties: Mitonnée fondante de joues du cochon, filet de fera eb croûte de sésame, moelleux chaud au chocolat. **Credit cards** Visa, Eurocard and MasterCard. **Pets** Small dogs allowed (+30F). **Facilities** parking. **Nearby** Conflans, fort du Mont, château of Miolans – 27-hole Giez-Faverges golf course. **Open** Mid. Apr – Nov 1.

This beautiful 14th-century watchtower, standing in the middle of the countryside on a hilltop at the foot of the Alps, has been converted into a charming small country hotel. A magnificent spiral staircase of black stone leads to the bedrooms. All different, they are regularly redecorated, prettily furnished, and comfortable. The ground-floor rooms form several attractive dining rooms, and just next to them, the garden-terraces offer a splendid view. Here, in the shade of the wisteria or the parasols, dining tables are laid, inviting the first arrivals to have lunch or dinner facing the snowy Alps and overlooking the Isère River as it snakes through the valley. When we stayed here, we took special note of the excellent cuisine and the staff's kind hospitality.

***How to get there*** *(Map 27): 19km southwest of Albertville via N90 towards Montmélian until Pont-de-Grésy, then D222 and D201 towards Montailleur.*

## Hôtel Adray-Télébar

73550 Méribel-les-Allues (Savoie)
Tel. (0)4.79.08.60.26 - Fax (0)4.79.08.53.85
M. Bonnet

**Category** ★★ **Rooms** 24 with telephone, bath or shower (24 with WC). **Price** Single and double 550-750F. **Meals** Breakfast 60F, served 8:00-11:00; half board 620-750F, full board 670-800F (per pers., 3 days min.). **Restaurant** Service 12:00-16:00, 20:00-22:00; menu 190F, also à la carte. Specialties: Escalope à la crème, steak au poivre, tarte aux myrtilles, fondue savoyarde, raclette. **Credit cards** Visa, Eurocard and MasterCard. **Pets** Dogs allowed. **Nearby** Skiing from hotel, Les Trois Vallées, mountain excursions – 9-hole Courchevel golf course, 18-hole Méribel golf course. **Open** Dec 20 – Apr 24.

This pretty chalet is only a few steps from the chairlift and the ski runs but it is well located above the valley, with spectacular views of pinewoods and mountains. You reach it via Méribel 1600, where you must leave your car; the hotel staff meets you and to take you to the chalet. The Adray is unrivalled at Méribel, and at lunchtime the large sunny terrace is invaded by skiers. The atmosphere is cheerful and the home cooking excellent. The bedrooms are simple but welcoming, with comfortable rustic furniture. The service is friendly and attentive. This is the place for making the most of the mountains without paying the higher prices of hotels in the village center.

***How to get there*** *(Map 27): 39km south of Albertville via N90 and D95, then D90.*

## Le Yéti

73553 Méribel-les-Allues (Savoie)
Tel. (0)4.79.00.51.15 - Fax (0)4.79.00.51.73
M. and Mme Saint Ghilhem

**Category** ★★★ **Rooms** 37 with telephone, bath, WC and satellite TV. **Price** Room with half board in winter 830-990F, in summer 540-750F (per pers.). **Restaurant** Service 12:00-14:30, 19:30-22:00; menus 98-235F, also à la carte. **Credit cards** All major. **Pets** Dogs not allowed. **Facilities** Swimming pool, sauna. **Nearby** Skiing from hotel, Les Trois Vallées, mountain excursions – 9-hole Courchevelle Golf Course, 18-hole Méribel Golf Course. **Open** All year except Apr 21 – June 30 and Oct 1 – Dec 16.

This chalet-hotel is located on the western slopes of Méribel, just next to the ski runs. Sophie and Frédéric Saint Ghilhem, who are both mountain guides, have decorated the hotel lovingly, and it shows. The walls are panelled in rough, hand-polished wood; the handsome furnishings include pretty objects, kilims, and comfortable armchairs in the bar and in front of the fire-place. The view is magnificent from all vantage points. The bedrooms are extremely comfortable and furnished in the loveliest mountain-chalet style. The panoramic restaurant has a terrace facing due south over a small swimming pool. Finally, when you set out for the lofty summits, Frédéric is there to advise you and to share the adventure.

***How to get there*** *(Map 27): 39m south of Albertville via N90 and D95, then D90.*

## Le Relais du Lac Noir

Tioulévé 73220 Montsapey (Savoie)
Tel. (0)4.79.36.30.52 - Fax (0)4.79.36.37.80
M. Caulliez

**Rooms** 8 (5 with bath, WC). **Price** Single 150F, double 220F. **Meals** Breakfast 35F; half board 240F, full board 310F (per pers.). **Restaurant** Service 12:30-15:00, from 20:00; menus 95-120F. Specialties: Gibier, diots (saucisses savoyardes), tartiflette, fondues, raclettes, magret, truite, tome chaude. **Credit cards** Visa, Eurocard and MasterCard. **Pets** Small dogs allowed. **Nearby** massif of the Lauzière, mountain excursions at Lac Noir (2000m) and at Grand Arc (2500m). **Open** 16 Dec – Nov 14.

The Relais du Lac Noir is located at the very end of a small, winding road which climbs up the mountainside to an altitude of 1030 meters in the heart of a natural cirque. It is surrounded by others chalets, some of which are very old. After having admired the splendid view, guests enter a large room with light-wood paneling. A corner bar, tables on a dais and a piano occupy a central foyer in front of which several comfortable chairs are arranged. M. and Mme Caulliez oversee everything, including mouthwatering mountain cuisine, and the friendly atmosphere which prevails here is due largely to them. The bedrooms, located on two floors, are small and well kept. Children will love the painted-wood closed beds upstairs, while their parents will prefer the rooms with a double bed (near the floor in some rooms); from all the rooms, you will enjoy silence, fresh mountain air and a beautiful view. The decoration is charming throughout, with old pine furniture and traditional objects contributing to an authentic and warm atmosphere. This is a special place, ideal for marvelous long walks (including, of course, a hike to Lac Noir), and there is excellent value for the money.

***How to get there*** *(Map 27): 75km north of Grenoble, toward Aiguebelle; via A43, Aiton exit.*

## Les Châtaigniers

Rue Maurice-Franck
73110 La Rochette (Savoie)
Tel. (0)4.79.25.50.21 - Fax (0)4.79.25.79.97 - Mme Rey

**Rooms** 3 and 1 suite and 1 apartment with telephone, bath, WC (2 with TV). **Price** Single and double 350-490F, suite 600-950F. **Meals** Breakfast 65F, served 7:45-10:00; half board from 3 night min. **Restaurant** Service 12:00-13:30, 19:45-21:30; menus 125-275F, also à la carte. Specialties: Foie gras mi-cuit au torchon maison, fish, tempura de homard, andouillette de saucisson chaud maison. **Credit cards** All major. **Pets** Dogs not allowed. **Facilities** Swimming pool, parking. **Nearby** Saint-Pierre-de-Chartreuse, château of Miolans, Charmant Som, belvédère des Sangles, la Grande Chartreuse convent, Wine Route of Savoie – 18-hole Aix-les Bains golf course. **Open** Jan 21 – 2 Jan closed 8 days in Sept and Nov (closed Saturday noon, Sunday evening and Wednesday in low season).

Between Savoie and Dauphiné at the foot of the mountains, this small hotel is a special place with a personality of its own. The lounge and the dining rooms all have an original, romantic, warm decor; the crystal sparkles, decorative objects abound, and several pieces of antique furniture remind us that we are in a former family home at Les Châtaigniers. The hospitality is on a par with the place, thanks to Philippe Roman, a former actor, a poet and a cook, who creates excellent cuisine with great respect for the products used; and Madame Rey, a charming, polyglot hostess with fine good taste. The atmosphere is lively, lighthearted, and don't be surprised if the evening ends with a poetry reading. The bedrooms have a kind of old-fashioned elegance (some carpets are a bit "tired".) The excellent breakfasts include marvelous hot pastries fresh out of the oven.

***How to get there*** *(Map 27): 30km north of Grenoble via A41, exit pontcharra, then D925; in La Rochette, in front of the "Hôtel de Ville" (town hall), to Arvillard.*

# Hôtel Le Calgary

73620 Les Saisies (Savoie)
Tel. 04 79 38 98 38 - Fax 04 79 38 98 00
M. Berthod

**Category** ★★★ **Rooms** 38 with telephone, bath, TV and minibar - 2 for disabled persons. **Price** Double and triple in half board 285-590F, full board 365-670F (per pers.). **Restaurant** Service 12:15-13:30, 19:15-21:00; menu 140-230F, also à la carte. Specialties: Le nougat de chevreau au miel des fleurs des montagnes, omble chevalier fumé par nos soins avec sa crème fouettée au genépi, parmentière de filet mignon de veau "de pays" au beaufort, chiboust aux poires caramélisées. **Credit cards** All major. **Pets** Dogs allowed (+50F). **Facilities** Swimming pool, hammam, sauna, garage (50F per day). **Nearby** Skiing from hotel, Olympic cross-country stadium at 200m – 18-hole Mont d'Arbois golf course in Megève (15 km). **Open** All year except May, Oct and Nov.

Le Calgary was built in Tyrolean style by the French ski champion Frank Piccard, who returned from Austria in love with the hotels there. Thus the reason for the flower-covered balconies which run along the façades and the two traditional oriel windows. Inside, the lounge recalls an Austrian pub and the dining room, with its colorful tablecloths, is very cheerful. Although the bedroom decor is somewhat standard, the rooms are spacious, and some can accommodate three people. All have a balcony with a lovely view over Beaufort and the ski trails of Les Saisies. In summer, the hotel offers a large choice of study sessions, including some for children. Le Calgary, by the way, is named after the town where Frank Piccard won an Olympic medal.

***How to get there*** *(Map 27): 31km northeast of Albertville via D925, towards Beaufort, and D218, towards Col des Saisies.*

1998

## Les Campanules

Le Rosset, BP 32
73320 Tignes (Savoie)
Tel. (0)4.79.06.34.36 - Fax (0)4.79.06.35.78 - MM. Reymond

**Category** ★★★ **Rooms** 33 and 10 suites with telephone, bath, WC and satellite TV - Elevator - 1 for disabled persons. **Price** Single and double 350-750F, 600-1060F; suite 800-1350F. **Meals** Breakfast incl., served 7:30-9:30; half board 430-720F, in suite 560-850F (per pers., 2 days min.). **Restaurant** "Le Chalet". Service 12:30-13:45, 19:30-21:45; menus 120-280F, also à la carte. Regional cooking. **Credit cards** Amex, Visa, Eurocard and MasterCard. **Pets** Dogs not allowed. **Facilities** Sauna, hammam, whirl pool. **Nearby** Skiing, Vanoise Park. **Open** Nov – May and June – Aug.

After a complete face lift, the Campanules today is truly a hotel of character and charm. The decorative scheme behind the renovation put priority on a return to tradition and improved modern amenities. The walls are panelled in blond wood, the furniture is of Savoyard inspiration, including enclosed beds and sculptured doors in several bedrooms, while shades of beige, brown, and red add a note of cheerful gaiety throughout the hotel. We also appreciated the little extras that make a return from the ski slopes so pleasant: individual slots for arranging our skis and drying our ski boots; a relaxing, well-equipped bathroom; a large choice of television programs; a sauna...not to mention the hotel's lovely Chalet restaurant, which serves elegant regional cuisine. Last but not least, the location is very special, in summer and winter alike, with the nearby lake and the Espace Killy.

***How to get there*** *(Map 27): 85km southeast of Albertville, highway to Moûtiers, N90 to Bourg-Saint-Maurice and Tignes.*

# Le Blizzard

73150 Val-d'Isère (Savoie)
Tel. (0)4.79 06 02 07 - Fax (0)4.79 06 04 94
M. Cerboneschi

**Category** ★★★★ **Rooms** 74 including 14 suites with telephone, bath or shower, WC and TV, minibar in suite - Elevator. **Price** Single and double 660-1390F (485-575F in summer). **Meals** Breakfast incl.; half board 485-850F per pers. (385-490F in summer per pers.). **Restaurant** Service 12:30-15:00, 19:30-22:00; menu from 160F, also à la carte. Specialties: Regional cooking. **Credit cards** All major. **Pets** Dogs allowed (+50F). **Facilities** Swimming pool, sauna, hammam, jacuzzi, parking. **Nearby** Ski lift (100m), Parc de la Vanoise, riding, mountain bikes, tennis. **Open** All year except May – June and Sept – Nov.

This has long been "the" hotel of Val d'Isère. Frequented by a chic clientele of habitués, there is nevertheless a sporty atmosphere marked by everyone's passion for skiing; if guests stay late at the bar, they are ready to go the next morning when the cable cars start up. Le Blizzard has just had a face lift. All the bedrooms have been redone in a style which is both modern and warm. Those on the south side are quieter and have a large balcony with a beautiful view. A large swimming pool has been built and is be open in both winter and summer. The restaurant serves excellent cuisine – on the terrace in summer and winter. Note also *La Luge*, the restaurant which is open until 2 AM.

***How to get there** (Map 27): 85km southeast of Albertville, highway towards Moûtiers, then N90 to Bourg-Saint-Maurice, then D902 to Val-d'Isère. Airport: Genève, Lyon Satolas, Chambéry. SNCF: TGV every Fridays Paris-Bourg-Saint-Maurice.*

## Hôtel Fitz Roy

73440 Val Thorens ( Savoie )
Tel. (0)4.79 00 04 78 - Fax (0)4.79 00 06 11
Mme Loubet

**Category** ★★★★ **Rooms** 30, 3 apartments, 3 mezzanines (with fireplace) with telephone, bath, hairdryer, TV and minibar- Elevator. **Price** Double in half board 800-1700F, full board 1000-1900F (per pers.). **Meals** Breakfast incl., served 7:00-11:00. **Restaurant** Service 12:00-15:00, 19:00-22:00; menu 220-500F, also à la carte. Specialties: Regional cooking. **Credit cards** Amex, Visa, Eurocard and Mastercard. **Pets** Dogs allowed (+90F). **Facilities** Covered swimming pool, sauna, health center, beauty salon, parking. **Nearby** Skiing from hotel. **Open** Dec 1 – May 6.

In the heart of Val Thorens, the Fitz Roy is a luxurious modern chalet. The interior is decorated very elegantly, with blond woodwork, predominantly white and pastel fabrics, and tasteful furniture. The large lounge, where vast sofas surround the fireplace, looks out due south over the ski runs. The bedrooms, which are all different, are spacious, with very refined decor and accommodations. Each has a balcony and a bathtub with whirlpool. In the evening, enjoy traditional Savoyard country cooking and professional service by candlelight. From the large terrace-solarium, you will also enjoy the superb sunsets over the resort. For l'après-ski, there is a swimming pool and excellent exercise equipment. In a resort which can be criticized for being artificial, the Fitz Roy has successfully combined luxury, modernity and the finest hotel tradition.

***How to get there*** *(Map 27): 62km southeast of Albertville via N90 to Moûtiers, then D915 and D117.*

## Chalet Rémy

Le Bettex
74170 Saint-Gervais (Haute-Savoie)
Tel. (0)4.50.93.11.85 - Mme Didier

**Rooms** 19 with basin. **Price** Double 250F. **Meals** Breakfast 35F, served 8:00-10:00; half board (obligatory in winter) and full board 300F and 350F (per pers., 3 days min.). **Restaurant** Service 12:00-14:00, 19:00-21:30; menu 95F, also à la carte. Specialties: Family cooking. **Credit cards** Visa, Eurocard and MasterCard. **Pets** Dogs allowed. **Nearby** Ski lift (300m), Chamonix, Megève – Mont-d'Arbois golf course in Megève (15km). **Open** All year.

This exceptional hotel is housed in an 18th-century farmhouse which through the centuries has preserved all its old woodwork. Panels, ceilings, moldings and the staircase leading to the superb gallery serving the bedrooms, all create a lovely harmony of dark red tones. The dining room is set with small tables lit by candles, and the family cuisine is excellent. Mme Didier loves classical music, which accompanies meals. It is the simplicity of the bedrooms that makes them charming; and though the bathroom facilities are merely basic, the bedrooms are absolute jewels with their lovely wood walls, floors and ceilings.The location of the Chalet Remy is another major asset. It is on the outskirts of Saint-Gervais and is reached by a winding road surrounded by pine woods and meadows facing the impressive snowy peaks of Mont Blanc.

***How to get there*** *(Map 27): 50km northeast of Albertville via N212 and D909 to Robinson and Le Bettex. By A40, Le Fayet-Passy exit.*

1998

# Chalet Hôtel L'Igloo

3120, Route des Crêtes
74170 Saint-Gervais (Haute-Savoie)
Tel. (0)4.50.93.05.84 - Fax (0)4.50.21.02.74 - M.Chapelland

**Category** ★★★ **Rooms** 11 with telephone, bath, WC, satellite TV, 9 with minibar. **Price** Double with half board 600-950F (per pers., discount in summer). **Meals** Breakfast 70F, served 8:00-10:00. **Restaurant** Service 12:00-16:00, 19:00-21:00; menus from 130F, also à la carte. **Credit cards** Amex, Visa, Eurocard and MasterCard. **Pets** Dogs allowed (+50F). **Facilities** Swimming pool. **Nearby** Skiing, Chamonix, Megève - Mont d'Arbois golf course in Megève (15 km). **Open** Dec 16 – Apr 19 and June 16 – Sept 19.

When the evening sun gilds the mountain peaks and the last skiers have disappeared behind the snowdrifts and into the valley, it's lovely to sit in silence and contemplate the gorgeous mountain scenery. The Igloo, located just at the arrival of the chairlift, makes the dream reality for the few lucky people who can do just that and then stay overnight in one of its eight comfortable bedrooms. The contrast is striking between the agitation of the daytime, with customers constantly coming in and out of the restaurant, the cafeteria or the bar, and the pastoral quiet which descends on the chalet at six in the evening. Then, you can quietly enjoy a drink on the terrace facing Europe's highest peak, before going into the restaurant to enjoy its excellent gastronomic cuisine.

***How to get there*** *(Map 27): In winter, access only by the Mont d'Arbois chairlifts leaving from Megève; in summer, via Saint-Gervais, dir. Alberville.*

## Hôtel La Savoyarde

28, route des Moussoux
74400 Chamonix (Haute-Savoie)
Tel. (0)4.50.53.00.77 - Fax (0)4.50.55.86.82 - M. and Mme Carrier
E mail: savoyarde@silicone.fr - Web: http://www/silicone.fr/savoyarde

**Category** ★★★ **Rooms** 14 with telephone, bath, WC and TV. **Price** Double 400-580F. **Meals** Breakfast 46F, served from 7:00. **Restaurant** Service 12:00-14:00, 19:30-21:30, menu 88F (38F child), also à la carte. Specialties: Raclette, tartiflette, fondue. **Credit cards** Visa, Eurocard and MasterCard. **Pets** Dogs allowed. **Facilities** Garage (+50F), parking. **Nearby** Skiing, mountain excursions – 18-hole Praz golf course. **Open** All year except May 11 – 28 and Nov 30 – Dec 17.

This hotel at the foot of Mount Brévent is surely one of the best located hotels in Chamonix. It overlooks the village and has a superb view of the Aiguille du Midi. Refurbished in the last two years, its style evokes both an English country cottage and an Alpine chalet. There are two adjoining buildings, both well cared for and, in summer, surrounded by flowers. The attractive entrance hall sets the tone of the house: painted ceilings, white walls and a cozy atmosphere. The owners have resisted the temptation to go in for a pseudo-rustic decor. The bedrooms are light and airy and have specially designed furniture. All have balconies or terraces and only two are at the back of the hotel. Among our favorites are Room 5, which has a large balcony, and Room 14, with its exposed beams. One drawback: in the bedrooms near the stairs, early-morning skiers can sometimes wake guests who are less enthusiastic early risers. Good mountain specialties are served by the fireside or on a terrace facing Mont Blanc.

***How to get there*** *(Map 27): 67km northeast of Albertville via N212 to Saint-Gervais, then N205. By A40, Le Fayet exit.*

## Résidences Les Balcons du Savoy

179, rue Mummery
74400 Chamonix (Haute-Savoie)
Tel. (0)4.50.55.32.32 - Fax (0)4.50.53.56.03 - M.Barlet
E-mail: balcons-du-savoy-chamonix@laposte.fr - Web: http://www.les-balcons-du-savoy.com

**Apartments** 67 with telephone, bath or shower, WC, satellite TV - Elevator. **Price** Apart. (2 pers.) 360-860F, 4 pers. 560-1145F, 6 pers. 745-1570F, 8 pers. 1072-2072F. **Meals** Breakfast 65-85F, served from 7:00. No restaurant. **Credit cards** Amex, Visa, Eurocard and MasterCard. **Pets** Dogs allowed (+40F). **Facilities** Covered swimming pool, hammam and parking. **Nearby** Skiing lift (50 m), mountain excursions - 18-hole Praz golf course. **Open** All year.

This hotel is somewhat in a category of its own because the Balcons de Savoie offers various kinds of apartment accommodations: You can rent an apartment and receive regular hotel services; for longer periods, you can enjoy the privacy and other advantages of a regular rented apartment; or you can combine the two arrangements according to your needs. The studios and the apartments are spacious, comfortably equipped, and well furnished (beige carpets, pine paneling, kilim-style fabrics, balconies...). All overlook an immense lawn, the arrival point for skiers in winter. Crowning the panorama is the majestic sight of Mont Blanc, its icy slopes plunging down to the foot of the small town of Chamonix. This large, modern complex is obviously not decorated in a terribly personal style, but the facilities available are a big plus. Several restaurants for the local fondues, raclettes and Savoyard products: *Le Chaudron, L'Impossible, Le Peter Pan* and *La Crèmerie des Bossons* in Les Houches.

***How to get there*** *(Map 27): 67km northeast of Albertville via N212 to Saint-Gervais, then N205. Via A40, exit Le Fayet.*

# Hôtel du Jeu de Paume

705, route du Château - Le Lavancher
74400 Chamonix (Haute-Savoie)
Tel. (0)4.50.54.03.76 - Fax (0)4.50.54.10.75 - Mme Prache

**Category** ★★★★ **Rooms** 22 with telephone, bath, shower, WC, TV, hairdryer and minibar. **Price** Single and double 890-1080F, suite 1390F. **Meals** Breakfast 65F, served 7:30-10:30; half board 585-635F (per pers.). **Restaurant** Service 12:00-14:00, 19:30-21:30; menu 170-300F, also à la carte. **Credit cards** All major. **Pets** Dogs allowed (+50F). **Facilities** Swimming pool, tennis, sauna, car rental, parking. **Nearby** Skiing in Argentières (Les Grands Montets, 3km), and in Chamonix – 18-hole Praz golf course. **Open** Dec 5 – Sep 10.

Elyane and Guy Prache, who own the elegant Hôtel du Jeu de Paume in the heart of the Ile Saint-Louis in Paris, have just opened this delightful chalet-hôtel at Lavancher, 7km from Chamonix, on the edge of a pine wood overlooking the Argentière Valley. The hotel is luxurious, refined and very comfortable; it is the chalet "re invented", with wood playing a major role in the decor. The bedrooms are all very functional and furnished with warmth and good taste; nearly all have balconies. There is the same comfortable coziness in the bar and lounges. Throughout the hotel there are lovely pieces of antique furniture, mirrors and paintings. The traditional cooking is excellent and is served in a convivial atmosphere. The staff is very welcoming and in winter the hotel car will take you to the departure points for the ski runs.

***How to get there*** *(Map 27): 67km northeast of Albertville via N212. By A40, Le Fayet exit.*

## Chalet-Hôtel Beausoleil

74400 Chamonix - Le Lavancher ( Haute-Savoie )
Tel. (0)4.50.54.00.78 - Fax (0)4.50.54.17.34
M. Bossonney

**Category** ★★ **Rooms** 15 with telephone, bath or shower, WC and TV. **Price** Single 265-300F, double 278-580F. **Meals** Breakfast 45F, served 7:30-10:00; half board 300-420F, full board 360-480F (per pers., 3 days min.). **Restaurant** Service 12:30-13:30, 19:30-20:30; menu 90-150F, also à la carte. Specialties: Entrecôte sauce morilles, escalope de veau savoyarde, filet de truite au Crepy, fondue, raclette. **Credit cards** Visa, Eurocard and MasterCard. **Pets** Dogs allowed in rooms. **Facilities** Tennis. **Nearby** Ski lift (3 km), overland skiing from hotel – 18-hole Praz golf course. **Open** Dec 20 – Sept 20.

This peaceful hotel has been run by the Bossonney family for fifty years. Lying at the foot of the Aiguille du Midi and Mont Blanc, it is surrounded by gentle fields and peaceful tranquility. The recently renovated bedrooms are small but all offer modern accommodations and pleasant bathrooms; the rooms upstairs have balconies. The dining room opens onto a terrace which in turn gives onto a lovely flower garden bordered with evergreens. You will enjoy good family cooking at the Beausoleil, along with a friendly welcome.

***How to get there*** *(Map 27): 67km northeast of Albertville via N212. Via A40, Le Fayet exit. (4km north of Chamonix via N506, toward Argentière).*

## Hôtel Le Labrador

101, route du Golf
74400 Chamonix - Les Praz (Haute-Savoie)
Tel. (0)4.50.55.90.09 - Fax (0)4.50.53.15.85 - M. Bartoli
E-mail: labrador@cyberaccess.fr - Web: http://www.montblanconline.fr

**Category** ★★★ **Rooms** 32 with telephone, bath, WC, TV and minibar. **Price** Double 555-800F. **Meals** Breakfast incl., served until 10:30; half board 398-670F, full board 560-795F (per pers., 3 days min.). **Restaurant** Service 12:00-22:30; menu from 85F, also à la carte. Specialties: Saumon fumé maison, côte de bœuf gros sel. **Credit cards** All major. **Pets** Dogs allowed. **Facilities** Sauna, fitness center, whirlpool, parking. **Nearby** Skiing from hotel, Alpine skiing: La Flégère (250 m), Chamonix (3 km) – 18-hole Praz golf course. **Open** Dec 15 – Oct 15.

Built on the Chamonix Golf Course facing Mont Blanc, the Labrador enjoys an outstanding location. A combination of Scandinavian and Savoyard architecture, the various buildings of the hotel fit harmoniously into the natural setting. The bedrooms are not very large but they are comfortable, and those on the front have balconies. The restaurant, La Cabane, is more typically Finnish, with a traditional kelo roof which is made of actual turf. (It is mowed every week!) La Cabane offers simple, hearty cuisine with specialties which vary with the seasons. (Try the roast beef ribs with coarse salt). The only drawback is its large size, which makes it somewhat lacking in intimacy. The service is attentive. And the hotel will also suggest ski, golf or mountain package trips if you wish.

***How to get there*** *(Map 27): 67km northeast of Albertville, via N212. Via A40, exit Le Fayet. (3km north of Chamonix via N506, toward Argentière; on the golf course).*

## Chalet-Hôtel Peter Pan

74310 Les Houches (Haute-Savoie)
Tel. (0)4.50.54.40.63
M. and Mme Bochatay

**Rooms** 13 (2 with bath, 4 shower and 2 with WC). **Price** Double 200-270F. **Meals** Breakfast 38F, served 8:00-10:00; half board 255-275F, full board 295-310F (per pers., 3 days min.). **Restaurant** Service at 12:30 and 19:30; menus 95F lunchtime - 145F, also à la carte. Specialties: Crépinette de pied de porc aux cèpes, bourguignon de canard à la crème de cassis, cake au chocolat. **Credit cards** Not accepted. **Pets** Dogs allowed. **Facilities** Parking. **Nearby** Ski lifts (1km) – 18-hole Praz golf course in Chamonix (7km). **Open** All year except in May and Oct 15 – Dec 15.

Michel Bochatay and his wife have been in this beautiful converted 18th-century farm for seventeen years. It is on a hilltop near Les Houches and has a superb view of the valley of Chamonix. In this delightful place the owners have created an original and welcoming ambience, with excellent food at reasonable prices. The two chalets are constructed entirely of wood and are veritable small museums. Meals are served by candlelight on prettily set little wooden tables bright with bouquets of flowers. The bedrooms vary in size and style. Rooms 1 and 2 are spacious (2 has a bathroom) and Room 6 on the top floor is more intimate; the three look out on the valley. The rooms in the annex are smaller and four of them have only a washbasin. Nevertheless, thanks to the tranquillity, the charming ambience and the warm welcome, the Peter Pan is a great place to stay.

***How to get there*** *(Map 27): 59km northeast of Albertville via N212, then N205. By A40, Le Fayet exit. 7km west of Chamonix.*

1998

## Le Montagny

490, Le Pont 74310 Chamonix - Les Houches (Haute-Savoie)
Tel. (0)4.50.54.57.37 - Fax (0)4.50.54.52.97
M. Ravanel

**Category** ★★ **Rooms** 8 with telephone, bath, WC and TV. **Price** Double 360F. **Meals** Breakfast 42F, served 7:30-10:30. No restaurant. **Credit cards** Visa, Eurocard and MasterCard. **Pets** Dogs not allowed. **Facilities** Parking. **Nearby** Skiing lift (3 km) - 18-hole Praz golf course in Chamonix (7 km). **Open** All year except in Nov.

One of the oldest families in the valley here has just opened this welcoming small chalet-hotel behind which the slope leads up to the Dôme du Goûter peak. Its location and the small number of rooms make the Montagny marvelously quiet, an impression heightened by the crystal-clear mountain air for which we would travel kilometers. We took an immediate liking to the interior with its light pine panelling, the green tartan fabric upholstery on the benches in the room where breakfast (delicious) is served, as well as on those in the lounge (where there is often an open fire, a must for a mountain evening.) We found the bedrooms just as inviting, with modern amenities and very pretty blue and white fabrics beautifully complementing the honey-colored panelling and the bathroom tiling. Room 104 is ideal for families; Numbers 206 and 207, located beneath the angular eaves of the roof, are equipped with charming alcove bathrooms. We can heartily recommend all the rooms. It's no wonder the delightful little Montagny already has its regular customers. Several restaurants for *fondues*, *raclettes* and Savoyard products: *L'Impossible* and *Le Peter Pan* in Les Houches.

***How to get there*** *(Map 27): 59km northeast of Albertville via N212, then N205. A40 Le Fayet exit (5km before Chamonix).*

1998

# Les Chalets de la Serraz

Rue du col des Aravis
74220 La Clusaz (Haute Savoie)
Tel. (0)4.50.02.48.29 - Fax (0)4.50.02.64.12 - Mme M.- C.Gallay

**Category** ★★★ **Rooms** 12 with telephone, bath, WC and satellite TV - 1 for disabled persons. **Price** Single and double 450-650F, 450-750F; suite 520-850F. **Meals** Breakfast 60F, served 8:00-10:30; half board 385-595F (per pers., 3 days min.). **Restaurant** Service 12:00-14:30, 19:15-21:30; menus 125-165F. Specialties: Péla traditionnelle au roblochon des Aravis, poissons de lac: féra, omble chevalier, perche. **Credit cards** Amex, Visa, Eurocard and MasterCard. **Divers** Dogs allowed (+55F). **Facilities** Swimming and garage (65F). **Nearby** Skiing; lake of Annecy **Open** All year except in May and Oct.

Leaving La Clusaz in the direction of the Col des Aravis, you will come to this group of traditional chalets on the picturesque route through the summer mountain pastures. The site itself, a valley dotted with spruce and traversed by a small river, ensures each bedroom of a lovely view. You have a choice of the small, individual *mazot* farmhouses with kitchenettes and lofts (ideal for families), or the bedrooms in the main building: a renovated old Savoyard farmhouse with a roof of wooden tiles. Their furnishings, including mountain furniture and red-and-white checked fabrics, are very much in keeping with the chalet style. (Only the bathroom fixtures are somewhat sad.) All the bedrooms, some with ground-floor terraces, are well-kept and comfortable. At dinner, we admired the elegance of the dining room and its pale panelling, and we enjoyed the cuisine, which alternates between dishes with a delicate gourmet touch and, once a week, Savoyard specialties, which are served at a communal table.

***How to get there** (Map 27): 5km of Chambéry.*

## Au Cœur des Prés

74920 Combloux (Haute-Savoie)
Tel. (0)4.50.93.36.55 - Fax (0)4.50.58.69.14
M. Paget

**Category** ★★★ **Rooms** 34 and 1 suite with telephone, bath, WC and TV. **Price** Single and double 400-550F. **Meals** Breakfast 48F, served from 7:30; half board and full board 410-480F (per pers.). **Restaurant** Service 12:30-14:00, 19:30-20:30; menu 155-190F, also à la carte. **Credit cards** Visa, Eurocard and MasterCard. **Pets** Dogs allowed. **Facilities** Tennis, sauna, whirlpool, garage (35F), parking. **Nearby** Ski lifts (1km), Megève, Chamonix – 18-hole Mont d'Arbois golf course in Megève. **Open** May 20 – Sept 25 and Dec 19 – Apr 15.

This hotel has the advantage not only of a superb view of Mont Blanc and the Aravis Mountains, but it is also surrounded by a large, quiet meadow. Most of the bedrooms overlooking Mont Blanc have a balcony; they are comfortable and all have now been renovated. Those on the troisième étage, which have mansard ceilings, are the most charming. The lounge has comfortable armchairs and a big fireplace, and the dining room is charming with its tiled floor, exposed beams, pink tablecloths and panoramic view. Guests very much enjoy chef Nicolas' cuisine. The hotel has been awarded prizes by the community for its summer flower display and is ideal for those who like peace and tranquillity amid impressive scenery. During the winter-sports season, the hotel has a shuttle to take clients to the various ski areas.

***How to get there*** *(Map 27): 36km northeast of Albertville via N212 to Combloux through Megève. Via A40, Le Fayet exit.*

# Les Roches Fleuries

74700 Cordon (Haute-Savoie)
Tel. (0)4.50.58.06.71 - Fax (0)4.50.47.82.30
J. and G. Picot

**Category** ★★★ **Rooms** 28 with telephone, bath, WC and satellite TV. **Price** Double 460-650F, suite 750-950F. **Meals** Breakfast 60F, served 7:30-10:00; half board 410-600F (per pers.). **Restaurant** Service 12:30-14:00, 19:30-21:30; menus 140-295F also à la carte. Specialties: Tartiffle de lapin au Beaufort, pigeon fermier mi-cuit aux pousses d'épinard, "la boite à fromages". Regional restaurant 160F. **Credit cards** All major. **Pets** Dogs allowed (+45F). **Facilities** Heated swimming pool, health center, ranning salon, whirlpool, hammam, Mountain bikes rental, mountain guides, parking, garage (30F). **Nearby** Ski lifts (700m), Megève, Chamonix – 18-hole Mont d'Arbois golf course in Megève. **Open** Mai 13 – Oct 1 and Dec 17 – Apr 8.

Cordon lies between Combloux and Sallanches on the threshold of Mont Blanc and is a delightful village all year round. In summer the chalets nestle among cherry and walnut trees, and in winter there are sensational views of the Aiguilles de Chamonix and the Aravis Mountains. The bedrooms are prettily furnished and most have terraces on which you can enjoy the magnificent view, the peace and the sun. Like the bedrooms, the lounge and dining room are furnished in a comfortable rustic style. In winter the blaze in the fireplace creates a warm and cozy ambience. The cuisine is light and elegant, and you can also enjoy regional specialties in the hotel's second restaurant, *La Boîte à Fromage*.

***How to get there*** *(Map 27): 40km northeast of Albertville via N212 to Combloux, then D113. Via A40, Sallanches exit.*

1998

## L'Ancolie

Cruseilles
Lac des Dronières 74350 (Haute-Savoie)
Tel. (0)4.50.44.28.98 - Fax (0)4.50.44.09.73 - M. Lefebvre

**Category** ★★★ **Rooms** 10 with telephone, bath WC and satellite TV. **Price** Single and double 350-445F. **Meals** Breakfast 45F, served 7:30-10:30; half board 400-445F (per pers., 3 days min.). **Restaurant** Service 12:00-14:00, 19:00-21:15; menus 120-360F, also à la carte. Specialties: Foie gras frais de canard landais, Rissoles de reblochon fermier, croustillant de pigeon de la ferme de monsieur Trottet. **Credit cards** All major. **Pets** Dogs allowed (+30F). **Facilities** Parking and garage (30F). **Nearby** Annecy Lake, Le Semnoz by the ridgeway, gorges of Le Fier, Genève - 18-hole Bossey golf course, 18-hole Annecy golf course in Talloires. **Open** All year except Oct 24 - Nov 4 and Feb 18 - March 4 - Sunday evening

Recently built in the style of a mountain chalet, the Ancolie stands facing Mount Salève and is reflected in the waters of a small artificial lake with newly landscaped banks. The location could be splendid if only Electricité de France had not put up three giant steel girders!...This reservation aside, the hotel is still greatly enjoyed by hikers and mushroom gatherers. We also love the interior decoration of the Ancolie, where waxed pine furniture, thick carpets and ravishing coordinated fabrics form an ensemble which is comfortable and smartly kept, as are the bedrooms; some have a terrace and all are well soundproofed. Our favorites are those on the lake. Yves Lebvre directs the hotel's hospitable staff and the kitchen, whose menu is highly tempting. While waiting for the opportunity to taste his cuisine, we will rely on his fine reputation to recommend it to you.

***How to get there*** *(Map 27): 20km from Annecy*

## Marceau Hôtel

115, chemin de la Chappelière
74210 Doussard (Haute-Savoie)
Tel. (0)4.50.44.30.11 - Fax (0)4.50.44.39.44 - M. and Mme Sallaz

**Category** ★★★ **Rooms** 16 with telephone, bath or shower, WC and TV. **Price** Double 480F, suite 700F, apart. 880F. **Meals** Breakfast 50F, served 7:30-10:00. No Restaurant. **Credit cards** All major. **Pets** Dogs allowed (+50F). **Facilities** Tennis, parking. **Nearby** Lake of Annecy, le Semnoz by the ridgeway, gorges of Le Fier – 18-hole Annecy golf course in Talloires. **Open** All year.

In one of the most touristic areas of France, how lovely it is to find a peaceful haven well off the beaten track! Set in the middle of the countryside with a beautiful view of the lake and valley, this elegantly comfortable hotel is precisely that and much more. In the dining-room, subtle shades of pink blend perfectly with the colors of the wood, and large windows open onto beautiful surroundings. There is an attractive lounge for watching television or reading by the fireside. In summer, both view and sunshine can be enjoyed on a delightful terrace next to the kitchen garden. The bedrooms are tastefully decorated, with carefully chosen furniture. There are fresh flowers everywhere and the welcome is warm.

***How to get there*** *(Map 27): 20km south of Annecy via N508 towards Albertville, Doussard and Marceau-Dessus.*

1998

## Hôtel des Cimes

Le Chinaillon 74450 Le Grand-Bornand (Haute-Savoie)
Tel. (0)4.50.27.00.38 - Fax (0)4.50.27.08.46 - M. and Mme Losserand
E-mail : http:/www.hotel.les cimes.@ msn.com

**Category** ★★★ **Rooms** 10 with telephone, bath, WC, TV and minibar. **Price** Double 395-650F, in Jan week 3400F per pers. **Meals** Breakfast incl., served 8:00-11:00. Meal trays 70-120F. **Credit cards** Visa, Eurocard and MasterCard. **Pets** Small dogs allowed. **Facilities** Sauna, parking and garage (2 places). **Nearby** La Clusaz, col des Aravis, gorges of the Fier, Annecy Lake. **Open** Dec 2 – Apr 30 and June 16 – Sept 14.

Le Grand Bornand: 200z0 inhabitants, 2000 cows, and a landmarked site where you can admire several magnificent old chalets including, nearby, this marvelous small hotel run by Kiki and Jeannot, a young couple from the mountains who have the gift of hospitality and good taste. From the entrance, we were charmed by the few pieces of old furniture from the area, decorative objects, bouquets of dried flowers. Fragrant with roses and lily-of-the-valley, the hotel has walls covered with broad golden pine boards; furniture and doors decorated with friezes or painted motifs by Kiki or an artist friend. We loved the bedrooms with their checked eiderdowns and their small bathrooms. There is a table here and there for the delicious breakfasts or the dinner trays (the family's kitchen is occasionally open to guests in the hotel.) The Hôtel des Cimes is one of our most beautiful recent discoveries. Reserve now!

***How to get there*** *(Map 27): 35km east of Annecy. On A3 Annecy-nord exit, then towards Thones and Saint Jean de Six; On A10, Bonneville exit to Le Grand-Bornand.*

# Hôtel de La Croix Fry

Manigod - 74230 Thônes (Haute-Savoie)
Tel. (0)4.50.44.90.16 - Fax (0)4.50.44.94.87 - Mme Guelpa-Veyrat
Web: http://www.oda.fr/aa/croix-fry

**Category** ★★★ **Rooms** 12 with telephone, bath (1 with balneo), WC and satellite TV. **Price** Double 500-1500F (suite). **Meals** Breakfast 80F, served 8:00-11:00; half board 550-900F (per pers., 3 days min.). **Restaurant** Service 12:30-13:30, 19:30-20:45; menus 145-385F, also à la carte. Specialties: Tartifflette maison, viande et omelette avec bolets et chanterelles, foie gras cuit maison, desserts aux fruits sauvages. **Credit cards** Amex, Visa, Eurocard and MasterCard. **Pets** Dogs allowed (+26F). **Facilities** Heated swimming pool, tennis, fitness room, parking. **Nearby** Skiing in La Croix-Fly/l'Etoile (1km), La Clusaz, Manigod valley, village of Chinaillon, gorges of Le Fier, Annecy lake – 18-hole Annecy golf course in Talloires. **Open** June 15 – Sept 15, Dec 15 – Apr 15.

This is the kind of hotel we would like to find more often in the French Alps without having to go to the five-star establishments. It is comfortable and cozy and its bedrooms – all named after mountain flowers – have had great care lavished on them over the years: beamed ceilings and old furniture create a snug chalet atmosphere. The ones facing the valley have breathtaking views and are very sunny. All have either a balcony, a terrace or a mezzanine to make up for the tiny bathrooms. (Some have balneotherapy bathtubs.) The former stables, converted into a bar with seats covered in sheepskin, lead into the dining-room, which faces the Tournette Mountains. This is a great spot in summer or winter, and you are strongly advised to reserve well in advance, for the hotel has a large and faithful following.

***How to get there*** *(Map 27): 27km east of Annecy via D909 to Thônes, then D12 and D16 to Manigod, then La Croix Fry.*

## Le Mont Blanc

Place de l'église, rue Ambroise Martin
74120 Megève (Haute-Savoie)
Tel. (0)4.50.21.20.02 - Fax (0)4.50.21.45.28 - M. Sibuet
Web: http://www.skifrance.fr/-hoyel-montblanc-megeve - E-mail: mtblanc@internet-montblanc.fr

**Category** ★★★ **Rooms** 40 with telephone, bath, WC, TV, minibar and safe. **Price** Single and double 1050-2790F (per pers.). **Meals** Breakfast incl. No restaurant. **Credit cards** All major. **Pets** Dogs allowed (extra charge). **Facilities** Steam bath, sauna, jacuzzi, health center. **Nearby** Ski lifts (50m), Chamonix valley – 18-hole Mont d'Arbois golf course. **Open** June 15 – May 1.

Successful, talented Jocelyne and Jean-Louis Sibuet are in charge of the Mont Blanc's «new life». The Mont Blanc! This was one of the symbolic places of the prosperity and carefree spirit of the 1960s when anybody who was a celebrity emigrated from Saint Tropez to Megève for the winter. Guests came down to enjoy the hotel's cozy comfort late in the day because most had spent the wee hours in Les Enfants Terribles, the hotel's famous, sophisticated bar which was decorated by Jean Cocteau. Reviving this spirit was a difficult challenge: Times have changed and most guests no longer have the whimsical insouciance of that Golden Age. Today, the Mont Blanc has taken on a very beautiful look, happily marrying English, Austrian and Savoyard styles. Everything is luxuriously perfect: every modern amenity, fine service...as well as the luxury and discretion which are appreciated by the hotel's international clientele.

***How to get there*** *(Map 27): 34km northeast of Albertville via N212. Take A40, exit Sallanches. (Megève exit via Albertville).*

## Les Fermes Marie

Chemin de Riante Colline
74120 Megève (Haute-Savoie)
Tel. (0)4.50.93.03.10 - Fax (0)4.50.93.09.84 - M. Sibuet
E-mail: fdemarie@internet-montblanc.fr - Web: http://www.skifrance.fr/-fermesdemarie

**Category** ★★★ **Rooms** 68 with telephone, bath, WC and TV. **Price** Single and double in half board 800-1470F (per pers.). **Restaurant** Service 12:00-14:00, 19:30-22:30; carte 250F. Specialties: Regional cooking, fish. Cheeses restaurant: Menu 220F. **Credit cards** Amex, Visa, Eurocard and MasterCard. Pets dogs allowed (extra charge). **Facilities** Steam bath, fitness center, sauna, jacuzzi, health center, swimming pool. **Nearby** Ski lifts (500m), Chamonix valley – 18-hole Mont d'Arbois golf course. Open Dec 17 – Apr 15 and June 23 – Sept 15.

"Marie's Farms" actually make up a Savoyard hamlet consisting of chalets reconstructed from old *mazots*—traditional tiny mountain chalets. The reception, the three restaurants, the library, and the bar occupy the large main chalet. All the bedrooms face due south and are beautifully fitted out in the best mountain style, with comfortable amenites, a balcony/terrce, and a small lounge. Jocelyne scoured the region for all the antique furniture in the hotel. You can enjoy three restaurants: a *rôtisserie,* another specializing in cheese, and finally, the restaurant serving regional gastronomy. Similar care has been given to the breakfast, which includes delicious homemade preserves, good country bread, and crusty *baguettes.* The Beauty Farm offers one-week beauty and fitness treatments with special rates in January, July, and September.

***How to get there*** *(Map 27): 34km northeast of Albertville via N212. Take A40, exit Le Fayet. (The hotel is on the road to Rochebrune).*

## Le Coin du Feu

Route de Rochebrune
74120 Megève (Haute-Savoie)
Tel. (0)4.50.21.04.94 - Fax (0)4.50.21.20.15 - M. and Mme Sibuet

**Category** ★★★ **Rooms** 23 with telephone, bath, WC and TV. **Price** Single and double 800-1050F. **Meals** Breakfast 35F; half board 680-840F (per pers.). **Restaurant** Service 19:30-22:30; menu 250F, also à la carte. Specialties: Regional cooking and fish from the lake. **Credit cards** Amex, Visa, Eurocard and MasterCard. **Pets** Dogs allowed (extra charge). **Nearby** Ski lifts (200m), Chamonix valley – 18-hole Mont d'Arbois golf course. **Open** Dec 20 – Apr 5 and July 25 – Aug 31.

This hotel has long been known to those who like tradition as the most appealing place to stay in Megève. Its success lies in its handsome pine furniture, oak panelling, the flowered fabrics and above all its welcoming fireplace. The hotel's restaurant, the Saint-Nicholas, attracts Megève regulars who come here for its simple but delicious cuisine or the traditional raclettes and fondues. The bedrooms are cheerful and pretty and you will receive a very friendly welcome.

***How to get there*** *(Map 27): 34km northeast of Albertville via N212. By A40, Le Fayet exit. (The hotel is on the road to Rochebrune).*

## Le Fer à Cheval

36, route du Crêt-d'Arbois
74120 Megève (Haute-Savoie)
Tel. (0)4.50.21.30.39 - Fax (0)4.50.93.07.60 - M. Sibuet

**Category** ★★★ **Rooms** 41 with telephone, bath, WC, satellite TV and minibar. **Price** Double with half board 595-900F (per pers.). **Meals** Breakfast 60F, served 7:45-11:30. **Restaurant** Service 19:30-21:30; menu savoyard, also à la carte. **Credit cards** Amex, Visa, Eurocar and MasterCard. **Pets** Dogs allowed (+45F). **Facilities** Swimming pool, sauna, whilpool, hammam, health center, parking, garage. **Nearby** Ski lifts (450m), Chamonix valley – 18-hole Mont d'Arbois golf course. **Open** Dec 14 – Easter and July 1 – Sept 11.

This is one of the most charming hotels in Megève, from every point of view. The chalet has been very well refurbished; exposed beams and lovely wood panelling create a warm and comfortable decor, as do the patinated and polished antique furniture and the variety of fabrics and *objets d'art.* We can't recommend any particular bedroom – they are all delightful and any variation in price is only due to size. In winter, meals are served by the fireplace in the dining room, and in summer by the swimming pool. The hotel shuttle can take you to the slopes and in the summer, you can spend a day in the *Les Moliettes* mountain pasture, lying at an altitude of 4680 feet, to which you can climb in a four-wheel drive or on foot (one hour), followed by lunch and a discovery of the local flora and fauna.. Guests receive a warm welcome.

***How to get there** (Map 27): 34km northeast of Albertville via N212. By A40, Sallanches exit.*

# Hôtel Le Mégevan

Route de Rochebrune
74120 Megève (Haute-Savoie)
Tel. (0)4.50.21.08.98 - Fax (0)4.50.21.79.20 - M. Demarta
Web: http://www.netarchitects.com/megevan

**Category** ★★ **Rooms** 11 with telephone, bath, WC, minibar and TV. **Price** Double 350-350F. **Meals** Breakfast incl., served from 7:30 No restaurant. **Credit cards** Amex, Visa, Eurocard and MasterCard. **Pets** Dogs allowed. **Nearby** Skiing from hotel with Rochebrune chairlift, valley of Chamonix – 18-hole Arbois golf course. **Open** All year.

Frequented largely by faithful clients, the Mégevan is a small, unpretentious hotel, very refined, but a true hotel of character and charm. There are no rigid hotel rules here, refusing you breakfast service at 10:03: hours are flexible and the staff is pleasant. Down from the Rochebrune road, the Demartas' old family house has eleven very beautiful bedrooms. All have a small balcony in the larches; the bedrooms are spacious and discreetly decorated in a 1930s style with pretty engravings, wood, soft carpets and charming bathrooms. The salon-bar with its deep sofas is an invitation to after-ski relaxation around the fireplace. The Rochebrune chairlift is only 100 meters away. The hotel has no restaurant but the choice is vast in Megève. Nearby, try the fondue at *Le Chamois* in the village or *Le Saint-Nicolas*, which is more «in»; for lunch, there is the beautiful terrace of *L'Alpette* in Rochebrune.

***How to get there*** *(Map 27): 34km northeast of Albertville via N212. Via A40, exit Le Fayet. The hotel is on the road to Rochebrune.*

## La Bergerie

Rue de Téléphérique
74110 Morzine (Haute-Savoie)
Tel. (0)4.50.79.13.69 - Fax (0)4.50.75.95.71 - Mme Marullaz

**Category** ★★★ **Rooms** 27 rooms, studios or apartments with telephone, bath, WC, TV (21 with kitchenette). **Price** Room 400-600F, studio 500-800F, apart. (4-6 pers.) 600-1000F. **Meals** Breakfast 60F, served 7:00-11:00. **Restaurant** Evening meals 1 day by week. **Credit cards** Visa, Eurocard and MasterCard. **Pets** Dogs allowed. **Facilities** Swimming pool, sauna, solarium, health center, games room, garage. **Nearby** Ski lifts (50m), Avoriaz, Evian – 9-hole Morzine golf course, 18-hole Royal Hôtel golf course, Evian. **Open** Dec 20 – mid. Apr and end Jun – mid. Sept.

This is the favorite hotel of Morzine residents, although it has changed somewhat. There are now studios and apartments as well as individual bedrooms, all sharing the hotel's services. The Mourgues armchairs and the orange-and-yellow check fabrics on the Knoll-style chairs in the lounge make for a delightful 1970s style. The best bedrooms are those facing south which look out over the garden and the swimming pool. The restaurant offers a small menu and once a week, a *table d'hôtes* dinner is served, featuring Savoyard specialties. In winter, the heated outdoor swimming pool is accessible via a covered passageway. The most popular restaurants with the resort's regulars are *Le Cherche Midi* on the road to Les Gets, or *La Crémaillère* in Les Lindarets-Montrionds, which you can also get to in winter via the ski trails.

***How to get there*** *(Map 27): 93km northeast of Annecy via A41 and A40, Cluses exit, then D902. The hotel is near the E.S.F (ski school).*

## Hôtel Beau Site

74290 Talloires (Haute-Savoie)
Tel. (0)4.50.60.71.04 - Fax (0)4.50.60.79.22
M. Conan

**Category** ★★★ **Rooms** 29 with telephone, bath or shower, WC and TV (10 with minibar). **Price** Single and double 450-825F, suite 900-1000F. **Meals** Breakfast 60F, served 7:30-10:30; half board 450-700F, full board 500-700F (per pers., 2 days min.). **Restaurant** Service 12:30-14:00, 19:30-21:15; menus 170-280F, also à la carte. Specialties: Fish from the lake. **Credit cards** All major. **Pets** Dogs allowed. **Facilities** Tennis (+65F), private beach, parking. **Nearby** Ermitage Saint-Germain, château de Menthon-Saint-Bernard, Thorens and Montrottier, château, lake, museum and olg city in Annecy – 18-hole Annecy golf course in Talloires. **Open** May 11 – Oct 12.

With grounds reaching right down to the banks of Lake Annecy, the Hôtel Beau Site is reminiscent of a hotel on the Italian lakes. A family estate converted into a hotel at the end of the 19th century, it has retained many gracious features: a vast, sunny dining-room-cum-verandah decorated with old plates; a delightful lounge with period furniture; and lawns well provided with deck chairs. The charming bedrooms have been completely refurbished; they have a terrace and many look out on the lake. Some are decorated with antiques, others are more modern, and some have a mezzanine. The food is excellent. The hotel is specially noted for its warm and friendly welcome.

***How to get there*** *(Map 27): 13km from Annecy via A41, Annecy exit. At Annecy, take east bank of lake towards Thônes until Veyrier, then Talloires.*

# INDEX

* Contents: Mountain Chalets--Hotels (see p. 597)
* Hotels in Paris (see contents)

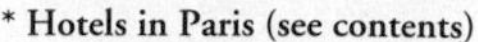

## C

## D

## N



## O



## P

## Q



## R

S



T

# CONTENTS: MOUNTAIN CHALETS-HOTELS

## *South-Alps*

**Praloup** *(Alpes-de-Haute-Provence)* 1600-2500 meters

**WINTER** – *Alpine skiing: 28 skiing tracks – Connection with La Foux-d'Allos (65 skiing tracks) – Ski-Pass: Pra-Loup-La Foux d'Allos – Hiking: 5km – Ice rink, 2 covered tennis – Cinema.* **SUMMER** – *Tennis, riding, hang gliding.*

**Tourist Office:** 04 92 84 10 04 - ESF: 04 92 84 11 05 / 15 15



**Super-Sauze** *(Alpes-de-Haute-Provence)* 1400-2450 meters

**WINTER** – *Alpine skiing: 35 skiing tracks – Hiking: 5km – Connection by shuttle between Barcelonnette and Pra-Loup – Covered swimming pool, walk with rackets and dogs sledge, hang gliding – Cinema.* **SUMMER** – *Hiking: 30km – Tennis, riding, ULM, mountain bikes, climbing.*

**Tourist Office:** 04 92 81 05 61 - ESF: 04 92 81 05 20



**Serre-Chevalier** *(Hautes-Alpes)* 1350-2800 meters

**WINTER** – *Alpine skiing: 93 skiing tracks – Cross-country skiing: 45km – Connection with Alpe-d'Huez, Deux-Alpes, Puy-Saint-Vincent, Voie Lactée, Bardonnecchia and Serre-Chevalier – Ski-Pass: Grand Serre-Che – Hiking: 20km – 3 ice rinks, covered swimming pool, ULM, hang gliding, trips in sledge– Cinemas.* **SUMMER** – *Hiking: in the Ecrins Park – Climbing, hang gliding, ULM, riding, tennis, rafting.*

**Tourist Office**: Monêtier: 04 92 24 41 98, Villeneuve-la-Salle: 04 92 24 71 88 - ESF: 1350 m: 04 92 24 17 41, 1400 m: 04 92 24 71 99, 1500 m: 04 92 24 42 66



## *Dauphiné*

**Corrençon-en-Vercors** *(Isère)* 1111-2287 meters

**WINTER** – *Alpine skiing: 15 skiing tracks– Cross-country skiing: 130km with the "Centre Nordique de Bois-Barbu", tel. 04 76 95 03 30 and "Centre Nordique de Corrençon-en-Vercors", tel. 04 76 95 06 24 – Connection with Villard-de-Lans, Lans-en-Vercors, Méaudre – Ski-Pass: Vercors 4 montagnes (46 skiing tracks) – Tennis – In Villard-de-Lans (6km): ice rink, covered swimming pool, covered tennis, luge.*

**SUMMER** – *Hiking: 270km – Corrençon golf course (18-hole), tel. 04 76 95 80 42 – Tennis in Villard-de-Lans (6km).*

**Tourist Office** – tel. 04 76 95 81 75 - ESF – tel. 04 76 95 83 46

## Les Deux-Alpes *(Isère)* 1650-3600 meters

WINTER – *Alpine skiing: 75 skiing tracks– Cross-country skiing: 20km – Connection with La Grave – Ski-Pass: Super-ski – Connection in helicopter with Alpe-d'Huez, tel. 04 76 80 58 09 – Ice rink, covered swimming pool, squash. Cinema* SUMMER – *Hiking: walk in Ecrins Park – Skiing in summer, tennis, fencing, golf course (4-hole), riding, hang gliding.*

**Tourist Office**: 04 76 79 22 00 - ESF: 04 76 79 21 21



## Villard-de-Lans *(Isère)* 1050-2170 meters

WINTER – *Alpine skiing: 36 skiing tracks – Connection with Corrençon, Lans-en-Vercors, Autrans, Méaudre (79 ski tows) – Ski-Pass: Vercors 4 montagnes – Cross-country skiing: 120km with the "Centre Nordique de Bois-Barbu", tel. 04 76 95 03 30 and the "Centre Nordique de Corrençon en Vercors", tel. 04 76 95 06 24 – Ice rink, covered swimming pool, covered tennis, luge. Cinema.*

SUMMER – *Hiking: 270km – Climbing, swimming pool, riding, mountain bikes, archery, pony-club. Corrençon golf course (18-hole) at 6km, tel. 76 95 80 42*

**Tourist Office** – tel. 04 76 95 10 38 - ESF – tel. 04 76 95 10 94



# *North-Alps*

## Courchevel *(Savoie)* 1300-2707 meters

WINTER – *Alpine skiing: 92 skiing tracks – Cross-country skiing: 50km – Connection with Méribel, La Tania, Les Menuires and Val-Thorens (610 skiing tracks) – Ski-Pass: Les 3 Vallées – Hiking: 30km – Ice rink, swimming pool, squash, trips in sledge, and with rackets – Cinema.* SUMMER – *Hiking: in the Vanoise Park. Tour des glaciers – Tennis, riding, ULM, hang gliding.*

**Tourist Office:** 04 98 80 00 29 - ESF: 1550 meters: 04 79 08 21 07, 1650 meters: 04 79 08 26 08, 1850 meters: 04 79 08 07 12



## Méribel *(Savoie)* 1450-2910 meters

WINTER *Alpine skiing: 65 skiing tracks – Cross-country skiing: 33km – Connection with Mottaret, Courchevel, La Tania, Les Menuires, Val-Thorens, (200 ski tows, 260 skiing tracks) – Ski-Pass: Les 3 Vallées – Hiking: 20km – Covered swimming pool – Cinema.* SUMMER – *Hiking: 31km – Golf course (18-hole) – Tennis, riding, ball-trap, archery, pony-club.*

**Tourist Office**: 04 79 08 60 01 - ESF: 04 79 08 60 31



## Les Saisies *(Savoie)* 1650-1950 meters

WINTER – *Alpine skiing: 28 skiing tracks – Cross-country skiing: 100km – Connection with Espace Cristal, Les Saisies, Crest-Voland, Cohennoz (48 skiing tracks) – Ski-Pass: Espace Cristal – Hiking: 3km – Cinema.* SUMMER – *Hiking: 105km – Tennis, climbing, hang gliding, riding, archery, mountain bikes.*

**Tourist Office:** 04 79 38 90 30 - ESF: 04 79 38 90 40



## Val-Thorens *(Savoie)* 2300-3200 meters

WINTER – *Alpine skiing: 55 skiing tracks – Cross-country skiing: 3km – Connection with Les 3 Vallées: Courchevel, La Tania, Méribel and Les Ménuires (500 skiing tracks,*

*2500ha) – Ski-Pass: Les 3 Vallées – Hiking: 7km – In Val-Thorens center: 2 covered swimming pools, 6 covered tennis, squash, climbing, sauna, fitness center, ice rink – Cinema.* **SUMMER** *– Hiking: 90km – Skiing in summer, hiking, swimming pool, tennis, hang gliding, canoeing/kayaking– Méribel golf course (18-hole) at 60km, tel. 04.79 08 61 33*

**Tourist Office** – tel. 04 79 00 08 08 - ESF – tel. 04 79 00 02 86



## Val d'Isère *(Savoie)* 1850-3300 meters

**WINTER** *– Alpine skiing: 70 skiing tracks – Cross-country skiing: 15km – Connection with Tignes (107 ski tows, 129 skiing tracks) – Ski-Pass: Espace Killy – Hiking: 10km – Ice rink, covered swimming pool – Cinema.* **SUMMER** *– Skiing in summer at Formet and on the Pissaillas Glacier – Mountaineering, climbing, tennis, riding, hang gliding.*

**Tourist Office**: 04 76 06 10 83 - ESF: 04 79 06 02 34



## Tignes *(Savoie)* 1550-3656 meters

**WINTER** *– Alpine skiing: 125 skiing tracks (Espace Killy) - 66 skiing tracks (Domaine Super Tignes) – Cross-country skiing: 44km – Ski-Pass: Espace Killy (Tignes/Val d'Isère) - Ski-Pass: Haute Tarentaise (Espace Killy + 2 days La Plagne/Les Arcs/Peisey/Vallendry) - Ski Pass: L'Olympic (Espace Killy + Haute Tarentaise + Les 3 Vallées) – Ice rink, Tignes Espace Forme (fitness center), hang gliding –* **SUMMER** *– Ski in summer from June 21. – Mountaineering, climbing, tennis, riding, hang gliding.*

**Tourist Office**: 04 79 40 04 40 - ESF: 04 79 06 30 28



## La Clusaz *(Haute-Savoie)* 1100-2600 meters

**WINTER** *– Alpine skiing: 72 skiing tracks – Cross-country skiing: 60km – Hiking: 20km – Ice rink, swimming pool – Cinema –* **SUMMER** *– Tennis, climbing, riding, hang gliding, swimming pool*

**Tourist Office** – tel. 04 50 02 60 92 - ESF – tel. 04 50 02 40 83



## Chamonix *(Haute-Savoie)* 1035-3275 meters

**WINTER** *– Alpine skiing: 55 skiing tracks – Cross-country skiing: 40km – Connection with 13 stations (206 ski tows, 600km with skiing tracks) – Ski Pass: Mont Blanc – Hiking: 17km – 2 ice rinks, swimming pool, covered tennis, squash, trips in sledge – Cinema* **SUMMER** *– Hiking: 300km – Tour du mont Blanc, Le Lac Blanc, Les Dents Blanches – Climbing - Trips: cableway Plan des Aiguilles, 1st station before Aiguille du Midi, (3842 m) to La Pointe Helbronner (3466 m) in Italy. Le Brevent, Le Montenvers, La Mer de Glace – Golf course (18-hole) – Tennis, riding, mountain bikes, hang gliding, archery.*

**Tourist Office**: 04 80 53 00 24 (Chamonix), 04 50 54 02 14 (Argentière) - ESF: 04 76 89 94 25 - MountainGuides Office: 04 50 53 00 88



## Les Houches *(Haute-Savoie)* 1008-1960 meters

**WINTER** *– Alpine skiing: 19 skiing tracks – Cross-country skiing: 30km – Connection with Megève, Chamonix, Argentière, Saint-Gervais, Les Contamines – Ski Pass: Mont Blanc, Grand ski Vallée Chamonix – Hiking: 20km – Ice rink, trips in dogs sledge, with rackets.* **SUMMER** *– Hiking: 100km – Tennis, archery, hang gliding.*

**Tourist Office**: 04 50 55 50 62 - ESF: 04 50 54 42 96



## Megève *(Haute-Savoie)* 1113-2350 meters

**WINTER** – *Alpine skiing: 61 skiing tracks; the night skiing in Jaillet – Cross-country skiing: 65km – Connection with Saint-Gervais-Les-Contamines, Saint-Nicolas-de-Veroce, Praz-sur-Arly – Ski Pass: Mont Blanc. Shuttle in the station for connection with Rochebrune, Le Jaillet, Le mont d'Arbois, La Côte 2000 and La Princesse. Shuttle for connection with Megève in Saint-Gervais, les Contamines, Chamonix, Combloux – Hiking: 50km – 2 ice rinks, 2 covered swimming pools, covered tennis, riding, luge, climbing, walk with rackets and trips in dogs sledge – Cinemas.* **SUMMER** – *Hiking: 150km – Mont d'Arbois golf course (18-hole), tel. 04 50 21 29 79 – Tennis, riding, rafting, hang gliding, pony-club, archery, ice rink – All sports in "Palais des Sports" and "Palais des Congrès".*

**Tourist Office**: 04 50 21 27 28 - ESF: 04 50 21 00 97



## Combloux *(Haute-Savoie)* 1000-1853 meters

**WINTER** – *Alpine skiing: 31 skiing tracks – Cross-country skiing: 15km – Connection with 4 stations (75 ski tows, 194km with skiing tracks) – Shuttle in Combloux with connection with Sallaches, Megève, Saint-Gervais, Chamonix. Ski-Pass: 4 C – Hiking: 20km – Trips in slegde* **SUMMER** – *Tennis, mountain bikes, archery, hiking, rafting and canoeing/kayaking at 8km.*

**Tourist Office**: 04 50 58 60 49 - ESF: 04 50 58 60 87



## Saint-Gervais - Le Bettex *(Haute-Savoie)*

**WINTER** – *Alpine skiing: 44 skiing tracks – Cross-country skiing: 30km – Connection with Saint-Nicolas, Megève, Demi-Quartier (78 ski tows, 180km with skiing tracks) – Ski-Pass: 4 C – Hiking: 30km – Ice rink – Cinema.* **SUMMER** – *Tennis, riding, golf course, mountain bikes, hang gliding, canoeing/kayaking.*



## Cordon *(Haute-Savoie)* 870-1600 meters

**WINTER** – *Alpine skiing: 9 skiing tracks – Cross-country skiing: 10km – Ice rink (4km) – Megève: 16km, Chamonix: 30km - Cinema.* **SUMMER** – *Walk, tennis.*

**Tourist Office:** 04 50 58 01 57 - ESF: 04 50 58 13 63



## Le Grand Bornand - Chinaillon *(Haute-Savoie)* 1000-2100 meters

**WINTER** – *Alpine skiing: 42 skiing tracks – Cross-country skiing: 22km – Ski-Pass: Aravis (Le Grand Bornand/La Clusaz/Manigod), connection with shuttle (free). - Rackets - Ice rink - Hang gliding - Cinema.* **SUMMER** – *Climbing, tennis, mountain bikes, hang gliding, hiking, golf course: golf practice green and 9-hole, archery, canyoning, trampoline, tumbling - Reblochon market - Festival "Au bonheur des Momes" in August.*

**Tourist Office**: Grand Bornand 04 02 78 00 / Chinaillon 04 02 78 02- ESF: 04 50 02 70 10

**Manigod** *(Haute-Savoie)* 1480-1810 meters

WINTER – *Alpine skiing: 27 skiing tracks– Cross-country skiing: 3km – Connection with La Clusaz by shuttle (free, 1 km) – Hiking, ice rink in La Clusaz.* SUMMER – *Hiking: 135km – Climbing, pony-club.*

**Tourist Office**: 04 50 44 92 44 - ESF: 04 50 44 92 04 / 04 50 02 54 29



**Morzine** *(Haute-Savoie)* 1000-1200 meters

WINTER – *Alpine skiing: 72 skiing tracks – Cross-country skiing: 60km – Les Portes du Soleil, connection in France with Morzine, Avoriaz, Les Gets, Montriond, Abondance, la Chapelle-d'Abondance, Aulps and Châtel. In Switzerland with Torgon, Morgins, Champoussin, Val d'Iliez, Les Crosets, Champéry and Planachaux – Ski-Pass: Les Portes du Soleil – Hiking: 25km – Ice rink – Cinema.* SUMMER – *Hiking: 34km – Tennis, riding, hockey on ice, archery, pony-club.*

**Tourist Office**: 04 50 79 03 45 - ESF: 04 50 79 13 13



## *Jura*

**Les Rousses** *(Doubs)* 1120 meters

WINTER – *Alpine skiing: 50km access by shuttle (3km) – Cross-country skiing: 450km, connection with La Zone Nordique Les Rousses-Haut Jura: Belle Fontaine, Bois d'Amont, Lamoura, Longchaumois, Morbier, Morez, La Mouille, Prémanon, Les Rousses – Hiking: 3km – Ice rink, bowling.* SUMMER – *Golf course (18-hole) in mont Saint-Jean, Les Landes, tel. 03.84 60 09 71, hang gliding, archery, riding, tennis.*

**Tourist Office**: 03 84 60 02 55 - ESF: 03 84 60 01 61



## *Vosges*

**Gérardmer** *(Vosges)* 666-1150 meters

WINTER – *Alpine skiing: 19 skiing tracks – Cross-country skiing: 40km – Hiking: 50km – Luge, ice rink, covered swimming pool, covered tennis, squash – Cinema.* SUMMER – *Hiking: 300km – Climbing, tennis, riding, squash, mountain bikes.*

**Tourist Office**: 03 29 63 33 23 - ESF: 03 29 63 33 23



**Le Thillot - Ventron** *(Vosges)* 900-1100 meters

WINTER – *Ventron at 15km - Alpine skiing: 8 skiing tracks – Cross-country skiing: 35km – hang gliding.* SUMMER – *Hiking: 50km – Tennis, climbing, riding, hang gliding.*

**Tourist Office**: 03 29 24 05 45 - ESF: 03 29 24 05 45

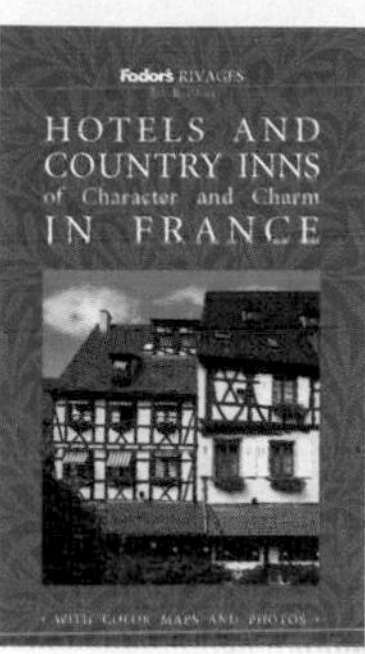
Fodor's RIVAGES
HOTELS AND
COUNTRY INNS
of Character and Charm
IN FRANCE
• WITH COLOR MAPS AND PHOTOS •

Fodor's RIVAGES
BED AND
BREAKFASTS
of Character and Charm
IN FRANCE
• WITH COLOR MAPS AND PHOTOS •

Fodor's RIVAGES
3RD EDITION
HOTELS AND
COUNTRY INNS
of Character and Charm
IN ITALY
• WITH COLOR MAPS AND PHOTOS •

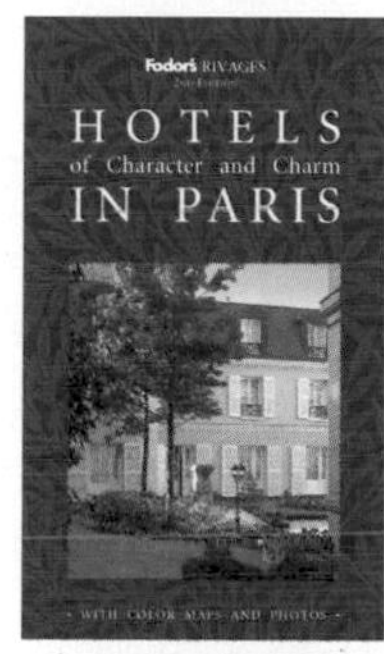
Fodor's RIVAGES
HOTELS
of Character and Charm
IN PARIS
• WITH COLOR MAPS AND PHOTOS •

Fodor's RIVAGES
HOTELS
of Character and Charm
IN SPAIN
• WITH COLOR MAPS AND PHOTOS •

Fodor's RIVAGES
HOTELS
of Character and Charm in
PORTUGAL
• WITH COLOR MAPS AND PHOTOS •

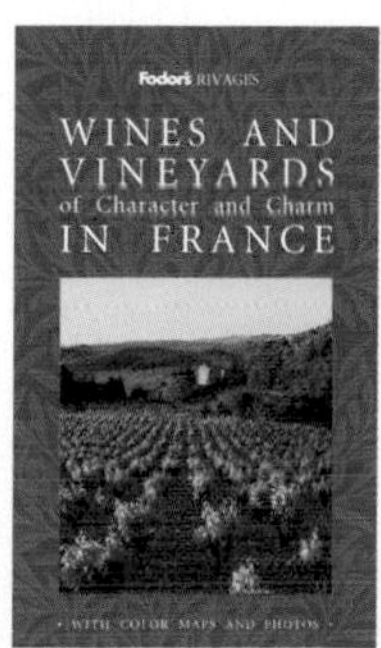
Fodor's RIVAGES
WINES AND
VINEYARDS
of Character and Charm
IN FRANCE
• WITH COLOR MAPS AND PHOTOS •